The

HOPE
FULFILLED

O. PALMER ROBERTSON

As Portrayed by His Daughter, Jane Kincannon Robertson Dodds

The HOPE FULFILLED

Essays in Honor of

O. PALMER ROBERTSON

EDITED BY

ROBERT L. PENNY

P&R
PUBLISHING

P.O. BOX 817 • PHILLIPSBURG • NEW JERSEY 08865-0817

Unless otherwise indicated, Scripture quotations are from The Holy Bible, English Standard Version, copyright © 2001 by Crossway Bibles, a division of Good News Publishers. Used by permission. All rights reserved.

Scripture quotations in chapters 2, 7, and 13 are from the HOLY BIBLE, NEW INTERNATIONAL VERSION®. NIV®. Copyright © 1973, 1978, 1984 by International Bible Society. Used by permission of Zondervan Publishing House. All rights reserved.

Scripture quotations in chapter 14 are from the NEW AMERICAN STANDARD BIBLE®. ©Copyright The Lockman Foundation 1960, 1962, 1963, 1968, 1971, 1972, 1973, 1975, 1977. Used by permission.

Scripture quotations in chapter 15 are from the NEW AMERICAN STANDARD BIBLE®. Copyright © 1960, 1962, 1963, 1968, 1971, 1972, 1973, 1975, 1977, 1995 by The Lockman Foundation. Used by permission.

Scripture quotations in chapter 9 are from the Authorized (King James) Version.

Italics within Scripture quotations indicate emphasis added.

Printed in the United States of America

Library of Congress Cataloging-in-Publication Data

The hope fulfilled : essays in honor of O. Palmer Robertson / edited by Robert L. Penny.
    p. cm.
Includes bibliographical references.
ISBN 978–1–59638–115–5 (pbk.)
1. Reformed Church—Doctrines. 2. Theology. I. Robertson, O. Palmer. II. Penny, Robert L.
BX9422.5.H67 2008
230′.42—dc22

                 2008009677

Contents

v

Preface

And thus the Word of God, presented by Erasmus to the learned in 1516 was given to the people by [William] Tyndale. In the parsonages and in the monastic cells, but particularly in shops and cottages, a crowd of persons were studying the New Testament. The clearness of the Holy Scriptures struck each reader. None of the systematic or aphoristic forms of the school were to be found there: it was the language of human life they discovered in those divine writings: here a conversation, there a discourse; here a narrative, and there a comparison; here a command, and there an argument; here a parable, and there a prayer. It was not all doctrine or all history; but these two elements mingled together made an admirable whole. Above all, the life of our Saviour, so divine and so human, had an inexpressible charm which captivated the simple. One work of Jesus Christ explained another, and the great facts of redemption, birth, death, and resurrection of the Son of God, and the sending of the Holy Ghost, followed and completed each other.[1]

One of the valuable gems Providence put on the path of my life was the experience of being a student, friend, and co-laborer of Dr. Owen Palmer Robertson. That remarkable stone first appeared at Reformed Theological Seminary, Jackson, Mississippi, in 1968, and he has been cherished ever since because of the single-minded orientation of the man. When Robertson arrived fresh from a south Mississippi pastorate, one quickly sensed in his class on the Epistle to the Hebrews his orientation to the whole Word of God, Old Testament as well as New. There was a reason for this and he showed

---

1. J. H. Merle d'Aubigne, *The Reformation in England* (Edinburgh: Banner of Truth, 1977), 1:107.

us day after day in class: Christ may be perceived, heard, and seen, from all parts of the Bible. Quite simply, the Bible in its entirety is about Christ! Thus a hearty amen to Tyndale's early efforts and, additionally, Augustine before him: *Novum Testamentum in Vetere latet, Vetus in Novo patet.*[2]

In this manner, Robertson has spent his life, as long as I have known him, preaching, teaching, and writing books to declare "the unsearchable riches of Christ" as they are highlighted from all those points, beginning with Moses and going through all the prophets. Now it is one thing to be deft in this exercise in the academic classroom, but it is quite another to take it to the pulpits and university campuses of America, the antebellum homes of north Mississippi, the university campus of the Mississippi Delta, the streets of suburban Washington or Philadelphia, and the refugee villages of East Africa. Additionally, Robertson teaches men to present Christ near Lake Victoria in Africa, the shores of which can be seen from a Kampala vantage, a short walk from the campus of African Bible College in Uganda.

Robertson was immersed early in a context of Reformational preaching in his home church, First Presbyterian of Jackson, Mississippi. It continued in his career as a youth assistant at First Presbyterian Church in Hattiesburg, Mississippi, and to his current vice-chancellorship and classroom at African Bible College, Uganda. His goal, observed as recently as one year ago, has been to teach the Bible to all classes of people to be applied to all of life because it declares the lordship of Christ over all of human experience on all its pages.

For this reason we have chosen as our theme for this honorary volume Christ's words: *"Then he said to them, 'These are my words that I spoke to you while I was still with you, that everything written about me in the Law of Moses and the Prophets and the Psalms must be fulfilled' "* (Luke 24:44). In the classroom these were frequent words from Robertson's mouth. His students, former colleagues, friends, and administrators of institutions where Robertson served or is highly regarded were asked to participate and to reflect on Robertson's reliance on this passage of Scripture. As one will quickly discover from the essays, Robertson's thesis (first Christ's) is not difficult to prove.

---

2. Augustine, *Quaestiones in Heptateuchum* (Questions on the First Seven Books of the Old Testament) 2.73. "The New Testament is in the Old concealed and the Old is in the New revealed." I want to credit my friend, colleague, and fellow contributor to this volume, Dr. Guy Waters, associate professor of New Testament at Reformed Theological Seminary, Jackson, Mississippi, for this reference and the original Latin version of the popular translation in English.

But more than just proving a thesis, our goal in this volume is to celebrate and to relish the truth of Christ's words. We also want to demonstrate publicly how this theme has enriched our understanding of the Scriptures and the worth of teaching others the same. This is our way of doing what Tyndale began for us centuries ago and what we pray will be done in new ways for centuries to come until Christ returns triumphantly.

Again,[3] our goal has been fourfold: the glory of God, the honoring of one of Christ's faithful teachers and authors in the church, the edification of the church through a useful volume of instructional essays, and the enjoyment of God's people through their celebration of the faithful life of one of His servants. *Soli Deo Gloria.*

ROBERT L. PENNY

---

3. See two other volumes in which former Reformed Theological Seminary professors have been honored with *festschrift* presentations: Joseph A. Pipa and C. N. Willborn, eds., *Confessing Our Hope: Essays in Honor of Morton Howison Smith on His Eightieth Birthday* (Taylors, SC: Southern Presbyterian Press, 2004); and Robert L. Penny, ed., *Interpreting and Teaching the Word of Hope: Essays in Honor of Jack Brown Scott on His Seventy-Seventh Birthday* (Taylors, SC: Southern Presbyterian Press, 2005). Both are still in print and available.

Acknowledgments

BY THE VERY NATURE of this book, there are many people whose contribution and help I want to recognize.

First, I want to thank the session of First Presbyterian Church in Hattiesburg, Mississippi, with whom I served happily for a five-year period ending in June 2007, for allowing me to work on this project and use their fine word-processing and mailing services. They are a fine "band of brothers" who will be my friends for life.

I also want to thank others: the session of First Presbyterian Church in Jackson, Mississippi, and many anonymous individuals who contributed to this project. I also want to thank the board of Reformed Theological Seminary. They are responsible for establishing an institution forty years ago—we are joyfully marking the occasion with "Ebenezers" on all our campuses—that brought this perceived "new" thing (i.e. the Reformed faith) to the modern South. Their founding the seminary many years ago has contributed to the spread of the Reformed faith all over the world, and they have allowed me to bring this incomplete project to full fruition.

Then there are the contributors: amazingly, the initially penciled "wish list" was about 95 percent of what you see in the table of contents. This project began in early 2006, and the contributors have been patient through the entire publication process. Our desire was to have men participate who had Palmer as a colleague or who knew something of his writings, and I believe we met that goal. We also sought to include tributes from administrators of all the institutions in which Palmer served.

Our fond hope was to have P&R Publishing take our efforts and bring them to the public, since P&R has published so many of Palmer's works.

Marvin Padgett and his staff, I feel, were wonderful to work with and have been cordial to come through for us.

Finally, I would like to thank Sara Sealy, office manager at First Presbyterian Church in Hattiesburg, Mississippi, for her indispensable help in handling the finances and other related details involved in the production of this book. Then also, I must thank our word processor, Michelle Robinson, Sara's daughter, who formatted all the pieces for me in preparation for the publisher. I am grateful to have had superlative help in those areas.

In the content of the essays, we sought to embody both the Reformation and Westminster theological flavors of Old Princeton, with a pinch of Old Southern Presbyterianism, and to demonstrate how these flavors affect a range of topics, including biblical interpretation, theological formulation, ecclesiastical life, pastoral ministry, and worldwide impact. We felt that such a collection of essays would accurately represent the broad impact of the man who is to be honored here. Further, we believe that the truths present here are, as Paul explained to Timothy, the "pillar and buttress of the truth" that will capture and conquer the world for Christ, even if slowly as the yeast in the flour.

In all of this, we sought to present the true flavor and the savor of the Christ. You will now have the opportunity to judge our efforts.

Sola Deo Gloria.

ROBERT L. PENNY

Biographical Sketch:
O. Palmer Robertson, the Sojourner

JANE KINCANNON ROBERTSON DODDS

WHAT I KNOW about my father's childhood and youth is based on memories my father shared with me. Owen Palmer Robertson was born in Jackson, Mississippi, on August 31, 1937, the fourth child of his parents' five children. I never met Bess Kincannon, my grandmother, but I believe she was the one who raised her daughter and four sons with faithful teaching from the Word. She was softhearted and had trouble catching her mischievous boys, who at least once almost burned down the woods near their house. She and her husband, Jack Robertson, lost their fourth child to a drowning accident in his teen years.

At the age of 15 my father heard the preaching of Billy Graham and received the gift of Christ's salvation. Soon afterward he felt God's call to become a pastor. He then used his skills as state yo-yo champion to tell the gospel with his yo-yo to the poor in the African-American neighborhoods.

He first met my mother, Julia Ruffin, when she was a senior in high school. Daddy would give her rides to youth group at First Presbyterian Church in Jackson.

Eight years later, in October 1963, I was born while my father was finishing doctoral studies at Union Theological Seminary in Richmond, Virginia. Not long afterward we moved to Picayune, Mississippi, where my father pastored his first church. My sister, Virginia "Jennie" Buchanan, was born there in May 1966. In 1967 we moved to Clinton, Mississippi, where my father taught at Reformed Theological Seminary. I believe my father enabled the students at RTS to become acquainted with the ministry of an African-American pastor in Jackson. Our family visited this black pastor's church, and it made a wonderful impression on me.

In 1971 my father was asked to teach at Westminster Theological Seminary near Philadelphia. So we made the dramatic move from the known South to the unknown North. When my father first walked into a Philadelphia sub shop, he asked for one "Hoa-a-gie, please" and was almost laughed out of the shop. The seminary soon cured his accent. I believe he was asked to speak strange sentences while holding his nose to get rid of his nasal twang.

My mother's mother and bed-ridden grandmother came to live with us at this time and stayed until my mother became pregnant with my sister Gwenette Orr, who was born in January 1971, a delightful addition to our family.

My father taught at Westminster for nine years. He seemed always to be involved with the students. While teaching Hebrew, he invented "happy Hebrew," a method of learning Hebrew phrases through song. I still can sing a couple of these tunes, including the Hebrew alphabet. He was also famous for answering precocious students' questions by saying "I don't know." Despite not knowing everything, my father was already well-known for his interpretations of the Epistle to the Hebrews and the Old Testament.

Around his fifth year at Westminster, my father started the first PCA church north of the "Mason-Dixon" line, in Malvern, Pennsylvania. We moved there, about an hour from Westminster. Many of the students from Westminster were involved in this new church. Although I was unaware of it at the time, I'm sure commuting to teach and planting a new church was a major undertaking. My memories of that little family of believers planted in me a love for the church and its vital worship. I especially learned from my father's weekly sermons and the popcorn and fellowship of Sunday evening services in our home. Daddy even pioneered a "Vespers" service which met in a wooded park complete with a pump organ and the beauty of sunset.

In 1979 my father accepted a position at Covenant Theological Seminary in St. Louis. In twelve years of teaching he had never received a sabbatical. Covenant Seminary graciously gave him a half-year sabbatical to

Cambridge, England, before coming to teach. So while packing and sending our things to St. Louis, we were also packing for an extended stay in England. That summer, we kids stayed with our aunt and uncle and their four girls in Amsterdam, the Netherlands, while our parents visited Italy, which I am sure was my mother's dream. She had finished her BA in art history while we were living in Philadelphia.

We moved into a house in a little town called Histon, outside Cambridge. My sister Jennie and I rode our bikes to the village college while Daddy rode his bike to Cambridge University. He must have been writing his book, *Christ of the Covenants* during that time, but of course I have my own memories. Daddy and I were able to ring the bells in the Norman Church down the street, which had eight bells—for which it is still well known among English bell-ringers. I rang the smallest bell and stood on a box to reach the cord. But Daddy rang one of the bigger bells and had his arms pulled out of joint! He didn't continue as a bell ringer, but the intrigue kept me climbing those steeple steps every week. We worshipped in this Anglican church for the remainder of our time in England.

Regretfully, we had to leave that romantic place and come back to America. But my parents seemed happy in St. Louis. They bought a little brick house in University Park. I finished my last two years of high school and went off to college. While teaching, again my father's love for the church led him to become the associate pastor of a Presbyterian church in the Washington University area.

I believe that my father's original call to the ministry continued to pull him, and in 1985 he received a surprise call to pastor a church in the Maryland suburbs of Washington, DC. At first he wasn't sure and specified that he needed to be able to continue writing books. Wallace Memorial Presbyterian wasn't sure about that, but I guess the church realized it was calling an incurable academic, and agreed. Of course Daddy was more than an academic and soon jumped into that pastoral position wholeheartedly. I felt, in that church, that the preaching we received was overflowing with the treasures of Scripture, both from my father and from the associate pastors.

My parents realized the need in the community for a Christian high school and started one, using the church facilities. My mother was the first principal and my sister Gwenette was one of their first seventh graders. As Wallace Memorial Presbyterian grew, my father had the vision to begin two new sister churches in the outer suburbs. These churches grew beautifully and all three churches are still doing well.

In 1992 my father and mother were called to join my father's sister and brother-in-law, Nell and Jack Chinchen, in Malawi, East Africa, to teach in the African Bible Colleges. When they returned to the USA to raise support for their missionary work in Africa, Daddy was also asked to teach Old Testament at Knox Theological Seminary in Florida. The seminary was willing to hire him for fall and January terms so that he could also continue in his position at African Bible College in Malawi for the second semester each year. This dual relationship between the college and seminary turned out to be beneficial to both institutions, as several American seminary professors came to Malawi to teach courses. My father had always had a passion for missions and had already traveled overseas to speak at many conferences all over the world. Teaching in Malawi seemed a natural fit for Daddy. He has a love for the African Christians and often speaks of their enthusiasm for learning. My mother, who had received a master's degree in Education while in Maryland, was also ready for a new stage of service to students. In her kind-hearted way, she saw the need for married student housing and was the primary cause for raising money for these buildings.

This chapter of my parents' lives was not to last long. In 1994, my mother was diagnosed with cancer, requiring them to remain in Florida for treatment. In early 1995 the cancer went into remission, so my parents returned to Africa for another academic term. But by the fall of 1995 my mother was severely ill again. She went to be with the Lord on Thanksgiving Day 1995. This was clearly a time of suffering and loneliness for my father. He was with my family during the birth of my fourth child, our first boy, whom we named Michael Owen, after his father and his grandfather. Daddy then went back to Malawi and continued teaching.

While in Africa, my father visited the Nairobi Evangelical Graduate School of Theology in Kenya, where an English woman 34 years old was studying to be a missionary with Wycliffe Bible Translators. Her name was Joanna Reilly. My father felt she was the only woman he had met who would fit well into our family. Well, that's how he described her to me, but what won me over was her charm and devotion to Christ and others, not to mention her commitment to tea-time. So he proposed to Joanna and, after considering how her own plans would be altered, she prayed and considered again and, after several weeks, agreed to marry my old dad. They were married in both England and America around Christmas of 1996. Joanna *was* perfect for our family and for the college, where she began to teach Bible Translation courses. By 2003 Joanna and my father had three little boys: Murray, born 1999, Elliot, born 2001, and Daniel, 2002; my brothers and the uncles to my five children!

Soon after the birth of Daddy and Joanna's first child, they became full-time teachers in Malawi. Then, in 2004, they moved to Uganda to help start another African Bible College. Presently this college is in its third year and has a growing student body and faculty and a fine campus.

As a child, my father's creative bedtime stories inspired and enlightened my own creativity and faith in a caring Father with a consistent plan to save; and later, his many theological writings and sermons did the same. Yet this quiet, productive part of his life never seemed to take away from his external relationships as a professor, pastor, or father. The only time I was aware he was writing or in private prayer was in the wee hours of the morning, if I should ever be awake then. He was available to create many wonderful memories, of which these are only the beginning.

Abbreviations

BAGD	W. F. Arndt and F. W. Gingrich, with F. Danker. *A Greek-English Lexicon of the New Testament and Other Early Christian Literature*. 2nd ed. Based on the 5th ed. of the German lexicon of Walter Bauer, 1958. Chicago: University of Chicago Press, 1979.
BDB	Francis Brown, S. R. Driver and Charles A. Briggs. *A Hebrew and English Lexicon of the Old Testament*. Oxford: Clarendon, 1957.
BT	*Biblical Theology* (Vos)
DJG	*Dictionary of Jesus and the Gospels*. Joel B. Green and Scot McKnight, editors. Downers Grove, IL: InterVarsity, 1992.
ESV	English Standard Version. Wheaton, IL: Good News, 2001.
GGBB	Daniel B. Wallace. *Greek Grammar beyond the Basics*. Grand Rapids: Zondervan, 1996.
HALOT	L. Koehler and W. Baumgartner, *The Hebrew and Aramaic Lexicon of the Old Testament*. Translated and edited under supervision of M. E. J. Richarson, 4 vols. (Leiden: Brill, 1994–99).
IB	C. F. D. Moule. *An Idiom Book of New Testament Greek*, 2nd ed. Cambridge: Cambridge University Press, 1959.
LXX	Septuagint
MT	Massoretic Text, in *Biblia Hebraica Stuttgartensia*, ed. Karl Elliger and Wilhelm Rudolph, 1967 and 1977.

NASB	New American Standard Bible: Updated Edition, 1995.
NEB	New English Bible
NICNT	New International Commentary on the New Testament
NICOT	New International Commentary on the Old Testament
NIV	New International Version
NJB	New Jerusalem Bible
NKJV	New King James Version
NRSV	New Revised Standard Version
NT	New Testament
OT	Old Testament
REB	Revised English Bible
s.v.	*sub voce,* "under a (given) word"
TC	Bruce Metzger. *A Textual Commentary on the Greek New Testament.* 2nd ed. United Bible Societies, 1994.
WCF	Westminster Confession of Faith
WSC	Westminster Shorter Catechism
WTJ	*Westminster Theological Journal*

PART I

Old Testament

Academical explanations were not necessary to those noblemen, farmers, and citizens. It is to me, for me and of me that this book speaks, said each one. It is I to whom all these promises and teachings concern. This *fall* and this *restoration* . . . they are mine. That old *death* and this new *life* . . . I have passed through them. That *flesh* and that *spirit* . . . I know them. This *law* and this *grace*, this *faith*, these *works*, this *slavery*, this *glory*, this *Christ* and this *Belial* . . . are all familiar to me. It is my own history that I find in this book. Thus by the aid of the Holy Ghost each one had in his own experience a key to the mysteries of the Bible.[1]

—J. H. MERLE D'AUBIGNE

1. J. H. Merle d'Aubigne, *The Reformation in England* (Edinburgh: Banner of Truth, 1977), 1:247–48.

I

Biblical Theology in
Southern Presbyterianism

C. N. Willborn

BIBLICAL THEOLOGY as a discipline has something of a checkered past. This past has been studied from various perspectives with much profit to the church.[1] The focus of this paper, however, is not to deal with the checkered past of the discipline but to expose a much-neglected sector of American Reformed biblical scholarship. The lacuna to which I refer is the contribution of Presbyterians in the southern United States to biblical interpretation in general and biblical theology in particular. In this chapter I hope to show that the labors of Geerhardus Vos and O. Palmer Robertson find considerable resemblance to an old perspective on biblical theology as promoted and practiced among some nineteenth century Southern Presbyterians. Ideas fundamental to the biblical theology of both Vos and particularly Robertson can be found in major (yet neglected) works from Southern Presbyterian theologians.

1. Good historical treatments of the discipline are Gerhard Hasel, *Old Testament Theology: Basic Issues in the Current Debate*, 4th ed. (Grand Rapids: Eerdmans, 1991) and *New Testament Theology: Basic Issues in the Current Debate* (Grand Rapids: Eerdmans, 2003).

PRINCETON AND BIBLICAL THEOLOGY

In the Reformed community, labors in biblical theology often center upon the noted Princeton scholar Geerhardus Vos (1862–1949). One assumes that any biblical theology course will have as one of its textbooks Vos's *Biblical Theology*. Furthermore, it is often thought that "Vos's work in biblical theology is largely without direct antecedents and indicates the originality with which he wrestled with the matter of biblical interpretation in the Reformed tradition."[2] Vos is also considered somewhat original in his attention to the "organically unfolding historical process"[3] of revelation and its theological significance.

There can be little doubt that Vos has been quite influential within the Reformed community of exegetes over the past sixty years;[4] however, to assume that Vos is unique in "the matter of biblical interpretation in the Reformed tradition" is a considerable overstatement. Indeed, the nineteenth century boasted a number of men on American soil who labored in the Holy Scriptures from a biblical-theological perspective, with an emphasis on the "organically unfolding historical process" of revelation. Peter Wallace has ably shown the important contributions of three nineteenth century Princeton scholars—Charles Hodge (1797–1878), J. A. Alexander (1809–60), and William H. Green (1825–1900)—toward establishing the Bible as normative, possessing an organic unity amidst its historical development, and "the centrality of redemptive history."[5]

The net result at Old Princeton was a growing recognition and use of the structure of biblical history as a hermeneutical and theological tool. When Vos, therefore, defines biblical theology as a linear approach to Scripture or the study of Scripture with an eye on its historical flow,[6] he is saying nothing that he did not learn from Old Princeton concerning the progressive nature of revelation within history and its organic unity. When he says that biblical theology "deals with the process of the special revelation of God

2. Richard B. Gaffin Jr., "Introduction," *Redemptive History and Biblical Interpretation* [hereafter *RHBI*] (Phillipsburg, NJ: Presbyterian and Reformed, 1980), xii.

3. Ibid., xv.

4. This is owing to the publication of Vos's lecture notes as *Biblical Theology* [hereafter *BT*] (Grand Rapids: Eerdmans, 1948).

5. Peter J. Wallace, "The Foundations of Reformed Biblical Theology: The Development of Old Testament Theology at Old Princeton, 1812–1932" [hereafter "Foundations"], in *Westminster Theological Journal* 59, no. 1 (Spring 1997): 42.

6. Geerhardus Vos, "The Idea of Biblical Theology," in *RHBI*, 15; *BT*, 16.

deposited in the Bible,"[7] he is affirming the normative role of the Bible for theology—something Hodge, Alexander, and Green made a hallmark of Princeton biblical scholarship in the previous century.

Vos's unique contribution within the Princeton tradition, admits Wallace, is when he took the labors of his predecessors and "combined their insights with traditional federal theology to connect the redemptive plan of God with the flow of history in the person and work of Christ."[8] Old Princeton labored cognizant of the historical focus of revelation and the organic unity of progressive revelation. Vos joined these foci with a federal or covenantal consciousness. It was Vos's contention that "the Bible is . . . conscious of its own organism" and he believed the "principle of successive Berith-makings (Covenant-makings), as marking the introduction of new periods, plays a large role in this, and should be carefully heeded."[9] Here Vos offers a vital principle to understanding the flow of history and the unfolding of revelation; history and revelation expand with "successive Berith-makings." In other words, the historical covenants—Adamic, Noahic, Abrahamic, Mosaic, Davidic—aid the exegete in his understanding and application of Scripture.

While Vos infused covenantal consciousness into the biblical theology of old Princeton, the idea of "successive Berith-makings" marking historical epochs of revelation was not original to Vos. Gustave Oehler, the German practitioner of biblical theology, argued that his discipline was "*the historical exhibition of the development of the religion contained in the canonical books of the Old Testament.*"[10] The basis of the religion that is developed or gradually unfolded to the people of God in the Bible "is the *covenant* with the chosen people."[11] The covenant as it was revealed in Mosaic literature (Adam to Moses) and the Prophetic literature (all OT literature from David to the period of silence) was the basis or foundation for OT religion as it developed under each revelatory epoch.

7. Vos, *BT*, 5.

8. Wallace, "Foundations," 42.

9. Vos, *BT*, 16.

10. Gustave Freidrich Oehler, *Theology of the Old Testament* (1883; repr., Grand Rapids: Zondervan, n.d.), 5. At the same time as Vos, the German OT scholar Walther Eichrodt was writing his *Theology of the Old Testament* (1st ed. 1933–35) committed to the covenant as the central theme. See Walther Eichrodt, *Theology of the Old Testament*, 6th ed. (Philadelphia: Westminster Press, 1961), 1:17.

11. Ibid., 43.

The idea that divine revelation was given gradually within historical periods and that divinely-initiated covenants marked the introduction of each new period did not find its final and most consistent expression in Vos. Both the "principle of historic progression" of special revelation and the organic "principle of successive Berith-makings," for which Vos is most notable, find equal or greater prominence, however, in the exegetical and biblical-theological fruit of Palmer Robertson.[12] Indeed, Robertson plied Vos's emphases to produce *The Christ of the Covenants* (1980) and *The Christ of the Prophets* (2004).[13]

It should also be noted that these two ideas—the principle of progressive revelation and that of successive divine covenants—were not first bound together in the theological enterprise of Geerhardus Vos. Among those who recognized these truths in Scripture earlier than Vos and most conspicuously incorporated these truths as interpretive concepts into their theological enterprise were Charles Colcock Jones (1804–63) and Stuart Robinson (1814–81). From these two men and other Southern notables, I hope to show how they anticipated the labors of Vos and Robertson.

A SOUTHERN BRAND OF BIBLICAL THEOLOGY

Biblical theology in the nineteenth century was largely an exercise among German theologians. Yet, as shown above, the discipline was pursued at old Princeton. It was also a discipline that a number of Southern Presbyterians discussed and practiced. In a review of Heinrich Ewald's *Old and New Testament Theology*, John Girardeau[14] revealed Southern awareness of the discipline and its relation to other departments of theology. The review

12. Robertson set forth his commitment to biblical theology and the historical nature of the discipline as early as 1971 in an essay entitled "The Outlook for Biblical Theology" in David F. Wells and Clark Pinnock, eds., *Toward a Theology for the Future* (Carol Stream, IL: Creation, 1971), 65–92.

13. O. Palmer Robertson, *The Christ of the Covenants* [Hereafter *Christ*] (Phillipsburg, NJ: Presbyterian and Reformed Publishing Co., 1980) and *The Christ of the Prophets* (Phillipsburg, NJ: P&R, 2005). I should say that followers of Vos include other notables like Richard B. Gaffin Jr., John Murray, Meredith Kline, and Willem VanGemeren, but none, I think, apply the major emphases to their biblical-theological enterprise as consistently and thoroughly as Robertson.

14. John L. Girardeau was the noted pastor to slaves in Charleston, SC (1854–74), and theologian in the Theological Seminary at Columbia, SC (1875–95). For a brief account of his ministry see Douglas Kelly, *Preachers with Power* (Edinburgh: Banner of Truth, 1992), and for an extended historical-theological treatment see C. N. Willborn, "John L. Girardeau: Pastor to Slaves and Theologian of Causes" (PhD diss. Westminster Theological Seminary, 2003).

exposed a number of points worth noting about theological academia in post-bellum Southern Presbyterianism. First, they were very much aware of biblical theology as a discipline. Second, Southerners labored, not as academic isolationists, but cognizant of an increasingly dismissive attitude toward systematic theology. Third, though they held systematic theology to be the "Queen of the Sciences,"[15] they were fully conscious of the component parts that ultimately produced a systematic statement of what the Bible teaches. They understood the importance and role of exegetical and biblical theology.

Girardeau applauded the German theologian for upholding "the principle upon which Systematic Theology proceeds," namely, "of comparing all the parts of the Scriptures together in order to grasp their catholic teachings."[16] Ewald applied his biblical theology with an eschatological tension. That is, he did not practice a biblical theology that isolated or excluded earlier historical epochs from later ones or vice versa. On the contrary, "the earliest movement is made in the light of the latest, and each stage of the progress takes place with relation to all that succeeds it."[17] History is made with an eye on the future; likewise, OT revelation was given with anticipation of further revelation.

What Girardeau was commending in Ewald was the German scholar's attempt to execute an exegetical, biblical, and systematic theology without showing inordinate deference to one or the other. "Every part of Scripture," explained Girardeau, " . . . ought to be studied in its immediate relations and in view of its own particular environment of circumstances and conditions [i.e., exegetical and biblical theology], but every part is to be contemplated in its catholic connection with the whole [i.e., systematic theology]."[18] Here Girardeau acknowledged the place of biblical theology and its linear-historical approach to Scripture—Scripture "studied in its immediate relations and in view of its own particular environment of circumstances and conditions"—but he also acknowledged the organic unity of Scripture and its role in the interpretive process.

---

15. An example of Southern commitment to the concept can be found as late as R. A. Webb, "The Adamic Principle in Theology," in *The Presbyterian Quarterly* 59 (July 1902): 29.

16. John L. Girardeau, "Criticisms and Reviews: *Old and New Testament Theology*. By Heinrich Ewald, late Professor in the University of Göttingen," in *The Presbyterian Quarterly* 6 (October 1888): 481.

17. Ibid.

18. Ibid., 482.

This principle—acknowledging the linear progress of history and revelation, while not excluding the organic unity of the whole of revelation from the interpretive process—is central to O. P. Robertson's hermeneutic as seen when he says, "This organic relation of the new covenant to the covenants of Abraham, Moses, and David finds explicit development both in the Old Testament prophecies concerning the covenant and in the New Testament realizations of this consummating covenant."[19]

THE COVENANTAL-CUMULATIVE PRINCIPLE

The Southern school was very much aware of biblical theology as a discipline and exegetical tool. They believed it should be used toward the end of properly understanding the Holy Scriptures and producing ultimately a statement of what the Scriptures say *in toto* with perspicacity. With considerable respect and acknowledgement of the primacy of revelation and the principle of progressive revelation, they also worked ever conscious of the linear-historical unfolding of revelation. With Vos and Robertson they also acknowledged and applied the essential principle of "covenant" to their theological pursuits. Like Vos and Robertson, one finds the Southern theological aristocracy weaving the revelation thread together with the historical thread *and* that of the federal principle. That is to say, "the principle of successive *Berith*-makings," played a large role in nineteenth-century Southern theology.

Before illustrating the presence of what I call the covenantal-cumulative view of revelation, it should be said that this principle was largely neglected before Vos. The federal or covenantal principle, as Peter Wallace has shown us, did not pervade the consciousness of the old Princeton scholars' view of revelation.[20] Indeed, by 1881 there were those who "feared that indications are beginning to manifest themselves of a growing tendency towards a departure from [federal theology]."[21] The indications were evidently clear

19. Robertson, *Christ*, 41.

20. Wallace, "Foundations," 61. While they did not fully wed the covenantal motif with the exegetical enterprise, Wallace is also quick to point out that the Princetonians were true to the federal principle and it does find a place in their final expressions.

21. John L. Girardeau, *The Federal Theology: Its Import and Its Regulative Influence*, ed. J. Ligon Duncan (1882; repr., Greenville, SC: Reformed Academic, 1994), 16. The content of this reprint originally appeared as an essay in *Memorial Volume of the Semi-Centennial of The Theological Seminary at Columbia, S.C.* (Columbia, SC: Presbyterian Publishing

and eventually confirmed, thus making Vos's emphasis on "successive *Berith*-making" a most significant rediscovery in his generation.

However, prior to 1881, Stuart Robinson of Kentucky produced two volumes which strongly anticipated Vos. Robinson was a prominent pastor and professor with R. J. Breckinridge in the Danville (KY) Theological Seminary. In 1867, Robinson placed before the American public "specimens" of his biblical expositions, which considered "a logical development of the gospel in the order of its communication."[22] In this brief description of his book one learns that redemption ("the gospel") was in view as it was progressively unfolded ("in the order of its communication"). In short, Robinson was presenting to the public the Scriptures as redemptive history, showing sensitivity to the linear-historical nature of revelation. In the mid–nineteenth century, therefore, we have a Southern theologian expounding "the centrality of redemptive history" just as the Princeton men were. However, where Princeton left off, the scholar-pastor of the South recognized and applied the principle of "periodicity" wherein God unfolded his special revelation within history *and* the periods of history as marked by "successive *Berith*-makings."[23]

Robinson explained "the mode of its [i.e., the Bible's] revelation is through a series of *covenants*, each one a larger development of that which precedes it."[24] Successive covenants mark the expansion of revelation as it flows from the gracious hand of God. This idea seems also to have guided Robinson ten years earlier when he published his work on ecclesiology.[25] Each period of revelation is marked by a divine covenant—Adamic pre-lapsarian, Adamic post-lapsarian, Noahic, Abrahamic, Mosaic, Davidic, and Messianic (new covenant). During each of these periods there was a

---

House, 1884)—a collection of essays first given in 1881 to raise support for the beleaguered Theological Seminary at Columbia, South Carolina. See also the Scottish theologian Hugh Martin, *The Atonement: In Its Relation to The Covenant, The Priesthood, The Intercession Of Our Lord* (1870; repr., Greenville, SC: Reformed Academic, n.d.), 24, for the same expressed concern.

22. Stuart Robinson, *Discourses of Redemption* [hereafter *Discourses*], Second American Edition (Louisville, KY: Davidson and Robinson, 1867), v. For an account of Stuart Robinson's life see Preston Graham, *A Kingdom Not of This World* (Macon, GA: Mercer University Press, 2002).

23. Vos, *BT*, 16.

24. Ibid., 23.

25. Stuart Robinson, *The Church of God As An Essential Element Of The Gospel* (Philadelphia: Joseph M. Wilson and Louisville, KY: A. Davidson, 1858; repr., Greenville, SC: GPTS Press, 1995).

9

development and accumulation of revelatory data regarding what man was to believe concerning God and what God demanded of man.

Robinson's utilization of a covenantal-cumulative approach to revelation and redemptive history is echoed in Vos, as we have seen, and again by E.J. Young: "He [God] chose to give His saving revelation in progressive stages."[26] The progressive and developmental and cumulative nature of revelation was acknowledged and stressed by Young when he wrote, "The OT revelation required supplementation, but it did not require correction."[27] Young stated the cumulative factor in terms of "supplementation." Robinson's biblical theological model, echoed in the twentieth century by Young, is perhaps most clearly and consistently exercised by Palmer Robertson in *The Christ of the Covenants*. A glance at Robertson's table of contents— "Covenant of Commencement," "Covenant of Preservation," "Covenant of Promise," and so on—confirms our claim.

Revelation and Covenant

Robinson expressed the importance of his biblical theological model when he developed three classes of truths, which emerge from revelation analyzed: "First, the record of historic events which prepared the way for certain *covenants*: next, the covenant and revelation connected to it; and next the history and revelations connected with the development of that covenant."[28]

The first class of truth addresses the perennial issue of historicity. Laboring at a time when a distinction between *historie* (facts of the world as studied by the historian) and *geschichte* (revelation as conveyed through the facts but not to be equated with the factual nature of an event, story, or narrative) was gaining prevalence, Robinson was pressing for the historicity (factuality) of biblical revelation. For Robinson, it would be bogus to view revelation as legitimate apart from its relation to true history. In other words, shady claims or factual inaccuracies do not make for proper modes of revelatory conveyance. Jehovah is God of and over history. Robinson labored under the conviction that E. J. Young expressed many years later when Young

---

26. Edward J. Young, *Old Testament Theology Today* [hereafter *OTT*] (New York: Fleming H. Revell, 1959), 36.

27. Ibid., 38

28. Robinson, *Discourses*, 23.

said, "it is necessary to insist upon the historicity of the patriarchs. . . . The unfolding of the covenant of grace has to do with historical events."[29]

Therefore, true history functioned to prepare the way for the various and successive divine covenants in history. In the first chapters of Genesis, for example, history unfolds in such a way as to prepare the citizens of the garden for God's gracious exercises in Genesis 3:15. Creation, divine institutions, and sovereign mandates all spoke to man as covenant creature in Genesis 1–2. As a creature made for covenantal union, the stage is set for the covenant of works. Robinson's fellow Southern pastor-scholar Charles Colcock Jones (1804–63) expressed this point cogently when he said: "By the very conditions of his origin and existence, he was under obligations of supreme love and obedience to God his creator, preserver, and benefactor. And in His sovereign pleasure, God put him upon the trial, whether he would fulfil [sic] these obligations or not, and this prohibitory command covered over the love and obedience which he owed to God in all things and forever."[30] Within this historical and covenantal epoch Adam, through disobedience, fell into an estate of sin and misery. Guilt and fear and misery set the stage for the marvelous and voluntary and gracious condescension on God's part in Genesis 3 when God came to Adam with words of rebuke, but also of grace and hope. With this one sees what Robinson meant when he said that one class of truth gleaned from revelation is that historical records prepared the way for each successive covenant.

Of course Robinson moves quickly to illustrate that all history and revelation from Genesis 3:15 forward "are to the end of preparing the way of the Lord's coming, as the king of a universal kingdom; and for the new covenant in his blood, under which his commissioned agents shall 'go into all the world and preach the gospel to every creature.' "[31] Here we see the

29. Young, *OTT*, 81. See Vos, *Discourses*, 66ff. for a defense of the historicity of the patriarchal figures and biblical narrative in general.

30. Charles Colcock Jones, *The History of the Church of God During the Period of Revelation* (New York: Charles Scribner & Co., 1867), 29. Charles C. Jones was from Liberty County, Georgia, and studied at Andover and Princeton Seminaries. His labors among the slaves of coastal Georgia are largely known and have earned him the title of "Apostle to the Negro Slaves." Jones was also widely respected as a churchman, which gained him appointment as general secretary of domestic missions for the PCUSA and professor of ecclesiastical history and polity in the Theological Seminary in Columbia, SC. A sizeable portion of his family correspondence is documented in the award-winning *The Children of Pride* by Robert Manson Myers (New Haven, CT: Yale University Press, 1972).

31. Robinson, *Discourses*, 24.

ever expanding revelation, marked by a succession of divine covenants, concerning redemption and the Redeemer, Immanuel. A hundred years after Robinson, O. P. Robertson traced this same theme similarly under the "Immanuel Principle."

The next class of truth Robinson finds in Scripture is that of "covenant and revelation connected with it." With the preponderance of theologians prior to the Barthian revolution, Robinson, Jones and the other Southern theologians held the nature of a covenant to be "contract." The contractual nature of covenant is clearly seen and readily acknowledged in the case of "equals"—as in the case of David and Jonathan in 1 Samuel 20.[32] However, when the case involves unequal parties—man and God—there is often some reservation about speaking of covenant as contract. For the pre-Barthian scholars, however, covenant as contract in the case of God's divine covenants was understood in terms of the unilateral act of God in voluntarily condescending to man, or the binding of God to execute his redemptive purposes with and toward man. There was, in Robinson and his predecessors' minds, no concept of man wrangling with God and working out an agreeable contract. No, God, who bound himself in covenant, sovereignly dispensed the covenant. Perhaps the passage that most clearly illustrates this point is Genesis 15 where God binds himself to death if what was said is not done: the maledictory oath, God binding himself to do all that he promised he would do upon pledge of death *if* the oath is not kept by the parties. This was at the heart of the covenant ratification in Genesis 15 and is the nature of the covenant as Robinson understood it. Thus, he could consider covenant as contract.

With this said, the Southern theologians recognized the need to understand divine revelation as it was given in history, within the parameters of the specific covenantal epoch to which the revelation was associated. This may be illustrated in any covenantal-revelatory period, but consider the case of Adam and Eve. In the garden prior to sin and death, God enjoined man to obedience (Gen. 2:16, 17). God bound man to perfect obedience *and* himself to administer judgment against disobedience and blessing toward obedience. Then came Eve, and Adam was blessed with companionship and help (Gen. 2:18–24). Adam was also given one for

32. The case of David and Jonathan is confirmed as a binding oath or covenant in 2 Samuel 21:7, where we read: "But the king spared Mephibosheth, the son of Saul's son Jonathan, because of the oath of the LORD that was between them, between David and Jonathan the son of Saul."

whom he was to act responsibly, representatively, federally. The representative or federal role of Adam is clearly seen in God's address to Adam (Gen. 3:9) after Eve had initiated the rebellion against Jehovah (Gen. 3:1–6). Adam and Eve enjoyed the purest intimacy without the hint of shame (Gen. 2:24–25) before sin entered. Furthermore, they enjoyed the closest of communion with Jehovah. His face was familiar to the first couple prior to sin. He walked with them and talked with them in the cool of the day. There was nothing intruding upon the original fellowship between Jehovah and his image bearer.[33]

Sin, however, did come and man entered a new and different estate, "the estate of spiritual death under a broken covenant." The holy records of divine revelation must now be considered as they detail "the workings of the human soul under this new phase." First, as Robinson outlines the revelation, there is an "experimental knowledge of evil" that has not been known before—"The eyes of both of them were opened, and they knew . . ." (Gen. 3:7). Next, Adam and Eve, we are told in revelation, "knew that they were naked" (Gen. 3:7). There was a relational shift. Their standing before Jehovah *and* with each other was different. Third, revelation tells us that a broken covenant generates fear (Gen. 3:10). What previously had been a joyous event, Jehovah's voice and presence in the delightful environs of Eden, is now filled with fear and avoidance (Gen. 3:8). Revelation further informs us that one's standing at odds with a divine covenant produces blame shifting—"they seek to evade and palliate the sin."[34]

Thus, within the earliest period of revelation and the epoch of the covenant of works we learn something of man's original happiness and holiness and the resultant sin and misery due to failure under the original covenant between God and man. The revelation of each period also anticipated and prepared the way for each successive covenant. Therefore, the fall anticipates redemption and, in what seems to have been an almost immediate response to Adam's plight, Jehovah responded with hope for Adam and his progeny. "On careful analysis of these words [Genesis 3:15]," writes Robinson, "and deducing the truths embodied by implication in them," the gospel is set forth in an eight-point "gospel creed," which,

33. In Genesis 3 we learn that Jehovah came in the cool of the day and they hid. They hid due to their knowledge of sin (Gen. 3:7, 8). Prior to sin entering in they were not fearful of Jehovah. It was their sin that separated them from God and hid his face from them (Isa. 59:2).

34. Robinson, *Discourses*, 64.

although appearing "in germ," is the full gospel.[35] C. C. Jones unfolded Genesis 3:15 more simply than Robinson, but with a similar conclusion— "Herein we have the first proclamation of the glorious Gospel of the grace of God, made by the Lord Jehovah himself!"[36] In Genesis 3:14–19, therefore, we have the initial time-space expression of the covenant of grace or, as Palmer Robertson tags it, the Covenant of Commencement.[37]

Revelation, Covenant, and the Church

Within the discipline of biblical theology there is ongoing discussion regarding the "center" of the discipline.[38] Is there a "center" to biblical theology? If so, is the center redemption? Is it kingdom? Is it covenant? Is it God's sovereign lordship? Is it the new creation? With the expanding clarity of the gospel in the OT, one finds an emphasis, which is related and parallel to those (i.e., redemption, covenant, kingdom, etc.) in the OT literature, the issue of redemption and gospel related to a people, a distinct people, the church of God. A number of Southern biblical theologians found the center or, perhaps better, the heart of their discipline in the church.[39] Stuart Robinson traced the line or history of the church through each successive period of revelation. Within the epoch of the Covenant of

35. Ibid., 65. While I do not follow Robinson completely in his deductions from Genesis 3:15, I do agree with his general assessment that the gospel is revealed in germ form, thus making this passage the *protoevangelium*.

36. Jones, *The History of the Church of God*, 65.

37. See Robertson, *Christ*, chapter 6.

38. In this essay I do not wish to enter the fray on whether there is a center to biblical theology. I am content here to simply set forth what appears to be a center for the Southern Presbyterian paradigm I am describing. It may well be the case that D. A. Carson was correct with his assessment of the search for a center when he concluded, "pursuit of a center is chimerical," in D. A. Carson, "NT Theology," in *Dictionary of the Later New Testament and Its Developments*, ed. R. P. Martin and P. H. Davids (Downers Grove, IL: InterVarsity, 1998), 810. For brief discussions of this topic see related chapters in Hasel, *Old Testament Theology: Basic Issues in the Current Debate* and *New Testament Theology: Basic Issues in the Current Debate*; Willem VanGemeren, *The Progress of Redemption*; and for a collection of essays on the topic see Scott J. Hafemann and Paul R. House, eds., *Central Themes in Biblical Theology*. There are also numerous references to this topic in Scott J. Hafemann, ed., *Biblical Theology: Retrospect and Prospect*.

39. Gerald Wilson, "Psalms and Psalter," in *Biblical Theology: Retrospect and Prospect*, 110, accepts "a plethora of centers" in BT, concluding that the literature of the Psalms has a "heart" rather than a "center." That heart, for Wilson, is the kingship of Jehovah. Similarly, it may well be that I would argue for the self-revelation of God as the center (a la Geerhardus Vos) and the church (a la Robinson et al) as the heart of the theological discipline.

Commencement Abel worshipped God through "a more excellent sacrifice" (Heb. 11:4) and, according to Robinson, "there and then began the visible Church on earth."[40]

C. C. Jones understood "that the true history of the Church lies within the inspired pages of the Old and New Testaments." Furthermore, Jones argued that the covenant of works and covenant of grace "lie at the foundation of the Church."[41] From these comments and the very title of Jones' long-forgotten book—*The History of the Church of God through the Period of Revelation*—one can clearly see that this nineteenth century Southern Presbyterian believed the church to be at the center of his endeavor and God's design. Nowhere is this more fully stated than in the following explanation of his intentions for his book.

> Our design is, in humble reliance upon Divine aid, to carry out this idea by beginning with the earliest existence of the Church, and thence, proceeding by regular steps downward through the entire Scriptures to their close, cover the period of revelation only; and we shall endeavor to determine the Origin, the Covenants, the Doctrines, the Rites, Ceremonies, Ordinances, Members and Officers, Order and Discipline of the Church; and, briefly, the principal events of her progress, and especially her passage out of the Old into the New Dispensation, and show what of the Old found accomplishment as type, or shadow, or prophecy, and passed away in the New, and what remained afterward that pertained to the necessary existence and constitution of the Church; and what was the final and perfect state in which our Lord and His Apostles left the Church when the canon of Scripture closed.[42]

The Bible, according to Jones, chronicles God's redemption of a people—the church—through the various periods of history. Through a linear-historical study of revelation Jones sought out answers to questions concerning the origin of God's church, the covenants that lie at the foundation of the church, and much more. What is important for us, however, is to recognize that for both Jones and Robinson, our representative Southern Presbyterians, the church was at the center of biblical theology.

40. Robinson, *Discourses*, 72,
41. Jones, *The History of the Church of God*, viii.
42. Ibid., ix.

15

Stuart Robinson argued that the mode of communication by which God spoke to man is "through successive covenants." Here, again, we see agreement between Robinson, writing in 1858, and Vos and Robertson in the twentieth century. That such a mode is chosen and utilized by Jehovah suggests "the idea of a distinct body of people with whom, as contracting parties with God, the covenants are made."[43] This "distinct body of people" is no other than the visible church of God throughout the various covenantal epochs. "The idea," continues Robinson, "which underlies all these covenants alike is of a separated portion of the race entering into contract with God."[44] The covenant, in Robinson's scheme, is sovereignly initiated and detailed by God, but is contractually binding on man nevertheless.

While Vos emphasized "successive *Berith*-makings" early in his BT, the concept soon falls into the background. With Robertson, however, the covenant motif remains central and visible, as with Robinson and Jones. When it comes to the "center" of Vos's BT, the church does not find the same prominence as in the Southern Presbyterians. In Robinson the church is visible from the time of Adam's and Eve's effectual calling in the garden, finding greater development as revelation is unfolded. With the Abrahamic covenant the church finds such definition as to be distinguished from locality and family—"The covenant with Abraham is specifically with him, as representative and head of a separate society."[45] In the Abrahamic epoch of revelation the church takes on expansive, even global dimensions, so that Robinson can refer to it as the ecclesiological covenant.[46] "This covenant with Abraham," explained Robinson, "is, therefore, the divine charter of the visible Church as heretofore and still existing. There is no other charter found in Scripture."[47]

Jones takes up the same Southern mantra late in his treatise on the church when he expounds on the Abrahamic covenant not as a "renewal of the covenant of grace, but rather a carrying out and a fuller unfolding of the precious promises and provisions of that covenant." The precious promises include, of course, the seed promise of a Redeemer and the restoration of paradise. The peculiarity of the ecclesiological covenant "consists in the

43. Robinson, *Church of God*, 47.
44. Ibid., 49.
45. Ibid.
46. Robinson, *Church of God*, 50.
47. Robinson, *Discourses*, 80.

separation of himself [i.e., Abraham] and his seed to be the only visible and organized body of God's people, which should be the depository of God's truth, and the heir of the promises and blessings of the covenant for all nations and all time. . . . It is a covenant enduring while the Church endures."[48]

For Vos, Abraham "was the father of the faithful, the nucleus of the Church,"[49] and he admits an "Old Testament Church"[50] existed. However, the Old Testament church had to give way "to make place for the Messiah's Church."[51] In these brief statements from Vos one realizes just how little attention is given to the institutional church in Vos's development of a biblical theology. Where in the Southerners the church is at the center of unfolding revelation and, therefore, at the center of redemptive history, that same center is not evident in Vos's biblical theology.

Reminiscent of Vos, Palmer Robertson developed his biblical theology with minimal reference to the church.[52] In the two chapters devoted to the Abrahamic covenant, there are but general references made to "the people of the covenant,"[53] "the externally organized community of Israel,"[54] "the community of Israel,"[55] and "the covenant community."[56] In his dealing with NT theology, Robertson continues to use terms such as "a community of people."[57] In his chapter on the new covenant, one might have expected to see "the church" figuring into the answer to the question, "Who is the corporate community called 'Israel'?"[58] Yet, the answer relates more to the question of ethnicity and the Jewish people. For all this one might assume that Robertson errs on the side of individualism, but this would be an incorrect assumption. There is plenty in his discussion on corporateness and the proper relationship between the corporate people of God and the

48. Jones, *History of the Church of God*, 553.
49. Vos, *BT*, 67.
50. Ibid., 400.
51. Ibid.
52. My point here is that the church finds no prominent place in *The Christ of the Covenants*. For further discussion of the people of God in Robertson's paradigm see O. Palmer Robertson, *The Israel of God* (Phillipsburg, NJ: P&R, 2000).
53. Robertson, *Christ*, 150.
54. Ibid., 153.
55. Ibid., 154.
56. Ibid., 158.
57. Ibid., 290.
58. Ibid., 288.

individual believer. Corporateness, argued Robertson, "must be understood first of all as an essential reality of the covenant."[59]

It seems that the "center" for Vos's BT is "the self-revelation of God,"[60] while Robertson's "center" is "covenant."[61] Each recognize the important role that successive historical covenants play in the proper handling of revelation, particularly as revelation is progressively unfolded on the time-space continuum. Robertson, certainly more consistently and fully than Vos, utilizes the covenant motif in his biblical theological endeavor. In so doing, Robertson presents, in my opinion, a less tedious and more fluid portrait of redemptive history.

The Southerners, on the other hand, found their center for biblical theology in the church. In so doing, they weaved from and through their biblical theology a portrait of what man is to believe concerning God, what God requires of man, the redemption that comes through Christ Jesus, which redemption or salvation is ordinarily found in the church.[62] Having traced out the revelation of the Old Testament along a linear-historical method, C. C. Jones concluded his 558 page treatment by saying,

> Finally we have the visible church—purged from her dross of idolatry and iniquity by the captivity, as well as by the subsequent revivals and reforms—once more settled in the holy land, a godly seed; blessed with temple, and priesthood, and all the service of God; with the canon of the Old Testament completed and left in her hands—a lamp unto her feet and a light unto her path; looking for and hastening unto the coming of her great Redeemer.

In these final words of his work on *The History of the Church*, as revealed in OT revelation, the "visible church" is once again the refrain. At the heart of the history of the church is "the coming of her great Redeemer." So, we see the history of redemption and the church organically wed.

Southern-styled biblical theology recognized the organic relationship between revelation, covenant, and the church. Divine revelation was

---

59. Ibid., 289.

60. Vos, *BT*, 5.

61. It could possibly be argued that Robertson's "unifying principle" is "covenant" and his "center" is "Immanuel Principle," Robertson, *Christ*, 46.

62. The latter point is drawn from the Westminster Confession of Faith 25.2, where the importance of the church is seen, "out of which there is no ordinary possibility of salvation."

integrally related to the successive historical covenants, and the redemptive or gospel orientation of the covenants was likewise related to the church. Robinson summarized it when he said:

> The fundamental error of many of the Protestant theories of the Church lies in overlooking the fact that the doctrine of the Church is the fundamental truth of the gospel, and is entitled to the same sort of consideration as other articles of theology. Nay more, that not only is this doctrine intimately connected with the other articles of Protestant theology, but it enters as an element into all those doctrines, and to a large extent moulds and shapes the scientific statement of them.[63]

There can be little doubt of the center of biblical theology within the Southern school—the church as the "pillar and buttress of the truth" (1 Tim. 3:15) from which the gospel flows and into which the redeemed flee for refuge and sustenance, with praise for their Redeemer.[64]

BIBLICAL THEOLOGY AND THE CONSUMMATION

The history of God's self-disclosure, man's plight, and God's redemptive purposes was unveiled progressively and gradually woven into the fabric of human events. The basic truths were supplemented to tell more and more of God, his redemption, and his church. C. C. Jones illustrated this briefly when he wrote:

> What is the Abrahamic covenant but the reiteration and continuation of the covenant of grace first made with Adam [i.e., Gen. 3:15], and to which other matter was then added, giving the covenant more visibility and fixedness in the world? What is the Mosaic Covenant? Indeed nothing more than a gathering up of all God's previous revelations of the covenant of grace, and His arrangements concerning it, with many things added for its still clearer manifestation.[65]

63. Robinson, *Discourses*, 454.
64. Here thanks are due to my dear friend, Dr. Mark Herzer, for some stimulating discussion on the topic of the center of BT and a fine young scholar and student of mine, Roland Mathews, for bibliographic assistance.
65. Jones, *The History of the Church*, 99.

19

The gradual, historical supplementation of truth grows, therefore, throughout the epochs of Abraham, Moses, and David, but culminates in the new covenant or Covenant of Consummation, as Palmer Robertson labeled it.

The importance of the church to the covenant ratified by Christ's blood is clearly established in the NT, and the Southern theologians did not miss the opportunity to express, once again, the center of their biblical theology—the church. With no intentions to short shrift the NT, but for space and time, I shall refer to one NT book to illustrate the relation of the church to the gospel and the consummation—the book of Revelation. In the final chapter of that consummating book of Holy Scripture we read the words of our Lord when he said,

> "I, Jesus, have sent my angel to testify to you about these things for the churches. I am the root and the descendant of David, the bright morning star." The Spirit and the Bride say, "Come." And let the one who hears say, "Come." And let the one who is thirsty come; let the one who desires take the water of life without price. I warn everyone who hears the words of the prophecy of this book: if anyone adds to them, God will add to him the plagues described in this book, and if anyone takes away from the words of the book of this prophecy, God will take away his share in the tree of life and in the holy city, which are described in this book. (Rev. 22:16–19)

Stuart Robinson, laboring to expound the revelation of God in its linear, historical context, fixes his attention on these four verses as he concludes his *Discourses of Redemption.*

Robinson developed a number of biblical theological themes from these verses. First, it is the ascended Lord who speaks the gospel. Several years after his ascension to the right hand of the Father, sitting in session with the Father in eternity, "there is no abatement of his interest in that wonderful scheme of redemption, which he had been gradually developing, through the revelations 'of sundry times and divers manners,' under successive covenants for four thousand years."[66] In this one statement we recognize the consistency in Robinson's biblical theology—he was committed to divine revelation, as it unfolds in linear, historical fashion, according to the divine covenants which expound the covenant of grace. He further

66. Robinson, *Discourses*, 431–32.

promoted the covenantal cumulative model as he draws his readers' attention to the Lord's self-disclosure as "the root and descendant of David." As the ascended and enthroned King he speaks as the fulfiller and fulfillment of the Davidic covenant.

I might also add that the very words of Revelation 22:17 reflect a continuity-fulfillment theme for they are the words of our preincarnate Lord: "Come, everyone who thirsts, come to the waters; and he who has no money, come, buy and eat! Come, buy wine and milk without money and without price" (Isa. 55:1). The "waters" (Isa. 55:1) and "water of life" (Rev. 22:17) are certainly self-referential as our Lord speaks. After all, he had declared himself to be the "living water" that assuages the need of the thirsty when he addressed the woman at the well (John 4:14). The "one who is thirsty" (Rev. 22:17) is parallel to "everyone who thirsts" (Isa. 55:1). The "thirsty" are those with need, but specifically they are sinners in need of the living water. To the thirsty sinners the call of the covenant LORD is to "come" (Isa. 55:1; Rev. 22:17) drink of the water, drink of it freely, "without price," (Isa. 55:1; Rev. 22:17). Interestingly, and not insignificantly, the Lord's call to a general, indiscriminate population of sinners in Revelation is the very same call he issued within the covenant community in Isaiah.

The thirst (sinner)-water (Savior) scheme is not simply a Davidic-Christ message, but Robinson traces its existence through the revelation of successive-covenant makings, noting both Exodus 17 (revelation under the Abrahamic covenant) and Numbers 20 (revelation under the Mosaic covenant). The same theme could be traced out variously in revelation under the Davidic covenant (e.g., Ps. 36:7–9; Jer. 2:12–13; Zech. 13:1). With this scheme ever at work in revelation, Robinson concludes that there is a general truth that is "too much overlooked"—thirst is "the general want, felt by humanity at large, of something analogous to the provision of the gospel."[67] In other words, spiritual "thirst" is the general condition of humanity and that can only be satiated by Jesus Christ, the living water. Thus, the recognition of this thirst-water scheme in each revelatory period of history aids the student of Scripture in seeing the development of the gospel germ from Genesis 3:15 to Revelation 22:17.

The final biblical-theological theme developed by Robinson is that of the church. The exalted Lord says, "The Spirit and the Bride say, 'Come,' "

67. Ibid., 443.

(Rev. 22:17). The Spirit appeals immediately to the sinner to come to that which refreshes and saves. The Spirit mediately calls sinners to the loving Savior through the ministerial and declarative offices of the bride or the church. Once again, the biblical-theological center of Robinson, Jones, and other Southerners is evident as Robinson expounds the doctrine of the church and her central role in the gospel-theological enterprise. "The results of this scheme of salvation," Robinson explains as he moves from Jesus as the water of life, "are organized by Christ into a great body, whose chief function it is, to extend the invitation. The church of God, the bride of the Lamb, saith, 'Come.'"[68]

From these final words of divine revelation under Christ's covenant/ new covenant, the church is seen to be vitally related to the gospel or the redemptive purposes of God in history. "The one grand mission of the Church on earth," explains Robinson, "is to holforth [sic] this water of life in the view of perishing sinners, and cry 'Come.'"[69] Thus, we have contained in these words at the end of divine revelation the emphases of a Southern-styled biblical theology—revelation, successive-cumulative covenants, and the church.

Stuart Robinson was not the only Southern theologian to deal with the book of Revelation from the revelation-covenant-church schema. Thomas Peck bequeathed to the church a sampling of his biblical theological commitment in two lectures on "The Apocalypse."[70] The first of the lectures deals with the historical-covenantal context of the revelation. The book of Revelation "is designed to set forth the general features of the history of the church."[71] Thus, we see in the very beginning of the professor's discourse a commitment to the church as the "center" of his theological enterprise. Initially, Peck opens his discussion with "the church's king, under whose

---

68. Ibid., 447.

69. Ibid. Here we have a hint of another biblical-theological theme held forth by Southern theologians like Thornwell, Girardeau, and Robinson—the spirituality of the church. This doctrine of the church's spiritual independence from all other institutions was carried over into the Presbyterian Church in America, which sets forth its commitment to this biblical teaching in its Book of Church Order 1.2—"The Church which the Lord Jesus Christ has erected in this world for the gathering and perfecting of the saints is His visible kingdom of grace, and is one and the same in all ages."

70. Thomas E. Peck, "The Apocalypse," *Miscellanies of Rev. Thomas E. Peck* [reprinted as *The Writings of Thomas E. Peck*], 3 vols. (Richmond: Presbyterian Committee of Publication, 1895–97; repr., Edinburgh: Banner of Truth, 1999), 2:167–201.

71. Ibid., 2:167.

administration the battles [of the church] are to be fought, and the victory achieved."[72] The church's king is none other than the "son of man" (Rev. 1:13), a term of self-disclosure used by our Lord. Laboring at a time when the Ritschlian school was humanizing Christ, Peck sought to flesh out "son of man" to show its biblical (not pagan) origin and its extra-human significance. "Son of man" did not simply speak to the humanity and humiliation of the Incarnate One, but it was "the description of a king chiefly"; as well as of a conquering man—the fulfillment of Adam's original "dominion" mandate; and, thirdly, the term means that Jesus was "more than man; that he is also God. He is the proper object of John's worship. He holds the keys of hades and of death."[73]

Peck's discussion of "son of man" is the product of his careful consideration of divine revelation. "It is in the Old Testament, and especially in the prophecies of Daniel," Peck argued, "that the full significance of this denomination is to be sought."[74] Peck's interest and emphasis on the OT and, particularly, Daniel find the same careful consideration in Geerhardus Vos many years later. One word from Vos will suffice to substantiate the similarity of appeal: "In the sayings about 'saving' and 'ministering' the condescension is fitly measured only if 'Son of man' connotes the innate majesty of our Lord. There is no reason, then, to assume that for Jesus the name [i.e., son of man] had ceased to possess the same glorious significance that had once for all been stamped upon it through the vision in Daniel."[75] Here Vos made "innate majesty" (which equates to Peck's "he is God") a vital element of the "son of man" designation and Daniel a necessary source for understanding the self-designation of Jesus. While the literary approach of each man was somewhat different, the commitment to revelation as the proper source for determining the meaning of "son of man," and the commitment to the concept of "periodicity," as Vos puts it, was common to both men, and the outcome was almost exactly the same.

Finally, Peck surveyed the remainder of "The Apocalypse," from the "seven churches" (Rev. 2–3) to the gospel call (Rev. 22). His center was the church, the church through her earthly labors culminating in her final state

---

72. Ibid.
73. Ibid., 2:169.
74. Ibid., 2:167.
75. Geerhardus Vos, *The Self-Disclosure of Jesus*, ed. Johannes G. Vos, 2nd edition (1953; repr., Phillipsburg, NJ: P&R, 2002), 237.

of "safety and comfort," "and of the greatest splendor and glory."[76] Thus, with Jones and Robinson, Peck is an example of the Southern Presbyterian commitment to a biblical theology grounded in divine revelation in its historical *milieu*, unfolding in successive-cumulative covenants, with God and his people, the church, as the focal principle.

CONCLUSION

Any time one writes about biblical scholarship from bygone days, there is the tendency to read it as simply "history." This tends to happen especially when the bygone scholarship is anti-critical; the mind seems to go into an avoidance or denial mode when offered information from anti-critical scholars. The Southern Presbyterians represented herein were not disposed to the critical approach to Holy Scripture that so character-ized biblical scholarship in the nineteenth century. Robinson, Jones, Peck, and numerous others, like their contemporaries at old Princeton, were all committed to the Bible as the authoritative, infallible, and inspired word of God and were committed to a confessional orthodoxy as set forth in the Westminster Confession Faith. For these two reasons, Presbyterian students, ministers, and scholars ought to be interested in the old perspective on biblical theology practiced by the Southern Presbyterians.

In addition to the old perspective's commitment to the sole authority and unique inspiration of Holy Scripture and confessional orthodoxy, it has been shown that successive generations have found much agreement with the perspective of the old Southern Presbyterians. Vos acknowledged the vital "principle of successive *Berith*-makings (Covenant-makings), as marking the introduction of new periods." This principle of "periodicity" was overtly applied by Robinson when Vos was a precocious five-year old. The "covenantal-cumulative" principle which Palmer Robertson plied so ably in *The Christ of the Covenants* was consistently utilized in the exegeti-cal-theological work of both Jones and Robinson,[77] but one hundred years

---

76. Peck, *Miscellanies*, 2:200.

77. I want to take this opportunity to refer readers to a sermon preached by the man we happily honor in this collection of celebratory essays. In "The Covenant of Law," January 5, 2004, http://www.sermonaudio.com/sermoninfo.asp?SID=12604192942, Dr. Robertson acknowledged both what I call the "cumulative-covenant" principle—the continual expan-sion of doctrinal content with each successive berith-making—and his indebtedness to C. C. Jones when he said, "We could go even further into this to show that the law is present

earlier. Finally, the old perspective on biblical theology found the church a vitally important part of its schema.

With their commitment to the Holy Scriptures and confessional orthodoxy, their adroit anticipation of so much of what made Reformed biblical theology special in the twentieth century, and their high esteem for the church—the bride of Christ, the pillar and buttress of truth—the old perspective laid a strong foundation for those who followed. It is always good to reexamine your foundation from time to time; and this old perspective of the Southern Presbyterians—revelation-covenant-church—is worthy of further consideration and utilization, especially in a day of non-absolutes, covenantal nomism, and rampant individualism.

---

in the period preceding Moses, but [I] simply refer you to a good, old Southern Presbyterian whose volume has been long forgotten, dusty on the shelf, C. C. Jones, *The History of the Church of God* . . . . C. C. Jones shows very effectively that each one of the Ten Commandments has various manifestations in all the periods preceding Moses." I wish to thank one of my diligent students, Nick Batzig, for locating this sermon and the reference to Jones.

2

Christ in the Psalms

BRUCE K. WALTKE

IN ONE OF JESUS' post-resurrection appearances to his disciples, he said to them, "This [my resurrection] is what I told you while I was still with you: Everything must be fulfilled that is written about me in the Law of Moses, the Prophets and the Psalms" (Luke 24:44). Although he had to open their minds so they could understand the Scriptures that Messiah will suffer and rise from the dead (24:45), he earlier rebuked the men on the Emmaus road: "How foolish you are, and how slow of heart to believe all that the prophets have spoken! Did not the Christ have to suffer these things and then enter his glory" (24:25–26)? In other words, the supernatural opening of their minds did not contradict the plain teaching of the Law, the Prophets, and the Psalms. This paper argues that the accredited grammatico-historical method of interpretation of the Psalms leads readers who are not hard-hearted to the gospel of Jesus Christ.

I will develop my argument in three steps. First, arguing as an exegetical theologian, and leaning heavily on John Eaton,[1] I mount evidence beyond reasonable doubt for an extensive royal interpretation of the Psalms. By

---

1. John Eaton, *Kingship and the Psalms* (Naperville, IL: Alec R. Allenson, 1976), 20–26.

"royal" I mean that prominent figure in the Psalms, often the speaker or the object of petition and praise, is David and his sons who are the heirs of the covenant God made with the David.

Second, I develop as a biblical theologian the unfolding concept of Messiah, beginning with David and ending with the gospel of Jesus Christ. In the course of that study I aim to show the role of the Psalter in developing the doctrine of Messianism and its relationship to the gospel of Jesus Christ.

Third, mostly following Gerald Wilson, I argue that in the Second Temple period, the editors of the Psalter fashioned it with reference to Messiah.

Finally, in conclusion, following Delitzsch, I will note the four ways in which the Psalms speak of Jesus Christ.

AN EXTENSIVE ROYAL INTERPRETATION OF THE PSALTER

Although the "I" in post-monarchic psalms (e.g., Ps. 137) refers to an anonymous leader or personifies Israel, the "I" of many pre-exilic psalms is the king; and if so, why not David? The following arguments support the thesis that most psalms—perhaps all the pre-exilic psalms—refer to the house of David, and if so, refer at least indirectly refer to Jesus Christ as member of that house.

First, the superscripts of seventy-three psalms name David as their author, and two other psalms are ascribed to Solomon (72, 127).[2] The *lamedh* in the phrase *ldwd* signifies authorship, as in many Semitic languages.[3] This is clearly its meaning in Isaiah 39:9, Habakkuk 3:1, and Psalm 18 (cf. 2 Sam. 22:1). In sum, half of the psalms identify the speaker as the king from the house of David.

Second, even psalms by the sons of Korah (cf. Pss. 44, 84) and by Ethan (cf. Ps. 89) pertain to the king. We will return to Psalm 44 below. While Psalm 84 is a pilgrimage psalm, upon the pilgrim's arrival at Jerusalem, he prays for the king:[4]

2. In Book I:3–41 (except 33; Psalm 10 is part of Psalm 9); Book II (51–65, 68–71; Psalm 71 is part of Psalm 70). Book III (86); Book IV (101, 103); Book V (108–10, 122, 124, 131, 133, 138–45).

3. *Gesenius' Hebrew Grammar*, ed. E. Kautzsch, trans. A. E. Cowley, 2nd English edition (Oxford: Clarendon, 1909), 419–20, §129c. Bruce K. Waltke and M. O'Connor, *Introduction to Biblical Hebrew Syntax* (Winona Lake, IN: Eisenbrauns, 1990), 206, § 11.2.l0d.

4. In chapter 2, the tetragrammaton is rendered as "I AM."

> Hear my prayer, I AM God Almighty;
>> listen to me, God of Jacob.
> Look on our shield, God;
>> look with favor on your anointed one. (Ps. 84:8–9 [9–10])

Psalm 89 is all about the Davidic covenant:

> Indeed, our shield belongs to I AM,
>> our king to the Holy One of Israel.
>
> Once you spoke in a vision,
>> to your faithful people you said:
> "I have bestowed strength on a warrior;
>> I have exalted a young man from among the people.
> I have found David my servant;
>> with my sacred oil I have anointed him.
> My hand will sustain him;
>> surely my arm will strengthen him.
> No enemy will subject him to tribute;
>> no wicked man will oppress him.
> I will crush his foes before him
>> and strike down his adversaries.
> My faithful love will be with him,
>> and through my name his horn will be exalted.
> I will set his hand over the sea,
>> his right hand over the rivers.
> He will call out to me, 'You are my Father,
>> my God, the Rock my Savior.'
> I will also appoint him my firstborn,
>> the most exalted of the kings of the earth.
> I will maintain my love to him forever,
>> and my covenant with him will never fail.
> I will establish his line forever,
>> his throne as long as the heavens endure.
>
> "If his sons forsake my law
>> and do not follow my statutes,
> if they violate my decrees
>> and fail to keep my commands,
> I will punish their sin with the rod,

their iniquity with flogging;
but I will not take my love from him,
    nor will I ever betray my faithfulness.
I will not violate my covenant
    or alter what my lips have uttered.
Once for all, I have sworn by my holiness—
    and I will not lie to David—
that his line will continue forever
    and his throne endure before me like the sun;
it will be established forever like the moon,
    the faithful witness in the sky." (Ps. 89:18–37 [19–38])

Third, temple music as a whole took its rise from the king (see 1 Chron. 15–16; 2 Chron. 29; Isa. 38:20). Moreover, throughout the ancient Near East the king took responsibility for worship. In Mesopotamia the petition psalms were royal.

Fourth, the subject's enemies are frequently nations. Psalm 20 draws to a conclusion with a prayer for the king as he goes forth to war:

"I AM, give victory to the king!
    Answer us when we call." (Ps. 20:9 [10])

Psalm 21 opens with the king rejoicing for the victory God gave him:

O I AM, the king rejoices in your strength.
    How great is his joy in the victories you give!
You have granted him the desire of his heart
    and have not withheld the request of his lips.
You welcomed him with rich blessings
    and placed a crown of pure gold on his head.
He asked you for life, and you gave it to him—
    length of days, for ever and ever.
Through the victories you gave, his glory is great;
    you have bestowed on him splendor and majesty. (Ps. 21:1–5 [2–6];
        see also Psalms 18:43 [44]; 28; 61; 63; 89; 144)

Fifth, the royal interpretation gives integrity to psalms that otherwise lack unity. For example, Psalm 4 hangs together when it is understood that the king is petitioning God for rain. In that light one can understand his accusation against the highborn men for tarnishing his glory as I AM's elect king by turning to pagan fertility deities—"How long, highborn men,[5] will you turn my glory into shame? How long will you love delusions and seek false gods" (Ps. 4:2 [3])? This situation explains his petition: "Fill my heart with joy when their [the many people] grain and new wine abound" (4:7 [8]).

Sixth, Eaton notes: "the only 'situation' that is certainly attested is that of the king; . . . he is the subject in a number of psalms, and the dispute is only about how many. This cannot be said of the other suggested usages."[6]

Seventh, the representative character of the king explains the special problem presented by the psalms where 'I' (i.e., the king) and 'we' (i.e., the people/army) alternate (cf. 44, 60, 66; 75; 102). Note the alternation [marked in bold] in Psalm 44:

> You are **my** King and my God,
>> who decrees victories for Jacob.
> Through you **we** push back our enemies;
>> through your name **we** trample our foes.
> **I** do not trust in my bow,
>> **my** sword does not bring me victory;
> but you give us victory over **our** enemies,
>> you put **our** adversaries to shame.
> In God **we** make our boast all day long,
>> and **we** will praise your name forever.
> But now you have rejected and humbled **us**;
>> you no longer go out with **our** armies. . . .
> You have made **us** a byword among the nations;
>> the peoples shake their heads at **us**.
> **My** disgrace is before **me** all day long,
>> and **my** face is covered with shame
> at the taunts of those who reproach and revile **me**. . . (Ps. 44:4–9 [5–10],
>> 14–16 [15–17])

Eighth, throughout the "psalms of the individual" there occur about twenty four motifs or expressions which are specifically appropriate for a king. Here we content ourselves with only five Gunkel[7] identified:

---

5. Heb. *bene 'ish* not *bene ha'adam* (see Pss. 49:2 [3]; 62:9 [10]).

6. J. H. Eaton, *Kingship and the Psalms* (Naperville, IL: Alec R. Allenson, 1976), 22.

7. H. Gunkel, *Einleitung in die Psalmendie Gattungen der religiösen Lyrik Israels* (Göttingen: Vandenhoeck and Ruprecht, 1933), 147f.

1. All Nations Attend to His Thanksgiving:

> Therefore I will praise you among the nations, I AM,
>> I will sing praises to your name
> He gives his king great victories;
>> he shows unfailing kindness to his anointed,
>> to David and his descendants forever.
>>> (Ps 18:49–50 [50–51]; cf. 57:9 [10]; 119:46)

2. His Deliverance Has Vast Repercussions:

> From you comes the theme of my praise in the great assembly;
>> before those who fear you will I fulfill my vows.
> The poor will eat and be satisfied;
>> they who seek I AM will praise him—
>> may your hearts live forever!
> All the ends of the earth
>> will remember and turn to the I AM,
> and all the families of the nations
>> will bow down before him,
> for dominion belongs to I AM
>> and he rules over the nations. (Ps. 22:25–28 [26–29])

3. He Invokes a World-Judgment to Rectify His Cause:

> Arise, I AM, in your anger;
>> rise up against the rage of my enemies.
>> Awake, my God; decree justice.
> Let the assembled peoples gather around you.
>> Rule over them from on high;
>> let the I AM judge the peoples.
> Judge me, I AM, according to my righteousness,
>> according to my integrity, O Most High. (Ps. 7:6–8 [7–9])

4. He Depicts Himself as Victorious over the Nations through God's Intervention:

> All the nations surrounded me,
>> but in the name of I AM I cut them off.
> They surrounded me on every side,
>> but in the name of I AM I cut them off. (Ps. 118:10–11)

31

5. He Is Like a Bull Raising Horns in Triumph

> You have exalted my horn like that of a wild ox;
>> fine oils have been poured upon me. (Ps. 92:10 [11])

In other words, the psalms are about the king, not about Mr. Everyman—that is to say, they are about the house of David. And if they are about the house of David, they are about Jesus Christ, who is the heir to David's throne. Matthew begins his gospel of Jesus Christ to establish this connection by tracing the lineage of Jesus back to David: "A record of the genealogy of Jesus Christ the son of David, the son of Abraham" (Matt. 1:1), and Matthew concludes his genealogy of Jesus by featuring David: "Thus there were fourteen generations in all from Abraham to David, fourteen from David to the exile to Babylon, and fourteen from the exile to the Christ" (Matt. 1:17).

MESSIANISM IN BIBLICAL THEOLOGY

Let us now interface this royal interpretation of the Psalter into the developing concept of Messiah (i.e., the Anointed). We begin with the term and then trace the development of the concept from the Davidic covenant into the New Testament.

The Term "Anoint" or "Anointed"

The term "Messiah" (Heb. *mashiah*) derives from the root *mashah*: "to paint, smear, sprinkle, daub" > "anoint" (Pss. 45:7; 89:20). The one "anointed" (*mashiah*, a passive participle of *mashah*) is designated and appointed publicly for divine status with divine authority (1 Sam. 10:1; 15:1, 17; 16:1–13; 2 Sam. 2:4, 7; 5:3, 17) and consecrated as God's property (Ex. 29:7; 40:9–11; Lev. 8:10–11; Num. 7:10–11), and this entails his invincibility and divine protection (1 Sam. 24:6–11; 26:9–24; Ps. 2:10–12; Ps. 105:15; Lev. 10:1–2) and his being qualified and equipped for the task by I AM's Spirit (1 Sam. 10:6; 16:13; Isa. 61:1–3). Those considered to be *meshiah Yhwh* ("anointed by I AM in the Old Testament included the patriarchs (Ps. 105:15 [1 Chron. 16:22]), priests (Lev. 4:3, 5, 16; Num. 3:3; Dan. 9:26), and especially the king (e.g. Saul [1 Sam. 24:6, 10], 26:16; 2 Sam. 1:14, 16]; David [2 Sam. 15:22; 23:1] and Zedekiah [Lam. 4:20]). Sometimes the king is called with reference to I AM "my anointed" (1 Sam. 2:35; Ps. 132:17); "your anointed" (Hab. 3:13; Pss. 84:10; 132:10; 2 Chron. 6:42 [2x]); and "his anointed" (1 Sam. 2:10; 12:3, 5; 16:6; 2 Sam. 22:51 [=Ps. 18:50 (51); Isa. 45:1; Pss. 2:2; 20:6 (7)]; 28:8), or the "anointed of the God of Jacob" (2 Sam. 23:1).

Other terms for I AM's ideal king or Messiah at the end of the ages are: 1) *hoter* "shoot" (Isa. 11:1); 2) *hotham* "signet ring" (Hag. 2:23); 3) *moshel* "ruler" (Mic. 5:2 [1]); 4) *tsemah tsadiq* "righteous shoot" (Jer. 23:5), "true shoot" Zech. 3:8; 6:12; and 5) *melek* "king" (Ezek. 37:22, 24).

Development of Concept of "Messiah" in the Old Testament

1. In the Davidic Covenant. The concept of an ideal king who will rule Israel in the eschaton is rooted in the Davidic covenant that promised David an eternal house, kingdom and throne (2 Sam. 7:16, see above). Israel's king is superhuman, a son of God, who represents I AM before the people. By divine anointing and the gift of the God's Spirit, the anointed king becomes a superhuman divine being filled with superhuman power and wisdom, but in the Old Testament he is not equated as one with God. Endowed with righteousness (i.e., with ability to rule), he defends the people and relieves the oppressed (Ps. 21:9–12); he is the people's source of strength and life (Lam. 4:20; 2 Sam. 21:7; Hos. 3:4; Ps. 72:6, 16). As a priest he is in corporate solidarity with the people and represents them before I AM. The concerns of the king are the people's concern; his sin infects the whole nation; he should bear Israel's religious and moral ideals and convey I AM's blessing on the people according to his obedience.

2. In the Prophets. Although the prophets did not use the term "the Messiah," they contributed significantly to the doctrine of a future king that would rule Israel and the world in the last days. For example, Isaiah saw a glorious future son of David ruling over Israel in contrast to corrupt Ahaz (ca. 735 B.C.). This coming king, born of a virgin, would be called "Immanuel" ("God with us," Isa. 7:14). His name would also be "Wonderful Counselor, Mighty God, Everlasting Father, Prince of Peace" (Isa. 9:6 [7]). Micah 5:2–6 announces the birth of the humble Messiah at inauspicious Bethlehem and his glorious reign. Commenting on Micah 5:4, I write:

The reigning Messiah will stand (i.e., endure forever; cf. Ps. 33:11) and shepherd his flock, providing for their every need, including spiritual food, and protecting them (Jn. 10; Heb. 13:20; 1 Pet. 5:4). Through faith he will rule "in the strength of the LORD," not through human engineering and manipulation (cf. 5:10–15). His subjects will live securely for, conquering Satan (Matt. 12:22–29; Rom. 16:20), he will extend his kingdom to the ends of the earth" (4:3–4; Matt. 28:18–20; John 17:2).[8]

Some have been troubled by God's judgment on Jehoiachin son of Jehoiakim. Regarding that king I AM swears, "even if you . . . were a signet ring [i.e., a representation of the owner] on my right hand I would still pull you off [i.e. revoke the Davidic covenant in your case]" (Jer. 22:24). As for Jehoiachin's children I AM prophecies, not swears, "Record this man as if childless, . . . for none of his offspring will sit on the throne of David or rule anymore in Judah," yet Jeconiah (i.e., Jehoiachin) is in the lineage of Jesus Christ (Jer. 22:30). I AM, in keeping with his character to change his prophecies according to the righteousness or unrighteousness of a person, graciously reversed this judgment.[9] He offered to make his servant Zerubbabel son of Shealtiel son of Jehoiachin his signet ring (Hag. 2:23), but this did not take place until Jesus (Matt. 1:12).

Isaiah prophesying to the exiles foresaw an anonymous suffering Servant who gives his life as an atonement for sin and after his resurrection assumes his glorious throne (42:1–7; 49:1–6; 50:4–11; 52:13–53:12). God says of him in 52:13, "See my servant will act wisely; he will be raised and [then] lifted up and [then] highly exalted." Since the rest of the oracle features his atoning death—I AM makes his life a guilt offering (53:10)—"he will be raised" must refer to his resurrection from the dead. His resurrection is then followed by his ascension ("lifted up") and glorification ("highly exalted"). This is explicitly stated in the rest of vv. 10b–11: "he will see his offspring and prolong his days. . . . After the suffering of his soul, he will see the light of life." In other words, Messiah must first die a vicarious death bearing the iniquities of Israel and then be raised from the dead to his glory.

8. Bruce K. Waltke, *An Old Testament Theology: An Exegetical, Thematic and Canonical Approach* (Grand Rapids: Zondervan, 2007), 888.

9. See Richard L. Pratt Jr., "Historical Contingencies and Biblical Predictions," in *The Way of Wisdom: Essays in Honor of Bruce K. Waltke*, ed. J. I. Packer and S. K. Soderlund (Grand Rapids: Zondervan, 2000), 180–203.

3. In the Psalms. First, the concept of Messiah was also augmented in the royal ideology of the Psalter. The Psalter's royal ideal was not due to the *Hofstil* of the ancient Near East, as Gunkel claimed, but Israel's genuine hope applied to reigning kings. The Psalms represented the king visually and *ideally* to the people and were always pregnant with Messianic expectations. Some royal psalms contain ideals that surpass historical reality and give birth to the Messianic expectation: the "anointed" rules to the ends of the earth (Ps. 2:7–8) and as long as the sun and moon endures (Ps. 72:5). David salutes this king who is his sovereign and who sits at God's right hand as his lord (Ps. 110:1). On the other hand, some royal psalms—such as the penitential psalms—contain elements that are less than ideal. This is so because discontinuity is a necessary dimension of typology for history to progress. Sacred history progressively rises from the less than ideal to the ideal. The outward, carnal forms of the Abrahamic and Davidic covenants had to fail to make way for the fulfillment of their inward, spiritual perfections.

Israel draped these magnificent royal psalms as robes on each successive king, but generation after generation the shoulders of the reigning monarch proved too small and the robe slipped off to be draped on his successor. Finally, in the exile, Israel was left without a king holding a wardrobe of royal robes in their hymnody. On the basis of I AM's unconditional covenants to Abraham and David, faithful Israel knows that Israel's history ends in triumph, not in tragedy. The prophets, as noted, envisioned a coming king that would fulfill the promise of these covenants.

Haggai and Zechariah, who prophesied in ca. 520 when the returnees had no king, fueled the prophetic expectation of the hoped for king by applying it to Zerubbabel, son of David, and to Joshua, the high priest. When this hope fell through, Israel pinned its hope on a future Messiah. It was in that context, when Israel had no king, the Psalter was edited with reference to the king. Accordingly, the editors of the Psalter must have resignified the psalms from the historical king and draped them on the shoulders of Messiah. Samuel Terrien, commenting on Psalm 21, agrees: "The theology of kingship and divine power had to be re-examined in the light of the historical events. Psalm 21 needed to be interpreted eschatologically. The Anointed One began to be viewed as the Messiah at the end of time."[10] In

---

10. Samuel Terrien, *The Psalms: Strophic Structure and Theological Commentary* (Grand Rapids: Eerdmans, 2003), 223.

short, in light of the exile and the loss of kingship, the entire Psalter was tinctured with a Messianic hue.

More specifically, in the petition psalms the Messiah must first suffer before he triumphs. In that light the true Jews at the advent of Jesus Christ should have anticipated from the "lament" motif of these psalms that Christ would first suffer before entering his glory depicted in both the praise motifs of these psalms and in the praise psalms. Satan understood Psalm 91, a psalm of confidence, as referring to Messiah and Jesus did not correct him. Moreover, the so-called enthronement psalms in Book IV must refer in the context of the Psalter's editing to Messiah. I AM reigns at the ends of the ages in Messiah, not apart from a human agent. In Book V exemplary David finds his fulfillment in Messiah.

Second, we can see the concept of "Messiah" in the editing of the Psalter. Gerald Wilson in his suggestive thesis on the editing of the Hebrew Psalter, has argued that certain royal psalms—in particular Psalms 2, 72, and 89—have been used as the editorial 'seams' of the first three books of Psalms. These, he argues, have shaped the understanding of these segments of the Psalter as an exilic response to the loss of the Davidic monarchy.[11] Let us look at this thesis more closely.

Books I and II (Psalms 1–72). With regard to Psalm 2, this coronation liturgy introduces the principal subject, the king in prayer. At the king's coronation he recites a poetic variation of a decree in the Davidic covenant (cf. 2 Sam. 7:14): "Ask of me my son, and I will give you the heathen for your inheritance and the ends of the earth for your possession" (Ps. 2:8). In the rest of the Psalter the reader hears the petitions and praises of David's heir.

With regard to Psalm 72, Wilson says: "The presence in 72:20 of the postscript announcing the conclusion of 'the prayers of David, son of Jesse' suggests Books One and Two may have combined to form an earlier collection introduced and concluded by 'Royal' psalms, a collection which because of its high Davidic content (60 of 70 psalms) might well justify the description 'prayers of David.' "[12] Within these books he notes a progression of thought. Psalm 2 introduces the idea of the Davidic covenant, Psalms 3 and 41 speak of the king's assurance of I AM's protection and security in the face of his enemies, and Psalm 72 contains multiple petitions for the

---

11. Gerald H. Wilson, "The Use of Royal Psalms at the 'Seams' of the Hebrew Psalter," *Journal for the Study of the Old Testament* 35 (1986) 85–94.

12. Ibid., 208.

king's son: "May he rule justly; may his domain be secure from his enemies; may he live long and be blessed." "So the covenant which YHWH made with David (Ps. 2) and in whose promises David rested secure (Ps. 41) is now passed on to his descendants in this series of petitions in behalf of thee king's son (Ps. 72)."[13]

Book III (Psalms 73–89). With Book III and its concluding hymn, Psalm 89, a new perspective is achieved. This is the dark book of the Psalter. The Davidic covenant is viewed as established in the dim past, and more importantly, it is considered as fractured: "At the conclusion of the third book, immediately preceding the break observed separating the earlier and later books, the impression left is one of a covenant remembered, but a covenant *failed*. The Davidic covenant introduced in Ps. 2 has come to nothing and the combination of three books concludes with the anguished cry of the Davidic descendants."[14] But there is hope!

Book IV (Psalms 90–106). With Book IV yet another perspective is achieved. Without a king, Israel falls back upon its heritage. They look back to Moses, who is now mentioned seven times (90:1; 99:6; 103:7; 105:26; 106:16; 23, 32), whereas heretofore he was mentioned only once (77:20 [21]). Moses' only song in the Psalter introduces Book IV. Moreover, Israel now looks back to their eternal king, I AM: "O God our help in ages past, our hope in years to come" (cf. 90:1–2). In Psalms 93–99 one finds the so-called Enthronement Psalms: I AM is king! He has been Israel's refuge in the past, long before monarchy existed; he will continue to be Israel's refuge now that monarchy is gone; and blessed are they that trust in him.

4. Book V (Psalms 107–150). Book V is clearly linked with Book IV. Ps 106:47 concludes Book IV with the prayer, "Save us, I AM our God, and gather us from the nations." Book V begins by viewing this act of gathering as an established fact: "he gathered us from the lands." The troubles of the Exile have been overcome. Two groups of Davidic collections are found in this book, 108–10; 138–45. The redactor intends to set up David as a model in response to the concerns of the psalms which precede them:

> Thus, in Psalms 108–110, David emerges as the 'wise man' (107:43) who 'gives heed' to the cautions of 107:39–42 and relies wholly on the steadfast love of YHWH. His willingness to sing the praise of YHWH 'among the

13. Ibid., 211.
14. Ibid., 213.

nations' (108:3) becomes a paradigm of action to be followed, whether by those yet in exile or among those vulnerable returnees surrounded by their foes. David knows that only reliance on YHWH is effective ... (108:12)....In like fashion to the first group of Davidic psalms, David serves as an example in Psalms 138–144 following the plaintive cry of the exiles expressed in the words of Psalm 137 which immediately precedes.[15]

Jamie Grant argues more convincingly that we see the return of the Davidic king in Psalms 101–3, as well as the strongly eschatological presentation of the Davidic monarch in Psalm 110, which is very reminiscent of Psalm 2. The last voice heard in the Psalter, prior to the doxology of Psalms 146–50, in Psalms 138–45, is also that of David.[16]

Moreover, there is a prominent Messianic hope in some of these Davidic psalms. In Psalm 110:1a David, using distinctively prophetic language,[17] foresees a King greater than himself: "I AM says (ne'um, in divine spirit speech) to my lord." Jesus pressed home the argument that Messiah is greater than David's son for David calls him "my lord" (Matt. 22:41–46). This King will be a warrior King-Priest after the order of Melchizedek. With himself at God's right hand (v. 1b) and God at his right hand (v. 5a), he and his army will crush rebellious kings and rule the earth (vv. 5b–7). In Psalm 118 Israel shouts to the King whom the builders rejected, but whom I AM made the capstone (vv. 22–23), "Blessed is he that comes in the name of I AM" (v. 26).

Messiah in Later Judaism

The terms *hammashiah* "the anointed" and *meshiha'* in Aramaic > *Christos* (Greek) for the eschatological king originates in later Jewish literature. The concept of the Messiah intensified in apocalyptic literature.[18] In the apocalyptic literature the righteous future kingdom of heaven under

15. Ibid., 221.

16. Jamie A. Grant, "The Psalms and the King," in *Interpreting the Psalms: Issues and Approaches,* ed. David Firth and Philip S. Johnston (Downers Grove, IL: IVP Academic, 2005), 108–9.

17. John Hilber, "Cultic Prophecy in the Psalms," *Beiheft zur Zeitschrift für alttestamentlich Wissenschaft* (Berlin: Walter de Gruyter), 352:76–88.

18. Daniel the man (ca. 550 B.C.); 1 Enoch (just before 161 B.C.); the Syriac Apocalypse of Baruch (after the destruction of Jerusalem in A.D. 70); Apocalypse of Abraham (some time after A.D. 70); 4 Ezra (= 2 Esdras) (ca. A.D. 100?). See Marinus de Jonge, "Messiah," in *Anchor Bible Dictionary*, ed. David Noel Freedman (New York: Doubleday), 4:785–86.

Messiah is seen as imminently breaking into the evil kingdoms of earth. Here the Messiah becomes strikingly profiled as Israel's coming king who ushers in the righteous kingdom of God at the end of the ages.

The central figure of 1 Enoch is "the Son of man" (cf. Dan. 7:9–14), referred to in 1 Enoch 46:1–3; the chosen One (cf. Isa. 42:1) or the Righteous One (38:2), and the "Anointed One" (52:6). This heavenly figure, who is regarded as having been with God from the beginning (48:3, 6) and remains in God's presence, reveals all things to the elect, is the judge of the world, and the champion of righteousness, who destroys the enemies of the righteous.

The Syriac Apocalypse of Baruch refers "my Anointed" (39:7; 40:1; 72:2), "my servant, the Anointed One" (70:9), and "the Anointed One" (29:3; 30:1) to a royal figure introducing a limited period of time of complete bliss and incorruptibility. "That time marks the end of what is corruptible and beginning of what in incorruptible" (74:2). The Messiah will reign over the remnant of God's people in the place God has chosen (40:2): "His kingdom will stand forever, until this work of corruption come an end and the time appointed are fulfilled" (40:3). When the Messiah's presence on earth has come to an end, he will return in glory, and general resurrection will follow.

In 4 Ezra (= 2 Esdras) the divine agent who finally ushers in after his death the new eon of incorruptibility, bringing with it resurrection and judgment (7:30–44), is called "my/the Anointed One." In another vision he is likened to a lion, "The Anointed One whom the Most High has kept back to the end of days, who will spring from the seed of David."

Other Second Temple Jewish literature from 200 B.C.–A.D. 100, although preoccupied with the priesthood, also makes its contribution to a royal Messiah.[19] Ben-Sirach is clearly interested in God's promises concerning the (high) priesthood in the line of Aaron. He does not neglect God's promises to David, but they do not seem to be relevant. The book of 1 Maccabees was written to legitimize the Hazmonean's leadership in cultic and political matters as high priests and princes. The Jews and their priests make Simon their leader (*hegoumenos*) and high priest forever (vv. 14:35, 41; vv 42 47), and "commander" (*strategos*) and v. 47 "ethnarch." This arrangement will last "until a trustworthy prophet

19. Ibid., 4:781–83.

should arise" (v. 41). The book of 2 Maccabees features the intrigues to replace Onias, son of Simon, and his murder. He is clearly thought to be with God in heaven.

The Book of Jubilees features Jacob's blessings of Levi and Judah in 31:13–17 and 18–20 respectively. These passages emphasize the functions to be exercised by the two patriarchs and their descendants on behalf of Israel. Of Judah it is said: "A prince shall you be, you and one of your sons." Not only the patriarch and tribe are in view but also David and/or a future ideal Davidic king.

The extant "Testaments of the Twelve Patriarchs" achieved its final shape in the hands of Christians; isolating the earlier traditions upon which it is based remains a hazardous undertaking. The Testaments in their present form are interested in the juxtaposition of Levi and Judah and of the priesthood and of kingship, but the former is superior to the latter. Levi's descendants are, however, singled out as sinners against Jesus Christ (T. Levi 4:4; chaps. 10, 14–15 and 16). In 5:2 Levi's priesthood will be limited to the period before God's decisive intervention in the history of Israel. Whenever the Testaments mention an agent of the divine deliverance in connection with these two tribes or with one of them, they mean Jesus.

The Qumran community represented in the writings that were discovered in the caves at Qumran was a priestly sect led by Zadokite priests. Under the leadership of their "Teacher of Righteousness" they separated from the Jerusalem temple and the Hasmonean priesthood officiating there. The people at Qumran looked forward to the time when the meaning of the Law would be fully clear and when God's catechism would be obeyed completely. Then a duly appointed high priest and a Davidic prince would discharge their respective functions properly. As may be expected from a priestly community, of these two the future high priest is the most important figure. When God brings about this decisive turn of events, the final battle against the demonic forces and human enemies would be won.

The authors of the *Psalms of Solomon*, which were written about 50–40 B.C., were clearly opposed to the Hasmoneans, who had not discharged their priestly duties properly and had usurped the high priesthood (8:11) as well as royal authority (17:5–6). They anticipate God's deliverance from a Davidic king (e.g. Pss. Sol. 17:21): "Behold, Lord, rule over Israel your servant." This king will rule as God's representative forever and ever and will free Israel from its enemies, the people in the dispersion will return, and the nations will serve God. The king will serve the Lord as the ideal pious, obedient, and wise man. In 17:32 and 18:5, 7 he is called "The Anointed" and in 18:7 "the anointed of the LORD." The "anointed of the LORD" has become a fixed expression denoting the Davidic king appointed by God to bring about a turn in the fate of Israel.

The Messiah and the New Testament

Jesus of Nazareth and his apostles identified the Lord Jesus as the Messiah, combining in his one person the future prophet, priest and king. He is the king worthy to wear the Psalter's royal robes. With his death, resurrection, and ascension the temple and its priesthood cease, but he is now exalted on David's throne at God's right hand. This is the true throne of which David's throne in Jerusalem heretofore was only a shadow. Jesus is a priest-king after the order of Melchizedek and the prophet to come like Moses. In fact, he is greater than Moses because Jesus is identified with I AM himself.

The New Testament regards David and Israel, including the priesthood, the representatives of the kingdom of God under the old covenant, as types of Christ and his church, the quintessential representatives of the kingdom under the new covenant arrangements. Of the 283 direct quotes from the Old Testament in the New Testament 116 (41 percent) are from the Psalter. Jesus Christ alluded to the Psalms over 50 times (see Luke 24:44). The New Testament introduces a realized eschatology, an already and a not yet. The Messianic expectation is *fulfilled* in Jesus Christ and his church (cf. Matt. 28:18–20; John 17:2) and *will be consummated* after his parousia (second coming) and the resurrection of his saints in the new heaven and the new earth (cf. 1 Cor. 15:23–28). The sufferings of the Christ at his first advent are clearly distinguished from his glory to follow his resurrection and ascension at his second advent.

The specific predictions of some psalms that find their fulfillment in Jesus Christ combined with the use of the Psalter in the New Testament suggest that the entire Psalter pertains to Jesus Christ and his church.

Christ and his apostles, however, radically transform the notion of Messiah from a superhuman human figure to one who is united with God from eternity past to eternity future. He is the one-of-a-kind Son of God. He fulfilled Israel's expectations and exceeded them by as much as the heavens

41

are higher than the earth.[20] Moreover, he did not come to satisfy Israel's cravings for a national, political, and even military Jewish restoration, but to radically transform the spiritual temper of the nation by repentance from confidence in both their corrupt priesthood and temple and also their self-righteousness, to trust in him. The people's concept of Messiah differed so radically from Jesus' understanding that the title "Messiah" is the one Jesus used *least*, preferring instead the title "Son of Man." Christopher J. H. Wright explains:

> The term "Messiah" had become so loaded with the hopes of a national, political and even military, Jewish restoration that it could not carry the understanding of messiahship which Jesus had derived from a deeper reading of his scriptures. A public proclamation of his own messiahship would have been "heard" by his contemporaries with a load of associations that were not part of Jesus' concept of his mission.[21]

The New Testament cites explicitly psalms[22] in which Jesus fulfills David's sufferings (cf. 2:1 with Acts 4:25–26; Ps. 6:3 [4] with John 12:27; Ps. 22:2 with Matt. 27:46; Ps. 22:18 with John 19:24; Ps. 31:5 [6] with Luke 23:46; Ps. 34:20 with John 19:36; Ps. 35:19 with John 15:25; 40:6 with Heb. 10:5–10; Ps. 41:9 [10] with John 13:18; Ps. 41:9 with John 13:18; 42:6 with Matt. 26:38; Ps. 69:22 with Matt. 27:34,48; Ps. 109:25 with Matt. 27:39; Ps. 109:8 with Acts 1:20).[23]

The anointed's *fervor* (Ps. 69:9) typifies the Anointed's (John 2:17). The *authoritative teaching* of the psalmist presages the authoritative teaching of Jesus Christ (cf. Ps. 37:11 with Matt. 5:5; Ps. 48:2 with Matt. 5:36; Ps. 78:2 with Matt. 13:35; Ps. 78:24 with John 6:31; Ps. 82:6 with John 10:34). The *glory* of the anointed king in the Old Testament becomes the glory of the Anointed King in the New Testament (cf. Ps. 2:6 [7] with Acts 4:25–28; Ps. 8: with Heb. 2:5–10 and 1 Cor. 15:27; Ps. 16:9 with

---

20. Frank Thielman, *Theology of the New Testament* (Grand Rapids: Zondervan, 2005), 150–62, 182–84.

21. Christopher J. H. Wright, *Knowing Jesus through the Old Testament* (Downers Grove, IL: InterVaristy, 1992), 145.

22. In the discussion that follows I cite references of David in lower case and to Messiah in upper case.

23. For a helpful discussion of Jesus's rejection by the Jewish leaders see Thielman, *Theology of the New Testament*, 185–96, but Thielman fails to distinguish sharply enough between the Jewish leaders and the Jewish people. Many of the latter, especially in Galilee, believed in him.

Acts 2:25–31; Ps. 18:49 [50] with Rom. 15:9; Ps. 22:22 [23] with Heb. 2:10–12; Ps. 45:6[7] with Heb. 1:8–9; 110:1 with Matt. 22:44; 110:3 with Heb. 1:5; 5:5; 118:22–23 with Matt. 21:42.

KINDS OF MESSIANIC PSALMS: HOW THE NEW TESTAMENT USES THE PSALTER

Indirect and Typical

Some of the psalms cited above are so indirectly typical that the New Testament use of them strongly suggests that all the psalms are a type of Christ. For example, select psalms that indirectly speak of Christ are: "my soul is troubled" (Ps. 6:3 [4]), "into your hands I commit my spirit" (31:5 [6]), "they hated me without reason" (35:19), and "my soul is downcast" (42:6). Derek Kidner says: "But a closer look at the way these psalms are handled will suggest that they are regarded as samples of a much larger corpus. It would scarcely seem too much to infer from this treatment that wherever David or the Davidic king appears in the Psalter . . . , he foreshadows to some degree the Messiah."[24] Of course, the anti-type must be greater than the type in order for history to advance. Whereas the psalmist, the type, confesses his sins, the anti-type is without sin. Moreover, whereas the type is the son of God as the heir of the Davidic covenant (cf. John 1:49), Christ is additionally the Son of God by virgin birth (Luke 1:34–35) and by his pre-incarnate glory with the Father (John 17). In Psalm 2:6 on the historical horizon "son" is a type in lower case, but on the prophetic horizon "Son" is uppercase.

Typico-Prophetic

David's sufferings and glory typifies Jesus Christ, but sometimes his language transcends his own experience and finds its fulfillment in Jesus Christ (e.g. Psalms 2, 22). Select psalms that are clearly predictive are: "they divided my garments among them and cast lots for my clothing" (22:18); "he protects all of his bones, not one of them will be broken" (34:20).

24. Derek Kidner, *Psalms 1–72*. Tyndale Old Testament Commentary (London: InterVarsity, 1973), 23–24.

Unfortunately, under the impact of historical criticism, academics restrict the prophetic gift and often undermine the New Testament. For example, Peter, following the Septuagint, interprets Ps. 16:10b to mean, "you will not let your Holy One see decay." On this basis he argues that since David's body decayed, David was a prophet and predicted the resurrection of the Christ, who "was not abandoned to the grave, nor did his body see corruption" (Acts 2:24–32). The New Revised Standard Version, however, undermines Peter by rendering the 16:10b "or let your faithful one see the Pit" (Heb. *shahath*). BDB[25] allows "pit" as the only meaning of *shahath* and *HALOT*[26] invests it with this meaning in Ps. 16:10b. The evidence, however, does not sustain their interpretation.

According to G. E. Whitney,[27] Reinke's defense of *shahath* meaning "decay" is even more thorough than that given by P. A. Vaccari.[28] Building on their studies, I argued in 1993 as follows:

> The noun shahath occurs 25x in the Old Testament, always in poetry. It can be derived from the verb shwh "to sink down" or from the verb shahath "to go to ruin." Nouns of the pattern shahath derived from II waw roots (e.g., shuah) are feminine (i.e., final t is the feminine suffix); nouns derived from the latter kind of verb are masculine (i.e, the t is part of the root). As a result homonyms, a masculine and a feminine forms, are possible. Nahath (feminine.),[29] a derivative from nuah, means "quietness/rest," but nahath (masculine)30 from nahath means "descent/descending." All the ancient versions understood shahath as a homonym.[31]

None denies *shahath* sometimes means "pit," but the Septuagint and Vulgate understood it to mean "corruption" in Psalms 9:16; 29 [30]:10; 34

25. F. Brown, S. R. Driver, and C. A. Briggs, *A Hebrew and English Lexicon of the Old Testament* (Oxford: Clarendon, 1907), 1001.

26. L. Koehler and W. Baumgartner, *The Hebrew and Aramaic Lexicon of the Old Testament*, trans. and ed. under supervision of M. E. J. Richarson, 4 vols. (Leiden: Brill, 1994–99), 1473.

27. G. E. Whitney, "Survey of the History of the Interpretation of Prophecy: How Interpreters Deal with Peter's Use of Psalm 16 in Acts 2," *Evangelical Theological Society* (Eastern Regional Conference, April 3, 1987, Myerstown, PA), 15.

28. P. A. Vaccari, "Salmo 16" and "Il Salmo della Risurrezione," *La Redenzione* (Rome, 1934), 165–90.

29. Brown, Driver, and Briggs, *A Hebrew English Lexicon*, 629.

30. Ibid., 639.

31. Bruce K. Waltke, "Psalms; Theology of," in *New International Dictionary of Old Testament Theology and Exegesis*, ed. Willem A. Van Gemeren (Grand Rapids: Zondervan, 1993), 4:1113.

[35]:7; 48 [49]:10; 54 [55]:24; 102 [103]:4. Symmachus so understood it in Psalms 35:7; 55:24; Aquila in Psalms 7:16; 30:10; Theodotion in Job 33:22, 30. In addition to the Septuagint, Jerome and Syriac understood it this way in Psalm 16:10. M. Pope, seemingly unaware of *shahath* (masc.), recognizes that it must mean "filth" in Job 5:31 and tries to explain it as due to the netherworld's putrescent nature.[32]

A clear example, however, of masculine *shahath* is found in Job 17:14: "If I say to . . . *shahath* 'You are my father,' and to the worm (*rimmah* [feminine collective for 'worms']), 'My mother' or 'My sister' " (NRSV). Karl Brugmann showed at the end of the nineteenth century that grammatical gender guided the poetic imagination in personification.[33] "Worm" (*rimmah*) is feminine, hence its personification by "mother" and "sister." We may confidently infer, therefore, that *shahath* personified as "father" is the masculine form, "decay/corruption."

Moreover, it can be established that the masculine form, "corruption," not the feminine form, "pit," is in view is Ps. 16:10 by the verb "to see" (*lir'oth*), which may express figuratively the ideas of "experiencing," "enduring," "proving" and the like, and takes for its object a noun indicative of *state* of the soul or of the body: e.g. "to see death" (Ps. 89:48 [49]), "to see trouble/evil" (Ps. 90:15), "to see sorrow" (Jer. 20:18), "to see famine" (Jer. 5:12), "to see affliction" (Lam. 3:1). On the contrary, when indicating the idea of *place* (e.g. pit, grave, *sheol*, gates of death, etc.), the Hebrew authors use a verb of motion; e.g. "to come" (Job 5:26), "to go" (Isa. 38:10; Eccl. 9:10), "to draw near" (Ps. 88:3 [4]; 107:18), "to descend" (Job 21:13), "to fall" (Pss. 7:15 [16]; 57:6 [7]). The expression "to go down to the pit" occurs four times in the Psalter and nine times in Ezekiel (cf. Isa. 38:18; Prov. 1:12). In this case, the ancient versions, not modern lexicographers, have the better of the argument, and so does the New Testament.

Prophetic

David predicts the reign of his Greater Son. Psalm 110 (see Matt. 22:41–46) envisions him as seated at God's right hand. Ehrlich argues:

---

32. M. Pope, *Job: Introduction, Translation and Notes*, The Anchor Bible (Garden City, NY: Doubleday, 1973), 75.

33. See Waltke and O'Connor, *Introduction to Biblical Hebrew Syntax*, 100, §6.3.1e.

"from the OT point of view it was wholly unthinkable, even in metaphor, to describe a mortal as seated on Yahweh's right hand."[34]

Enthronement (Psalms 93–99) and Other Psalms

These psalms, celebrating I AM's coming universal, righteous kingdom find their fulfillment in the church and their consummation in the coming reign of Jesus Christ in the new heaven and the new earth. The specific predictions of some psalms that find their fulfillment in Jesus Christ, combined with the use of the Psalter in the New Testament, suggest that the entire Psalter pertains to Jesus Christ and his church. The New Testament identifies the everlasting Creator with Jesus Christ (cf. Ps. 102:25–27 [26–28] with Heb. 1:10–12). The apostles did not hesitate to use the Psalter with reference to today (cf. Ps. 34:12–16 with 1 Peter 3:10–12; Ps. 55:22 [23] with 1 Peter 5:7; Ps. 90:4 with 2 Peter 3:8; Ps. 4:4 [5] with Eph. 4:26; Ps. 112:9 with 2 Cor. 9:9; Ps. 116:10 with 2 Cor. 4:13; Ps. 24:1 with 1 Cor. 10:26; Ps. 146:6 with Acts 4:24).

---

34. A. B. Ehrlich, *Die Psalmen: neu uebersetzt und erklaert* (Berlin: M. Poppelauer, 1905), 278. Author's translation.

3

On Reading Ecclesiastes

BENJAMIN SHAW

READING A BOOK may be an easy task, or it may be very difficult. Most fiction, for example, is easy to read. It follows a straight historical narrative sequence, starting at the beginning and developing the story through to the end. If the reader is forced to stop for a time and pick up the book again later, he can usually reorient himself to the place in the story. However, some fiction is more difficult to read. The novels of William Faulkner, for example, have a stream-of-consciousness narrative with fragmented and multiple perspectives. This manner of story-telling is more demanding for the reader, who must work harder to put the pieces of the story together. The level of difficulty for the reader can thus vary not only from author to author, but also from reader to reader. The beginning reader would be hard put to make any sense out of one of Faulkner's novels, while the advanced reader might find Faulkner a much easier read.

This same diversity of reading difficulty is found in the books of the Bible. The narratives of Genesis or 1 Samuel, for example, present the reader with straightforward story-telling. While the reader may miss some details of the story, or lack a familiarity with certain ancient practices, he will generally get the point of the account. This is not the case with Ecclesiastes. Even most scholarly readers struggle with this book, unclear about how the various parts of it fit together, and what the overall message of the book is. There are four considerations however, that if properly understood can make the task of reading Ecclesiastes more profitable even for the lay reader. These considerations are the structure of the book, the key terms and themes of the book, the larger Old Testament context of the book, and the New Testament context of the book.

THE STRUCTURE OF ECCLESIASTES

Linear Structure

For the most part Western readers are used to a linear structure in the books they read. That is, most books follow the general structure of a novel. The movement is along a straight line, building through the course of the book until the conclusion, which wraps everything up. This is the case not only for novels, but for histories as well. It is also the usual sort of structure for other types of non-fiction. That is, the goal is presented to the reader at the beginning. The author then adds arguments to one another until, at least to his satisfaction, he has demonstrated the truth of what he intended to prove. At that point he makes his conclusion, perhaps summarizing his arguments as he presses his point upon the reader. In modern books, such devices as a table of contents, chapter headings, and subdivisions within the chapters outline this structure for the reader. For older books, such as the books of the Bible, the structure of the books must be teased out by paying attention to the details of the book itself. Thus the structure of the books of Samuel can easily be shown by noticing the changes in the content of the books, giving the following structure:

I. The rule of Samuel, judge and prophet (1 Sam. 1–8)

II. The appointment and rise of Saul as king (1 Sam. 9–14)

III. The decline of Saul and the rise of David (1 Sam. 15–17)

IV. Saul versus David (1 Sam. 18–31)

V. David's move from king of Judah to king of all Israel (2 Sam. 1–5)

VI. The consolidation of David's reign (2 Sam. 6–10)

VII. The dissolution of David's reign (2 Sam. 11–24)

The two books present a straightforward historical narrative that takes the reader from the period of the judges to the end of David's reign.

Since many books of the Bible also follow such a linear structure, the tendency for the reader is to assume that all the biblical books follow that sort of structure. However, when that assumption has been applied to the book of Ecclesiastes, the results have been less than impressive. In fact, one nineteenth-century commentator despairingly concluded, "All attempts to show, in the whole, not only oneness of spirit but also a genetic progress, an all-embracing plan, and an organic connection, have hitherto failed, and must fail."[1] Wright then goes on to specify twenty-three commentators who have been in essential agreement with Delitzsch. He then lists another dozen commentators who have attempted to delineate the structure of Ecclesiastes. There is little agreement among these authors, and none of the proposed outlines has resulted in any general agreement among scholars. At this point, one must face the question as to whether there is a structure to Ecclesiastes, and if so, of what sort is that structure.

Chiastic Structure

It must be recognized that, while linear structure is perhaps the most familiar, it is not the only way in which a book may be structured. In Old Testament literature one commonly finds another type of structure. It is found at the level of the individual verse, in longer passages, and in the outline of whole books. This type of structure is called *chiastic*, from the Greek letter *chi*, which looks like an X. It can be demonstrated in the following short form:

a   b

b'   a'

---

1. Franz Delitzsch, cited in Addison G. Wright, "The Riddle of the Sphinx: The Structure of the Book of Qoheleth," in *Reflecting with Solomon: Selected Studies on the Book of Ecclesiastes*, ed. Roy B. Zuck (Grand Rapids: Baker, 1994), 46.

If a line is drawn to connect the two a's, and another to connect the two b's, an X shape is the result, hence again the name *chiastic*. A concrete example can be helpful here. Psalm 90:7 reads, "For we are brought to an end by your anger; by your wrath we are dismayed." Note that the verse has essentially four elements: 1) "we are brought to an end," 2) "by your anger," 3) "by your wrath," and 4) "we are dismayed." Notice that the first and fourth elements are roughly parallel, as are the second and third elements. If the first element is labeled *a*, the fourth element is labeled *a'*, the second element is labeled *b*, and the third element is labeled *b'*, the result matches the chiastic structure shown above. This type of chiasm at the verse level is very frequent in the book of Psalms, though often the English versions do not reflect it.

Chiastic structures are not limited to four elements, nor are they limited to an even number of elements. For example, a chiastic structure of six elements would be a-b-c-c'-b'-a'. A structure of seven elements would be a-b-c-d-c'-b'-a'. The repeated elements are roughly parallel. Any non-repeated element (such as *d* in the second example) is found at the center of the chiasm, representing the point at which the two lines of the X cross. Usually this center element represents the main point of the argument.

As mentioned above, chiasm is not limited to single verses. It can be found at larger levels of text as well. The story of the Tower of Babel is familiar to most readers, though they are usually unaware that the story follows a chiastic pattern. This chiasm can be shown as follows:[2]

a—introduction: *all the earth* had one language (Gen. 11:1)

  b—people settle together in Shinar (11:2)

    c—the people resolve to build (11:3–4)

      d—Center: Yahweh comes down (11:5)

    c'—Yahweh resolves to stop the building (11:6–7)

  b'—Yahweh scatters the people (11:8)

a'—conclusion: *all the earth* has many languages (11:9)

2. See David Dorsey, *The Literary Structure of the Old Testament: A Commentary on Genesis-Malachi* (Grand Rapids: Baker, 1999), 53.

Here the structure indicates that the focus is on Yahweh and his action, rather than the intended actions of the people. Nothing really happens in the story until Yahweh acts.

Another example of chiastic structure, this time at the book level, is the book of Isaiah. Isaiah is another Old Testament book that has proven difficult to outline, and many readers attempting to read through the book find themselves lost. The proposed outline of the book from the commentator E. J. Young runs some twenty-one pages. It is not easy to follow and is no real help for the reader in dealing with the book. But if the reader considers the possibility of a chiastic structure, the development and interrelationships of the parts of the book fall into place, indicating a structure that is very helpful in reading the book. That structure is as follows:

a—Introductory messages of condemnation, pleading, and future restoration (1–12)

  b—Oracles to nations: the proud king of Babylon humiliated (13–27)

    c—Woes: Don't trust earthly powers (28–35)

      d—Center: Showing Yahweh's supremacy over earthly and divine powers (36–39)

    c'—Yahweh's supremacy over idols: Don't trust idols (40–48)

  b'—Servant messages: Humble servant of Yahweh exalted (49–54)

a'—Concluding messages of condemnation, pleading, and future restoration (55–66)

Notice how this outline makes good sense of the whole book, is easy to follow, and is easy to remember.[3]

Chiasm and Ecclesiastes

Given that chiasm is found in many places in the Old Testament, at all levels of text, and given that Ecclesiastes has not previously given up the secret of its organization to linear analyses, it makes sense to try a chiastic

---

3. Ibid., 234. I would recommend that the reader examine Dorsey's entire discussion of Isaiah (217–35), as he lays out there the details that support his analysis.

analysis of the book. Dorsey has done this with considerable success in making sense out of the book. His chiastic outline is as follows.[4]

Title: 1:1

a—The brevity of life considered (1:2–11)

    b—Wisdom's failure to make sense of life (1:12–2:26)

        c—Time and human inability to see the "big picture" (3:1–15)

            d—Center: fear God (3:16–6:12)

        c'—Time revisited, with practical advice (7:1–14)

    b'—Wisdom's failure revisited, with practical advice (7:15–10:19)

a'—Life's brevity reconsidered, with practical advice (10:20–12:8)

Conclusion: the main point of the book restated (12:9–14)

The reader should notice that the book alternates between long and short sections (a, a', c, and c' are all short, while b, b', and d are long). Recognizing this order to the book goes a long way in helping the reader make sense of it as he reads, and shows the general unity of purpose to the book, something that many commentators have doubted.

KEY TERMS AND THEMES OF THE BOOK

Vanity

The most obvious term in Ecclesiastes is "vanity." Since the word appears 38 times in the book (about once in every six verses), understanding what this word means is a major key to understanding the message of the book. The KJV and translations descending from it (ASV, RSV, ESV) use "vanity" to translate the Hebrew word *hebel*. However, since the spate of new translations began appearing in the 1960s, many different terms have been used. The Modern Language Bible (1959) used "futility." The Good News Bible used "useless." The NIV uses "meaningless." In part these words are an attempt to translate the Hebrew word, but it may also be that they intend to give some meaning to the English word "vanity," a word that is simply not in common use any more.

4. Ibid., 198.

Unfortunately, the modern renditions are not only no improvement on "vanity"; they are actually misleading, based more on a skeptical understanding of the teaching of the book than on the meaning of the Hebrew word.

The word *hebel*, when used concretely, means a puff of wind, or a breath of air. It is used this way in Isaiah 57:13 speaking of the idols being carried away by the wind, taken away by a breath (*hebel*). Most of its uses, however, are figurative, and in order to understand the figurative meaning, it is necessary to understand what a breath of air or a puff of wind indicates. Perhaps the most obvious meaning is that it refers to something that is temporary, short-lived, or evanescent. This is perhaps the most common sense in which Ecclesiastes uses the term. The emphasis throughout the book is that man's existence and all aspects of that existence are temporary. They do not last. That which is temporary has no permanence, so in a derived sense *hebel* can refer to something that is without weight or substance.

The modern tendency to use "meaningless" or "futile" for *hebel* is misdirected. It turns the book into a skeptic's textbook. This in turn has contributed to much misunderstanding of the book's message among modern evangelicals. Instead, as Cover notes, "Qoheleth deliberately chose a word with a calculated ambiguity; he skillfully employed it in a variety of contexts so that several associated meanings could be communicated without the use of synonyms."[5] This is another characteristic of Hebrew composition, the repetition of a key term used with different connotations throughout a section in order to tie the section together. Another place in which this can be seen is in Genesis 2–5, where the word "know" in both its verb and noun forms is used a number of times to emphasize the theme of knowledge in that section. English translations have recognized the importance of *hebel* in Ecclesiastes, and so have tried to find one English word that will be roughly suitable for all its uses in the book. "Vanity" probably works better than almost anything else, since it has roughly the same range of meanings as does *hebel*.

Under the Sun

This phrase is used almost thirty times in the book or roughly once in every seven verses. This frequency, as with *hebel*, indicates its importance to

---

5. "*Hebel* in Ecclesiastes" (ThM thesis, Dallas Theological Seminary, 1978), 76, cited in M. James Sawyer, "The Theology of Ecclesiastes," http://www.bible.org/page.php?page_id=1632 (accessed January 22, 2008).

the thought of the book. The point the author is making with his use of this phrase is the identification of his sphere of investigation. Many commentators have argued that Ecclesiastes has no understanding of an afterlife. This would certainly be unusual. All ancient Near Eastern cultures, so far as we can determine, had notions of an afterlife. In both Egypt and Mesopotamia this area of thought was quite developed. Though in the Old Testament the theology of the afterlife is not as explicit as some would wish, it is indeed present throughout. Ecclesiastes' vagueness about the afterlife is not due to a disbelief in it, but rather due to the fact that he has limited his investigation to life "under the sun," that is, the sphere of this present life, the life of the "here and now."

There are other terms important to the book as well. Such words as "profit," "labor," and "chasing the wind" all contribute to the focus on this life, showing its difficulties and frustrations. What the author finds as a result of his investigation is that this life is temporary. It is filled with frustration. It is filled with puzzles and paradoxes. Man's work has no permanence. What is certain is that God controls all things and works them for his own purposes, but man, because of his limitations, cannot figure out all that God is doing. One can more clearly see the significance of these conclusions when the book is considered in its larger Old Testament context.

THE LARGER OLD TESTAMENT CONTEXT

Wisdom Literature

Scholars generally class Ecclesiastes with Proverbs, Job, and some of the Psalms as "wisdom literature," a category of literature also found in Mesopotamian and Egyptian culture. Though there are thematic connections between the Old Testament and ancient Near Eastern (ANE) literature, the Old Testament wisdom literature is set apart by two primary considerations. First, the Old Testament literature is determinedly monotheistic, in stark contrast to the ANE wisdom material. Second, the gods in the ANE literature are at best marginally involved in the lives of men. This is contrary to what we find in the Old Testament, where even Ecclesiastes, often considered the most "secular" book in the Old Testament, affirms the active involvement of God in the everyday lives of men.

In the Old Testament itself, these three books are probably intended to be understood as complementary, as are the four gospels, or the parallel histories of Samuel-Kings and Chronicles. This can be seen through the clear thematic similarities of the three books, as well as by the fact that there are a number of rare Hebrew words (that is, they do not occur often in the Old Testament) that occur in Proverbs, Job, and Ecclesiastes, but rarely if ever outside of those books. Thus Ecclesiastes is not to be understood as teaching anything essentially contradictory to those things taught by Proverbs and Job, but may deal with issues from a different perspective. To begin with, Proverbs is generally understood (and rightly so) as a guide book for the young. This is clear from the opening verses of the book (1:1–7). But the occasional difficulties of the book make it clear that it is indeed instruction in understanding "the words of the wise and their riddles" (1:6). In short, Proverbs responds to Francis Schaeffer's question, "How should we then live?" with the answer, "This is how you should live."

Job is perhaps the most complex book in the Old Testament. As such it is a bit difficult to pin it down in a few sentences. But it would be fair to say that the message of Job is that God is God, man is not God, and the ways and purposes of God, albeit perfectly wise, are often inscrutable to man.

Ecclesiastes provides a balance to both Proverbs and to Job. With regard to Proverbs, it would be easy for the reader to reach the conclusion that "if I behave the way this book directs, I will live a blessed life." That is, in fact, how many modern readers view the book of Proverbs. They seem to think that each proverb is a promise and then become angry with God when things do not work out the way they expected. Ecclesiastes tells the reader of Proverbs, "That book tells you how to live. My book tells you what to expect from life." There will be injustice. There will be frustration. There will be oppression. There will be times when it all seems meaningless. But fear God, because he is the judge of all things, and the judge of all the earth will do right.

Job can leave the reader with the sense that he is in the hands of a capricious deity, from whom anything might be expected. Ecclesiastes comforts the reader of Job with the reminder that Job's case is an exceptional one. God gives man many pleasures in life, most often of the simple sort, such as the love and enjoyment of family and friends. Not only that, but God also keeps close accounts, and everything will be properly weighed and measured.

55

Ecclesiastes and Genesis[6]

Outside of the wisdom books, the most important source for Ecclesiastes is the opening chapters of Genesis (1–5). This appears in both obvious and subtle ways. For example, the mention of "your creator" (12:1) uses the verb *bara'*, which mostly occurs in Genesis and in Isaiah 40–66. The mention of man's returning to dust (3:20; 12:7) echoes Gen. 3:20. The word "toil" (Heb. *'amal*) which appears frequently in Ecclesiastes, does not occur in Genesis 3, but is very close in meaning to Genesis 3:17–19. It is laborious toil, toil characterized by difficulty and frustration, just as promised in the judgment pronounced on Adam. Even the noun "man" (Heb. *'adam*) occurs forty-nine times in Ecclesiastes, again, drawing the reader's attention to the book of Genesis.

Ecclesiastes also presses the fallenness of the present human state on the reader in more subtle ways. The statement in 7:29 that "God made man upright, but they have sought out many schemes" is a clear allusion to the Fall. The inability of human wisdom to accomplish a full understanding of all that transpires hints at the failure of man to succeed at what he attempted in eating the fruit of the tree of the knowledge of good and evil. The "tree was to be desired to make one wise" (Gen. 3:6), but man's wisdom and knowledge are limited both in their scope and in their ability, something that Ecclesiastes repeatedly makes clear.

Finally, it should be noted that the second son of Adam and Eve, Abel, shares much with the book of Ecclesiastes. His name is the noun *hebel*, which is the key term of Ecclesiastes. It may be suspected that, as Eve named Cain in hope that he was the promised seed of 3:15, so she named Abel in recognition of the fact that it was not so, and that they would know the vanity of life before their own death.

What Ecclesiastes sets before the reader is what he can expect from life in a fallen world. It has its sorrows, and it has its joys. It has its frustrations, and it has its successes. It is beyond man's comprehension, but all things are accounted for by God. This is sound advice for the unbeliever, who must be directed to fear God. It is also sound advice for the believer, who must be reminded that this world is not his final home.

---

6. See also Charles C. Forman, "Koheleth's Use of Genesis," *Journal of Semitic Studies* 5 (1960): 256–63. I came across this article rather late in my investigation. Some of my conclusions are similar to those of Forman, but they were reached independently.

New Testament Context

There are two particular New Testament passages that are helpful in understanding the message of Ecclesiastes (though more could be mentioned). The first is James 4:13–15. In this passage James reminds man that he is "a mist that appears for a little time and then vanishes." And because he is this impermanent creature, he must submit himself to the will of God in all things. This is an effective summary of the message of Ecclesiastes: man is a creature of time, subject to vanity (that is, he is here and then he is gone) who must remember that in all things he is subject to the will of God and accountable to the judgment of God.

The second New Testament passage for understanding Ecclesiastes is Romans 8:18–21. This passage reminds the believer that this life has a fair amount of suffering, but that it is not comparable to the glory to be revealed. Not only the human race, but the whole creation waits for that revelation. The present time is a time of futility, purposely brought about by God (because of man's disobedience) to direct his creation to await "the freedom of the glory of the children of God." The word translated "futility" in the ESV is the Greek word *mataiotēs*. It is the same word that the Septuagint uses to translate *hebel* in the book of Ecclesiastes. Thus Paul affirms that vanity characterizes this present life, that this vanity is brought about by the purposeful action of God, and that this vanity is designed to point the believer to that which is to come—the glorious revelation of the children of God. This is no more the view of an unbelieving skeptic than is the view of Ecclesiastes. In fact, the reader may consider Ecclesiastes to be an extended set of reflections on the truth set forth so succinctly by Paul.

CONCLUSION

The reader of Ecclesiastes needs to keep a number of things in mind as he reads the book. First, the seemingly negative evaluation on much of life found in the book is simply putting this life in its proper perspective. He should not expect more from this life than it is intended to give. Second, life is lived subject to the will of God and accountable to his judgment. Third, the Christian especially must remember that life in Christ does not deliver one from the vanities of this life. Those vanities serve to remind him that to die and be with Christ is far better; for the time being, however, a faithful life in this world is necessary.

Those readers who want further help in understanding Ecclesiastes would do well to consult Michael Eaton's commentary in the Tyndale Old Testament Commentaries,[7] as well as Derek Kidner's *A Time to Mourn, and a Time to Dance: Ecclesiastes and the Way of the World*, in The Bible Speaks Today series.[8]

7. Michael Eaton, *Ecclesiastes: An Introduction and Commentary*, Tyndale Old Testament Commentaries (Downers Grove, IL: InterVarsity, 1983).

8. Derek Kidner, *The Message of Ecclesiastes*, The Bible Speaks Today (Downers Grove, IL: InterVarsity, 1984).

PART 2

New Testament

Such at that period were the hermeneutics of England. Tyndale had set the example himself by explaining many of the words which might stop the reader. "The New Testament!" we may suppose some farmer saying, as he took up the book; "what Testament is that?"—"Christ," replied Tyndale in his prologue, "commanded his disciples before His death to publish all over the world *His last will*, which is to give all his goods unto all who repent and believe. He bequeaths them his righteousness to blot out their sins—His salvation to overcome their condemnation; and this is why that document is called the *Testament* of Jesus Christ."[1]

— J. H. MERLE D'AUBIGNE

1. J. H. Merle d'Aubigne, *The Reformation in England* (Edinburgh: Banner of Truth, 1977), 1:247–48.

4

"For Our Sakes Also": Christ in the Old Testament in the New Testament

RICHARD B. GAFFIN JR.

CHRIST IN ALL OF SCRIPTURE is a theme so all-encompassing and multifaceted that it has to be addressed from a great variety of angles.[1] Even when we narrow our attention to the place of Christ in the Old Testament, numerous approaches are still in order. The interest of this chapter is Christ in the Old Testament from the vantage point of the New, that is, Christ in the Old Testament as seen by Jesus during his earthly ministry and by the New Testament writers.

There are two basic ways to approach this topic. On the one hand is the New Testament use of the Old, the specific and varied ways in which Jesus and the New Testament writers quote, appeal to, and otherwise utilize the Old. On the other hand, to be distinguished from this actual usage, are New Testament statements, often of a more general sort, about the

---

1. Christ in all of Scripture, in the Old Testament in particular, has been a primary and pervasive theme, addressed so eloquently and with such edification over the years, in the preaching, teaching, and writing of Palmer Robertson. See the selected bibliography of his works in this volume.

Old Testament, whether as a whole or in part. Obviously, neither of these approaches excludes the other. In fact, they are complementary. Each informs the other and both need to be explored. To ignore or otherwise obscure either approach will undoubtedly result in a distorted understanding of the place and function of the Old Testament in the New.

Priority, however, belongs to the latter approach, to New Testament statements, especially overall generalizations, *about* the Old Testament. That is, instances of specific Old Testament usage are properly understood as one's understanding is controlled by the generalizations, rather than the sense of the generalizations being largely determined and perhaps unduly limited by conclusions drawn from considering instances of specific usage.

The situation here is akin, and materially not unrelated, to the fundamental distinction that B. B. Warfield, especially, highlighted and employed so incisively and effectively about a century ago in the debate over the inspiration of the Bible.[2] Warfield has permanently identified a basic issue we must confront in formulating a doctrine of Scripture, especially since the time of the Enlightenment with its increasingly widespread commitment to the autonomy of human reason in studying the Bible. Two approaches, mutually exclusive, are in conflict. The one approach, faithful to the Bible, begins with its explicit self-witness, the Bible's statements about itself, and develops the heart of the doctrine of Scripture from that self-witness. In the light of that doctrine, a doctrinal core intact and impervious to change other than by exegetical reconsideration of that self-witness, this approach then proceeds to deal with the so-called phenomena of Scripture, including whatever problems one encounters.

The other approach adopts the reverse procedure. It begins with the phenomena and problems and then proceeds to develop a doctrine of Scripture, to arrive at an overall assessment of what the Bible is. Accordingly, its self-witness is discounted and then inevitably, at least as it has so far worked out in practice, is in effect negated. The one approach begins with the divine authorship of Scripture and considers its humanity in that light. The other approach begins with the human authors, and the resulting assessment of that humanness becomes the controlling factor for understanding whatever divine aspects may be attributed to Scripture.

2. See esp. B. B. Warfield, "The Real Problem of Inspiration," *The Inspiration and Authority of the Bible* (Philadelphia: Presbyterian and Reformed, 1948), 131–241 [reprinted from *The Presbyterian and Reformed Review*, 4 (1893): 177–221], esp. 174–75, 201–8.

Similarly, then, in considering the Old Testament in the New, including Christ in the Old Testament according to the New, it is essential that the New Testament statements about the Old control one's understanding and that the numerous citations and other uses of the Old Testament throughout the New be understood in the light of those statements, together with the implications that follow from them, rather than reversing that procedure. This is a point that needs stressing because of a current tendency, animated often by the quite commendable concern that adequate due be given to the "humanity" of the Bible, to be occupied with the ways the Old is used by the various New Testament writers, especially the perceived similarity of their usage to contemporary non-Christian Jewish (Second Temple) hermeneutical methods. The result, in some instances perhaps unintended, is that the more general declarations about the Old in the New are neglected or at least do not exercise the control in understanding due them.

My interest in what follows here, then, is these overarching New Testament declarations. With limited space, I will deal with those passages and other lines of evidence that, it seems to me, are the most important. What is notable in them is the centrality of Christ.

Preliminary to examining these key texts, we may note that according to Romans 4:23, what Genesis 15:6 says about the righteousness God imputed to Abraham was "written . . . for our sakes also."[3] Christian readers of Romans, Paul says in effect, are among the intended addressees of the Genesis passage. Similarly, in 1 Corinthians 10:1–13 the events of Israel's wilderness generation in view, as they were recorded in the Pentateuch, "were written down for our instruction," for those "on whom the end of the ages has come" (v. 10), that is, for the new covenant people of God. These are but two instances that make explicit the well-known and sweeping assertion in 2 Timothy 3:16 that for the New Testament church, until Jesus returns, the entire Old Testament, as "breathed out by God," is "profitable for teaching, for reproof, for correction, and for training in righteousness . . . ."

Such passages, and others like them, prompt the following observations. The intent or design of the Old Testament expressed in these New Testament passages is ultimately that of God, as its primary author. That is to say, the varied intentions of Moses and the other Old Testament writers, along with those emerging with whatever subsequent traditioning process

---

3. The English Standard Version (ESV) will be cited throughout, unless, as here, I modify it.

may mark Old Testament documents in their final form, are certainly hermeneutically relevant, but they are hermeneutically subordinate. Specifically, their intention in writing does not exhaust the intention of what they wrote. What they wrote for their contemporaries is what, in the final analysis, God has written and so involves an intention that transcends theirs. In fact, at times that intention may even be beyond the writers' own comprehension as well as that of their original readers.

Further, this divine authorial intent of the Old Testament documents, just as it encompasses Christian readers in its purview, provides the proper sense of any Old Testament passage as addressed to its original recipients. The sense of an Old Testament passage is the same for both the original and subsequent old covenant readers as well as new covenant readers, no matter what may have been the understanding of the passage by old covenant readers (their "reader response") or even by its human author. The question before us, then, becomes this: what, according to the New Testament, are the scope and basic dimensions of this divine authorial intention of the Old Testament, largely considered? Several passages provide an answer to that question.

Luke 24:44–47

> Then he said to them, "These are my words that I spoke to you while I was still with you, that everything written about me in the Law of Moses and the Prophets and the Psalms must be fulfilled." Then he opened their minds to understand the Scriptures, and said to them, "Thus it is written, that the Christ should suffer and on the third day rise from the dead, and that repentance and forgiveness of sins should be proclaimed in his name to all nations, beginning from Jerusalem."

On the issues before us, probably no passage is more frequently cited or discussed than this, and with good reason, for none is more important.

1. The immediate context unit, verses 44–49, is of particular interest and value because the Gospel records tell us relatively little about what went on between the resurrection and ascension. This period is in a certain sense anomalous: the Messiah, now resurrected, has entered into his state of exaltation but has not yet gone, by ascension, to his place of exaltation. But this

interlude in the history of redemption is not for that reason nonessential. Particularly with our interest in these verses in view, it is important to see them as providing a generalized or cross-sectional view of what went on throughout this forty-day interim (see Acts 1:3). They give "an extremely succinct account of that happened further."[4]

What disposes us to this reading is that on the one side, everything up through verse 43 is explicitly tagged as taking place on the day of the resurrection (vv. 1, 13, 33, 36), while on the other side, beginning at verse 50, we are at the ascension, forty days later. The intervening verses, however, lack any such temporal indicator. In view is what took place at an unspecified time in between, and this indefiniteness supports taking verses 44–49 as presenting what was typical or particularly characteristic of the forty days as a whole.

2. Verses 44–47 show that this period was marked largely by instruction in which the resurrected Christ, having triumphed over death by his labors and found rest from his sufferings, now, from that vantage point, discloses and explains to his disciples the significance of this suffering and consequent glory. We might fairly picture the situation as a kind of forty-day intersession in which Jesus gave an intensive course in Old Testament hermeneutics and theology from a post-resurrection perspective. He showed these disciples how the history of redemption, having at last reached that point, is to be understood from the Old Testament.

More particularly, looking into verse 44, Jesus, from his newly achieved post-resurrection perspective, recalls to the eleven (and perhaps others, cf. v. 33) his teaching during the period of his ministry prior to his death and resurrection, "while I was still with you." This expression, quite striking, is an indication of the decisive redemptive-historical significance of the resurrection. From the vantage point of his ministry prior to the resurrection, it is as if now, in view of what has taken place in the resurrection and because of who he now is as resurrected, he is no longer "with them."

Further, the object clause at the end of verse 44 summarizes the content of this pre-resurrection teaching of Jesus. This clause in effect also summarizes what was the characteristic content of his teaching between

---

4. J. N. Geldenhuys, *Commentary on the Gospel of Luke* (Grand Rapids: Eerdmans, 1951), 641. "The activities of the 40 days are here compressed into the span of a few verses" (R. P. Martin, as I recall, in a reference I am no longer able to document).

the resurrection and ascension. Jesus is teaching them now what he taught them then: the necessary fulfillment of everything written in the law of Moses, the prophets, and the Psalms (Writings) concerning himself. His teaching, both pre- and post-resurrection, was concerned with what the Old Testament in all its parts, indicated here in its standard three-fold division, teaches about him. This content is virtually identical to the summary characterization of his earlier instruction to the two men on the road to Emmaus, "And beginning with Moses and all the Prophets, he interpreted to them in all the Scriptures the things concerning himself" (v. 27).

In the overall presentations of the teaching of Jesus in Luke, as well as the other Synoptic Gospels, the kingdom of God/heaven is the theme that is both central and all-encompassing.[5] From this we may infer in verse 44 that the comprehensive focus of the teaching of Jesus, pre- as well as post-resurrection, concerned the necessary fulfillment of the whole Old Testament that has been inaugurated in the arrival of the kingdom in his person and work. For his post-resurrection teaching this inference is made explicit in the passage that overlaps Luke 24:44–52 at the beginning of part two to Theophilus, Acts 1:3–11. What characterized the forty days between the resurrection and ascension in terms of teaching was that, all told, to the apostles (v. 2) Jesus was "speaking about the kingdom of God . . ." (v. 3; literally, "the things concerning the kingdom of God"). To speak of the necessary fulfillment of everything written in Scripture about him is to speak about the kingdom of God.

3. A key question for our reflections is the force of the preposition in the phrase, "in the Law of Moses and the Prophets and the Psalms" in verse 44, a question that applies as well to "in all the Scriptures" in verse 27. Is the "in" here all-inclusive or exclusive? That is, is the prepositional phrase comprehensive or partial? Does it refer to everything "in the Law of Moses and the Prophets and the Psalms" or only to some things in each of these three parts? Does it circumscribe the entire Old Testament, in all its parts and with no remainder, or does it refer only to certain strands of teaching or to a quantity of material in each of the three major sections of the Old Testament, excluding or leaving out of view other materials from the same part of the canon?

5. See, e.g., the still valuable overview of G. Vos, *The Teaching of Jesus Concerning the Kingdom of God and the Church* (Nutley, NJ: Presbyterian and Reformed, 1972).

The answer is almost certainly the former of these alternatives. At least two considerations within the immediate context (vv. 44–49) support this conclusion. First, these verses, as noted, are best understood as Luke's way of summarizing what went on during the entire forty days and so suggest that the instruction that took place was comprehensive. Put negatively, it would seem highly unlikely to suppose that throughout this period only certain parts of the Old Testament were discussed and the rest, in effect, was kept a closed book.

This observation is confirmed at a point of some dispute. The overlap to these verses at the beginning of Acts shows that the teaching of Jesus during this period included the relationship of Israel as a nation and the status of the old covenant promises given them as a people to the kingdom inaugurated in his work. Specifically, his teaching was such that it prompted the question of the apostles in 1:6, "Lord, are you at this time restoring the kingdom to Israel?"—a question that he answers, and obliquely corrects, in verses 7–8.[6]

Second, and even more decisive, is verse 45, "Then he opened their minds to understand the Scriptures"—the same description of his dealings earlier with the two men on the Emmaus road (v. 32). The connection in thought with verse 44, as far as this mind-opening is concerned, is surely this: what Jesus had all along taught the disciples throughout his ministry prior to the resurrection—the necessary fulfillment of everything in the Old Testament concerning himself—is now clear to them in a way it was not before. They finally comprehend or have a depth of comprehension of what previously they did not and were even afraid to ask about (e.g., 9:45; 18:34).

The description of what they now comprehend is "the Scriptures." Not, "these Scriptures" in distinction from others, not a specific set of Scriptures or a particular aspect of Old Testament revelation but simply "the Scriptures." This conventional designation in contemporary Second Temple Judaism and the New Testament (in the latter, Matt. 22:29; John 5:39; Acts 17:2, etc.) always refers to the Old Testament, whatever its exact extent at this time, as a whole, indicating the plurality of documents seen as a single entity.

In the light of the fulfillment brought by the resurrection, the disciples are now brought to an "opened" understanding of what Jesus had been

---

6. The apostles have the question wrong. Its terms need to be reversed. They should have asked, "Lord, when are you restoring Israel to the kingdom?" As the New Testament answers elsewhere, notably Romans 9–11, yes, ethnic Jews do have a kingdom future, the same future as that of the non-Jews—through the gospel and in the church.

saying previously during his earthly ministry about the necessary fulfillment of everything written about him in the Old Testament, and this new
understanding is said to be an understanding not just of certain parts of
Scripture but of Scripture, of the Old Testament as a whole, in its unity, in its
pervasive meaning, its full, overall sense. Jesus opened their minds to grasp
how the various parts of the Old Testament in its entirety cohere. They now
have a dawning deepened understanding of "the consent of all the parts,
the scope of the whole" (Westminster Confession of Faith 1.5).

In answer to the question posed above, then, we may conclude that
in verse 44 the reference of the prepositional phrase, "in the Law of Moses
and the Prophets and the Psalms" (and the similar phrase in v. 27), is all-
inclusive. Nothing in the Old Testament, seen in its basic three-fold division, is excluded. There is nothing in the Old Testament that is not "about"
Christ. The Old Testament as a whole is essentially forward-looking and
in that sense prophetic, and the focus of that fundamentally prophetic
outlook is Christ.

4. If "the Scriptures" in verse 45 is all-inclusive, verses 46–47 are best
read as specifying what is at their heart, taken as a whole, and what is central in the disciples' mind-opening experience. "It is written," Jesus says,
using a standard expression for citing Scripture within Greek-speaking
Judaism and the New Testament (in the latter, Mark 1:2; Acts 13:33; Rom.
1:17, etc.). Here the construction that directly follows this introductory
formula specifies the content of what is said to be written: the Messiah's
suffering, his resurrection and, syntactically coordinate as a third element, world-wide preaching of the gospel, characterized as the message of
"repentance for the remission of sins."[7] In other words, Jesus affirms here,
the central message of the Old Testament in its comprehensive totality is
messianic suffering and glory, the Christ's death and resurrection, and,
as a consequence, it should not be missed, universal gospel proclamation.
Linking this to the terms of verse 44, "everything about me" written in
the law, prophets and Psalms, Jesus now says, has its central focus in his
death, his resurrection and the consequent world-wide preaching of the
gospel in his name.

---

7. If in this expression one decides for the variant reading "and" (instead of "for"), the sense
is materially the same. On the textual issue, see B. M. Metzger, *A Textual Commentary of the
Greek New Testament* (London: United Bible Societies, 1994), 161.

Because gospel proclamation is inherently efficacious, to speak of it is necessarily to speak of its result or intended outcome—the church. So the primary effect of the gospel's universal proclamation is the church universal, the repentant not just from one but every nation. Jesus could hardly be clearer than he is here that the New Testament church, made up both Jews and non-Jews, is at the heart of the Old Testament taken as a whole. The focus of the fulfillment of all God's old covenant promises to Israel as a nation includes the church.

This passage tells decisively against dispensational constructions, older or progressive, that dichotomize in Scripture, particularly with an eye to the Old Testament, by distinguishing to a greater and lesser extent and in a more or less nonintersecting, parallel fashion between God's "theological" purposes for Israel among the nations and his "soteriological" purposes realized in the Jew-Gentile composition of the New Testament church. God's eschatological promises to the fathers are both: theological and soteriological, and they are that indivisibly, theological-soteriological, because their fulfillment is christological. As Paul says—and the immediate and larger context makes no qualifications on his sweeping declaration—"Whatever may be the promises of God, in him [the crucified and resurrected Christ] they have their Yes, . . . their Amen to God" (2 Cor. 1:20).

5. Verses 46–47 prompt the question, where in the Old Testament do we find Christ's death, his resurrection, and the church mentioned together? In what sense are they there? In fact, when we search the Old Testament, we fail to find a particular verse or passage that expresses these three elements, places that include the triad that is said here to be written there. To be sure, various passages come to mind as pertinent, especially certain psalms like 16 and 22, and the latter part of Isaiah. But that is already to point us in the direction of taking "it is written," regularly elsewhere a standard formula for introducing direct quotations, in a looser and more general sense here.

But how much looser and more general? The answer to that question appears to lie along the lines of what we have already noted in this passage, namely Christ as giving coherence and unity to the entire Old Testament in its various parts, Christ as providing "the consent of all the parts, the scope of the whole." Verses 46–47, then, specify his death, his resurrection, and the church as being at the core of what is "written" in the Old Testament in all its parts.

To summarize our reflections on this passage, the Old Testament in all its parts and without residue has an essentially anticipatory, prophetic orientation that, all told, is about Christ, and the triad of his death, his resurrection, and the church is at the center that unifies its diverse teaching.

APOSTOLIC PREACHING IN ACTS

Luke's accounts of apostolic preaching are instanced, representatively as he likely intends, by Peter and Paul. He also surely intends these representative accounts to be read in the light of the words of Jesus, just considered, at the close of part one to Theophilus. A couple of factors are prominent in his summaries of that preaching. Characteristically, it culminated in a call to repentance and faith, following out of a focus on the death, but especially the resurrection, of Christ (cf. Acts 2:32–36, 38; 3:13–15, 19; 4:32–33; 10:39–43).[8] Further, a repeated emphasis is that this gospel, centered in the death and resurrection, was preached from Scripture. What is notable is just how comprehensive some of these references to this Old Testament basis are.

Peter, for instance, within the temple precincts in Jerusalem, is especially, even emphatically, sweeping. Without specific Old Testament citation, the suffering of God's Christ is said to be "foretold through the mouth of *all the prophets*" (3:18). Again without any specific references, in verse 24 he declares, "these days"—the days of Jesus, the appointed Christ (v. 20), the final prophet Moses promised (v. 21), culminating in his death and resurrection—"*all the prophets from Samuel on down, as many as have spoken, have also proclaimed.*" In 10:43 the account of his proclamation to the Gentiles gathered in the house of Cornelius ends on a similar note, "To him *all the prophets* bear witness that everyone who believes in him receives forgiveness of sins through his name."

The same sweeping accent is present in the preaching of Paul. In Acts 26, in the audience granted him before the governor, Festus, and King Agrippa, he is intent on surveying his life's ministry coming toward its close. According to verses 22–23, all that he has stood for and has all along been saying ("testifying") is "nothing but what the prophets and

---

8. In the alternative references to repentance or to faith in these passages, the one is best taken as entailing the other; cf. the general characterization of Paul's preaching in 20:21, " . . . repentance toward God and faith in our Lord Jesus Christ"; see also Luke 24:47.

Moses said would come to pass: that the Christ must suffer and that, by being the first to rise from the dead, he would proclaim light both to our people and to the Gentiles." Assuming that here "the prophets and Moses" is likely synecdochic for the whole Old Testament, it is noteworthy that this is virtually the same sweeping encapsulation that we find for the post-resurrection teaching of Jesus in Luke 24:46–47: in its entirety the Old Testament witnesses to the Messiah's suffering and resurrection and, inseparably connected with that, to the church-establishing world-wide proclamation of gospel light.

A similar sweeping outlook on the Old Testament marks Paul's missionary activity from the outset. In Acts 13:27, in the course of his comments in the synagogue in Pisidian Antioch, he makes the negative point that those in Israel who have rejected God's promised savior, Jesus (v. 23), have done so "because they did not recognize either him or the utterances of the prophets." Further, by "condemning him" they "fulfilled" these utterances, not as they are heard only infrequently on this or that occasion but as they are said to be "read every Sabbath."

At a later point, at Thessalonica during the course of his second missionary journey (17:2–3), Paul, in what is said was customary for him, entered the synagogue and there, on three different, perhaps successive, Sabbaths "reasoned with them from the Scriptures." This reasoning is further described as consisting in "explaining and providing evidence" from Scripture "that the Christ had to suffer and rise again from the dead" and, with that, in declaring, "This Jesus whom I am proclaiming to you is the Christ."

To the same effect is Luke's description of Paul's final activity in Rome. On at least one occasion there, while under house arrest, he was extensively preoccupied ("from morning till evening") with expounding Scripture to local Jewish leaders. This exposition was marked particularly by the effort "to convince them about Jesus both from the Law of Moses and from the Prophets" (28:23–24). The note on which Acts closes suggests that this expository strategy was characteristic of the entire two years he was in Rome (28:30–31).

At an earlier point Luke presents the activity of Apollos in a similar vein. After he had been instructed "more accurately" in "the things concerning Jesus" by Priscilla and Aquila, he powerfully refuted the opposition in "showing by the Scriptures that the Christ was Jesus" (18:25–26, 28).

This survey of Lucan instances of preaching during the church's apostolic era suffices to show that it primarily took the form of biblical exposition, and that such exposition was in the interests of showing that the old covenant Scriptures, not just in part but taken in their entirety, establish with divine authority that Jesus is the Christ and, in particular, the attendant necessity of his death and resurrection.

For our interests, what is particularly noteworthy is the reciprocal movement that marks these accounts taken as a whole. In them the direction is not only from the fulfillment that has taken place in Christ back to the Old Testament and its previously obscure but now properly clarified understanding, but, conversely, from the Old Testament to Christ. The argument runs both ways, but it is the latter that is predominant and invariable: from the Old Testament Scriptures to Christ and a proper understanding of who he is.

Certainly it is the case that the apostles, including Paul, as well as others of their generation, were brought to faith in Christ from their personal contacts with him, whether before or after his resurrection. They became Christians from encountering him in his deeds and words while he was on earth. Further, based on these encounters, especially with Christ as resurrected, the apostles were appointed by him primarily to be his authorized witnesses (cf. Acts 1:21; 2:32; 3:15; 4:33; 10:40–41; for Paul, 1 Cor. 9:1; 15:8–9). Accordingly, as these references in parentheses show, they offer this eyewitness as a ground for their summons to repentance and faith in him.

But that is not always or solely the case. The descriptions of preaching in Acts may sometimes include appeals to apostolic eyewitness as a basis for faith in Christ. But present in all of them is a biblical basis; they are essentially preaching of what now has become the Old Testament.

Surely we may say, and it is most important to say, that Christ in his death and resurrection is the "key" to all of Scripture. Surely, too, the unfolding redemptive or covenantal history that gave rise to the Old Testament as the revelatory attestation of that history is an incomplete history, a history short of its consummation. In terms currently in vogue, the Old Testament is a "story" lacking its ending.[9] It is one large promise looking

---

9.One ought to be cautious about this use of "story." Too often its current widespread use, applied to narrative material in the Bible, especially in the Old Testament, masks indifference, sometimes deliberate, to issues of historical reliability or even to any sort of historical reference.

for its fulfillment. It is, using a grammatical analogy, one long protasis without an apodosis. Christ in his exalted glory is that consummation, that ending, that fulfillment, that apodosis. Accordingly, the apostles and others undoubtedly came to understand the Old Testament in an unprecedented and fuller way in the light of what had taken place in Christ, his death and resurrection, and they preach from the Old Testament in the light of that fulfillment. Luke 24:45, for one, demands that we say that.[10]

But, on the other hand, to say that Christ is the key to the Old Testament is not to say that its meaning was largely closed and inexplicable prior to his death and resurrection. Whether considered by themselves or as a whole, these documents are not ambiguous or confused or confusing. Neither do they comprise multiple trajectories of meaning, each more or less valid in itself but only one of which may be properly construed as relevant to the eventual death and resurrection of Christ and universal spread of the gospel.

Again, the actual fulfillment in Christ does provide the apostles and, based on their teaching, all New Testament believers with clarity both concerning his person and work and the attendant meaning of the Old Testament that those under the old covenant did not possess, including the Old Testament writers themselves. Psychological content (the "reader response") concerning Christ and, correlatively, the meaning of the Old Testament are hardly identical for Old and New Testament believers. That is beyond question and not at issue here.

But what is at issue is the importance for sound biblical interpretation of recognizing that this difference in clarity is only relative and involves continuity in understanding the text of the Old Testament. At issue here as well is the essential and pervasive clarity of the Old Testament documents in their unified divine-human intention and meaning. This continuity and implied clarity are evident, for instance, in the words of Jesus concerning the arrival of the eschatological kingdom in his person and work, "But your eyes are blessed, for they see, and your ears, for they hear. Truly, I say to you, many prophets and righteous people longed to see what you see, and did

---

10. This "opened" understanding of Scripture, however, no matter how unprecedented, was at the same time relative—relative to the biblical understanding they already had before the resurrection and relative to the growth and even correction in their understanding still needed subsequently, as, for instance, Acts 1:6 and, in the case of Peter, Acts 10:13–17, 34; 11:7–10, and Galatians 2:11–14 all show.

73

not see it, and to hear what you hear, and did not hear it" (Matt. 13:16–17; cf. Luke 10:21–22). This normative old covenant longing, however inchoate and imperfectly formed, as it was prompted by and mediated through the Old Testament Scriptures, was intent on and satisfied by the fulfillment eventually realized in Christ, and by nothing else.

This unmistakable Christ-focused desire of the Old Testament, however shadowy and limited in its seed form, provides the point of departure for apostolic preaching, assuming that Acts provides an accurate profile of that preaching as a whole. Characteristically, that preaching did not offer an eyewitness message about Christ and then seek to show Jewish listeners in particular how the Old Testament could or even should now be read in the light of that message. Rather, it began with the Old Testament, confident in its overall clarity as God's word, and, in the light of the fulfillment that had arrived in Christ, established that fulfillment from this biblical basis. It was pervasively Old Testament-based reasoning that took the form of "explaining and proving ["from the Scriptures"] that it was necessary for the Christ to suffer and to rise from the dead" (Acts 17:2–3).[11]

So, anecdotally, the greater nobility of the Jews in Berea who received this apostolic word did not consist in their new understanding of the Old Testament in the light of that word, although they no doubt did gain such insight. Rather they were "more noble" because, reciprocally, they were eagerly "examining the Scriptures daily to see if these things [Paul proclaimed] were so" (Acts 17:11). Here, the validity of the apostolic proclamation of Christ is plainly tethered to the resident truth and authority of the Old Testament.

The dealings of Jesus with the two men on the road to Emmaus on the day of his resurrection are instructive at this point. As he travels along with them, Jesus eventually reproves them for being "foolish and slow of heart" (Luke 24:27). Why? Not because they failed to recognize him in his newly emergent resurrection glory. As if to exclude this as a factor, we are told explicitly that "their eyes were kept from recognizing him" (v. 16).[12] Nor did he reprimand them for failing to comprehend who he was during his pre-resurrection ministry, though on the way at least one of them evidenced exposure to or at least an awareness of that ministry in some detail

11. See the apposite comments in this regard of Dennis E. Johnson, *Him We Proclaim: Preaching Christ from All of Scripture* (Phillipsburg, NJ: P&R, 2007), 150n28.

12. The verb here is a divine passive. God, or Christ specifically, is surely the active agent of the veiling that took place.

(vv. 18–24). Rather, his admonition addresses their culpability at what Jesus sees to be its primary level. What underlies their failure to recognize him for who he was, whether in encountering him before or after his resurrection, was their failure "to believe all that the prophets have spoken" (v. 25).

In a similar vein, previously, in John's gospel, Jesus had rebuked Jewish leaders even more severely. Their failure to believe him, he stipulates, is predicated on their antecedent and underlying failure to believe Moses and the rest of Scripture, "If you believed Moses, you would believe me; for he wrote of me. But if you do not believe his writings, how will you believe my words?" (5:46–47; cf. verse 39, "You search the Scriptures because you think that in them you have eternal life; and it is they that bear witness about me."). Here Jesus affirms the relative overall clarity and independence of Moses (the Old Testament), as a witness to himself, distinct from his own teaching (and so, by implication, of the New Testament). So much is the case that this Old Testament witness to Christ serves as an adequate basis for the just condemnation of those rejecting him (verse 45), in itself and independent of his own self-witness.

What the two men had to say, when they eventually recognized Jesus and he had left them, reinforces these observations. Remarkably, they do not mention that they have just met the living Christ, as memorable and moving as that encounter of itself no doubt was. Rather, what they experienced as particularly affecting and riveting ("our hearts burned within us"), and especially worth mentioning, was that in talking to them, "he opened to us the Scriptures" (Luke 24:32; cf. v.27, "And beginning with Moses and all the Prophets, he interpreted to them in all the Scriptures the things concerning himself."). This is what is ever at stake in the use that Jesus, the apostles, and the New Testament writers make of the Old Testament: its basic and pervasive clarity and, by implication, its didactic unity, its doctrinal harmony as God's word, across the face of its diverse historical and human-authored contents. As the apostolic preaching in Acts shows, faith in Christ and the stability of that faith depend on that divinely-authored, God-breathed Old Testament unity and clarity.

1 PETER 1:10–12

Concerning this salvation, the prophets who prophesied about the grace that would come to you searched and inquired carefully, inquiring what person or time the Spirit of Christ in them was indicating when he predicted the sufferings of Christ and the glories to follow. To them it was revealed that they were serving not themselves but you, in the things that have now been announced to you through those who preached the gospel to you by the Holy Spirit sent from heaven, things into which angels long to look.

In the section immediately preceding these verses, Peter eloquently describes the salvation predicated on Christ's resurrection (v. 3), salvation that is already present for believers but embracing as well their future inheritance (v. 4) at his return (= his "revelation," v. 7). What Peter goes on to say concerning that salvation prompts the following observations pertinent to our interests.

First, this salvation, the grace that has come to New Testament believers, is said to be the concern or preoccupation of the prophets (v. 10). This reference to the prophets is best taken as a synecdoche for the entire Old Testament. For one, the related and almost certainly synecdochic occurrences of "the prophetic word," "every prophecy of Scripture," and "prophecy" in 2 Peter 1:19–21 point to that conclusion.

Several things are immediately apparent about this prophetic preoccupation. For one, given the scope of the salvation Peter has in view, comprehending the future as well as the present, that preoccupation is similarly comprehensive. Also, considering the compound Greek verbs Peter uses in verse 10, their concern was thorough; they "searched intently and with the greatest care" (NIV). The Old Testament preoccupation in view is as intensive as it is comprehensive.

In looking at the Old Testament writers in terms of their searching activity, these verses provide a definite indication of their intention as human authors. We are told here of what the Old Testament text says in a way that at the same time shows that content to be the dominating interest of its various authors. Clearly in contradiction to this passage is any notion that their human intention is in conflict or irresolvable tension with God's intention, properly understood, or with the Old Testament understood in the light of the New. With all that was undoubtedly limited and shadowy about their understanding, these verses point to an essential and pervasive continuity between their understanding and the divine intention of what they wrote, to the organic flow there is from their seed-like comprehension to the final and fuller revelation of the New Testament.

Pertinent in this regard is the evangelist's comment in John 12:41 on Jesus' citing Isaiah 53:1 and 6:9–10 concerning Israel's unbelief (vv. 38–40), "Isaiah said this because he saw Jesus' glory and spoke about him." In view is not only what Isaiah said (wrote) but also what, in so doing, he himself saw or understood. He saw the glory of Jesus as well as spoke about it. In fact, with an eye to the syntax of verse 41, he spoke, "because he saw"; he said it because he saw it. The implied continuity of this prophetic perception with the climactic revelation of that glory, in view in 1:14 and elsewhere throughout John's gospel, is unmistakable. The thrust of what Isaiah wrote had Christ as its goal only because of the christological understanding granted to him (and to his original and all subsequent readers, at least potentially). This we may take as just one instance about which Peter generalizes for all the Old Testament authors.

Second, what the various prophets say is unified and harmoniously integrated. Why? Because ultimately it is a matter of what the one Spirit, as "the Spirit of Christ"[13] was indicating and predicting though each of them (v. 11a). This overarching activity of the Spirit explains why in the Old Testament as such "the consent of all the parts, the scope of the whole" is present and discoverable. The multi-authored diversity and varied genre of the Old Testament constitute an organically unfolding and divinely determined didactic unity.

Third, at the center of the comprehensive and integrated body of Old Testament prophecy is "the sufferings of Christ and the glories to follow" (v. 11b). The focus of its overall consent and scope is messianic humiliation and exaltation, Christ's death and resurrection. Present here, then, is the same centering outlook on the Old Testament as a whole that we find in the post-resurrection teaching of Jesus in Luke 24 and in the apostolic preaching in Acts.

Fourth, verse 12 confirms what have already observed about the intention of the Old Testament writers and the continuity of that intention with the New Testament. In ministering as they did in the circumstances peculiar to each in his own time and place, they understood, by revelation, that ultimately they were not serving themselves and their contemporaries

---

13. As the subject of the verb in its clause, this expression is best taken as referring to the unified activity of the preincarnate Christ along with the Holy Spirit under the old covenant (cf. 1 Cor. 10:4), adumbrating their conjoint post-Pentecost activity, based on the cross and resurrection (e.g., Acts 16:7; Rom. 8:9–10; 1 Cor. 15:45; 2 Cor. 3:17; Eph. 3:16–17).

but New Testament believers. Affirmed here is continuity between their ministries, including the Scriptures they wrote, and the post-Pentecostal, Spirit-empowered proclamation of the gospel.

Romans 16:25–26

> Now to him who is able to strengthen you according to my gospel and the preaching of Jesus Christ, according to the revelation of the mystery that was kept secret for long ages but now has been manifested and, through the prophetic Scriptures, has been made known, according to the command of the eternal God, to all the nations in order to the obedience of faith.

This overarching doxological perspective on his ministry with which Paul brings Romans to a close reinforces a key point present in other passages we have been considering. Here the controlling notion, "the revelation of the mystery" (see also Col. 1:26; cf. Eph. 3:3–6), specifies the central content of Paul's gospel preaching. This revelation is not a purely noetic or cognitive category; it is not referring to verbal revelation, although that is involved derivatively. Rather, the "mystery" is such as it refers to God's saving purpose in Christ rooted in the ultimate hiddenness of his eternal counsel, and its revelation, in turn, is the actual realization of that purpose in history. Previous to that realization it was "kept secret" in the sense of not yet having happened. In other words, "the revelation of the mystery" is a redemptive-historical reality, the salvation finally revealed in Christ. Christ himself, preeminently in his death and resurrection, is God's mystery revealed, his open secret (cf. Col. 2:2–3).[14]

Pertinent to our interest is the way the three participial clauses Paul predicates of the mystery, particularly the last, reinforce this reading. It (1) has been kept secret or silent from eternity, (2) has been manifested or revealed now, at last (the "now" here has eschatological force), and, as such, (3) has been made known or declared universally "through the prophetic Scriptures," that is, the Old Testament. This last qualification shows that the mystery and its revelation do not have to do with hidden or arcane information. Nor is it a matter of verbal revelation previously unknown.

---

14. On this interpretation see further, esp., H. Ridderbos, *Paul: An Outline of His Theology* (Grand Rapids: Eerdmans, 1975), 46–49.

In that sense, as verbal revelation, it has already been revealed in the Old Testament. Accordingly, Paul is saying in describing his ministry as a whole, he proclaims the salvation revealed in Christ by using the Old Testament as the revelatory medium for making that salvation known. The instances in Acts examined above show something of how this "through the prophetic Scriptures" functioned for Paul.

For Paul, the exalted Christ, the mystery now revealed through apostolic witness to that mystery, is the key that serves to clarify the meaning of the Old Testament. Reciprocally, however, apostolic proclamation of the Old Testament makes clear the meaning of Christ as the revealed mystery. Here, in Romans 16:26, and as Paul considers his ministry as a whole, he accents the latter: from the Old Testament, in its presupposed divine authority and pervasive clarity, to Christ.

CONCLUSION

The interest of this chapter has been Christ in the Old Testament from the vantage point of the New. Specifically, we have paid attention to New Testament passages that generalize about the Old, rather than the actual and varied usage of the Old in the New. We may easily summarize the results of this study. For Jesus and the New Testament writers the Old Testament is one large prophetic and promissory witness to Christ, a diverse but unified witness that centers in his sufferings and consequent glorification. The Old Testament has its overall integrity, its various parts cohere, in terms of this death-and-resurrection focus.

Put negatively, the Old Testament does not have multiple and discordant trajectories of meaning, but only one. That is the unidirectional path that leads to Christ, however obscure and difficult it may be for us to follow that path at points along the way. To be sure, many and multivalent trajectories may appear to be the case when the Old Testament documents are read "on their own terms." But such a reading is precluded as illegitimate for new covenant readers faithful to both the Old and New Testaments as the word of God. This is so not only because the Old Testament is to be read in the light of the New, but also because Jesus and the New Testament writers are clear about the continuity in intention and meaning there is between themselves and the various Old Testament writings in their own time and place. To seek to read the various Old Testament writers for themselves and apart from the vantage point of the New exposes one ultimately to misunderstanding them.

Of a great deal more to be said beyond what I can here about a sound use of the Old Testament in the church today, including proper assessment of the actual use of the Old Testament in the New, two extremes are to be avoided. On the one hand, in the light of the passages we have considered, it would be clearly wrong to restrict reference to Christ to a limited number of passages perceived to be clearly messianic, as if the rest of the Old Testament has little or nothing to do with them and offers a message that is largely, if not entirely, unrelated.

The opposite extreme is to view each and every Old Testament text, however factored, as having a christological message of its own, as teaching in its own terms some specific point about Christ's death and/or resurrection. This approach disposes toward and, where forced inevitably results in, more or less uncontrolled allegory always looking behind everything in the Old Testament for a presumed "deeper" meaning. On this approach Old Testament interpretation tends to devolve into a kind of hermeneutical scavenger hunt, a contest in discovering ever more subtle and strained christological types and allusions.

We may highlight a useful guideline for maintaining requisite balance by addressing the proposition, "Christ is in every sentence of the Old Testament." Is that so? The answer is yes and no. If one intends this statement in the extreme, atomistic sense just noted, that every sentence has a specific Christological message all its own, then the answer is clearly no.

However, every Old Testament sentence or text is in a context, and that context is a history, the ongoing history of God's dealings with his covenant people Israel. That history, in all its twists and turns, has only one direction and serves only one controlling purpose. That overall purpose, qualifying every part without exception, comes to a focus, as Peter says, in "the sufferings of Christ and the glories to follow." So, in that context-qualified sense, we not only may but must say, Christ is in every sentence of the Old Testament.

Every sentence or text has its intended meaning as it is embedded in and qualified by the flow of redemptive history. That is so, for instance, inclusive of a genre like Proverbs. No matter how much such so-called Wisdom Literature may leave the impression of being largely made up of aphorisms that are "timeless" in the sense of being devoid of narrative considerations and largely indifferent to specific historical qualification and change, Proverbs, all told, is a statement for wise living in covenant with the God of Israel, the life, in whatever time and place, that is dependent on, as it has its consummate realization in, the now exalted Christ, "in whom are hidden all the treasures of wisdom and knowledge" (Col. 2:3).

Finally, seeing the entire Old Testament as concerned with the history of God's covenant that reaches it culmination in the salvation brought by Christ in "the fullness of time" (Gal. 4:4; Eph. 1:10), as Jesus and the New Testament writers plainly do (!), in no way need result in an undue redemptive narrowing of the message of the Bible. For that message, as a message of salvation, is simply unintelligible unless it is set against the background of the covenant history of the original creation, with everything about it "very good" (Gen. 1:31), which subsequently has become subject to corruption and death due to human sin. The redemption accomplished in Christ's death and resurrection, as glimpsed from afar by "the many prophets and righteous people" of the Old Testament (Matt. 13:17), has kingdom proportions, dimensions on the order of the eschatological kingship of God in Christ already established over the entire creation (cf. Matt. 28:18; Eph. 1:21) and awaiting its full manifestation at this return (cf. 1 Cor. 15:23–28; Heb. 2:7–8). This cosmic and creation-renewing scope of salvation is very clear, for instance, in Romans 8:18–25, including Paul's implicit commentary on Genesis 3 in verses 20–22. "Redemption restores and perfects creation," nothing less.

5

The Significance of "Israel" in
the Usage of the New Testament

George W. Knight III

WRITERS ON THE THEME of "Israel" in the New Testament are significantly in debt to O. Palmer Robertson in view of his wide-ranging work on *The Israel of God: Yesterday, Today, and Tomorrow*. So much are we in debt to this work, and especially to his exposition of "the Israel of God" in Galatians 6:16, that this article might seem to unneeded. But this article seeks to cover ground not covered in detail in Dr. Robertson's book, as able as his work is, namely, the occurrences of the term "Israel" in the entire corpus of the New Testament in their various and specific contexts. This research is necessary to determine the significance of each occurrence and then to attempt to come to a conclusion about the various usages of "Israel" in the NT and about any overarching conclusion(s) that may be drawn.

Old Testament Background

The first occurrence [of 2566 times[1]] of the name "Israel" in the Scriptures is in Genesis 32:28 in the midst of the account of Jacob wrestling with

1. The name appears 2498 times in the Hebrew Old Testament, and 68 times in the Greek New Testament.

82

God at a place which Jacob latter called Peniel. The person wrestling with Jacob asks him "What is your name?" in answer to which he responds with "Jacob" (v. 27). But God responds by giving him a new name and says: "Your name shall no longer be called Jacob, but Israel, for you have striven with God and with men, and have prevailed" (v. 28). God is so intent on giving Jacob this new name that he appears to him again and at that appearance again gives him the name "Israel" (Gen. 35:9–15, esp. v. 10, "no longer shall your name be called Jacob, but Israel shall be your name. So he called his name Israel."). Conjoined with this naming, "God Almighty" gave to Israel the blessings of fruitfulness, and to him and his offspring, as to Abraham and Isaac, God promised a land.

Because of this designation of the patriarch Jacob as Israel, we find that his twelve sons designated collectively are called the "people of Israel"[2] (or "tribes of Israel," cf. Gen. 49:16), with the first occurrence coming in Genesis 32:32 where they are called "the sons of Israel." Thereafter the community of people is designated as simply "Israel" when the text speaks of the thing as having been done "in Israel" (Gen. 34:7). So the term comes over into the New Testament as a designation of the people that God had called unto himself, or as the religious designation of the covenantal grouping known as the Hebrews. The prophet Amos is an example of a number of Old Testament prophets who regard "Israel" in this sense when he relates that God says, "I will restore the fortunes of my people Israel . . . says the LORD your God" (Amos 9:14–15). And these words are found in a passage that is quoted in part by James as being fulfilled in the New Testament age (cf. Amos 9:11–12 cited in Acts 15:15–19).

THE FOUR GOSPELS

Of the sixty-eight times that the word "Israel" appears in the NT, nearly half of them, thirty occurrences, occur in the four Gospels (with twenty-six in the Synoptics). The most frequent of the occurrences (16 times) is "Israel" without qualification, followed by the "kingdom of Israel" (4 times), and then followed by five combinations each occurring

---

2. So translated in the English Standard Version (ESV), which is used throughout this article except where indicated that another version, such as the New American Standard Bible (NASB), is used. Rendered by other translations as "children of Israel," or more literally as "sons of Israel" (because of the fact that the twelve sons of Israel were the originators of the twelve tribes).

only twice, "land of Israel," "God of Israel," "people of Israel," "house of Israel" and "people (children or sons) of Israel."

Mark

We begin with Mark's gospel, where the word occurs twice (12:29; 15:32). In answer to a question from a scribe about "Which commandment is the most important of all?" (12:28), Jesus answered, "The most important is, 'Hear, O Israel: The Lord our God, the Lord is one'" (12:29; quoting Deut. 6:4 quite precisely, where the word Israel is found).

The second occurrence is in 15:32. The background for this occurrence is of some significance as is the change made by the religious leaders in their use of the term. Pilate has asked about and referred to Jesus as "the King of the Jews" (15:2, 12), and the soldiers pick up this description (15:18). Mark says "the inscription of the charge against him read, 'The King of the Jews'" (15:26; cf. also Matt. 27:37; Luke 23:38; John 19:19). But the chief priests and scribes when they mock Jesus by saying, "He saved others; he cannot save himself. Let the Christ, the King of Israel, come down from the cross that we may see and believe" (15:31b–32; cf. also Matt. 27:42–43), use the word "Israel" instead of the word Jews. These religious leaders used the significant religious term "the King of Israel" even though the inscription read "the King of the Jews," and even though in Luke's gospel the soldiers joining in the mocking still use "the King of the Jews" (Luke 23:37).

Matthew

The most frequent usage of "Israel" among the gospel writers is found in the 12 occurrences in Matthew (2:6, 20–21; 8:10; 9:33; 10:6, 23; 15:24, 31; 19:28; 27:9, 42). Here we find the word 3 times in chapter 2, and 2 times each in chapters 10, 15, 27, as well as once each in chapters 8, 9 and 19.

The first three occurrences virtually set the parameters for the usage elsewhere in the Gospel. Matthew 2:6 quotes from the prophecy of Micah which says that from Bethlehem (where Jesus is to be born) will come forth one who "will shepherd my people Israel." This Christ (v. 4) is prophesied to be one who will shepherd or care for God's ("my") "people." So the first usage refers to Israel as God's people (for a fuller treatment of people and Israel together, see Acts 4:10).

The next two occurrences use the word "land" before "Israel" and thus speak of the "land of Israel" (2:20–21). This is the land that now bears the name of the patriarch and the nation/people named after him because the Lord promised it to him and them. So when God instructs Joseph to return to Israel from Egypt, there is no question about where he is to take Jesus and his mother (the land of Judea and Galilee).

The "in Israel" references of 8:10 and 9:33 refer either to the boundaries of the nation or to those regarded as the people of God ("with no one in Israel have I found such faith"; "Never was anything like this seen in Israel"; for 8:10, see Luke 7:9 below).

Even though the words "through all the towns of Israel" (10:23) seem to describe towns in a nation, the earlier statement of Jesus that he was sending the twelve "to the lost sheep of the house of Israel" (10:6; cf. Jer. 50:6 and Isa. 5:7) speaks of them more in their spiritual condition than simply of their geographical boundaries.

Likewise, Jesus' statement to the Canaanite woman concerning her daughter that he was "sent only to the lost sheep of the house of Israel" (15:24), must be seen in its entire context where Jesus admits that, even though he is on this directed mission to them (at that moment of his ministry), there are crumbs of bread from the children's table for one who believes on him (15:25–28), as his "Great Commission" makes clear in the light of his death and resurrection with its words "make disciples of all nations" (Matt. 28:18–20). The usage in 8:10 and 15:24 make clear that Jesus is using "Israel" in a sense that distinguishes those who had been gathered by God and the non-Israelites, like the centurion and the Canaanite woman, who are desiring the good news of the gospel and its benefits (see also Luke 4:23–30 below).

In 15:21, the crowd that had witnessed and wondered about the many healings of all sorts of ills that Jesus had done "glorified the God of Israel," and thereby acknowledged that Jesus had been sent by him and was his representative.

Matthew 19:28 correlates the twelve tribes of Israel and the twelve apostles and it does so by Jesus telling them that they "who have followed me will also sit on twelve thrones, judging the twelve tribes of Israel." In this same gospel Jesus also tells his Jewish hearers and their religious leaders that "the kingdom of God will be taken away from you and be given to a people producing its fruits" (21:43). What Jesus here prophesies is stated as an already accomplished fact by Paul when he recounts the image of the olive tree and its natural branches broken off, wild branches grafted in, and also natural branches grafted back in (Rom. 11:17–24). What is seen in both Jesus and Paul is that there is and will be a remnant, so that both Jesus' promise to the apostles and his threat to the religious leaders are the two sides of one truth and this truth in its two-sidedness is spelled out further by Paul in Romans 11.

In 27:9–10, Matthew alludes to the fulfillment of what had been spoken by the prophet Jeremiah (cf. Jer. 19:1–13) and also paraphrases Zechariah[3] 11:12b–13: "And they took the thirty pieces of silver, the price of him on whom a price had been set by some of the sons of Israel, and they gave them for the potter's field, as the Lord directed me." The relevance of this reference is that it is a quotation using the phrase "sons of Israel," a description which itself points back to the origin of the word "Israel" as the title of the Jews as the people of God.

Finally, the last usage in Matthew is 27:42 in which "the chief priests, with the scribes and elders, mocked" Jesus with a saying almost identical to that of Mark 15:31–32 (which see for the words and explanation; Matthew omits "the Christ").

Luke

We now turn to Luke's gospel with its twelve occurrences (1:16, 54, 68, 80; 2:25, 32, 34; 4:25, 27; 7:9; 22:30; 24:21).

The first six occurrences (or half of the total) are in the first two chapters and occur in the statements to or from individuals with reference to the birth of John the Baptist and Jesus. An angel tells Zechariah that John "will turn many of the children of Israel to the Lord their God" (1:16). Mary magnifies the Lord for causing her to bear Jesus and says that he does so to help "his servant Israel, in remembrance of his mercy, as he spoke to our fathers, to Abraham and to his offspring forever" (1:54–55). Zechariah prophesied by the Holy Spirit and began his words by saying, "Blessed be the Lord God of Israel, for he has visited and redeemed his

---

3. For this practice of citing two prophets and using only the name of the longer and best known one, see D. A. Carson, "Matthew," in *The Expositor's Bible Commentary*, ed. Frank E. Gaebelein (Grand Rapids: Zondervan, 1984), 8:562–66, and Douglas J. Moo, "Tradition and Old Testament in Matt 27:3–10," in *Gospel Perspectives*, ed. R. T. France and David Wenham (Sheffield: JSOT, 1983), 3:157–75.

people and raised up a horn of salvation for us in the house of his servant David" (1:68–69). Zechariah goes on to say that God's work of giving John is "to show the mercy promised to our fathers and to remember his holy covenant, the oath that he swore to our father Abraham ..." (vv. 72–73), and that his "child will be called the prophet of the Most High: for you will go before the Lord to prepare his ways" (v. 76). Luke ends this account saying that John "grew and became strong in spirit, and he was in the wilderness until the day of his public appearance to Israel" (v. 80). All these references ("the children of Israel," "his servant Israel," "the Lord God of Israel," and "his public appearance to Israel") speak of the people with whom God had entered into fellowship with a covenant of promise, whether looking back to the fathers, Abraham and David, or to the present moment where the Lord God of Israel is at work through John and Jesus in the midst of this people called Israel.

In his second chapter, the gospel writer continues in the same vein when he describes Simeon as one who is "waiting for the consolation of Israel" (2:25; cf. Isa. 40:1 and Luke 2:38, "to all who were waiting for the redemption of Jerusalem"). He declares that this Jesus is "a light for revelation to the Gentiles, and for glory to your people Israel" (2:32), and says directly to Mary that her "child is appointed for the fall and rising of many in Israel" (2:34). Like the preceding verses, but even more prophetically looking forward to his day, Simeon uses "Israel" of the Jewish people seen as the ones to whom God has come in promise and now comes to both them and the Gentiles with his light for revelation to the Gentiles and for glory to his people Israel. The Old Testament pattern is clearly in place in Simeon, one of the great Old Testament saints awaiting the consolation of Israel, and yet he also comments that this Jesus is also for the Gentiles, as he said in this statement and in his preceding words, "for my eyes have seen your salvation that you have prepared in the presence of all peoples" (2:30–31).

Jesus, in Luke 4:25, 27, makes a point to the Israelites that just as there were many widows (v. 25) and lepers (v. 27) "in Israel," and that Elijah and Elisha were sent to believers elsewhere, so also in Jesus' day and ministry it is not their being in Israel that elicits from Jesus God's blessing but only faith like in those he has mentioned. Thus also Jesus marvels at the faith of the centurion who says that Jesus need not come to heal his servant but only "say the word, and let my servant be healed" (7:7), and so he says to the crowd following him, "I tell you, not even in Israel have I found such faith" (7:9; see also Matt. 8:10 above).

In 22:30 (as in Matt. 19:28; see much more fully above) Jesus promises his apostles that he has assigned to them, as his Father assigned to him, "a kingdom," and that they "may eat and drink at my table in my kingdom and sit on thrones judging the twelve tribes of Israel." This unified expectation of the apostolic leaders and the twelve tribes of Israel are sketched together in this promise of Jesus, and Paul spells out some aspects of it further in Romans 11.

The last reference to Israel in Luke's gospel is on the lips of the two disciples on the way to Emmaus in 24:21. In answer to Jesus' inquiry about what they were talking about when he joined them, they say that they had hoped that Jesus "was the one to redeem Israel." Here they use Israel to designate a people that they had hoped that Jesus would, in some way, redeem.

John

To conclude our survey of the Gospels, we turn to John's gospel with its 4 occurrences (1:31, 49; 3:10; 12:13). John the Baptist, in bearing witness to Jesus as the Lamb of God (1:29) and the Son[4] of God (1:34), says that "for this purpose I came baptizing with water, that he [Jesus] might be revealed [made known] to Israel" (1:31). In his great surprise that Jesus had seen him under the fig tree, "Nathanael answered him, Rabbi, you are the Son of God! You are the King of Israel!" (1:49). Like John, he declares that Jesus is the Son of God, and also declares him as the King of Israel, perhaps referring to the promise to David being fulfilled in Jesus with reference to this people. In doing so he may be most influenced by Psalm 2 where the anointed Messiah of God is called both his Son (vv. 7, 12) and also the King on his holy hill, Zion (v. 8). For both John and Nathanael the word Israel is used with reference to their contemporaries. In 3:10 Jesus answers Nicodemus' inquiry about the new birth in a human by the work of the Spirit (3:3–8), stated incredulously with "How can these things be?" (3:9), by questioning Nicodemus for being "the teacher in Israel and yet you do not understand these things?" Again, Jesus used Israel to refer to a contemporary people.

Finally, we find the large crowd crying out as Jesus comes into Jerusalem riding on a young donkey, "Hosanna! Blessed is he who comes in the name of the Lord, even the King of Israel!" (12:13). Only John reports the

---

4. Unless we follow the Greek manuscripts that read "Elect" (or "Chosen") instead of "Son."

crowd calling Jesus "the King of Israel." Likely they did so because the text from Zechariah 9:9 is referred to in a closely following verse (12:15) which says, "Fear not, daughter of Zion; behold, your king is coming, sitting on a donkey's colt!" This verse also uses Israel with a contemporary reference and describes Jesus as "King of Israel," as Nathanael had done.

The gospel writers use the word "Israel" to refer to the people in the Old Testament, to those contemporary with Jesus, and also to a people who would be present with Jesus and the apostles in the future.

THE ACTS OF THE APOSTLES

The Acts of the Apostles contains more occurrences of the term "Israel" (15 times) than any one of the Gospels and is only exceeded in the New Testament by the Pauline letters. This section of the New Testament should prove to be a significant contributor to our understanding of the usage of "Israel" in the New Testament. The occurrences are 1:6; 2:36; 4:10, 27; 5:21, 31; 7:23, 37, 42; 9:15; 10:36; 13:17, 23, 24; 28:20.

The book of Acts places on its first pages a question coming from Jesus' disciples, namely, "Lord, will you at this time restore the kingdom to Israel?" (1:6). This question about restoring the kingdom to Israel is similar to that question of James and John (and their mother for them) asking to sit on Jesus' right hand and left hand in his kingdom (cf. Matt. 20:20–28; Mark 10:35–45). Perhaps these disciples had forgotten Jesus' parable of the tenants (Matt. 21:33–46) where he had said to his Jewish hearers that "the kingdom of God will be taken away from you and given to a people producing its fruits" (21:43). Whatever they were thinking and however they asked their question, Jesus simply responded to them that such future matters should be left to the Father's knowledge and control (Acts 1:7). But he goes on to say that they, laboring with the power of the Holy Spirit, should witness about Jesus throughout the surrounding area "and to the end of the earth" (1:8). Perhaps he is implying to them (and to us) by this command that which he had taught them in his earthly ministry, "And this gospel of the kingdom will be proclaimed throughout the whole world as a testimony to all nations, and then the end will come" (Matt. 24:14).[5]

---

5. See for this question of the disciples and all that we can learn from Jesus' answer in its context the fine fuller treatment given by O. Palmer Robertson in *The Israel of God: Yesterday, Today, and Tomorrow* (Phillipsburg, NJ: P&R, 2000), 127–37.

In 2:36 Peter addresses his Jewish hearers (cf. v. 22 earlier in his speech where he addresses the crowd, "men of Israel," literally, "men, Israelites;" cf. also 2:14) as "all the house of Israel" informing them so that they can "know for certain that God has made him both Lord and Christ, this Jesus whom you crucified." Luke uses this phrase "house of Israel" both here and in 7:42, just as Matthew used it in 10:6 and 15:24 and the writer to the Hebrews used it in Hebrews 8:8 and 10. The usage of the phrase in the New Testament finds its rootage in the Old Testament, especially in the passages quoted where this phrase is used (cf. Acts 7:42–43 where the phrase is in Amos 5:25–27 which is cited, and Hebrews 8:8 and 10 where the phrases are in Jer. 31:31–34 which is cited in Heb. 8:8–12).

In 4:10 and 27, Luke uses the expression "the people(s) of Israel," an expression used 6 times in the New Testament and all except one are in the gospel of Luke and the book of the Acts (Matt. 2:6; Luke 2:32; Acts 4:10, 27; 13:17, 24). There are several differences that may be noted. Matthew's account (2:6) has the qualifier "my" before "people" in the cited prophecy of Micah 5:2, Simeon qualifies "people" with "your" (Luke 2:32), and Paul qualifies it with "this" (Acts 13:17). These three (Matthew [citing Micah], Simeon, and Paul) all use "Israel" in apposition to the word "people" in their passages. In the remaining 3 occurrences in Acts (4:10, 27; 13:24), "Israel" is in the genitive qualifying "people." Acts uses "all" with the phrase in Acts 4:10 and 13:24, and the plural, "peoples," in used only in Acts 4:27. The usage of the phrase "the people of Israel" in the prophecy of Micah 5:2 (cited in Matt. 2:6) and in the blessing of Simeon (Luke 2:32) show the influence of the Old Testament, as does also its usage by others in their speeches to the Jews (4:10; 13:17, 24) and prayers to God (10:27) in the early and middle portions of the book of Acts. The possessive pronouns "my" and "your," referring to God and thus identifying "the people" as His, demonstrate that this usage of Israel in apposition to the "people" presents Israel as the people of God. The genitive structure, "the people(s) of Israel," can be assumed to do the same.

The context of each occurrence is impressive. In answer to their question, "By what power or by what name did you do this?" (4:7), Peter answers, ". . . let it be known to all of you and to all the people of Israel that by the name of Jesus Christ of Nazareth, whom you crucified, whom God raised from the dead—by him this man is standing before you well"

(4:10). 4:27–28 is equally awesome and impressive as the believers lift their voices to the Sovereign Lord and say, "for truly in this city there were gathered together against your holy servant Jesus, whom you anointed, ... the Gentiles and the peoples of Israel, to do whatever your hand and your plan had predestined to take place." The people(s) of Israel were responsible and so were the Gentiles and all occurred as God had predestined.

The Jewish religious leaders meeting with the high priest are designated in their called gathering as "the council and all the senate of Israel" (5:21b), that is, the reputed rulers of the people of Israel. Brought before this gathering to give answer for their continued teaching about Jesus, which this council had forbidden them to do, Peter and the apostles answered them that "the God of our fathers raised Jesus" (5:30) and that "God exalted him at his right hand as Leader and Savior, to give repentance to Israel and forgiveness of sins" (5:31). Peter and the apostles tell the gathered religious leadership that God raised and exalted Jesus so that he can give to the very people Israel (who in 4:27 are named among others as responsible for the things that had happened to Jesus) repentance and forgiveness of sins.

In the seventh chapter there are three references to Israel in Stephen's speech before the council. In 7:23 Stephen relates that Moses, when he was about forty years old, desired "to visit his brothers, the children of Israel." Stephen introduces Moses with the following words: "his brothers, the children of Israel," referring to the Hebrews, or Jewish people, living in Egypt, and perhaps because Stephen is so taken with the fact that they are all descendents of the patriarch Israel. He also presents Moses addressing them as the "sons [or, children] of Israel" in 7:37 for a similar reason. Last of all, Stephen cites Amos 5:25–27 in Acts 7:42–42 with its occurrence of "O house of Israel" in verse 42: "Did you bring to me slain beasts and sacrifices, during the forty years in the wilderness, O house of Israel?" For the phrase "house of Israel," see the fuller treatment under Acts 2:36.

The Lord's call to Saul (by means of Ananias) is presented in 9:15 in these words: "Go, for he is a chosen instrument of mine to carry my name before the Gentiles and kings and the children of Israel." The Lord himself uses the Old Testament designation of "the children of Israel" as an appropriate way to communicate to Saul (the converted Pharisee) his duty and responsibility to the Jews (as well as the Gentiles), who are still remembered by God because of his promise to Abraham and Israel by the phrase "the children of Israel."

91

In 10:36 Peter presents what God had been doing through Peter's ministry, which he describes as "the word that he sent to Israel," and then explains its content in this and the following verses, speaking of "preaching good news of peace through Jesus Christ (he is Lord of all)." This content ("he is Lord of all") is so relevant everywhere that he preaches the same message to Cornelius the God-fearer and those gathered with him in his house because he understands, as he has just said, "that God shows no partiality, but in every nation anyone who fears him and does what is right is acceptable to him" (10:34–35). This "to Israel," describes people in a particular place, and this is summarized later as being "both in the country of the Jews and in Jerusalem" (v. 39). But equally so, Peter says, in view of his understanding of God's outlook on people everywhere, that the Old Testament bears witness in all the prophets "that everyone who believes in him [Jesus Christ] receives forgiveness of sins through his name" (10:43).

Paul in his exhortation to the Jews in the synagogue in Antioch in Pisidia uses the term Israel three times (Acts 13:17, 23, 24). He begins by addressing them as Israelites and God-fearers (v. 16), and begins his message with the words "The God of this people Israel chose our fathers and made the people great during their stay in the land of Egypt, and with uplifted arm he led them out of it" (13:17). He speaks to the assembled group as part and parcel of "this people Israel." He depicts in a wonderful and compact way how God has kept his promise to David and Israel by saying, "Of this man's [David's] offspring God has brought to Israel a Savior, Jesus, as he promised" (13:23). And he follows this statement by saying that "Before his [Jesus'] coming, John had proclaimed a baptism of repentance to all the people of Israel" (13:24). John's hearers were of that group called "all the people of Israel." Jesus was brought by God and repentance was proclaimed by John, in both cases "to Israel," and in so doing God has kept his promise to David and to "this people Israel" (cf. esp. vv. 26, 32–33). Paul speaks of "Israel" with a sweep that goes back to their fathers and continues until the day of his ministry (cf. esp. vv. 32–33, "And we bring you the good news that what God promised to the fathers, this he has fulfilled to us their children by raising Jesus . . .").

In Paul's address to the local leaders of the Jews in Rome, he explains his imprisonment to them in these words, "it is because of the hope of Israel that I am wearing this chain" (28:20). Paul uses the word "hope" in the phrase "hope of Israel" to describe that which Israel has been looking forward to and which he now finds fulfilled in the person and work of Jesus. Paul uses this word "hope" in a Jewish context three other times in Acts (23:6; 24:14–15; 26:6ff.). In 23:6 Paul speaks of his being on trial "with respect to the hope and the resurrection of the dead." What the believing Jew looked forward to was a resurrection hope and the Christian relied upon that hope also as it is found in the reality of Christ's resurrection as the basis for his own salvation and resurrection (cf. 1 Cor. 15:12–21). Similarly, in 24:14–15 Paul uses hope and resurrection in close proximity when he says that he and others, "having a hope in God, which these men themselves accept, that there will be a resurrection of both the just and the unjust." He also uses hope in the midst of the Jews he is addressing in Jerusalem to speak of his being on trial "because of my hope in the promise made by God to our fathers to which our twelve tribes hope to attain . . . And for this hope I am accused by Jews, O king! . . ." And he concludes by asking why it should be thought incredible "that God raises the dead?" (26:6–8). The hope in 28:20 most likely (from this brief survey of Paul's other uses in Acts) includes both salvation and the resurrection in the light of Jesus as the crucified and risen Messiah.

The book of Acts uses "Israel," as do the four Gospels, to refer to the people in the Old Testament, to those contemporary with the apostles, and also to a people who would be present with Jesus and the apostles in the future.

THE LETTER TO THE HEBREWS

We turn to the letter to the Hebrews (and then to the book of Revelation) before dealing with some of the most significant usages in the letters of Paul. Hebrews contains three occurrences of the term "Israel" (8:8, 10; 11:22). All three have an Old Testament setting. The first two occur in a citation of Jeremiah 31:31–34 which, however, points to the future of "the house of Israel" which the writer says is fulfilled now in Christ. The third occurs in a mention of the exodus of Israel (see Acts 2:36 for a survey of the phrase "house of Israel").

Let us take note of the first two (8:8, 10) in their contextual settings. "Behold, the days are coming, declares the Lord, when I will establish a new covenant with the house of Israel and with the house of Judah. . . . For this is the covenant that I will make with the house of Israel after those days, declares the Lord: I will put my laws into their minds, and write them on their hearts, and I will be their God, and they shall be my people." This quotation is premised on the remarks about Christ mediating a covenant that "is better, since it is enacted on better promises" (8:6). With other transitional remarks, the writer then quotes from Jeremiah the promise from God for this "new covenant with the house of Israel" (8:8, 10). The writer then seals this reference to Christ in the ninth chapter when he writes in verse 15, "Therefore he [Christ] is the mediator of a new covenant, so that those who are called may receive the promised eternal inheritance, since a death has occurred that redeems them from the transgressions committed under the first covenant." Who is this "house of Israel" to which Jeremiah looked forward, and about which the writer of Hebrews says has received this "new covenant" with its "promised eternal inheritance"? The writer concludes the ninth chapter with his implied answer: "so Christ, having been offered once to bear the sins of many, will appear a second time, not to deal with sin but to save those who are eagerly waiting for him" (9:28). It is for those "many" whose sins he bore and who "are eagerly waiting for him" that he enacted this new covenant. And these "many" [not, "all," implies an election on the part of God; cf. 9:15, "those who are called may receive the promised eternal inheritance"] are "the house of Israel" to whom the promises of a new covenant were given long ago, i.e., they are the Christians who "are eagerly waiting for him." So we have "the house of Israel" used in prophecy to apply in a future date to Christians, whether Jew or Gentile.

Hebrews 11:22 uses "Israel" as an item of historical identification as it expresses the expectation of Joseph's faith: "By faith Joseph, at the end of his life, made mention of the exodus of the Israelites [literally, "the sons of Israel"] and gave directions concerning his bones."

The letter to the Hebrews uses Israel to describe the Old Testament people (11:22) and, in fulfillment of God's promise, to designate those to whom the second and new covenant was promised, whom the letter argues are New Testament believers (8:8, 10; cf. also 8:13).

REVELATION

In the book of Revelation, the term "Israel" also occurs 3 times in the phrase "the sons of Israel" (2:14; 7:4; 21:12). The term is used in 2:14 as a historical designation, and in 7:4 and 21:12 as a historical designation with a heavenly reference.

In the letter to the church in Pergamum God states what he has against it. There are some in the church "who hold the teaching of Balaam, who taught Balak to put a stumbling block before the sons of Israel, so that they might eat food sacrificed to idols and practice sexual immorality" (2:14). The reference "the sons of Israel" used with Balak is used as an Old Testament identification of the Hebrew people. In 7:4, the phrase is used again to identify those who are the "servants of our God" who are sealed on their foreheads (7:3). So the quotation reads, "And I heard the number of the sealed, 144,000, sealed from every tribe of the sons of Israel" (7:4). Those that are thus sealed are those living in the future, about which John writes in this book, and they are sealed to be protected from the harm produced on the earth in that future time (cf. 7:3). Finally, the holy city, Jerusalem, coming down out of heaven from God, is described as having on the gates of its wall "... the names of the twelve tribes of the sons of Israel ... inscribed—on the east three gates, on the north three gates, on the south three gates, and on the west three gates" (21:12–13). This is quite significant in that it is one of the chief marks of the wall of that great and holy city. But even more so is it significant that the other great mark of the wall were the foundations marked with "the twelve names of the twelve apostles of the Lamb" (21:14). This city is marked by the twelve tribes of the sons of Israel and by the twelve apostles of the Lamb. These are there, and they are marking the wall, because they, like others that are therein, are there only because they are "those who are written in the Lamb's book of life" (21:27).

THE LETTERS OF PAUL

The letters of Paul also contain the most occurrences of the usage of "Israel" in the New Testament under any one author in any one corpus, i.e., 17 occurrences (if Luke-Acts is taken together it has the most occurrences, 27 in all; while the four Gospels together have 30). These occur in Romans (11 times), 2 Corinthians (2 times) and 1 Corinthians, Galatians, Ephesians, and Philippians (one occurrence each). Since Romans has the most frequent, and one or more of the most important, occurrences, we will take it next to last, with special attention being given to Romans 9–11 (where 11 of the 17 references to Israel occur) and especially to Romans 11:26. Last of all, we will consider Galatians 6:16 where the very significant occurrence of "the Israel of God" occurs (the only occurrence of this phrase, with its addition "of God," in the New Testament). The occurrences are as follows: Romans 9:6, 27 (2 times), 31; 10:19, 21; 11:2, 7, 25, 26; 1 Corinthians 10:18; 2 Corinthians 3:7, 13; Galatians 6:16; Ephesians 2:12; Philippians 3:5

We will deal with the letters in the order that Paul wrote them, except for Romans and Galatians.

In the only occurrence in 1 Corinthians Paul uses Israel in an unusual way. He speaks of it as "Israel according to the flesh" and asks the Corinthian church to "consider" it as teaching a lesson for us with regard to the Lord's Supper and the table of demons. He says, "Consider Israel according to the flesh: are not those who eat the sacrifices participants in the altar?" (10:18; the ESV uses "the people of Israel"). Just as surely as "Israel according to the flesh" who eat the sacrifices are participants in the altar, so also those who partake of the Lord's Supper have a participation in the blood and body of Christ (10:16–17), and also those who participate at the demons' table are participating with the demons (10:20–22).

Twice in 2 Corinthians Paul contrasts the glory and effectiveness of the ministry of the Spirit in this Messianic age with that of Moses to "the sons of Israel." "Now if the ministry of death, carved in letters on stone, came with such glory that the Israelites [literally, the sons of Israel] could not gaze at Moses' face because of its glory . . . will not the ministry of the Spirit have even more glory" (3:7–8)? And, "Since we have such a hope, we are very bold, not like Moses, who would put a veil over his face so that the Israelites [literally, "the sons of Israel"] might not gaze at the outcome of what was being brought to an end" (3:12–13).

Paul speaks in Ephesians of the past status of the Gentiles and asks them to "remember that you were at that time separated from Christ, alienated from the commonwealth of Israel and strangers to the covenants of promise, having no hope and without God in the world" (2:12). He also affirms in the following verse: "But now in Christ Jesus you who once were far off have been brought near by the blood of Christ" (2:13). And now they, both the Gentiles who "were far off" and the Jews "who were near" (2:17), "are fellow citizens with the saints and members of the household of God" (2:19). Paul describes the Gentiles' plight as that of one shut off from the spiritual reality of relationship with Christ and with God because they did not know the covenants of promise and had no place in the commonwealth of Israel. But all that is changed for them through the blood of Christ and his proclamation of peace to them (2:13–18, which they have embraced by faith, cf. 2:8–10). These Gentiles are not brought into the commonwealth of Israel but with the believing Jews into "the household of God, built on the foundation of" "Christ Jesus . . . the cornerstone" and of "the apostles and prophets" (2:19–20).

Paul reminds his readers in Philippians that their status of salvation is all accomplished by the work of Christ and that they should not hark back to their Jewishness or any other thing of their own (3:3). Paul makes that point by pointing to himself and to his heritage which he does not boast of or rest in but in fact counts as loss (3:7), and that therefore they should follow his example. In the midst of his statement of what he could boast in but does not, he lists "of the people of Israel." "If anyone else thinks he has reason for confidence in the flesh, I have more: circumcised on the eighth day, of the people of Israel, of the tribe of Benjamin, a Hebrew of the Hebrews . . ." (Phil. 3:4–5). These things are even now his current status, that is, he is currently an Israelite, but they count for nothing to gain Christ.

Paul in 1 and 2 Corinthians, Philippians, and Ephesians uses the word "Israel" to refer to the Old Testament community which is now replaced by the "household of God," the body of Christ, the church (cf. Eph. 2:13–22).

Romans 9–11

We now turn to the longest discussion of Israel found in the NT, *Romans 9–11*. Paul begins chapter nine by saying that he wishes that his kinsmen, the Israelites, to whom God gave so many spiritual blessings, would embrace Jesus who was born as a member of their race.

In fact, the paucity of response by the Israelites to Jesus as the promised Messiah brings Paul to assert that "it is not as though the word of God has failed" (9:6). He gives as the reason for this assertion the following: "For not all who are descended from Israel belong to Israel, and not all are children of Abraham because they are his offspring . . ." (9:6–7). Here we have Israel used in two different senses in the same sentence. The first occurrence is used of those who are the physical descendents, or offspring. The parallel statement in the joining verse which says "not all are children of Abraham" in the spiritual sense "because they are his offspring" makes this evident. Paul explicates this by a further assertion in verse 8: "This means that it is not the children of the flesh who are the children of God, but the children of the promise are counted as offspring." And Paul refers to Isaac and Jacob in distinction from Ishmael (understood) and Esau (stated) as two cases immediately evident in the lineage and promise to Abraham.

The second occurrence of "Israel" is in 9:6: "for not all who are descended from Israel belong to Israel . . ." and it is used in the sense of the spiritual "children of God" or "the children of the promise" (both statements of description are given in 9:8). These children of the promise "are counted as offspring," that is, they are the ones to whom God's promise was given and for whom it was intended, as indicated by Isaac (9:7). And all this takes place, as exampled further in the children of Isaac, "in order that God's purpose of election might continue, not because of works but because of his call" (9:11) in which God says to Rebecca, "The older will serve the younger" (9:12). The second Israel consists of those elected by God, called by God, and those to whom his promise was given and intended, and thus those who are the children of God.

This concept of the remnant is identified as such in the two occurrences of the term in Romans 9:27, where Isaiah 10:22–23 and Hosea 1:10 are merged in a citation: "And Isaiah cries out concerning Israel: 'Though the number of the sons of Israel be as the sand of the sea, only a remnant of them will be saved.'" The people that Isaiah cries out to is the nation or people of Israel who are then also referred to as "the sons of Israel." And this remnant is a remnant of the entirety of the whole of Israel, i.e., those referred to by Paul in Romans 9:6–13. This remnant is one of God's election and calling (cf. 9:11) as the following verse citing Isaiah again (1:9) indicates in its wording, "If the Lord of hosts had not left us offspring, we would have been like Sodom and become like Gomorrah."

Again in 9:31 the mass of Israel is reproached for not accepting the good news of a righteousness received by faith, which the Gentiles have attained (9:30), but rather have sought a righteousness based on works: "but that Israel who pursued a law that would lead to righteousness did not succeed in reaching that law. Why? Because they did not pursue it by faith, but as if it were based on works" (9:31–32). God's children are elected and called, and attain the promise by faith.

In these verses from Romans 9 Paul uses the term "Israel" to refer to the Jewish people in general, with only the second usage in 9:6 and the remnant in 9:27 referring to spiritual Israel.

Israel is used in that same general way in the two occurrences in the tenth chapter as well. First, we read in 10:19, "But I ask, did Israel not understand?" Here Paul is speaking of the good news of the gospel (cf. 10:14–17, esp. v. 15). He answers his own question in part in two Old Testament citations that follow in the next verses. He then concludes his answer with another citation from Isaiah (65:2) in verse 21 which says, "But of Israel he says, 'All day long I have held out my hands to a disobedient and contrary people.' " They heard (cf. 10:18), but they did not respond in faith, and so were disobedient to the call to believe (cf. 16a and 21b with 16b and 17).

"Israel" occurs four times in Romans 11 (vv. 2, 7, 25, 26). Paul picks up the conclusion of Romans 10 and poses the question, "has God rejected his people?" He is quite forthright in saying "By no means! For I myself am an Israelite, a descendant of Abraham, a member of the tribe of Benjamin" (v. 1). Paul indicates that "his people" in the question is the people "Israel" (understood spiritually), as he responds with the answer "I myself am an Israelite." He reinforces that in verse 2 by declaring again that "God has not rejected his people whom he foreknew," and by answering the appeal of Elijah against Israel ("how he appeals to God against Israel," also v. 2). That answer is given in verses 4 and 5 ("But what is God's reply to him?"): First, that he still had a remnant in Elijah's day (the 7000), and, second, "So too at the present time [in the New Testament age] there is a remnant, chosen by grace." "What then," asks Paul (v. 7a)? The answer may seem bleak, but it is not when one hears the rest of God's plan. Paul begins and ends his answer with the bleak part: "Israel failed to obtain what it was seeking. The elect obtained it, but the rest were hardened" (v. 7b and c). The "elect" [remnant] of Israel understood and obtained it, but Israel seen in the whole "failed to obtain" it, and they "were hardened."

Paul enlightens us that this hardening is a means by which Gentiles are hearing the gospel and being brought into the church. He writes in verse 25: "Lest you be wise in your own conceits, I want you to understand this mystery, brothers: a partial hardening has come upon Israel, until the fullness of the Gentiles has come in." Here, again, he uses Israel as the Old Testament people of God, still regarded as such because of their election through their forefathers, which is irrevocable. ("But as regards election, they are beloved for the sake of their forefathers. For the gifts and the calling of God are irrevocable" [11:28b–29].)

This brings us to the significant statement of Romans 11:26: "And in this way all Israel will be saved, as it is written, 'The Deliverer will come from Zion, he will banish ungodliness from Jacob'; 'and this will be my covenant with them when I take away their sins'" (Paul citing Isaiah 59:20–21). There are two questions we must pose about this statement. First, when does what is stated in it occur, and second, what is the meaning of "Israel" in this statement?

We will deal with the time factor first. There are those, among whom Dr. Robertson is a worthy example, who argue that the time reference is to that which is going on now in the New Testament age as Jews, like Paul, are being brought into the kingdom by their conversions so that when the last one is brought in, all Israel (both Jews and Gentiles) will be saved. There are others who expect a large ingathering of the Jews in a yet future time as the meaning of "all Israel will be saved" (including the current ingathering as playing a part).

For the current ingathering of Jews as the proper and entire understanding of the passage, Dr. Robertson points to several references in Romans 11 that certainly seem to be *prima facie* indications of that understanding. "In answer to the question, 'Has God rejected his people?' [Rom. 11:1] Paul identifies himself as living proof that God's purposes for Israel are being realized in the present era."[6] With these words of Paul, Robertson expounds Romans 11:1 by arguing from Paul's response, namely, that he not only denies the question but also points to himself as part of the answer with his words "For even I am an Israelite."

He also argues from the words "at the present time" in Romans 11:5 which read, "So too at the present time there is a remnant, chosen by grace."[7] God is presently dealing with Israel by saving this remnant, and Dr. Robertson affirms that this is the group he has always determined to save. Dr. Robertson also argues from Romans 11:13–14 that Paul says he intends by his ministry to the Gentiles "to make my fellow Jews jealous, and thus save some of them" (11:14). He states that this "must be understood in the context of God's present dealing with the nation."[8] He argues further that this "present saving of some in Israel . . . is immediately connected with the 'receiving' of the Jews in the following verses (vss. 15–16). The

6. Robertson, *Israel*, 168.
7. Ibid., 169.
8. Ibid.

'for if' . . . of verse 15 connects the 'receiving' of the Jews with the present ministry of the apostle Paul in the gospel era."[9]

But one may respectfully differ with this understanding of the way verse 15 connects to the preceding verses and how it affects our understanding of the receiving or acceptance of the Jews. It is true that the "for if" connects verse 15 to that which precedes, but it may be to verse 12 rather than to verses 13–14. At any rate, the "for if" is saying that "their rejection means the reconciliation of the world," the first part of verse, and the "what" of the second part of the verse asks "what will their acceptance mean but life from the dead" (v. 15). So it seems that verse 15 is reiterating verse 12 which focused first on the significance of "their trespass" and "their failure," and then on their "full inclusion," which is the same pattern as verse 15 except for "for if" taking the place of "now if" in verse 12 and "what" taking the place of "how much more" in verse 12. But be that as it may, the "for if" does not focus on their "acceptance" but upon their "rejection." But "since the provoking to jealousy is a factor in the conversion of Israel (vs. 11) and since Paul pursues his ministry to that end, his saving some no doubt contributes to the 'fullness' of Israel. But this he does not say."[10] This agreement by Murray to the fact that Paul's then present ministry had a part in bringing in Jews only means that it contributes to the "fullness" yet to be manifested but does not say that it is that "fullness."

Dr. Robertson also discusses possible references in Romans 11 which might seem to imply dealing with Israel in the future.[11] And he comes to the conclusion that they do not point in that direction.

Now it is best for us to summarize those arguments that would seem to indicate that Paul has in view God's special dealing with Israel in the future and only as needed refer to Dr. Robertson's alternative perspective.

First, the overall contents of Romans 11. Paul seems to be writing Romans 9–11 with the redemptive-historical perspective that God dealt primarily with the Jews in the Old Testament, then primarily with the Gentiles in the New Testament because the Jews rejected Jesus as their promised Messiah, and that he will yet deal with Israel as a whole after the fullness of the Gentiles has come in (cf. 11:30–31). Thus he speaks of Israel's "stumble," "trespass," "failure" (11:11–12) and even of their being "broken off because

---

9. Ibid.
10. John Murray, *The Epistle to the Romans*, NICNT (Grand Rapids: Eerdmans, 1965), 2:80n25.
11. Robertson, *Israel*, 171–82.

of their unbelief" (11:19–21). "A partial hardening has come upon Israel" (11:25). Yes, the dire strait of Israel is moderated by the absolute truth that God has not rejected his people and that the present remnant is a clear indication of that fact (11:1–2, 5). Yet to this truth must be added the terrible "but": "but the rest were hardened" (11:5–10). Does this terrible stumble mean that Israel has completely fallen from God's plan (11:11a and b)? No, it does not, but rather that salvation has come to the Gentiles so as to make Israel jealous (11:11c). But now we can look forward to God's bringing about a "full inclusion" of Israel (11:12). "For God has the power to graft them in again" (11:23).

This brings us, secondly, to verses 25–26a and the citation of the Old Testament in verses 26b–27. Paul places in his remarks in verse 25 the purpose clause "lest you be wise in your own estimation" (NASB). Here Paul is warning the Gentiles with his use of "you" harkening back to the "you" which he introduced in verse 13 with its coordinate "Gentiles" and which he also used in verse 17 and continues throughout the passage concluding in the "you" of verse 24. That "you" is the "wild olive branch" (v. 17; cf. v. 24) or, as originally designated in verse 13, "Gentiles." He warns them not to be "wise in their own estimation."

With this term "estimation" Paul summarizes for them what he has warned them about in verses 17–24. The Gentiles were inclined to be wise in that way as Paul relates them saying in verses 19–20: "Then you will say, 'Branches were broken off so that I might be grafted in.' That is true. They were broken off because of their unbelief, but you stand fast through faith. So do not become proud, but stand in awe." It is this tendency to become proud that Paul warns them about when he urges them not to be wise in their own estimation. Do not be arrogant about the church being now predominantly Gentile, but remember that you were "grafted, contrary to nature, into a cultivated olive tree" (v. 24), and that you "now share in the nourishing root of the olive tree" (11:17). To keep you from being arrogant toward the broken off branches, "remember it is not you who support the root, but the root that supports you" (11:18).

Paul writes verse 25, and also the beginning of verse 26, to help them not to be wise in their own estimation. He describes what he writes, as a "mystery," indeed as "this mystery" (11:25). By "mystery" Paul usually understands that which man has not discovered by himself but which is now being set forth by means of revelation. And he writes to them that they may not "be uninformed of this mystery" (NASB).

He begins by saying "a partial hardening has come upon Israel" (11:25). He describes the hardening as "partial." Here he returns to the hardening by which he had described Israel and now speaks of it as "partial." He had spoken of the rest of Israel as being "hardened" using the cognate verb in verse 7. Now he uses the noun in verse 25. One of the nuances of this term as both a verb and a noun is "difficulty in understanding or comprehending," or "complete lack of understanding, dullness, insensibility."[12] Mark 6:52 says that Jesus' disciples "did not understand about the loaves, but their hearts were hardened," but when their eyes were opened by Jesus then they understood (cf. the use of hardened with reference to them in Mark 8:17, and Jesus' question in Mark 8:21, "Do you not yet understand?"). Similarly, Paul describes the Gentiles as "alienated from the life of God because of the ignorance that is in them, due to their hardness of heart" (Eph. 4:18). The disciples are also said to have once been like them until God made them "alive together with Christ" (Eph. 2:1–6, esp. v. 5). So also with Israel. "The hardening of Israel is partial not total." "The last clause in this verse [25] should surely be taken as referring to a point of eventuation that brings the hardening to an end." "Until the fullness of the Gentiles be come in" indicates that the hardening is "temporary not final."[13]

This "partial hardening" is said to be "until [*achri hou*] the fullness of the Gentiles has come in" (11:25). The significance of "until" is important to gain an understanding of the significance of this concluding statement. Does it imply until the end of time,[14] or does it imply the ending of the partial hardening? It needs to be noted that the usage in the statement after the words "a partial hardening has come upon Israel" imply a *prima facie* understanding that the conjunction used after it, "until," will indicate when the partial hardening ceases. A consideration of the use of the Greek phrase "until" [*achri hou*] elsewhere in the New Testament strengthens this understanding. The phrase *achri hou* with the relative pronoun following it

12. BDAG, 900.

13. Murray, *Romans*, II, 92, 92n45, & 92 again. Similarly, Cranfield, Hodge, Moo, Sanday and Headlam, Schreiner, and Stott.

14. Robertson, *Israel*, 150, "The phrase implies not a new beginning after a termination, but the continuation of a circumstance until the end of time," (i.e., the "eschatological termination," "until the final return of Christ"). "In any case, 'hardening until' does not by itself indicate that in a subsequent period of time the partial hardening of Israel will be lifted."

is the short form for "until the time to which," [*achri tou chronou ho*],[15] so that the addition of the relative pronoun "of which" to "time" [understood] focuses on that moment expressed afterwards, i.e., "until the fullness of the Gentiles has come in." This is borne out by the usage of *achris* in a number of cases elsewhere in the New Testament. Of particular notice is that 25 of the 37 temporal usages "rather clearly denote a period of time that will come to an end and be followed by a change of those circumstances denoted. Significantly, 14 of these are followed by an aorist verb (as in Rom. 11:25), while only two of ten occurrences of *achris* where it means 'right up to' use the aorist."[16] It seems to me that the ending of the partial hardening is in view with the word "until." That time is when "the fullness of the Gentiles has come in," i.e., when God has gathered that vast and completed number of the Gentiles that he is saving, and caused them to "come in," i.e., to enter into his kingdom.[17]

This brings us to verse 26a, "And in this way all Israel will be saved." The Greek underlying "in this way" is used to indicate the manner in which all Israel will be saved and to do so by linking this statement to the preceding verse. That which will be saved is presented as "all Israel." Paul has used Israel ten times so far in Romans 9–11 and each of these refers to the ethnic entity whether referring to all those born of that line, or to those elected and chosen by God to be the recipients of his promise to their forefathers (cf. 9:6b [2 times], 27 [2 times], 31; 10:19, 21; 11:2, 7, 25).

In effect this is the conclusion of the entire section of Romans 9–11 dealing with Israel. Romans 9:6 began the discussion by saying that God's word had not failed because the promise was intended for God's elect (9:11), so that Paul could write, "For not all who are descended from Israel belong to Israel" (9:6b). The passage progressed further by saying that God had always saved a remnant who seek him by faith and that Israel, in the main, had not done that (9:30–33). In fact he says that they did not understand (10:19–21). But he wants to say most emphatically that God has not rejected his people (11:1). Here he introduces the concept of remnant most explicitly (11:5), even though at the same time he says that "the rest were hardened" (11:7). But there is a reason for this hard-

---

15. BDAG, 160.

16. See Moo, *Romans*, 717n30, where the passages are given and detail is provided.

17. For the significance of this Greek verb, "to come in," "to enter," compare the absolute uses of it in, e.g., Matt. 7:13; 23:13; Luke 13:24.

ening from God's perspective, namely that the Gentiles may be brought in (11:11–12). At the same time he reminds us that Israel has not fallen away never to be rescued (11:11). He is an example of that fact, and the full inclusion of Israel will be a further example of that fact (11:12–13). It is of that "full inclusion" that he speaks when he says "all Israel" will be saved, that is, not just the remnant or himself, but that number that God will call from ethnic Israel to fill out his elect and to keep his promise to the forefathers that the coming of Jesus was to accomplish this purpose. So it is that he quotes from Isaiah 59:20–21 in 26b–27 where this promise was made concerning Jacob [Israel]: "The Deliver will come from Zion, he will banish ungodliness from Jacob'; 'and this will be my covenant with them when I take away their sins' " (11:26–27).

So it is that we must have two perspectives on the Jews [Israel]. And to make this clear he writes two seemingly (on the surface) different perspectives on Israel for the Christians. "As regards the gospel, they are enemies of God for your sake. But as regards election, they are beloved for the sake of their forefathers. For the gifts and the calling of God are irrevocable" (11:28–29). So "now" from the perspective of redemptive history given to us in these chapters (Rom. 11:31, "they also may now receive mercy"), we may expect this outcome and not be proud of our current standing as if it were the end of the story without them. In fact, Jews and Gentiles will be treated the same. Both will have been saved from disobedience and both will have mercy: "For God has consigned all to disobedience, that he may have mercy on all" (11:32).

Regardless of the exegetical outcome reached about these verses, i.e., whether it is the final and complete gathering of the elect among ethnic Israel (as I and others would suggest), or both Jews and Gentiles all together and finally gathered (as Dr. Robertson and others with him), when we come to this point of our study we can only be brought to our knees to join with Paul in saying, "Oh, the depth of the riches and wisdom and knowledge of God! How unsearchable are his judgments and how inscrutable his ways! . . . To him be glory forever. Amen" (11:33, 36b).

In Romans 9–11 Paul primarily uses "Israel" to refer to the external entity of the Hebrew people, but in two very important places, 9:6 and 11:26, he uses it to refer to spiritual Israel. In 9:6 he contrasts spiritual Israel, used to refer to the elect and believing ones among external Israel, with earthly Israel. He also uses "Israel" in a similar way in 11:26.

Galatians 6:16

We turn to our final source for Israel in the pages of the New Testament, namely, Galatians 6:16: "And as far all[18] who walk by this rule, peace and mercy be upon them, and upon the Israel of God."

The first question we must ask of this passage is what is "this rule," or standard, by which "all" should walk and which also elicits Paul's blessing upon them? The broadest context of this reference is of course the entirety of this letter and its message. As true as this may be, it seems that Paul intends for the reference to point back to what he has written in the preceding verse, "For neither circumcision counts for anything, nor uncircumcision, but a new creation" (v. 15). And this verse, by its introductory "for," is dependant on the verse preceding it, "But far be it from me to boast except in the cross of our Lord Jesus Christ, by which the world has been crucified to me, and I to the world" (v. 14). And so it is in the spiritual reality of knowing and boasting of the cross of our Lord Jesus Christ that one comes to death to the world and recognizes that all that counts for anything in one's life is the new creation in Christ. Thus Paul has already drawn the conclusion that "neither circumcision counts for anything, nor uncircumcision, but a new creation" (v. 15). It is by this rule that one is to walk or live his life. No external entity is determinative of this new life (neither circumcision nor uncircumcision); it is only the new creation which our Lord Jesus Christ has wrought in us. This then is the rule or guiding standard by which one lives. The old distinctions are no longer that rule, but only the new creation in Christ. Thus, as Dr. Robertson so clearly articulates the significance of this truth, "a canon or rule of conduct related to the identity of the people of God has been established. . . . That rule is that no distinction may be made between circumcised or uncircumcised people when identifying the people of God."[19] And thus this benediction of Paul is given to "all" who are "a new creation," whoever they may be (whether circumcised or uncircumcised, whether Jew or Gentile), who walk by this rule.

That benediction is "peace and mercy be upon them." To this benediction Paul adds the phrase which contains our word Israel, "the Israel of God," apparently to identify those that are in view in his phrase "upon them."

18. The Greek correlative is the plural *hosoi* from *hosos* which even without "all" being used with it has the meaning, as here, of "all who," BGAD, 729.

19. Robertson, *Israel*, 40.

We need now to understand the verse as a whole with the phrase "the Israel of God" as part of it. The problems that remain for one who has gotten this far are as follows: How one understands and translates verse 16 depends upon whether one sees one or two groups in view, how one understands the last Greek *kai* to be rendered (either as "and" or as "even"), and how one understands the phrase "the Israel of God." The alternative for the phrase "the Israel of God" is that it is understood as some sort of reference to the Hebrew people whether seen more narrowly as the elect or more broadly as the community.

Rather than going through each of these questions independently,[20] we will look at them as a whole as seen in the light of the context. Thus if our understanding of the verses that have preceded verse 16 are correct, and if the connection of verse 16 with verse 15 and then verse 14 is also correct, then the conclusion which we reached in the end of the paragraph before the last is correct, and the words "apparently" can be removed, so that the statement would read "to identify those that are in view in his words 'upon them.' " Assuming that our understanding has been correct, we see one group, and not two, and we are inclined to understand the last Greek *kai* as signifying "even," that is, to be used in an explanatory sense (technically in an epexegetical sense) to explain who the "them" are, rather than just as "and." With the use of "even" the phrase "the Israel of God" is understood to be a delineation of who the "them" are.

Two other considerations corroborate this view. First, the context of the letter. Paul throughout this letter is arguing against those that say that Gentiles need to circumcised to be become members of the people of God (Gal. 2:3–5,14; 5:1–6; 6:12–15), and he calls Gentile believers the sons of Abraham (Gal. 3:7, 29; 4:31; cf. Rom. 4:11–12). Second, "Israel" in this context is used with the addition of the words "of God," a phenomenon which is not found elsewhere in Paul or the New Testament. Some have suggested that the Judaizers or false teachers used it as a catch phrase to describe the identity which they were trying to create, namely, the people of God who manifest that they are such by the fact that they are circumcised. If this is the case, and we can only speculate that this might be the case, then Paul is taking the phrase they have coined and indicating that only those of the "new creation" in Christ are truly "the Israel of God," and not those who

---

20. For a fuller treatment of these questions and alternatives, and for interaction with those espousing alternative positions, see Dr. Robertson's fine contribution in *The Israel of God*, 39–46.

depend upon an external sign. But it is even more likely that this phrase was produced by Paul himself for this particular situation and that it is done so because he wants to delineate that being in the true Israel "of God" is accomplished by the act of Jesus Christ making us a "new creation," and not by the external rite of circumcision.

Thus Paul in this letter to the Galatians, over against the false teaching of those who would demand that Gentiles be circumcised to become members of the people of God, has indicated that the true "Israel of God" are those of the "new creation," those who have trusted in Jesus Christ alone for salvation, and who are not distinguished by circumcision or uncircumsion.

Conclusion

The witness of the entire New Testament is that the writers use the word "Israel" in three different senses: (1) to designate the Hebrews (in Paul generally, and also in Romans 9:6 [the first occurrence], 31, 10:31, 11:7; so also in the Gospels and partially in Acts); (2) to designate the elect, believing, and spiritual entity, to be distinguished from the external but not elect or believing entity (cf. Rom. 9:6 [the second occurrence], 11:26 and also elsewhere in the New Testament); (3) "the Israel of God" as all those who are united to Christ by faith and who belong to God as his "new creation" (Gal. 6:16; cf. also "the olive tree" of Rom. 11:17–24, and other allusions in Paul such as Eph. 2:19–21, cf. vv. 11–12, Phil. 3:3, and also Heb. 12:22–24 and 1 Peter 2:9–10).

Thus the church in the New Testament period may use these designations as the New Testament does. In doing so, it must recognize that circumcision or being Jewish does not distinguish between those that are in "the Israel of God," but at the same time recognize that God has made two correlated promises to Abraham which he has fulfilled in Jesus Christ, namely, those descended from Abraham who are elect and believing in Jesus Christ and whose ancestors are the very root of the olive tree (i.e., believing Jews), and those from every nation (the wild olive branches) who also are being blessed and brought in and are fellow-members with the natural olive branches (i.e., believing Gentiles). We must not distinguish between these two groups who are united as one in the church (Gal. 6:15–16), and we also must not forget that God remembers his promises to them both which he made to Abraham and which he fulfills in Jesus Christ, in one spiritual body, the church (Rom. 11:25–32).

6

The Prophecy of Zechariah in Matthew's Passion Narrative

J. Knox Chamblin

I AM GRATEFUL for the invitation to contribute to this volume of essays in honor of my longtime friend, Palmer Robertson.[1]

Zechariah consists of two major sections, chapters 1–8 and 9–14. The Gospel according to Matthew contains three quotations from the prophecy. They all come from Zechariah 9–14, and all appear in Matthew's Passion Narrative, chapters 21–28: see 21:5 (Zech. 9:9); 26:31 (Zech. 13:7); and 27:9–10 (Zech. 11:12–13). We will also discover noteworthy allusions to Zechariah 9–14 in these closing chapters of Matthew.[2]

1. Most of the material in this essay is drawn from my forthcoming commentary on Matthew, and is used with permission from the publisher, Christian Focus. Palmer and I were raised together in the First Presbyterian Church of Jackson, MS. I was one of his groomsmen when he wed his first wife Judy; he was one of mine when I wed my wife Ginger. Both weddings were on September 10 (in different years!). I am not sure Palmer will agree with all the views expressed in this essay; but it is offered to him with deep affection and high esteem.

2. For this analysis of Zechariah, see Joyce C. Baldwin, *Haggai, Zechariah, Malachi: An Introduction and Commentary.* Tyndale Old Testament Commentaries (Downers Grove, IL: InterVarsity, 1972), 85–86. On the unity of Zechariah 1–14 in face of arguments to the contrary, see ibid.,

A. Zechariah in Matthew 21:1–11

Matthew's Passion Narrative opens with Jesus' entry into Jerusalem. According to verses 4 and 5, "This happened in order that what was said through the prophet might be fulfilled, saying: 'Say to the daughter of Zion, "Behold, your king is coming to you, meek and mounted on a donkey, and on a colt, the foal of a beast of burden." ' "[3]

The Preface to the Quotation from Zechariah

While this scriptural citation anticipates the entry itself, the opening "this" (*touto*) points to the instructions of verses 2–3, and thus shows that these preparations are integral to the prophecy's fulfillment. Already in verse 2 Jesus has spoken of a "donkey" (*onos*) and a "colt" (*pōlos*); and the "king" (*basileus*) of verse 5 matches the "Lord" (*Kyrios*) of verse 3.

The quotation is said to have been spoken "*through* [the preposition *dia*] the prophet," and so (by implication) "*by* [the preposition *hypo*] the Lord." Compare Matthew 1:22 and 2:15, where the latter phrase is explicit. Moreover, says Matthew, this prophecy is now being *fulfilled* (the verb *plēroō*)—here in Jesus and nowhere else.[4]

Most of 21:5 is devoted to Zechariah 9:9. Yet the opening of that verse—"Rejoice greatly, O daughter of Zion!"—is here replaced by Isaiah 62:11b, "Say to the daughter of Zion" (*tē thygatri Ziōn*), a poetical address to the city of Jerusalem and its inhabitants.[5] According to this text, (i) Yahweh comes to Zion with a message of salvation (62:11c); (ii) the saved are identified as "the redeemed of Yahweh" (62:12); and (iii) this gospel is "proclaimed to the end of the earth" (62:11a).[6] Given the change from

---

62–70. Like chaps. 1–8, chaps. 9–14 consist of two main sections, 9:1–11:17 and 12:1–14:21. The opening words of 9:1 and 12:1 are identical: "The burden of the word of Yahweh . . ."

3. All translations are my own, unless otherwise noted.

4. The verb *plēroō* appears only in prefaces to Old Testament quotations peculiar to Matthew, one of which is 21:5.

5. BAGD s.v. *Ziōn*, 2. a. (cf. Zech. 9:9, "O daughter of Zion . . . O daughter of Jerusalem"). In the parallel text of John 12:15 the words "Fear not, daughter of Zion" (probably an allusion to Isa. 40:9) preface the quotation from Zech. 9:9. Such "conflation of texts was common practice." Craig S. Keener, *A Commentary on the Gospel of Matthew* (Grand Rapids: Eerdmans, 1999), 493n99.

6. News of Zion's salvation (Isa. 62:11c) "does not retreat from the universal proclamation" of 62:11a, "for Zion's salvation (54:1) is the world's salvation (55:1)." J. Alec Motyer, *Isaiah* (Downers Grove, IL: InterVarsity, 1999), 383. The LXX of 62:12 contains the verb *lytroō* ('redeem'): see Matt. 20:28 for the cognate noun *lytron*.

Zechariah's "Rejoice" to Isaiah's "Say," the rest of the quotation becomes an evangelistic appeal to unbelieving Israel.[7]

Zechariah 9:9 in Its Original Setting

Lessons from Israel's past, Zechariah 1:1–6, are followed by eight visions and explanatory oracles, 1:7–6:15. A question about fasting prompts further disclosures from Yahweh, 7:1–8:23, which amplify those of chapters 1–6. The prophecies of 9:1–8 open the next major section and preface our text. Given the content of 9:9 (together with v. 10), several themes from the preceding passages are to be noted. There Yahweh (i) warns of judgment upon both Israel and the nations, and urges Israel to repent of her sins and to return to him; (ii) demonstrates his steadfast love as the covenant-keeping God even in face of Israel's infidelity, and promises to save and prosper a people from among both Israel and the nations; and (iii) honors the high priest Joshua and the royal governor Zerubbabel, who together prefigure the Messiah by whom Yahweh will establish justice and accomplish salvation.[8] Then in 9:9 Messiah's own coming is announced: "Rejoice greatly, O daughter of Zion! Shout aloud, O daughter of Jerusalem! Behold, your king is coming to you, righteous [*tsaddiq*] and victorious [*nosha'*] is he, humble [*'ani*] and riding on a donkey [*khamor*], and on a colt [*'ayir*], the foal of a donkey ['*athon*]."

Zechariah proclaims, to the city where David reigned, the Messiah of David's line (12:8)—the "Branch" (*tsemakh*) (3:8; 6:12), whose rule is prefigured in both Joshua and Zerubbabel (4:1–14).[9] The term *nosha'* (a Niphal

---

7. This change "makes the following an evangelistic challenge to unconverted Israel," notes Robert H. Gundry, *Matthew: A Commentary on His Handbook for a Mixed Church under Persecution*, 2nd ed. (Grand Rapids: Eerdmans, 1994), 408. Matthew's opening "makes plain that the entrance and acclamation demand a response from Jerusalem." W. D. Davies and Dale C. Allison Jr., *The Gospel According to Saint Matthew* (Edinburgh: T & T Clark, 1997), 3:118–19, referring to N. Lohfink.

8. For (i), see 1:2–6, 18–21; 5:1–11; 7:1–14; 9:1–8; for (ii), 1:12–17; 2:1–13; 8:1–23; 9:7; for (iii), 3:1–10; 4:1–14; 6:9–14.

9. The high priest Joshua is himself a royal figure (3:7; 6:9–14). Zerubbabel, the governor, is a descendant of king David (see Matt. 1:12–13). Eschatological hopes attached to Joshua and Zerubbabel will be fulfilled in Messiah "the Priest-King." Willem A. VanGemeren, *Interpreting the Prophetic Word* (Grand Rapids: Zondervan, 1990), 201. Throughout Zechariah "the union of the two offices of priest and king in a single figure takes on a prominence not found . . . in the previous prophets. . . . [Zech. 6:11–12] is clearly messianic in its intent." O. Palmer Robertson, *The Christ of the Prophets* (Phillipsburg, NJ: P&R, 2004), 386, 388. Cf. Jer. 23:5, "I will raise up

participle of the verb *yasha'*) (9:9b), is better translated "victorious" (BDB, NJB, NRSV) than "having salvation" (LXX, ESV, NIV). "The king has been through some ordeal in which he has experienced the Lord's deliverance, and so is *victorious*."[10] He is thus honored because he willingly underwent that ordeal to serve Yahweh's purpose: that is, the king shows that he *is* righteous (*tsaddiq*) (9:9b), by *doing* righteousness (*tsedeq* and *tsedaqah*).[11]

The king enters Jerusalem (9:9b) as one whom Yahweh has already vindicated; the city celebrates a victory that has already been won (9:9a). The choice of mount does not obscure the *fact* of the rider's kingship but reveals its *character*: how fitting that the humble king (*'ani*) should ride on a lowly beast of burden—a donkey (*khamor*), further identified as a colt (*'ayir*), a mere *child* of the species.[12] Moreover, the king hereby bears visible witness that he is embarking on a mission of peace; for going into battle, a "proud war horse" (10:3, NRSV) would be the proper mount. Yet precisely by means of this lowly king astride a donkey Yahweh "will cut off the chariot from Ephraim and the war horse from Jerusalem" (9:10a; under his benevolent rule the people of Israel shall at last be reunited. Not only so: according to 9:10b the Hebrew Messiah will "speak peace [*shalom*] to the nations"—including those formerly under judgment (9:1–8)—and will establish his reign universally.[13] This

for David a righteous [*tsaddiq*, as in Zech. 9:9] Branch [*tsemakh*, as in Zech. 3:8; 6:12]"; Isa. 11:1, "a shoot from the stump of Jesse, and a Branch [*netser*] from his roots."

10. Baldwin, *Haggai, Zechariah, Malachi*, 165. (In LXX *nosha'* is rendered *sōzōn*, "saving.") "The picture is of a humble and gentle king, who, like the Servant of Yahweh, is victorious only because God has vindicated and delivered him." R. T. France, *Jesus and the Old Testament* (Downers Grove, IL: InterVarsity, 1971), 105–6. Cf. 11:7–14 and 13:7–9, where Zechariah "intimates that this Messiah is to suffer as the smitten shepherd." VanGemeren, *Interpreting the Prophetic Word*, 201.

11. In Zech. 9:9, as in Isa. 9:7; 11:4–5, the Messianic king's inherent righteousness finds expression in his just and righteous deeds. Cf. Baldwin, *Haggai, Zechariah, Malachi*, 165. Yahweh likewise saves his Servant (Isa. 53:10–12; cf. Ps. 28:8), because the Servant himself has achieved a saving work (53:4–12 and Matt. 20:28). O. Palmer Robertson, *The Books of Nahum, Habakkuk, and Zephaniah*, NICOT (Grand Rapids: Eerdmans, 1990), 230, 238, renders Hab. 3:13a "You go forth for (the) salvation of your people, for salvation with your anointed," and takes this as a dual reference to Cyrus (Isa. 44:27–45:7) and the Servant (Isa. 42:1–4; 49:1–6).

12. All three terms used for the animals in Zech. 9:9 appear in other Old Testament references to royal figures: for *khamor* (donkey), see 2 Sam. 16:2; for *'ayir* (colt), Judg. 10:4; 12:14; for *'athon* (the colt's mother), Gen. 49:11 and Judg. 5:10. Early rabbis applied Zech. 9:9 to the Davidic Messiah, and stressed not his triumph but his lowliness: see France, *Jesus and the Old Testament*, 189 (with references).

13. Already 9:7 promises that Philistia will be "a remnant for our God" and "like a clan in Judah." The good news of 9:9–10 is strongly anticipated in 2:10–11. For further references to Yahweh as both judge and Savior of the nations, see note 8 above, (i) and (ii).

prophecy recalls Jacob's words about his son Judah in Genesis 49:8–12. A descendant of Judah is destined to rule in Israel (49:8, 10a; cf. Zech. 9:9a, 10a). "The obedience of the peoples" will be his as well (49:10b; cf. Zech. 9:10b). His reign brings peace and prosperity, one sign of which is that he binds "his colt [*'ir*] to the vine," and "the foal of his donkey [*bene 'athono*] to the choice vine" (49:11a; cf. Zech. 9:9), with "colt" (*'ayir*) and "foal of a donkey" (*ben 'athonoth*).[14]

Zechariah 9:9 in Its Present Setting

The quotation in Matthew 21:5 reflects Matthew's awareness of both the MT (Hebrew) and the LXX (Greek) of Zechariah 9:9, so it will be helpful to have all three texts before us. *MT*: "[i] Behold, your king is coming to you, [ii] righteous and victorious is he, [iii] humble and riding on a donkey, [iv] and on a colt, the foal of a donkey." Lines two and three of the Hebrew text (the portion from which Matthew draws) are here translated as before, and divided in accord with the MT's punctuation. *LXX*: "[i] Behold, your king is coming to you, [ii] righteous and saving is he, [iii] meek and mounted on a beast of burden [iv] and a young colt." All four parts of the MT are translated; part iv. is abbreviated. The participle "saving" in part ii. is slightly misleading (see the previous section). Parts iii. and iv. together mention only one animal, whereas MT speaks of both the donkey (= the colt) and its mother. Matthew: "[i] Behold, your king is coming to you, [iii] meek and mounted on a donkey, [iv] and on a colt, the foal of a beast of burden." Part ii. is lacking. Parts i., iii. and iv. are all true to the MT. Part i. is identical to the LXX; so is part iii., except for the name of the animal (LXX, *hypozygion*, "beast of burden"; Matthew, *onos*, "donkey"). Part iv. is closer than the LXX to the MT.

---

14. The NIV renders Gen. 49:10a, "The scepter will not depart from Judah, nor the ruler's staff from between his feet, until he comes to whom it belongs." The Hebrew for this last clause is much disputed; for support of this translation, see Gerhard Von Rad, *Genesis*, trans. John H. Marks, rev. ed. (Philadelphia: Westminster Press, 1972), 425. Gen. 49:11 describes both prosperity and conquest: see ibid.; Iain Duguid, "Messianic Themes in Zechariah 9–14," in *The Lord's Anointed*, ed. Philip E. Satterthwaite and others (Carlisle: Paternoster, 1995), 268; Bruce K. Waltke, *Genesis: A Commentary* (Grand Rapids: Zondervan, 2001), 608–9. The masculine noun *'ir* (colt) (49:11) is the root of *'ayir* (Zech. 9:9). The feminine noun *'athon* (donkey) is singular in 49:11, plural in Zech. 9:9. There are both Jewish and Christian sources that connect Zech. 9:9 to Gen. 49:10–11. See France, *Jesus and the Old Testament*, 189 and Davies and Allison, *Gospel according to Saint Matthew*, 116.

To judge from Matthew's careful quotation of parts i., iii., and iv., he has deliberately omitted part ii., "righteous and victorious is he." In this case the reason for the omission is that Zechariah 9:9, in its original setting, announced an accomplished victory (see above). To be sure, Jesus does righteous deeds and achieves great victories from Matthew 3–4 onwards. Yet when he enters Jerusalem, his foremost righteous act (his death) and his finest victory (his resurrection) have yet to occur. That acclamation—"righteous and victorious is he"—is rightly reserved for Matthew 28 and beyond. The parallel text of John 12:15–16 is illuminating: here too the quotation from Zechariah 9:9 lacks the above words; and John expressly states that Jesus is yet to be glorified. One effect of that omission is to accentuate the lowliness of the coming king.[15]

Whereas the other evangelists report that one animal is brought to Jesus (Mark 11:2–3; Luke 19:30–31; John 12:14), Matthew speaks of two—a "donkey" (*onos*) and her "colt" (*pōlos*) (21:2–3). Matthew, having himself witnessed these events, and anticipating the quotation from Zechariah, presents the fuller account of what happened.[16] The other Gospels do not deny the presence of the second animal but simply focus on the one that Jesus rode. Yet both Mark 11:2 and Luke 19:30, by saying that this is "a colt [*pōlos*]...on which no one has ever sat," help to explain why Jesus has its mother brought as well.[17] Using synonymous parallelism, the MT of Zechariah 9:9 prophesied that the king would come riding "on a donkey" (*'al khamor*), that is, "on a colt" (*'al 'ayir*), "the foal of a donkey" (*ben 'athonoth*). Correspondingly, Matthew 21:5 declares that Jesus is mounted "on a donkey" (*epi onon*), that is, "on a colt" (*epi pōlon*), "the foal of a beast of burden" (*huion hypozygiou*). Like Zechariah, Matthew uses three terms to describe the animal on which Jesus rides (*onos*, *pōlos* and *huios*, matching *khamor*, *'ayir* and *ben* respectively);

15. The omission "puts all the emphasis upon Jesus' meekness and the animals and, in view of upcoming events, mutes any notion of triumphalism" (Davies and Allison, *Gospel according to Saint Matthew*, 119). In view of the argument (ibid., 121) that Matthew's quotation of Zech. 9:9 alludes to Ex. 4:19–20, where Moses and his family return to Egypt on donkeys, it is to be noted that this journey presages great victory for Moses and Israel.

16. The same holds true for 8:28–34, which reports the healing of two demoniacs (whereas Mark and Luke speak of only one). Zechariah 9:9 is cited in John's account of the entry (12:15, though this quotation is shorter than Matthew's), but not in Mark or Luke.

17. See e.g. Donald A. Hagner, *Matthew 14–28* (Dallas: Word, 1995), 594: "the tumult with which Jesus would enter Jerusalem would make such accompaniment all the more necessary." Keener, *Commentary on the Gospel of Matthew*, 491. In John 12:14–15 Jesus' mount is called *onarion* (a diminutive of *onos*), "little donkey, young donkey" (BAGD s.v.), as well as *pōlos*, "colt."

and a fourth term to describe that animal's mother (*hypozygion*, matching *'athon*).[18] The *onos* of 21:2 is therefore to be distinguished from the *onos* of 21:5. In the first instance, *onos* is feminine (the colt, *pōlos*, is "with her," *met autēs*, v. 2b); in the second, it is masculine (the parallel nouns *pōlos* and *huios* are both masculine).[19]

The quotation in 21:5 rests upon Jesus' own "acted quotation" of Zechariah 9:9. He deliberately enters Jerusalem in fulfillment of this prophecy, as is already clear from his instructions in 21:2–3 and from the quotation's preface in verse 4 ("This happened in order that what was said through the prophet might be fulfilled").[20] "Behold" (*Idou*, for Hebrew *hinneh*), begins the quotation: i.e., "Daughter of Zion [21:5a], pay close heed." What then does Jesus want witnesses to learn from this event? *a.* Let Israel acclaim Jesus as her promised Messiah: "*your* king is coming *to you*" (21:5a; cf. 2:2). He is the promised "Son of David" (1:1) whom the Lord God has appointed to reign from David's throne forever (Luke 1:32). *b.* Let Israel perceive the true character of Jesus' kingship: "*meek* and mounted on a *donkey*, and on a *colt*" (21:5b). He, the royal Son, is also the gentle and lowly Servant of Yahweh (3:17; 11:29; 12:18–21). The nation is currently threatened with the severest judgment (as the rest of Matthew 21 clearly shows). For that very reason Messiah—himself Yahweh incarnate—comes with overtures

18. *Huios*, like *ben*, is literally "son." *Hypozygion* (lit., "under the yoke") was used of beasts of burden besides donkeys (BAGD s.v.); in 2 Peter 2:16, the one other New Testament instance, it again denotes a donkey. In the LXX of Zech. 9:9 *hypozygion* denotes the animal on which the king rides (see the above translation). As noted, the Hebrew noun *'athon* is plural in Zech. 9:9b.

19. On *onos* as both masculine and feminine, see BAGD s.v. While in Matthew's quotation of Zech. 9:9, *onos* is masculine, in John 12:15 it is probably feminine (*epi pōlon onou*, "on a donkey's colt"). In the LXX *onos* translates both the masculine *khamor* (e.g. Gen. 12:16) and the feminine *'athon* (e.g. Num. 22:21). According to another view, Matthew (i) mistakenly thinks the "donkey" and the "colt" of Zech. 9:9 are two animals, and (ii) therefore adds the second animal (the mother donkey) to the record (21:2) and depicts Jesus as riding on two animals instead of one (21:7). For support of my exegesis, see e.g., D. A. Carson, "Matthew," in *The Expositor's Bible Commentary*, ed. Frank E. Gaebelein (Grand Rapids: Zondervan, 1984), 8:438; R. T. France, *Matthew* (Grand Rapids: Eerdmans, 1985), 298; Gundry, *Matthew*, 409; Hagner, *Matthew 14–28*, 594–95. Several views are surveyed in Davies and Allison, *Gospel according to Saint Matthew*, 120–21.

20. The quoted phrase is from France, *Jesus and the Old Testament*, 205. Matthew is "making explicit Jesus' own allusion" to the prophecy (ibid., n. 143). France speaks earlier of "the deliberately significant nature of the acts themselves" (ibid., 105). Was not Zech. 9:9 one of the prophecies about which Jesus instructed his disciples, including Matthew, following his resurrection (see Luke 24:44–49; cf. John 12:15–16)? That Zech. 9:9 speaks of both the colt and its mother, helps to explain why Jesus instructs the disciples to bring both animals.

of peace: he enters *Yerushalaim* on a mission of *shalom*, to offer the grace of salvation to his rebellious and refractory people.[21] To win that peace, the Son of David will indeed wage war—but not as envisaged by those who ascribe this name to him in 21:9. Instead, he will achieve his triumph through defeat: at the cost of his own life he will save his people from their sins (1:21; 26:28) and rescue them from the evil one (6:13).[22] *c.* Let Israel recognize Messiah to be the Savior of the world: he came to give his life "as a ransom *for many*" (20:28), for Gentiles as well as Jews. He will "speak peace to the nations" (Zech. 9:10b) rather than declare war on them. Compare his words in Matthew 24:14 ("this gospel of the kingdom will be preached . . . to all the nations") and 28:19 ("make disciples of all the nations").[23]

The Present Witness to Jesus

Having gone (the verb *poreuomai*) and done what Jesus commanded, the two disciples bring (the verb *agō*) the mother donkey (*onos*) and her colt (*pōlos*) to him (21:6–7a: all four of these Greek words are so used in v. 2). We thus come to the entry itself, and to the actual fulfillment of Zechariah's prophecy.

The first visible witness comes from Jesus himself: "they placed garments on them [*ep autōn*], and he sat on them [*epanō autōn*]" (v. 7b). *a.* The single mount. The two disciples place their garments (*ta himatia*) on the

21. In this respect as in others, the original setting of Zech. 9:9 is illuminating (see above). In light of Zeph. 3:14 (whose language is very similar to Zech. 9:9), see Zeph. 3:15–16 (with the repeated promise that Yahweh will banish fear from Jerusalem; cf. John 12:15, "Fear not, daughter of Zion") and 3:17a ("Yahweh your God is in your midst, a mighty one who saves"). It is Jesus, the God-man, who fulfills these promises. See Robertson, *Nahum, Habakkuk, and Zephaniah*, 338. On Yahweh's offer of salvation to Israel, see also Isa. 62:11–12.

22. Jesus makes peace "through the blood of his cross" (Col. 1:20); there he conquers the demonic powers (2:15). Cf. below on the relation of Matt. 26:28 to Zech. 9:11. In *The Man Born To Be King*, one of the magi (Balthazar) says of the King they seek: "The greatest of warriors; yet he shall be called the Prince of Peace. He will be victor and victim in all his wars, and will make his triumph in defeat." Dorothy L. Sayers (London: Gollancz, 1943), 54.

23. The Hebrew for "nations" in Zech. 9:10 is *ethne*, for which LXX has *ethnos*, the term used in Matt. 24:14 and 28:19. Given the theme of Gentile salvation in this gospel, it is highly probable that the quotation of Zech. 9:9 in Matt. 21:5 points to 9:10. On Old Testament quotations as pointers to their contexts, see C. H. Dodd, *According to the Scriptures* (London: Nisbet, 1952), 126, 132. In John's account of Jesus' entry into Jerusalem, the Pharisees exclaim, "Behold, the world [*kosmos*] has gone after him" (12:19b); thereafter "certain Greeks" seek an audience with Jesus (vv. 20–21), and Jesus declares, "And I, when I am lifted up from the earth, will draw all people [*pantas*] to myself" (v. 32).

two animals mentioned in verse 7a—the mother donkey (*onos*) and her colt (*pōlos*). Some, contending that *onos* and *pōlos* likewise denote two animals in the prophecy of verse 5, take the close of verse 7 to mean that Jesus sits on both *animals*. A preferable view is that he sits on the *garments* that are placed on the colt: a person's sitting on two animals is hard to imagine (and according to the other three accounts, Jesus mounts one animal: Mark 11:7; Luke 19:35; John 12:14); *onos* and *pōlos* denote the same animal in 21:5; and the genitive plural *autōn* at the close of verse 7 refers as easily to the preceding *ta himatia* as to the preceding *autōn*.[24] *b. The lowly king.* Unlike the normal pilgrim, "Jesus does not approach the city on foot. Instead he rides. This reflects his extraordinary status: the king sits."[25] Yet his appearance offers no encouragement to fervent nationalists: "an unarmed, plainly clad civilian riding a donkey contrasts sharply with an armed soldier astride a war horse."[26]

The pilgrims' visible witness begins with their very number: it is "a very large crowd" (*ho pleistos ochlos*) that accompanies Jesus (v. 8a; in John 12:12–13 a "huge crowd," *ho ochlos polys*, goes out to meet him). That they both precede and follow Jesus (v. 9a) places him at the center of a regal procession. They offer him two further visible tributes, which are featured alongside each other in verse 8.[27] The garments (*ta himatia*, as in v. 7) which they spread on the road (v. 8a) are themselves testimony to Jesus' royalty.[28] The branches (*kladoi*) which others spread on the road (v. 8b)—identified

24. The plural *autōn* can denote the neuter *himatia* as well as the masculine/feminine *onos* and the masculine *pōlos*. The Greek word order of 21:7b is *ep autōn ta himatia . . . epanō autōn*: Is not the second *autōn* more likely to refer to the relatively near *himatia* (garments) than to the relatively distant first *autōn* (animals)? Does the change of preposition (from *epi* to *epanō*) signal a change of object (from animals to garments)? For this reading of 21:7b, see e.g. Gundry, *Matthew*, 410 and Craig L. Blomberg, *Matthew* (Nashville: Broadman, 1992), 313. See also the above comments on 21:5.

25. Davies and Allison, *Gospel according to Saint Matthew*, 123. They note that the verb behind "sat" in 21:7, *epikathizō*, is used of Solomon in the LXX of 1 Kings 1:38, 44 (where he is anointed king). Cf. Matt. 19:28 and 25:31, where Jesus speaks of the Son of Man's sitting (*kathizō*) on his glorious throne.

26. Blomberg, *Matthew*, 312.

27. Both v. 8a and v. 8b contain the phrase *en tē hodō* ("on the road") and the verb *strōnnyō* ("spread"). The adjective *pleistos*, a superlative of *polys*, is probably elative in 8a (though it could mean "the greatest part of the crowd," in view of *alloi*, "others," 8b): see BAGD s.v. *polys*, III.; *IB*, 98.

28. In 1 Kings 9:13 those who proclaim Jehu king place their garments (LXX *himation*) beneath his feet. For further references see Davies and Allison, *Gospel according to Saint Matthew*, 123. Since by synecdoche clothes represent their wearers (cf. 1 Sam. 24:4–5), "their position

in John 12:13 as branches (*baia*) of palm trees—signal hopes that Israelite prestige and power will be renewed under this awaited Son of David, and may also reflect the influence of Psalm 118, which the crowd quotes in 21:9.[29]

In Matthew's account, preparations for the entry are dominated by Jesus' words (21:2–3), but in the entry itself Jesus' testimony is wholly visible.[30] The verbal witness comes from the huge crowd: in acclaiming Jesus, they employ the text of Psalm 118 (21:9) and a confession of their own (21:11). The pilgrims' shouts serve the Christology of the evangelist Matthew. Jesus is rightly praised as "Son of David" (1:1); homage has been due him as "king of the Jews" since the time of his birth (2:2). He is the descendant of Judah promised in Genesis 49, and he the messianic Priest-King prefigured by Joshua and Zerubbabel in Zechariah 4 and 6. And Jesus indeed comes "in the *name* of the Lord" (*en onomati kyriou*): he wields Yahweh's very *power*, and he himself is Yahweh visibly *present*.[31] His words, his works, and he himself are therefore cause for highest praise and deepest joy both on earth and in heaven, both now and hereafter. Moreover, says Matthew, Jesus' rule over the nations will far surpass what David was ever able to achieve.[32]

Those of Matthew's readers who know the rest of this story (chaps. 21–28), who have been granted insight into the secrets of the kingdom (13:11), and whom Jesus has saved from their sins (1:21), can exclaim as no others, "Praise to the Son of David!" and "Blessed is he who comes in the

---

beneath another's feet means submission." Ibid. Most of the *himatia* of Matt. 21:7–8 are doubtless outer garments, i.e. cloaks or robes (so e.g. ESV, NIV and NRSV). Cf. 5:40.

29. For palm branches as signs of Jewish nationalism, see 1 Macc. 13:51 (Jews hail the capture of Jerusalem "with acclamations and carrying palms" NJB); 2 Macc. 10:7 (to celebrate the cleansing of the temple, they carry "leafy boughs and palms" NJB). "The crowd's use of palm branches, an allusion to Maccabean triumphs, implies that they still see [Jesus] in more revolutionary messianic terms." Keener, *Commentary on the Gospel of Matthew*, 494. Many of these pilgrims journeyed from Jericho (20:29), "city of palms," where such trees were plentiful (c.f. Rev. 7:9). As Ps. 118:25–26 is quoted in Matt. 21:9, note 118:27b in NRSV: "Bind the festal procession with branches, up to the horns of the altar." But the exact sense of the Hebrew is uncertain. Cf. ESV: "Bind the festal sacrifice with cords, up to the horns of the altar," NIV text and margin, and the commentaries.

30. But see Luke 19:40–44, verses peculiar to Luke.

31. Yahweh's name signaled his "invocable presence" and his "accessible power." Richard L. Pratt Jr., *1 and 2 Chronicles* (Fearn, Ross-shire: Christian Focus, 1998), 180, 178.

32. See e.g. 12:18–21; 24:14; 25:31–32; 28:18–20. 2 Sam. 22:44 (David as "head of nations") and 51 (Yahweh's "steadfast love to his anointed, to David and his descendants forever") are "a preview and pledge of the day when all kings will bow down and all nations (will) serve David's royal Descendant (Ps. 72:11)." Dale Ralph Davis, *2 Samuel: Out of Every Adversity* (Fearn, Ross-shire: Christian Focus, 1999), 242. The crowd speaks in Mark 11:10 of "the coming kingdom of our father David."

name of the Lord!" *Like* the high priest Joshua in Zechariah, this "Joshua" (1:21) was victorious over Satan (4:1–11; Zech. 3:1–2). *Unlike* that Joshua, this royal priest had no need to be saved from sin (Heb. 4:15; Zech. 3:4); and he sacrificed his own life, not that of animals, to redeem a sinful people (Matt. 20:28; Heb. 10:11–14). In thanksgiving for his sacrifice, they now celebrate a Passover of their own (Matt. 26:26–28; 1 Cor. 5:7). Still, like those earlier pilgrims (Ps. 118:25), they cry "Yahweh, save, we pray!" "Let your kingdom come" (Matt. 6:10); satisfy our longing for lasting righteousness (5:6); deliver us forever from persecutions and from all the devices of "the evil one" (5:10–12; 6:13); usher us into life eternal (25:46); and hasten the day of Messiah's final triumph (16:27; 26:29).

B. ZECHARIAH IN MATTHEW 21:12–22

This passage records Jesus' cleansing of the temple, his cursing of the fig tree, and teachings related to both events. It is probable that each episode alludes to Zechariah, especially to chapter 14.

The Cleansing of the Temple

Like the pilgrims of Psalm 118, Jesus comes into the temple (*hieron*) (v. 12a).[33] He, the Son of David (v. 9) and a descendant of Judah (1:2), now behaves as a Levite—not strange for one prefigured by the high priest Joshua (Zech. 3 and 6). More importantly, the actions of 21:12–16 reveal Jesus to be the rightful Lord of the temple. Even his departure (v. 17) is an act of judgment.

Jesus finds persons "selling [the verb *pōleō*] and buying [the verb *agorazō*] in the temple," (v. 12a). The scene is the court of the Gentiles, an enclosure of some thirty-five acres which surrounded, and was separated from, the precincts of the temple open to Jews—the court of the women, the court of Israel (of the men) and the court of the priests. The merchants in question first *buy* the requisites for sacrifice (animals, wine, oil, salt, etc.), then *sell* them to the worshipers—most of whom, having come from afar, could not bring their offerings with them. Verse 12 speaks also of "money

---

33. Many mss. add "of God" to "temple" at v. 12a, perhaps to stress the holiness of the place and the rightness of Jesus' act (Hagner, *Matthew 14–28*, 598, note a.; see also Bruce Metzger, *TC*, 44). *Hieron* (also in vv. 12b, 14, 15) denotes the whole temple complex; *naos* is normally used of the inner shrine, the sanctuary itself (e.g. 23:16–17; 27:51).

changers" (*kollybistai*). In the Palestine of Jesus' day the main currency was Roman; but all payments to the temple, notably the annual tax (17:24), had to use Greek coinage (from Antioch or Tyre), which provided the closest equivalent to the old Hebrew shekel.[34]

Jesus opposes *sinful practices* within the established system. Both groups he addresses in verse 13 *handle money*; and he accuses them of making God's house "a den of *robbers*," language drawn from a passage that condemns *theft*, Jeremiah 7:9, 11. Jesus hereby protests "exorbitant rates of exchange for foreign currency and high prices for sacrifices."[35] And if Jesus verbally recalls Jeremiah 7, he visibly witnesses to Malachi 3—which rests on the indictment of priestly corruption in Malachi 1 and 2. Was not the governing priesthood at least partly to blame for commercial corruption within its precincts? Were not the priests themselves threatened with slavery to wealth (Matt. 6:24), owing to the enormous sums of money entrusted to the temple?[36]

Jesus also combats a *sinful presence*. It is not commerce *per se* he opposes: both merchants and money changers met legitimate needs. Nor is Jesus protesting primarily against commercial malpractice: were all these people scrupulously honest in their dealings, his actions would still be explicable.[37] It is commerce *in the temple* that he opposes: this is evident from the juxtaposition of "house of prayer" and "den of robbers" in verse 13, and

34. See Herbert Danby, *The Mishnah. Translated from the Hebrew with Introduction and Brief Explanatory Notes* (London: Oxford University Press, 1964), 541. *Bekhoroth* ["Firstlings"] 8:7; William L. Lane, *Commentary on the Gospel of Mark* (Grand Rapids: Eerdmans, 1974), 405. So the reason for this stipulation was not that Roman coins bore heathen symbols (such as the emperor's image), for such symbols were found on Grecian (Tyrian) coins as well. Leon Morris, *The Gospel according to John*, rev. ed. (Grand Rapids: Eerdmans, 1995), 170, following Israel Abrahams.

35. Gundry, *Matthew*, 413, with references.

36. Cf. Keener, *Commentary on the Gospel of Matthew*, 501 (temple authorities as "the real bandits"). "The Temple was the most important factor in the commerce of Jerusalem," says Joachim Jeremias. *Jerusalem in the Time of Jesus*, transl. F. H. and C. H. Cave (Philadelphia: Fortress, 1969), 57. On the temple's wealth, see Emil Schürer, *The History of the Jewish People in the Age of Jesus Christ*, ed. Geza Vermes *et al.* (Edinburgh: T & T Clark, 1979), 2:257–74 ("the priestly dues").

37. "The dealers and money-changers were performing an essential service for pilgrims and other worshippers. . . . Indeed, without their infrastructure of services, it would be difficult to see how the Temple sacrifices could have continued. Moreover, the money-changers charged a modest commission to convert currency into the Tyrian coinage required by the Temple, and the dealers in sacrifices provided unblemished and ritually acceptable victims." W. R. Herzog II, in *DJG*, 818. It is most unlikely that business was always conducted as described in this closing sentence; but even if it was, there were still good reasons for Jesus' action.

from Jesus' expulsion of *both* sellers *and* buyers in verse 12. The holy temple is being converted in to a marketplace: cf. John 2:16, "Take these out of here! Stop making the house of my Father [*ton oikon tou patros mou*] a house of trade [*oikon emporiou*]!"[38] As Jesus enacted Zechariah 9:9 by entering Jerusalem, (Matt. 21:5–11), so here in 21:12–13 he keeps the promise of Zechariah 14:21b, "And there will no longer be a trader [*kenan'ani*] in the house of Yahweh of hosts on that day." The Hebrew *kenan'ani* is sometimes literally translated "Canaanite" (NASB, NIV, NKJV); but "trader" or the equivalent (ESV, NJB, NRSV) is preferable. The term "Canaanite" in some contexts denotes not a race of people but a class of merchants; and the rule of Israel's promised Messiah will embrace rather than exclude Gentiles (Zech. 9:9–10).[39] Both in entering Jerusalem and in cleansing the temple, Jesus declares himself to be the Son of David who inaugurates the Day of Yahweh (Zech. 14:1 *et seq*).[40]

There is another reason why Jesus, in Matthew 21:13, places quotations from Isaiah 56:7 ("My house shall be called a house of prayer") and Jeremiah 7:11 ("a den of robbers") beside each other. Crowning his promises to Gentiles in Isaiah 56:3–7b, Yahweh declares in verse 7c that his house—his temple—"shall be called a house of prayer for all peoples." As noted, the merchants and the money-changers did their work in the Court of the Gentiles. The Gentiles had few privileges in the temple; but they were permitted, in this relatively remote area, to worship Israel's God. And

38. Here in John 2:16 "the objection is not to [the traders'] dishonesty, but to their presence." Morris, *John*, 172. "It seems," says France, "that it is not [i] any specific malpractice that Jesus rejects, but [ii] the whole system of sacrificial worship which had developed into big business, and particularly the temple authorities who had allowed its commercial aspect to become enshrined within the temple precincts." *Matthew*, 301. I would rather say, especially ii., but also i.

39. BDB s.v. *kena'ani*, II., "trader, merchant," cites Zech. 14:21 and Prov. 31:24 (so too NIV for the latter). BDB s.v. *kena'an*, II., "merchant(s)," cites Zeph. 1:11 (note the parallel "dealers in silver"); Ezek. 16:29; 17:4 (note the parallel "merchants" or "tradesmen"). Cf. Baldwin, *Haggai, Zechariah, Malachi*, 180 (on Zech. 11:7), 208 (on 14:21; here "the word applies, not to a particular nationality, but to those who make extortionate profits out of the worshippers"); Robertson, *Nahum, Habakkuk, and Zephaniah*, 279 (on Zeph. 1:11). See also Hagner, *Matthew 14–28*, 600, and the article by Cecil Roth to which he refers. Duguid thinks that Jesus also fulfills Zech. 9:8 ("I will encamp at my house as a guard")—"ironically not by driving out the oppressive Romans but by evicting the home-grown merchants." "Messianic Themes," 277. But "my house" here may denote the whole land (Baldwin, *Haggai, Zechariah, Malachi*, 161).

40. Note "a day for Yahweh" (Zech. 14:1); "on that day" (14:4, 6, 8, 9, 13, 20, 21; see also 12:3–11; 13:1–4). On Jesus' fulfillment of Zech. 14:21, see F. F. Bruce, *This Is That: The New Testament Development of Some Old Testament Themes* (Exeter: Paternoster Press, 1968), 113; Morris, *Gospel According to Matthew*, 526; Davies and Allison, *Gospel According to Saint Matthew*, 138.

now even that space is being usurped: these installed tradesmen are *robbing Gentiles* of their place of worship. So Israel's Messiah, the one appointed to proclaim peace to the nations (Matt. 21:5; Zech. 9:9–10), now exercises his authority as Priest-King on their behalf. The preface to the quotation—"It has been written [*Gegraptai*]" (21:13a), shows that the prophecy of Isaiah 56:7 remains in force until it is fully realized (cf. later comments on 26:31, where *gegraptai* recurs). Integral to that fulfillment is Jesus' present action. In light of Zechariah 14:21, let us notice the promise of 14:16 that survivors from the nations "will go up year after year to worship the King, Yahweh of hosts, and to keep the Feast of Tabernacles."

"And the blind [*typhloi*] and the lame [*chōloi*] came to [Jesus] in the temple, and he healed them," reports Matthew 21:14. Having been acclaimed "Son of David" by those blind men he cured outside Jericho (20:29–34), Jesus here acts in that same capacity (cf. 21:9), and shows that he is indeed the promised Messiah (cf. 11:2–6, especially v. 5a, "the blind [*typhloi*] receive their sight, and the lame [*chōloi*] walk"). David marched with an army on Jerusalem to conquer the Jebusite stronghold (2 Sam. 5:6–7). Many of the Jebusite "lame and blind" who opposed him (5:8a) were doubtless maimed or killed; and a false application of David's words barred such people from the temple (5:8b). Now David's greater Son enters Jerusalem on a mission of peace; and he welcomes the blind and the lame who come to him in the temple. Far from assaulting them, he—the Servant-King—*heals* them, which David would not, and could not, have done for his Jebusite enemies.[41] Moreover, the compassion of Yahweh's Shepherd-King (Zech. 9:9 with 12:10; 13:7), stands in stark contrast to the cruelty of the foolish shepherd who "does not . . . heal the maimed" (Zech. 11:16).

Lessons about Prayer

Following Jesus' judgment on the fig tree (21:18–19), his astonished disciples ask a question (v. 20), focusing on the miracle itself rather than its parabolic significance. In response Jesus teaches a lesson about prayer; in so doing, he takes account of the question, the immediate surroundings and the parable he has just enacted. "Truly I say to you, if you have faith

41. "David was using 'the lame and the blind' as a figurative epithet for the Jebusites. By healing the blind and the lame right within the Temple, Jesus denies the Jews' false deduction from David's statement." Gundry, *Matthew*, 413.

and do not doubt, not only will you do what was done to the fig tree; but also if you say to this mountain, 'Be removed and be thrown into the sea,' it will happen. And all things, whatever you ask in prayer, believing, you will receive" (vv. 21–22).

The weighty preface (*Amēn legō hymin*, as in 5:18 *et seq.* and most recently in 19:28) underscores the truth of what follows, and applies most directly to the conditional clause *ean echēte pistin kai mē diakrithēte*. Not only are the disciples to have faith (the noun *pistis*): they must believe without doubting (a passive of the verb *diakrinō* with the negative particle *mē*); i.e., let their faith not be mingled with doubt, let them not be double-minded.[42] Echoing the accent on faith in 21:21a is the participle "believing" (*pisteuontes*, from the verb *pisteuō*) in verse 22.

One expresses that faith by *praying* (the noun *proseuchē*), by asking God (the verb *aiteō*) to take particular actions and to meet certain needs. There are countless subjects for such requests: "And all things, whatever you ask" (*kai panta hosa an aitēsēte*) (v. 22a). From his two examples—the withering of a fig tree and the removal of a mountain—it is clear that Jesus wants disciples to pray audaciously, to ask God for the seemingly impossible.

When you pray that way, says Jesus, "you will receive" (*lēmpsesthe*, from the verb *lambanō*) from God (v. 22b)—a promise as extensive as the requests (v. 22a). When in faith disciples tell a mountain to be thrown into the sea, "it will happen" (*genēsetai*, from the verb *ginomai*)(v. 21b). Jesus thus underscores some of his earlier teachings about prayer: see 7:7–8 (with *aiteō* and *lambanō*); 17:20 (the removal of a mountain by means of the smallest faith); and 18:19 (with *aiteō* and *ginomai*). In light of Jesus' promises to the "two or three" who pray (18:19–20), notice his consistent use of the second person plural in 21:21–22. May not the Christian *community* make a request of God with yet greater confidence than the lone *individual*?

Another prior text on which this passage builds is the prayer of 6:9–13. That prayer too is to be offered in faith; and the requests Jesus urges disciples to make in 21:21–22 cannot be understood apart from the content of that foundational prayer. *a.* "Our Father in heaven." Jesus here encourages disciples to bring their every request to God ("all things, whatever you

---

42. Cf. BAGD s.v. *diakrinō*, 2. b. "be at odds with oneself, doubt, waver"; also the adjective *dipsychos*—"doubting, hesitating," literally, "double-minded" (BAGD s.v.)—in James 1:8 and 4:8; and the verb *diastazō* ("doubt") in Matt. 14:31; 28:17. The "pure in heart" (Matt. 5:8) are single-hearted in their devotion to God (cf. Ps. 86:11).

ask," 21:22a); and he assures them of God's favorable response to every such request ("it will happen," 21b and "you will receive," v. 22b). Yet those teachings are qualified by Jesus' stress on faith in verses 21 (the noun *pistis*) and 22 (the verb *pisteuō*). And what good is faith unless its object is the all-sovereign God—the Father *in heaven*? And what is prayer but the reliance of a powerless human being upon the omnipotent God? Who but he could make a fig tree suddenly wither, or hurl a mountain into the sea?[43] *b.* "Your kingdom come." Jesus speaks in 21:21 of disciples' achieving what he himself has just done—caused a fig tree suddenly to wither (v. 19). That act was a sign of Jesus' own trust in God: he was assured that the Father would *both* supply the power needed to kill the tree *and* execute the judgment on Israel here symbolized.[44] That is, Jesus is certain that God's rule is coming. Disciples can pray in the same confidence (cf. 6:10; Luke 18:7–8). In 21:21 Jesus also assures disciples that God will remove mountains in response to the prayer of faith. This promise may be claimed in face of innumerable obstacles (17:20). Yet here Jesus may well be urging disciples to pray specifically for the coming of God's kingdom. In the present context "*this* mountain" must be the Mount of Olives. It is probable that Jesus here alludes to Zechariah 14:4, "On that day his feet will stand on the Mount of Olives . . . and [it] will be split in two from east to west. . . . " The prophecy of Zechariah is a strong influence elsewhere in the Passion Narrative (beginning in 21:5); the day of Yahweh (Zech. 14:1) and the rule of God are two expressions for one reality; and Jesus' action in the temple (21:12–17) alludes to Zechariah 14:21. If Zechariah 14:4 is in view, then Jesus is teaching *both* that God alone is mighty enough to establish his rule *and* that disciples are to pray fervently to that end. On this reading of the evidence, Jesus' pictures of the fig tree and of the mountain serve the same pedagogical purpose.[45]

---

43. The passive verbs in 21:21—*arthēti* ("be removed") and *blēthēti* ("be thrown")—signal divine activity. The parallel to *genēsetai* ("it will happen") (v. 21) in Mark 11:23 is *estai autō* ("it will be done [by God] for him"). As is often said, "prayer is impotence grasping hold of omnipotence."

44. Cf. Chamblin, *Matthew* (Fearn, Ross-shire: Christian Focus, forthcoming), on 21:18–19.

45. Some who suggest a link with Zech. 14:4 are Alfred Plummer, *An Exegetical Commentary on the Gospel according to St. Matthew*, 3rd ed. (London: Robert Scott, 1911), 292; William Manson, *Jesus the Messiah* (London: Hodder & Stoughton, 1956), 29–30, 39–40; Bruce, *This Is That*, 107–8; Lane, *Commentary on the Gospel of Mark*, 410. Some who doubt this link are France, *Matthew*, 304; and Gundry, *Matthew*, 418. David Hill, *The Gospel of Matthew* (Grand Rapids: Eerdmans, 1972), 295, thinks Matt. 21:21 may refer to the temple mount. Keener, *Commentary on the Gospel of Matthew*, 505, suggests an allusion to Zech. 4:6–9, "where Zerubbabel's obstacles

C. ZECHARIAH IN MATTHEW 24:30

We approach this text by way of Matthew 23:35, which refers to "the blood of Zechariah son of Barachiah, whom you murdered between the temple and the altar." Some believe this to be the prophet "Zechariah, the son of Berechiah, son of Iddo" (Zech. 1:1). Yet in all probability Jesus is speaking of "Zechariah, the son of Jehoida the priest" (2 Chron. 24:20), who pronounces Yahweh's judgment on the people and is then stoned to death "in the court of the house of Yahweh" for his prophetic words (24:21; cf. Matt. 23:35b). In this case Matthew 23:35 encompasses the whole Hebrew Bible, which opens with Genesis and closes with 2 Chronicles.[46]

In Matthew 24:30 Jesus says, "Then will appear in heaven the sign of the Son of Man, and then all the tribes of the earth will mourn, and they will see the Son of Man coming on the clouds of heaven with power and great glory" (ESV).

One Reading of Matthew 24:30

In this verse Jesus alludes to Zechariah 12:10–14, which foretells a time of great mourning for families of Israelites in Jerusalem and elsewhere in the land. In the LXX of these verses, *phylē* ("tribe") translates the Hebrew *mishpakhah* ("family, clan"); *gē*, the Hebrew *'erets* (in this context both nouns mean "land" rather than "earth"); and *koptomai*, the Hebrew *saphad* (both verbs mean "mourn").

Some believe that Jesus retains that very sense of the prophecy; that he has in view the unbelieving Jews in Jerusalem and Judea whom he will come to judge in A.D. 70; and that Matthew 24:30b should be translated "And then all the tribes [*pasai hai phylai*] *of the land* [*tēs gēs*] will mourn [*kopsontai*]." Says one scholar: "If . . . the reference is to the coming destruction of Jerusalem, seen as a specific act of judgment by the vindicated and exalted Jesus on the people who had rejected him (*cf.* Zc. 12:10, 'they shall look on me whom they have pierced'), the appropriateness of the quotation is clear. A destruction of the city could hardly fail to produce such a lamentation by the Jews."[47]

---

in building the temple are compared to a mountain (perhaps the old Zion). . . . That is, like his Davidic ruling ancestor Zerubbabel, . . . Jesus was to prepare a new temple (21:42)."

46. Matt. 23:35 is discussed more fully in Chamblin, *Matthew*.

47. France, *Jesus and the Old Testament*, 237, with 90, 236–38. Cf. J. Marcellus Kik, *An Eschatology of Victory* (Phillipsburg, NJ: Presbyterian & Reformed, 1971), 139–40.

Another Reading of Matthew 24:30

In my judgment it is preferable to see the entirety of this verse as a reference to Jesus' final *parousia*—his second advent—and to translate verse 30b as the ESV has done (above).[48] In favor of this view several points may be made. *a.* The peoples of all the nations will actually *see* the Son of Man at that time (v. 30c), whereas in A.D. 70 he manifests himself by his work of judgment, not by his visible presence (cf. Acts 1:11; Rev. 1:7). *b.* The angels' universal mission (24:31) accords better with this final coming than with the localized events of A.D. 70.[49] *c.* That the Jewish Messiah should transpose *gē* (and *'erets*) from "land" to "earth" accords with his mission to save a people (1:21), not only from Israel (15:24) but from all the nations (24:14; 28:19). Thus too in 5:5 he declares that the meek will inherit *tēn gēn*—no longer meaning "the land" (cf. ESV at Ps. 37:11) but "the earth."[50] *d.* As Israel remains one of the nations to be evangelized (10:23), so the original meaning of Zechariah 12:10–14 is not abandoned but incorporated into a larger reality. On the one hand, the meaning of *phylai* is enlarged to embrace "tribes" of other nations, just as the term *mishpakhah* is applied to Israel in Zechariah 12:10–14 but to "all the families of the earth" in Genesis 12:3. On the other hand, Jesus' use of the term *phylai* in 24:30 suggests that the destiny of *Israelites* is here especially, though not exclusively, in view. So it was in 19:28 (which contains the only other instance of *phylē* in Matthew), where Jesus speaks specifically of the judgment in store for "the twelve tribes of Israel," though "all the nations" will then be gathered before him (25:31–32).[51] At the end Israelites will mourn for different reasons: for some it will be a mourning of *despair*, because they have persisted in their rejection of Jesus the Messiah; for others it will be a mourning of *repentance* (in keeping with Zech. 12:10–14) joined to *joy* over the advent of the one

48. NASB, NIV, and NRSV also translate "all the tribes of the earth." NIV has "all the nations of the earth"; NJB has "all the peoples of the earth"; REB, "all the peoples of the world."

49. Compare 24:31b ("from the four winds, from one end of heaven") to Zech. 2:6b ("as the four winds of the heavens").

50. Where *gē* occurs in Matthew, usually the context makes it plain if "land" as a political or territorial entity is meant (cf. 2:6, 20–21; 4:15; 9:26, 31; 10:15; 11:24; probably 27:45). Elsewhere *gē* denotes "land" as distinct from water (14:24, 34); "soil" (13:5, 8, 23); "ground" (10:29; 15:35; 25:18, 25; probably 27:51); and "earth" as distinct from heaven or as the inhabited globe (5:5, 13, 18, 35; 6:10, 19; 9:6; 10:34; 11:25; 12:40, 42; 16:19; 17:25; 18:18–19; 23:9, 35; 24:35; 28:18). Cf. BAGD s.v., 1., 2., 4., and 5.

51. Cf. Chamblin, *Matthew*, on 19:28.

who has forgiven their sins.[52] So it will be for the people of the nations in general: those who face eternal punishment (25:46a) for their unbelief and relentless iniquities against Jesus and his people (24:4–5, 9–12) will despair; the godly sorrow of those who repent in response to the gospel (24:14) will be turned into joy when they enter life eternal (25:46b).[53]

D. ZECHARIAH IN MATTHEW 26:14–16 AND 27:6–10

Both passages feature Judas Iscariot and the Jewish authorities. In the first, Judas agrees to deliver Jesus over to them. The second follows his act of betrayal.

Judas and the Thirty Silver Coins (26:14–16)

In 26:14 the name Judas Iscariot (*Ioudas Iskariōtēs*) appears for the first time since 10:4. Here, as there, he is identified as one of the twelve. Verse 14 also relates his going to the chief priests, the first conspirators named in 26:3. The adverb "then" that opens verse 14 links Judas' action both to that plot and to the woman's "good work" which he had strongly opposed (vv. 8–10; cf. John 12:4–5).

Having come to the chief priests, Judas asks, "What are you willing to give me so that I will hand him over to you?" (26:15a). In response to Judas' inquiry, the chief priests "weighed out [*estēsan*] for him thirty silver coins [*triakonta argyria*]" (v. 15b). Matthew is the only evangelist who records the amount given to Judas (cf. 27:3–10, where *triakonta argyria* occurs twice). These two passages recall Zechariah 11:12–13. Here the prophet (v. 4), representing the Shepherd-King, the promised Messiah, reports that when he spoke to the people about payment for his services, "they weighed out [*yishqelu*] for my wage thirty pieces of silver" (v. 12b).[54] The parallel

---

52. See Zech. 13:1; and Chamblin, *Matthew*, on Matt. 23:39. Judas mourned in despair (27:3–5); Peter, in repentance (26:75). Cf. 2 Cor. 7:10; James 4:8–10; Kik, *Eschatology of Victory*, 139–40.

53. The *erchomenon* of 24:30c is a present participle of *erchomai*. Forms of this verb also occur in 10:23 and 16:27–28. Chamblin (in his *Matthew*) argues that Jesus speaks in 10:23 both of his imminent coming (his judgment on Israel in A.D. 70) and of his ultimate coming; and again of both in 16:27 (ultimate coming) and 28 (imminent coming).

54. The rejected shepherd of Zech. 11:12 "was a Messianic figure." France, *Matthew*, 364. Zechariah "intimates that this Messiah is to suffer as the smitten shepherd (11:7–14; 13:7–9)." VanGemeren, *Interpreting the Prophetic Word*, 201.

to 26:15b in Mark 14:11b states that the chief priests "promised [the verb *epangellomai*] to give him money [*argyrion*]." The reason Matthew chooses *estēsan* (from *histēmi*) instead, is that the LXX of Zechariah 11:12 uses this very term to translate the Hebrew verb *shaqal* ("weigh out"). In that light, it is preferable to translate the *estēsan* of 26:15 as "weighed out" rather than "set" or "fixed." The Markan parallel indicates that the authorities would not actually pay Judas until he had delivered Jesus into their hands.[55]

By all indications, the silver coin taken from the temple treasury to pay Judas (cf. 27:6) was the *statēr* or *tetradrachmon* ("four drachma piece"), which in Jesus' day was equivalent in value to the Hebrew shekel of Old Testament times. As a Greek *drachmē* was roughly the value of a Roman *dēnarion*, thirty staters would amount to wages for 120 days' manual labor.[56] This was a sum large enough to appeal strongly to Judas' avarice. "Persian governors before Nehemiah had exacted forty shekels in tax (presumably *per annum*), and the amount is quoted as burdensome [Neh. 5:15]. The fact that in the Mosaic law [Ex. 21:32] thirty shekels was demanded in compensation for the death of a slave indicates the high value set on human life."[57] But from another standpoint, a wage of thirty silver coins was a paltry amount, evidence of the people's low esteem for Yahweh's shepherd. Thus the irony of Zechariah 11:13a, "And Yahweh said to me, 'Throw it to the potter,' this princely sum at which they valued me!" (cf. NJB). For a *mere* thirty pieces of silver, Judas betrays Yahweh's Shepherd-King, and thus betrays Yahweh himself (Matt. 1:23),

55. For the instance of *histēmi* in 26:15, BAGD include both "set, fix," and "weigh out," but prefer the latter (s.v., 2. c.). Cf. NASB ("weighed out"), NIV ("counted out"), ESV ("paid"). Yet as Hagner notes, "it seems unlikely that the authorities would have paid in advance" (so he translates *estēsan* "set with"). *Matthew 14–28*, 760. I believe that the money was "weighed out" on this occasion, and set aside for later payment. *Argyrion* can denote silver in particular or money in general (BAGD s.v., 1. a., b.). The word for silver in the LXX of Zech. 11:12–13 is *argyros*. Matthew uses this term once, in 10:9, where Jesus tells the twelve, including Judas, to acquire no silver for their belts; Davies and Allison think there is possibly an "intratextual link" between 26:15 and 10:9. *Gospel according to Saint Matthew*, 453. Mark 14:11 also reports that the chief priests *rejoice* (the verb *chairō*) over Judas' initiative; they realize how important he is for the success of their plan.

56. See Chamblin, *Matthew*, on 17:24–25. The Hebrew noun *sheqel* (originally a unit of weight) is a cognate of *shaqal* ("weigh out"), the verb used in Zech. 11:12.

57. Baldwin, *Haggai, Zechariah, Malachi*, 184, on Zech. 11:12. On *dēnarion*, cf. Chamblin, *Matthew*, at 20:2. "Judas has the same name as Judah, one of the twelve sons of Jacob, who in Gen 37:26–28, rather than shed his brother Joseph's blood, sold him for twenty (or thirty) pieces of silver." Raymond E. Brown, *An Introduction to the New Testament* (New York: Doubleday, 1997), 201, n. 69; he apparently includes the number "thirty" in light of Ex. 21:32. Cf. Lev. 27:1–8.

rejects the Father who sent him (cf. 10:40), and commits blasphemy against the Holy Spirit (12:32).

"And from then on [*apo tote*] he sought for a favorable opportunity to betray him," concludes the passage. "Just as in 4:17 this phrase [*apo tote*] indicated the beginning of Jesus' Galilean ministry and in 16:21 indicated the beginning of his teaching the disciples about the coming passion and resurrection, so here it indicates the beginning of the passion-cum-resurrection itself."[58] The "favorable opportunity" (*eukairia*) that Judas seeks (the verb *zēteō*) will entail the absence of a crowd, as noted in the parallel of Luke 22:6. In the meantime Judas must act by stealth (*dolos*) (26:4), and "exercise a hunter's patience"—which will in the end be rewarded (26:47–56).[59]

The Blood Money and the Field of Blood (27:6–10)

Judas having departed to hang himself (vv. 3–5), the chief priests take up the thirty silver coins (v. 6a) that Judas scattered in the temple (v. 5a).[60] Then they say, "It is not lawful [*ouk exestin*] to put them into the treasury [*eis ton korbanan*], since this is blood money [*timē haimatos*]" (v. 6b). The closing two Greek words are literally "the price of blood" (so NASB)—that is, "the money paid for a bloody deed," "the price paid to secure a death."[61] The text indicts the chief priests for their double-mindedness. On the one hand, their statement honors Deuteronomy 23:18, which prohibits offering to God money obtained by sinful means (in this case prostitution).[62] On the other hand, the priests show not the slightest awareness that they have sinned by taking this money from the temple treasury to secure the arrest and execution of Jesus.[63] Is not this the most appalling case imaginable of

58. Gundry, *Matthew*, 523. These are the only three instances of *apo tote* in Matthew.

59. Davies and Allison, *Gospel according to Saint Matthew*, 453.

60. In light of v. 5a, the aorist participle *labontes* (from *lambanō*, "take, receive"), v. 6a, may be translated "having taken up" (Hagner, *Matthew 14–28*, 810) or "picked up" (NIV).

61. The first quotation is from BAGD s.v. *timē*, 1.; the second from Morris, *Matthew*, 696.

62. On Deut. 23:18–19, see Peter C. Craigie, *The Book of Deuteronomy*, NICOT (Grand Rapids: Eerdmans, 1976), 302. *Korbanas* translates an Aramaic term for the "temple treasury" (BAGD s.v.). Correspondingly, the term *korban* denotes a "gift" consecrated to God: see Mark 7:11, with Matt. 15:5. Neither term occurs elsewhere in the New Testament. John 8:20 states that Jesus taught in the temple at the treasury (*gazophylakion*): apparently he stood in the court of the women (cf. Mark 12:41–44, where this noun denotes a receptacle for money) at a place adjacent to one such treasury (for there were probably several).

63. Morris remarks that "apparently they had not scrupled to take the money out of the temple treasury to bring about Jesus' death, but they now had tender consciences about putting it

adhering to the letter of the law while violating its weightier matters, of straining out a gnat while swallowing a camel (Matt. 23:23–24)?

"So, having taken counsel, they bought with them the potter's field as a burial place for aliens. Therefore that field has been called the Field of Blood to this day" (vv. 7–8). The opening words (*symboulion . . . labontes*) recall verse 1, where chief priests and elders "took counsel" (*symboulion elabon*) to have Jesus put to death. Now, with the very coins used for that purpose, they purchase "the potter's field" (*ton agron tou kerameōs*), which probably lay south-southwest of Jerusalem, across the Hinnom Valley (cf. Jer. 19:2), and which perhaps contained (as the name suggests) rich deposits of clay.[64] Moreover, the acquired land is to be used as a burial plot (*taphē*): "unclean money buys an unclean place."[65] The aliens (*xenoi*) in question are resident Gentiles, "who were not allowed to be buried in the same cemetery with Jews."[66] In Matthew the name "Field of Blood" (*Agros Haimatos*) (27:8) is related to its purchase with "blood money" (*timē haimatos*) (27:6). Acts connects the name (*Chōrion Haimatos*) (1:19), to Judas' death there (1:18).[67]

That brings us to Matthew 27:9–10, "Then what was spoken through Jeremiah the prophet was fulfilled: 'And they took the thirty silver coins, the price of him on whom a price had been set by some of the sons of Israel, and they gave them for the potter's field, as the Lord commanded me.'" Showing his skill as an interpreter of truth both new (the coming of Jesus) and old (prophecies of his coming) (13:52), Matthew here employs language from both Jeremiah and Zechariah under the name of the more prominent prophet.[68] Discussion of texts from Jeremiah (19:1–13 and 32:6–9) is mostly

---

back! To them it was no crime to use it to bring about a death, but it was a crime to put it into their treasury when it had been used for the purpose for which they expended it." *Matthew*, 696.

64. On the name and location, see Davies and Allison, *Gospel according to Matthew*, 567.

65. Ibid. Cf. 23:27.

66. Hagner, *Matthew 14–28*, 813.

67. Ibid. See Chamblin, *Matthew*, on 27:5, where 27:3–10 is compared to Acts 1:15–20.

68. Raymond E. Brown calls 27:9–10 a "mixed citation" with words from Zechariah and Jeremiah. *The Death of the Messiah* (New York: Doubleday, 1994), 651. So too Douglas J. Moo, "Tradition and Old Testament in Matt. 27:3–10," in *Gospel Perspectives 3: Studies in Midrash and Historiography*, ed. R. T. France and David Wenham (Sheffield: JSOT Press, 1983), 161 ("this complex citation"). Moo says that Jeremiah is expressly mentioned because this is the less obvious reference. Matt. 21:4–5 speaks of what God spoke "through the prophet," but cites both Isa. 62:11 and Zech. 9:9. Mark 1:2–3 contains quotations from Malachi and Isaiah but only names the latter. The name Jeremiah appears three times in Matthew (2:17; 16:14; 27:9) and nowhere else in the New Testament. To be rejected is the view, first propounded in defense of Matt. 27:9, that Zechariah 9–11 was the work of Jeremiah (noted in Baldwin, *Haggai, Zechariah, Malachi*, 63).

reserved for my forthcoming commentary. We focus mainly on Matthew's indebtedness to Zechariah.

Three features of 27:9–10 recall the prophecy of Zechariah 11:12–13. *a.* Both texts refer to "thirty silver coins": *ta triakonta argyria* (the Greek of Matt. 27:9); *sheloshim kaseph* (the Hebrew of Zech. 11:12, 13).[69] *b.* In both passages the money serves a sinful purpose. In Zechariah the Israelites show their contempt for Yahweh's appointed Shepherd, the promised Messiah, by paying him this paltry wage. In Matthew some of the sons of Israel, namely the chief priests, promise thirty pieces of silver to Messiah's betrayer.[70] *c.* Each text speaks of a "potter": *kerameus* (the Greek of Matt. 27:10); *yotser* (the Hebrew of Zech. 11:13).[71] In Zechariah, in obedience to Yahweh's command, the Shepherd threw the thirty silver coins "into the house of Yahweh, to the potter" (11:13b).[72] In Matthew the thirty coins are first thrown (by the betrayer) into the temple (the house of Yahweh), and then given (by the chief priests) for the potter's field (so, in a sense, to the potter).[73]

69. The reading in Zech. 11:13 is *shelosim hakeseph*. In the LXX of 11:12–13 this term is rendered *triakonta argyrous*. This noun for silver, *argyros*, is much less common than *argyrion*, the one Matthew consistently uses for the money paid to Judas. *Argyros* occurs once in Matthew, in 10:9.

70. For this reading of Zech. 11:12–13, see above on Matt. 26:14–15 and below on 26:31.

71. The term *hayotser* ("the potter") occurs twice in 11:13. Some English translations, following the Syriac version of the OT, opt instead for *ha'otsar* ("the treasury"): so NRSV, REB. But the latter "seems to be the result of a scribe's ingenuity, accommodating the reading to what he took to be the sense" (Baldwin, *Haggai, Zechariah, Malachi*, 185, following M. Delcor). So the preferable reading is "the potter": so ESV, NIV. But see the next note.

72. The verb *yatsar* (of which *yotser* is a participle) basically means to "form" or to "shape," so it can apply to working with both clay and metal. Some think the latter sense is meant at 11:13b. In the LXX the closing phrase is rendered *eis to chōneutērion* ("into the furnace" or "into the foundry"); in the NJB, "for the smelter." Bruce, *This Is That*, 109, while noting that *yotser* normally means "potter," believes that "here it denotes the man who melted down precious metal in the temple mould or foundry." "M. Delcor links the verse with Judges 17:4, where two hundred shekels of silver were made into a molten image. By comparison thirty shekels would make only a figurine, and in this detail, he thinks, lies the irony. If they will not have the Lord's shepherd to rule them the only alternative is to have a little god made from the silver pieces." Baldwin, *Haggai, Zechariah, Malachi*, 185; she favors this view. Yet (i) as Bruce acknowledges (above), *yatsar* more readily suggests the work of a potter than of a smelter (cf. BDB s.v.); (ii) the noun *kerameus* (Matt. 27:7, 10) must denote a worker in clay (cf. "ceramic"); and (iii) in any case Matthew's references to a potter are mainly related to Jeremiah.

73. Of course Matthew does not say that the thirty coins are paid to a potter. But at least the grammar of 27:7, 10, identifies the field as the potter's possession: in both verses the noun *kerameus* appears as the possessive genitive *kerameōs*. See Daniel B. Wallace, *GGBB*, 81–83. The historical link between the temple *treasury* (*korbanas*) (27:6) and the field of the *potter* (*kerameus*) (27:7, 10) invites a word play upon *'otsar* and *yotser*, the Hebrew terms for "treasury"

Matthew, the well-trained scribe (13:52) begins with "things new," the events of 27:3–8. Then in 27:9–10 he draws from his treasury "things old," and shows how prophecies in Zechariah and Jeremiah are fulfilled (the verb *pleroō*, v. 9a) in those events. Linguistic and conceptual parallels serve Matthew's theological purpose.[74] Jesus is the Shepherd-King promised in Zechariah, the One whom Israel rejects, and whom Yahweh will soon strike down (26:31, quoting Zech. 13:7). Jeremiah witnesses to Jesus by both his word and his life. By the shedding of Jesus' innocent blood (Matt. 27:4; cf. Jer. 19:4), the new covenant foretold in Jeremiah 31:31–34 will be established (Matt. 26:28). Moreover, the prophet himself is a type of Jesus: for Jeremiah too was maltreated by the Jewish authorities; he too was a man of sorrows and acquainted with grief; he too was despised and rejected by his people (cf. Isa.53:3).[75] If the contemporaries of Jeremiah and Zechariah spurned the witness of these prophets, how much greater the guilt of the generation that repudiates the words and works of Messiah himself (Matt. 11:16–24; 12:38–45; 16:1–4; 21:33–46; 23:37–38). Both Zechariah and Jeremiah declare that Yahweh will surely punish those who disobey his word and reject his servants (see e.g. Zech. 11:1–17; Jer. 18:1–19:15). Yet the judgment that awaits the Judea and Jerusalem of Jesus' own generation will be far more calamitous than the one Jeremiah foretold (see Matt. 24:15–21).

E. ZECHARIAH IN MATTHEW 26:28

Jesus here speaks of "my blood *of the covenant* [*to haima mou tēs diathēkēs*], which is poured out . . . *for the forgiveness of sins* [*to . . . ekchynnom-enon eis aphesin hamartiōn*]*." This is the sole instance of the noun *diathēkē* in Matthew. The translation "this is my blood of the covenant" (ESV) is to be preferred over "this is My blood of the new [*kainēs*] covenant" (NKJV); the same holds true for Mark 14:24 (again ESV and NKJV).

---

and "potter" noted earlier. There is a corresponding word play on *yotser* itself if this term is understood to refer to both the *smelter* in the temple treasury and the *potter* of the field (see note 72).

74. Matthew's use of the Old Testament in 27:3–10 is "the result of a careful theological study which takes account not only of superficial verbal 'coincidences,' but of underlying themes of prophetic expectation." France, *Matthew*, 388.

75. While Zechariah "supplied a whole chain of texts" that helped the early Christians to understand Jesus, "that prophet in his book had no personal story. Jeremiah both in his message and in his personal 'passion' was a more vivid introduction to God's plan for the Messiah." Brown, *Death of the Messiah*, 652.

It is probable that "my blood of the covenant" alludes to both Exodus 24:8 and Zechariah 9:11. In the first one Moses, having sprinkled half the blood on the altar (v. 6), sprinkles the other half on the people and says, "Behold, the blood of the covenant [*dam haberith*] which Yahweh has made with you . . ."; in the LXX that Hebrew phrase is translated *to haima tēs diathēkēs*, the terms of Matthew 26:28. These same nouns, *dam* and *haima*, *berith* and *diathēkē*, recur in Zechariah 9:11. Here Yahweh says, "As for you also, because of the blood of my covenant with you, I will set your prisoners free from the waterless pit" (ESV)—a text all the more notable given its proximity to the prophecies about the Davidic king in 9:9–10.[76] But the words of Luke 22:20 and 1 Corinthians 11:25, "This cup is the *new* covenant [*hē kainē diathēkē*] in my blood,"[77] together with those of Matthew 26:28b, "for the forgiveness of sins," show that Jesus is referring primarily to Jeremiah 31:31–34, and that he views his death as crucial for the fulfillment of this prophecy.

"The blood of the covenant" in Exodus 24:8 (together with the kindred phrase of Zech. 9:11) reflects the Old Testament *type*; and "my blood of the covenant" in Matthew 26:28, the New Testament *antitype*. The latter *intensifies* the former: whereas Moses *sprinkled* the blood of *animals* on the people, Jesus voluntarily pours out his *own* blood, and commands his followers to *drink* a cup signifying that sacrifice.[78]

76. In Ex. 24:8, as in Lev. 8:22–24 and 14:14, 25 (the only other Old Testament texts that speak of sprinkling people with blood), "it seems that the action signifies cleansing from earlier defilement and consecration to a new life of service to God." Morris, *Matthew*, 660. Dodd notes that Zech. 9:11 continues the prophecy of 9:9–10, and "is probably one of the scriptures underlying" Mark 14:24 and Matt 26:28. *According to the Scriptures*, 64. Cf. Baldwin, *Haggai, Zechariah, Malachi*, 167.

77. It is easy to understand later scribes' importing the adjective from Luke and Paul into Matthew and Mark. But if it was original to the latter two, "there is no good reason why anyone would have deleted it." Metzger, *Textual Commentary*, 54; cf. ibid., 95, on Mark 14:24).

78. The typology of these texts is well noted by Davies and Allison, *Gospel according to Saint Matthew*, 473, and by Clay Ham, "The Last Supper in Matthew," *Bulletin for Biblical Research* 10 (2000), 64–65. In each case a biblical covenant is "a bond-in-blood sovereignly administered." O. Palmer Robertson, *The Christ of the Covenants* (Phillipsburg, NJ: Presbyterian & Reformed, 1980), 15, a truth that comes to supreme expression in Jesus' death. In the LXX of Ex. 24:8 and in Matt. 26:28 *diathēkēs* is a genitive of *product*: i.e., the shedding of blood is essential for establishing, for producing, the given covenant (see Ham, "Last Supper in Matthew," 58; *GGBB*, 106). God forgave his people in Old Testament times on the basis of the atonement his Son would provide (see Rom. 3:25–26; Heb. 8:1–10:18, including the quotation from Jer. 31:31–34 in 8:8–12 and 10:16–17).

F. ZECHARIAH IN MATTHEW 26:31–32

On the way to the Mount of Olives and the Garden of Gethsemane, Jesus says to his disciples, "All of you will fall away because of me tonight. For it has been written, 'I will strike the shepherd, and the sheep of the flock will be scattered.' But after I have been raised, I will go before you into Galilee." Yet again Matthew's passion narrative is illuminated by a prophecy from Zechariah, this time from 13:7.

Zechariah 13:7 in Its Original Setting

The verse reads, " 'Awake, sword, against my shepherd, against the man who is my companion,' declares Yahweh of hosts. 'Strike the shepherd, and the sheep will be scattered, and I will turn my hand against the little ones.' " This is the same shepherd whom the people reject in 11:4–14 and whom Yahweh therefore replaces with a worthless shepherd (11:15–16). Zechariah the prophet represents the first shepherd (11:4) and impersonates the second (11:15). But the first shepherd himself is a ruler—indeed *the* ruler, the promised Messiah, the coming Shepherd-King.[79] In 13:2–6 Yahweh promises to banish uncleanness from the land and to deal severely with false prophets; so had 13:7 spoken of his entrusting his sword to the Shepherd-King for judgments against false prophets and worthless shepherds (cf. 10:2–4; 11:17), we would not have been surprised. But we are shocked by what Yahweh actually does: he commands his sword to strike his own close companion, the good Shepherd.[80]

Once the shepherd is smitten, his sheep are scattered. God, having ordered the shepherd's death, now turns his hand against the young of the flock.[81] Two thirds of the land's inhabitants will perish, but one third will be kept alive (13:8). Yahweh wills that the latter suffer great trial, that they may be refined, and his covenant with them renewed (13:9). A comparison with Jeremiah 31:31–34 (Yahweh forgives sins under the new covenant) and

79. See above, A. (on Matt. 21:5) and D. (on 26:15); Bruce, *This Is That*, 100–114 ("The Shepherd King"); Duguid, "Messianic Themes," 266–75.

80. The father and the mother of a false prophet are commanded to put him to death by "piercing him through" (Zech. 13:2–3; cf. Deut. 13:1–11). Yahweh calls upon his sword to "strike" (i.e. to pierce) his own close relation. Cf. Baldwin, *Haggai, Zechariah, Malachi*, 197, following D. R. Jones.

81. The Hebrew *tso'arim* ("little ones") is better translated "lambs" (REB; BDB s.v.) than "shepherd boys" (NEB).

Isaiah 53:5, 10 (Yahweh crushes the Servant for his people's sins) suggests that the covenant is renewed because the Shepherd has died.[82]

Zechariah 13:7 in Its Present Setting

"I will strike the shepherd [*pataxō ton poimena*], and the sheep of the flock will be scattered [*kai diaskorpisthēsontai ta probata tēs poimnēs*]," runs the quotation in Matthew 26:31b. This Greek text agrees with one version of the LXX, except for the opening word: the LXX uses an aorist imperative of the verb *patassō* (*pataxate*, "strike"), in agreement with the Hebrew; Matthew (like Mark) uses a future indicative. The imperative voices Yahweh's sovereign initiative: it is he who commands the sword to strike (as we saw above). From that we may infer that this is Yahweh's own sword; yet only the indicative expressly states that he himself will strike the shepherd.[83] Jesus will indeed be murdered by his enemies (26:4). Yet the deepest and most mysterious explanation of his death is that God wills that it should happen, and that the Son, the sin-bearer, should there become the object of the Father's wrath. The Shepherd-King "also fulfills the role of priestly sacrifice." No wonder Jesus dreads the cross (26:36–46).[84]

The quotation is prefaced by the words "For it has been written," *gegraptai gar*. The verb, a perfect passive indicative of *graphō*, indicates that the prophecy has lost none of its authority—that it remains in force, that it "stands written" till the time appointed for its fulfillment.[85] In the case of this prophecy that time has come. In less than twenty-four hours, the Shepherd

---

82. See Matt. 26:28. The verb *nakah* occurs in Zech. 13:7 as a *hiphil* imperative ("strike"), in Isa. 53:4 as a *hophal* participle ("smitten"). In the latter text, "the sufferings are misunderstood as . . . a disfavour of God directed personally against the Servant" (Motyer, *Isaiah*, 334).

83. The indicative *pataxō* "is best explained not as a variant text [of *pataxate*] but as a grammatical adaptation necessitated by the abbreviated quotation, which does not include the explicit mention of the 'sword' in the opening line of the oracle, to which the command is addressed." R. T. France, *The Gospel of Mark* [Grand Rapids: Eerdmans, 2002], 575, n. 73. Matthew follows LXX^A (Codex Alexandrinus), which is closer to the MT than LXX^B (Codex Vaticanus): see Davies and Allison, *Gospel according to Saint Matthew*, 485.

84. Robertson, *The Christ of the Prophets*, 385. Robertson continues: "Jesus himself modifies the form of the Old Testament's wording [Zech. 13:7] to underscore the fact that God himself originates the deathblow to the Good Shepherd: '*I* will smite the shepherd . . . .' The gentle king of his people has become the priest sacrificed at the hands of the Lord himself. Only in this manner could actual redemption be accomplished." Ibid., 386. See Acts 2:23; Rom. 8:32; Isa. 53:5–10; and Chamblin, *Matthew*, on 26:1–5, 36–46.

85. The *gegraptai* shows that the following quotation has "present and binding authority." Wallace, *GGBB*, 576. Cf. the use of *gegraptai* in 21:13 (under B. above).

will have been put to death. And this very night, when the disciples fall away (v. 31a, with the future passive *skandalisthēsesthe*), the prediction about the sheep's being scattered (v. 31b, with the future passive *diaskorpisthēsontai*), will come true: the *gar* ("for") in the preface to the quotation expressly links the disciples' flight (cf. v. 56) to the prophecy.[86]

"But after I have been raised [*meta . . . to egerthēnai*], I will go before you into Galilee," says Jesus in verse 32. He thus declares that Zechariah 13:9 will be fulfilled as surely as 13:7. The understood subject of the passive verb (from *egeirō*) is "God": the very one who strikes down the Shepherd will raise him from the dead. The Father will thus honor his Son for accomplishing his mission and for inaugurating the new covenant by his shed blood (26:28; cf. Heb. 13:20). As a mark of the forgiveness thereby provided, the risen Shepherd will restore his scattered disciples. Their falling away will be a terrible sin; but unlike Judas they will not perish. "They will fall to rise again," now refined for the work to which Jesus will commission them (28:10, 18–20).[87]

G. CONCLUSION

Our study has shown that Matthew's Passion Narrative is illuminated by several texts from Zechariah—notably by 9:9–11 (sections A. and E.); 11:12–13 (D.); 12:10–14 (C.); 13:7 (F.); and 14:21 (B.). As the last Matthean text to be considered was 26:31–32, and as the theme of this festschrift is the Old Testament's witness to Jesus Christ, it is fitting that we conclude with some words of Jesus at the scene of his arrest. "How then [*pōs oun*] would the Scriptures be fulfilled [*plērōthōsin hai graphai*], that it must happen thus [*hoti houtōs dei genesthai*]" (26:54)? "But all this has happened [*touto de holon gegonen*] in order that the Scriptures of the prophets may be fulfilled [*hina plērōthōsin hai graphai tōn prophētōn*]" (26:56). Each statement (i) is conclusive (the first is Jesus' closing word to Peter, the second his final word to the crowd); (ii) speaks of what is happening (forms of *ginomai*) now (*houtōs*, "thus"; *touto . . . holon*, "all this"); and (iii) recognizes that

---

86. Passive forms of *skandalizō* can denote taking offense at Jesus, or falling away, or falling into sin, on his account: see the instances in 11:6; 13:21, 57; 15:12; 24:10; 26:33. Active forms of *diaskorpizō* ("scatter") appear in 25:24, 26. Cf. the passive of *skorpizō* in John 16:32.

87. France, *Mark*, 575. On 26:32, see Chamblin, *Matthew*, on 28:7.

the Scriptures (*hai graphai*) are being fulfilled (identical forms of *plēroō*) in these events.[88]

Jesus refers mainly to prophecies of his own suffering and death. In light of the repeated *graphai* ("Scriptures" or "writings") in these two verses, note the use of the cognate verb *graphō* in 26:24a, "the Son of Man is going as it has been written [*gegraptai*] about him," and 26:31, "for it has been written [*gegraptai*], 'I will strike the shepherd, and the sheep of the flock will be scattered.'" Verse 56 speaks of "the Scriptures *of the prophets*"; so attention may especially be drawn to Isaiah 53:11–12 (to which Jesus alludes in Matt. 20:28 and again in 26:28); to Jeremiah 31:31–34 (to which he alludes in 26:28); and to Zechariah 13:7 (which he quotes in 26:31, and which is partly fulfilled in 26:56b). Matthew 26:54b, "that it must [*dei*] happen thus," recalls the language of 16:21, "that it was necessary [*dei*] for him to go to Jerusalem and to suffer . . . and to be killed."

I give thanks to God that Palmer Robertson committed his life to Christ the Redeemer at the Billy Graham crusade in Jackson, Mississippi, during the summer of 1952, and that he has served him faithfully ever since. May the faithful, covenant-keeping God who has brought Palmer to his seventieth birthday (Ps. 90:10), now satisfy him with yet longer life (Ps. 91:16), and enable him to bear much fruit in the years to come (Ps. 92:14).

---

88. *Genesthai* (v. 54) is an aorist infinitive, and *gegona* (v. 56) a perfect indicative, of *ginomai*. *Plēroō* appears in both verses as the aorist subjunctive *plērōthōsin*. The adverb *houtōs* ("thus") is closely akin to the pronoun (and adjective) *houtos* ("this"), whence the neuter pronoun *touto*.

7

Psalm 110 in the Epistle to the Hebrews

SIMON J. KISTEMAKER

OF ALL THE NEW TESTAMENT books, the Epistle to the Hebrews features the most Old Testament quotations and allusions. Some of the chapters in this epistle are filled with biblical passages taken directly or indirectly from the Old Testament.[1] Just as Romans highlights more quotations than the rest of the Pauline corpus and the Apocalypse has more allusions to the Old Testament than John's gospel and epistles have, so Hebrews excels in its quotations from and allusions to these Scriptures.[2]

The apostle Paul relied heavily on the Old Testament Scriptures that he generally quoted from memory. For example, in Romans most of them derive from Isaiah's prophecy (sixteen quotations) and the Psalter (fourteen instances). Also note that Clement of Rome quoted from the Psalter more than from any other Old Testament book.[3]

---

1. L. Venard, "L'utilisation des Psaumes dans l'Épitre aux Hébreux," *Mélanges E. Podechard*, (Lyon: Facultés Catholiques, 1945), 253–64.

2. Simon Kistemaker, *The Psalm Citations in the Epistle to the Hebrews* (Amsterdam: Van Soest, 1961), 13.

3. Consult the *Index Locorum Veteris Testamenti* in *Patrum Apostolicorum Opera* (ed. O. de Gebhardt, A. Harnack, Th. Zahn), 144–45. Clement quoted from and referred to the Psalms 34

The unknown writer of the Epistle to the Hebrews quoted from the Psalter and from the larger hymn of Moses (Deut. 32). It is obvious that the author uses psalms and hymns with which his readers were familiar for the purpose of conveying to them his message. There are a total of 26 direct quotations in Hebrews with another 6 that are more indirect to bring the total to 32.[4] If we take the psalms as units, we note that the author quotes ten psalms from the Psalter (2, 8, 22, 40, 45, 95, 102, 104, 110, and 118). Some of the quotations are short, others are long. Some occur only once, others frequently because they function as a basis for the author's theology. The sequence of seven biblical quotations in Hebrews 1 begins with Psalm 2:7 and ends with Psalm 110:1. Both passages stress the kingship of God's Son.

Note also that Psalm 110:1 appears in Hebrews 1:13 while Psalm 110:4 functions as a necessary part of teaching the high priesthood of Christ in Hebrews 5:6; 6:20; 7:17, 21. Thus, after introducing the Son of God as king, the writer stresses his eternal priesthood.[5] In fact, he stresses both the kingship and the priesthood and applies this dual office to the one Person, Jesus Christ. The Qumran documents also mention the two offices but apply the teaching to two individual persons: a king and a teacher. By contrast, one of the Minor Prophets writes, "Here is the man whose name is the Branch . . . who will build the temple of the LORD . . . and will sit and rule on his throne. And he will be a priest on his throne" (Zech. 6:12–13).[6] The person called the Branch serves as both priest and king.

The Jews in the second century applied Psalm 110 to King Hezekiah (see Justin Martyr in his Dial. 33, 83) and they also related the psalm to Melchizedek who blessed Abram. But how did Jews and Christians at the time of the apostles understand this psalm? The answer is that they understood it to refer to the Messiah. But when the conflict between Judaism and Christianity became divisive, for the next few centuries a

---

times (Genesis 17 times, Isaiah 14 times, Job 11 times, and all other Old Testament books less than 10 times).

4. Compare B. F. Westcott, *The Epistle to the Hebrews* (1892; repr., Grand Rapids: Eerdmans, 1952), 469–71, who counts a total of 29 quotations. Paul Ellingworth notes, "Fourteen of the 35 quotations are drawn from the Psalms." See his *The Epistle to the Hebrews: A Commentary on the Greek Text* (Grand Rapids: Eerdmans; Carlisle: Paternoster, 1993), 39.

5. O. Palmer Robertson, *The Christ of the Covenants* (Phillipsburg, NJ: Presbyterian & Reformed, 1980), 236. Also consult David G. Dunbar, "The Relationship of Christ's Sonship and Priesthood in the Epistle to the Hebrews." (ThM thesis, Westminster Theological Seminary, 1974).

6. All Scripture quotations in this article are taken from the New International Version (NIV).

messianic interpretation among the Jews was forbidden.[7] During the first century Jewish scholars considered this psalm to be messianic, because the apocalyptic literature speaks of the Chosen One who sits on the throne of glory.[8]

The early church fathers (Clement of Rome, Justin Martyr, and Irenaeus) repeatedly allude to Psalm 110 in a messianic setting and do so in connection with the Epistle to the Hebrews.

The author quotes Psalm 110:4 to stress the priesthood of Christ. This verse is pivotal in his epistle, for it proves from the Old Testament Scriptures that Jesus as the Son of God functions as a priest forever in the presence of God who swore an oath that can never be revoked. With it God sealed the Messiah's priesthood, which differed from the Aaronic priesthood. Aaron and his successors were appointed by law but not by oath. Also, the Old Testament priesthood lasted only a few decades while the priesthood in the order of Melchizedek was everlasting.

PSALM 110:1

> The LORD says to my Lord,
>   "Sit at my right hand
> until I make your enemies
>   a footstool for your feet."

The author of Hebrews stresses the term *Son* at the beginning of his epistle (1:2, 5a, 5b, and 8). The Son has spoken the last word of God over against the Old Testament prophets who received revelation by dreams, visions, and appearances. The Son of God is unique and has no one as his rival; he surpasses angels, Moses, Aaron, and Melchizedek. The Son is the Messiah, the King, the heir, and the ruler of the universe. He occupies the seat of honor at the right hand of God the Father. David composed the words, "Sit at my right hand until I make your enemies a footstool for your feet" (Ps. 110:1).

At Jesus' trial before the Sanhedrin, the high priest asked him whether he was the Christ, the Son of the Blessed One. Jesus replied, "I am," ... "And

---

7. Hermann L. Strack and Paul Billerbeck, *Kommentar zum Neuen Testament aus Talmud und Midrasch* (München: C. H. Beck, 1961), 4, 1, 452–65.

8. Enoch 45, 3; 51, 3; 55, 4; 61, 8; 62, 3–5; 69, 27–29.

you will see the Son of Man sitting at the right hand of the Mighty One and coming on the clouds of heaven" (Mark 14:62).[9]

Hebrews 1:3 has an indirect reference to this psalm that stresses Christ's kingship, namely, "he sat down at the right hand of the Majesty in heaven." But this reference is preceded by the clause, "after he had provided purification for sins." By implication, the task of Christ being priest precedes that of his being king. In other words, his humiliation in his priestly task is antecedent to his exaltation as king. His humiliating suffering goes before his royal enthronement.

The author elaborates the motif of Christ's humiliation in the succeeding chapter (2:9) where he portrays Jesus as one who was made "a little lower than the angels, now crowned with glory and honor because he suffered death."

At the beginning of the seven Old Testament quotations in Hebrews 1, the writer takes the wording of Psalm 2:7, "You are my Son; today I have become your Father" to establish Jesus' sonship.[10] The last of the quotations is Psalm 110:1, which he uses to link it to the kingship of Jesus that was explicitly expressed in Psalm 2. The writer of Hebrews refrains from mentioning Jesus' use of Psalm 110:1 in his dispute with the Pharisees two days before his death on the cross. In that debate Jesus silenced his opponents, namely, the Jewish clergy, by pointing out that David called the Messiah Lord (see Matt. 22:41–45). This was the correct interpretation and application of the psalm, which the Pharisees were unable to refute; thus, they left Jesus without giving him an answer.

The author of this epistle assumes that his readers understand that Psalm 110 cannot apply to David. The early Christian church knew that David as the writer of this psalm pointed to the Messiah. "The messianic interpretation of the text, and more specifically its application to Christ as Lord, are presupposed in Hebrews."[11] With this psalm citation, the author firmly establishes the fact that the Son who was God's agent in creating the universe (1:2) rules supreme over the angel world. This means that the psalm

9. Refer to W. R. G. Loader, "Christ at the Right Hand—Ps. CX.1 in the New Testament," *New Testament Studies* 24, 2 (1978), 200. Thomas G. Smothers notes, "No Old Testament passage was used as often in the New Testament as Psalm 110." See his article "A Superior Model: Hebrews 1:1–4–13," *Review and Expositor* 62, 3 (1985), 337.

10. Also see 2 Samuel 7:14, "I will be his Father and he will be my Son."

11. Ellingworth, *Hebrews*, 130. He notes, "The psalm itself contains slight elements of royal messianism."

citation actually sounds a note of triumph as Peter put it in his reference to Christ's ascension, "[Jesus] is at God's right hand—with angels, authorities and powers in submission to him" (1 Peter 3:22).

PSALM 110:4

The LORD has sworn
  and will not change his mind:
"You are a priest forever,
  in the order of Melchizedek."

The wording of this psalm citation speaks volumes about Jesus' priestly office. The author of Hebrews uses Psalm 2:7 to illustrate his kingly office in 1:5. He quotes this text a second time, when he links it to Christ's priestly office five chapters later (5:5). Here he sets forth Jesus' high priesthood in the order of Melchizedek by subtly mentioning this name that dates from the time of Abraham. The Jewish clergy could relegate the priesthood of Melchizedek to ancient times and claim that it was superseded by the Aaronic priesthood. But when King David mentions Melchizedek some 500 years after Moses, the name could no longer be consigned to ancient history and be forgotten. King David composed it approximately a thousand years later than the era of Melchizedek.

Jewish rabbis had not explained this Scripture passage at all; it appears that because of the name Melchizedek they had relegated it to a distant past and perhaps blamed their neglect on forgetfulness. Nevertheless, the message of the passage is sufficiently clear in its designation of a king who is also a priest "in the order of Melchizedek."

HISTORICAL BACKGROUND

Although the prophet Zechariah (6:13) had mentioned the twofold office of king and priest in the Messiah, the Jews had failed to pay attention to the scriptural teaching about him. Even Jeremiah in 30:21 had prophesied that the future leader of Israel would be one who was allowed to come near to God—a distinct reference to a person of priestly status (Num. 16:5).

In effect, the royal function overshadowed the Messiah's priestly office. The gospel accounts feature him as king at the beginning and at the end of his earthly life (Matt. 2:2 and 27:11, 37, 42; see also the parallels). Jesus was known as king and as prophet but never as priest. He was born into the tribe of Judah, which was the royal tribe (Matt. 1:3 and Heb. 7:14).

The writer of Hebrews reminds his readers that verses 1 and 4 of Psalm 110 apply to Jesus and describe him as king and priest. He teaches the recipients of his letter to study these two verses instead of neglecting them. To be sure, they accepted him in his royalty but they approached his priesthood much the same as their forefathers had done: they neglected to accept the promised Messiah as priest. Among the writers of the New Testament, the author of Hebrews is the only one who calls the Christ a priest.[12] He highlights the fourth verse of Psalm 110. He does this repeatedly as he builds up to the climax where he compares the priesthood of Aaron to the priesthood of Melchizedek and points out the difference of time versus eternity.

This king of Salem and priest of God Most High was a mere man. Though highly esteemed by Abraham, Melchizedek had no pedigree of father or mother, no lineage, and no successor.[13] All the descendants of Levi had to prove identity by means of their family tree to enter the priesthood of Aaron. However, here is a person mentioned in antiquity but who lacks any form of identification. Nonetheless he was called by God Most High to serve him as priest. In addition, his priesthood had no temporal restrictions, for "he remains a priest forever" (Heb. 7:3).

TEXTUAL DIVISION

The author of Hebrews begins chapter 7 with the word *Melchizedek*, which he had mentioned without explanation in 5:11 and 6:20. This term is the last word in the quotation of Psalm 110:4, "You are priest forever in the order of Melchizedek," which means "king of righteousness." Then he divides chapter 7 into two distinct parts: verses 1–10, in which he explains the phrase "priest in the order of Melchizedek," and verses 11–25, in which he provides an exegesis of the phrase "you are a priest forever."

In the first part he points out the greatness of Melchizedek who excelled the patriarch Abraham. First, the king of Salem collected a tenth part from

12. Geerhardus Vos, *The Teaching of the Epistle to the Hebrews* (Grand Rapids: Eerdmans, 1956), 91.
13. Consult John Owen, *Exposition of Hebrews* (Evansville, IN: Sovereign Grace, 1960), 3:298.

the best of the booty Abraham had taken from the battlefield, and then he blessed him (Gen. 14:19, 20). He concludes that the one who blesses is greater than the one who receives the blessing. And next, the one who collects a tithe is superior to the one who pays it.

The second part (vv. 11–25) reveals four concise summaries that relate to Christ's priesthood.[14] In verses 12–14, the author gives the first summary and states that a change in the priesthood necessitates a change in the Mosaic Law. It is clear that Jesus belonged to the tribe of Judah from which the kings descended and not to that of Levi who functioned as the head of the priestly clan. In fact, Jesus is called priest in the order of Melchizedek not according to the Mosaic Law but in the power of an endless life.

The next conclusion (vv. 15–19) states that if Jesus is priest forever, he is in another order—one that disannuls the law. That is to say, God who enacted the law has revoked it now that Christ has assumed his priesthood in Melchizedek's order.

Thirdly, the author states conclusively in verses 20–22 that the introductory sentence speaks about God having uttered an oath in Psalm 110:4a, "The Lord has sworn and will not change his mind." The readers should know that the word *oath* spoken by God calls to mind the image of unchangeableness. A law, when it is enacted, can be repealed at any time, but an oath, once it is sworn, remains in effect forever. By the way, the writer of Hebrews in 3:11, 13 and 4:3 had quoted Psalm 95:11 where God said, "So I declared on oath in my anger, 'They shall never enter my rest.'" And in a positive sense he wrote about Abraham's test of faith. He said that God swore by himself, blessed the patriarch with the promise of giving him many descendants, and then confirmed it with an oath (6:13–17). An oath that is sworn denotes permanence.

The fourth conclusive summary (vv. 23–25) states that Christ's priesthood is forever, inviolable, and unchangeable. Here is the assurance that Christ in the capacity of high priest not only saves his people but also intercedes for them.

Theological Motifs

The book of Genesis is known for its genealogies that list the names of persons and their ages and descendants. God's people are listed in the

14. Refer to Kistemaker, *Psalm Citations*, 118–19.

covenant line with their ages at the time of death,[15] but those outside of that line are devoid of any reference to their age, for instance, the descendants of Cain, Ishmael, and Esau.[16]

What does that say about Melchizedek? This person is unique because he is identified with Christ. "Like the Son of God he remains priest forever" (Heb. 7:3). This means that Melchizedek's priesthood, not the man, is eternal. His priesthood was a priesthood of dedication to God Most High, while the Aaronic priesthood was one of consecration. Melchizedek dedicated his priesthood to serve God and thus he was like the Son of God. By contrast, Aaron's priesthood had to do with bloody sacrifices, atonement, forgiving sin, intercession, and comfort. These sacrifices had to be repeated again and again. Also, the period of service for an individual priest lasted only a few decades at most. The consecration of priests was an ongoing ritual in Israel because illness and death were contributing factors to ending the service of a priest.

The Jewish people of the first century were only acquainted with and accustomed to the Levitical priesthood that had been enacted by law (Num. 18:23).[17] That law had been irrevocably linked to Israel's priestly hierarchy and no Jew would dare to challenge the Law of Moses. Therefore, the author's statement that the priesthood in the order of Melchizedek is hard to explain (5:11) should not be surprising at all.

As the author introduces the name Melchizedek, Jewish people would think first of the historical account of Genesis 14:18 and then of Psalm 110:4.[18] They would have difficulty incorporating that priesthood into the Levitical framework. Only the sons of Aaron might serve as priests in the sacrificial system, and they formed a close-knit community which could never be violated.[19] Members of the community had been given the distinct privilege of being intermediaries between sinful human beings and a holy God. "Thus a priest is one who brings men near to God, who leads them into the presence of God."[20]

While the Genesis account provides the historical setting of the priest-king, Melchizedek, who blessed the patriarch Abraham, the wording of

15. Gen. 5; 11; 23:1; 35:28; 47:28; 50:26

16. Gen. 4:17–22; 25:13–16; 36:1–43.

17. There are many other references: Ex. 28–29; Lev. 8–10; Num. 16–18; Ezra 2:61–63; Neh. 7:63–65.

18. Ellingworth, *Hebrews*, 300.

19. Kistemaker, *Psalm Citations*, 121.

20. Vos, *Teaching*, 94.

Psalm 110:4b caused uncertainty in the minds of Jewish Christians: "You are a priest forever in the order of Melchizedek." We assume that these people were acquainted with the incident in which Jesus confronted the Pharisees by pointing out to them that David in Psalm 110:1 spoke about the royal Messiah, the Christ. The first readers of the Epistle to the Hebrews would have no difficulty accepting Jesus as king, but they could not understand that he also filled a priestly role.

The Jewish rabbis had never explained the meaning of Psalm 110:4. To them it was a mystery that advisably would be better ignored. The writer of Hebrews, however, takes up the challenge of applying the priesthood of Melchizedek to Jesus and portraying him as an eternal priest. He refers to Melchizedek twice (5:10 and 6:20) before he comes to a protracted explanation (7:1–3). He wants to make sure that the readers comprehend that Psalm 110 is first of all a messianic prophecy; secondly, verse 4 once more introduces the name Melchizedek now for the purpose of showing that this figure from the ancient past is a prototype of Christ's priesthood. He notes that in the historical description of this man, the kingly office precedes the priestly office. "Then Melchizedek king of Salem brought out bread and wine. He was priest of God Most High" (Gen. 14:18). Composing Psalm 110, David follows this trend by mentioning first his kingship in verse 1 and then his priesthood in verse 4.

This royal priest is the forerunner of Jesus the Messiah. He too claims royalty and a priesthood that is not based on a Levitical genealogy but is like that of the ancient figure Melchizedek. Jesus Christ is the greater of the two, however, for the author of Hebrews uses the word *like* twice in chapter 7 when he compares the two persons Melchizedek and Christ. "Without father or mother, without genealogy, without beginning of days or end of life, like the Son of God he remains a priest forever" (v. 3). "And what we have said is even more clear if another priest like Melchizedek appears" (v. 15). Note that in these two verses the Son of God is superior to Melchizedek just as the Son is superior to angels, to Moses, and to Aaron.

MESSIANIC FULFILLMENT

The writer compares the superiority of Christ's priesthood to that of Aaron's and does this twice. First, he uses the example of taking tithes in the Levitical system. The Levites taxed their own countrymen; this means that the one who received the tithe was greater than the one who paid it. Abraham paid Melchizedek a tenth of the spoils the patriarch had taken from the battlefield, which proves that this royal priest was the greater of the two (7:5, 6). Second, the Levites did their work on the basis of the Mosaic Law, but they were figuratively speaking represented by Abraham who paid the tithe to Melchizedek. They collected the tithe but were subject to death, but the one who received Abraham's tithe is described as alive without temporal limitations (7:8). The Levites would display genealogies to prove their priestly status, but Melchizedek had none of that. The descendants of Aaron were subject to death and would pass away. But Melchizedek's priesthood is declared to be without beginning and without end. Levites derived their priestly office that was handed down by physical descent (Ex. 29:9; Num. 25:13), but Christ received his priesthood, which had its prototype in Melchizedek—not on the basis of law by a divine oath. He as the Son of God fills an eternal priesthood in the order of Melchizedek.[21]

Christ fulfilled the priesthood of Aaron and of Melchizedek yet he has his prototype in the latter. Sacrifices offered by Levitical priests were unable to cleanse the soul, because the shedding of animal blood was an external rite that made the sinner outwardly clean. On the other hand, Christ by shedding his blood on Calvary's cross purifies believers inwardly and cleanses their soul. The shedding of Christ's blood signifies the end of the old covenant and introduces the new covenant. In the words of the writer of Hebrews, "By calling this covenant 'new', [Christ] has made the first one obsolete; and what is obsolete and aging will soon disappear" (8:13). In short, the order of Melchizedek is superior to that of the Levitical order.

In the Epistle to the Hebrews, Christ is called both priest and high priest. The word *priest* occurs in the quotation from Psalm 110:4, "You are a priest forever in the order of Melchizedek." But the writer generally designates him as high priest and even calls him the "great high priest" (4:14) as well as "a merciful and faithful high priest" (2:17) to mention no more. Is it possible that the author uses the terms *priest* and *high priest* at random? The answer is that the evidence disproves this exegesis. Geerhardus Vos writes, "When Psalm 110 is quoted, it is necessary to speak of Christ as *priest*, with reference to Melchizedek. Only in one passage, 5:10, is the quotation given more freely: here He is called *high priest*, but this may be explained in the

---

21. Compare Ronald E. Clements, "The Use of the Old Testament in Hebrews," *Southwestern Journal of Theology* 28, 1 (1985), 41.

context; the reference is a prelude to the subsequent argument. In that argument Christ is contrasted both with Melchizedek and Aaron. Where a comparison with Aaron is expressed or implied, Christ is called *High Priest* (2:17; 4:14; 5:1; 7:26, 28; 8:13; 9:11, 12). When the comparison is between Christ and the Levitical order, He is called *priest*." The author of Hebrews quite consciously made a distinction between the word *priest* and the term *high priest* and shows that the two terms are not used arbitrarily.[22]

Let us look once more at the prophecy in Zechariah 6:12–13, where Joshua (Jesus), the son of Jehozadak, at God's command had "to build the temple of the LORD. It is he who will build the temple of the LORD, and he will be clothed with majesty and will sit and rule on his throne. And he will be a priest on his throne. And there will be harmony between the two." This is a foreshadowing of Jesus the high priest who sits on the throne to rule in glory. This same Joshua was put to shame by Satan accusing him in the presence of God, because the high priest Joshua was dressed in filthy garments. He is told to take off his dirty clothes, which are a symbol of sin. Then God put clean garments on him and a clean turban on his head (Zech. 3:1–5). These things point to the prophecy in Zechariah 6:12–13. Joshua could never fulfill that prophecy of building a temple, bearing glory, sitting and ruling on the throne, and fulfilling the position of a priest. Not Joshua the high priest but only Jesus the king and priest could fulfill this prophecy. Joshua merely foreshadowed his namesake, Jesus the Son of God.

Did Jesus fulfill the Aaronic priesthood? An affirmative answer can be given to this query. Jesus shed blood twice: in Garden of Gethsemane and on the cross. The Aaronic high priest sprinkled blood on the ark twice: once for himself and family, and the second time for the people. Jesus brought the Aaronic priesthood to an end by shedding not animal blood but his own. Having done so, Jesus continued in the priesthood of Melchizedek for ever.

Conclusion

Only the author of the epistle to the Hebrews discusses the priesthood of Christ. He does this exclusively by quoting and applying Psalm

22. Vos, *Teaching*, 94.

110:4 to Jesus. Although Paul in Romans 8:34 alludes to Jesus as interces-
sor, he does not mention the word *priesthood*. With respect to Hebrews,
the writer fully explains that Jesus Christ fulfilled the priesthood in the
order of Melchizedek. "Psalm 110 *is* the primary priestly contribution
to the Book of Hebrews."[23]

---

23. David R. Anderson, *The King-Priest of Psalm 110 in Hebrews* (New York: Peter Lang,
2001), 239 (his italics). Theo de Kruijf comes to the same conclusion in "The Priest-King
Melchizedek: The Reception of Gen 14, 18–20 in Hebrews mediated by Psalm 110." *Bijdragen
tijdschrift voor filosofie en theologie* 54 (1993), 400. He writes, "One can even say that the main
body of the epistle is contained in the quotation of Ps 110,4 and enclosed by Ps 110,1 (Heb
1, 13–12, 2)."

PART 3

Theology

"The law and the gospel," says a citizen of London, in his shop, *"what is that?"*—*"They are two keys,"* answered Tyndale. *"The law is the key which shuts up all men under condemnation, and the gospel is the key which opens the door and lets them out. Or, if you like it, they are two salves. The law, sharp and biting, driveth out the disease and killeth it; while the gospel, soothing and soft, softens the wound and brings life."* Everyone understood and read, or rather devoured the inspired pages; and the hearts of the elect (to use Tyndale's words), warmed by the love of Jesus Christ, began to melt like wax.[1]

—J. H. MERLE D'AUBIGNE

1. J. H. Merle d'Aubigne, *The Reformation in England* (Edinburgh: Banner of Truth, 1977), 1:247–48.

8

Systematic Theology and a Burning Heart

R O B E R T   L .   R E Y M O N D

IT WAS WITH HEARTFELT alacrity that I agreed to write this essay for this honorary volume celebrating the life and ministry of my dear friend, O. Palmer Robertson. He was my colleague at both Covenant Theological Seminary and Knox Theological Seminary, and we stood together "in the trenches" at several defining moments in our shared histories, not the least of which was the Shepherd affair that troubled Westminster Theological Seminary in the 1970s over the issue of whether one is justified before God by faith alone in Christ, the position that we espoused, or by one's obedient faithfulness to Christ, the position that Dr. Norman Shepherd espoused.

I want to begin my essay with a small touch of personal history. The reader will quickly see my reason for doing this. For a good many years now when signing my books for those who request it of me I have placed under my signature the biblical reference Psalm 71:17–18, which reads:

> O God, from my youth you have taught me,
> and I still proclaim your wondrous deeds.

So even to old age and gray hairs,
O God, do not forsake me,
until I proclaim your might to another generation,
your power to all those to come.

I have thought for some time that the psalmist's words could describe my experience. They certainly express the desire of my heart. You see, for ninety-three semesters now, not counting winter and summer terms, and in five American and about a dozen international seminaries I have taught the Reformed faith. But I have not taught the Reformed faith simply because it is a hobby of mine. No, I have not been simply riding a hobby these last forty-two years. Rather, the wondrous, dread, and awesome Reformed faith, while I admit it is the love of my spiritual and professorial life, is also, I am convinced, the teaching of the Lord God himself and therefore its propagation is for me both a *passion* and a *mission*. I view the five great *sola*'s of the Magisterial Reformation—*Grace* alone, *Christ* alone, *Faith* alone, *Scripture* alone, with our salvation redounding to the *Glory* of God alone—as matters of eternal life and eternal death for the peoples of this world. Agreeing with the Magisterial Reformers I came to understand early on in my seminary days and professorial career, by the grace of God, of course, the following truths:

1) The *only* man with whom the infinitely holy God can have *direct* fellowship is Jesus Christ, the only mediator "between God and man" (1 Tim. 2:5), and that it is only as sinful people such as you and I place their trust in Christ's saving cross-work and are thereby regarded by God as no longer "in Adam" but "in Christ" that the triune God can have any fellowship with them (this is the *solus Christus* or "Christ alone" principle of salvation).

2) The only way to protect the *solus Christus* and the *sola gratia* ("grace alone") of salvation is to insist upon *sola fide* ("faith alone") as the instrumental means of justification, and the only way to protect *sola fide* as the instrumental means of justification is to insist upon the *solus Christus* and the *sola gratia* of salvation.

3) The only way to protect both the *solus Christus* and the *sola gratia* of salvation and the *sola fide* of justification is to insist upon *sola Scriptura* ("Scripture alone") as the church's sole authority in such matters.

154

4) Justification by faith is not to be set off over against justification by works as such but over against justification by *our* works, for justification is indeed grounded in Christ's alien preceptive and penal obedience to the Law of God in our stead, whose obedience we receive through faith alone.

5) Saving faith is to be directed solely to the doing and dying of Christ alone and never in any sense to the good works or inner experience of the believer.

6) The Christian's righteousness before God today is *in heaven* at the right hand of God in Jesus Christ and *not on earth* within the believer.

7) The ground of our justification is the vicarious work of Christ *for* us, not the gracious work of the Spirit *in* us.

8) The faith-righteousness of justification is

- not personal but vicarious,
- not infused but imputed,
- not experiential but forensic,
- not psychological but legal,
- not our own but Christ's alien righteousness, and
- not earned but graciously given through faith in Christ, which faith in Christ is itself a gift of grace.

9) The salvation of the elect is to be credited to God's grace alone (*sola gratia*) to whom alone belongs all the praise for their salvation (*soli Deo gloria*).

But because I was seriously challenged early on in my career to do so, I also came to understand that these great Reformation truths and the Reformation *sola*'s require that the entire Christian system of which they are a central part must be justified as an intellectual discipline before a critical world. Thus I was forced to face the more ultimate issue of the need to justify the Christian theological enterprise as such, including my involvement in it. But how was I to do this? I realized that an appeal to extra-biblical data—data that I am very willing to use in *ad hominem* arguments in accordance with Proverbs 26:5, "Answer a fool [the unbeliever] according to his folly, lest he be wise in his own eyes," to show the non-Christian that he cannot consistently live with his world-and-life-view—could never in themselves make the justification of Christian theology as such logically or apodictically demonstrative. I knew that such an appeal would at best advance only possibilities, including the possibility that my conclusions were themselves in error, and would end up suffering the fate of total and unrelenting skepticism. So I sought the justification of Christian theology as an intellectual discipline, including my engagement in it, where there could be no question regarding its validity or certitude—an Archimedean point of reference, so to speak, outside the universe. And where was that? In the data of God's inspired, inerrant Word to us from another world and by good and necessary inferences drawn therefrom.

It is this issue of justifying our theology as such that I want to develop in this essay, for in such a setting as this "honor volume" it is appropriate to explain why we believe we may legitimately do what we do in our Reformed seminaries. As we begin let us face some hard questions. Many new seminary students have often wondered after a few weeks of study:

> What am I doing at seminary? Why should I study theology? Am I wasting my time and money studying *Christian* theology? Does Christian theology serve any useful purpose in today's world? Was moving my family here a rash act? And why should I make the arduous sacrifice that I am asking of myself and of my family in order to attend seminary?

Such questions, I would argue, are not a waste of time to consider since we must admit that Christian theology has fallen upon hard times in our generation. Let me make clear what I mean by recounting two events, one borrowed and one personally experienced.

First, the borrowed event. In one of Dr. Martyn Lloyd-Jones's books he tells of a large religious conference he attended which was being held in the city of Glasgow in Scotland. As is often done, for some extraordinary reason when such conferences are held, the Lord Provost of the City had been invited to attend the inaugural meeting and to welcome and address the conference for a few minutes. As reported by the "Doctor," here is the essence of what he said:

156

All of you men assembled here today are very learned theologians, and confessedly I am not. I am a plain man. I am a man of affairs and I do not understand your theology and all these church things. In fact, I am not interested in your theology, and personally I believe you are wasting a lot of time when you argue among yourselves about your theology. What *I* want to know—in fact, what a lot of people like me want to know—is simply this: How can I love my neighbor? That is what we want to know from you. We are not interested in your great theology. We just want to know—indeed, the common man simply wants to know—How can I love my neighbor?

If one has had a course in Christian personal and social ethics in a good Reformed seminary, he will immediately recognize that man's total doctrinal illiteracy, for he knows that the Bible and theology are directly related to his interest in love for one's neighbor. In fact, he knows that unless a transcendent and absolute Authority requires us to love our neighbors and to do so in such a way that we will do it even to our own hurt, no other reason can possibly be given to obligate any of us to do anything at all for anyone else other than for ourselves. But this is not the reason behind my citing this illustration at this moment. It is to illustrate my present point. For this man, the church with its Bible and its theology was completely irrelevant unless it could address what *he* wanted to know, that is, what for him was the wholly secular matter of "how to live at peace with one's neighbor."

Now the second and directly personal event: Several years ago my wife and I decided we would drive down to Key West for a day or two of relaxation. The Orthodox Presbyterian Church has a church there, and its preacher, Bill Welzien, a chalk-talk artist, goes to Mallory Pier on the west side of the island on Monday, Wednesday, and Friday evenings (he has trained a church member to go on Tuesday, Thursday, and Saturday, but quite often on these evenings he also attends) when the hundreds of tourists gather to watch the sun set in the West, attracts a crowd with his artistry, and then preaches the gospel. Knowing this, we made it a point to be there on Friday evening and we stood in the crowd and prayed for him as he limned his drawing and proclaimed the gospel to the crowd. In the middle of his presentation, a man who was pushing through the crowd in his attempt to get to an attraction farther down the pier, yelled to this preacher with a great deal of huff: "What do you think you are doing here? Why don't you go out and get yourself a real job?" I hope you see my point:

This man's remarks dripped with stinging sarcasm. To this man, and to many people like him, Pastor Welzien was an irrelevancy. He was suggesting that Bill would have spent his time much more profitably studying to become a doctor, an engineer, a school or business administrator, a chef, an environmental designer, an educator—yes, even a lawyer—than studying to enter the Christian ministry.

Then there is Søren Kierkegaard's lampooning definition of a theologian as "a professor of the fact that *Another* [that is, Someone else] has suffered" but not he,[1] while Jaroslav Pelikan, professor of church history at Yale Divinity School, reminds us that the nearest equivalents to the term "theologian" in the New Testament are "scribes and Pharisees."[2] Such reminders do not make the work of the theologian very appealing either to the church or to the world at large. Indeed, as the Western world has become increasingly a "secular city" more and more men and women within as well as outside the church argue that it is impossible even to say anything meaningful about God. Accordingly, Gordon H. Clark began his book *In Defense of Theology* with the following assessment:

> Theology, once acclaimed "the Queen of the Sciences," today hardly rises to the rank of a scullery maid; it is often held in contempt, regarded with suspicion, or just ignored.[3]

If Clark's judgment is correct, and it would seem in this post-Christian age that it is, seminary students might well conclude that they should be done with Christian theology as an intellectual discipline altogether and devote their time to some mental pursuit holding out promise of greater esteem among men. But I hope to show in this essay that such a conclusion would be singularly wrongheaded. The issue can be pointedly framed: How are Christian theology, construed as an intellectual discipline that deserves the church's and the world's highest interest and respect, and one's lifelong occupation as a preacher and/or teacher of that theology to be justified? Still more pointedly: Why should a Christian engage himself for a lifetime in scholarly reflection on the content and on the proclamation of the Christian

1. Søren Kierkegaard, *Journals*, trans. and ed. Alexander Dru (Oxford: University Press, 1938), no. 1362.

2. Jaroslav J. Pelikan, "The Function of Theology," in *Theology in the Life of the Church*, ed. Robert M. Bertram (Philadelphia: Fortress, 1963), 3.

3. Gordon H. Clark, *In Defense of Theology* (Milford, MI: Mott, 1984), 3.

message? And why should he engage himself in the particular way that the church in its best moments, in my opinion, has worked out its theology in the past, namely, by means of the historical/grammatical canons of interpreting the Scriptures of the Old and New Testament? I would offer the following five pillars upon which, in my opinion, the justification of Christian theology as an intellectual discipline securely rests, pillars that lead me to conclude that *every* Christian should continue in his engagement in the theological enterprise.

CHRIST'S OWN THEOLOGICAL METHOD

The first pillar upon which the justification of Christian theology as an intellectual discipline rests is Christ's own theological method. Because of the significance of his testimony, I will treat this pillar more extensively than the others.

All four Evangelists depict Jesus Christ who after rising bodily from death on the third day after his crucifixion showed himself alive by "many convincing proofs" (Acts 1:3 NIV), and upon whose earthly ministry God the Father placed his *imprimatur* by raising him from the dead (Gal. 1:1; Rom. 8:11), thereby both declaring him powerfully to be the divine Son of God (Rom. 1:4) and vouchsafing to us his Son's every word as true—all four Evangelists, I say, depict the divine Christ as being deeply engaged throughout his earthly ministry in heart and mind with the Old Testament Scriptures.[4]

Jesus' Attitude toward the Historicity of the Old Testament

It is popular to criticize the historicity of the Old Testament today and to reconstruct it along critical lines. Martin Noth, for example, contended that nothing can be known with certainty of Israel's past prior to her entrance by various stages into Canaan and that the twelve tribes were not unified prior to the making of the covenant at Shechem in Joshua 24.[5] John Bright, professor of Old Testament at Union Theological Seminary, Virginia, though more moderate in his reconstruction of Old Testament

---

4. Critical scholars acknowledge that even their so-called original sources of the Gospels, *Ur-Markus*, Q, M, L, and John represent Jesus as teaching the reliability, authority, and inspiration of the Old Testament with unabridged and utter seriousness.

5. Martin Noth, *The History of Israel* (New York: Harper & Row, 1960).

history than Noth, nonetheless questioned the historicity of the pre-patriarchal period of biblical history.[6] But this was not Jesus' attitude toward the historicity of the Old Testament. In fact, J. W. Wenham, vice-principal of Tyndale Hall, Bristol, observed, ". . . the narratives that proved least acceptable to what was known a generation or two ago as 'the modern mind' are the very ones that [Jesus] seemed most fond of choosing for His illustrations."[7] For example, if we consider only Matthew's gospel Jesus refers therein to the following historical events and in every instance it is plain that he viewed the history of the Old Testament as unimpeachable:

- The creation of Adam and Eve by a direct act of God (19:4–5)
- The murder of Abel (23:23)
- The times of Noah and the Genesis flood (24:37)
- The destruction of Sodom and Gomorrah (10:15)
- Moses as the lawgiver (8:4; 19:8)
- David's eating the bread of the presence (12:3–4) and his writing of psalms (22:43)
- The queen of Sheba's visit to Solomon (12:3–4)
- The sufferings of the prophets (5:12; 13:57; 21:34–36; 23:29–37)
- The stoning of Zechariah (23:35)
- The great fish's swallowing of Jonah (12:40)
- Jonah's preaching and Ninevah's repentance (12:39–41)
- Allusions to other Old Testament characters such as Abraham, Isaac, Jacob, Solomon, Isaiah, and Daniel (8:11; 13:14; 15:7–8; 24:15)

Jesus' Attitude toward the Inspiration of the Old Testament

There are several indications in Matthew's gospel that Jesus believed and taught that the Old Testament Scriptures were the very words of God. In Matthew 19:5 Jesus taught that words spoken in Genesis by either Adam or Moses (probably the latter) proceeded more ultimately from God ("he created . . . and said. . . ."). In his argument with the Sadducees regarding the resurrection of the body (Matt. 22:31–32) Jesus asked them, ". . . have you not read what was said *to you* [*humin*] by God: 'I am the God of Abra-

---

6. John Bright, *A History of Israel* (Philadelphia: Westminster, 1959).

7. J. W. Wenham, *Our Lord's View of the Old Testament* (London: Tyndale, 1953), 9.

ham, and the God of Isaac, and the God of Jacob'?" He then cited words that God addressed *to Moses* (Ex. 3:6). Thus Jesus regarded these words of Scripture as the Word of God addressed both to Moses and to his contemporaries. Moreover, Jesus hung his case for the resurrection of the body on the present tense of the verb "to be": "I *am* [*eimi*] the God of Abraham," not "I was the God of Abraham," implying thereby, first, that Abraham was still alive and would be resurrected someday from death and, second, that the words of Scripture were so carefully superintended by God that one can hang an argument on the tense of a verb. In Matthew 22:43–45 Jesus based his argument that he is the Son of God on David's calling his son according to the flesh his Lord "in the Spirit." That is to say, the words of Psalm 110, although penned by David, originated from the Spirit of God, thereby highlighting the remarkable concurrence of God and man in the production of Scripture (see 2 Peter 1:20–21). And again Jesus' argument here hung on one word—David's employment of the word "Lord" (*'adhon*) to describe his son.

Jesus' Attitude toward the Authority of the Old Testament

No one can seriously question that the Old Testament was for Jesus authoritative in all that it affirmed. In his Sermon on the Mount Jesus taught his disciples, "Do not think that I have come to abolish the Law or the Prophets; I have not come to abolish them but to fulfill them. For truly, I say to you, until heaven and earth pass away, not an iota, not a dot, will pass from the Law until all is accomplished" (Matt. 5:17–18). In Luke 16:17 he also declared that the tiniest portion of the written letters of Scripture would never fail (*pesein*). Again and again he refers to "the Law and the Prophets" (Matt. 5:17; 7:12; 11:13; 22:40), often citing them to settle an issue (Matt. 12:5; 15:3–6; 21:31, 42; 22:42–43). He implies by this phrase a fixed canon of authoritative material, intending by it the entire Old Testament. In Matthew 4:4–10 he repulsed the Tempter by citing Deuteronomy 8:3, 6:16, and 6:13 in that order, each time demonstrating his belief in the finality of the Old Testament's authority by prefacing his citation by the Greek perfect (or its Aramaic "force equivalent"), "It is written [and continues to stand so]" (see also Matt. 11:10; 21:13; 26:24, 31). Setting "the Word of God" off over against Jewish tradition in Mark 7:13 Jesus implied that God was the authority behind the entire Old Testament.

161

Repeatedly he asked his interrogators, "Have you not read?" (Matt. 12:3; 19:4; 21:16; 22:31). He ordered the cleansed leper to obey the Mosaic legislation pertaining to cases of cleansing (Matt. 8:4). He charged the Sadducees with error concerning the resurrection of the body because they did not know the Scriptures (Matt. 22:29). He approved the scribes' and Pharisees' obedience to the law of the tithe though he denounced them for neglecting the weightier matters of the Law—justice, mercy, and faith (Matt. 23:23). In Matthew 26:53–56 Jesus revealed his great esteem for the prophetic Scripture when he declined the aid of more than twelve legions of angels to deliver him from the cross, saying, "Do you think that I cannot appeal to my Father, and he will at once send me more than twelve legions of angels? But how then should the Scriptures be fulfilled, that it must be so?" And at his death his thoughts were centered on Scripture, for he cited Psalm 22:1 just moments before he died (Matt. 27:46). This Matthean material—and the other three Gospels make the same case—proves beyond all controversy that for Jesus the Old Testament was unimpeachably authoritative.

Jesus' Attitude toward the Predictive Character of Old Testament Prophecy

Jesus constantly emphasized the predictive character of Old Testament prophecy. In Matthew 11:10 he taught that John the Baptizer's ministry fulfilled Malachi 3:1. He warned that Daniel's prophecy concerning the abomination of desolation would soon be fulfilled (Matt. 24:15). His own death he viewed as the inaugurating event fulfilling Jeremiah's prophecy of the "new covenant" (Matt. 26:28). But most significantly Jesus drew from the Old Testament Scriptures fascinating theological deductions about himself. On forty-nine different occasions by my count, discounting Gospel parallels, Jesus in the Gospels cited or referred to the Old Testament and many of these citations he applied to himself as evidenced by the following examples:

According to Luke 4:16–21,

> [Jesus] came to Nazareth, where he had been brought up. And as was his custom, he went to the synagogue on the Sabbath day, and he stood up to read. And the scroll of the prophet Isaiah was given to him. He unrolled the scroll and found the place where it was written,

> "The Spirit of the Lord is upon me,
>> because he has anointed me
>> to proclaim good news to the poor.
> He has sent me to proclaim liberty to the captives
>> and recovering of sight to the blind,
>> to set at liberty those who are oppressed,
> to proclaim the year of the Lord's favor."

And he rolled up the scroll and gave it back to the attendant and sat down. And the eyes of all in the synagogue were fixed on him. And he began to say to them, "Today this Scripture has been fulfilled in your hearing."

Here Jesus claimed to be the Old Testament Messiah.

According to John 5:46–47 Jesus expressly affirmed to the Jewish religious leadership of his day on another occasion, "If you believed Moses, you would believe me; for he wrote of me. But if you do not believe his writings, how will you believe my words?" Here Jesus claimed to be the prophet like Moses. And in John 10:35 Jesus declared, after citing Psalm 82:6 in defense of his claim to divine sonship, "Scripture cannot be broken [*ou dunetai luthēnai*]," that is, cannot be nullified—a striking declaration regarding the extent to which Jesus thought Scripture spoke truth concerning him.

According to Luke 18:31–33 on still another occasion Jesus informed his disciples, "See, we are going up to Jerusalem, and everything that is written about the Son of Man by the prophets will be accomplished. . . ." He also taught in Matthew 26:24, 31, 53–56: "The Son of Man goes as it is written of him. . . . You will all fall away because of me this night. For it is written, 'I will strike the shepherd, and the sheep of the flock will be scattered.' . . . Do you think that I cannot appeal to my Father, and he will at once send me more than twelve legions of angels? But how then should the Scriptures be fulfilled, that it must be so?"

According to Luke 22:37 on yet another occasion Jesus, citing Isaiah 53:12, "And he was numbered with the transgressors," declared, "This Scripture must be fulfilled in me. . . . For what is written about me has its fulfillment." Here Jesus claimed to be the suffering Servant of the so-called Fourth Servant Song of Isaiah.

Then, according to Luke 24:27, on the road to Emmaus the evening of his bodily resurrection from the dead, Jesus "beginning with Moses and all the Prophets . . . explained to [two of his disciples] what was said in all the Scriptures concerning himself" (NIV; see also John 13:18; 19:24, 28, 36–37; 20:9). Such an extensive engagement of his mind in Scripture exposition involved our Lord in theological activity in the highest conceivable sense. I would say in passing that Christians have often expressed the wish that they could have heard Jesus' Emmaus road discourse. They can be assured, however, that both the apostles' sermons recorded in Acts and their apostolic letters bear the stamp of the major features of Christ's exposition in the way in which they interpret the Old Testament christologically. So we know essentially what Jesus said, and our hearts should burn within us as the hearts of those two disciples did as his Spirit opens the Scriptures about him to us. Then, according to Luke 24:44, that same evening Jesus declared to the disciples who had gathered in the upper room along with others with them, "This is what I told you while I was still with you: Everything must be fulfilled that is written about me in the Law of Moses, the Prophets and the Psalms" (NIV). By these claims Jesus taught that the entire Old Testament spoke about him as the Seed of the Woman, the unique Seed of Abraham, Moses' Prophet, David's Priest after the order of Melchizedek, Isaiah's virgin-born Immanuel, his Child of the exalted titles "Wonderful Counselor," "Mighty God," "Everlasting Father," and "Prince of Peace," and his Suffering Servant, Jeremiah's Branch, Daniel's Son of Man, Malachi's Messenger of the Covenant, and in sum God's Messiah, all which meant that for him, and therefore for us, the Old Testament, if read aright, *must* be read in light of his ministry as the prophetic fulfillment of the Old Testament age of prophetic promise.[8]

---

8. I must say in passing that world Jewry's rejection today of Jesus as the Christ is precisely the reason that it does not understand its own Scriptures correctly. Paul declared in 2 Corinthians 3:7–16 that an unlifted "veil" (*kalumma*) covers the hearts of unbelieving Jews when they read Moses, that is, the old covenant, a veil that can only be removed by Christ. The blindness that Israel experienced when beholding the radiant face of Moses, Paul writes, continues "to this day" as a veil over their hearts when they read the old covenant, so the Jewish people do not today and never will read aright the Old Testament as long as they read it apart from its fulfillment in Jesus Christ and his saving work. They do not understand that the glory of God that they seek in Torah has been surpassed by the greater glory found in Christ who is the image of God, and that therefore the Old Testament must be read christologically, that is, from the present perspective of its fulfillment in Christ. The real truth of the matter is that no one—neither Jew nor Gentile—who has heard of the Messiah and his atoning work and then rejects him understands the Old Testament.

Jesus' Pre-Authentication of the New Testament Writers as Authoritative Teachers of Doctrine

Finally, Christ pre-authenticated his apostles as authoritative teachers of doctrine when he declared to them, "But the Helper, the Holy Spirit, whom the Father will send in my name, he will teach you all things and bring to your remembrance all that I have said to you." (John 14:26), and then he taught them, "I still have many things to say to you, but you cannot bear them now. When the Spirit of truth comes, he will guide you into all the truth, for he will not speak on his own authority, but whatever he hears he will speak, and he will declare to you the things that are to come [here Christ pre-authenticates the prophecies of the New Testament]. He will glorify me, for he will take what is mine and declare it to you" (John 16:12–14).

It is Christ himself then who established for his church the pattern and end of all proper theologizing. The *pattern*? What should it be? To make sound exposition of Scripture the basis of our theologizing. And the *end* of all our theological labors? What should it be? To arrive by our exegetical labors finally at him![9]

9. Since the only Christ about whom one knows anything with confidence is the Christ about whom the Old and New Testament Scriptures speak, one must never separate the testimony of the Old and New Testament Scriptures about him from the testimony of the divine Christ concerning them or the testimony of the divine Christ concerning them from the testimony of the Old and New Testament Scriptures about him. They belong together—the Bible as the word of the self-authenticating Christ and the Christ of the self-authenticating Bible—and they must be kept together.

In addition to Christ's divine testimony concerning Holy Scripture there are other authenticating lines of evidence by which the Bible "doth *abundantly evidence itself* to be the word of God"—what Benjamin B. Warfield calls the Bible's own intrinsic divine *indicia*—such as "the heavenliness of the matter, the efficacy of the doctrine, the majesty of the style, the consent of all the parts, the scope of the whole (which is to give all glory to God), the full discovery [disclosure] it makes of the only way of man's salvation, the many other incomparable excellences, and the entire perfection thereof" (Westminster Confession of Faith, 1.5, emphasis supplied). That is to say, the Bible is self-evidencingly, self-validatingly, self-authenticatingly, self-attestingly the Word of God, and in turn it witnesses to the self-authenticating Christ (see John 8:14). For one to disagree with this statement he would need to possess some authoritative source of information about God other than the Bible. Take, for example, the Bible's doctrine of the atonement. If one does not have another authoritative source of information about it, how could one know that the Bible's teaching is wrong? But someone may ask, "How does one know that the Bible's doctrine is right?" The first answer the Confession gives is as follows: "The authority of the Holy Scripture, for which it ought to be believed, and obeyed, dependeth not upon the testimony of any man or Church, but wholly upon God (who is truth itself), the author thereof; and, therefore, is to be received, because it is the word of God" (I/iv). Its second answer, in the following article, is as follows: "Our full persuasion and assurance of the infallible truth and divine

CHRIST'S MANDATE TO HIS CHURCH TO TEACH THE NATIONS

The second pillar upon which the justification of Christian theology as an intellectual discipline rests is the risen Christ's mandate to his church to teach the nations. After determining for his church the pattern and end of all proper theologizing, the glorified Christ commissioned his church to disciple the nations, baptizing and teaching his followers to obey everything that he had commanded them (Matt. 28:18–20). And his promise to be with his disciples "always, to the end of the age" implies that he expected this mandate to continue in force beyond the lives of his contemporaries. Thus Christ's Great Commission placed upon his church three continuing *intellectual* requirements, namely, the *evangelistic* requirement to reach effectively every generation and every culture with its message about Christ, the *didactic* requirement to correlate the manifold data of Scripture into a coherent system and to apply this systematized knowledge to all phases of humankind's thinking and conduct in keeping with the cultural mandate, and the *apologetic* requirement both to justify before this hostile world the existence of Christianity as alone the revealed religion of God and to protect its message from adulteration and distortion (see Titus 1:9).

To meet these concrete requirements of the Great Commission—no small task I assure you—Christian theology as an intellectual discipline arose in and has continued throughout the life of the church. I will mention here only a few people who responded to Christ's command, namely, the *Apostolic Fathers* (Barnabas of Alexandria, Hermes, Clement of Rome, Polycarp, Papias of Hierapolis, and Ignatius of Antioch), the *Apologists* (Justin Martyr, Tatian, Irenaeus, Athenagoras, and Theophilus of Antioch),

---

authority [of the Old and New Testaments] is from the inward work of the Holy Spirit, bearing witness by and with the Word in our hearts." That is to say, it is God himself who causes one to believe that the Bible is his Word. This faith he works in the hearts of his elect, and by this faith "a Christian believeth to be true whatsoever is revealed in the Word, for the authority of God himself speaking therein" (Confession, 14.2). The psalmist declared: "Blessed is the one you choose and bring near, to dwell in your courts" (Ps. 65:4).

Gordon H. Clark correctly notes in his *What Do Presbyterians Believe?* (Philadelphia: Presbyterian and Reformed, 1965), 18, "Logically the infallibility of the Bible is not a theorem to be deduced from some prior axiom. The infallibility of the Bible is the axiom from which the several doctrines are themselves deduced as theorems. Every religion and every philosophy must be based on some first principle. And since a first principle is first, it cannot be 'proved' or 'demonstrated' on the basis of anything prior." The first principle of Christianity then is this: God is there and he has spoken to us in and by his Word.

and the *Antignostic Fathers* (Irenaeus and Tertullian), followed by Origen of Alexandria, Athanasius, the "three great Cappadocians"—Basil, Gregory Nazianzus, and Gregory of Nyssa—and Augustine, bishop of Hippo. Then in the Middle Ages came the Augustinians Gottschalk and Thomas Bradwardine, followed by the pre-Reformers John Wycliffe and Jan Hus. Then appeared in the *sixteenth* century the great Magisterial Reformers Martin Luther, Philip Melanchthon, William Farel, John Calvin, Martin Bucer, Ulrich Zwingli, Johann Heinrich Bullinger, Theodore Beza, John Knox, Casper Olevianus, and Zacharias Ursinus. In the *seventeenth* century appeared Francis Turretin, Johannes Cocceius, and Herman Witsius, in the *eighteenth* century came Jonathan Edwards who dominated the theological scene, in the *nineteenth* century James Bannerman, James Buchanan, William Cunningham, Robert Lewis Dabney, James Henley Thornwell, Charles and A. A. Hodge, and in the *twentieth* and *twenty-first* centuries Abraham Kuyper, Herman Bavinck, Benjamin B. Warfield, Geerhardus Vos, Gerrit C. Berkouwer, Louis Berkhof, John Murray, Lorraine Boettner, Gordon H. Clark, Carl F. H. Henry, Roger Nicole, James Packer, Henri Blocher, Gerald Bray, Donald A. Carson, and the Old Testament scholar whom we honor by this volume, O. Palmer Robertson.

Space would fail me were I to mention more than a handful of the deserving thousands of pastor-theologians such as Charles Spurgeon, Martyn Lloyd-Jones, and James Montgomery Boice and the untold numbers of missionaries who responded to Christ's Commission during the modern missionary movement in the nineteenth century such as William Carey and the Baptists in England, Henry Venn and the Church of England, Adoniram Judson, Hudson Taylor, David Livingston and the Church of Scotland, and in our day D. James Kennedy, founder of Evangelism Explosion, most of whom, by the way, were Calvinistic in their theology as well as being great soul winners.

Who would be so brash as to suggest that these theological giants ignorantly wasted their time and talents as servants of Christ? No one reading this volume I am sure. So standing on the shoulders of these people in continuing obedience to Christ's Commission we today must acquire, explicate, proclaim, propagate, and defend in a logical and coherent manner the truth that God has revealed in Holy Scripture about himself, the world he has created, and the people who inhabit it. And to do this is to do Christian theology.

The Apostolic Model

The third pillar on which the justification of Christian theology as an intellectual discipline rests is the apostolic model. Such activity as eventually led to the church's engagement in theology is found not only in the teaching and example of Jesus Christ and in his Great Commission to his church but also throughout the *entirety* of the New Testament. The apostles all theologized. Peter inferred from his vivid memory of the risen Christ breathing upon his disciples fifty days earlier in the upper room that it was the ascended Christ who had breathed by his Holy Spirit upon his church on the day of Pentecost. Paul wasted no time after his baptism but set out immediately to "prove" to his fellow Jews from the Old Testament that Jesus is the Son of God and the Old Testament Messiah (Acts 9:20–22). Later, as a seasoned missionary he entered the synagogue in Thessalonica and on three Sabbath days he "reasoned" with them *from the Scriptures*, explaining and proving that the Messiah had to suffer and rise from the dead (Acts 17:2–3). The learned Apollos vigorously refuted the Jews in public debate, proving *from the Scriptures* that Jesus was the Messiah (Acts 18:18).

Nor was Paul's evangelistic theologizing limited to the synagogue. While waiting for Silas and Timothy in Athens, Paul "reasoned" not only in the synagogue with the Jews and God-fearing Greeks but also in the marketplace with all those who happened to be there about Jesus and his resurrection (Acts 17:17–18). This got him an invitation to address the Areopagus, which he did in a "big picture" way that could be understood by the Epicurean and Stoic philosophers gathered there but without any accommodation of his message to what they were prepared to believe. Then, in addition to that three-month period at Ephesus during which he spoke boldly in the synagogue, arguing persuasively about the kingdom of God (Acts 19:8), Paul dialogued daily in the lecture hall of Tyrannus, not hesitating as he would say later to the Ephesian elders at Miletus both to preach everything that was helpful to them and to teach them publicly and from house to house the whole counsel of God, declaring to both Jews and Greeks that they must turn to God in repentance and to Jesus Christ in faith (Acts 20:20–21). Paul was clearly not just an apostle but a missionary theologian as well!

We also see in Paul's letter to the Romans both his theological exposition of the doctrine of justification by faith alone and the theologizing method that he employed. Note should be taken of the brilliant "theological flow" of his letter to the Roman church, how he moved logically and systematically from the dire plight of the human condition (Rom. 1:18–3:20), employing the Old Testament to drive home his point (Rom. 3:10–18), on to God's provision of salvation in Christ, namely, justification by faith alone in Christ apart from works of law (Rom. 3:21–31), in connection with which he used Abraham as the best Old Testament example (Rom. 4); then, in turn, to the results of justification (Rom. 5) and to the two major objections he constantly faced regarding his doctrine of justification, namely, that his doctrine of justification by faith alone granted license to sin (Rom. 6–8) and that his doctrine of justification by faith alone nullified the promises made to Israel as a nation (Rom. 9–11), both of which he addressed through his exposition of Old Testament Scripture, and finally on to the Christian ethic that flows out of this central doctrine of the Christian faith (Rom. 12–16).

It detracts in no way from Paul's "inspiredness" (see 1 Thess. 2:13; 2 Tim. 3:16; 2 Peter 3:15–16) to acknowledge that he reflected upon and bolstered his theological conclusions along the way by appeals to earlier conclusions, Old Testament history, and even his own personal relationship to Christ as he laid out his doctrinal perceptions of the gospel of God under the Spirit's superintendence. One finds these theological reflections and logical deductions embedded in Romans in the very heart of some of the apostle's most radical assertions. For example, ten times, after reaching a specific point in his argument's development, Paul asks, "What shall we say" (Rom. 3:5, 9; 4:1; 6:1, 15; 7:7; 8:31; 9:14, 30; 11:7), and he then proceeds to deduce by good and necessary inference theological conclusions that he desires his readers to adopt. Also in Romans 4 he draws the theological conclusion that circumcision is unnecessary to the blessing of justification and that Abraham is the spiritual father of the uncircumcised Gentile believer from the simple observation based on Old Testament history that "Abram believed the Lord, and he credited it to him as righteousness" (Gen. 15:6 NIV) some fourteen years *before* he was circumcised (Gen. 17:24) and before God changed Abram's name to Abraham—*striking* theological deductions to draw in his particular religious and cultural milieu simply from the "before and after" relationship between two historical events! Then, to prove that "at the present time there is a [Jewish] remnant chosen by grace" (Rom. 11:5) Paul simply appeals to his own status as a Christian Jew (Rom. 11:1), again a striking theological assertion to derive from the simple fact of his personal faith in Jesus.

This apostolic model of theological exposition of, theological reflection upon, and theological deduction from Scripture supports our current need for engagement in the theological enterprise. If we are to help our generation understand the Scriptures and their saving message, we too must arrange and deduce theological conclusions from what we gain from our exegetical labors in Scripture interpretation, frame them both didactically and sermonically, and be ready to "dialogue" theologically with this generation. When we do these things we are doing theological work!

THE APOSTOLICALLY APPROVED EXAMPLE AND ACTIVITY OF THE NEW TESTAMENT CHURCH

The fourth pillar upon which the justification of Christian theology as an intellectual discipline rests is the apostolically approved example and activity of the New Testament church in its creation of extrabiblical, *uninspired* confessions and creedal statements. The New Testament by its descriptive terms and phrases such as "the traditions" (2 Thess. 2:15), "the pattern of doctrine" (Rom. 6:17), "the faith once for all delivered to the saints" (Jude 3), "the deposit" (1 Tim. 6:20), and the five "faithful sayings" of Paul's pastoral letters (1 Tim. 1:15; 3:1; 4:7–9; 2 Tim. 2:11–13; Titus 3:4–8) indicates that already in the days of the apostles the theologizing activity had begun of reflecting upon and comparing Scripture with Scripture, collating, deducing, and framing doctrinal statements into creedal formulae approaching the character of later church confessions. Examples of these early Christian creedal formulae may be seen in the following verses:

- Romans 1:3–4: "Concerning his Son, who was descended from David according to the flesh and was declared to be the Son of God in power according to the Spirit of holiness by his resurrection from the dead, Jesus Christ our Lord."
- Romans 10:9: "If you confess with your mouth that Jesus is Lord and believe in your heart that God raised him from the dead, you will be saved."
- 1 Corinthians 12:3: "Jesus is Lord."

- 1 Corinthians 15:3–5: "that Christ died for our sins in accordance with the Scriptures, that he was buried, that he was raised on the third day in accordance with the Scriptures, and that he appeared to Cephas, then to the twelve."
- 1 Timothy 1:15: "The saying is trustworthy and deserving of full acceptance, that Christ Jesus came into the world to save sinners."
- 1 Timothy 3:1: "The saying is trustworthy: If anyone aspires to the office of overseer, he desires a noble task."
- 1 Timothy 3:16: "Great indeed, we confess, is the mystery of godliness: He was manifested in the flesh, vindicated by the Spirit, seen by angels, proclaimed among the nations, believed on in the world, taken up in glory."
- 1 Timothy 4:7–9: ". . . train yourself for godliness; for while bodily training is of some value, godliness is of value in every way, as it holds promise for the present life and also for the life to come. *The saying is trustworthy and deserving of full acceptance.*"
- 2 Timothy 2:11–13: "*The saying is trustworthy,* for if we have died with him, we will also live with him; if we endure, we will also reign with him; if we deny him, he also will deny us; if we are faithless, he remains faithful—for he cannot deny himself."
- Titus 3:4–8: ". . . when the goodness and loving kindness of God our Savior appeared, he saved us, not because of works done by us in righteousness, but according to his own mercy, by the washing of regeneration and renewal of the Holy Spirit, whom he poured out on us richly through Jesus Christ our Savior, so that being justified by his grace we might become heirs according to the hope of eternal life. *The saying is trustworthy,* and I want you to insist on these things."[10]

All of these primitive creedal formulae the New Testament church developed with the full knowledge and approval of Christ's inspired apostles. Indeed, the apostles were personally involved in this "creedalizing" activity. For example, at the Jerusalem Council in Acts 15:1–16:5—that I believe may be justifiably designated the "first General Assembly of the Presbyterian Church in the World"—the apostles, laboring not as apostles but as elders

---

10. An excellent survey of this material may be found in J. N. D. Kelly, "Creedal Elements in the New Testament," in *Early Christian Creeds* (London: Longmans, Green, 1950).

together with other elders, prepared for the church's guidance, through the activity of deliberation and debate, a written counciliar response that addressed the issue they were confronting at that time, namely, whether the church would require of Gentiles for church membership faith in Christ alone or faith in Christ plus circumcision and observance of the law of Moses. "It seemed good to the Holy Spirit and to us," they wrote, to opt for the former position. Clearly, then, the church did not err when it wrote creeds; frankly, it errs when it ceases to write them.

Thus when we today, under the guidance of the Spirit of God and in faith, come to Holy Scripture and, working with our best intellectual tools and the canons of grammatical/historical exegesis, make the effort to explicate the Bible's propositions and precepts by our exegetical theology, trace their workings in the world by our historical theology, systematize them into creeds and confessions by our systematic theology, and propagate their systematized message to the world by our practical theology, we are standing squarely in the theologizing process already present in and conducted by the church of the apostolic age under the sanctions of the apostles themselves.

THE IMPLICIT DEMAND OF HOLY SCRIPTURE AS THE REVEALED WORD OF GOD

The fifth pillar upon which the justification of Christian theology as an intellectual discipline rests is a particularly striking one, namely, a good and necessary inference from the very nature of Holy Scripture as the revealed Word of God (2 Tim. 3:16–17; 2 Peter 1:20–21). I have presumed throughout this essay that the Bible is the revealed Word of God. However, I have presumed this because, among other reasons that could also be adduced, the divine Christ himself, the Lord of the church, regarded it as such and gave his church ample reason as well so to regard it. This means that the triune God about whom the Bible speaks is "really there and he has spoken." Now if this God is really there and if he has spoken to us in Holy Scripture as the divine Christ and his inspired apostles taught, then he is someone about whom we and all mankind *ought* to want to know. This fact alone provides sufficient warrant to study the Old and New Testament Scriptures. It is as simple as this: *If the one living and true God has revealed propositional truth about himself, about us, and about the relationship between himself* and us in Holy Scripture alone, then we and all mankind ought to want to know, indeed, we must know Holy Scripture. If we take seriously the biblical truth that only in the light of God's Word will we come to understand for sure anything as we should (Ps 36:9), then we *must* study his propositional revelation to us, or what amounts to the same thing, we *must* engage our minds in the pursuit of theological truth exegetically drawn from the written Oracles of God.

Now I am going to say something that may shock. Here it is: *Not to be intensely interested—and this is true for clergy and laity alike—I repeat, not to be intensely interested in the study of Holy Scripture if the one living and true God has revealed himself therein is the height of spiritual folly, indeed, such disinterest is a form of insanity.* I characterize such disinterest this way with no hesitation because Jesus taught it before I did. In his parable of the prodigal son Jesus taught that the son in the far country away from his father's house, representing all of us in our raw natural state, was not just in great physical need; *he was mad!* This is clear from Jesus' statement that the son, destitute in the far country and in great peril, finally "came to himself" and said: "I will arise and go to my father" (Luke 15:18). Jesus' descriptive expression "came to himself" means literally, "came to his senses," which means that he was *out of his mind* to think that he could find lasting fulfillment and live happily out of fellowship with his father. Paul affirms the same thing when he states in 2 Timothy 2:25–26 that the servant of the Lord must "in humility teach those who oppose him, that God may grant them 'a change of mind' with reference to a knowledge of the truth, that *they may regain their senses and escape [ananēpsōsin]* from the snare of the devil." Indeed, because of fallen mankind's refusal to retain God in their knowledge, declares Paul, God abandoned the peoples of this world in their rebellion against him to a debased mind (Rom. 1:28) and they are "darkened in their understanding, alienated from the life of God because of the ignorance that is in them, due to their hardness of heart" (Eph. 4:18). And God himself infers that there is something epistemically bizarre about mankind's rebellion against him for even the dumb ox knows his owner and the ass his master's crib but "my people do not understand [who it is who made them, who owns them, and who daily feeds them]" (Isa. 1:3). Now *that* is grotesque ignorance, to say the very least! So I say again, for a person to have no interest in what the one living and true God thinks and says about him and no interest in discovering the remedy that God has provided to reverse the human plight reflects the fact that his is an insanity of the first order. He is, spiritually and mentally speaking, more than an ordinary fool; he is a deranged madman!

This pillar stands even if one is not sure that the Bible is the Word of God, for if the Bible even *might be* the Word of God, as Christ and his apostles declare that it is, then the obligation is upon the doubter to determine whether it is or not. If he refuses to study the evidence that supports the divine nature of the Bible or if after considering the evidence he wrongly rejects it, well, he will remain in the far country of his spiritual insanity at the peril of his soul. But if, by the grace of God, his study leads him to conclude rightly that the Bible is God's Word, then he will want to know everything he can about what God thinks about him as taught therein and he will engage himself in the theological enterprise. But *to possess no interest in the teaching of Holy Scripture whatsoever is simply sheer spiritual madness.*

CONCLUSION

Well, there it is: Christian theology as an intellectual discipline supported by five unassailable pillars provided by Holy Scripture—the intellectual discipline that supports in turn the great salvific *sola*'s of the Reformation faith that the Magisterial Reformers derived from Scripture by careful exposition and then proclaimed to their world.

So why should *we* bother with Christian theology today? Because Christ the Lord of the church did so, because Christ's Great Commission mandated it, because the apostles did so, because the New Testament church under the sanctions of the apostles did so, and because the very nature of Holy Scripture as God's revealed Word lays the responsibility upon people to do so. I commend these five pillars to you for your careful consideration and submit that they provide more than ample justification for the church to remain committed to the theological enterprise as an intellectual discipline. And it can remain so committed with the full assurance that its labors will not be a waste of time and energy. And these pillars give those who have involved themselves in theological training in Reformed and evangelical seminaries the assurance that their labors will not be in vain in the Lord. I will even state categorically that no intellectual pursuit will prove more rewarding ultimately than the acquisition of a knowledge of God and of his ways and works based upon Holy Scripture.

So clear is the Bible's mandate for the theological enterprise, since the Lord of the church and his apostles leave us with no other viable option, that actually the church's primary question should not be whether or not it should engage itself in the theological task. *Of course it should*, and it will if it is faithful to Christ and his apostles as authoritative teachers of doctrine. Rather, what should ever be of even greater concern to the church than the engagement itself is *whether in its engagement in theology as an intellectual discipline it is listening as intently and submissively as it should to its Lord's voice speaking to his church in Holy Scripture.* And in light of the five pillars I have set forth in this essay our *primary* concern should be, not whether we should engage ourselves in the theological enterprise—of course we should—but whether the theology we are acquiring is correct? Is it orthodox? Better still, is it *biblical?* And this is where our Reformed seminary faculties come into the picture. They take sacred vows to do all they can to make certain that their students acquire a theology that will pass biblical muster.

Now I invite you, the readers of this festschrift, to join O. Palmer Robertson in that theological task and to seek to rekindle the Reformation in our time with its five great *sola*'s. I urge you to dedicate yourself to the oft-times arduous study that the acquisition of a great theology that is worthy of God will demand of you, for make no mistake about this: Your theological activity is an act of worship whatever it may be. So as I close I will ask you two questions:

- Is your theological activity as an act of worship worthy of your God? It will be only if it is informed by Holy Scripture alone.
- Is your God worthy of your theological activity as an act of worship? He will be only if he is the sovereign triune God of Holy Scripture.

You must also remember that you are laboring to hear your blessed Savior say to you someday, "Well done, good and faithful servant. You have been faithful over a little; I will set you over much. Enter into the joy of your master" (Matt. 25:21). Moreover, you have done "your best to present yourself to God as one approved, a worker who has no need to be ashamed, rightly handling the word of truth" (2 Tim. 2:15). May he say such to each of us in the great day of judgment, I pray in his name. Amen.

9

"Of Christ the Mediator" in the
Westminster Confession of Faith

D OUGLAS F. K ELLY

THE LATE PROFESSOR R. A. Finlayson of the Free Church College in
Edinburgh, a grand old Calvinist theologian, whom I often heard with pleasure when I was a student, once asked this question: "What is the difference
between heaven and hell?" He answered: "Hell is eternity in the presence of
God; heaven is eternity in the presence of God with a Mediator."

Yes, the Mediator and only the Mediator is what makes heaven possible for us hell-deserving sinners. As Paul tells us in 1 Timothy 2:5, "For
there is one God, and one mediator between God and men, the man Christ
Jesus." Thus, when we think of the Mediator, we are turning our thoughts
to the most important issue that we will ever face—salvation or damnation,
eternal loss or eternal gain; heaven or hell. No issue in all of my brief human
life and no issue in the endless ages of eternity so concerns me as this one:
Who is the One Mediator, and what does he mean for me?

I know of no other passage in all of theological literature, in any language, that is such a wonderful exposition of Christ our Mediator, as the
eighth chapter of our Westminster Confession of Faith. It takes us from

eternity into time and back into eternity with the profoundest and truest biblical survey of who Jesus Christ, Messiah of Israel and Savior of the world is, and what it means for us. In this glorious sweep of saving truth, we are translated out of our darkness into his eternal light. It well behooves us to bathe in this serene light, and never to leave it very far from our minds.

Let me summarize the eight paragraphs of this amazing chapter under three major points. (1) In order to be the one Mediator between God and men, Christ had to be fully man; (2) In order to be the true Mediator, Christ had to be fully God; and (3) In order to be the Mediator of his people, Christ had to be man and God together at the same time.

THE MEDIATOR HAD TO BECOME MAN IN ORDER TO REDEEM HIS PEOPLE

Hebrews 2:17 states, "Wherefore in all things it behooved him to be made like unto his brethren, that he might be a merciful and faithful high priest in things pertaining to God, to make reconciliation for the sins of the people." Hence, to fulfill his priesthood in which he takes his once sinful people into the place of eternal salvation in the Father's favorable presence, into the holiest place of all, he had to become one of them. Thus, "it behooved him to be made like unto his brethren."

Earlier in Hebrews 2, it states that Christ did not become an angel (v. 16). Angels are not redeemable; their number is fixed as either elect or reprobate. Angels do not die. But Christ became a man, "taking on the seed of Abraham" in order to die. The Christ child is one baby that was born specifically so that he could die! Hebrews 2:14, 15 explains why his death in human nature was essential to the salvation of the elect portion of the human race: "Forasmuch then as the children are partakers of flesh and blood, he also himself likewise took part of the same; that through death he might destroy him that had the power of death, that is, the devil; And deliver them who through fear of death were all their lifetime subject to bondage." In other words, since sin was committed in the human race, he had to become human (though without ceasing to be God at the same time) so as to live a holy life in our flesh, thus fulfilling the covenant of God with man his creature, and to die in our flesh—in order to atone for our sins in the place where they were committed, and in the very place that was to be

177

redeemed, thereby paying the penalty due to a broken covenant. He had to be fully man in order to accomplish this essential side of his saving work.

Few have brought out the necessity of Christ's true humanity so well as Professor T. F. Torrance (in his unpublished class notes for Edinburgh University on "The Hypostatic Union"), from which I quote.

> If Jesus Christ were not Man as well as God, that would mean that God had not actually come all the way to man, that He had not really got a foothold in our creaturely world, as it were, within the time-series in which we are, and that God would still be far away from us, as far as the heaven is from the earth, as far as Creator is from creature. Any docetic view of the Humanity of Christ snaps the life-line between God and man, and destroys the relevance of the divine acts in Jesus for men of flesh and blood. . . . The stark actuality of Christ's humanity, His flesh and blood and bone, guarantees to us that we have God among us. If that manhood were in any sense unreal, God would be unreal for us in Him. The full measure of Christ's Humanity is the full measure of God's reality for us, God's actuality to us, in fact the measure of God's love for us. If Christ is not Man, then God has not reached us, but has stopped short of our humanity—then God does not love us to the uttermost, for His love has stopped short of coming all the way to where we are, and becoming one of us. But Christ's Humanity means that God's love is now flesh of our flesh, and bone of our bone.

John Calvin makes the same points very powerfully in his *Institutes of the Christian Religion*, Book 2, Chapter 12, from which I extract some brief quotations.

> The situation would surely have been hopeless had the very majesty of God not descended to us, since it was not in our power to ascend to him. Hence, it was necessary for the Son of God to become for us "Immanuel, that is, God with us" [Isa. 7:14; Matt. 1:23], and in such a way that his divinity and our human nature might by mutual connection grow together. . . . Even if man had remained free for all stain, his condition would have been too lowly for him to reach God without a Mediator. . . . Therefore, lest anyone be troubled about where to seek the Mediator, or by what path we must come to him, the Spirit calls him "man", thus teaching us that he is near us, indeed touches us, since he is our flesh. . . . Who could have done this had not the self-same Son

178

of God become Son of man, and had not so taken what was ours as to impart what was his to us, and to make what was his by nature ours by grace? . . . Ungrudgingly he took our nature upon himself to impart to us what was his, and to become both Son of God and Son of man in common with us . . .

The second requirement of our reconciliation with God was this: that man, who by his disobedience had become lost, should by way of remedy counter it with obedience, satisfy God's judgment, and pay the penalties for sin. Accordingly, our Lord came forth as true man and took the person and the name of Adam in order to take Adam's place in obeying the Father, to present our flesh as the price of satisfaction to God's righteous judgment, and in the same flesh to pay the penalty that we had deserved. . . .

When he himself appeared, he declared that the reason for his advent was by appeasing God to gather us from death unto life . . . Here [referring to John 12:27–28] he clearly indicates why he assumed flesh: that he might become a sacrifice and expiation to abolish our sins.[1]

Saint Irenaeus of second century Lyon, whom Calvin liked to quote, had said much the same thing over 1,300 years earlier about the necessity of the Son of God taking on our humanity. According to Irenaeus:

Therefore . . . He caused man (human nature) to cleave to and to become one with God. For unless man had overcome the enemy of man, the enemy would not have been legitimately vanquished. And again: unless it had been God who had freely given salvation, we could never have possessed it securely. . . . For in what way could we be partakers of the adoption of sons, unless we had received from Him through the Son that fellowship which refers to Himself, unless His Word, having been made flesh, had entered into communion with us? Wherefore also he passed through every stage of life restoring to all communion with God . . . .[2]

Later in his book, Irenaeus speaks against those who deny that Christ became a real man:

But if he pretends that the Lord possessed another substance of flesh, the sayings respecting reconciliation will not agree with that man. For that

---

1. John Calvin, *Institutes of the Christian Religion*, ed. John T. McNeill, trans. Ford Lewis Battles, Library of Christian Classics (Philadelphia: Westminster Press, 1960), 2.12.1–4.

2. Irenaeus, *Adversus Haereses*, 3.18.7.

thing is reconciled which had formerly been in enmity. Now, if the Lord had taken flesh from another substance, He would not, by so doing, have reconciled that one to God that had become inimical through transgression. But now, by means of communion with Himself, the Lord has reconciled man to God the Father, in reconciling us to Himself by the body of His own flesh, and redeeming us by His own blood, as the apostle says to the Ephesians, "In whom we have redemption through his blood, the remission of sins . . ." And in every Epistle, the apostle plainly testifies, that through the flesh of our Lord, and through His blood, we have been saved.[3]

The Mediator Had to Be God in Order to Redeem His People

T. F. Torrance in his paper on "The Hypostatic Union" rightly notes that

the Deity of Christ . . . is the guarantee that in Jesus Christ we have to do with the reality of God Himself. What Jesus does in forgiveness is not just the work of man but also the work of God, and is therefore of final and ultimate validity. Only God against whom we sin can forgive sin, but the Deity of Christ is the guarantee that the action of Christ in the whole course of his life is identical with the action of God toward us. It is not something of God that we have in Christ, but God Himself, very God of very God. . . . The Deity of Christ is thus the guarantee that the actions of Christ are not in time only, not just temporary or temporal actions, but the eternal action of God, eternally real in the Godhead.

In what I consider to be one of the most significant passages in contemporary theological literature, Torrance shows the disaster of denying the deity of Christ. He writes:

Thus the weakening in the affirmation of the Deity of Christ, results in indecision and uncertainty. It is indeed because of this weakness that men are engulfed in relativity, and are not sure about what they believe. How do you know that you are right and you are not wrong? Such is the uncertainty that is born of clouded vision of the Deity of Christ. When the Deity of Christ is denied, the bottom falls out of Christianity. When the Deity of Christ is denied, His Humanity is denied as well, because Jesus

3. Ibid, 5.14.3.

is made out to be a liar, and if Jesus is cut adrift from the Truth, then we are all hopelessly at sea.[4]

I might add here that this is the tragedy of Western culture since the eighteenth-century humanistic Enlightenment. When the intelligentsia of our culture denied the deity of Christ in order to enthrone man, everything went relativistic, and finally we have wound up by losing man as well (for we can abort him, subject him to euthanasia, and make him a meaningless cipher subservient to economic and governmental purposes). When our leadership denied the deity of Christ, they looked in other areas to replace him, and one by one the replacements have failed: Darwinian evolutionism, Marxism, and now passé Freudian psychotherapy. All that is now left standing is sheer materialism (the absolutely unrestrained rule of money) and raw government power, with few humane restraints upon either. And in addition to these two frightful powers, we now find a third factor entering the world scene: resuscitated Islam, funded by seemingly endless barrels of oil.

We turned out Christ and opened the door to false religions. The basic motivation of Western pluralism is simple: any religion (even Islam or Satanism) has to be better than Christianity. "Anything but Christ!" is the cry of millions of the most privileged people in our culture. I suspect that that is why the youth (and many middle-aged folk) have enslaved themselves to the destructive demons of drugs and pornography. That is why so many who teach English, history, and religion at our most prestigious universities hate and seek to denigrate their own culture. They are really saying "Anything but Christ!"

Torrance goes on to say, "It is important to see that if the Deity of Christ is denied, then the Cross becomes a terrible monstrosity. If Jesus Christ is man only and not also God, then we lose faith in God and man . . . for that means that man is such that when he sees the very best, the very highest and noblest the world has ever known, he crucifies it in spite, and will have nothing to do with it except to hate it. Put God in heaven and Jesus a man only on the cross, and you destroy all hope and trust, and preach a doctrine of the blackest and most abysmal despair. . . . But put God on the cross, and the cross becomes the world's salvation. . . ."[5]

4. T. F. Torrance, "The Hypostatic Union." In the same line of thought see the remarkable article by Pierre Courthial, "Actualité de Chalcédoine", in *Foi et Vie*, 1 (Jan.-Feb. 1976), 59–66.
5. Ibid.

A glaring illustration of this denial that the Man of Sorrows on the cross is none less than the eternal Son of God, a denial that leads to hatred of the cross and hatred of everything else that matters most, was seen in some of the reactions to Mel Gibson's film *The Passion of the Christ*. What seems to have upset some of our so-called intellectual leadership the most was the graphic portrayal of the horrendous flogging of the back of Jesus by the cruel Roman cat-of-nine tails. In the largest newspaper in North Carolina, *The Charlotte Observer*, a professor of religion from a prestigious college that was started by the Presbyterians long ago, wrote a very angry letter denouncing the film, and especially the portrayal of the violent beating of Christ by the Romans. The professor said something more or less like this: "If Christianity involves this kind of violence visited upon Jesus, then I want nothing to do with Christianity or its God."

What was his problem? For after all the four Gospels clearly teach that Jesus willingly bore such horrid violence in order to cleanse us from our sins. But this well-educated man assumes that the scriptural testimony to the divinity of Jesus cannot be true, because his Enlightenment philosophy puts a deistic disjunction between God upstairs and the real world of history below. Thus, Jesus was only a good man, and he does not wish to be graphically reminded of what the human race (which he probably considers to be essentially good, and certainly not guilty of infinite sin against its Creator) did to the only really good man who ever lived. So, he puts God in heaven and Jesus a mere man on the cross and bitterly (and dare I say "violently") opposes the tender grace and infinite mercy of God to sinners in his beloved Son. That is where the modernism that denies the Deity of Christ will finally land you. That is why the main-line churches are largely emptying out. I can only pray that the PCA will not follow them, but there does seem to be a kind of second law of thermodynamics in most denominations.

Now let us take another illustration of the consequences of denying Jesus' deity from the opposite point of view. The very popular book of Dan Brown, *The Da Vinci Code*, has been made into a film by Ron Howard, who used to play "Opie" on "The Andy Griffith Show." Many of you have read the book or will see the film. When the book was published in 2003, it quickly became number one with every major bookseller list in the USA, has sold over six million hardback copies, and has been translated into some forty languages. Why has it become so amazingly popular? It is not great literature. There is very little character development in it; the story line is fairly thin, and over 20 percent of it (according to a critique by Roman Catholic authors Olson and Miesel) consists basically of preaching or lecturing.[6] Fine novels do not get their message across by preaching!

Yet it has sold extremely well in spite of its very poor literary quality. Why? Yes, it did hold my attention because of its interesting and exciting escape scenes of the heroes from the French police and from a crazed assassin. But that quality alone would not have been sufficient to make it so widely acceptable. Perhaps a contrast with another recent film will make clear the real reason for its popularity.

It is interesting to contrast *The Da Vinci Code* with Mel Gibson's *The Passion of the Christ*. The mainstream media, including all of Hollywood, fiercely opposed the making of Gibson's film, a film that (to a very considerable degree) worked on the basis of the deity of Christ and the truth of the Scriptures. Most of academia was against it. But on the contrary, the mainstream media seems to have done all it could to push Dan Brown's novel and newly made film. Could the reason be that it is based on a flat denial of the deity of Christ; that it sets him forth only as a mere man, and perhaps one of questionable ethical standards at that? *The Da Vinci Code* openly denies the antiquity and authenticity of the canon of the New Testament, and attempts to replace it with the kind of pagan, feminist, pansexuality of ancient (and modern) Gnosticism. Nearly all of that twenty percent of the novel, which is sheer lecturing or preaching is pushing this message, so welcome to humanists who want some kind of religion without having to bow before the Lord Jesus Christ as Son of God and only Lord and Savior of the world. That is why so many love it.

I think that Dr. Peter Jones is right to have noted in his *Cracking Da Vinci's Code* that the theology of Dan Brown is the theology of the so-called "Jesus Seminar."[7] This "Seminar" is a group of modernist scholars who basically throw out anything in the New Testament that speaks of miracles, so that their Jesus is a mere man; a sort of cynic, left-wing philosopher: not surprisingly, rather like themselves! What the "Jesus Seminar" does next is very interesting; at this point they have gone beyond traditional liberalism. It is nothing new to attempt to cut miracles out of the Bible. Thomas Jefferson

6. Carl E. Olson and Sandra Miesel, *The Da Vinci Hoax: Exposing the Errors in the Da Vinci Code* (San Francisco: Ignatius Press, 2004).

7. James L. Garlow and Peter Jones, *Cracking Da Vinci's Code* (Colorado Springs: Victor, 2004), 159.

did that long ago in his own edition of the Bible (although not many people followed him)! Not content with that, the "fellows" of the Seminar take an even more radical step to get rid of the divinity of Jesus. They *add in* new books to the New Testament! They take the Gnostic writings with their weird sexualized paganism, humanistic mysticism, and silly magical practices, and add them in to their version of the New Testament. Dan Brown actually claims in *The Da Vinci Code* that these heretical Gnostic writings discovered at Nag Hammadi in 1945 are the earliest Christian records![8]

Bertrand Rickenbacher of Lausanne recently noted that older liberalism attacked *the content* of Scripture, whereas the newer liberalism attacks *the canon* of Scripture. [9] Or as T. F. Torrance once said, it is as though the Jesus Seminar (and perhaps Elaine Pagels, popular author of *The Gnostic Gospels*) consider themselves "a new apostolate" who have far more authority than the ancient church to determine what is inspired by the Holy Spirit and what is not, and thus to set new limits to the ancient canon of the historic Christian church!

How could some of the most intelligent and educated people in our country be so blind? I think the basic explanation is to be found in an insight from E. Michael Jones, a traditionalist Roman Catholic who has no use for Protestants. Nonetheless, truth came out of the mouth of Balaam's ass, and we need to receive the truth from whatever quarter. Jones' hard-hitting book, *Modern Degenerates*, holds that the intellectual heroes of modern secularist culture, such as Margaret Mead, Lord Keynes, Sigmund Freud, Picasso and others, were enthroned as the new priesthood of the West in the twentieth century because their message allowed people to escape the sexual restraints imposed by traditional Christianity without feeling guilty any longer about their immorality. Here is Jones' central insight: there are only two ways to relate to the truth. Either you conform your desires to the truth, or you conform the truth to your desires.

Now do you see the connection here? Gibson's *The Passion of the Christ* confronted our culture with the God/man, who as such, deserves and requires the total trust and loyalty (including sexual obedience) of all who shall be saved. This is not a popular message in a culture sold out to

8. Dan Brown, *The Da Vinci Code* (New York: Anchor, 2003), 245.

9. See here Louis Gaussen's masterpiece, *The Canon of the Holy Scriptures Examined in the Light of History* (Boston: American Tract Society, 1862).

every possible kind of sexual practice, a culture that would far rather deny who God is than to split with their sins.

But the Jesus of *The Da Vinci Code* is a mere man, who requires no such forsaking of the autonomous self-life with its sexual preoccupations; innocent and personal choices which are wickedly labeled "sins" by the Christian church, an institution that was dishonestly and violently foisted on the public by Emperor Constantine. I suspect that far more people in the apostate West will choose the option of conforming the truth to their desires than of conforming their desires to the truth. To do the latter would require the intervention of God's sovereign grace, creating a broken heart and a renewed spirit in the self-satisfied multitudes. God can and will accomplish this renewal of faith and repentance in his good time. But until then, millions are delighted over the direct denial of the deity of the Lord Jesus Christ in Dan Brown's novel and film. It allows them to keep their sins and still feel good about themselves.

Ah, yes, but what a price they will pay later! For Jesus says in Luke 12:9 that those who deny him now before men will be denied by him as they stand before Jehovah's awesome judgment seat on that last momentous day. Particularly is that so of those who had privileged information and thus knew better, but denied the Lord's deity in order to nourish to the very end their soul-destroying sins!

If you want to do these people any good in the light of their own certain death and eternal existence somewhere, then you must seek to tell them who Jesus really is. HE is their only hope! Confront them with him. Romans 10:9 shows that to acknowledge him is the only way to be saved for an endless eternity: "That if thou shalt confess with thy mouth the Lord Jesus, and shalt believe in thine heart that God hath raised him from the dead, thou shalt be saved." I hope that this study in Chapter VIII of our Westminster Confession may encourage you to do just that, perhaps in a fresh way.

THE MEDIATOR HAD TO BE GOD AND MAN AT THE SAME TIME IN ORDER TO REDEEM HIS PEOPLE

Now we turn to the second paragraph of the eighth chapter of the Confession. I do not know of any other piece of theology anywhere which provides such eternally massive truth with such exquisite biblical and theological balance, and which so fruitfully uses the history of the ancient creeds of the church in such a short and luminous compass.

"The Son of God, the second person in the Trinity, being very and eternal God, of one substance, and equal with the Father, did, when the fullness of time was come, take upon him man's nature, with all the essential properties and common infirmities thereof, yet without sin; being conceived by the power of the Holy Ghost, in the womb of the virgin Mary, of her substance. So that the two whole, perfect, and distinct natures, the Godhead and the manhood, were inseparably joined together in one person, without conversion, composition, or confusion. Which person is very God and very man, yet one Christ, the only mediator between God and man."

Now let us look more closely at the significance of the second long sentence, which states that the divine and human natures (thus, two natures) were inseparably joined together in one Person. The way this joining is described requires careful thought, for in it our whole eternal felicity lies, for in it—and in no other way—was God's eternal plan of salvation accomplished in space and time. Here, other than the Trinity, is perhaps the hardest, most mind-stretching question ever faced by a rational being: how can one person have two natures; how could Jesus Christ be fully God and fully man at the very same time? Nearly all the soul-destroying heresies of all the ages are rooted in wrong approaches to this question. This is no small matter. Some things in theology are not very important; but this is so crucial, that few things beyond this really matter. And that is why Satan so constantly in every generation opposes a sound view of the person of the Mediator. He will do everything he can to get the church off track here, for if they miss this, then all else is lost.

But the eighth chapter of the Westminster Confession keeps us on track. This is one train that I do not intend to leave! So how could the Lord Jesus Christ, one person, have a divine and human nature together at the same time without constituting a merely superficial linking—in schizoid fashion—of two persons, or a total merging and dissolving of one nature into the other, so that he is neither really God nor man? Our Confession goes back to the grand Chalcedonian Creed of A.D. 451, which explicates this union of two natures in one person with such consummate biblical balance that it has never been equaled, much less excelled! The Fathers of Chalcedon probably take us as far as the human mind can ever go in grasping something of this miraculous joining, which enters into the substance of our salvation.

It is instructive to note how they do it. They were at the same time too pious, too humble, and too intelligent to think that they could ever understand or explain such an infinite mystery; something bigger than creation out of nothing (for in this action of incarnation the Creator becomes a creature without ceasing to be Creator). So they do not explain it, but they do cast much light upon the union of two natures in one person. As I said, the fathers of Westminster thought you could not—and need not—go any further than Chalcedon went.

What they did was to summarize the essential aspects of this incarnate union between God and man in terms of four negatives (called in Greek the four "alpha privatives"). If one can avoid these four negatives (which are mistaken ways of thinking about how Christ is both God and man at the same time), then one is likely to possess a sound and saving knowledge of who our Mediator is. Chalcedon states that the two natures of Christ were joined together in one person, "without confusion," "without conversion," "without division," and "without separation." The Westminster Confession boils these four negatives down to three: "without conversion, composition, or confusion." The same truths are equally well safeguarded in both Confessions, for Westminster simply joins together the two Chalcedonian alpha privatives "without division" and "without separation" into one term that encompasses them both: "without composition," that is without the combination of parts or elements of a whole.

For the sake of greater simplicity, and I hope, clarity, let us let us summarize these three (or four) alpha privatives under two main headings: (1) "without confusion" of the two natures, or (2) without separation of the two natures, that is, "without composition." Essential gospel truth is safeguarded by these two negative statements about who Jesus is.

(1) "Without confusion" of the two natures of Christ into one another, so that the human is no longer human, and the divine is no longer divine. Chalcedon here was safeguarding against the tendency of the ancient theological school of Alexandria, some of which merged the humanity into the deity and the deity into the humanity. What difference does this make?

T. F. Torrance states it clearly, "It is such a union [i.e. the hypostatic union] that true godhead and true manhood are joined together

187

in such a way . . . that they can never be confused, and so that one does not absorb the other, or that both do not combine to form a third entity which is neither divine nor human."[10] In other words, if Jesus' humanity took on divine attributes in itself, then it was no longer human, and thus he could not really represent us in what he was doing on the cross, the empty tomb, and on the Father's throne. For in that case he would represent some "third thing" somewhere between God and man, and thus our manhood would not have been atoned for and lifted up into resurrection life. Hence, we humans would still not have been redeemed if his humanity had become merged or transmuted into something else, even if it were something higher.

There are other deleterious implications that flow from merging or converting Christ's true humanity into some kind of deified "third thing." Karl Barth was right, I think, when he pointed out that the Lutheran error of attributing the divine attribute of "ubiquity" to Jesus' humanity, as a way of backing their view of the physical presence of the body of Christ in the Lord's Supper, is what finally lay behind the development of German Romantic Pantheism and Idealism. German Idealism, nourished by Lutheran concepts of the deifying of Christ's physical body, eventually resulted in the deification of humanity as a whole, and especially—with Hegel, and consequently Marx and Communism—resulted in seeing the highest form of deified humanity as the German or Soviet State, which was said to be "God walking on the earth." The direction in which that led Russia and Germany in the first third of the twentieth century was tragic beyond words, because the State replaced God, and thus could declare an entire class of persons as having no rights (for the state, not a transcendent God, gives and takes "rights" at its will).

We will do well to remember here that human states almost always have the temptation to deify themselves, and Germany is not the only one. The functional replacement of God by the human state and its consequent confusion of the temporal and spiritual powers is the source of totalitarianism, ancient and modern. What safety and happiness there is in refusing to allow the very concept of human nature, or any human institution, to take on divine attributes! Human institutions that try to take on divine attributes become horrendous monsters.

10. T. F. Torrance, "The Hypostatic Union."

188

As far back as the last half of the sixteenth century, the Lutheran theologians were soundly warned of how this severe Christological mistake (putting divine attributes into the human nature of Christ) was a sin against the biblical balance found in Chalcedon, and of how far afield it could lead them. The successor of John Calvin in Geneva, Theodore Beza, did some excellent writing to the Lutherans on this point that the two natures must not be merged or converted into one another.[11] Also the great antagonist against the Reformation, Robert Cardinal Bellarmin, who disagreed with Calvin and Beza on huge issues, and who constantly fought against them, did in fact agree with them against the Lutheran doctrine of ubiquity, and did some very insightful writing on the terrible mistake of transmuting Christ's humanity into some kind of deity. He, along with Beza, sought to bring the Lutherans back to the fine balance of the Chalcedonian alpha privatives.[12] But Beza and Bellarmine had no influence on the Germans, and we know what happened there some three centuries later.

By the way, I do not point this out in order to make an example of the Germans. We face such problems ourselves, though in a very different kind of context, as our culture foolishly seeks by its messianic democratic secularization of the Puritan hope to turn humanity (and its institutions) into God. R. J. Rushdoony's book *The One and the Many* is helpful on this issue, and one does not have to agree with all of his viewpoints in that book to feel that he is on to something important; something that we need to hear in order to prevent human culture (and not least the modern humanistic state) from becoming a monster that will finally eat up every human and religious value.

In addition to protecting us from totalitarian statism, the "no confusion" of Chalcedon and Westminster, also precludes today's popular "New Age" pantheism, according to which, since everything is God, then I am God, and hence, there is no transcendent, infinite Person above me to dictate to me! The impersonal, evolutionary world-system is complete within itself,

---

11. See Jill Raitt, *The Eucharistic Theology of Theodore Beza: Development of the Reformed Doctrine* (Chambersburg, PA: American Academy of Religion, 1972), *The Colloquy of Montbéliard: Religion and Politics in the Sixteenth Century* (New York: Oxford University Press, 1993), and Jean-Marc Berthoud, "Theodore de Beze, Pasteur et defenseur de la Foi (1519–1605)," (unpublished paper, Lausanne, Switzerland, 2006).

12. See Christian David Washburn, *St. Roberto Bellarmino's Defense of Catholic Christology against the Lutheran Doctrine of Ubiquity* (PhD diss., Catholic University of America, 2004). I owe this reference to the fine essay of Jean-Marc Berthoud, listed immediately above.

and needs no outside personal God. Therefore, the natural realm is the substance of God, and since I am part of the natural realm, my substance is part of the substance of God. But as John Calvin noted, we can never accept a viewpoint of our union with Christ in the Holy Spirit that would involve "a gross mixture" between the substance of God and the substance of mankind.[13] For that did not happen even in Christ, the Mediator between God and man! Even in our closest union with God in Christ through the Holy Spirit, the essential distinction of Holy Scripture between Creator and creature is always preserved. This divinization of nature is at the same time a negation of creaturely reality.

The exquisite biblical balance found in Chapter VIII of the Westminster Confession, which enshrines the necessary refusal of Chalcedon to transmute Christ's human nature into deity, must be our guide today more than ever before. Torrance summarizes it well:

> It is such a union that the presence of full and perfect humanity does not impair or diminish or restrict the presence of full and perfect Deity, and the presence of full and perfect Deity does not impair or diminish or restrict the presence of full and perfect humanity. . . . In this union God has become Man without ceasing to be God, and man is taken up into the very being of God without ceasing to be Man. That is the mystery of Jesus Christ in whom we have communion through the Holy Spirit.[14]

(2) The second side of the Chalcedonian (and Westminsterian) formula is: "without separation" (that is, "without composition"). Just what does this mean, and why is important for our salvation?

The Fathers of Chalcedon were safeguarding here against the tendency of many in the other ancient theological school, that of Antioch, of whom some (such as Nestorius, or at least his followers) basically separated the human and divine natures of Christ in such a way that Christ was finally two persons, somehow linked together, without a true incarnation of God in the flesh ever having occurred. Here is the fatal problem with that theory for our own salvation.

As Torrance writes, "If we could divide between the two natures of Christ, his divine and his human nature, into a nature of a divine person

---

13. Calvin, *Institutes*, 3.11.10.
14. Torrance, "The Hypostatic Union."

and a nature of a human person, then the human acts would not be acts of the divine person, and the divine acts would not be in the human person. In the event, the accomplishment of reconciliation would be illusory, for its ultimate achievement would not have been carried through. . . ."[15]

That means, for instance, that if the human nature of Jesus were not personally united with God the eternal Son, then the shedding of his blood would have no infinite value to forgive our infinite sins, and thus we would still have to pay for our own sins. For as Anselm rightly pointed out, sin against an infinite Person (God) is infinite sin, and only the sufferings of an infinitely holy Person would avail to purge away such sin.[16] Thus, keep the human nature of Christ from being personally (hypostatically) united to God the eternal Son, and you keep his death and resurrection from availing for the redemption of elect humanity. That would be a high price to pay for such a crucial theological error!

All honor to the fathers of Chalcedon and Westminster for helping us to avoid such fatal error!

Let me make only one other point about the tendency to separate Christ's humanity and deity. To refuse to appreciate that Christ's humanity (in which he thoroughly and perfectly represents all of us) is personally united to his eternal and infinite deity, is to fail to appreciate the beauty of the new humanity that Christ has provided for us in his incarnation, atoning death, and life-giving resurrection. He is the head of a new humanity, a resurrection race. Because of the church's spiritual union with the God/man in the glory, we Christians are available here below to take part in the transformation in some measure of God's good creation, pock-marked though it is by sin. The enlightenment given by the written Word of God to the souls of believers, and the constant empowerment of the church by the Holy Spirit who inspired that Word, mean that (unlike Eastern thought), instead of fleeing the creation—including embodied humanity—we appreciate its God-given marvels, fight against its sins, and seek to transform it to the glory of the one who created and redeemed it. Abraham Kuyper of the Netherlands set the right tone on this subject in his famous *Lectures on Calvinism*, delivered at Princeton in 1898.

My assessment here may be misguided, but I think that a certain kind of Protestant evangelical pietism, in some respects the heir of certain "other worldly" tendencies of some of our Puritan forebears, especially after the

---

15. Ibid.
16. See Anselm's *Cur deus homo.*

fundamentalist/modernist debates of the 1920s, tended so to emphasize Christ's deity that it feared to affirm enthusiastically his humanity; his true incarnation. Without meaning to do so, not a few of the fundamentalists (whose hearts were certainly in the right place on the "five fundamentals") all but abandoned human culture, and seemed almost ashamed of our embodied existence as human (and not least, validly sexual) personalities. It apparently became pious to speak only of church services and individual, personal salvation, while serious engagement with God-created aspects of culture such as education, health, politics, art, literature, etc. was more or less "worldly", and unworthy of much Christian effort. Thus, as Francis Schaeffer frequently pointed out, in this way evangelicals tragically lost Western culture.

It is my belief that we would not have done so had we kept to the truth of the eighth chapter of Westminster (which follows Chalcedon so faithfully) that the two natures of Christ are not separate or divided, but are personally united. We will never even begin to regain our rotting, secularist culture until we return to the God-given christological truth that as Paragraph 2 of Chapter VIII of Westminster says, "So that two whole, perfect, and distinct natures, the Godhead and the manhood, were inseparably joined together in one person, without conversion, composition, or confusion. Which person is very God and very man, yet one Christ, the only mediator between God and man."

Let me conclude these thoughts on our noble Mediator with some lines from an old Southern gospel hymn. These lines constitute a prayer. "O Jesus, blest Redeemer, sent from the heart of God; hold us who wait before Thee, near to the heart of God." What is God's response? Surely it is "Yes, yes, always yes! I gave that prayer to the saved soul, to all of my true church, and I will give you its glorious answer!" I am loosely paraphrasing here—or at least meditating upon—Romans 8:15-17:

> For ye have not received the spirit of bondage again to fear; but ye have received the Spirit of adoption, whereby we cry, Abba, Father. The Spirit itself beareth witness with our spirit that we are the children of God: And if children, then heirs; heirs of God, and joint-heirs with Christ; if so be that we suffer with him, that we may be also glorified together.

This, I think, is what old Professor Finlayson meant when he said that "heaven is eternity in the presence of God *with* a Mediator." May it be true for you; may it be true for me!

IO

"Baptism" in First Peter 3:21:
A Study in Sacramental Theology

RICHARD D. PHILLIPS

Baptism, which corresponds to this, now saves you, not as a removal of dirt from the body but as an appeal to God for a good conscience, through the resurrection of Jesus Christ. (1 Peter 3:21)

It has been aptly observed that the history of theology consists of a flight from one error or extreme to another. The evangelical movement's approach to the sacraments in the late twentieth and early twenty-first centuries is a classic example of this phenomenon. Reacting against Roman Catholic sacerdotalism and influenced by revivalism, twentieth-century evangelicalism looked upon the sacraments with suspicion at best and loathing at worst. Many evangelicals considered it a great heresy to suggest that God conferred any grace via the sacraments: they were human acts of memorial and nothing more.

Isaac Newton taught us that every action has an equal and opposite reaction. The reaction to anti-sacramentalism is occurring now, especially among younger believers who were spiritually impoverished in churches devoid of mystery and transcendence. This is a significant impulse in the current flight of some evangelicals to the sacramental world of Roman Catholicism. A number of books chronicle this movement, including one titled *Born Fundamentalist, Born Again Roman Catholic.* In the first chapter, the author recounts the impeccable dispensationalist credentials of his father, a Bible-church pastor, along with expressions of admiration for his dad's inspiring faith and godliness. One might expect such a son to enroll in Dallas Theological Seminary, which his father was attending at the time of his birth. Chapter 2 explains why he did not, recounting the quest that led to Rome. The chapter is titled "The Real Presence," and it outlines a fundamentalist's child's quest for mystery and sacramental grace. From the perspective of Reformed theology, this journey from anti-sacramental Dallas to sacerdotal Rome presents a classic instance of the tendency to flee one extreme into the arms of another.

This phenomenon provides at least some of the background for the renewed interest in sacramental grace among many Reformed Christians. Reacting strongly against anti-sacramentalism, many Reformed Christians are rethinking and re-emphasizing the sacraments. This renewed interest has raised important questions of late and sparked new controversies. Among the questions are "What kind of grace is conveyed via the sacraments? In what manner is sacramental grace conveyed? How do the sacraments function as 'signs' and 'seals' of the covenant of grace? More generally, what is the proper role of the sacraments in our theology of salvation?" Historically, the Reformed community stands between evangelical anti-sacramentalism and Romish sacerdotalism. But recent experience suggests that our ability to answer questions like those above will determine whether Reformed churches offer a biblical solution to this timely concern or whether Reformed churches are torn asunder by the competing sacramental poles.

"BAPTISM NOW SAVES"

The question of sacramental grace pertains to both baptism and the Lord's Supper, but because the former serves as our rite of initiation, questions regarding baptism are particularly urgent. A favorite passage of those promoting high views of baptism is 1 Peter 3:21. Having compared out salvation to that experienced by Noah through the flood, the apostle states, "Baptism, which corresponds to this, now saves you, not as a removal of dirt from the body but as an appeal to God for a good conscience, through the resurrection of Jesus Christ."

I would like to consider this passage as an inroad to the recent discussion of sacramental grace. Peter has exhorted Christians to suffer well, giving a witness in suffering like that of our Lord and rejoicing in our hope of resurrection. When Jesus was put to death, his good behavior put his tormentors to shame. Relying on God the Father, he was "put to death in the flesh but made alive in the spirit" (1 Peter 3:18). After this, our Lord "went and proclaimed to the spirits in prison" (3:19), a statement I will leave unexplored in this study. It is certain, however, that Peter turns to the example of Noah in the flood because this is an earlier example of a righteous person being reviled by the world, but saved through judgment into a new life. It is evidently Peter's statement that Noah was thus "brought safely through water" (3:20) that brings baptism into his mind. The apostle states that baptism "corresponds to this"—that is, Noah's deliverance through the flood, as well as Christ's deliverance through the cross. Peter's teaching that "baptism . . . now saves you" challenges us to incorporate a fully biblical doctrine of the sacrament to which he refers.

The first point to consider, and one that bears directly on today's debate, is the relationship of the sign of baptism to the reality it signifies. In brief, in referring to baptism, does the apostle make a simple reference to the sacramental rite of baptism as something that saves us? Or, does he employ the sign as a way of referring to the thing signified, namely, the deliverance of those who humbly rely on God through death and resurrection?

This verse is of central importance to our sacramental debates today, because it is the best passage to provide a rule by which we will normally consider similar references to baptism in the New Testament. When we read Peter's use of *baptisma*, should we understand the rite itself as the primary reference? Or are there occasions when biblical writers use the sign as shorthand for the thing signified? Many who espouse a renewed emphasis on the sacraments consider that whenever the New Testament uses the noun *baptisma* or the verb *baptizo*, the primary reference is to the rite of baptism. Peter Leithart, for instance, argues that the rite of infant baptism involves God's public declaration of the child's justification. To support this position, Leithart refers to Romans 6:1–11 and 1 Corinthians 12:12–13, both among the numerous instances where the apostle Paul uses *baptizo* in the context of his description of salvation, references which Leithart understands as designating the rite of baptism as the vehicle by which salvation is conferred.[1] The question at hand, illustrated by Leithart's interpretation, is this: when Peter or Paul employs the words *baptisma* or *baptizo* in their discussion of salvation, is it always or even normally the case that they are directing us to the sign or to the thing signified?

First Peter 3:21 is an important verse in treating this subject, for it provides a clear statement regarding baptism and salvation, one to which high sacramentalists have regularly referred to prove their view of baptism as the vehicle of salvation. "Does not Peter plainly state that 'baptism now saves?'" they argue. But what really is the apostle's thinking? Does he posit that having a minister pour water over your head while repeating the baptismal formula accomplishes salvation? Or is Peter employing the sacramental act of baptism as shorthand for the whole drama of redemption, the latter of which should occupy our foremost attention?

John Calvin, whom no one can accuse of a low sacramentology, takes the latter view, namely, that the apostles employed *baptizo* in order to refer to the thing signified rather than to the sign itself. First, Calvin makes the kind of statement that sacerdotalists love to cite: "Noah was saved by water, in a figure of baptism." But he goes to specify his meaning: "As Noah obtained life through death, when he was buried in the ark just as if in a grave, and among the total ruin of the world he was preserved together with his small family, so today the death which is set forth in baptism is to us an entrance into life, and no salvation can be hoped for, unless we be separated from the world."[2] In other words, Calvin argues that Peter speaks of the sign of baptism in order to refer us to the salvation in Christ that separates us from the world through death.

We need not rely on Calvin, however, for Peter himself provides a definitive caveat regarding his use of *baptisma*. Having written that "baptism . . . now saves," the apostle provides a qualification that limits our understanding of his reference to "baptism."

---

1. Peter J. Leithart, "Baptism and Justification," on-line at http://www.leithart.com/archives/001238.php. Here, as in other writings, Leithart and others who argue for baptismal regeneration, baptismal justification, and so on simply assume that the New Testament use of *baptizo* and *baptisma* refers primarily to the rite—that is, to the sign and not the thing signified.

2. John Calvin, *The Epistle of Paul the Apostle to the Hebrews; The First and Second Epistles of St. Peter*, ed. David W. Torrance and Thomas F. Torrance, trans. William B. Johnston, Calvin's New Testament Commentaries 12 (Grand Rapids: Eerdmans, 1994), 295.

First, Peter tells us what he does not mean: "Not as a removal of dirt from the body." It is hard to see how one might deny that Peter is referring to the outward act of washing with water, and, hence, to the rite of baptism itself. As Karen Jobes warns us, Peter means that "water baptism is not a 'ticket to heaven' that exempts them from subsequent issues of morality."[3] Peter Davids adds, "While baptism does consist in a washing in water, it is not this outward washing . . . that is salvific. The water does not have a magical quality; neither does the outward ritual."[4] This answers an important question: Are there instances when the New Testament speaks of baptism but does not want us to focus on the external rite itself? Not only does 1 Peter 3:21 show that there is at least one instance, so that we may rightly ask this question about other verses, but this is the occasion when an apostle most directly addresses this concern. Peter is quick to say, "No, not the rite itself!" If anything, this should constitute a rule and not an exception regarding the New Testament use of *baptisma* and *baptizo* in the context of teaching on salvation. Indeed, the concern that many pastors and scholars share today about an excessive reliance on sacramental grace seems validated by the apostle's own concern. Why else is Peter so quick to point us away from the outward act? Alexander Nisbet states the concern eloquently:

> There is no small hazard of people's placing too much in the external and outward part of the ordinances, as if that of itself were of some efficacy for salvation; against which the ministers of Christ have no less need to guard in their doctrine, than against peoples' undervaluing of the ordinances: for after that the Apostle has asserted baptism to be the means of our salvation answerable to the Ark, lest any might persuade themselves of salvation because they had received the external baptism, he adds as a guard, not the putting away of the filth of the flesh.[5]

This consideration explains the consternation of many today when neo-sacerdotalists trumpet Peter's statement, "baptism . . . now saves," as grounds for excessive teaching regarding the sacraments.

3. Karen Jobes, *1 Peter* (Grand Rapids: Baker, 2005), 255.
4. Peter H. Davids, *The First Epistle of Peter* (Grand Rapids: Eerdmans, 1990), 144.
5. Alexander Nisbet, *1 & 2 Peter* (1658; repr., Edinburgh: Banner of Truth, 1982), 149–50.

Secondly, we should ask what Peter does mean by writing that "baptism . . . now saves." He is not, he insists, referring to "a removal of dirt from the body," so what does Peter mean?

As Peter proceeds, he qualifies "baptism" positively: "but as an appeal to God for a good conscience, through the resurrection of Jesus Christ" (3:21). This expression also raises questions. There are two main options for Peter's meaning, both of which may be right. First, ancient baptismal rites involved the taking of pledges (the word "appeal" in the English Standard Version often being rendered as "pledge" in other translations). Davids explains, "Baptism is a response to God in answer to questions placed by the baptizer (e.g., 'Do you commit yourself to follow Christ?')."[6] Secondly, Peter refers here to salvific blessings that flow from faith in Christ. When we pledge ourselves to Jesus, receiving his saving work in faith, we are delivered from judgment and death and inwardly renewed with a good conscience, just as Noah was saved from the flood through faith. Baptism signifies and seals the reality of believers coming "to God to give them a good conscience and cleanse them from the guilt of sin."[7]

Peter's key statement is the one that comes last in verse 21: "through the resurrection of Jesus Christ." The apostle's careful construction links Christ's resurrection not to our baptism but to the water that saved Noah. Noah was "brought safely *through water*," and we are delivered "*through the resurrection* of Jesus Christ." As Noah's flood meant life to him and death to his tormentors, so does Christ's resurrection deliver us from the wicked world into eternal life. Christ's resurrection serves as a synecdoche for his entire redemptive achievement in the covenant of grace—death, resurrection, and ascension. As baptism draws our attention to water, it signifies the resurrection as that through which the believer is saved.

REGENERATION OR SANCTIFICATION?

These considerations give us a biblical entry into many questions today regarding sacramental grace. Are the sacraments for regeneration or sanctification? The question itself needs some elaboration. Another way to state this is to ask, "For what purpose did Christ institute the sacraments? Did he give us baptism to *effect* our salvation in Christ or to *signify* and *seal*

6. Davids, *The First Epistle of Peter*, 145.
7. Jobes, *1 Peter*, 255.

our redemption in Christ? Does God communicate his grace to us in the sacraments so as to *cause* our salvation or rather does sacramental grace *strengthen* us *in* our salvation?"

The very language of 1 Peter 3:21 introduces us to a terminological difficulty. Peter says, "baptism . . . now saves." But, in *ordo salutis* terms, what does he mean by "saves"? Should we think of regeneration or justification or sanctification? Salvation is a broad term into which these may all fit. But are they all appropriate when relating the sacraments to salvation? The same situation occurs in the Westminster Standards, where the Larger Catechism says, "The sacraments become effectual means of salvation" (WLC 161).

This situation has occasioned considerable debate. In the 2003 colloquium between advocates and critics of the "Auburn Avenue Theology," or "Federal Vision," I had the task of responding to Douglas Wilson's paper on the sacraments. Citing the above statement in the Larger Catechism, Wilson agreed that baptism does not "automatically or inexorably" save. But he did insist that the Confession's language requires its subscribers to assert that in the case of those who are saved—that is, the elect—baptism is the effectual means of their salvation. In doing so, he appealed to 1 Peter 3:21, a proof text to Larger Catechism 161, noting the language "baptism . . . now saves" without Peter's obvious caveat. Using the example of a man who was baptized as a child and then came to saving faith later in life, Wilson argued that we must understand that his infant baptism was the cause of his later salvation. Wilson explains, "He got saved because the grace of his baptism was finally kicking in."[8]

In response to Wilson, I noted my concern that Peter's and the Confession's general term "saves" or "salvation" was being appropriated without discrimination. Let me quote from my paper:

> Wilson contends that we should assert that the sacraments convey saving grace. That is an unfortunate designation, lacking the specificity our debate requires. We use the term salvation for all the benefits conveyed to believers in Christ. Salvation includes justification and sanctification. So we may all agree that saving grace is involved, without getting to the point. The issue at hand is whether or not the sacraments convey a grace

8. Douglas Wilson, "Sacramental Efficacy in the Westminster Standards," in E. Calvin Beisner, ed., *The Auburn Avenue Theology: Pros and Cons* (Ft. Lauderdale, FL: Knox Theological Seminary, 2004), lines 107–242.

that initiates salvation, that is, one that involves initial regeneration or otherwise creates a saving relationship with God that did not exist prior to the grace conveyed by the sacrament.[9]

We both will agree that baptism conveys grace to believer. But the question at hand concerns the effect of the grace conveyed through baptism. More succinctly, does baptismal grace "kick in" prior to belief, so that "baptism . . . now saves" in the sense of bringing the sinner from death into life, or does baptismal grace "kick in" in response to faith, so that it strengthens the faith by which alone the sinner comes to eternal life?

So far as the Westminster Standards are concerned, the answer is that while in some places the broad term "salvation" may suggest an unqualified endorsement of "saving grace" in the sacraments, the Standards elsewhere place clear limits on the nature of this efficacious grace. The clearest instance is in the Confession's treatment of saving faith. Here, primacy is given to the instrumentality of God's Word over that of the sacraments in conveying "the grace of faith":

> The grace of faith, whereby the elect are enabled to believe to the saving of their souls, is the work of the Spirit of Christ in their hearts, and is ordinarily wrought by the ministry of the Word, by which also, and by the administration of the sacraments, and prayer, it is increased and strengthened. (14.1)

This paragraph states the case for sanctifying grace only via the sacraments. Faith is "ordinarily wrought by the ministry of the Word." But such faith is then "increased and strengthened" by the Word, the administration of the sacraments, and prayer. In other words, the faith that saves results from the Spirit's work of applying God's Word to our hearts. This paragraph elegantly sums up many statements in the Westminster Standards that insist "that the sacraments convey only what may be called *sanctificational* grace, or . . . *edifying* grace."[10] Michael Horton explains, "Through them, God strengthens the faith that he creates through the

9. Richard D. Phillips, "Response to 'Sacramental Efficacy in the Westminster Standards,'" in E. Calvin Beisner, ed., *The Auburn Avenue Theology: Pros and Cons* (Ft. Lauderdale, FL: Knox Theological Seminary, 2004), lines 88–95.

10. Ibid., lines 98–99.

preaching of the gospel."[11] Therefore, just as Peter's caveat should shape our understanding of baptismal teaching throughout the New Testament—referring "not as the removal of dirt from the body, but as an appeal to God for a good conscience, through the resurrection of Jesus Christ"—so also the clear teaching of the Westminster Confession in 14.1 ought to shape our reading of "baptism" and "salvation" throughout the Standards.

Moreover, the unbiased reader of the New Testament is bound to draw the same conclusion as that of the Westminster Confession. Over and again, we are taught that salvation comes through believing the Bible's testimony concerning Jesus Christ. John writes, "to all who did receive him, who believed in his name, he gave the right to become children of God" (John 1:12). Paul answered the Philippian jailor's question by saying, "Believe in the Lord Jesus, and you will be saved" (Acts 16:31). Peter himself assigns the beginning of salvation life by writing, "You have been born again, not of perishable seed but of imperishable, through the living and abiding word of God" (1 Peter 1:23). This is not to denigrate sacramental grace, thus falling into the error so common in recent evangelicalism. It is true that God provides saving grace through baptism: the increase and strengthening of faith that pertains to sanctification. But to fail to make this distinction is no less an error than to emphasize Peter's teaching that "baptism . . . now saves," without including his urgent caveat that directs us away from an unbalanced emphasis on ritual religion.

SIGNS AND SEALS OF THE COVENANT OF GRACE

In the context of this specific debate, the distinction between *regenerating* or *sanctifying* grace is a serviceable one, the point being that sacramental grace does not *cause* or *initiate* our salvation, but rather strengthens that faith through which we are saved. But these terms suffer from imprecision when we turn from the theological questions to the biblical data. The terms *regeneration, justification,* and *sanctification* belong to the *ordo salutis*: the description of the way salvation comes to us in Christ. More accurately, though, the sacraments relate to the *historia salutis*—not to what God does

11. Michael S. Horton, *Covenant and Eschatology* (Louisville: Westminster John Knox, 2002), 270.

in us, but God did in his redemptive-historical work through Jesus Christ.[12] We see this clearly in 1 Peter 3:21, where Peter relates baptism to salvation not in terms of either our *regeneration* or *sanctification*, but in terms of Christ's *resurrection*. Biblically, the manner in which sacraments convey God's grace is as *signs* and *seals* of God's redemptive work for us in the covenant of grace.

This is, in fact, the Westminster Confession's primary description of the sacraments: "Sacraments are holy signs and seals of the covenant of grace, immediately instituted by God, to represent Christ, and His benefits; and to confirm our interest in Him" (27.1). This is precisely how we see baptism functioning in 1 Peter 3:21. Baptism is a sign—that is, it points to something—and that something is salvation through the death and resurrection of Jesus Christ. This is why Noah's story serves Peter's purpose so well. The way that Noah was saved—passing through judgment by entering the death of the ark's dark interior and emerging into new life through the flood waters—is a reminder of how we are saved in Christ. Peter says, "Baptism . . . corresponds to this." Baptism signifies now the same thing that Noah's salvation signified then: "For Christ also suffered once for sins, the righteous for the unrighteous, that he might bring us to God, being put to death in the flesh but made alive in the spirit" (1 Peter 3:18). Moreover, baptism is a seal. It is not just a sign that is posted somewhere "out there" but is applied personally to us by God's appointed ministry. As we pledge ourselves to him in faith, seeking cleansing from sin and a renewing of our conscience, baptism seals to us God's promise of salvation through Jesus Christ.

There is much confusion today regarding the word "seal." Sacerdotalists use it in almost a mystical sense, as if God's saving grace were being infused into us or impressed upon our souls the way wax paper is melted onto a leaf in a child's school project. But, instead, the Bible speaks of sacraments as a seal in the way Peter does: as a pledge certifying the receipt of saving blessings. Michael Horton explains that the sacraments serve as means of grace "not in terms of the analogy of infusion, but in terms of the analogy of declaration."[13] The apostle Paul gives this same understanding of sacramental grace: as a sign and seal of what we take possession of by faith alone. Writing of Abraham and the sacrament of the old covenant, Paul says, "He

---

12. I am indebted to Michael Horton for this observation, in a personal critique of the Auburn Avenue Theology debate.

13. Horton, *Covenant and Eschatology*, 270.

received the sign of circumcision as a seal of the righteousness that he had by faith" (Rom. 4:11).

It is in these terms that we must understand God's effectual grace for us in the sacraments: as *signs* and *seals*. We do not receive the saving benefits of the covenant of grace by baptism, but rather through faith alone as it believes the Word of God concerning Jesus Christ. So what role does the sacrament play? The Westminster Larger Catechism explains, "A sacrament is a holy ordinance instituted by Christ in his church, to signify, seal, and exhibit unto those that are within the covenant of grace, the benefits of his mediation" (WLC 162). In other words, the benefits of Christ's mediation are received through faith alone, but then these benefits are signified, sealed, and exhibited to us in the sacraments. To some, this may seem to be no grace at all, or very little at most. They may think, "We don't get anything from the sacraments; we are only shown what we already have." That is the memorialist position that has so impoverished evangelical religion. Such a view can only happen in a culture that knows nothing of the Bible's covenant theology. If you understand that we are saved through faith into an unbreakable covenant bond, then you will think differently. It is possible to recognize baptism as a dramatic representation of the gospel, but still to think that it matters little whether you get wet or stay dry in the pews. But when you realize that baptism is not only a sign, but also a seal by which God covenantally pledges all that he has promised through the mediation of Christ, then you will assault the chancel so that it may be applied by God's minister personally to you. Then, recognizing the privileges that confer to your children through your covenant headship, you will bring your children with you, just as the Philippian jailer did after he was justified through faith alone and then received the covenant seal of baptism.

In his sermons on Ephesians, John Calvin offers an illustration that helpfully relates saving faith and God's sovereign election. He notes that we are saved because of God's sovereign decree in election. But then he observes that we know that this is true of us personally through our faith in Christ. Calvin writes, "God has his eternal counsel, and he always reserves to himself the chief and original record of which he gives us a copy by faith."[14] So our possession of saving faith serves as the certificate given to us by God of our sovereign election. But if you have ever traveled abroad, you know that

---

14. John Calvin, *Sermons on Ephesians* (Edinburgh: Banner of Truth, 1973), 47.

a passport is made official by the seal stamped upon it. It may be genuine without it, but this cannot be objectively attested. The same may be said of the sealing grace of the sacraments, received through saving faith in Christ. It means everything for us to have saving faith, for which the Bible itself provides tests of genuineness. Ultimately, it is through the validity of our faith that we gain assurance that we possess an unbreakable bond to Christ and his benefits. But when it comes to the increase and strengthening of our faith, and our precious assurance of God's mercy and love, we are further blessed by the seal of baptism, administered to those either raised in or received into the covenant community of the Church of Jesus Christ. The same may be said of the Lord's Supper and its sealing grace. It is one thing to consider yourself a believer, and it is another to be admitted to Christ's covenant meal to be assured of your participation in his body and blood and to be fed by the grace of his Holy Spirit.

What does this have to say about the idea of baptismal regeneration? Certainly the above considerations must cause us to reject the idea that those who are spiritually dead enter into spiritual life through the bare ritual of baptism. But it is interesting to note that the term "regeneration" admits of both an initiatory meaning and an on-going meaning. We were made alive in our conversion and believers continue to be made more and more alive to God throughout our Christian experience. This is why Calvin favored the term *vivification*, since it combines the once-for-all new birth and its never-ending progress in our lives that we refer to as sanctification. The fruit of God's life-giving Spirit is always life and holiness through faith in Christ, and as faith is increased and strengthened by the Word, the sacraments, and prayer, this work is mightily advanced. In this latter sense, that of the increase of faith and spiritual life, we may rightly relate regeneration to the grace of the sacraments. As the administration of baptism and the Lord's Supper signifies and seals the benefits of Christ's saving work to the believer's soul, existing faith is increased and strengthened with untold blessings in our lives.

HAVEN'T YOU BEEN BAPTIZED?

In conclusion, let us return to Peter's exhortation so that we do not fail to appropriate his purpose in saying that "baptism . . . now saves." It is important that we avoid sacerdotal errors that threaten us with a reliance on external rites, so that our sacramentology finds itself in accord with the Scriptures. But Peter's concern was not merely, or even primarily, related to doctrinal apprehension. Peter did not bring up baptism in hopes that his readers would be saved that way, since he addresses them as those already saved. Nor did he intend merely that his reference to baptism and the salvation it signifies and seals should warm our hearts with assurance of salvation. Peter brought up the topic as a battle cry for our conflict with both the world and the sinful tendencies within our own hearts. In fact, Peter's reference to baptism serves as a motivation within the long section that runs from 2:13 to 4:19 in which the apostle exhorts Christians to live joyfully under affliction in submissive reliance on God.

"Haven't you been baptized?" Peter asks. By this, he means, "Haven't you pledged yourself to Jesus Christ, entering into his deliverance from this wicked world through death and into resurrection life?" If so, he argues, let us not merely be saved with Christ from this world, but let us also live like Christ in this world. The center of his appeal is found in 2:21–25:

> For to this you have been called, because Christ also suffered for you, leaving you an example, so that you might follow in his steps. He committed no sin, neither was deceit found in his mouth. When he was reviled, he did not revile in return; when he suffered, he did not threaten, but continued entrusting himself to him who judges justly. He himself bore our sins in his body on the tree, that we might die to sin and live to righteousness. By his wounds you have been healed. For you were straying like sheep, but have now returned to the Shepherd and Overseer of your souls.

How does this apply to us? Peter calls us to live in submission to Christ in whatever place we are found and in whatever role God has assigned us for the display of his glory. Are you under civil authority? Regardless of what the emperor does, he says, "Be subject for the Lord's sake to every human institution . . . that by doing good you should put to silence the ignorance of foolish people" (2:13–15). Are you an employee? "Be subject to your masters with all respect, not only to the good and gentle but also to the unjust. . . . If when you do good and suffer for it you endure, this is a gracious thing in the sight of God" (2:18–20). Are you a wife? "Be subject to your own husbands, so that even if some do not obey the word, they may be won without a word by the conduct of their wives" (3:1). Are you a church member? "Have unity of mind, sympathy, brotherly love, a tender heart, and a humble mind. . . . Bless, for to this you were called, that you may obtain a blessing" (3:8–9). Are you living in the midst of dark and unbelieving world? Then, "In your hearts regard Christ the Lord as holy, always being prepared to make a defense to anyone who asks you for a reason for the hope that is in you" (3:15).

Thus we see the meaning of Peter's teaching as it relates to baptism. The grace of Christ is to characterize our lives—not merely in some ideal world but in *this* world. We are to pattern ourselves on Christ in a world like Noah's world—a dark world under judgment and imminent destruction. How? Why? Because God has provided an ark for you, the cross of Jesus Christ. The cross means death to this present world, on which the floods once roared and on which the fires soon will burn. But as the ark floated above those judging waters, carrying Noah and his family into a bright, new world, the cross of Christ will bear you to the empty tomb and into the resurrection light of the new creation. Thus, he concludes:

> Baptism, which corresponds to this, now saves you, not as a removal of dirt from the body but as an appeal to God for a good conscience, through the resurrection of Jesus Christ, who has gone into heaven and is at the right hand of God, with angels, authorities, and powers having been subjected to him. Since therefore Christ suffered in the flesh, arm yourselves with the same way of thinking, for whoever has suffered in the flesh has ceased from sin. . . . The end of all things is at hand; therefore be self-controlled and sober-minded for the sake of your prayers. Above all, keep loving one another earnestly, since love covers a multitude of sins. Show hospitality to one another without grumbling. As each has received a gift, use it to serve one another, as good stewards of God's varied grace: whoever speaks, as one who speaks oracles of God; whoever serves, as one who serves by the strength that God supplies—in order that in everything God may be glorified through Jesus Christ. To him belong glory and dominion forever and ever. Amen. (1 Peter 3:21–4:11)

II

The Theology of Norman Shepherd: A Study in Development, 1963–2006

GUY PRENTISS WATERS

THE LIFE AND MINISTRY of Dr. O. Palmer Robertson will be rightly remembered for his classroom instruction while on the faculties of Westminster, Covenant, and Reformed Theological Seminaries; for his many books, reviews, and articles; and for his pioneering work with the African Bible College. One of Dr. Robertson's most important services to the church is among his least recognized contributions: his labors on the faculty of Westminster Theological Seminary during the controversy relating to Professor Norman Shepherd. In the course of this controversy (1975–1982), Robertson determinedly maintained that Shepherd had departed from the confessional standards he had sworn to uphold. Specifically, Shepherd's formulations of the doctrine of justification were incompatible with those of the Westminster Standards. There has been a recent resurgence of Shepherd's views concerning not only justification but also covenant, election, and baptism. The Federal Vision, while not to be identified with the theology of Shepherd, is nevertheless sufficiently indebted to that theology as to bring Shepherd's doctrine before the attention of the church once again.

We will therefore pursue an historical overview of the development of Norman Shepherd's theology and the controversy that surrounded his teaching at Westminster Theological Seminary (Philadelphia) in the 1970s.[1] We can examine Shepherd's writings in three groupings: before, during, and after the seminary controversy.

Before the Controversy: 1963–1973

Having completed a ThM thesis under professor John Murray on the "Image of God," and having undertaken post-graduate study in the Netherlands, Shepherd returned to Philadelphia to teach systematic theology in 1963. Within the first decade of his teaching career, there is nothing in his published output that would alert the reader to the positions that Shepherd began to propound in the mid–1970s. Most of his writings are book reviews, whether of such modernist authors as Karl Barth, Hendrikus Berkhof, John Macquarrie, or of such evangelical and Reformed writers as Ernest Kevan and Robert Lightner. With the benefit of hindsight, we are able to see two concerns that Shepherd expresses in this time period which will underlie his later controversial positions.

First, we find within Shepherd an express dissatisfaction with traditional systematic theological formulations and an interest in reshaping the theological project by means of distinctly biblical-theological categories. In 1962–63, Shepherd published a review of the first volume of J. Oliver Buswell's *A Systematic Theology of the Christian Religion.*[2] It is clear from this review that Shepherd is disappointed in Buswell's work, both in terms of some of its conclusions, and in terms of its usefulness as a Reformed response to modern theology. Part of Shepherd's disappointment also stems from the manner in which Buswell had undertaken his project.

---

1. Two of the most helpful and comprehensive surveys of this controversy are to be found in O. Palmer Robertson, *The Current Justification Controversy* (Unicoi, TN: The Trinity Foundation, 2003) and A. Donald MacLeod, *W. Stanford Reid: An Evangelical Calvinist in the Academy* (Montreal: McGill-Queen's University Press, 2004), 257–79. An earlier survey, contemporary to the Shepherd controversy at Westminster Theological Seminary, is contained within "Reasons and Specifications Supporting the Action of the Board of Trustees in Removing Professor Shepherd," 1–11.

2. Review of James Oliver Buswell Jr., "A Systematic Theology of the Christian Religion. Volume One: Theism and Biblical Anthropology." *Westminster Theological Journal* (hereafter *WTJ*) 25 (1962–63): 68–73.

[T]his reviewer suggests that there is still need for a Reformed Systematic Theology giving much more space than the present volume does to a painstaking derivation of the doctrines of the faith through the exegesis of Scripture. That will necessitate bringing to bear the insights of Biblical Theology upon the choice, organization, and development of materials included in the systematic treatment. Such a Systematic Theology will give evidence of an awareness of the dogma-historical and contemporary problems involved, but will not allow these to control the discussion. The net result should be an entirely new work, most likely departing more radically from established patterns than Buswell has done, but only for the sake of a more faithful exposition of biblical truth, which is, after all, its best defense.[3]

It is unclear from this comment whether Shepherd faults Buswell's work with a lack of exegesis *simpliciter*, or a lack of exegesis as the discipline of biblical theology has conceived the task of exegesis. It is clear, however, that Shepherd is proposing a new way of proceeding with the theological project, a way that will likely reconfigure the "choice, organization, and development of materials included in the systematic treatment." While he does not elaborate how he conceives such a project, it is fair to say that Shepherd nevertheless regards at least some fundamental components of the traditional systematic theological enterprise to be negotiable.

This concern finds a parallel in another review from this period. In a 1965 review of Kevan's *The Grace of Law*, Shepherd quotes Kevan saying that the contemporary church needs to "listen . . . again to the voice of the Puritans and receiv[e] the truth to which they bore testimony."[4] Shepherd vehemently dissents from advocating that "masses of people . . . read Puritan writings," which, he concedes, "Kevan does not say."[5] While the Puritans "serve to help us see that truth," Shepherd says, "we are most in harmony with the Puritans when we seek to find answers where they found them, in the Word of God, and not in the tradition of the elders."[6] Shepherd is by no means categorically dismissing the insights or conclusions that Puritan

---

3. Ibid., 72–73. Emphasis mine.
4. Kevan, *The Grace of Law* (London: Carey Kingsgate, 1964) 13, cited in Norman Shepherd, Review of Ernest Kevan, "The Grace of Law." *WTJ* 27 (1964–65): 214.
5. Ibid.
6. Ibid., 215.

theology reached. His concern reflects, however, a biblicism that is natively suspicious of "tradition."[7]

We must note, however, that Shepherd is ready to defend the Protestant Scholastics as true heirs of Calvin and to accept the legitimacy of scholastic categories. This is nowhere more evident than in his 1973 response to Otto Gründler's attempt "to seek respectability for a radical departure from orthodoxy by means of an appeal to the Reformers, and to find in classic Reformed theology a rapid deterioration of Reformed principles."[8] The difference between Calvin and Zanchius, Shepherd concludes, may be defined not as fundamentally theological but as terminological.[9] In conclusion, then, we may observe that Shepherd, in a polemical context, is unwilling to shed scholastic language (thereby conceding a "Calvin versus the Calvinists" hypothesis). We may also observe, however, that Shepherd, in a non-polemical context, expresses varying degrees of discomfort with the use of tradition in Reformed theology and the traditional systematic-theological project.

A second area that anticipates a concern reflected in Shepherd's controversial writings is also broached in his review of the first volume of Buswell's *Systematic Theology*. This concern addresses the relationship between the decree of election and the mandate of evangelism. Shepherd reflects on the significance of Buswell's contention that God has savingly revealed himself to men outside the Scripture and of Buswell's claim that "the reason and ground for the punishment of *any* individual is his rejection of the love of God in Christ"[10]:

> There is no reason why the fact that God has elected certain men to salvation, and also ordained the means thereto, should cause any embar-

7. One might compare the later and sharper comments directed against the Puritans in Shepherd's Review of Helmut Thielicke, "The Evangelical Faith, Volume I." *WTJ* 38 (1976): 368–71. Here he suggests that contemporary interest in the "Puritan pietistic literature within the orthodox Reformed community" may be indicative of "a spirit very much attuned to the modern world in spite of appearances to the contrary," *viz.* the emphasis on anthropology in theology undertaken in the tradition of the Enlightenment, 369.

8. Norman Shepherd, "Zanchius on Saving Faith." *WTJ* 36 (1973–74): 47.

9. "It appears, therefore, that as with the object of faith, so also with the nature of faith, the distance between Zanchi and Calvin is not as great as the difference between the terminology of illumination/trust and habit/act might initially suggest," ibid., 42. Compare Shepherd's defense of Turretin and other Reformed theologians within the Protestant Scholastic tradition in his Review of James Daane, "The Freedom of God. A Study of Election and Pulpit." *WTJ* 36 (1973–74): 305–33.

10. Shepherd, "Review of Buswell," 71.

rassment. What should cause the embarrassment is the fact that we have been commissioned to preach the gospel to every creature, and we have not done it. If men do not have the gospel it is squarely our fault. . . . It is not the decree of God but the written Word by which we are to judge the competence of our missionary endeavor.[11]

Shepherd expresses here a defense of the Reformed doctrine of election against charges that it is at cross purposes with evangelistic effectiveness or the project of evangelism. In so doing, he maintains the doctrine in its integrity. By 1975, Shepherd's defense of election had changed considerably. That later defense entails substantial reworking of the doctrine, as we shall see. Shepherd's defense of the Reformed doctrine of election, in response to Buswell's concerns, informs us that, as early as 1965, the attack on this doctrine was a matter of concern to him and required defense.

In 1973, Shepherd mounted another defense of the Reformed doctrine of election in an extensive review-article outlining and criticizing James Daane's *The Freedom of God: A Study of Election and Pulpit*.[12] Like his defense of election eight years earlier, and unlike his defense of election two years later, Shepherd upholds the Reformed doctrine of election. In *The Freedom of God*, Daane argues that "the doctrine of election is a central and indispensable element of the Reformed faith," but is "not being preached from Reformed pulpits."[13] Shepherd agrees with Daane in that observation, but dissents from Daane's assessment of the reasons behind the absence of election from within the Reformed pulpit. Daane contends that "the reason for the silence . . . is simply that the doctrine of election as traditionally formulated and understood cannot be preached."[14]

Shepherd's response to Daane consists largely of two parts. First, Shepherd attempts to vindicate the formulations of the Protestant Scholastics against Daane's attacks. He argues that Daane's efforts to understand the Canons of Dordt apart from the scholastic theological matrix in which they were conceived are ill-grounded.[15] Contending that the Protestant Scholastics were not guilty of "rationalistic determinism," Shepherd attempts to show the essential continuity existing between Calvin and his theological

11. Ibid.
12. Shepherd, Review of Daane, "The Freedom of God."
13. Ibid., 305.
14. Ibid.
15. Ibid., 307–10.

211

successors concerning the decree.[16] Positively, Shepherd observes that "the appreciation of the historical covenants arose in the context of decretal theology, not in the context of Lutheranism. . . ."[17] One may not, therefore, pit "decree" against "history." There is nothing necessarily incompatible between them.

Second, Shepherd devotes the remainder of his review to citing problems and contradictions within Daane's own conception of the decree. One matter to which Shepherd devotes particular attention is Daane's contention that the proper and "interchangeable" objects of election are "Christ, Israel, and Church."[18] Specifically Daane argues that "the Bible knows nothing of an individual election with a direct reference to eternity; it knows only of a divine election that is historical, one that moves and is actualized in the continuity of father and son, family and nation."[19] This is, as Daane contends, a non-numerical conception of election, and it is to this conception that Shepherd responds in defense of the biblical and confessional doctrine.

Two issues or criticisms raised by Shepherd in his review of Daane are as follows: (1) Daane's charge that the decree and history (covenant) are necessarily incompatible, and (2) Daane's charge that a decretal and individual or "numerical" doctrine of election is incompatible with faithful gospel preaching. Shepherd never concedes the truth of either of these criticisms. In 1973, his response to Daane evidences complete sympathy with what the Reformed have confessionally affirmed concerning the decree, individual election, and the covenants. In 1975, however, it will become evident that these same concerns have occasioned significant and unorthodox reformulations in Shepherd's "Covenant Context of Evangelism." In other words, Shepherd would in 1975 express dissatisfaction with the traditional responses to Daane that he had advanced in 1973.

YEARS OF CONTROVERSY: 1974–82

The years 1974 through 1982 reflect the emergence of Shepherd's controversial formulations concerning election and reprobation, covenant, baptism, and justification.

16. Ibid., 316, 310–11.
17. Ibid., 318.
18. Ibid., 324.
19. Daane, *The Freedom of God*, 14, 115, cited in ibid., 327.

We may divide these years into two main groupings. First, 1974–76 evidence important changes in Shepherd's thought, evidenced by two critical transitional articles and addresses, the first published in 1974, and the second written in 1975 and published in 1976. Second, 1976–1982 witnessed the public controversy within Westminster Seminary and the Orthodox Presbyterian Church that resulted in Shepherd's removal from his theological chair at the seminary and his withdrawal from the OPC into the Christian Reformed Church.

1974–76

The first published evidence of Shepherd's deviation from historic Reformed theology surfaced in the 1974 article, "The Resurrections of Revelation 20."[20] Although this article is rarely, if ever, cited in discussions of Shepherd's theology, it is a crucial and transitional piece. "The Resurrections of Revelation 20" appeared amidst a series of pieces published in the *Westminster Theological Journal* between 1972 and 1977 addressing the "resurrections" of Revelation 20:4–6.[21] Strikingly, Shepherd's thesis attracted little notice within this discussion and, for all intents and purposes, appears to have been largely ignored.[22]

In this article, Shepherd mounts a response to one of the strongest *prima facie* arguments for premillennialism, *viz.* the "two resurrections" of Revelation 20. Shepherd's concerns, however, are greater than a narrow exegetical treatment of three verses from Revelation. He sets forth a program that he cautions is "programmatic rather than definitive," and is designed to produce a "more unified conception of . . . 'individual eschatology' and 'general eschatology,' as well as a more unified conception of soteriology and eschatology."[23] In this respect, Shepherd is telegraphing to the readership of the *Journal* a slice of a larger project in the works.

20. Norman Shepherd, "The Resurrections of Revelation 20." *WTJ* 37 (1974–75): 34–43.

21. James A. Hughes, "Revelation 20:4–6 and the Question of the Millennium." *WTJ* 35 (1972–73): 281–302; Meredith G. Kline, "The First Resurrection." *WTJ* 37 (1974–75): 366–375; J. Ramsey Michaels, "The First Resurrection: A Response." *WTJ* 39 (1976–77): 100–109; Meredith G. Kline, "The First Resurrection: A Reaffirmation." *WTJ* 39 (1976–77): 110–119; Philip Edgcumbe Hughes, "The First Resurrection: Another Interpretation." *WTJ* 39 (1976–77): 315–18.

22. The only noticeable mention of Shepherd's article appears to be a reference in a footnote within Kline's first contribution noting "the negative conclusion at least that 'the first resurrection' is not a bodily resurrection," "The First Resurrection," 366, n.1.

23. Shepherd, "The Resurrections of Revelation 20," 43, n.9.

"The Resurrections of Revelation 20" begins with an exposition of Revelation 20:4–6. Shepherd sets out to answer precisely who are the participants in this "first resurrection," and what is the precise nature of the movement from "death" to "life" described by the apostle. Shepherd argues that the two resurrections of Revelation need to be correlated with the two resurrections mentioned elsewhere in the Johannine and Pauline literature. When we do so, he concludes, we find, against pre-millennial interpreters, that the "first resurrection" does not "refer to the moment of physical death." Against many Reformed interpreters, however, Shepherd refuses to identify the "first resurrection" with " 'conversion' to which baptism is later appended." [24] Rather, Shepherd argues, this phrase refers to the "experience of baptism." [25] In fact, he says, this "baptism is even more properly resurrection than is the resurrection of the body." [26]

Shepherd proceeds to argue that "baptism" is an architectonic component of New Testament theology. Because the "first resurrection" entails movement from "death" to "life," the Johannine language of "new birth" and the Pauline language of "new creation" therefore need to be understood as specifically referring to the "origin of new life which the baptized have in Jesus Christ as arising from the will of God." [27]

This relationship among first resurrection/birth/creation is parallel to a similar relationship in the New Testament: second resurrection/new birth/new creation. The former categories refer to "personal" realities, and the latter categories refer to "cosmic" realities. [28] Both conceptual clusters (first and second resurrection/birth and new birth/creation and new creation) are to be understood as "grounded in union with Christ." [29] It is this common foundation that establishes a genetic tie

24. Ibid., 36.

25. Ibid., 37, 36.

26. Ibid., 37. Shepherd continues, "The just who are alive at the return of the Lord will not be resurrected in the body but will be transformed. The righteous dead who do rise bodily at the last day do not again assume mortality but immortality. Not resuscitation but transformation is the leading feature of resurrection, and the foundational transformation and transition takes place at baptism, the first resurrection. The ordinal number may suggest eminence as well as sequence. Christ was raised from the dead in the fullest sense of the word, although his body saw no corruption. Those joined to him by baptism experience resurrection with him before their bodies see corruption," ibid., 37–38.

27. Ibid., 38.

28. Ibid., 41.

29. Ibid.

between the "personal" and "cosmic" transformations envisioned within both sets of categories.

> The cosmic resurrection, or creation, or birth, toward which all things are pressing is really cosmic salvation in union with Christ. It is a definitive baptism into Christ, cosmic in scope, of which the baptism at the time of Noah and the repeated baptisms administered in the church are but anticipations.[30]

This creative proposal yields two important implications that Norman Shepherd is careful to delineate in this article. First, one implication of the relationship between resurrection and baptism is that they are mutually explanatory. Shepherd concludes, then, that "not resuscitation but transformation is the leading feature of resurrection, and the foundational transformation and transition takes place at baptism, the first resurrection."[31] He speaks, as a result, of "the transformation and transition wrought in baptism," arguing that Scripture elsewhere speaks of this "transformation and transition . . . as creation and as birth."[32]

Shepherd, however, will demur from applying the language of "regeneration" to the event of baptism. He prefers the term "begetting or generation" because of Scripture's application of the language of "regeneration" exclusively to the "end-time cosmic cataclysm" (Matt. 19:28).[33] Shepherd is undoubtedly driven by a biblicistic concern to limit modern theological vocabulary strictly to the biblical incidences of those words. It is clear, however, that Shepherd's understanding of what happens at an individual's baptism is what Reformed theology has historically called "regeneration." In his understanding of baptism as a transformational event whereby the believer is inwardly or morally changed, Shepherd does not entirely shed traditional language.

Shepherd's proposal raises a second concern. In his judgment, the Reformed *ordo salutis* requires revisiting. Shepherd insists that because of the parallel relationship between "cosmic salvation" and "personal salvation," we expect, and in fact find, a single *ordo salutis* shared between them.[34] He

30. Ibid.
31. Ibid., 38.
32. Ibid.
33. Ibid., 39.
34. Ibid., 42.

argues that in Ephesians 1:1–10, Paul "lead[s] up to the climactic affirmation of cosmic union with Christ," and in so doing, presents an order of sancti fication—adoption—justification, citing Eph. 1:4, 5, and 7, respectively.[35] Consequently, as "this order appears appropriate to the order of cosmic salvation" it is "perhaps . . . not wholly inappropriate to the order of personal salvation."[36] Having proposed this revision, Shepherd observes "of course, not sanctification, but Jesus Christ is the foundation of justification; and by the same token, not justification but Jesus Christ is the foundation of sanctification. . . . Each of the benefits of Christ is related directly to Christ."[37] Shepherd does not elaborate this statement. It is unclear whether he is simply attempting to clear a perceived misunderstanding concerning the *ordo* that he proposes, or whether he is problematizing the concept of the *ordo* altogether. At the very least, we may conclude that Shepherd evidences a marked departure from the conventional Reformed *ordo salutis* maintained by his predecessor at Westminster Theological Seminary.[38]

The second transitional piece that Shepherd drafted during this period is his "The Covenantal Context of Evangelism," initially presented in May, 1975, before a ministerial conference sponsored by the Reformed Presbyterian Church of North America, and published the next year.[39] This piece attracted the attention of Sinclair B. Ferguson, whose review of the volume in which this article appeared substantially concentrated on Shepherd's article.[40] Ferguson's review prompted Shepherd's rejoinder, published in a subsequent issue of *The Banner of Truth*.[41]

Several issues were raised in these articles which formally launched the question of Shepherd's orthodoxy before the attention of the broader Reformed community. We will presently identify two primary areas of concern and comment briefly on them.

35. Ibid.

36. Ibid., 42, n. 8.

37. Ibid.

38. See John Murray, *Redemption Accomplished and Applied* (Grand Rapids: Eerdmans, 1955).

39. "The Covenant Context of Evangelism," in *The New Testament Student*, vol. 3, *The New Testament Student and Theology*, ed. John H. Skilton (Philipsburg, NJ: Presbyterian and Reformed, 1976), 51–75.

40. Sinclair B. Ferguson, Review of John H. Skilton, ed. "The New Testament Student and Theology," *The Banner of Truth* 166–67 (Jul-Aug 1977): 59–63.

41. Norman Shepherd, "More on Covenant Evangelism: A Reply from Norman Shepherd" *The Banner of Truth* 170 (Nov 1978): 22–26.

Election and covenant. Norman Shepherd is explicit about the concerns that prompt him to address the manner in which "election" and "covenant" ought to be addressed from the Reformed pulpit. He observes, on the one hand, the charge of some that "evangelistic zeal and the Reformed faith appear to be related antithetically."[42]

> Some would argue that the particularism of the Reformed faith—election, limited atonement, irresistible grace, not to mention reprobation—makes it inherently impossible to present the gospel was good news to modern man. The gospel would hardly appear to be good news to the reprobate; and since no one knows who the elect are, no word can be addressed directly to them as such. The result is that the gospel tends to be spoken about in the third person in terms of what Christ has done for "his own." But the question is, what good news can be given to this or that particular man?

Shepherd likely has in mind James Daane's objection that the doctrines of election and reprobation destroy preaching. Shepherd rejects the acceptability of the solution to this "problem" posed by "the theology of Karl Barth," much less the conclusions of individuals who see the issues as "inexplicable paradoxes."[43] He concludes that "not all of the resources of the Reformed faith have been brought to bear in seeking a resolution of" this matter, and that the solution is to be found in the "doctrine of the covenant of grace."[44]

Shepherd argues that the Reformed have succumbed to a truncated version of the application of their theology to the work of preaching. He calls this "election evangelism" or "regeneration evangelism."[45] One's starting point, Shepherd argues, determines a particular methodology of evangelism and preaching. To make one's starting point "election" or "regeneration" is to commit oneself to a methodologically faulty mode of evangelism. Such preaching is unable to tell the sinner that Christ has died for him personally. In contrast to this "election evangelism" or "regeneration evangelism," Shepherd proposes that we adopt "covenant evangelism."[46] In so doing, he concedes the charge that the traditional or

42. Shepherd, "Covenant Context," 51.
43. Ibid., 52, 53.
44. Ibid., 53.
45. Ibid.
46. Ibid.

non-covenantal understanding of the Reformed doctrine of election and reprobation eviscerates preaching to the sinner.

How does "covenant evangelism" differ from "election" or "regeneration evangelism?" Shepherd argues from Deuteronomy 29:29 that we must be careful to distinguish the "decree" from the "covenant." Only God has access to the knowledge of which individuals are elect or reprobate. We must therefore employ "covenant language" for "covenant language is simply language which is appropriate to describe [the] unique relation" between God and man.[47] In other words, one cannot *and ought not* speak of a divine-human relationship without recourse to covenantal language.[48] This is to follow the pattern of the Scripture, for "all of Biblical [*sic*] language is covenant language."[49]

What does this mean in practice? We should address men, not in terms of decretal election or reprobation, but in terms of their covenant faithfulness. When one adopts and applies covenant evangelism, then he will address men *not* as "elect" and "reprobate," but as "covenant breakers" and "covenant keepers." Consequently, Shepherd argues, "the Reformed evangelist can and must say on the basis of John 3:16, Christ died to save you. . . . He died for people, for you and for me." While from "the perspective of election," *viz.* "election as God views election," this statement "is at best only possibly true, and may well be false," yet when understood as "covenant truth," we may address men individually in these terms.[50]

Shepherd's proposal raises two related questions. First, precisely how are we to understand the place of the decree in what is said to be the covenant language of Scripture? Shepherd allows us to say from Scripture that the decree exists, but little more. The decree has no meaningful connection with or relationship to Shepherd's covenantal perspective.

Second, how are we to reconcile Shepherd's covenant evangelism with historic Reformed theology? On the face of it, Shepherd has denied particular redemption. His response is that to speak covenantally differs from, but is nevertheless compatible with, speaking decretally. It is not sufficient, however, to assert that these two modes of speaking are compatible. It must be demonstrated. But it is precisely such a demonstration that Shepherd fails to provide.

47. Ibid.
48. Ibid., 60.
49. Shepherd, "More on Covenant Evangelism," 22.
50. Shepherd, "Covenant Context," 61–62.

Baptism and regeneration. Shepherd's formulation of covenant and election prompts him to address a second and related coupling of doctrines: baptism and regeneration. Shepherd faults what he terms the "regeneration/election" model of evangelism with a number of problems and errors: (1) use of the law of God within the context of an "impossible salvation by works" in order to drive the sinner to Christ; (2) an irresolvable tension between the inability of the sinner to believe and obey and the demands of the gospel to believe and repent; (3) a stress on indwelling corruption and a corresponding minimization of "new obedience"; (4) an inability, therefore, to offer a substantial and enduring assurance to the believer.[51] These problems have as their common denominator an inordinate "focus on man and his experience."[52]

Shepherd calls for preaching that is less focused on "experience" and more focused on "Christ." Such preaching will be "oriented to the covenant structure of Scripture."[53] How is this non-experience-focused and covenantal preaching evidenced? Shepherd affirms that "baptism rather than regeneration is the point of transition from lostness in death to salvation in life," qualifying this affirmation by asserting without argument "the position here advocated should not be confused with the sacramentalist doctrine of baptismal regeneration."[54] In response to Ferguson's criticism, Shepherd later retracted this statement,[55] and reformulated it, "baptism marks the transition from death to life."[56]

In his exchange with Ferguson, Shepherd retreats from his affirmation of baptismal regeneration. What complicates analysis of this retraction is that, even prior to this exchange, Shepherd did not understand himself to be advancing baptismal regeneration. It is, nevertheless, difficult to read Shepherd's statements here and in his 1974 *Westminster Theological Journal* article in any other way.

51. Ibid., 67–70.
52. Ibid., 70.
53. Ibid., 71.
54. Ibid., 66.
55. "I now sincerely regret that the antithetical way in which I stated my third thesis . . . gave reasonable grounds for the criticism that on the one hand baptism was isolated from faith and conversion, and on the other the sign and the thing signified were confused with each other." Shepherd, "More on Covenant Evangelism," 25.
56. Ibid.

What then are we to make of Shepherd's reformulation? If we examine it in light of his proposed decree/covenant distinction, then we are in a position better to understand what he intends to say. From the perspective of the decree, Shepherd claims that regeneration "may take place before, or after, or in conjunction with baptism; it may never take place at all."[57] From the perspective of the covenant, however, we may affirm that a man "becomes a Christian . . . when he is baptized."[58] Shepherd's formulation only successfully addresses Ferguson's concern, if the decree/covenant distinction for which Shepherd pleads is a legitimate one. It is on this very point, however, that Shepherd's retraction proves unsuccessful.

What, for Shepherd, is the place of baptism in covenant evangelism? Baptism is an appropriate emphasis within "covenantal evangelism" not only because it is commanded by Jesus in the Great Commission but also because, unlike "regeneration [which] is one of the secret things that belong to God," it is "open and obvious to all."[59] Echoing the argument in his 1974 *Westminster Theological Journal* article, Shepherd claims that baptism is "to be understood as of a piece with the total transformation which is salvation. It is the sacramental side of a total renewal (regeneration in the broad sense) of both the inner and outer man."[60] In the Great Commission, it is "coupled directly with instruction in obedience to the commands of Christ," ensuring that "covenant evangelism" will never "isolate . . . faith . . . from the call to obedience."[61] In any pastoral theology informed by covenant evangelism, baptism is going to occupy center stage.

1976–82

At this point in time, it becomes impossible to disentangle the development of Norman Shepherd's distinctive views from the controversy that attended them within Westminster Seminary and the Orthodox Presbyterian Church.[62] In 1975, the year in which "The Covenant Context of Evangelism" was drafted and delivered, reports began to surface from presbyteries that former students of Shepherd were, in their examina-

---

57. Ibid., 25.
58. Ibid.
59. Shepherd, "Covenant Context," 72.
60. Ibid., 73.
61. Ibid., 74.
62. The following account is dependant upon Robertson, *The Current Justification Controversy.*

tions, promoting an unorthodox doctrine of justification.[63] Discussions between Shepherd and other members of the faculty of Westminster soon unearthed a number of concerns regarding Shepherd's teaching. These concerns centered on the doctrine of justification. Having been charged by the faculty the previous spring to do so, Shepherd produced and presented a substantial paper before the faculty in October, 1976. In the paper, "The Relation of Good Works to Justification in the Westminster Standards," Shepherd outlined and defended his formulations concerning justification.[64] Shepherd defended these formulations in faculty discussions over a period of a year and a half, and made only cosmetic changes to the paper as a result of these discussions.[65] He has not substantially revised his conclusions in subsequent publications.

Precisely what formulations did Shepherd put forward that have proven to be so controversial? Shepherd contrasts his view of justification with one that he claims not only prevails within American evangelicalism, but also has had its origins with Luther. The prevailing evangelical doctrine of justification is said to suffer from at least three problems. First, this doctrine can be formulated in an antinomian way. It is not uncommon to find its advocates teaching that repentance and good works are optional, or that they are temporally subsequent to justification. Second, this doctrine has formal parallel with Rome's understanding of initial justification by unformed faith. Both Rome and evangelicalism, Shepherd alleges, maintain justification, at least at the outset, by a faith that may be empty of good works. Third, "in the subsequent relating of good works to justification as evidence of a justifying verdict," an unwholesome "experiential focus" was introduced into the doctrine of justification.[66] This focus, Shepherd alleges, produced "despair" in the realm of "assurance" because "to say that

63. One such student reported that "he was presenting the doctrine he had been taught in Mr. Shepherd's class in the fall of 1974." "Reasons and Specifications Supporting the Action of the Board of Trustees in Removing Professor Shepherd," 3.

64. Norman Shepherd, "The Relation of Good Works to Justification in the Westminster Standards" (n.p., 1976). For Robertson's response to this paper, see "Nineteen Erroneous or Misleading Statements in Norman Shepherd's October 1976 paper, 'The Relation of Good Works to Justification in the Westminster Standards.'"

65. See Norman Shepherd, "Response to a Special Report of the Faculty to the Board on the Discussion on Faith and Justification" (n.p., January 3, 1978); "A Further Response to a Special Report of the Faculty to the Board on the Discussion of Faith and Justification" (n.p., March 1, 1978).

66. Shepherd, "The Relation of Good Works," 6.

works are the ground of assurance of justification is only a hair's breadth away from saying that they are the ground of justification."[67]

Before proceeding, we should observe that Shepherd's criticisms of the Reformational doctrine of justification fail to meet their mark. No magisterial Reformer or Reformational creed either conflated or separated faith and the good works produced by that faith. They did, however, distinguish them. Shepherd has undoubtedly criticized *distortions* of the Reformers' teachings on justification. He has not, however, successfully criticized the teachings themselves.[68]

Shepherd argued that when we adopt a "covenantal perspective on justification,"[69] however, we will have achieved a genuinely Reformed doctrine that escapes the pitfalls both of Rome and of antinomian evangelicalism. What does this entail? "Necessary for . . . justification is not faith-alone, but faith and repentance," as well as the "outward means of grace."[70] Earlier in the paper, Shepherd insists that the pairing of "faith" and "alone" in the Westminster Standards was intended simply to say that faith is the alone instrument of justification. In this statement, however, Shepherd's language assigns roles to repentance and the outward means of grace that are comparable to that of faith. In other words, the unique and instrumental office of faith in justification is at the very least obscured.[71] In a discussion answering the question "What do we say to a sinner on his knees asking what he must do to be saved?," Shepherd will furthermore affirm that "to ask for obedience is not a fundamentally different thing than to ask for faith, though faith and obedience may be distinguished as descriptive of a single total response from different perspectives."[72] It is from such statements as these that critics concluded that Shepherd's doctrine was unable to sustain the sole receptivity of faith in justification maintained by the Westminster Standards (WLC 73).

67. Ibid.

68. See here Robertson, "Nineteen Erroneous or Misleading Statements," Statement 1. It is telling to note that Shepherd introduces what he alleges to be a distinction between Luther's (antinomian) doctrine of justification, and the doctrine upheld by Calvin and the Westminster Assembly. For the essential continuity between Luther and Calvin on the doctrine of justification, see R. Scott Clark, "*Iustitia Imputati Christi*: Alien or Proper to Luther's Doctrine of Justification," *Concordia Theological Quarterly* 70: 269–310 (see especially 274n11).

69. Shepherd, "The Relation of Good Works," 6.

70. Ibid., 15.

71. See here Robertson, "Nineteen Erroneous or Misleading Statements," Statement 10.

72. Shepherd, "The Relation of Good Works," 51.

Shepherd also spoke of justification in this paper in such a way as to compromise its integrity as a grace distinct from sanctification. Shepherd, purposefully interchanging the terms "justification" and "salvation,"[73] argues that "in order to reach the heavenly city, we must enter upon the path of faith, repentance, and obedience to Christ; and we must stay on that path in order to reach the goal which is our justification and eternal life."[74] Such statements militate against the Standards' definition of justification as a complete, definitive, and unchangeable act at the outset of one's Christian experience (WLC 70–73, 77).

In this paper, Shepherd also queries whether the language of "instrument" and that language's "Aristotelian philosoph[ic]" background is appropriate to give expression to the biblical teaching on justification.[75] Its loss would "not [be] serious because instrument is not a biblical term."[76] Even to speak of the "priority" of faith to justification "results from the impact of Aristotelian presuppositions in the dogmatic structure" and not "analysis of the biblical language."[77] At the very least, Shepherd has questioned the propriety of longstanding theological terminology employed to sustain the distinctions found within the Bible's teaching on justification.

In the two responses drafted by Shepherd to the board and faculty of Westminster Theological Seminary in January and March, 1978, it is clear that the author's posture is a defensive one. We find in these articles no substantial reformulations of the doctrines propounded in the October 1976 paper. In April, 1978, Westminster's faculty concluded that while Shepherd's thought was "bound to create misunderstanding," it was not contrary to the Westminster Standards.[78] The next month, however, the board declined to concur with the faculty's judgment, charging Shepherd to revisit his formulations. In February, 1979, the board voted to concur with President Clowney's judgment that discussions cease concerning Shepherd's views. These views, Clowney maintained in 1977, were unclear but not contrary to the Seminary's confessional standards. In February, 1979, Shepherd

---

73. Ibid., 26.
74. Ibid., 24. See here Robertson, "Nineteen Erroneous or Misleading Statements," Statement 19.
75. Shepherd, "The Relation of Good Works," 45.
76. Ibid.
77. Ibid., 46.
78. "Report of the Faculty to the Board on Faith and Justification" (25 April 1978), quoted at Robertson, *Current Justification Controversy*, 26.

presented to the board a new and lengthy treatment of justification, "The Grace of Justification."

In the interim between Shepherd's discussions with the faculty and the release of this new paper, Shepherd offered two further statements of his views. In June, 1978, he delivered an address, "Reprobation in Covenant Perspective," before the Christian Reformed Ministerial Institute. In November, 1978, he presented "Thirty Four Theses on Justification," to the Presbytery of Philadelphia (OPC). Examination of these three works evidences that Shepherd had not substantially altered the views concerning covenant, election and reprobation, and justification that he had advanced in 1975 and 1976. One noticeable change, however, was the greater care exercised by Norman Shepherd to avoid the language of multiple and concurrent instruments of justification. This change is semantic, however, and does not reflect movement or transition from the doctrine that Shepherd advanced in 1976.[79]

The controversy developed along two parallel but inseparable tracks: church and seminary. First, in 1977, charges were filed against Shepherd in the Presbytery of Philadelphia (OPC), where Shepherd held his ministerial credentials. It was not until 1978, however, that the charges were considered at any length by the presbytery. Heavy debate centered around the question of which documents could be considered as evidence within the trial. The Presbytery settled its attention on the "Thirty Four" theses submitted by Shepherd. The matter came to a vote early in 1980, and Presbytery declined *either* to accept *or* to condemn Shepherd's formulations as (un)biblical or (un)confessional. An appeal to the 1981 General Assembly was unsuccessful. The following year (1982), charges were again filed before the Presbytery, but Shepherd concurrently transferred his ministerial credentials to the Christian Reformed Church, where he remained until his retirement.

The seminary controversy soon came again before the attention of the broader, international Reformed community. In May, 1979, the board chose to revisit its February decision to declare Shepherd's views unclear but within the bounds of the Westminster Standards. Consequently, a joint committee of members from both the board and faculty was created to "prepar[e] a study paper and statement on the doctrine of justification by

79. For analysis of the Thirty Four Theses, see Guy Prentiss Waters, *Justification and the New Perspectives on Paul* (Phillipsburg, NJ: P&R, 2004), 209–11.

faith."[80] In October, 1979, this committee distributed several relevant articles and papers pertaining to Shepherd to "various noteworthy theologians of the Reformed community."[81]

After collating these responses, meeting with Norman Shepherd, and drafting the document it was charged to produce, the joint committee, concluding its work in May, 1980, was unable to reach full consensus. In the same month, one year after the committee had been commissioned, and in the wake of the Presbytery of Philadelphia's actions earlier that year, the board appointed a "Commission on Allegations," whose membership was also drawn from both the board and the faculty. This commission was "to determine if charges should be brought against" Norman Shepherd.[82] After meeting with Shepherd and drafting several allegations, a majority of the commission proposed in November, 1980, that the allegations not be levied against Shepherd and that he be permitted to continue teaching at the seminary. The Board as a whole voted that same month neither to clear nor to dismiss Shepherd.

Over the next several months, two important events helped to call further attention to the controversy at the seminary. In May, 1981, forty-five leaders within the Reformed churches drafted and sent to the seminary's trustees a letter of concern regarding Shepherd's views.[83] Furthermore, joint discussions were being conducted in earnest in 1981 concerning ecclesiastical union between the Presbyterian Church in America (PCA) and the OPC. It is likely that the controversy surrounding Shepherd's views contributed to the ultimate failure of these two denominations to unite ecclesiastically.[84]

By the fall of 1981, President Clowney, hitherto a longstanding proponent for tolerating Norman Shepherd's views at the seminary, had now concluded that Shepherd's views stood outside the bounds of the Westminster Standards.[85] Through his leadership, notwithstanding the continued support of the faculty, Shepherd was removed by action of the board of trustees on November 20, 1981. His dismissal was effective

80. Robertson, *Current Justification Controversy*, 41. For the membership and work of the committee (of whom Robertson was a member), see ibid., 40–54.

81. Ibid., 46.

82. Ibid., 55.

83. For their names, see ibid., 62.

84. For a causal relationship between the failure of church union and the Shepherd controversy, see Robertson's argument in ibid., 63–66.

85. Ibid., 67.

on January 1, 1982. What prompted the board's decision undoubtedly involved an understanding of Shepherd's views as erroneous and outside confessional boundaries.[86]

The final phase in the Norman Shepherd controversy at Westminster Seminary entailed the appeal that Shepherd made of the board's decision. In response to this appeal, the board released in February, 1982 "Reasons and Specifications Supporting the Action of the Board of Trustees in Removing Professor Shepherd Approved by the Executive Committee of the Board." This statement explicitly stresses that proven theological error was not a reason for Shepherd's dismissal.[87] It nevertheless specifies several particular doctrinal matters of concern.[88] Shepherd subsequently retracted his appeal, and, so it seemed, the controversy surrounding Shepherd had come to a welcome end.

1982–2006

The controversy surrounding Shepherd's theology, however, has not come to an end. Shepherd's teachings concerning covenant, election, reprobation, and justification have gained adherents from a new and younger generation of Reformed ministers and elders.[89] This merits consideration of what Shepherd has authored and published in the quarter century since the conclusion of the seminary controversy.

In terms of publication, Shepherd produced very little between 1982 and 1999. In this period, he never published a defense of his doctrinal posi-

86. See the discussion in ibid., 69–73.

87. "The Board did not remove Mr. Shepherd on the ground of demonstrated errors in his teaching . . ." "Reasons and Specifications," 1.

88. For these specifications, see ibid., 11–18. Note in particular the following statement, "The Board has come to the decision that Prof. Shepherd's removal is necessary for the best interests of the Seminary with great regret, and only after seven years of earnest study and debate, because it has become convinced that Mr. Shepherd's teaching concerning justification, the covenant of works and the covenant of grace, and related themes, is not clearly in accord with the teaching of Scripture as it is summarized in the system of doctrine contained in the Westminster Standards," Ibid., 2.

89. This is evident from the writings of proponents of the "Federal Vision." On the theological indebtedness of Federal Vision proponents to Shepherd's theology, see Waters, *The Federal Vision and Covenant Theology: A Comparative Analysis* (Phillipsburg, NJ: P&R, 2006), 96–107. For an extended defense of Shepherd's doctrine of justification, see Mark Horne, "Justifying Faith: A *Prima Facie* Vindication of Norman Shepherd according to Reformed Orthodoxy" (n.p., 2005).

tions in view of the controversy within the seminary, the Orthodox Presbyterian Church, and the broader Reformed community. He did author, however, some articles addressing perseverance and repentance in *The Outlook*, and some reviews of books dealing with justification and the *ordo salutis*.[90] In these articles and reviews he has continued to promote his controversial views and concerns, but they will disappoint the reader searching for thorough exegetical or theological explanations or defenses of those views.

The period 2000–2006 has represented a relatively substantial literary output on the part of Shepherd. He has published a book: *The Call of Grace*, roughly half of which had been published in 1976 as "The Covenant Context of Evangelism."[91] He has also published several articles addressing the doctrine of justification.[92] These pieces are useful in confirming to the reader that Shepherd has not abandoned his distinctive views of election and reprobation, covenant, baptism, and justification. He has not, however, simply restated his earlier views. For instance, he has elaborated his understanding of the "works of the law" by which Paul denies that no man is justified.[93] He has furthermore made explicit his rejection of the imputation of the active obedience of Christ to the believer for his justification.[94]

90. Norman Shepherd, "Perseverance: The Gift (I)," *The Outlook* (1992): 10–11; "The Need to Persevere (II)," *The Outlook* (1992): 20–21; "A Ringing Call to Repentance," *The Outlook* (1997): 5–6; Review of Alister McGrath, *ARCIC II and Justification: An Evangelical Anglican Assessment of 'Salvation and the Church'*, *Calvin Theological Journal* 23 (1988) 271–72; Review of Anthony A. Hoekema, *Saved By Grace*, *Calvin Theological Journal* 26 (1991) 437–38.

91. Norman Shepherd, *The Call of Grace* (Philipsburg, NJ: Presbyterian and Reformed, 2000).

92. "Justification by Faith Alone." *Reformation and Revival Journal* 11/2 (2000): 75–89; "Law and Gospel in Covenantal Perspective." *Reformation and Revival Journal* 13 (2004/5): 73–88; "Justification by Faith in Pauline Theology," *Backbone of the Bible: Covenant in Contemporary Perspective* ed. Andrew Sandlin (Nacogdoches, TX: Covenant Media Foundation, 2004), 85–101; "Justification by Works in Reformed Theology," 103–20 in ibid.

93. Shepherd insists that "works of the law" refer to "the Mosaic covenant or the old covenant under which God's people (Israel) served the Lord from Mt. Sinai to the advent of Christ;" "obedience to a limited selection of laws found in the Scripture;" and what is done "in the strength of human flesh in order to obtain the justifying verdict of God," "Justification by Faith in Pauline Theology," 95, 97, 99. Compare Shepherd, "Response to a Special Report of the Faculty to the Board on the Discussion on Faith and Justification," January 3, 1978, 6–7.

94. This concern is evident in *The Call of Grace*, in which Shepherd categorically rejects "merit" from covenantal reflection. The implication of this rejection is that even Jesus' obedience during his estate of humiliation must not be described as "meritorious" in any sense. Shepherd's rejection of the imputation of Christ's active obedience for the believer's justification is made explicit in "Justification by Works in Pauline Theology." In this article, he argues that Luther, Calvin, and Ursinus maintained this same view. Shepherd understands an imputed

There is a third area in which Shepherd appears to have refined his views. In the February, 1982, "Reasons and Specifications," concerns were raised that Shepherd had compromised, if not denied altogether, the doctrine of the covenant of works.[95] These concerns had surfaced both from unpublished lectures and addresses and from institutional dialogue with Norman Shepherd. They were not documented from his published writings.

In recent years, it has become clear that this assessment of the board in 1982 comports with the teaching of Shepherd today. We may look at two examples. First, in *The Call of Grace*, Shepherd has offered a "revised form" of his article, "The Covenant Context of Evangelism," published initially in 1976. While most of the revisions are stylistic, there is a telling pattern of revision of "The Covenant Context of Evangelism." In the original article, Shepherd uses on seven occasions the phrase "covenant of grace." In each of those instances in the parallel sections of the revision, the words "of grace" have been excised.[96] Clearly, Shepherd has expressed discomfort with the language of the "covenant of grace," preferring to it the language of "covenant" *simpliciter*. The likeliest explanation is that Shepherd is uncomfortable with the traditional distinction between the "covenant of works" and the "covenant of grace."

Second, in Rowland Ward's *God & Adam: Reformed Theology and the Creation Covenant*, Shepherd offers an extended précis of his own under-

---

active obedience in justification to be a declension from this earlier view. This is attributable, he argues, to the Reformed's embrace of a "works /merit paradigm [that] is really a return to the same paradigm that Rome uses to structure its doctrine of justification," 113. See especially Shepherd's summary statement of justification at "Justification by Works," 118. More recently, see Shepherd's "Comments on the OPC Justification Report (4)." It should be noted that Shepherd affirms Christ's sinlessness. He also affirms Christ's obedience to the law as a necessary precondition for the sinner's justification. He denies, however, the imputation of that obedience to the believer for his justification.

95. See "Reasons and Specifications," 5, 12–15. The report concluded that "by rejecting the distinction between the covenant of works and the covenant of grace as defined in the Westminster Standards, and by failing to take account in the structure of the 'covenant dynamic' of Christ's fulfillment of the covenant by his active obedience as well as by his satisfaction of its curse, Mr. Shepherd develops a uniform concept of covenantal faithfulness for Adam, for Israel, and for the new covenant people. The danger is that both the distinctiveness of the covenant of grace and of the new covenant fullness of the covenant of grace will be lost from view and that obedience as the way of salvation will swallow up the distinct and primary function of faith," 15.

96. Compare "The Covenant Context for Evangelism," (CCE), 53 with *Call of Grace* (COG), 70; CCE, 60 (*tris*) with COG, 82, 83, 84; CCE, 61 with COG, 84; CCE, 65 (*bis*) with COG, 91 (*bis*).

standing of the Adamic covenant in Genesis 2.[97] In this outline, it becomes clear that the Adamic covenant is not generically different from the Abrahamic, Mosaic, or new covenant administrations. In other words, Shepherd does not appear to accept either the language or doctrine of the "covenant of works" and "covenant of grace," and understands the Scripture to teach a single monocovenantal scheme, extending from Genesis to Revelation.[98]

To summarize, Shepherd during this period has refined his thought in at least three areas. First, He has proposed definitions of the "works of the law" by which no one shall be justified. These definitions do not exclude what is said to be the non-meritorious obedience of the believer. Second, he has explicitly rejected the imputation of the active obedience of Christ to the believer for his justification. Finally, he advances a monocovenantal theology.

These three areas of refinement converge in one important area. In addressing the biblical doctrine of justification, Reformed theologians have often observed that "pardon would release from the punishment of its breach, but would not entitle to the reward of performance."[99] Pardon, in other words, renders one non-objectionable. It does not thereby render one acceptable.[100] The imputation of Christ's active obedience renders one acceptable in justification. Shepherd maintains, however, that Christ's obedience to the law is not imputed to the believer. What, for Shepherd, can render one acceptable? What fills the gap left by the absence of the imputation of Christ's active obedience? To fill this gap Shepherd offers only the works that one performs as a Christian. This is evident from his interpretation of Philippians 3:9:

> Through the revelation of Jesus Christ he realized that righteousness was not something to be achieved by works, but was a gift to be received by faith, the forgiveness of sins. Now with his sins forgiven by the death of Christ he longs for the power of Christ's resurrection. It is through union

97. Rowland Ward, *God & Adam: Reformed Theology and the Creation Covenant* (Wantirna, Australia: New Melbourne, 2003), 188–89.

98. "My difficulty with the covenant of works lies just at this point. There is no exegetical basis for it," Shepherd, "Some Comments on the OPC Justification Report (3)."

99. Robert L. Dabney, *Systematic Theology* (1871; repr., Edinburgh: Banner of Truth, 1985), 624–25, cited at "Report of the Committee To Study the Doctrine of Justification, Presented to Seventy-third General Assembly of the Orthodox Presbyterian Church," 22.

100. This terminology is drawn from Dr. John H. Gerstner, "Salvation: It's First Fruits" (audio recording, Montreat, NC: TRAV, 1965).

with Christ in his death and resurrection that he will enter into eternal life, not through the imputation of active obedience. There is nothing in Phil. 3:9 about the imputation of active obedience. The passage directs us to the death and resurrection of Christ as the source of life for us.[101]

The believer, then, finds himself in the place of Adam in the estate of innocency. To be sure, he is unlike Adam in one important regard—Adam is sinlessly upright, and believers are not. The believer's sins are pardoned on the basis of the work of Jesus Christ. He is like Adam, however, in that his entrance into life is contingent upon his own obedience. It is the assistance of divine grace that enables him to render this obedience. In this respect there is, for Shepherd, no qualitative difference between the covenant made with Adam in Genesis 2 and the covenant in which believers presently find themselves.

CONCLUSIONS

The renewed interest in Shepherd has not been without ecclesiastical response. One PCA presbytery and study committees of two Reformed denominations have proposed extensive and critical reflections on Shepherd's theology.[102] That one of these study committee reports should have come from a General Assembly-appointed committee of the OPC is striking. This committee had been charged by the Seventy-first General Assembly "to critique the teachings of the 'New Perspective on Paul,' 'Federal Vision,' and other like teachings concerning the doctrine of justification and other related doctrines . . . ."[103] The frequent and critical interactions with Shepherd's theology within the committee's report suggest that the committee understood criticisms of Shepherd's theology to be essential to its assigned task. Judging by the Seventy-third General Assembly's favorable reception of the report

101. Shepherd, "Comments on the OPC Justification Report (4)." Emphasis mine.

102. See "A Précis of the Theology of Norman Shepherd," 9–10 in the Study Report of the Mississippi Valley Presbytery (PCA); "Report of the Special Committee to Study Justification in Light of the Current Justification Controversy Presented to 258th Synod of the Reformed Church of the United States, May 10–13, 2004, 1–56; "Report of the Committee to Study the Doctrine of Justification," Presented to the 73rd General Assembly of the Orthodox Presbyterian Church, 2006.

103. For a fuller statement of the background to the formation of the committee, see "Report of the Committee," i–ii.

as a whole,[104] it is evident that Shepherd's theology remains a matter of debate and concern within the OPC.[105]

The theology of Norman Shepherd, then, is very much a live issue within confessional Reformed churches. It is here that we may pause with renewed appreciation for the services of such men as Dr. O. Palmer Robertson. His tireless and sacrificial advocacy for the doctrines of the Westminster Standards during the Shepherd controversy has bequeathed a much-needed testimony to this generation. May the Reformed churches at the turn of the twenty-first century not only esteem but also profit from that legacy, and may the Holy Spirit be pleased to bless in our day the preaching of the God-exalting and soul-abasing gospel of grace.

104. The 73rd General Assembly "commend[ed] the report" to its presbyteries, sessions, and ministers," "Report of the Committee," ii. In so doing, it "approved the content and reasoning of the report" but did not "endorse every word of the report" or elevate the report to constitutional status, ibid.

105. Shepherd in turn has drafted four responses to the committee's report. Norman Shepherd, "Some Comments on the OPC Justification Report;" "Some Comments on the OPC Justification Report (2);" "Some Comments on the OPC Justification Report (3);" "Some Comments on the OPC Justification Report (4)," available online at http://www.federal-vision.com (accessed Feb. 2, 2008).

12

Calvin's Correspondence on Our Threefold Union with Christ

W. DUNCAN RANKIN

There is a sense, therefore, in which we must speak of all men as ingrafted into Christ in virtue of His incarnational and atoning work, and we must consequently speak of those who refuse Him and ultimately prove reprobate as those who break themselves off from Him. In Calvin's words, "that very relationship of the flesh, by which He has allied us to Himself, the ungodly break off and dissolve by their unbelief, so that it is by their own fault that they are rendered utter strangers to Him" (Comm. on Ps. 22:23).[1]

We know that the sons of God are born not of flesh and blood but of the Spirit through faith. The sharing of flesh alone does not produce brotherly communion.[2]

---

1. T. F. Torrance, *The School of Faith* (London: James Clark & Co., 1959), cxvi–cxvii.
2. John Calvin, *Calvin's Ecclesiastical Advice*, trans. Mary Beaty and Benjamin W. Farley (Louisville, KY: Westminster/John Knox, 1991), 39–40.

This article sets out Calvin's doctrine of union with Christ in an important set of correspondence brought again to light by a recent Calvin study. When exploring this correspondence, I will examine Calvin's doctrine in its several forms and facets, giving careful attention to the incarnation and union with Christ. At every step I will maintain sensitivity to historical context and development.

BACKGROUND

Princeton Professor David Willis highlights the importance of the doctrine of union with Christ to the Reformer:

> Calvin's doctrine of the union with Christ is one of the most consistently influential features of his theology and ethics, if not indeed the single most important teaching which animates the whole of his thought and his personal life.[3]

Other studies have long stressed the importance of the doctrine of union with Christ in Calvin's theology.[4]

Willis identifies two different yet related levels within Calvin's doctrine of union with Christ, the first of which is incarnational:

3.D. Willis-Watkins, "The Unio Mystica and the Assurance of Faith According to Calvin," in *Calvin: Erbe und Auftrag, Festschrift für W. H. Neuser*, ed. Willem van't Spijker (Kampen: Kok Pharos, 1991), 78.

4.For example, see John W. Nevin, *The Mystical Presence* (Philadelphia: J. B. Lippincott & Co., 1846), 54–58; Thomas Gregory, "Union to Christ the Ground of Justification," in *Opening and Closing Addresses to the New College Theological Society, Session 1882–83* (Edinburgh: Lorimer & Gillies, 1883), 33–50, especially 38–39; W. Kolfhaus, *Christusgemeinschaft bei Johannes Calvin*, in *Beiträge zur Geschichte und Lehre der Reformierten Kirche*, vol. 3 (Neukirchen: Buchhandlung des Erziehungsvereins, 1939); Karl Barth, *Church Dogmatics* IV/3.2, ed. G. W. Bromiley and T. F. Torrance, trans. G. W. Bromiley (Edinburgh: T. & T. Clark, 1962), 551–53; W. Niesel, *The Theology of Calvin*, trans. H. Knight (Philadelphia: Westminster Press, 1956), 120–26; Paul van Buren, *Christ in Our Place* (Edinburgh: Oliver and Boyd, 1957), 95–106; R. S. Wallace, *Calvin's Doctrine of the Christian Life* (Edinburgh: Oliver and Boyd, 1959), 17–27; W. Niesel, *Reformed Symbolics*, trans. D. Lewis (Edinburgh: Oliver and Boyd, 1962), 181–86; F. Wendel, *Calvin: Origins and Development of His Religious Thought*, trans. P. Mairet (New York: Harper and Row, 1963), 234–42; Kilian McDonnell, *John Calvin, the Church, and the Eucharist* (Princeton: Princeton University Press, 1967), 177–205; Charles Partee, "Calvin, Calvinism, and Philosophy: A Prolusion," *Reformed Review* 33 (1980): 129–35; Charles Partee, "Calvin's Central Dogma Again," *Sixteenth Century Journal* 18 (1987): 191–99; John H. Leith, *John Calvin's Doctrine of the Christian Life* (Louisville, KY: Westminster/John Knox, 1989), 98–103; Jean-Daniel Benoit, *Calvin in His Letters*, trans. R. Haig, in *Courtenay Studies in Reformation Theology*, no. 5 (Oxford: Sutton Courtenay, 1991), 73–81.

There is the incarnation, the hypostatic union of the eternal Word with the humanity which believers share with every other person. The "communication of properties" applies to this level, the hypostatic union. This level of union is primarily the subject in Institutes II, chapters 13 and 14.[5]

The second level of union with Christ is particular and limited to believers only.[6] But it does not stand on its own:

> This particular union—I repeat—presupposes the prior union. It is the way believers have applied to them the salvation wrought by "the whole course of obedience" (Institutes II 16, 5) of Jesus Christ, the eternal Word united to humanity.[7]

Although Willis' statement is grammatically ambiguous, the wider context makes it plain that for Calvin the particular union applies the salvation made possible only by the prior incarnation.[8] The limited scope of his Festschrift article prevents a detailed treatment, but Willis does note that it is important to recognize that the two levels function together in Calvin's theology.[9]

Professor T. F. Torrance, in the introduction to his book *The School of Faith*, touches upon the doctrine of union with Christ in response to George S. Hendry's analysis of Calvin. In his rebuttal to Hendry's analysis of Calvin, Torrance gives his own understanding of Calvin on union with Christ:

> There is a sense, therefore, in which we must speak of all men as ingrafted into Christ in virtue of His incarnational and atoning work, and we must consequently speak of those who refuse Him and ultimately prove rep-

5. Willis-Watkins, "Unio Mystica," 78.

6. "There is, secondly, the particular union of Christ with believers which comes about by the Holy Spirit who is the bond by which we are united to Christ (*Institutes* 3.1.1), the eternal Word made flesh. This is the reality which Calvin, in a subsequent section (3.11.10), calls "that conjunction of the Head and members, the indwelling of Christ in our hearts, the mystical union." Ibid., 78–79.

7. Ibid., 79.

8. Wilhelm Niesel put it memorably: "The miracle of Christmas must be followed by the miracle of Pentecost if the former is to reach its goal in us." Niesel, *Reformed Symbolics*, 184.

9. "To understand what Calvin means by it [i.e., union with Christ], we must note the difference between two levels of that union. The second or consequent level of union presupposes the prior or first level of union." Willis-Watkins, "Unio Mystica," 78.

robate as those who break themselves off from Him. In Calvin's words, "that very relationship of the flesh, by which He has allied us to Himself, the ungodly break off and dissolve by their unbelief, so that it is by their own fault that they are rendered utter strangers to Him" (Comm. on Ps. 22:23).[10]

Torrance sees in Calvin a universal union with all men via the incarnation whereby they are ingrafted into Christ.[11]

The most helpful study of Calvin's doctrine of union with Christ to date is by Dennis E. Tamburello.[12] Computer word searches of key terms in the 1559 *Institutes* provide the starting point of Tamburello's study.[13] In addition to this material, Tamburello takes many important cues from Kolfhaus's earlier study and the primary sources it cites.[14]

Wilhelm Kolfhaus's work covers John Calvin's doctrine of union with Christ in detail, making it the fullest single treatment to date.[15] After a

10. Torrance, *School of Faith*, cxvi–cxvii. Tony Lane takes exception with Torrance here, saying, "The idea of the headship of Christ over all men is a Barthian idea alien to Calvin." A. N. S. Lane, "The Quest for the Historical Calvin," *Evangelical Quarterly* 60 (1983), 113.

11. In an interview with this author, Torrance expanded on this theme: "Calvin . . . says there is a threefold ingrafting into Christ and a twofold cutting off, [which is] a very interesting expression. . . . Now, what is this threefold grafting in? One graft is Christ—we were just speaking about it—he became man and takes all humanity. That's a grafting into Christ, a fundamental grafting into Christ. The other one is baptism. . . . And following . . . faith" (Torrance, interview by author, January 29, 1990, Edinburgh, tape recording). Torrance mentions Calvin's doctrine of threefold ingrafting and twofold breaking off in T. F. Torrance, *Kingdom and Church* (London: Oliver & Boyd, 1956), 102, n. 3.

12. Dennis E. Tamburello, "Christ and Mystical Union: A Comparative Study of the Theologies of Bernard of Clairvaux and John Calvin" (PhD diss., University of Chicago, 1990). This dissertation was written under the supervision of Brian A. Gerrish at the University of Chicago Divinity School. This study was later published as *Union with Christ: John Calvin and the Mysticism of St. Bernard* (Louisville, KY: Westminster/John Knox, 1994). All further citations of Tamburello's study will be to the published work.

13. Ibid., 84, 141, n. 1. These word searches were performed on a database at the H. H. Meeter Center for Calvin Studies in Grand Rapids, Michigan, which was originally prepared by Ford Lewis Battles and later revised by Richard F. Wevers. The results of this search are contained in an appendix to the book, "Appendix: References to Union with Christ in the 1559 *Institutes* and Other Selected Calvin Texts." Ibid., 111–13.

14. On Kolfhaus, see footnote 4 above. Tamburello refers to Kolfhaus no less than 35 times in his 40-page chapter "John Calvin on Mystical Union." Kolfhaus's citations of Calvin's writings are included in Tamburello's word search list. Tamburello does not draw, however, uncritically from Kolfhaus's earlier work.

15. Kolfhaus's study has received wide attention. See, for example, Niesel, *The Theology of Calvin*, 120; Wallace, *Doctrine of the Christian Life*, 341; Wendel, *Calvin: Origins and Development*, 234; Partee, "Calvin's Central Dogma Again," 197; Willis-Watkins, "Unio Mystica," 78.

historical survey of German thought on Calvin's doctrine, Kolfhaus grapples with the question at hand—"Was ist Christusgemeinschaft?"[16]

Kolfhaus turns first to the primary source he considers to be most important—Calvin's letter of 8 August 1555 to Peter Martyr.[17] He devotes several pages merely to a German translation of a major extract from this Latin letter. The balance of the chapter marshals numerous other passages from Calvin's corpus to illustrate and clarify the letter to Martyr.[18] Tamburello also gives attention to Calvin's letter to Martyr, his original interest apparently stirred by Kolfhaus.[19]

The importance of this 8 August 1555 letter for Calvin's doctrine of union with Christ, however, does not appear to be widely appreciated in English language Calvin studies.[20] Perhaps this is because Beveridge's extract oddly omits the bulk of the letter which treats the doctrine.[21]

16. Other than references to a dozen notable German scholars, Kolfhaus only deals very briefly with the opinions of three Dutch writers on Calvin's doctrine of union with Christ—Abraham Kuyper, Herman Bavinck, and S. P. Dee. His list of German worthies includes Heinrich Heppe, Ernst Troeltsch, Wilhelm Niesel, and Reinhold Seeberg.

17. John Calvin, "2266. Calvinus Vermilio (August 8, 1555)," *Ioannis Calvini Opera Quae Supersunt Omnia*, vol. 15, ed. G. Baum, E. Cunitz, and E. Reuss, in *Corpus Reformatorum* (Brunsvigae: C. A. Schwetschke et Filium, 1876), 43:722–25. Hereafter all volumes in this series will be designated by *CO* followed by the volume and page numbers. For English translations of extracts of this letter, see John Calvin, "Calvin to Martyr, Geneva, August 8, 1555," in *Gleanings of a Few Scattered Ears*, ed. G. C. Gorham (London: Bell and Daldy, 1857), 349–52; and John Calvin, "To Peter Martyr," in *Selected Works of John Calvin: Tracts and Letters*, ed. Henry Beveridge and Jules Bonnet, trans. M. R. Gilchrist (Grand Rapids: Baker Book House, 1983), 6:217–18. Gorham's extract omits only Calvin's opening remarks and closing church news. All English citations of this letter will be drawn from Gorham and designated as "Calvin to Martyr," unless specified otherwise. Beveridge's extract only gives Calvin's closing church news.

18. Kolfhaus, *Christusgemeinschaft*, 24–35.

19. After quoting the Latin text of the letter, Tamburello references Kolfhaus. See Tamburello, *Union with Christ*, 87 and 143, n. 18. Only one other secondary source cited by Tamburello mentions this letter, and then just once in passing. See R. S. Wallace, *Calvin's Doctrine of the Word and Sacrament* (Edinburgh: Oliver & Boyd, 1953), 146, n. 5. Tamburello does not refer to this footnote in Wallace.

20. Other than Kolfhaus's German volume, none of the works on Calvin's doctrine of union with Christ cited in footnote 4 above mentions the letter. Although Kolfhaus's work itself is not unknown, the only other references to the letter in Calvin studies material in English that I have found are made by Tamburello and his academic supervisor. See B. A. Gerrish, *Tradition and the Modern World: Reformed Theology in the Nineteenth Century* (Chicago: The University of Chicago Press, 1978), 63. This is in a chapter on J. W. Nevin's treatment of Calvin on the Lord's Supper. See also the more recent volume, B. A. Gerrish, *Grace and Gratitude: The Eucharistic Theology of John Calvin* (Edinburgh: T. & T. Clark, 1993), 128–29. Professor Gerrish kindly first drew my attention to this letter while he was in Edinburgh delivering these Cunningham Lectures at New College in 1989.

21. It is not immediately obvious in Beveridge's edition that the letter as given is only a small extract. See Calvin, *Tracts and Letters*, 6:217–18. Gorham's 1857 volume is more

Calvin's letter to Martyr deals almost exclusively with the doctrine of union with Christ[22] and ends on this informative note:

Were I teaching any other person, I should follow up this subject more diffusely; in addressing you, I have glanced at it briefly, with the simple view of showing you that we entirely agree in sentiment.[23]

Thus, Calvin's letter dated as 8 August 1555 was in fact a response to Martyr's own views on the subject expressed at an earlier date.[24]

This fuller set of correspondence between Calvin and Martyr is better known in secondary works on Peter Martyr.[25] Only in the past few decades has there been a reawakening of scholarly interest in Peter Martyr Vermigli.[26] That

---

obscure than Beveridge's, and his fuller English extract consequently appears to be little known.

22. "Although I promised to write to you, on the secret Communion which we have with Christ, yet I shall not treat this subject so largely as you hoped: nevertheless, as the matter is one of vast importance, I think it may be profitable to state my opinion definitely in a few words." Calvin to Martyr, 349 [*CO* 15:722].

23. Calvin to Martyr, 352 [*CO* 15:724].

24. Kolfhaus, Tamburello, and Gerrish do not display any awareness of this fact. They fail to employ Martyr's letter as important background material for the interpretation of Calvin's response.

25. For example, see M. W. Anderson, *Peter Martyr: A Reformer in Exile (1542–1562)* (Nieuwkoop: B. De Graaf, 1975), 186–95, especially 187–89; M. W. Anderson, "Peter Martyr, Reformed Theologian (1542–1562): His letters to Heinrich Bullinger and John Calvin," *Sixteenth Century Journal* 4 (1973): 41–64, especially 58; J. C. McLelland, *The Visible Words of God* (Edinburgh: Oliver and Boyd, 1957), 88, 14–147, especially 143–46.

26. The first major study of Martyr in English was completed at the instigation and under the supervision of T. F. Torrance: Joseph C. McLelland, "The Doctrine of the Sacraments in the Theology of Peter Martyr Vermigli (A.D. 1500–1562)," (PhD diss., University of Edinburgh, 1953), which was later published under the title *The Visible Words of God* (Grand Rapids: Eerdmans, 1957). Philip McNair, *Peter Martyr in Italy* (Oxford: Clarendon Press, 1967), vii. On Martyr also see J. C. McClelland [sic], "The Reformed Doctrine of Predestination," *Scottish Journal of Theology* 8 (1955): 255–71; M. W. Anderson, "Peter Martyr, Reformed Theologian (1542–1562)," 58; M. W. Anderson, "Peter Martyr on Romans," *Scottish Journal of Theology* 26 (1973): 401–20; M. W. Anderson, *Peter Martyr: A Reformer in Exile (1542–1562)* (Nieuwkoop: De Graaf, 1975); John Patrick Donnelly, *Calvinism and Scholasticism in Vermigli's Doctrine of Man and Grace* (Leiden: E. J. Brill, 1976); J. C. McLelland, "Calvinism Perfecting Thomism? Peter Martyr Vermigli's Question," *Scottish Journal of Theology* 31 (1978): 571–78; J. C. McLelland, "Peter Martyr Vermigli: Scholastic or Humanist?" in *Peter Martyr Vermigli and Italian Reform*, ed. J. C. McLelland (Waterloo, ON: Wilfrid Laurier University Press, 1980); Robert M. Kingdon, *The Political Thought of Peter Martyr Vermigli* (Geneva: Librairie Droz, 1980). For a helpful new primary and secondary bibliography of Martyr, see J. P. Donnelly, R. M. Kingdon, and M. W. Anderson, *A Bibliography of the Works of Peter Martyr Vermigli* (Kirksville, MO: Sixteenth Century Journal Publishers, 1990).

John Calvin and Peter Martyr Vermigli held each other in highest esteem is now beyond question.[27]

Martyr's letter to Calvin that prompted the above reply is dated 8 March 1555.[28] After briefly discussing the tragic case of an unnamed theologian who "does not honestly admit the doctrine of Predestination," Martyr turns to union with Christ, inviting Calvin's own opinion on the matter.[29]

> Men do not all agree concerning the communion which we have with the Body of Christ and the substance of His nature; for what reason, I suppose you will hear. It is of much importance that he that is Christ's should understand the manner of His union with Him.[30]

Martyr concludes by kindly declining Calvin's previous offer of employment as pastor of the Italian congregation in Geneva.[31]

Peter Martyr may not, however, be the Reformer who first raised the issue of union with Christ that prompted this correspondence. As G. C. Gorham notes at the end of Martyr's 8 March 1555 letter to Calvin:

> There is a long and interesting letter, on the same subject, to Beza ... without date, but probably written at the same time as this to Calvin ....[32]

27. As Anderson puts it: "One must concur with Peter Martyr, that he and John Calvin were as closely joined in mind and judgment as was any other pair of theologians in sixteenth-century Europe" (Anderson, "Peter Martyr, Reformed Theologian [1542–1562]," 63). Anderson also notes that the 1576 Latin edition of Calvin's *Institutio Christianae Religionis* published by Thomas Vautrollerius includes marginal apparatus referring to Martyr! Ibid., 55.

28. Peter Martyr Vermigli, Letter to John Calvin, March 8, 1555, *Loci Communis Petri Martyris Vermilii Florentini Theologi Celeberrimi* (Geneva: Pierre Aubert, 1627), 767–69. All future citations from the *Loci Communis* will be taken from this edition and abbreviated *LC*, followed by the page number. An English edition is found in Peter Martyr Vermigli, *Common Places of the most famous and renowned Divine Doctor Peter Martyr, divided into foure principall parts*, with Appendix, trans. Anthony Marten (London: H. Denham and H. Middleton, 1583), 96–99. Anthony Marten's 1583 English edition, *Common Places*, will be used, as will his page numbering scheme. It will be abbreviated *CP*, followed by part number in brackets and then page number. A new translation of a major extract of the letter is also found in Peter Martyr Vermigli, "Martyr to Calvin, Strasburgh, March 8, 1555," in *Gleanings of a Few Scattered Ears*, 340–44. All English citations of this letter below will be taken from Gorham and designated as "Martyr to Calvin," unless specified otherwise.

29. Martyr to Calvin, 341–42.

30. Ibid., 342. The ambiguous double capitalization is Gorham's. Perhaps Andreas Osiander is the reason Martyr has in mind.

31. Martyr, *CP* [Appendix], 98–99.

32. Martyr to Calvin, 344 (editor's note). See *LC*, 777–78. A full English translation is found in *CP* [Appendix], 105–6. All English citations below will be taken from Marten's edi-

That Gorham associates Martyr's letter to Calvin with Martyr's letter to Beza is of little surprise.[33] Some internal evidence suggests that Martyr's letter to Beza antedates his letter to Calvin.[34]

Like Calvin, Peter Martyr did not offer his views on union with Christ unsolicited. It is clear from Martyr's letter to Beza that Beza first inquired of Martyr on the doctrine![35] Although one cannot conclude definitely that Beza's letter to Martyr preceded Martyr's letter to Calvin, the continuity between them makes both letters important background material for understanding Calvin's own comments and views on the doctrine of union with Christ.[36]

Building on Tamburello's study, I propose to re-examine Calvin's doctrine of union with Christ in light of Peter Martyr's fuller correspondence on the subject.[37] As previously mentioned, Kolfhaus and Tamburello consider the letter of 8 August 1555 from Calvin to Martyr to be perhaps the *most important* data available for unpacking Calvin's doctrine of union with Christ. In his study,

---

tion of the *CP* and designated as "Martyr to Beza," unless specified otherwise. The original Latin text may also be had in modern typeface. See Theodore Beza, *Correspondance de Théodore de Bèze*, ed. F. Aubert and H. Meylan (Geneva: Libraire E. Droz, 1960), 1:153–55.

33. In structure, content, and phrasing the two are remarkably similar. At the close of the letter, Martyr mentions his colleague Zanchius, suggesting a dating in his second Strasbourg period of 1553–56. See McLelland, *Visible Words of God*, 143, n. 11. Anderson agrees with Gorham's judgement by assigning to the letter from Martyr to Beza, based on internal criteria alone, a date of March 8, 1555. See Anderson, *Peter Martyr*, 475.

34. Martyr's letter to Calvin displays a tighter, crisper style. Near the end of his letter to Beza, Martyr repeats himself, giving extra illustrations in what appears to be an attempt to clarify his position. In the letter to Calvin, Martyr's critique of Cyril of Alexandria is more fully developed and substantial than in his letter to Beza. Perhaps these differences only reflect a greater degree of informality and familiarity with Beza. However, Martyr's letter to Beza appears to be more of a "first draft" on the subject.

35. Martyr begins confessing to Beza, "I should have long ago answered your two learned and courteous letters." After briefly criticizing a manuscript on predestination prepared by Beza as lacking sufficient scriptural documentation, Martyr devotes the bulk of the letter to union with Christ: "It now remains that I should answer those things which you demand as touching our communion with Christ" (Martyr to Beza, 105). Beza's original two letters of inquiry now unfortunately have been lost. See Beza, *Correspondance*, 155, n. 1.

36. Martyr forms something of an historical bridge between Calvin and Beza on the subject of union with Christ. As in Calvin's August 8, 1555 letter, Martyr ends his letter to Beza on an unmistakable note of continuity: "Between our two opinions there is but a little or no difference at all" (Martyr to Beza, 106.) Beza had obviously outlined his own understanding of the doctrine in his previous letter to Martyr, sadly no longer extant.

37. For an analysis of Martyr's letters to Calvin and Beza, as well as tracing of the themes in these letters through the balance of Martyr's corpus, see W. Duncan Rankin, "Peter Martyr Vermigli on Union with Christ," *Haddington House Journal* 7 (2005): 101–24.

Tamburello describes "a twofold communion with Christ" in Calvin's writings, especially in Calvin's 8 August 1555 letter.[38] These two kinds of union with Christ are mystical union and spiritual union. To these two we will turn first.

Mystical Communion with Christ

Tamburello notes that Calvin uses the term *unio mystica* in only two places in the *Institutes*.[39] The most important occurs in *Institutes* 3.11.10:

> Therefore, that joining together of Head and members, that indwelling of Christ in our hearts—in short, that mystical union—are accorded by us the highest degree of importance, so that Christ, having been made ours, makes us sharers with him in the gifts with which he has been endowed. We do not, therefore, contemplate him outside ourselves from afar in order that his righteousness may be imputed to us but because we put on Christ and are engrafted into his body—in short, because he deigns to make us one with him. For this reason, we glory that we have fellowship of righteousness with him.[40]

Although he does not use the title "mystical union," John Calvin opens his letter to Peter Martyr of 8 August 1555 with a detailed discussion of that communion which flows from his heavenly influence, and breathes life into us, and makes us to coalesce into one body with himself.[41]

It is clear that this section in Calvin's letter is describing what he later calls "mystical union."[42] As in Martyr, only the regenerate are said to enjoy this high level of union with Christ:

38. "Another important reference to this twofold communion is found in a letter of Calvin to Peter Martyr. Again Calvin speaks of two communions with Christ: the first communion is that Christ lives in us through the power of the Spirit. . . . [T]he second communion [is one] whereby Christ makes us rich in spiritual gifts. . . . It is interesting to note that this second communion grows whereas the first is total." Tamburello, *Union with Christ*, 86–87.

39. Ibid., 84.

40. Calvin, *Institutes* (1559) 3.11.10 (737). CO 2:540: "*Coniunctio igitur illa capitis et membrorum, habitatio Christi in cordibus nostris, mystica denique unio a nobis in summo gradu statuetur, ut Christus noster factus, donorum quibus praeditus est nos faciat consortes. Non ergo eum extra nos procul speculamur, ut nobis imputetur eius iustitia; sed quia ipsum induimus, et insiti sumus in eius corpus, unum denique nos secum efficere dignatus est, ideo iustitiae societatem nobis cum eo esse gloriamur.*" The other reference to "mystical union" is less descriptive: Calvin, *Institutes* (1559) 2.12.7 (473) [CO 2:258].

41. Calvin to Martyr, 349 [CO 15:722–23].

42. The section in the *Institutes* on mystical union quoted above was added to the 1559 edition and did not appear in earlier editions. In the French translation, Calvin does not call it a

But I affirm, that, as soon as we receive Christ by faith, as He offers Himself to us in the Gospel, we are truly made His members, and His life flows to us from Him as from our Head. For He reconciles us to God by the sacrifice of His death, in no other way than as He is ours and we are one with Him.[43]

It is "the faithful" who "are called into the Communion (*koinōnia*) of His [Son] . . . ."[44] Calvin does not leave the door open to a broadening of this level of union to include the unregenerate.

Calvin employs the Johannine imagery of a vine and branches to delineate mystical communion, just as Peter Martyr did before him.[45] The outcome of this ingrafting is that "He is ours and we are one with Him."[46] In direct effect of this incorporation into Christ, "life flows from Him to us in the same manner as the root transmits sap to the branches."[47] This is why mystical communion can only be posited of the regenerate—for the benefits of Christ's life and death only apply to those united to him by mystical communion.[48]

Calvin's main concern is to stress this life of Christ that becomes ours through mystical communion.[49] Christ's "life is transfused from heaven to

mystical union but a *union sacrée* (Calvin, *Institutes* [1559] 3.11.10, 737 n. 20; and *CO* 4:238). On the medical duress under which Calvin oversaw this translation and related issues, see Wendel, *Calvin: Origins and Development*, 118–19. In this letter Calvin describes this degree of union with Christ as the "sacred unity." Tamburello agrees that this first section in Calvin's letter to Martyr deals with mystical union (Tamburello, *Union with Christ*, 86–87). Did Martyr's prior designation of "mystical communion" in his letter of 1555 prompt Calvin's language in the 1559 *Institutes*? See footnote 41 above. Gerrish is convinced that Calvin's intent in using "mystical" is straightforward: "Calvin meant no more by the actual word *mysticus* than simply 'mysterious.' Hence he can equally well use the adjective 'secret' or 'wonderful' to characterize our communion with Christ. 'Mystical' was perhaps suggested to him by his favorite biblical proof for union with Christ: Ephesians 5:28–33. . . . This, I think, is all Calvin means by calling our union or communication with Christ 'mystical.'" Gerrish, *Grace and Gratitude*, 72–73. Gerrish's observation is not spoiled by the criticisms of his book by T. H. L. Parker, Review of *Grace and Gratitude: The Eucharistic Theology of John Calvin by B. A. Gerrish*, in *Journal of Theological Studies* 45 (1994): 771–75.

43. Calvin to Martyr, 349–50 [*CO* 15:723].

44. Ibid., 350 [*CO* 15:723].

45. Calvin denominates this image variously, but the language of ingrafting is one of his favorites. See ibid., 350–51 [*CO* 15:722–23], especially Calvin's phrases *facit ut in unum cum ipso corpus coalescamus and filius Dei nos in corpus suum inserit.*

46. Ibid., 350 [*CO* 15:723].

47. Ibid.

48. Hence, mystical union "breathes life into us." Ibid., 349 [*CO* 15:723].

49. While Calvin's letter includes a distinct section on mystical communion, does he not here threaten to get ahead of himself? No longer is he only pointing to the act of incorporation, by

earth" via mystical communion.[50] The redeemed enjoy that sacred unity by which the Son of God engrafts us into his body, so that he communicates to us all that is his. We so draw life from his flesh and blood that they are not improperly called our food.[51]

Calvin does not spell out the precise nature of this life. He does say, however, Christ comes "to dwell in us, to sustain us, to quicken us, and to fulfil all the offices of the Head."[52]

How does this mystical communion occur? Calvin leaves that question not fully resolved:

> How that is done, is, I confess, far deeper than the measure of my understanding; and, therefore, I rather receive this mystery, than labour to comprehend it . . . .[53]

He does, however, affirm the intimate involvement of the Holy Spirit in the event. It is the Spirit who transmits Christ's life in heaven down to earth.[54] The physical distance between the heavenly Savior and his people must, therefore, be overcome by the Holy Spirit.[55] Calvin goes so far as to say that Christ's very flesh would not be life-giving without the concomitant work of the Spirit.[56]

---

which Christ's life is made the believer's for the first time, but Calvin hints that this incorporation produces an ongoing effect, which he treats more fully in the next section of his letter when discussing spiritual communion. See ibid., 350–51 [*CO* 15:722–723].

50. Ibid., 350 [*CO* 15:723].

51. Ibid.

52. Ibid. Calvin's allusion to "the offices of the Head" may well refer to his doctrines of the Mediator and the *triplex munus*.

53. Ibid.

54. Ibid.: "life is transfused from heaven to earth by the Divine influence of the Spirit . . . ."

55. Ibid.: "nor could its efficacy reach as far as us, except through the immense operation of the Spirit." Calvin is here providing an alternative to the Lutheran notion of ubiquity.

56. Ibid.: "life is transfused from heaven to earth by the Divine influence of the Spirit; for, neither could the flesh of Christ be life-giving by itself, nor could its efficacy reach as far as us, except through the immense operation of the Spirit. Hence it is the Spirit who makes Christ to dwell in us, to sustain us, to quicken us, and to fulfil all the offices of the Head." Calvin does not say why the flesh of Christ could not be life-giving by itself. But it is clear that this limitation of the efficacy of Christ's flesh and dependence on the Spirit conflicts with the Lutheran concept of the ubiquity of Christ's body, as well as the Roman Catholic concept of transubstantiation, which places life-giving grace and the means of its conveyance in the physical flesh of Christ itself. See also John Calvin, *Tracts*, trans. Henry Beveridge, ed. Henry Beveridge and Jules Bonnet, vol. 2, *Containing Treatises on the Sacraments, Catechism of the Church of Geneva, Forms of Prayer, and Confessions of Faith* (1849; repr. as *Selected Works of John Calvin: Tracts and Letters*, Grand Rapids: Baker, 1983), 2:563 [*CO* 9:511–12].

Like Peter Martyr, John Calvin is convinced that any notion of a crass mixture of substance with Christ is wrong.[57] Calvin extends Martyr's criticism of Cyril of Alexandria for immoderately using "hyperbolical expressions" to also include Hilary of Poitiers:

> But though I see that the ancients, especially Hilary and Cyril were carried much too far, yet I am not disposed severely to censure their hyperbolas, except when it is sought to prop up error by their authority, an attempt to which I always distinctly oppose myself. . . . Still, provided these new fusionists do not thrust their authority upon us, I shall be satisfied in not subscribing, and I shall not voluntarily drag them into the arena.[58]

Clearly, Calvin was agreeing with Martyr that these Fathers had "afforded a large handle to many errors."[59] Calvin, however, appears reticent to disagree publicly with these Fathers, who "were carried much too far," unless driven to it by "these new fusionists."[60] Calvin is satisfied disagreeing with the "wretchedly obscure position that we also are of the same essence with Christ."[61]

Calvin and Martyr plainly saw eye-to-eye on mystical communion with Christ. Both affirm that it is a degree of union proper to regenerate Christians alone. Both agree in using Johannine ingrafting language for this level of union, firmly linking the efficacy of Christ's flesh to the spiritual status of the regenerate. Both point to the Holy Spirit as a key player in the mystical event. Both are opposed to notions of a mixture of substance between Christ and believers, even when found among certain Church

---

57. See also Calvin, *Tracts*, 2:535 [*CO* 9:490–91].

58. Calvin to Martyr, 350 [*CO* 15:723]. See also Calvin, *Tracts*, 2:540–41 [*CO* 9:494–95].

59. Martyr to Calvin, 344.

60. Calvin's hesitation to disagree publicly with these ancient authorities conspicuously contrasts with Torrance's assertions about Calvin's use of the Fathers. While Augustine was cited most frequently by Calvin, Torrance maintains that this was mainly for apologetic purposes, since he was the *magister theologiae* of his day. For the true source behind Calvin's teaching, Torrance points to the Eastern Fathers and those influenced by them, such as Hilary. See T. F. Torrance, "The Doctrine of the Holy Trinity, Gregory Nazianzen and John Calvin," *Sobornost* 12 (1990): 7–8; and T. F. Torrance, *The Hermeneutics of John Calvin* (Edinburgh: Scottish Academic Press, 1988), 82. The "fusionists" Calvin has in mind doubtless include Andreas Osiander and his followers, who opposed Melanchthon's doctrine of imputation, positing instead that the essential divine righteousness of Christ was the believer's. See Calvin, *Institutes* (1559) II.12.4–7 (467–74) [*CO* 2:342–47] and III.11.5–12 (729–43) [*CO* 2:536–45; and Calvin, *Tracts*, 2:535, 547.

61. Calvin to Martyr, 351 [*CO* 15:723].

Fathers. Neither sees this degree of communion with Christ as the only one operating in the lives of Christian believers.

SPIRITUAL COMMUNION WITH CHRIST

The second kind of union that Calvin discusses in his letter to Peter Martyr is also by action of the Holy Spirit and is closely related to the first. This level of communion is again only for regenerate believers. It cannot be separated from the former mysterious type, of which it is "the fruit and effect":

> For after that Christ, by the interior influence of His Spirit, has bound us to Himself and united us to His Body, He exerts a second influence of His Spirit, enriching us by His gifts.[62]

The balance of Calvin's treatment of spiritual union centers upon the gifts that believers enjoy through it.

Calvin weaves a list of spiritual gifts that the justified enjoy into a beautifully moving passage, doubtless the most memorable of the letter:

> Hence,—that we are strong in hope and patience,—that we soberly and temperately keep ourselves from worldly snares,—that we strenuously bestir ourselves to the subjugation of carnal affections,—that the love of righteousness and piety flourishes in us,—that we are earnest in prayer,—that meditation on the life to come draws us upwards,—this, I maintain, flows from that second Communion, by which Christ, dwelling in us not ineffectually, brings forth the influence of His Spirit in His manifest gifts.[63]

As a dynamic and progressive relation, spiritual union with Christ is clearly bound up intimately with the Christian walk. Such manifold blessings are not absurd, Calvin argues, because by mystical communion "we coalesce into His body": mystical communion is the rationale

---

62. Ibid. Because Calvin stresses that this second communion is by the action of the Holy Spirit, we shall designate it "spiritual communion." However, this should not be taken in an exclusive sense, as if mystical communion were not also accomplished by action of the Holy Spirit.

63. Ibid.

behind giving them.[64] Spiritual union is the means by which "the life of Christ increases" in believers and "He daily offers Himself to be enjoyed by them."[65] To this level of union with Christ, Calvin assigns the Lord's Supper.[66]

Though not every phrase and line of reasoning is identical, Calvin and Martyr do appear to coincide remarkably in their understanding of the believer's union with Christ. Both degrees of union are peculiar to Christians only. While Martyr emphasizes that spiritual union makes one "Christ-shaped," Calvin extends his Johannine ingrafting theme, stressing the sap—"the life of Christ"—that can be ours in greater measure through spiritual union.

Both Calvin and Martyr agree that mystical communion must lie behind the daily experience of spiritual communion with Christ in a believer's life. Mystical communion is a definitive event in the lives of the elect, while spiritual communion is an ongoing, progressive relation.[67] Thus, mystical communion grounds justification, while spiritual communion appears to ground sanctification.[68]

How successful is Calvin in distinguishing between these two types of communion with Christ? Admittedly, the terminology involved can be rather cumbersome. Mystical communion is no less "mysterious" than

---

64. Ibid. *CO* 13:722–23: "*Nam de ea tantum agendum est quae a coelesti eius virtute manat et nobis vitam inspirat, et facit ut in unum cum ipso corpus coalescamus.*" This is reminiscent of Martyr's argument that mystical union must be "prior, in nature at least, if not in time" to spiritual union. See footnotes 53 and 54 above.

65. Calvin to Martyr, 351–52 [*CO* 15:724].

66. Ibid., 352 [*CO* 15:724]: "This is the Communion which they receive in the Sacred Supper." Gerrish notes that here Calvin assigns the Eucharist more to spiritual communion rather than mystical communion: "Calvin does seem to intend at least a relative difference of function between preaching and the Eucharist: the first [mystical] communication is associated chiefly with the gospel, the second [spiritual communication] chiefly with the Sacrament." Gerrish, *Grace and Gratitude*, 129.

67. Tamburello has analyzed the correlation between this twofold communion and Calvin's doctrines of justification and sanctification (see Tamburello, *Union with Christ*, 86–87). "It is interesting to note that this second communion 'grows' whereas the first is 'total.' This corresponds exactly to Calvin's theology of justification and sanctification. Just as justification for Calvin is always total while sanctification is always partial, so our participation in Christ's righteousness is total while the union of regeneration is partial." Ibid., 87.

68. Calvin's famous statement in the *Institutes* on the *unio mystica* makes clear his intention to ground the imputed righteousness of Christ on mystical communion. See footnote 40 above; and Alister E. McGrath, *Iustitia Dei: A History of the Christian Doctrine of Justification*, vol. 2: *From 1500 to the Present Day* (Cambridge: Cambridge University Press), 1986, 36–38.

spiritual communion, and in turn, spiritual communion is no less "of the Spirit" than mystical communion![69] Nevertheless, it is clear that Calvin does distinguish between these two communions in his letter of 8 August 1555.[70] To his mind, they are distinct yet inseparable concepts, each brought about by a separate influence of the Holy Spirit.

Yet why does Calvin draw such a distinction between mystical and spiritual communion? He feels compelled by Scripture itself:

> Nor is it absurd, that Christ, when we coalesce into His Body, communicates to us His Spirit, by whose secret operation He first was made ours; since Scripture often assigns both offices to Him.[71]

While Calvin does not here specify the biblical passages that delineate these two offices to Christ, it is at least clear that Christ's headship and office as king are juxtaposed with his giving of the Holy Spirit and office as prophet.[72] He distinguishes between mystical and spiritual communion in the same way he distinguishes Christ and his gifts, or justification and sanctification.[73]

Both Tamburello and Willis notice two levels of union with Christ in Calvin; however, the levels they each notice are not identical. Tamburello points to the mystical and spiritual unions that we have treated above.[74] Willis,

69. Even Calvin stumbles over himself in discussing these two types of the believer's union with Christ. See footnote 49 above. Perhaps this awkwardness is the reason Calvin fails to strictly label these two communions in his letter. See footnotes 42 and 62.

70. He makes this abundantly evident when first introducing spiritual communion: "I come now to a second Communion, which, as I think, is the fruit and effect of the former. For after that Christ, by the interior of His Spirit, has bound us to Himself and united us to His Body, *He exerts a second influence of His Spirit, enriching us by His gifts.*" Calvin to Martyr, 351 [*CO* 15:723].

71. Ibid. [*CO* 15:723–24].

72. This distinction between Christ's offices of king and prophet is also made in Calvin's other writings. See, for example, Calvin, *Institutes* (1559) II.15.1–2 (494–96) [*CO* 2:361–63] and II.15.3–5 (496–501) [*CO* 2:363–66]. While Jansen discounts the use that Calvin makes of his *triplex munus*, his conclusions have not gone unchallenged. Compare J. F. Jansen, *Calvin's Doctrine of the Work of Christ* (London: James Clarke, 1956), 97, with R. A. Muller, *Christ and the Decree* (Grand Rapids: Baker, 1988), 31–33.

73. The contrast between mystical and spiritual communion is also clearly shown in *Institutes* (1559) 3.1.1–2 (537–39) [*CO* 2:393–95]. Here Calvin first treats the Holy Spirit as the bond that unites believers to Christ (which is an obvious prologue to his later teaching on the *unio mystica*) and then moves to discuss the benefits of Christ the Mediator giving the Holy Spirit.

74. Tamburello, *Union with Christ*, 86–87. Tamburello does develop these categories more fully, citing references quite widely in Calvin's corpus. He does not, however, display any aware-

in addition to mystical union, points to a union with Christ by virtue of the incarnation.[75] As I will show, each of these scholars has correctly described different portions of Calvin's overall position on union with Christ.

INCARNATIONAL COMMUNION WITH CHRIST

It is no wonder that Tamburello misses Calvin's reference to incarnational communion in his letter to Peter Martyr on 8 August 1555. Without previous knowledge of Martyr's own letter on the subject, Calvin's reference to incarnational communion is easily overlooked.[76] After brief introductory remarks, Calvin plunges into the requested topic of correspondence only with some hesitation:

> Although I promised to write to you, on the secret Communion which we have with Christ, yet I shall not treat this subject so largely as you hoped: nevertheless, as the matter is one of vast importance, I think it may be profitable to state my opinion definitely in a few words.[77]

In the next sentence the Genevan makes his fleeting comments about incarnational communion:

> That the Son of God put on our flesh, in order that He might become our Brother, partaker of the same nature,—is a Communion on which I do

---

ness of Peter Martyr's 8 March 1555 letter to Calvin nor use Martyr's teaching on the subject as background material for interpreting Calvin's views. The same is true of his academic supervisor. See Gerrish, *Grace and Gratitude*, 128–29.

75. Willis-Watkins, "Unio Mystica," 78–79. These categories are not developed more fully. Willis-Watkins only references Calvin's 1559 *Institutes* in this brief treatment.

76. In fairness, incarnational union does fall outside the scope of Tamburello's comparative study on mystical union in Calvin and Bernard. He does, however, only denominate two degrees of union with Christ when treating this material. His academic supervisor is perhaps more observant, when he describes mystical communion as "something subsequent to the union with Christ that was already effected by the incarnation, but antecedent to the communication of his benefits" (Gerrish, *Grace and Gratitude*, 128). He does not expand upon this theme.

77. Calvin to Martyr, 349 [*CO* 15:722]. Calvin's promise of brevity may be made more out of courtesy than consequence. After his generous treatment, Calvin concludes: "Were I teaching any other person, I should follow up this subject more diffusely; in addressing you, I have glanced at it briefly, with the simple view of showing you that we entirely agree in sentiment." Ibid., 352 [*CO* 15:724].

not mean to speak here: for I propose to treat only [mystic and spiritual communion].[78]

Calvin then begins his treatment of mystic communion, followed by instruction on spiritual communion.

With this passing reference, Calvin is acknowledging Martyr's fuller treatment of incarnational communion with Christ in his letter of 8 March 1555. While he obviously means what he says—he does not mean to expand on this kind of communion with Christ in this letter—Calvin does not leave us empty-handed. The very terms in which he avoids the subject give us a handle with which to grasp his meaning in other places: "carnem nostram induit, ut frater noster fieret eiusdem naturae particeps." Calvin's preferred terminology for this relationship, like Martyr's, is not incarnational "union" but "communion."[79] Calvin feels it sufficient to point out that an incarnational communion exists and to indicate that fact with a certain idiom.

Martyr's original request to Calvin was both polite and compelling:

I have discussed this matter more at large, I fear, than suits your occupation, and yet less copiously than may suffice to unfold my meaning. When you shall have leisure, do not, I pray, conceal from me any part of your opinion.[80]

Calvin in turn professes in the strongest terms consistency and continuity with Martyr's own position on the doctrine of union with Christ as stated in his letter:

78. The Latin reads: "*Quod filius Dei carnem nostram induit, ut frater noster fieret eiusdem naturae particeps, de illa communicatione dicere supersedeo.*" Ibid., 349 [*CO* 15:722]. Gerrish notes that later in this same letter, when referring to spiritual union, Calvin varies the terms *communio* and *communicatio* without any difference in meaning (see Gerrish, *Grace and Gratitude*, 129, n. 16). In this earlier instance, however, Calvin's use of *communicatio* when discussing the incarnation carries a more definite overtone—that of the *communicatio idiomatum*. Calvin's Reformed construction of this doctrine conflicted with that of his Lutheran counterparts who taught the ubiquity of Christ's body.

79. In the letters between them, the relationship between Christ and human persons based on the incarnation alone is not called a *unio*. For Martyr's use of both *communio* and *communicatio* when discussing natural communion in neighboring sentences, see *LC* 768. Calvin only uses *communication* for this relation. Could Martyr and Calvin be signaling a qualitative difference in this use of "communion" or "communication" rather than "union"? Did *unio* carry heavy ontological overtones that could too easily be confused with a mixture of essence when referring to this relationship?

80. Martyr to Calvin, 344.

Were I teaching any other person, I should follow up this subject more diffusely; in addressing you, I have glanced at it briefly, with the simple view of showing you that we entirely agree in sentiment.[81]

There is no hint of duplicity in Calvin's dealings with Martyr here. Calvin is comfortable passing over incarnational communion when answering Peter Martyr's plea for his own frank opinion on the doctrine of union with Christ. Martyr and Calvin were very close in their mutual theology, friendship, and regard at this point in their lives.[82] Thus, it is patently unreasonable to suspect that in passing over incarnational communion Calvin had something to hide.[83] In disregarding the topic, is Calvin not implying that the wider subject can be adequately treated without it?

Calvin's important correspondence with Peter Martyr highlights several key points about his doctrine of incarnational communion with Christ. First, Calvin is happy professing to "entirely agree in sentiment" with someone who describes incarnational "communion" as *debilis* and reserves Johannine ingrafting language for believers only. This same person explicitly points to a biological origin for this communion in men and women, rather than to an upholding of the cosmos or human flesh by the incarnate Savior. Finally, Calvin can contentedly pass over the whole subject of incarnational communion when discussing the believer's union with Christ. In our effort to probe Calvin's fuller views on incarnational communion, we must therefore look to his wider corpus for light, using the handle he gives in this letter to grasp the subject more firmly.

Conclusion

Calvin's use of Johannine ingrafting language and the biblical phrase "in Christ" is reserved for mystical and spiritual communion. Calvin does,

81. Calvin to Martyr, 352. *CO* 15:724: "*Apud alium quempiam, qui mihi docendus esset, fusius prosequerer quae breviter apud te hoc tantum consilio perstringo, ut nos idem prorsus sentire videas.*"

82. Calvin had just offered Martyr a job in Geneva, and Martyr had only a few months before given Calvin some quite frank advice that Calvin warmly appreciated (see Calvin, *Tracts and Letters*, vol. 6, 121–26) [*CO* 15:386–89]. Calvin continued to have a warm and open relationship with Martyr. See ibid., 313–14 [*CO* 16:403–4].

83. Even McLelland insists that Calvin is here professing continuity with Martyr's views on incarnational union, although McLelland inflates the place of incarnational union in Martyr's theology. McClelland [sic], "Reformed Doctrine of Predestination," 271, n. 3.

however, teach different degrees of union with Christ, which flow out of different kinds of communion or communication with Christ. Each involves different sets of persons, as becomes apparent from close examination of his correspondence with Peter Martyr. The hypostatic union and resultant incarnational communion involve the man Jesus, who in his humanity is a man just like other men, sin excepted. Mystic communion is a definitive sacred ingrafting into the life of Jesus Christ by the action of the Holy Spirit upon faith. Spiritual communion is the progressive enjoyment of the Spirit and blessings of Christ's life that flow from mystic union.

The marked difference between the status of unbelievers versus believers in their relationship to Christ—Calvin's acceptance of Martyr's *debilis* and *infirma*—puts a clear theological division between incarnational communion on the one hand, and mystical and spiritual communion on the other. For Calvin, the believer's spiritual union with Christ is another union in addition to our incarnational union with him.

PART 4

Practical Theology

One work of Jesus Christ explained another, and the great facts of the redemption, birth, death, and resurrection of the Son of God, and the sending of the Holy Ghost, followed and completed each other. The authority of Christ's teaching, so strongly contrasting with the doubts of the schools, increased the clearness of His discourses to His readers; for the more certain a truth is, the more distinctly it strikes the mind.[1]

—J. H. Merle d'Aubigne

1. J. H. Merle d'Aubigne, *The Reformation in England* (Edinburgh: Banner of Truth, 1977), 1:247–48.

13

Redemptive History and the Regulative Principle of Worship

DOMINIC A. AQUILA

WORSHIP IS CENTRAL to the Christian life. It is a task that brings us into one of the closest relationships with the living God. This is one reason why we must take it seriously and why we should be concerned to practice it with great care and propriety.

The Reformation took worship seriously. As a result there has been debate within Reformed churches since the Reformation about where to draw the line in applying the regulative principle of worship. There has not been unanimity of definition and practice. While there has been the desire to honor the regulative principle, its clear application has not been universal, and perhaps even elusive. It could be that none of us can remove ourselves completely from our historical context, even while affirming true and lofty biblical principles.

An important point in the study of history in general and church history in particular is that we must see and evaluate ideas and events in their immediate contexts. It should also be recognized that people and ideas are products of their times. In reviewing some of the thoughts and practices of the Reformers, we can make a good case that they, too, were influenced by their time and context. While the Reformers laid a good foundation for much of the theology that is important to us today, they were not completely free of the influences of their day.

Arguably, some of the views on worship practices coming out of the Reformation were influenced or affected, at least in part, by a reaction to the prevailing worship practices of the Roman Catholic Church, rather than just out of a desire to apply pure biblical principles. Luther grounded his Ninety-five Theses in justification by faith alone; he made a clear declaration of the authority of Scripture in his ringing comment, "My conscience is captive to the Word of God."[1] Zwingli, too, grounded his ministry on the authority of Scripture. Yet, when it came to the Lord's Supper each man applied this authority in different ways. Luther believed that Christ was present in such a way that he adopted consubstantiation. Zwingli, on the other hand, reacted strongly to the idea of Christ's physical presence in the Supper and adopted a memorial view.[2] The point is that both men were sincere in desiring reformation and honoring Scripture, but in different ways they were still products of their time. There is a principle to be drawn from this: No one group, person or theology is absolutely pure and without some effects of the times and context in which it lives.

We can study the regulative principle of worship from a number of perspectives. We do need to understand its development from its historical and theological contexts, especially as developed from the Reformation. It also needs to be reviewed and understood in the light of redemptive history, a process that will provide guidance in setting this principle in a biblical context. Worship is a major theme from beginning to end in God's redemptive history; the same principles of worship hold true for each period of this history. God mandated one set of truths or principles to govern worship in every stage of redemptive history, even though there are observable differences of worship practices in these various stages. In other words, the distinctive practices in these stages of redemption expressed the same principle of worship. God is the author of the whole of redemption and we find consistency of thought throughout these various periods. In

1. Roland H. Bainton, *Here I Stand: A Life of Martin Luther* (New York: Abingdon, 1950), 185.
2. Louis Berkhof, *Systematic Theology* (London: Banner of Truth, 1966), 651–54.

our study of Scripture, it is our responsibility to see the abiding principles behind the practices of these various redemptive periods.

Old covenant shadows and new covenant realities are distinct, yet related to one another. The Westminster Confession of Faith explains the relationship between old covenant and new covenant understandings of the use of the law: "To them [Israel] also, as a body politic, He gave sundry judicial laws, which expired together with the state of that people; not obliging any other now, further than *the general equity thereof may require*" (19.4, emphasis added). The phrase "general equity" is another way of expressing "principle."

The Scripture presents Israel as the church under a tutor, that is, under Mosaic legislation. This Mosaic legislation was given in exhaustive detail because the Israelites, the church under the old covenant, were "children" and placed under the supervision of a disciplinarian tutor,[3] which exercised exacting supervision and boundaries. This supervision included regulations for every area of life: worship, family, economics, justice, etc. Under the new covenant, and in its fulfillment and consummation in Christ, the exacting, supervisory nature of Mosaic legislation was abrogated. But the principle (the general equity) of Mosaic legislation was not abrogated. Under the new covenant we read the Old Testament with minds and eyes informed by the consummation that has come in Christ, we see the abiding principles, and we apply them in new covenant ways.[4] And even here we need to recognize that not all new covenant practices will look exactly the same, even among believers who hold tenaciously to the same truths.

Where does the regulative principle of worship fit into this framework? The regulative principle of worship is defined as the means by which the

3. "Before this faith came, we were held prisoners by the law, locked up until faith should be revealed. So the law was put in charge [*paidagōgos*] to lead us to Christ that we might be justified by faith. Now that faith has come, we are no longer under the supervision (*paidagōgos*) of the law" (Gal. 3:23–25).

4. "Preaching Christ from the Old Testament means that we preach, not synagogue sermons, but sermons that take account of the full drama of redemption, and its realization in Christ. To see the text in relation to Christ is to see it in its larger context. The context of God's purpose in revelation. We do not ignore the specific message of the text, nor will it do to write an all-purpose Christocentric sermon finale and tag it for weekly use.

"You must preach Christ as the text presents him. If you are tempted to think that most Old Testament texts do not present Christ, reflect on both the unity of Scripture and the fullness of Jesus Christ. Christ is present in the Bible as the Lord and as the Servant." Edmund Clowney, *Preaching Christ in All of Scripture* (Wheaton: Crossway, 2003), 11.

public worship of God should include only those elements that are instituted, commanded, or appointed by command or example in the Bible; that God institutes in Scripture everything he requires for worship in the church, and he prohibits everything else.

In contrast to the regulative principle of worship is the normative principle. The normative principle teaches that whatever Scripture does not prohibit in worship it permits, so long as it is agreeable to the peace and unity of the church. In other words, there must be agreement with the general practice of the church and no prohibition in Scripture for whatever we do in worship. The normative principle is the generally accepted approach to worship practiced by the Orthodox Churches, Roman Catholics, Lutherans, some Anglicans, and Methodists. The regulative principle of worship is generally practiced by those churches that consider themselves Reformed.

The Westminster Confession defines the regulative principle:

> The light of nature showeth that there is a God, who hath lordship and sovereignty over all, is good, and doth good unto all, and is therefore to be feared, loved, praised, called upon, trusted in, and served, with all the heart, and with all the soul, and with all the might. But the acceptable way of worshipping the true God is instituted by himself, and so limited by his own revealed will, that he may not be worshipped according to the imaginations and devices of men, or the suggestions of Satan, under any visible representation, or any other way not prescribed in the Holy Scripture. (21.1)[5]

What are the principles for worship that are common in every stage or period of redemptive history? They would include at least the following: worshiping in community (covenant people are the "assembled" ones, the "called out ones"); theocentricity (God is the one on the throne and in the center of the assembled ones); proclamation (God speaks propositionally in Scripture and must be heard; there is the announcement of the gospel);

5. The Presbyterian Church in America's Book of Church Order 47–1 states: "Since the Holy Scriptures are the only infallible rule of faith and practice, the principles of public worship, must be derived from the Bible, and from no other source. The Scripture forbids the worshipping of God by images, or in any other way not appointed in His Word, and requires the receiving, observing, and keeping pure and entire all such religious worship and ordinances as God hath appointed in His Word (WSC 51, 50)."

singing (songs of the various aspects of the redemption, highlighting the person and acts of God, personal reflections and questions to God; songs as expressed, for example, in the Psalms and in the Song of Moses, Ex. 15); offerings (we offer ourselves and our substance; the Old Testament language of sacrifice is used in the New Testament in non-bloody ways, e.g., Rom. 12:1–2); and praying (ascriptions of praise, thanksgiving, confession, requests, and petitions).[6]

Some have made distinctions between "elements" of worship and "circumstances" of worship. There are some, like John Frame, who have argued that the distinctions between elements and circumstances are not necessarily helpful or valid.[7] However, as commonly stated, the elements included in worship are like those listed in the Westminster Confession 21.3–5. The circumstances are items concerning where the church meets, the time it meets, how it sits, and so forth.[8]

6. The Westminster Confession of Faith 21.3–5 gives the following as the "elements" of worship:

"3. Prayer, with thanksgiving, being one special part of religious worship, is by God required of all men: and, that it may be accepted, it is to be made in the name of the Son, by the help of his Spirit, according to his will, with understanding, reverence, humility, fervency, faith, love, and perseverance; and, if vocal, in a known tongue.

"4. Prayer is to be made for things lawful; and for all sorts of men living, or that shall live hereafter: but not for the dead, nor for those of whom it may be known that they have sinned the sin unto death.

"5. The reading of the Scriptures with godly fear, the sound preaching and conscionable hearing of the Word, in obedience unto God, with understanding, faith, and reverence, singing of psalms with grace in the heart; as also, the due administration and worthy receiving of the sacraments instituted by Christ, are all parts of the ordinary religious worship of God: beside religious oaths, vows, solemn fastings, and thanksgivings upon special occasions, which are, in their several times and seasons, to be used in an holy and religious manner."

The Presbyterian Church in America's Book of Church Order 47–9 lists the following elements of worship: "The Bible teaches that the following are proper elements of worship service: reading of Holy Scripture, singing of psalms and hymns, the offering of prayer, the preaching of the Word, the presentation of offerings, confessing the faith and observing the Sacraments; and on special occasions taking oaths."

7. "In those discussions, Reformed thinkers have labored over concepts like *elements, parts, substance, essence, accident, forms, expressions,* and *circumstances* (further subdivided into circumstances with and without religious significance, and those necessary and unnecessary to the orderly conduct of worship). In my opinion, these concepts are not helpful, and using them to add further restrictions to the broad regulative principle is not scriptural. In this part of my essay, I will describe those additional restrictions and explain why I object to them." John Frame, "A Fresh Look at the Regulative Principle," *Reformed Perspectives Magazine,* 2005, http://reformedperspectives.org/newfiles/joh_frame/Frame.Ethics2005. AFreshLookattheRegulativePrinciple.html (accessed Feb. 2, 2008).

8. "Does this mean that there in *nothing* that may be done in a Reformed Church except what is commanded in the Bible? Not exactly. There are 'some circumstances concerning the

One of the difficulties in applying the regulative principle is that the distinctions between elements and circumstances can become confused or even melded together. The result is lack of distinctive clarity, which can result in both circumstances and elements being defined as elements. It is possible, also, to develop preferences for worship, which on the surface may be consistent with prescribed elements. If care is not taken, however, we can confuse our preferences with precepts. That is, we can raise preferences to the level of precepts and circumstances to the level of elements. If we raise circumstances to the level of elements and preferences to the level of precepts, then there will be confusion about the nature and practice of worship.

The regulative principle of worship emphasizes and focuses on the elements of worship; these principles are then to be applied to the specific contexts of worship and their circumstances. The regulative principle seen this way, and understood in light of redemptive history, does not so much restrict our worship as it directs its expansiveness. Worship is before God's throne and calls true worshipers to express and engage their whole being. While the elements of worship are always true and guide us, in the new covenant they do not restrict or bind us. New covenant believers are not under the old covenant and its modalities; they must express worship in and with new covenant modalities. Old covenant modalities directed the people how to live and worship with exacting detail. Under the new covenant, the old covenant forms have been abrogated, and new covenant believers live under the general equity of God's rule for life and worship.

How does the unfolding nature of redemptive history guide us in understanding and using the regulative principle of worship? Redemptive history is one way of speaking of God's work of redemption; it is God's redemptive plan unfolded through successive stages of biblical history and recorded in Scripture. Each stage builds progressively on and is connected to preceding and succeeding stages, finally culminating in the revelation found

---

worship of God . . . which are to be ordered by the light of nature and Christian prudence, according to the general rules of the Word' (WCF 1.6). These 'circumstances' are such as are 'common to human actions and societies.' But one must be careful to distinguish between the circumstances of worship and the worship itself. For example: Scripture does not prescribe the hour of the day at which public worship of the congregation is to be held. Neither has the Lord prescribed the shape, style, or size of the place of worship. In the nature of the case, such circumstances will vary from country to country, season to season, and place to place. There is the general rule, however, which requires that congregations assemble somewhere on the Lord's Day." G. I. Williamson, *The Westminster Confession of Faith for Study Classes* (Philadelphia: Presbyterian and Reformed, 1964), 160–61.

in Jesus Christ. Geerhardus Vos referred to this as the "History of Special Revelation": he recognized, however, that the term "Biblical Theology" was commonly used and defined it this way: "Biblical Theology is that branch of Exegetical Theology which deals with the process of the self-revelation of God deposited in the Bible."[9]

Vos drew a distinction between terms used to express different aspects of theological studies:

> Biblical Theology occupies a position between Exegesis and Systematic Theology in the encyclopaedia of theological disciplines. It differs from Systematic Theology not in being more Biblical, or adhering more closely to the truths of the Scriptures, but in that its principle of organizing the Biblical material is historical rather than logical. Whereas Systematic Theology takes the Bible as a completed whole and endeavors to exhibit its total teaching in an orderly, systematic form, Biblical Theology deals with the material from the historical standpoint, seeking to exhibit the organic growth or development of the truths of Special revelation from the primitive preredemptive Special revelation given in Eden to the close of the New Testament canon.[10]

In the flow of redemptive history, the pattern of the sanctuary God gave Moses was essential for that time, but when Jesus came he brought the superior covenant and the new tabernacle essential to reflect that new covenant. The first covenant was given with glory, but it was not the end of God's plan, and the glory was veiled. But when Christ came, the fullness of glory was revealed. Believers should expect the nature of worship under the fuller glory of the new covenant to be more glorious and unveiled than the nature of worship under the old covenant. And yet it appears that with certain definitions and applications of the regulative principle of worship, that believers are bound to old covenant realities and practices. We need

9. Geerhardus Vos, *Biblical Theology* (Grand Rapids: Eerdmans, 1948), 13.

10. Ibid., Preface. Vos observes further, "Both [Systematic Theology and Biblical Theology] equally make the truth deposited in the Bible undergo a transformation: but the difference arises from the fact that the principle by which the transformation is effected differs in each case. In Biblical Theology this principle is one of *historical*, in Systematic Theology it is one of *logical* construction. Biblical Theology draws a *line* of development. Systematic theology draws a *circle*. Still it should be remembered, that on the line of historical progress there is at several points already a beginning of correlation among elements of truth in which the beginnings of the systematizing process can be discerned." Ibid., 25.

to be careful not to impose old covenant anticipatory patterns, shadows, and types unto new covenant realities. The fuller glory of the new covenant has come in Christ and the lesser glory of the old has faded and no longer pertains, except for the general equity required thereof.

Paul highlights the greater glory of new covenant worship; he indicates that the old covenant came with glory, even though it was a ministry of death. If the old and that which was to fade away came with glory, how much more glorious will the ministry of the Spirit be?

> Now if the ministry that brought death, which was engraved in letters on stone, came with glory, so that the Israelites could not look steadily at the face of Moses because of its glory, fading though it was, will not the ministry of the Spirit be even more glorious? If the ministry that condemns men is glorious, how much more glorious is the ministry that brings righteousness! For what was glorious has no glory now in comparison with the surpassing glory. And if what was fading away came with glory, how much greater is the glory of that which lasts! (2 Cor. 3:7–11)

The writer of Hebrews calls believers to worship, not at Mount Sinai but at Mount Zion, in the heavenly Jerusalem. While believers worship in the earthly sphere, they join with the joyful assembly already taking place in the heavenly realm.

> You have not come to a mountain that can be touched [i.e., Mount Sinai] . . . But you have come to Mount Zion, to the heavenly Jerusalem, the city of the living God. You have come to thousands upon thousands of angels in joyful assembly, to the church of the firstborn, whose names are written in heaven. You have come to God, the judge of all men, to the spirits of righteous men made perfect, to Jesus the mediator of a new covenant, and to the sprinkled blood that speaks a better word than the blood of Abel. (Heb. 12:18, 22–24)

This heavenly sphere, where joyful assembly is being expressed, takes place in the perfect tabernacle/temple/sanctuary (Heb. 8:1–5). Moses was given the blueprint for the construction of the tabernacle (Ex. 25:40), which was to be erected exactly as God had given it to him. No building committee was to review, modify, or approve these plans. Why? Because the tabernacle was an earthly model of the heavenly and true sanctuary, and it was not to be adjusted by human ideas or designs. In essence, we can say that heaven came down to earth in the form of the tabernacle. And since God dwelt with his people in the Shekinah glory cloud, we can say that God "tabernacled" with his people. Later the temple would be built on the same pattern as the tabernacle.[11] The writer of Hebrews stated it this way:

> Every high priest is appointed to offer both gifts and sacrifices, and so it was necessary for this one also to have something to offer. If he were on earth, he would not be a priest, for there are already men who offer the gifts prescribed by the law. They serve at a sanctuary that is a copy and shadow of what is in heaven. This is why Moses was warned when he was about to build the tabernacle: "See to it that you make everything according to the pattern shown you on the mountain." But the ministry Jesus has received is as superior to theirs as the covenant of which he is mediator is superior to the old one, and it is founded on better promises. (Heb. 8:3–6)

The book of Revelation addresses believers in their present context; it is not a book just dealing with future events. The Lord gave John the Revelation to encourage believers in the first century as they faced persecution and tribulation. It is written in the present tense for the original readers in which Jesus Christ is shown as the Lamb who was slain yet is alive; he is the Lion of Judah who rules supremely over all things. It is a book intended to encourage each generation of the church, urging believers to live faithfully under every type of circumstance. Many of the scenes depicted in Revelation, including some of the heavenly ones, are contemporaneous

11. "The ministry of the levitical priests . . . is associated with *a copy and shadow of the heavenly sanctuary*, not with the true and eternal reality. But to call it 'a copy and shadow' does at least mean that the tent in the wilderness had a definite correspondence with the heavenly reality, though only to a limited degree. It was *a copy*, much as a drawing or plan of a building but is not the building itself . . . or as a model is not comparable in reality and splendor to the reality it portrays in miniature. It was also a *shadow* inasmuch as a shadow presupposes a body or substance which casts a shadow, though the shadow itself is incorporeal and insubstantial. There is, however, a real correspondence between a shadow and the substance of which it is the shadow.

"The important thing is to possess the substance, not the shadow, the reality, not the copy. Yet the very language our author uses serves to suggest that if, as has already been demonstrated, there are fundamental differences between the order of Levi and the order of Melchizedek, there are nonetheless significant affinities. . . . The type both points forward to and receives meaning from the antitype. But, as the context indicates, the complete perspective involves still more than this, for the antitype is also the archetype. The reality comes not only after but also before the copy and the shadow. Jesus Christ is the first as well as the last (cf. 13:8)." Philip Edgcumbe Hughes, *A Commentary on the Epistle to the Hebrews* (Grand Rapids: Eerdmans, 1977), 292–93.

with human history. As such, we should see the worship scenes as present scenes, not future ones.

The worship scenes in Revelation are instructive for our worship in this present age (e.g., Rev. 4; 5:8–14; 7:9–17; 11:15–19; 15:1–8; 19:1–10). The scenes, while heavenly, are contemporaneous with the time from Christ's ascension until his coming again. The worship in heaven is always in the present. When worship scenes are presented in Scripture, they show us worship as it is. When believers worship on earth they are joining the worship already taking place in heaven. Revelation 14:3 states, "And they sang a new song before the throne and before the four living creatures and the elders. No one could learn the song except the 144,000 who had been redeemed from the earth." Commenting on this verse Kistemaker indicates that the new song is being sung in heaven and on earth:

> Notice the special place the musicians and singers are allowed to occupy: they are in front of the throne, in the presence of God himself, and they stand in front of the four living creatures and the twenty-four elders who surround the throne (4:4–6). The identity of the singers is not revealed (compare 11:15; 12:10). Their voices sing a new song that arises from hearts filled with gratitude and love to God. We are not given the words of the song they sang, but we assume that they glorify the one sitting on the throne and extend thanks to the Lamb for the redemption he has accomplished on earth.
>
> "And no one could learn the song except the 144,000." If we put it in positive terms, the intent of this clause is to include all the saints, for they are able to sing this new song; no one of the saints in heaven and on earth is excluded from joining the chorus. But no unbeliever is able to learn a song of praise to God. The saints in heaven constantly sing their praises to God. Likewise, all God's people on earth sing his praises at worship, especially on the Lord's Day. Of course, the dividing line between heaven and earth continues to exist until the last day, yet the intent of the praises of thanksgiving is similar. The perfect song of the saints in heaven reverberates to the saints on earth and strengthens them in the battle against anti-Christian forces.[12]

It is obvious, then, that the glory of Christ is the center of worship. He is the Word made flesh who tabernacled among us and we beheld his

12. Simon J. Kistemaker, *Revelation*. New Testament Commentary (Grand Rapids: Baker, 2001), 402–3.

glory, the glory of the Father (John 1:14). Jesus also claims to be the new temple (John 2:11–22). His conversation with the Samaritan woman leads to a comment on the nature of true worship (John 4:19–26). Now that Jesus has come in the fullness of glory, worship is no longer bound to a particular location (this mountain or that one), but now worship can be anywhere under the direction of the Holy Spirit and consistent with God's truth.

Again, the writer of Hebrews issues a summons to worship not in the shadows of the old, but in the full light and reality of the new. It is because Christ has come in fullness that the invitation to worship can be made with great expectation:

> The law is only a shadow of the good things that are coming—not the realities themselves. For this reason it can never, by the same sacrifices repeated endlessly year after year, make perfect those who draw near to worship. . . . Therefore, brothers,
> - Since we have confidence to enter the Most Holy Place by the blood of Jesus, by a new and living way opened for us through the curtain, that is, his body, and
> - Since we have a great priest over the house of God:
>   - Let us draw near to God with a sincere heart in full assurance of faith. . . .
>   - Let us hold unswervingly to the hope we profess. . . .
>   - Let us consider how we may spur one another on toward love and good deeds. . . .
>   - Let us not give up meeting together. . . . (Heb. 10:1, 19–25)

When John was ushered into heaven to see what must take place (Rev. 4:1), he saw the true sanctuary, the same one that Moses saw when he met with God on the mountain and received the pattern or type of the tabernacle. This vision of heaven and the worship John observed was not a picture of worship in the distant future, of only what will be, but worship in the present time. Another way to state it is that John observed the nature of worship that is, has always been, and will always be before the throne. It was the same worship that Moses would have observed when he met with God. Because Jesus is the same yesterday, today, and forever (Heb. 13:8), he is to be worshiped according to the same principles in our time and in every generation.

What did John see when he was taken into heaven (Rev. 4–5)? He saw the true sanctuary, the real tabernacle that was the model for the earthly, temporary tabernacle. The throne is in the center of heaven; God is on the throne, and the Lamb is in the center of the throne. The Spirit was present in fullness (the seven-fold Spirit). Then, what to the human eye could be described as a perfect square (in the same way as the New Jerusalem is described as a perfect square—reflecting the order of and in God and of his heaven, Rev. 21:15–17), John saw the four living creatures, the twenty-four elders, six on each side of the square, the myriads of angles, and then the whole host of heaven surrounding the throne.

All of them: the four living creatures, the twenty-four elders, the myriad of angels and every creature, were focused on the throne. Their worship was directed to "him who sits on the throne and to the Lamb" (Rev. 5:13). This heavenly worship was not only the pattern for old covenant worship as represented through the tabernacle, it is also the pattern for new covenant worship that is expressed through the new temple, Jesus Christ.

How does all of this guide us in our worship for our present time? The church in every age is to use the full scope of redemptive history and the application that flows from this work of grace to direct its worship. All of the elements of worship are to assist us to see God and the Lamb on the throne.

A part of our worship includes the proclamation of the Scriptures; they are proclaimed prescriptively so that the whole counsel of God is declared (Acts 20:27). Christ is the center of redemptive history, and the revelation he brought is the controlling lens through which all Scripture must be seen (cf., Luke 24:27, 44). The "Scriptures" that Jesus used to explain himself to the disciples was the Old Testament: Law, Prophets, History, and Psalms.[13] For new covenant believers, we no longer interpret Old Testament passages only in light of their immediate context; we must now see them in the con-

---

13. "Greidanus trenchantly asks, 'Where did the New Testament writers, in contrast to their non-Christian Jewish counterparts, get the idea of interpreting the Old Testament from the reality of Christ?' He gives the obvious answer first. The disciples had been with Jesus and had and had met the risen Lord. 'But a more complete answer is that Jesus himself taught them to read the Old Testament in this way.' Here is the key to our interpretation of the Old Testament. Jesus gave it to his disciples on Easter morning." Then Clowney refers to both Luke 24:25–27 and 24:44–45. He continues, "Luke then reports his words. Jesus provided a summary of the gospel and its spread through the nations (vv. 46–47)—all from the Scriptures. This is to be the message of the disciples as his witnesses to all peoples. They are to wait for the empowering of the Spirit (vv. 48–49)." Clowney, *Preaching Christ*, 39–40.

text of the full revelation given in Christ. To preach Scripture faithfully is to preach Christ from every part of the Bible; Christ is the consummation of God's redemptive plan.

Singing is also a part of our worship. What is appropriate music or hymnody for worship? Here is a working principle for worship: We should sing only what is acceptable to preach. That is, the texts of hymns and songs should express biblical truths in the same way that sermons are to express biblical truths. We can speak the truth (sermons) and we can sing the truth (psalms, hymns, and spiritual songs, Eph. 5:19). If the human preacher can interpret, explain, and apply Scripture in human language, we can also sing scriptural concepts written by human authors. Whether it is spoken or sung, whether it is a direct quotation from Scripture or a faithful interpretation and application of Scripture, God's truth is being declared. Just as sermons should present Christ to worshipers from all of the Scriptures (which includes interpretation and application), so new covenant believers should sing about Christ and his redemptive work, whether directly from Scripture, like the Psalms, or with faithful interpretations of all parts of Scripture.

New covenant ministers are not to preach the Psalms or any other Old Testament texts only in their typological sense. The faithful preacher exposits, explains, and applies all of Scripture in light of the fullness that has come in Christ. This is one reason why singing only the Psalms in worship is deficient in that, while they do speak of Christ, they do so typologically. Since the consummation of God's redemptive revelation is in Christ, we need to speak and sing of Christ in all his fullness. Singing the Psalms is good but incomplete; we need to see and sing about the anticipation of Christ's coming, but in the fullness of Christ's completed redemptive work (Luke 24:44).

New covenant believers no longer live and worship under old covenant modalities. They speak and sing the same truths as old covenant believers, but they do so in light of the fuller revelation that has come in Christ. We are to preach the truth and we are to sing the truth.

Under the old covenant, earthly worship was centered in the tabernacle, which was a model or picture of heaven on earth (Heb. 8:5; 9:1). The tabernacle was always in the center of the camp, representing God in the midst of his people. Now that Christ, the true tabernacle, has come and is enthroned in heaven, our earthly worship is patterned after the new tabernacle (Heb. 8:1–2; 9:11, 23–24). The Spirit and the Scriptures reveal to us Jesus, the new tabernacle/temple, and we worship him by the Spirit and consistent with his revealed truth (John 4:24). Christ is the center of our worship, and when the people of God gather as the new covenant assembly, heaven comes down by the Spirit, and he ushers before the throne.

What, then, regulates our worship? It is always God's revelation. According to this revelation, Christ is truly present, we are gathered before him in the heavenly sanctuary, and we stand on holy ground. We also join the choruses of praise offered by the four living creatures, the twenty-four elders, the myriads of angles, and the host of heaven. Their worship is present and contemporaneous with our earthly time frame. This is one reason we can say that the regulative principle is not to restrict our worship but to expand it. Being in the presence of Christ, who is on the throne, will have the effect of regulating our worship.

New covenant believers do not live and worship under old covenant modalities. Old covenant modalities commanded the people how to live in specific detail. New covenant believers no longer worship at the base of Mount Sinai; they now come to the New Jerusalem, the city of the living God (Heb. 12:22–28). Old covenant forms have been abrogated and new covenant believers now live and worship under the general equity of God's eternal and abiding truths.

14

Exodus 20:4–6 and the
Regulative Principle of Worship[1]

JOSEPH A. PIPA JR.

SOME OF THE SADDEST words in the Bible are those that portray the condition of the church in the days of the judges, "Everyone did what was right in his own eyes" (Judg. 21:25). These words described a devastating spiritual anarchy. Our days are marked by the same anarchy, not only in the culture, but also in the church. Congregations and individuals are doing their own thing. One congregation excommunicates a man for immorality. He goes down the street, joins another congregation, which not only receives him, but also makes him an officer.

This spiritual anarchy is particularly evident in the area of worship. Not that long ago when visiting a Presbyterian or Reformed church, one would have found a basic uniformity in worship. It mattered not whether

---

1. I count it a great privilege to contribute to a book honoring Dr. Roberston. I am indebted to him in many ways, not the least is with respect to the regulative principle of worship. The article is adapted from a chapter I wrote, "Covenantal Worship," which is part of the book *Written for Our Instruction*, ed. by Joseph A. Pipa Jr. and J. Andrew Wortman (Greenville,SC: Southern Presbyterian Press [Greenville Presbyterian Press], 2001), 65–87.

one was in the United States, Mexico, or Korea. Today everyone is doing what is right in his own eyes. A multitude of diverse forms of worship confronts us under the guise of making worship understandable and contemporary. It seems that along the way people began to experiment and then began looking around for some theological justification of what they were doing. In the process some have redefined the principles that govern worship.

The earlier uniformity in worship grew out of a common commitment to the biblical foundation for worship. Today, many are altering or even denying this foundation. Two of the primary proponents of new principles for regulating worship are: John Frame, who redefines the regulative principle, and Steve Schlissel, who denies it. Although beginning with different presuppositions, both men argue in a similar fashion and reach similar conclusions. They claim that Scripture does not regulate worship in the manner stated in the Reformed Confessions. According to them, God requires certain basic things to be done in worship (e.g. preaching, singing, and prayer), but leaves it to the elders who oversee worship to determine the specific application.[2]

This chapter's purpose is to demonstrate the biblical basis for the regulative principle of worship. Before proceeding, let me define my terms. At the time of the Reformation, two principles developed with respect to the acts of worship. Luther taught that in worship one may do anything that the Bible does not forbid. This regulation is permissive: if something is not forbidden in Scripture, we may do it; hence, we may worship God according to the tradition of the church.[3]

As John Calvin studied the Scriptures, particularly the second commandment, he concluded that the Lutheran wing of the Reformation had not gone far enough. Calvin enunciated the principle that one may only offer to God in worship that for which one finds warrant in the Bible. He wrote:

> I know how difficult it is to persuade the world that God disapproves of all modes of worship not expressly sanctioned by His Word. The opposite persuasion which cleaves to them, being seated, as it were, in their very

2. John Frame, *Worship in Spirit and Truth* (Phillipsburg, NJ: P&R, 1996); Steve Schlissel, "My Back Pages," *Chalcedon Report* Nos. 404–9 (March-May 1999).

3. *Formula of Concord*, Article 10; *Augsburg Confession*, Article 15.

bones and marrow, is, that whatever they do has in itself a sufficient sanction, provided it exhibits some kind of zeal for the honour of God. But since God not only regards as fruitless, but also plainly abominates, whatever we undertake from zeal to His worship, if at variance with His command, what do we gain by a contrary course? The words of God are clear and distinct; 'Obedience is better than sacrifice.' 'In vain do they worship me, teaching for doctrines the commandments of men,' (1 Sam. xv. 22; Matth. xv. 9) [sic] Every addition to His word, especially in this matter, is a lie. Mere 'will worship' [Col. ii.23] . . . is vanity. This is the decision, and when once the judge has decided, it is no longer time to debate.[4]

This position, normally called the regulative principle of worship, is the position of the Westminster Standards.

According to Professor Frame's and Pastor Schlissel's new definitions, the church is free to determine the ways she will do the few things God has commanded (pray, preach, and praise). Frame states:

Typically, Scripture tells us what we should do in general and then leaves us to determine the specifics by our own sanctified wisdom, according to the general rules of the Word. Determining the specifics is what I call "application."[5]

He teaches that the elders may work out the manner in which the few required things are to be applied: "Human wisdom may never presume to *add* to its commands. The only job of human wisdom is to *apply* those commands to specific situations."[6] On the basis of his principle he allows for the use of dance and drama in corporate worship.

Pastor Schlissel denies the regulative principle and substitutes for it his Informed Principle of Worship. He writes:

All parties agree that what is forbidden must be excluded. But for the rest, what? High-churchers say, 'Not forbidden, then Fine.' Regulativists says, 'If it is not commanded, it is forbidden.' Both propositions fail to meet the

---

4. John Calvin, *Calvin's Selected Works*, ed. Henry Beveridge and Jules Bonet, vol. 1, *Tracts Relating to the Reformation*, ed. and trans. Henry Beveridge (1844; repr., Grand Rapids: Baker, 1983), 128–29.

5. Frame, *Worship*, 41.

6. Ibid., 43.

test of tota scriptura. We propose the IPW: What is not forbidden might be permitted. It depends.[7]

I will illustrate the three views of the regulation of worship with the use of Advent Candles. Many congregations have incorporated the use of special candles to celebrate the birth of Christ. On the Sundays leading up to Christmas, someone from the congregation will light a candle and read a portion of Scripture. According to the Lutheran principle, one would say of this practice, "no problem." One following the Calvinistic principle would say, "no way." An advocate of the new principle would say, "a way." By this he would mean that God's Word commands us to praise God, and the church may introduce a practice like "Advent Candles" to praise God for the incarnation. For all practical purposes, in application, the redefinition differs little from the Lutheran principle.

In this paper, I am seeking defend the Confession's position over against the Lutheran and new principles. This position is stated three places in the Westminster Confession of Faith:

> The whole counsel of God concerning all things necessary for his own glory, man's salvation, faith and life, is either expressly set down in Scripture, or by good and necessary consequence may be deduced from Scripture: unto which nothing at any time is to be added, whether by new revelations of the Spirit, or traditions of men. Nevertheless, we acknowledge the inward illumination of the Spirit of God to be necessary for the saving understanding of such things as are revealed in the Word: and that there are some circumstances concerning the worship of God, and government of the church, common to human actions and societies, which are to be ordered by the light of nature, and Christian prudence, according to the general rules of the Word, which are always to be observed. (WCF 1.6)

> God alone is Lord of the conscience, and hath left it free from the doctrines and commandments of men, which are, in anything, contrary to his Word; or beside it, in matters of faith or worship. (WCF 20.2)

---

7. Schlissel, "My Back Pages," No. 409, 33. Schlissel's application is more conservative than Frame's, but I find nothing in his principle that would dictate a more conservative application of the principle. Therefore, I deal with them as one principle.

But the acceptable way of worshipping the true God is instituted by himself, and so limited by his own revealed will, that he may not be worshipped according to the imaginations and devices of men, or the suggestions of Satan, under any visible representation, or any other way not prescribed in the Holy Scripture. (WCF 21.1)

I plan to demonstrate that God establishes the regulative principle in the second commandment. Remarkably, both Frame and Schlissel ignore the role of the second commandment in the development of the regulative principle. Nevertheless, the second commandment is the place we must begin in rightly understanding the regulative principle of worship.

The second commandment lays the foundation for worship by establishing the principle of the spirituality of worship. The Lord God says:

You should not make for yourself and idol, or any likeness of what is in heaven above or on the earth beneath or in the water under the earth. You shall not worship them or serve them; for I, the Lord your God, am a jealous God, visiting the iniquity of the fathers on the children, on the third and the fourth generations of those who hate Me, but showing lovingkindness to thousands, to those who love Me and keep My commandments. (Ex. 20:4–6)[8]

God prohibits two things: making a physical representation of God and giving worship to any object alongside God or to God through such an object. By forbidding any physical representation of himself, God establishes the spirituality of worship: "You shall not make for yourself an idol, or any likeness of what is in heaven above or on the earth beneath or in the water under the earth" (v. 4). Obviously we are not to make images of a false god or worship false gods through their images, but the particular focus of the second commandment is that we are not to make any physical representation of the true God. The Bible does not forbid art, not even some religious art (note the images used in the temple and tabernacle). What Scripture forbids is manufacturing any physical representation of the Godhead or of any of the three persons of the Godhead.[9]

God is a Spirit and we know him in a spiritual way. God reinforces this principle in Deuteronomy 4:15–19:

8. All Scripture quotation are taken from the NASB, 1977 edition.
9. See the Larger Catechism, 109.

> So watch yourselves carefully, since you did not see any form on the day the LORD spoke to you at Horeb from the midst of the fire, lest you act corruptly and make a graven image for yourselves in the form of any figure, the likeness of male or female, the likeness of any animal that is on the earth, the likeness of any winged bird that flies in the sky, the likeness of anything that creeps on the ground, the likeness of any fish that is in the water below the earth. And beware, lest you lift up your eyes to heaven and see the sun and the moon and the stars, all the host of heaven, and be drawn away and worship them and serve them, those which the LORD your God has allotted to all the peoples under the whole heaven.

In Exodus 33, when Moses wanted to see the glory of God, God reminded him that no man can see God's glory and live. God nevertheless promised to reveal his glory (vv. 20–23). He hid Moses in a rock (a type of Christ through whom we see the glory of God) and revealed his glory verbally:

> And the LORD descended in a cloud and stood there with him as he called upon the name of the LORD. Then the LORD passed by in front of him and proclaimed, "The LORD, the LORD God, compassionate and gracious, slow to anger, and abounding in lovingkindness and truth; who keeps lovingkindness for thousands, who forgives iniquity, transgression and sin; yet He will by no means leave the guilty unpunished, visiting the iniquities of the fathers on the children and on the grandchildren to the third and fourth generations." (Ex. 34:5–7)

Moses beheld the glory of God, not in what he saw, but in what he heard. The Lord God revealed himself to Moses through his names, works, and attributes. Thus, God forbids our manufacturing mental and physical images of him. He reveals his glory by verbal revelation.

Furthermore, he prohibits our using images in his worship. In this prohibition, God forbids three things. First, we may not supplement the worship of the true God by setting up images alongside him, as Manasseh did (2 Kings 21:7). Second, we may not offer worship to God through any physical likeness, as Jeroboam did (1 Kings 12:25–30). Third, we may not worship God according to the practices of idolaters (Deut. 12:29–32; cf. Jer. 7:31; Deut. 17:3).

By the twofold prohibition of Exodus 20:4, 5, God establishes the spirituality of worship, which leads to the regulative principle. Since God is a Spirit, we must worship him spiritually and not according to our imaginations. Therefore, we must worship him according to revelation.

In order to understand this development of thought, we must keep in mind two very important principles for interpreting the Law spelled out in the Westminster Larger Catechism, question 99. In answering the question "What rules are to be observed for the right understanding of the Ten Commandments?" the Catechism lists 8 principles that one should use in interpreting the Law of God. Two of these in particular are pertinent:

> [No.] 4 That as, where a duty is commanded, the contrary sin is forbidden; and, where a sin is forbidden, the contrary duty is commanded: . . . [6] That under one sin or duty, all of the same kind are forbidden or commanded; together with all the causes, means, occasions, and appearances thereof, and provocations thereunto.

The fourth principle teaches that the opposite of what is forbidden is required and the opposite of what is required is forbidden. For example, the first commandment states, "You shall have no other gods before me." When Moses applies the first commandment in Deuteronomy 6, he inculcates the positive duty that we are to have the Lord God as our God; thus, we are to worship and serve him alone. In other words, to abstain from the worship of false gods is not sufficient. God grants no neutrality. Christ says, either you are for me or against me. The only way to keep the first commandment is to have God as your God by faith in the Lord Jesus Christ and to worship and serve him alone as your God.

The sixth principle states: "That under one sin or duty, all of the same kind are forbidden or commanded; together with all the causes, means, occasions, and appearances thereof, and provocations thereunto." We may illustrate this principle from the seventh commandment. Under the prohibition of adultery in the seventh commandment, the Bible includes fornication and other forms of sexual impurity, as well as sins like drunkenness, which leads to sexual immorality.

When we apply these principles to the second commandment, we recognize that in forbidding us to worship him through images, God is forbidding our worshiping him according to our imaginations. By forbidding us to worship him according to our imagination, God requires us to worship him according to his revelation. Furthermore, we must avoid all occasions that tend to corrupt worship by inventing symbols or introducing liturgical devices and any other thing that would challenge God's proprietary rights in worship.

On the basis of these two interpretative principles the Shorter Catechism develops the regulative principle of worship:[10]

Q. 50 What is required in the second commandment?
A. The second commandment requireth the receiving, observing, and keeping pure and entire, all such religious worship and ordinances as God hath appointed in his word.

Q. 51 What is forbidden in the second commandment?
A. The second commandment forbiddeth the worshipping of God by images, or any other way not appointed in his word.

In these two statements we are reminded that neither may we make images, nor may we worship God in any way contrary to his Word. Furthermore, we are obligated to keep pure his worship as he has revealed it to us.

A wide range of commentators support this interpretation of the second commandment. The Presbyterian theologian William Plumer wrote:

While the second commandment, no less than all the other precepts of the decalogue, should be regarded as designed to regulate our tempers, it no doubt has special reference to the external worship of God. The things forbidden in it relate to outward acts. It is true the most gross form of violating God's worship is mentioned, just as the most flagrant form of sinning against our neighbour's life, and peace, and property are mentioned in the sixth, seventh and eight commandments.

Later he adds:

Our worship must be according to divine directions. Every sovereign, as every court, has a right to regulate the manner in which petitioners shall approach. Nothing more effectually destroys all acceptableness in worship than that our fear towards God be taught by the precept of men. . . . We may not, therefore devise any false worship, Num. xv.

10. Compare the Larger Catechism, 108 and 109.

37–40; nor recommend it to others, Deut. xiii. 6,7,8; nor enjoin it upon others, Hosea v. 11; nor use it ourselves, 1 Kings xi. 33; nor in any wise countenance it. Rev. ii. 14.[11]

Contrary to some modern claims, the Reformation church was unanimously committed to this interpretation of the second commandment. In what is otherwise a very fine book, *A Quest for Godliness*, J. I. Packer claims that the regulative principle was a Puritan innovation: "The idea that direct biblical warrant, in the form of precept or precedent is required to sanction every substantive item included in the public worship of God was in fact a Puritan innovation, which crystallized out in the course of the prolonged debates that followed the Elizabethan settlement."[12] Schlissel claims that very few in the Continental Reformed church, except those whom the Puritans influenced, embraced a version of the RPW (regulative principle of worship).[13] He quotes with approval a minister in the Orthodox Christian Reformed Church to substantiate that the regulative principle is really a Presbyterian distinctive and not part of the Continental Reformed tradition: "I must say that I never *heard* of the Regulative Principle of Worship until exposure to my ministerial colleagues here in the OCRC's who were from Presbyterian background."[14]

When one compares Packer's and Schlissel's claims with Reformation and post-Reformation statements, one quickly sees that their statements are erroneous. Consider what some of the Reformed creeds say:

The Heidelberg Catechism:
Q. 96 What does God require in the second commandment?
A. We are not to make an image of God in any way, nor to worship Him in any other manner than He has commanded in His Word.

The Belgic Confession, Article 32:
We believe that, although it is useful and good for those who govern the Church to establish a certain order to maintain the body of the Church, they must at all times watch that they do not deviate from what Christ, our only Master, has commanded. Therefore we reject all

11. William Plumer, *Law of God* (Harrisonburg, VA: Sprinkle Publications, 1996), 185, 187.
12. J. I. Packer, *A Quest For Godliness* (Wheaton: Crossway, 1990), 247.
13. Schlissel, "My Back Pages," No. 409, 32.
14. Ibid.

human inventions and laws introduced into worship of God which bind and compel the consciences in any way.

I quoted Calvin above on the regulative principle, but consider a couple of other statements:

I have also no difficulty in conceding to you that there is nothing more perilous to our salvation than a distorted and perverse worship of God. The primary rudiments by which we are wont to train those whom we wish to win as disciples to Christ, are these; viz., not to frame any new worship of God for themselves at random, and after their own pleasure, but to know that the only legitimate worship is that which He himself approved from the beginning. For we maintain what the sacred oracle declared, that obedience is more excellent than any sacrifice (1 Sam. xv. 22). In short, we train them by every means to be contented with the one rule of worship which they have received from His mouth, and bid adieu to all fictitious worship.[15]

In *The Necessity of Reforming the Church*, he said,

If it be inquired, then, by what things chiefly the Christian religion has a standing existence amongst us, and maintains its truth, it will be found that the following two not only occupy the principal place, but comprehend under them all the other parts, and consequently the whole substance of Christianity, viz., a knowledge, first, of the mode in which God is duly worshipped; and, secondly, of the source from which salvation is to be obtained.[16]

For the sake of those, like Schlissel, in the Continental Reformed tradition, I will quote three other sources. Zacharias Ursinus, one of the framers of the Heidelberg Catechism, wrote regarding the second commandment:

The true worship of God is, therefore, here enjoyed, and a rule at the same time given, that we sacredly and conscientiously keep ourselves within the bounds which God has prescribed, and that we do not add anything to

15. John Calvin, *A Reformation Debate*, ed., John C. Olin (Grand Rapids: Baker Book House, 1976), 59.

16. John Calvin, *The Necessity of Reforming the Church*, trans. Henry Veveridge, rev. ed. (1844; repr., Dallas: Protestant Heritage Press, 1995), 15.

that worship which has been divinely instituted, or corrupt it in any part, even the most unimportant; . . . To worship God truly, is to worship him in the manner which he himself has prescribed in his word.[17]

Á Brakel wrote on the second commandment at the end of the seventeenth century:

> The third sin is will-worship. This consists in serving God in a manner of our own devising, or in a manner which has been suggested to us by men—doing so without concern and investigation as to the manner in which God wants to be served. We then imagine that God will be pleased with our work as long as we have a good intent to serve Him by means of that activity. The Lord rejects this in Matthew 15:9.[18]

A modern example, R.B. Kuiper:

> What has been said constitutes a most important principle governing the content of worship in general and of corporate worship in particular. Sad to day, not all churches subscribe to it. The church of Rome takes the position that everything is permissible in public worship, which is not forbidden by the Word of God. . . . The Reformed churches have upheld the principle that only that is permissible in the content of public worship, which has the positive sanction of Holy Scripture. And that principle is biblical. It is plainly implicit in the second commandment of the moral law (Exodus 20:4–6). While the first commandment forbids the worship of false gods, the second forbids worship of the true God in a wrong way.[19]

I give these few quotations to illustrate that the regulative principle, as taught by the Westminster Divines, was not some peculiar English Puritan twist on worship, but was in fact the Reformed understanding of the second commandment.

17. Zacharias Ursinus, *The Commentary of Dr. Zacharias Ursinus on the Heidelberg Catechism*, trans. G. W. Williard (1852; repr., Phillipsburg, NJ: Presbyterian and Reformed Publishing Company), 517.

18. Wilhelmus à Brakel, *The Christian's Reasonable Service*, trans. Bartel Elshout from *Redelijke Godsdienst*, 3rd ed. (Pittsburgh: Soli Deo Gloria Publications, 1994), 3:114.

19. R. B. Kuiper, *The Glorious Body of Christ* (London: Banner of Truth, 1967), 349. Kuiper represents both the Continental and Presbyterian traditions. He was president of Calvin College [1930–33] and professor of practical theology at Westminster Theological Seminary [1933–52].

Since the principle is based on the second commandment, we rightly infer that it has continuing validity in the New Testament. Schlissel maintains that God carefully regulated the tabernacle/temple worship with its sacrificial system, but not the rest of old covenant worship or subsequently new covenant worship:

> The point, however, is that what is strictly regulated is the sacrificial system of worship, not worship per se. In fact 'mere' sacred assemblies are not covered by this rule. From the beginning God had made known that the path by which man might be restored to him is a path of shed, substitutionary blood. This was indicated in the animal sacrifice God had made when providing coverings for Adam and Eve, and again in his acceptance of Abel's blood offering brought in faith. The atoning path of blood was laid out by God.[20]

Note, however, that since God established the principle in the second commandment, it must apply to more than the tabernacle/temple. God has established the moral principle that the only way people may approach him in worship is in the way that he has revealed. We, therefore, do not need a specific New Testament commandment to regulate worship by the Word of God.

Professor Frame also claims to see a fulfillment of Old Testament types that negates the more narrow regulative principle in the New Testament:

> From a New Testament perspective, we can see all the various elements of Old Testament worship point to Jesus.[21]

> The great changes from the Old Testament to the New imply that there will be changes in worship. As the new Israel in Christ, the church worships in a way that is parallel to that of the Old Testament, in that every ordinance of the Old Testament is fulfilled in Christ. We too have a covenant, a priesthood, sacrifices, a tabernacle, circumcision, atonement, and feasts. But in our actual practice, there are great differences, for all of these institutions now exist in Christ and in him alone. And our worship in Christ presupposes the once-for-all accomplishment of the redemption to which the Old Testament Jews looked forward.

20. Schlissel, "My Back Pages," No. 406, 31.
21. Frame, *Worship*, 25.

One difference that should already be evident is that in the New Testament, the traditional terminology for worship is typically used in the broad sense. . . . Essentially, what is left is worship in the broad sense: a life of obedience to God's word, a sacrifice of ourselves to his purposes. All of life is our priestly service, our homage to the greatness of our covenant Lord.[22]

Assuredly, Christ fulfilled the Old Testament types. Frame, however, fails to distinguish between the ceremonial and typical elements of temple worship and the trans-covenantal elements like preaching, prayer, and singing. He also fails to prove that the broad sense is essentially all that is left. By failing to consider the trans-covenantal nature of corporate prayer, praise, preaching, and reading of Scripture, he is able to suggest the possibility that it is very difficult in the New Testament to distinguish between broad and narrow worship.[23]

John teaches us how Christ's fulfillment of the types and ceremonies applies to the new covenant in John 4:21–24. He shows that because Christ fulfilled the types and ceremonies, New Testament worship is not confined to any particular place. Rather, it is worship offered in spirit and truth; namely, it is worship freed from the external elements of the types and ceremonies, offered in Christ who is the fulfillment of them all, and governed by the truth of the Word of God. Hendriksen points out that such worship enforces the regulative principle: "In such a setting, it would seem to us, worshiping in *spirit and truth* can only mean a. rendering such homage to God that the entire heart enters into the act, and by doing this in full harmony with the truth of God as revealed in his Word."[24]

Consequently, the rule continues in the New Testament age. Calvin, commenting on the change in worship and the Jews' refusal to embrace Christ wrote:

The same is true of all who have left the pure faith of the Gospel for their own and other men's inventions. However much in their obstinacy those who worship God from their own notions or men's traditions flatter and praise themselves, this one Word thundering from heaven overthrows every

22. Ibid., 29–30.

23. Ibid., 30.

24. William Hendriksen, *Exposition of the Gospel According to John*, New Testament Commentary (Grand Rapids: Baker Book House, 1967), 167.

divine and holy thing they think they possess: Ye worship that which ye know not. And so, if our religion is to be approved by God, it must needs rest on knowledge conceived of His word.[25]

When we grasp the significance of the second commandment for the regulative principle, not only do we see the principle must continue in the New Testament, but also that it would have governed the synagogue worship in the Old Testament. Both Frame and Schlissel concede that the synagogue was of divine origin in the Old Testament institution. They assert, however, that its liturgy was unregulated:

And he (the regulativist) knows that he cannot find so much as a sliver of a divine commandment concerning what ought to be done in the synagogue. And, according to his principle, if God commanded naught concerning what ought to be done, then all was forbidden. And if all was forbidden then the whole of it—institution and liturgy—was a sinful abomination. But that brings him back to Christ's attending upon the service of God there and Christ's following its liturgy: did he sin by participating in an entire order of worship that was without express divine warrant? The thought is blasphemy![26]

I find two problems in Schlissel's assertion. First, we have good inference for the synagogues' divine establishment. In Leviticus 23:3 God commands the people to observe a "holy convocation" every Sabbath. They would have done this in all the cities of the land. Moreover, Psalm 74:8 states that when the Babylonians destroyed the temple, they also destroyed the meeting houses (synagogues).

Second, we rightly infer on the basis of the second commandment and the synagogues' close relation to the temple, that its worship was regulated. The synagogue was an extension of temple worship, without the sacrifices and other typical ceremonies. In fact, the synagogue service was organically related to the sacrifices of the temple. It should not be viewed as an independent institution. Synagogue worship was acceptable on the basis of the regular priestly service of the tabernacle/temple. No acts were performed at the synagogue that were not performed at the temple. Because

25. John Calvin, *Calvin's Commentaries: The Gospel According to St John 1–10*, trans. T.H.L. Parker (repr., Grand Rapids: Eerdmans, 1995), 99.
26. Schlissel, "My Back Pages," No. 406, 34. See Frame, *Worship*, 22, 23.

of the second commandment, no faithful Jew would have countenanced introducing something of human invention into the synagogue. God, therefore, prepared it as a pattern for New Testament worship.

In addition to the second commandment, the Bible gives several other reasons why one should worship God only according to his Word. We can summarize them under two headings: the sufficiency of Scripture and explicit statements regulating worship.

The doctrine of the sufficiency of Scripture demands the regulative principle. T. David Gordon applies this doctrine to worship. Commenting on WCF 1.6, he writes:

> The teaching of the Westminster Assembly both implicitly and expressly relates the regulative principle of worship to the doctrine of the Scripture's sufficiency. Implicitly it does so because the public worship of God must be "necessary for His own glory" and "man's . . . faith and life." Explicitly, this very passage, in which Scripture's sufficiency is asserted, qualifies the assertion expressly regarding worship, and yet mentions "circumstances common to human actions and societies" (not elements) as the only qualification to Scripture's sufficiency in this area. Those who would add elements to the biblically-instituted elements necessarily imply that the biblically-instituted elements are not sufficient guide to the elements of public worship. For the Reformed Christian, Scripture is a sufficient guide, providing "all things necessary" for God's glory and for our faith and life. To the natural mind, the simple ordinances of God may appear inadequate. To the redeemed mind, accustomed to the simplest, weakest, and most foolish things being employed by God's Spirit to enliven the dead, the ordinances of God are more than adequate.[27]

More specifically, Scripture throughout affirms that one is to worship God only according to his Word. Let us consider some examples. In Leviticus 10:1, 2, God strikes Nadab and Abihu dead with fire, because they offered incense with strange fire. Schlissel states this text does not prove the point, because they did not offer something in addition to God's Word, but rather disobeyed God's Word. He told them what kind of incense to burn (Ex. 30:9) and they broke his commandment by offering strange incense.[28]

---

27. T. David Gordon, "Presbyterian Worship: Its Distinguishing Principle" (unpublished paper, n.d.).

28. Schlissel, "My Back Pages," No. 404, 24, 25.

He, though, fails to read the text properly. God destroyed them with fire because they offered strange fire (not strange incense). They did not use the fire of the altar (for which there was no specific commandment) but brought their own fire.[29] Thus God enforces the principle that men may not worship him according to their imaginations.

One New Testament example affirming the regulative principle is Christ's quoting Isaiah 29:13 in Mark 7:6–8. The Pharisees rebuke the disciples for not observing the ceremonial washings (baptisms). Christ defends his disciples by showing that these were traditions of men and thus contrary to God's Word:

> Rightly did Isaiah prophesy of you hypocrites, as it is written,
>
> > "This people honors me with their lips,
> > But their heart is far away from me.
> > But in vain do they worship me,
> > Teaching as doctrines the precepts of men."
>
> Neglecting the commandment of God, you hold to the tradition of men.

The ceremonial washings of the Pharisees were not forbidden by explicit commandment, but Christ condemns the washings as the human traditions that cause men to neglect and eventually nullify the commandments of God. Schlissel, however, writes:

> Without doubt, our Lord condemned any human tradition which obscured, nullified, set apart or contradicted the Word of God (e.g., Mk. 7:9 and context). But there is no indication that He opposed traditions which supported, magnified or drew attention to the Word and works of God. It is not, for us, a question merely of whether an observance can be traced to 'human tradition,' but it is also a question of fidelity to Scripture, propriety in worship, and profitability to the people of God.[30]

This is a gross misunderstanding of the Savior's teaching. The ceremonial washings by nature did not contradict or nullify the Word of God.

---

29. For an excellent discussion of this passage see Jeremiah Burroughs, *Gospel Worship* (1648; repr., Ligonier, PA: Soli Deo Gloria Publications, 1990), 3–7.

30. Schlissel, "My Back Pages," No. 407, 38.

They were wrong because they were in addition to the Word. Christ's condemned all worship and acts of piety based on human tradition.

Building on his view of tradition, Pastor Schlissel maintains that Chanukah and Purim were festivals of Jewish tradition. Since Jesus observed them they must not be wrong.[31] Let us recall, however, that Purim was a thanksgiving feast called by the civil magistrate, and the Westminster Divines rightly inferred from its institution, recorded in Esther 9:29–32, that the magistrate may appoint special days of thanksgiving.

Chanukah was a commemoration of the victory of Judas Maccabaeus over Antiochus Epiphanes and of the cleansing and rededication of the temple. Obviously, this was a humanly invented feast. Since John tells us that Jesus was at the temple during this feast, Schlissel concludes that he observed it. "At that time the Feast of the Dedication took place at Jerusalem; it was winter, and Jesus was walking in the temple in the portico of Solomon" (John 10:22–23). We have no evidence, however, that Jesus participated in this feast. Hendriksen writes:

> The rainy season had arrived. Hence, it does not cause surprise that Jesus was waking in the covered colonnade that ran along the eastern wall of the temple. This portico is said to have been the only remnant of the original temple.[32]

Hence, we have no evidence that Jesus was at the temple for any other reason than to preach and teach. He would have been walking in the portico because of the rain.

We understand the reason God carefully regulates his worship when we ponder who he is and who we are. The very nature of God demonstrates the necessity of Scripture regulating worship (John 4:24). In Job 11:7–10 (I acknowledge that much of what Job's friends had to say was not true, but sprinkled through their speeches are some profound insights) we read,

> Can you discover the depths of God? Can you discover the limits of the Almighty? They are high as the heavens, what can you do? Deeper than Sheol, what can you know? Its measure is longer than the earth, And

31. Ibid., 37, 38.
32. Hendriksen, *John*, 120.

broader than the sea. If He passes by or shuts up, Or calls an assembly, who can restrain Him?[33]

Since God is infinite and transcendent, he must take the initiative. He must reveal himself to us; God must tell us who he is and what is pleasing to him. We cannot discover by our wisdom what pleases him; thus, he comes to us as a self-revealing God in covenant and teaches us how we are to respond to him.

The necessity of God's initiative in revelation is the essence of theism. T. David Gordon writes,

> Since there is a great gulf, however, between the being of God and the being of creatures, we cannot know, apart from revelation, what would be pleasing in God's sight. Even prior to the Fall, Adam would not have known what worship would be acceptable to God apart from positive institution from God.[34]

Because God is infinite, he is also sovereign. As the sovereign God, he alone is Lord of the conscience (WCF 20). What one does in corporate worship of necessity binds the conscience. When elders include things for which they have no biblical warrant, they compel worshippers to do that which is not dictated by Scripture; thus, binding their consciences.

Compounding the infinite distance between God and man is our sinfulness. The depravity of man necessitates the regulative principle. We are born dead in sins and trespasses and possess a remnant of sin. Calvin points out, "Such is our folly, that when we are left at liberty, all we are able to do is to go astray. And then when once we have turned aside from the right path, there is no end to our wanderings, until we get buried under a multitude of superstitions."[35] Bannerman adds:

> This addition of positive institutions of worship, and the express regulation of the manner of it, were more especially necessitated by man's fall. After the fatal separation between man and God occasioned by that event, it remained for God, and for Him alone, to say whether He would ever again permit the approach of man to Him in the way of worship;

33. Compare Isaiah 55:9, 10.
34. T. David Gordon, "Presbyterian Worship."
35. Calvin, *Necessity*, 128.

and if so, it remained for God, and for Him alone, to prescribe the terms and to regulate the manner of the approach. In regard to such a matter as either the conditions or the way of a sinner's approach to God in accepted worship, it was for the sinner not to devise his own method, but to receive submissively God's method.[36]

How foolish for us who possess a remnant of sin, which fuels our lusts and vain imaginations, to think that because something pleases us it pleases God.

We learn, therefore, that Scripture must be our absolute guide in worship. Having established this principle, let us consider the two areas in which God gives the church liberty to do things in worship without a specific scriptural warrant; namely, circumstances and forms. Regrettably, Professor Frame lumps circumstances and forms with elements in a confusing manner:

> Scripture is silent about many things that we do in worship. It doesn't tell us when or where to meet on Sunday, whether to sit on pews or chairs, how long the service should be, which hymns we may sing, or what text the pastor should preach on? Do we need human wisdom, in addition to Scripture, to plan our worship?[37]

By confusing circumstances and forms with elements, he is able to develop the principle that we may use our own judgment in determining what we should do in worship. Under his definition of circumstance, he teaches that God leaves broad areas in which the elders my apply the general principles of the Word and by their wisdom institute practices of worship:

> [A]pplications include such matters as the time and place of worship: Scripture tells us to meet, but not when and where—so we must use our own judgment. Similarly, Scripture tells us to pray, but does not dictate to us all the specific words we should use—so we need to decide."[38]

Professor Frame makes an elementary error, which we will see as we define "circumstance" and "form." First, what does the Westminster Confession of Faith means by circumstances of worship? The Confession states:

36. James Bannerman, *The Church of Christ* (Edinburgh: Banner of Truth, 1974), 1:326.
37. Frame, *Worship*, 40.
38. Ibid., 41.

Never the less we acknowledge the inward illumination of the Spirit of God to be necessary for the saving understanding of such things as are revealed in the word; and that there are some circumstances concerning the worship of God, and government of the Church, common to human actions and societies, which are to be ordered by the light of nature and Christian prudence, according to the general rules of the word which are always to be observed. (WCF 1.6)

What are circumstances? They are those things that enable us to perform the acts of worship (time, place, order, arrangement of pews and pulpit, sound system, etc.). The elders may order them then according to the general customs of the time and place and according to the general principles of the Word of God. Jeremiah Burroughs gives an excellent definition of circumstances:

It's true that there are some things in the worship of God that are natural and civil helps, and there we do not need to have a command. For instance, when we come to worship God the congregation meets. They must have a convenient place to keep the air and weather from them. Now this is only a natural help, and so far as I use the place of worship as a natural help, I need have no command. But if I will put anything in a place beyond what it has in its own nature, there I must look for a command, for if I account one place more holy than another, or think that God should accept worship in one place rather than another, this is to raise it above what it is in its own nature.[39]

Let us illustrate this definition with the use of candles. If the electricity went out and the elders determined to use candles to light the building, such use would be a circumstance, because that is the natural use of a candle. On the other hand, when we give some liturgical value to a candle (candle-light service or advent candles) we are not using them in their natural way and thus they are not circumstances, but rather elements of worship.

The second area in which God grants some liberty is in the use of "forms." Forms are the precise content of an element; e.g., which song is

---

39. Burroughs, *Gospel Worship*, 14. See also John Owen, *A Declaration of the Glorious Mystery of the Person of Christ—God and Man*. The Works of John Owen, ed. William H. Goold (1850–53; repr., Edinburgh: Banner of Truth, 1987) 1:3–4; James Henley Thornwell, *Church-Boards and Presbyterianism*. The Collected Writings of James Henley Thornwell, ed. B. M. Palmer (1873; repr., Edinburgh: Banner of Truth, 1986), 4:247; Bannerman, *Church of Christ*, 1:355–57.

to be sung or whether to use common prayer or free prayer. Of course, the content of our prayers must be in accord with the truth of Scripture; if we sing hymns they must be faithful to Scripture; and our preaching must focus exclusively on the truth of Scripture. This commitment to liberty in forms gave rise to the concept of a directory of worship rather than a book of common prayer. A directory gives us the guidelines and leaves a certain freedom in terms of how we express ourselves: the selection of hymns and psalms, the number of prayers and their content, the content of the sermon, and the order of the service. God thus grants some liberty to the elders in the circumstances and forms of worship. What we do, however, as acts of worship offered to God (the elements) must have biblical warrant.

Having established the regulative principle, let us briefly consider the manner by which we derive the elements. Although this task is difficult, the Scriptures are clear and there are relatively few areas of disagreement. Furthermore, any difficulty should not lead to the agnosticism expressed by Professor Frame: "Unfortunately, it is virtually impossible to prove anything is divinely required specifically for official services."[40] Bannerman reaches the opposite conclusion:

> The Scriptures are the only rule for worship, as truly as they are the only rule for the Church in any other department of her duties. And the Scriptures are sufficient for that purpose; for they contain a directory for worship, either expressly inculcated, or justly to be inferred from its statements sufficient for the guidance of the Church in every necessary part of worship.[41]

Admittedly, even those seriously committed to the regulative principle will differ with respect to some aspects such as the use of non-inspired hymns, choirs, or musical instruments. In the areas of difference, we are to be patient and humble as together we seek the mind of God.

How then do we go about the task? Bannerman offers three guidelines:

> There are, first, express precepts contained in Scripture, and designed to regulate the practice of Divine worship in the Church as to ordinances and services; second, There are particular examples of worship in its various

---

40. Frame, *Worship*, 44.
41. Bannerman, *Church of Christ*, 1:368.

parts recorded in Scripture, and both fitted and intended to be binding and guiding models for subsequent ages. And, third, When neither express precepts nor express examples are to be met with, there are general Scripture principles applicable to public worship, enough to constitute a sufficient directory in the matter. Anything beyond that directory in the celebration of worship is unwarranted and superstitious.[42]

When we apply these principles, we are able to determine the elements of worship. Frame, however, suggests that there is no Scriptural warrant for the task of determining elements: "The most serious problem is that there is no scriptural warrant for it! Scripture nowhere divides worship into a series of independent 'elements,' each requiring independent scriptural justification."[43]

In contrast Bannerman declares: "There is a sufficient directory for worship laid down in the Bible to furnish the church with those principles of order which enable it to regulate every new case occurring in regard to the outward worship of the church which requires to be regulated."[44]

Having seen something of the basis of the regulative principle and its method of application, let us note its importance. Earlier I quoted Calvin saying, "God not only regards as fruitless, but also plainly abominates, whatever we undertake from zeal to His worship, if at variance with His command, what do we gain by a contrary course?"[45]

God highlights the importance of the second commandment saying, "I, the LORD your God, am a jealous God, visiting the iniquity of the fathers on the children, on the third and the fourth generations of those who hate Me, but showing lovingkindness to thousands, to those who love Me and keep My commandments" (Ex. 20:5, 6). He reminds us that he is our covenant king, our husband, and we are his people, his subjects, and his bride. As our Lord, he is rightly jealous of his own glory and worship. In Deuteronomy 4:24, he teaches us that his jealousy applies to his worship: "For the LORD your God is a consuming fire, a jealous God." Thus if we are jealous for his glory, we shall desire that he be honored in a way that he has appointed.

---

42. Ibid. Early on Schlissel seems to caricature the principle by demanding an explicit commandment. A better way to express this principle is a Scriptural warrant.

43. Frame, *Worship*, 53.

44. Bannerman, *Church of Christ*, 1:345. The Westminster Confession of Faith gives us this Directory in 21.4.5.

45. Calvin, *Tracts*, 128, 129.

The Lord constrains obedience to the regulative principle with a threat and a promise. He threatens to visit the iniquity of the fathers on the children to the third and fourth generations of those who hate him. In a sense we can apply this threat to all the commandments, but we must note that he particularly applies it to the second commandment. If we grasp the seriousness of this threat, we can understand why Calvin said proper worship is essential to the salvation and the well-being of the people of God. "I have also no difficulty in conceding to you that there is nothing more perilous to our salvation than a distorted and perverse worship of God."[46] God does not take lightly non-regulated worship. True, he is long–suffering. He does not strike us dead as he struck Nadab and Abihu and Uzzah, but he will vindicate his honor. He will manifest his displeasure by cutting off subsequent covenant generations of those who abuse his worship.

The promise, on the other hand, tells us that when we seek to worship according to his Word, he blesses us in ways that defy description. He promises covenant blessings unto the thousands of generation of those who love him and keep his commandments. Herein lies the prosperity of the church, and you see why correct worship is important. The issue involved here is the well-being of the church. Therefore, let us be jealous for God's honor and zealous for him to regulate our worship by his Word. Christ's crown rights demand this commitment. The time for tolerance and a nonchalant attitude to worship has long since passed. We must not be obnoxious, but we must be strong and courageous. I fear that our denominations are already under God's anger, as we allow idolatrous worship to multiply in our day.

46. Calvin, *Reformation Debate*, 59.

15

The Ebb and Flow of *Lectio Continua* Bible Reading in the English-Speaking Reformed Churches, 1539–2000

TERRY JOHNSON

MANY OF THE MINISTERS of my generation look to Dr. Palmer Robertson as a mentor in Reformed pastoral ministry. His has been one of the clearest voices in advocating the distinctives of Reformed worship: expository preaching, classic hymnody, metrical psalmody, and Scripture-enriched prayer. J. Ligon Duncan acknowledges our indebtedness to Dr. Robertson in his introduction to Reformed Academic Press's edition of Matthew Henry's *A Method for Prayer*.[1] Robertson's powerful public prayers stimulated a desire in his students to pray with more proficiency and scriptural content. His recommendations led to the republication of Henry's work, an important milestone in the revival of traditional Reformed worship. What was true of prayer was also true of his influence on the other traditional elements of Reformed worship. The following

---

1. Matthew Henry, *A Method for Prayer* (1710; repr., Greenville, SC: Reformed Academic Press, 1994), vi.

essay is dedicated to Dr. Robertson as an expression of my gratitude for his faithfulness as a theologian, pastor, and missionary.

Sometime in the school year of 1977–78 I attended a Sunday evening service at St. Mary's Redcliffe, in Bristol, England. The church has had a long and varied history, including some notoriety for having once refused to allow George Whitefield to preach within its walls, though later, they reconsidered and received him with great effect.[2] The church was built before Columbus sailed and was a beautiful, spacious place in which to conduct a worship service.

At the time I was none too pleased with the *Prayer Book* service that was used. I was unaccustomed to reading prayers and responses, regularly got lost, and was typically confused. But one part of the service made a powerful impression. At the appropriate time a reader stood to read the Old Testament lesson, and later another to read the New Testament lesson. The readers read slowly, deliberately, and beautifully. The Old Testament text was from Isaiah. I recall being surprisingly moved by the power of the word skillfully read. I also recall thinking that the experience of hearing an extended reading of Scripture was new. I couldn't recall in twenty-two years of church-going at evangelical churches (whether Brethren, Baptist, Congregational, Independent Bible, or Presbyterian) of ever hearing a text of Scripture being read other than the few verses before the sermon. Obviously it made an impression. I can still speak of it over a quarter of a century later. Isn't it "funny," I thought, that these liturgical Anglicans read the Bible, and my "gospel-preaching" churches don't. With all their high-church regalia, with all the various postures and gestures of the priests, which my low-church self referred to as "bobbing and weaving" (thank you, Cassius Clay), they packed more Bible into their services than we did.

The disappearance of the public reading of Scripture in evangelical churches has been a gradual and disappointing development in Evangelical Protestantism since the time of the Reformation. Liturgist James F. White, addressing Protestantism more generally, calls the current situation of selective reading or minimal reading of the Bible "apostasy."[3] Aside from the couple of verses upon which the sermon is based, the Bible remains an unread book in the public gatherings of what we ironically call the

2. Arnold Dallimore, *George Whitefield* (Edinburgh: Banner of Truth, 1970), 1:253, 257.
3. James F. White, "Our Apostasy in Worship," *Christian Century* (September 28, 1977): 842.

"Bible-believing" churches. I can cite no empirical study upon which to base this claim, but personal experience and anecdotal evidence from the "Bible" churches, the seeker-friendly churches, the charismatic churches, the old revival-format churches, and the contemporary churches is overwhelming. The Bible simply is not being read, and has not been for a very long time.

This is surprising because the Reformers were unanimous regarding the value of public Bible reading, and Reformed Protestants were unanimous even with respect to the method by which texts were to be selected. Evangelical Christians, presumed theological heirs of the Reformation, have dropped a major plank in the Reformer's program of "church revitalization" (as we might call it today), without, one imagines, calculating the spiritual cost of omitting this public discipline. If it is true that faith comes by hearing the word of Christ (Rom. 10:17), that we are born again by the living and abiding Word of God (1 Peter 1:23), that we grow by the pure milk of God's Word (1 Peter 2:2), and that we are sanctified by the truth of God's Word (John 17:17), then this omission from the public worship of evangelical churches is a defect that begs to be corrected.

HISTORICAL & BIBLICAL BACKGROUND

The medieval practice, with which the Reformers were interacting, was to follow a program of selected Bible readings according to a pattern codified by Gregory the Great (c. 540–604) in the sixth century. The program, called a lectionary, was selective (determined mainly by the themes of the church calendar), not continuous, *lectio selecta* not *lectio continua*.[4]

The Reformers looked behind this medieval pattern of Bible reading to the practice of the patristic church, the apostolic church, and the synagogue before them. They found Moses reading Scripture to the people at Sinai (Ex. 24:7). They found Ezra setting the pattern of reading and explaining Scripture (Neh. 8:5–8ff). They found Jesus in the synagogue participating in the reading and explaining of Scripture. Luke describes the process:

4. R. H. Fuller, "Lectionary," in *The New Westminster Dictionary of Liturgy & Worship*, ed. J. G. Davies (Philadelphia: The Westminster Press, 1986), 297–99.

> He entered the synagogue on the Sabbath, and stood up to read. And the
> book of the prophet Isaiah was handed to Him. And He opened the book.
> (Luke 4:16b–17a)

The Reformers found the apostle Paul at Pisidian Antioch doing
the same.

> And after the reading of the Law and the Prophets the synagogue officials
> sent to them, saying, "Brethren, if you have any word of exhortation for
> the people, say it." (Acts 13:15)

Luke records that "after the reading of the Law and the Prophets"—note
that both the books of Moses and the prophetic books were normally
read—an exposition/explanation was expected. The synagogue officials
say, "if you have any word of exhortation for the people, say it." Customary practice was to read from the "Law" and the "Prophets" and to offer an
explanation or exhortation. Similarly, James asserted,

> For Moses from ancient generations has in every city those who preach
> him, since he is read in the synagogues every Sabbath. (Acts 15:21; cf. Acts
> 17:2–4, 11; 18:4; 18:19; 19:8)

James argues as a matter of accepted fact that in the synagogues of the
first century, Moses is "read" and "preach(ed)." This has been done, James
says, "from ancient generations." Hughes Old maintains that the primary
method of reading in the synagogue was *lectio continua*, or consecutive
readings of Old Testament texts (giving way to *lectio selecta* for feast days).
"The older approach," he says, "was to read a passage of appropriate length
each Sabbath, beginning with Genesis, continuing each Sabbath where one
left off the Sabbath before until one reached the end of Deuteronomy."[5]
Later, readings from the prophets were added.

The early church, the Reformers argued, adopted from the synagogue
the practice of sequential reading of Scripture with explanation, adding the
Gospels and the Epistles to the Scripture to be read. It was this pattern of the

---

5. Hughes O. Old, *The Reading & Preaching of the Scriptures in the Worship of the Christian Church*, vol. 1, *The Biblical Period* (Grand Rapids: Eerdmans, 1998), 99ff. Synagogue
pericopes were "chosen on the principle of *lectio continua* for ordinary Sabbaths." Fuller,
"Lectionary," 297.

"ministry of the Word" to which the early Christians were devoted (Acts 6:2, 4; 2:42; 17:11; 20:7, 27). The Reformers found further support for *lectio continua* Scripture reading and preaching in the writings of the church fathers, whom they valued as witnesses to the practice of the apostles. The sermons of Origen (c.185–c.254), Augustine (354–430), Chrysostom (c.347–407), Gregory of Nyssa (c.330-c.395), and Gregory the Great (c.540–604) provided confirming evidence of *lectio continua* rather than *lectio selecta* readings.[6] In pre-Nicene times, "For ordinary Sundays the principle of *lectio continua* was used," writes R. H. Fuller, confirming the findings of the Reformers, "a book being selected apparently at local discretion and read in successive pericopes until it was finished."[7]

Convinced that this was the *pattern* that they found the Scripture and the patristic church, the Reformers were also convinced for *prudential* reasons that the Bible should be read publicly in sequence, verse-by-verse, book-by-book. Their basic concern was that the Bible should be read consecutively so that it might be understood in context, and so that no section or genre of Scripture might be omitted. *Comprehension* and *comprehensiveness* were the two goals. Martin Bucer's *Strassburg Liturgy* (1539) explained in its rubrics the reasons for *lectio continua* reading and preaching:

> And the Minister goes to the pulpit and reads out of the Gospels as much as he proposes to expound in a single sermon, treating the book in succession . . . and they should be dealt with in their order, not as heretofore by picking out several pieces, often without particular skill, so that all the other things given in the Gospels have been withheld from the congregation. In the afternoon and other hours, the other biblical books are also expounded.[8]

Bucer and the Strasbourg Reformers were concerned that "all the other things given in the Gospels" not be "withheld from the congregation." They were eager to expose Christian congregations to the whole counsel of God.

6. Hughes O. Old, *The Patristic Roots of Reformed Worship* (Zurich: Theologischer Verlag, 1970), 194–95.

7. Fuller, "Lectionary," 298.

8. Bard Thompson, *Liturgies of the Western Church* (Philadelphia: Fortress Press, 1961), 170–71.

The Scots in their first *Book of Discipline* (1560), reasoned along similar lines:

> We think it most expedient that the Scriptures be read in order, that is, that some one book of the Old and the New Testament be begun, and orderly read to the end. In the same we judge of preaching . . . for this skipping and divagation (i.e. wandering about) from place to place of the Scripture, be it in reading or be it in preaching, we judge not so profitable to edify the church as the continual following of one text.[9]

Selective readings from Scripture are not so much sinful or unlawful as unwise, say the Scots. Skipping about is "not so profitable to edify the church as the continual following of one text." Thompson summarizes the Scottish Reformers' concerns:

> Scarcely anything was less appropriate of a minister than he presume to control or obscure God's way among men by parceling out the Scriptures in bits and snatches. On the contrary, the Scriptures should be expounded book by book, chapter by chapter, in a continuous and orderly fashion. This procedure also implied that the sermon was not precisely the preacher's device to warm hearts, win souls, inculcate piety for the oncoming week. It was the Word of God, made real, alive, and effective in the hearts of men through the action of the Holy Spirit.[10]

The First Book of Common Order, containing what is sometimes called the "John Knox Liturgy," codified Knox's *Form of Prayers*[11] in 1564, and according to D. B. Forrester, "provided the norm for Reformed worship in Scotland until well into the seventeenth century."[12] Thomas M'Crie, 19th century Scottish church historian, described worship in Scotland from 1564–1638 as beginning with the "reader" (a provision permitted by the *Book of Discipline* because of the prevalence of untrained ministers), "whose office it was to read the prayers from Knox's liturgy, and portions of Scripture, before the minister entered the pulpit." M'Crie outlines the service as follows:

9. Ibid., 291, English modernized
10. Ibid.
11. Ibid., 295–307.
12. D. B. Forrester, "Worship," in *Dictionary of Scottish Church History and Theology*, ed. Nigel M. de Cameron (Downers Grove, IL: InterVarsity Press, 1993), 896.

- prayer
- Psalm sung
- Scripture reading
- prayer
- Lord's prayer
- doxology
- Psalm sung
- prayer of illumination
- sermon
- prayer
- Psalm sung
- benediction[13]

The "portions of Scripture" read by the reader would no doubt be the *lectio continua* readings mandated by the first *Book of Discipline*.[14]

On the basis of several contemporary sources, William D. Maxwell in *A History of Worship in the Church of Scotland* describes the worship of Scotland from roughly 1600 to 1640 in similar terms.[15] The reader would lead the congregation in the confession of sin from Knox's liturgy, then lead the people in singing a psalm or psalms with doxologies, and reading "a chapter or chapters in course out of both the Old and New Testaments, possibly with further psalms or canticles sung between them."[16] The minister, once he arrived, "read a text of Holy Scripture, and preached his sermon upon it."[17]

The English Puritans' *Middleburg Liturgy* (1586) directed that "some chapters of the canonical books of Scripture" be read, and that they be read "in order as the books and chapters follow, that so from time to time the

13. Thomas M'Crie, *The Story of the Scottish Church* (1874; repr., Glasgow: Free Presbyterian Publications, 1988), 166–67; cf. Charles Greig M'Crie, *The Public Worship of Presbyterian Scotland* (Edinburgh: William Blackwood & Sons, 1892), 162ff.

14. "There is no mention of the public reading of Scripture" in the *Book of Common Order* (1564), concedes Forrester, but he agrees, "This seems to have been included in a preliminary service by a reader." "Worship," 85.

15. He mentions William Cowper, *Seven-Days Conference between a Catholic Christian and a Roman Catholic*; Sir William Brereton in Hugh Brown, *Early Travelers in Scotland*, and Alexander Henderson, *The Government of the Church of Scotland*.

16. William D. Maxwell, *A History of Worship in the Church of Scotland* (London: Oxford University Press, 1955), 95.

17. Ibid., 96.

Holy Scriptures may be read throughout."[18] They deemed exposure to the whole Word of God important.

Similarly the Westminster Assembly's Directory (1645), the classic expression of Puritan views of worship, required *lectio continua* readings.

> Reading of the word in the congregation, being part of the publick worship of God, . . . and one means sanctified by him for the edifying of his people, is to be performed by the pastors and teachers.
>
> All the canonical books of the Old and New Testament . . . shall be publickly read in the vulgar tongue, out of the best allowed translation, distinctly, that all may hear and understand.
>
> How large a portion shall be read at once, is left to the wisdom of the minister; but it is convenient, that ordinarily one chapter of each Testament be read at every meeting; and sometimes more, where the chapters be short, or the coherence of matter requireth it.
>
> It is requisite that all the canonical books be read over in order, that the people may be better acquainted with the whole body of the scriptures; and ordinarily, where the reading in either Testament ended on one Lord's day, it is to begin the next.[19]

Note the Reformers' and Puritans' concern that the whole Bible be read, including the Old Testament, which, according to Hughes Old, "had for all practical purposes been lost from the regular worship of the Western Church" in the Middle Ages.[20] With the exception of the chanting of the Psalms and bits and pieces of the Old Testament here and there in selected services, the Old Testament was not opened. "Normally," says Old, "the faithful did not hear the Old Testament read in worship."[21] The Reformation restored the regular reading of the Old Testament in public worship. Why? "That the people may be better acquainted with the whole body of the Scriptures," said the Westminster divines.

We may add Baxter's *Reformed Liturgy* (1661) and Cranmer's *Book of Common Prayer* (1549, 1662) to our list of witnesses, as each envisioned a chapter being read from each testament in the regular worship of the

18. Thompson, *Liturgies*, 322.
19. Ibid., 358.
20. Old, *Patristic Roots*, 203.
21. Ibid.

church, though not necessarily *lectio continua*.[22] Old summarizes in saying that the practice of reading a chapter from each testament in each service was "a major feature of English Protestant worship from the beginning of the Reformation" until well into the seventeenth century.[23]

DEVELOPMENT

Lectio continua Scripture reading from both testaments was practiced in the continental Reformed churches and among the Scots and Puritans from the seventeenth to the nineteenth centuries, though with significant adaptations. Over time the Scripture reading developed into a reading with commentary, an "expository reading," as we will call it, of a chapter from the Bible. This approach was recommended by Martin Bucer in his *Grund und Ursach* as early as 1524. His order of service for the Lord's Supper included the reading of "some sections of the writings of the Apostles," for which the minister "gives a very brief explanation of the same." This "expository reading" would precede the reading of the gospel and what he called the "sermon proper."[24]

The Westminster Directory further paved the way for expository readings by providing guidelines for a phenomenon no doubt already developing among the Scots, to whose practice the directory is responding:

> When the minister who readeth shall judge it necessary to expound any part of what is read, let it not be done until the whole chapter or psalm be ended; and regard is always to be had unto the time, that neither preaching, nor other ordinances be straitened, or rendered tedious. Which rule is to be observed in all other publick performances.[25]

Notice the distinction between the exposition of what is read and the preaching, which is not to be adversely affected by the amount of time given

22. See Thompson, *Liturgies*, 391, 392; Maxwell, *An Outline of Christian Worship: Its Developments and Forms* (London: Oxford University Press, 1952), 138. Cranmer addressed the weaknesses of a *lectio selecta* approach through a weekday lectionary which took readers through the Bible in a year. See Old, *The Reading & Preaching of the Scriptures in the Worship of the Christian Church*, Vol. 4, *The Age of the Reformation* (Grand Rapids: Eerdmans, 2002), 151–55).

23. Old, *The Reading & Preaching of the Scriptures in the Worship of the Christian Church*, Vol. 5, *Moderatism, Pietism, and Awakening* (Grand Rapids: Eerdmans, 2004), 219.

24. Ottomar Cypris, *Basic Principles: Translation and Commentary of Martin Bucer's Grund Und Ursach, 1524* (Ann Arbor, MI: University Microfilms, 1971), 149–50.

25. Thompson, *Liturgies*, 358.

to the reading. Among English-speaking Reformed churches in seventeenth and eighteenth centuries, close to a half hour would come to be given to an expository reading of a chapter or so, that is, a reading with commentary, prior to the sermon proper, which in turn might last for an hour or more. Sometimes called the "double sermon," this phenomenon can be found among the Puritans in England, New England, and the Presbyterians in Scotland.[26]

Regarding the English Puritans and Dissenters, Hughes Old finds evidence for the expository reading, or double sermon, in the writings of Matthew Henry. He argues that Matthew Henry's *Commentary on the Whole Bible* is essentially his Bible reading notes.[27] Similarly at Isaac Watt's Bury Street Independent Meeting House, London, in the early 18th century, the order of service, according to contemporary accounts, was as follows:

- Psalm singing
- invocatory prayer
- expository reading of Scripture
- psalm or hymn
- long prayer
- sermon
- concluding prayer

Notice the "double sermon," both the expository reading and the sermon. Eighteenth-century English dissenters still included "about a half hour in the exposition of some portion of Scripture," according to contemporary observers in the early 18th century, in addition to the sermon proper. This was true of the morning service but not of the evening.[28] The same would appear to be true of Baptists of the same era.[29]

John Cotton's writings make explicit reference to the "double sermon" in the New England churches of the first generation. Horton Davies, working from the same sources as Hughes Old (John Cotton's

26. Old, *Reading & Preaching*, 5:29.

27. Hughes O. Old, "Henry, Matthew (1662–1714)", in *Historical Handbook of Major Biblical Interpreters*, ed. D. K. McKim (Downers Grove: IL: InterVarsity Press,1998), 197.

28. Horton Davies, *Worship & Theology in England: From Watts & Wesley to Maurice, 1690–1850* (Princeton, NJ: Princeton University Press, 1961), 101–2.

29. Ibid., 133.

The New England Way, 60–70 and *The True Constitution*, 5–8), outlines the following order of service in Boston and throughout New England:

- Prayer
- Reading & exposition of a chapter of the Bible
- Psalm singing
- Sermon
- Psalm singing
- Prayer
- Blessing[30]

Note the distinction between the "reading and exposition" and the sermon proper.

Among the Scots similar developments took place as well. Patrick Fairbairn, writing in 1874, dates the "double sermon" to Commonwealth times (the 1650's), referring to the expository reading as a "lecture" or "expository discourse" prior to the sermon proper. This practice, he said, consisting of "expounding in order a few verses out of some book of Scripture" is one which he says "has long prevailed," and was "a recognized and established part of the ordinary worship service."[31] Forrester characterized eighteenth and nineteenth century worship in Scotland as marked by "long sermons being supplemented by almost equally lengthy 'lectures' or biblical expositions," that is, our "expository reading."[32] Hughes Old, citing the support of Philip Ryken's studies, points to the evidence of the expository reading in the ministry of Thomas Boston (1676–1732). "The regular (Sunday) Scripture lessons . . . followed the *lectio continua* and were accompanied by a detailed exposition," says Old.[33] Further support can be found in the General Assembly of 1694 urging the recovery (after the persecutions of the Covenanting era) of the directory's program of *lectio continua* reading and "opening up" (by exposition) of, "large and considerable portion(s) of

30. Horton Davis, *The Worship of the American Puritans, 1629–1730* (Morgan, PA: Soli Deo Gloria Publications, 1999), 8.

31. Patrick Fairbairn, *Pastoral Theology: A Treatise on the Office & Duties of the Christian Pastor* (1875; repr., Audubon, NJ: Old Paths Publications, 1992), 239–40. His verb tenses are interesting. Did he mean that the double sermon was still practiced in his day?

32. Forrester, "Worship," 896.

33. Old, *Reading and Preaching*, 5:448.

the word of God."[34] This clearly is the "expository reading," not the sermon, to which the General Assembly was referring.

Old summarizes the situation in Reformation and post-Reformation Scotland by saying that "The serious business of preaching in Scotland was to take a book of the Bible and to preach through it." This, he says, was true in the days of John Knox (c.1514–1572), when Thomas Chalmers (1780–1847) began his exposition of Romans in his new church in Glasgow, and when Alexander Whyte (1836–1921) began his exposition of the Psalms at the beginning of the twentieth century. For the Scots, Old continues, "It was because the Word was holy that their expository preaching had to preach the Word through in an orderly and complete manner. With the *lectio continua* one respected the order of the sacred book."[35] At times this conviction was maintained through the *lectio continua* expository sermon, and at other times through the *lectio continua* expository reading. Old advances his view of the "double sermon" as a "hypothesis," but as we have seen it has more than substantial support among English Puritans and Dissenters, New England Puritans, and Scottish Presbyterians.[36]

DECLINE

Despite the various authorized liturgies and directories of English-speaking Reformed Protestantism, over time the *lectio continua* was dropped in favor of thematic preaching, based upon a few verses which alone were read. What happened? It is difficult, frankly, to determine. There is no evidence of a denominational body ever issuing an official directive to reduce Bible reading. This is not the kind of issue about which public complaints were likely to be received. But we can say that Scripture reading did diminish, and nearly completely drop out, in American Protestant churches. Charles Baird, writing in 1855 in his ground-breaking book *Eutaxia* (later renamed *Presbyterian Liturgies*) lamented the current lack of Bible reading among Presbyterians called for a return to the principles of the Directory for Worship, "the regular and continuous reading of Holy Scripture, at every religious service, and in sufficient portions."[37] He called regular, sequential reading

---

34. Cited in Maxwell, *History of Worship*, 128.
35. Old, *Reading & Preaching*, 5:539.
36. Ibid., 629.
37. Charles Baird, *Presbyterian Liturgies*, (1855; repr., Grand Rapids: Baker, 1957).

of Scripture "rare," a fact "deeply to be deplored," and a development for which "there can be no justification."[38] Yet this is what had happened among Presbyterians by the mid–nineteenth century. Methodists similarly ignored John Wesley's liturgy (1784), with its Psalm, Old Testament and New Testament readings, for a hundred and fifty years.[39] The format of Methodist worship from the late eighteenth century until the middle of the twentieth century was that of revivalism. The same was true of the Baptists and the Congregationalists.

According to Maxwell, decline in the public reading of Scripture in Scotland began early, within seven years of the adoption of the Directory. Yet, the Church of Scotland remained committed to the *lectio continua* readings required by the directory, the General Assembly reaffirming the necessity of reading a chapter from each testament in each service in 1652, 1694, and as late as 1856. Maxwell prefers to interpret these reaffirmations as signs of decline. They might better be seen as signs of continued commitment. Still, by the latter date, significant decline had occurred.[40] Likewise in New England, public Scripture reading had sharply declined by the second and third generations (see below).

There are other indications of the decline of Scripture reading. For example, one will find no mention of Scripture reading, or even the mechanics of reading Scripture in the nineteenth-century pastoral theology texts by John Brown (1826), Charles Bridges (1830), W. G. T. Shedd (1867), Patrick Fairbairn (1874), or Thomas Murphy (1877),[41] or the preaching manuals written by Ebenezer Porter (1834), J. W. Alexander (1864), R. L. Dabney (1870), Henry Ward Beecher, (1872), R. W. Dale (1877), Phillips Brooks (1877), or C. H. Spurgeon (1881–1894).[42]

---

38. Ibid., 264.

39. Thompson, *Liturgies*, 263.

40. W. D. Maxwell, *An Outline of Christian Worship* (London: Oxford University Press, 1952), 132.

41. John Brown, *The Christian Pastor's Manual* (1826; repr. Ligonier, PA: Soli Deo Gloria, 1991); Charles Bridges, *The Christian Ministry; With an Inquiry into the Causes of Its Inefficiency; With an Especial Reference to the Ministry of the Establishment* (London: Seeley, 1849); William G. T. Shedd, *Homiletics and Pastoral Theology* (1867; repr., Edinburgh: Banner of Truth, 1965); Fairbairn, *Pastoral Theology*; Thomas Murphy, *Pastoral Theology: The Pastor in the Various Duties of His Office* (1877; repr., Audubon, NJ: Old Paths Publications, 1996).

42. Ebenezer Porter, *Lectures on Homilectics and Preaching, and on Public Prayer; Together with Sermons and Letters* (New York: Flagg, Gould and Newman, 1834); James W. Alexander, *Thoughts on Preaching: Being Contributions to Homiletics* (1864; repr. Edinburgh: Banner of Truth, 1975); Robert L. Dabney, *Sacred Rhetoric or A Course of Lectures on Preaching* (1870;

In the twentieth century some authors did give attention to the need to restore Scripture reading to regular public worship and to the art of reading. For example, by 1912 J. H. Jowett, in his Yale lectures entitled *The Preacher: His Life & Work*,[43] was calling for renewed attention to be given to the reading of Scripture. Let it be "lifted into primary significance," he said. "What we need . . . is to exalt the ministry of the lesson in public worship. . . . Let us magnify the reading of the Word."[44] No mention, however, was made of *lectio continua*. His concern was with the mechanics of good reading, not the method of text selection. John A. Broadus' *On the Preparation & Delivery of Sermons*,[45] at least in its revised, 1944 edition, reflects the renewed interest in the public reading of Scripture, devoting five pages to its consideration. Yet his priorities are those of Pietism, not the Reformation. He too is largely concerned with the mechanics of reading. Insofar as he provides a criteria for text selection, it is a passage's devotional usefulness not *lectio continua*. Texts are to be those which are "in a higher decree devotional" and will "awaken devout feeling." Selections are to be governed by "good taste and devout feeling."[46]

As we approach the contemporary scene, a cursory glance provides not much in the way of encouragement from the Reformed or broader Protestant community. No advocates for *lectio continua* Bible reading can be found anywhere from the mid to late twentieth century: not in the writings of Andrew Blackwood, professor of practical theology at Princeton Theological Seminary from 1930 to 1950[47]; not in Thomas Oden's encyclopedic *Pastoral Theology* (1983)[48]; not in the *Leadership Handbooks*

repr. Edinburgh: Banner of Truth, 1979); Henry Ward Beecher, *Yale Lectures on Preaching* (New York: Fords, Howard, and Hulbert, 1893); R. W. Dale, *Nine Lectures on Preaching* (London: Hodder and Stoughton [nd]); Phillips Brooks, *Lectures on Preaching Delivered before the Divinity School of Yale College In January and February* (1877; repr., New York: E. P. Dutton and Company, 1907); C. H. Spurgeon, *Lectures to My Students* (1881–94; repr., Fearn, Ross-shire: Christian Focus Publications, 2000).

43. J. H. Jowett, *The Preacher: His Life & Work* (New York: George H. Doran Company, 1912).

44. Ibid., 159, 161.

45. John A. Broadus, *On the Preparation & Delivery of Sermons* (1870; repr., Nashville: Broadman Press, 1944).

46. Ibid., 359.

47. Andrew Blackwood, *The Fine Art of Worship* (Nashville: Abingdon Press, 1939) and *Leading in Public Prayer* (Nashville: Abingdon Press, 1957).

48. Thomas C. Oden, *Pastoral Theology: Essentials of Ministry* (San Francisco: Harper and Row Publishers, 1983).

of *Practical Theology, Volume One, Word and Worship*[49]; not in William H. Willimon's *Preaching and Leading Worship*[50]; not in contemporary books on preaching by Lloyd-Jones, Adams, Still, Stott, Robinson, and Chapell[51]; not in the more recent serious books on Reformed worship[52]; not in the important volume honoring Edmund P. Clowney ambitiously entitled *Practical Theology and the Ministry of the Church*, 1952–84[53]; not in The Master's Seminary's *Rediscovering Pastoral Practice*,[54] which represents the thinking of serious, conservative non-charismatic, semi-Reformed evangelicals; and not in the evangelical and/or Reformed periodicals: *Leadership, Christianity Today, Reformation & Revival, Reformed Worship*; not in *The Journal of Pastoral Practice*, published at Jay Adam's initiation and editorial leadership by the Christian Counseling and Education Foundation from 1977–92, revamped and republished as *The Journal of Biblical Counseling* since 1992.

Worldcat (World Catalogue search of the Library of Congress) and Atla (American Theological Library Association search of over 600 journals of which 50 are full-text) search engines produced only a handful of books or articles mentioning the public reading of Scripture and even fewer men-

49. James D. Berkley, ed., *Leadership Handbooks of Practical Theology, Volume One, Word and Worship* (Grand Rapids: Baker, 1992).

50. William H. Willimon, *Preaching and Leading Worship* (Philadelphia: The Westminster Press, 1984).

51. D. Martyn Lloyd-Jones, *Preaching and Preachers* (Grand Rapids: Zondervan, 1971); Jay E. Adams, *Preaching with Purpose* (Phillipsburg, NJ: Presbyterian and Reformed, 1982); William Still, *The Work of the Pastor* (Aberdeen: Didasko Press, 1976); John R. Stott, *Between Two Worlds: The Art of Preaching in the Twentieth Century* (Grand Rapids: Eerdmans, 1982); Haddon W. Robinson, *Biblical Preaching* (Grand Rapids: Baker, 1980); Bryan Chapell, *Christ-Centered Preaching: Redeeming the Expository Sermon* (Grand Rapids: Baker, 1994).

52. Jean-Jacques von Allmen, *Worship: Its Theology and Practice* (London: Lutterworth Press, 1965); Maxwell, *An Outline of Christian Worship*; Robert Rayburn, *O Come Let Us Worship* (Grand Rapids: Baker, 1980); Donald Macleod, *Presbyterian Worship: Its Meaning and Method* (Richmond: John Knox, 1967); James Hastings Nichols, *Corporate Worship in the Reformed Tradition* (Philadelphia: Westminster Press, 1968); H. G. Hageman, *Pulpit & Table: Some Chapters in the History of Worship in the Reformed Churches* (Richmond: John Knox Press, 1962). Marva J. Dawn, *Reaching Out without Dumbing Down* (Grand Rapids: Eerdmans, 1995). John Frame, *Worship in Spirit & Truth* (Phillipsburg, NJ: P&R, 1996). We can add to the list Methodist James F. White, *Introduction to Christian Worship* (Nashville: Abingdon, 1980); D. A. Carson, ed., *Worship: Adoration and Action* (Grand Rapids: Baker, 1993), which includes essay by Edmund P. Clowney on "Presbyterian Worship," 110–22.

53. Harvey M. Conn, ed., *Practical Theology and the Ministry of the Church, 1952–1984: Essays in Honor of Edmund P. Clowney* (Phillipsburg, NJ: P&R Company, 1990).

54. John MacArthur, et. al., *Rediscovering Pastoral Ministry* (Dallas: Word Publishing, 1995).

tioning *lectio continua*. Of those only two could legitimately be considered advocating *lectio continua* as a method of Scripture selection. We may trace both to a single influence, Hughes O. Old.[55] *Lectio continua* preaching has its champions, *lectio continua* reading has not, save one.[56]

55. John P. Burgess, "Shaping a Congregation through *Lectio Continua*" in *Reformed Liturgy & Music*, 30, no. 1, (1996): 3–6. The author confesses that much of his account of the history of *lectio continua* he "gleaned from personal conversation with Hughes Oliphant Old," and from Old's *Worship That is Reformed According to Scripture* (note 8). The other advocate, not surprisingly, is Hughes O. Old, writing in *Reformed Worship*, 8 (Summer 1988): 24–25.

56. Where the reading of Scripture has been discussed in the late twentieth century literature, interest has been limited primarily to the "how-to's" of reading. Blackwood in *Fine Art of Worship* affirms that "the reading of the Scriptures is perhaps the most important part of public worship." He offers comments upon responsive readings, the pulpit Bible, the strengths of the King James Version, the "how-to's" of public reading, and the virtues of the lectionary" (128). An interesting aside: Writing in 1939, Blackwood says, "A generation ago the minister who wished to be up with the times was either using the responsive reading, or else wondering why he was not." While in the end he endorses its use, he speaks of the responsive reading as a passing fad, a view with which the present writer has some sympathy. Among the anti-arguments: "The Psalms were written to be sung, not read; that the responsive reading consumes valuable time, with no appreciable effect; and that it quickly becomes formal, almost perfunctory." Ibid.,128–29. H. G. Hageman recalls the Reformation era practice of *lectio continua*, acknowledges "there is more to be said for the custom than most of us are willing to admit," laments the current practice of a single lesson determined by the sermon, insists it "calls for correction," and concludes that church committees, lectionaries, or the Christian year may serve as guides in selecting which Scriptures shall be read. *Lectio continua* is, in most cases, impractical today, he says, because "many of our congregations would weary of it." *Pulpit & Table*, 123. Von Allmen devotes 7 pages to the subject, comparing *lectio continua* and *lectio selecta*. He notes that the *lectio selecta* has gradually come to prevail even in the Reformed churches, and says, surprisingly, "and we must rejoice about it," though he doesn't want *lectio continua* to be entirely superseded. *Worship*, 134. Donald Macleod is concerned about the growing ignorance of the Bible among Protestants. His answer is a calendar-based *lectio selecta* lectionary that he claims "covers the Bible in two years," which of course, it doesn't except highly selectively. *Presbyterian Worship*, 114. Rayburn urges both a Old Testament and New Testament reading, but never mentions *lectio continua*. Willimon, a Methodist, wants to see more Scripture read and urges three lessons every Sunday, as well as "the orderly reading of Scripture." *Preaching and Leading*, 19. *Preacher & Preaching*, a significant effort to promote biblical preaching, does have a promising chapter entitled "Reading the Word of God Aloud." Samuel T. Logan, Jr., ed., *The Preacher & Preaching: Reviving the Art in the Twentieth Century* (Phillipsburg, NJ: Presbyterian & Reformed Publishing Company, 1986). But, alas, it too turns out to be concerned only with the mechanics of reading. The same is true of Chapell, *Christ-Centered Preaching*, 337ff. The *Leadership Handbooks* devotes one and a half pages to "the public reading of Scripture" out of 500 in volume one on "Word & Worship." It recommends frequent use of "familiar texts and devotional texts" because "they create a spirit of warmth and gratitude" (188). *Worship in the Presence of God*, a collection of essays written by committed Presbyterian traditionalists, includes a chapter on "The Reading of Scriptures," by Louis F. DeBoer. Frank J. Smith and David C. Lanchman, eds., *Worship in the Presence of God* (Greenville, SC: Greenville Seminary Press, 1992). DeBoer says quite a bit about the importance of reading Scripture. He even urges the reading of two full chapters, one from each testament,

Let us restate what we have found: Among the books on pastoral theology, preaching, and worship; among the journals and magazines we can find no champions of *lectio continua* Scripture reading in the nineteenth and twentieth centuries, excepting Baird and Old. Increased *lectio selecta* Bible reading has had its advocates. Skillful Bible reading has had its advocates. *Lectio continua* preaching has had its advocates. *Lectio continua* reading has not, outside of Baird and Old.

As we push into the twenty-first century, the picture brightens only slightly. Clayton J. Schmit has written *Public Reading of Scripture: A Handbook.*[57] Its concern is with the training of lay readers, or lectors. How texts are selected to be read and how much is to be read is not discussed. As was true of works cited above, his concern is with the mechanics of public reading. The bad news is most of the books on worship written out of the evangelical and/or Reformed tradition (the lines between these two groups are fluid, hence my imprecision) still mainly ignore Scripture reading generally and *lectio continua* specifically. These include those books edited by D. A. Carson (with articles by R. Kent Hughes on "Free Church Worship," and by Timothy J. Keller on "Reformed Worship in the Global City"),[58] R. J. Gore,[59] D. G. Hart,[60] and D. G. Hart and John R. Muether.[61] Michael Horton recommends Old Testament and New Testament readings, the second reading determined by its relation to the theme of the

in each service. But his criteria of selection is not *lectio continua*, which goes unmentioned, but thematic connection with the theme of the preacher's sermon. Another collection of essays written in honor of Calvin Seminary's Old Testament Professor John H. Stek carries the hopeful title of *Reading & Hearing the Word*, Arie C. Leder, ed. (Grand Rapids: CRC Publications, 1998). Yet even in this volume, the subject of *lectio continua* reading is ignored, indeed, despite the title, the whole subject of the public reading of Scripture is omitted. No advocates of *lectio continua* Scripture reading are to be found. Even the esteemed Dr. Old limits his advocacy to *lectio continua* preaching and omits to press the case for reading in his *Worship That Is Reformed According to Scriptures*. Only with the publishing of his multi-volumed *The Reading & Preaching of the Scriptures in the Worship of the Christian Church* can we find positive advocacy for *lectio continua* reading of the Scripture (Grand Rapids: Eerdmans, Vol. 1–7, 1998–).

57. Clayton J. Schmit, *Public Reading of Scripture: A Handbook* (Nashville: Abingdon Press, 2002).

58. D. A. Carson, ed., *Worship by the Book* (Grand Rapids: Zondervan, 2002).

59. R. J. Gore, Jr., *Covenantal Worship: Reconsidering the Puritan Regulative Principle* (Phillipsburg, NJ: P&R Company, 2002).

60. D. G. Hart, *Recovering Mother Kirk: The Case for Liturgy in the Reformed Tradition* (Grand Rapids: Baker, 2003).

61. D. G. Hart and John R. Muether, *With Reverence and Awe: Returning to the Basics of Reformed Worship* (Phillipsburg, NJ: P&R Company, 2002).

primary reading, i.e. the text to be preached.[62] Meyer strongly commends extended Bible reading and includes four readings in his morning service (Old Testament, Epistle, Psalm, Gospel), but provides no criteria for selection except pragmatic considerations according to the wisdom of the ministers and elders.[63] Horace T. Allen compares and contrasts *lectio continua* and *lectio selecta* urging a combination of the two along the lines of the common lectionary in *Christian Worship in Reformed Churches Past & Present*.[64]

Among the books on worship published in the twenty-first century, we can turn only to Ligon Duncan in *Give Praise to God* to find positive advocacy for *lectio continua* Scripture reading in public worship.[65]

Among the magazines and journals, we find some encouragement of late. There has been some lamenting of the sorry state of Scripture reading and advocacy for its increase.[66] Several articles have even been written positively commending *lectio continua* public Scripture reading.[67]

So again we ask, what happened by the middle of the nineteenth century that led to the disappearance of Bible reading in general, and *lectio continua* reading in particular? Tracing this development is difficult and conjectural. Still, we can identify several trends and/or movements that influenced the shift away from the Reformation-era practice of extensive, whole-chapters per service readings.

62. Michael Horton, *A Better Way: Rediscovering the Drama of God-Centered Worship* (Grand Rapids: Baker, 2002), 89–90.

63. Jeffrey J. Meyers, *The Lord's Service: The Grace of Covenant Renewal Worship* (Moscow, ID: Canon Press, 2003), 156–62; 194–200.

64. Horace T. Allen, Jr., "Calendar & Lectionary in Reformed Perspective & History," in *Christian Worship in Reformed Churches Past & Present*, ed. Lukas Vischer (Grand Rapids: Eerdmans, 2003).

65. J. Ligon Duncan, "Reading & Praying the Bible in Corporate Worship," in *Give Praise to God: A Vision for Reforming Worship*, Philip G. Ryken, ed. (Philipsburg, NJ: P&R, 2003), 141–48.

66. Donald N. Bastian, "The Silenced Word," in *Christianity Today* 45, no. 4 (March 5, 2001): 92; Christopher K. Lensch, "The Public Reading of Scripture," *Western Reformed Seminary Journal* 7, no. 1 (February 2000): 19–22; Dwight A. Randall, "Scripture Reading & Worship," *Life News* (Internet Magazine, available at http://lifeministries.org.au/internal.php?content_id=139); Arthur Howe, "The Public Reading of the Scriptures," *The Banner of Truth Magazine* no. 499 (April 2005): 17–21.

67. David Jussley, "*Lectio Continua*: The Best Way to Teach & Preach the Bible," *The Banner of Truth Magazine* no. 499 (April 2005): 12–16); James C. Goodloe, IV, "Righteous Judgment," *The Presbyterian Outlook* (February 7, 2004).

Medieval Scholasticism

Hughes Old suggests that the first reason for the decline of *lectio continua* Scripture reading has to do with the manner in which Reform came to the English-speaking world. Continental Reformed Protestantism arose out of the new learning of the late Renaissance. It rejected the scholastic method in favor of a return *ad fontes*, to the original sources themselves, which were to be interpreted in their integrity. The preaching inspired by the new learning of Christian humanism was concerned to be textual. It drank deeply from the wells of biblical and patristic sources. It rejected medieval preaching methodology, with its reliance upon rhetorical tricks and gimmicks. The preaching of Zwingli, Calvin, Oecolampadius, Capito, and the whole host of continental Reformed Protestants was biblical rather than topical, expository rather than scholastic, simple and plain rather than ornate, *lectio continua* rather than *lectio selecta*.

But as Old points out, "The new learning of the Christian humanists had appeared in only a few churches in England; it had not produced an elite corps of biblical scholars all eagerly studying the original languages as it had, for example, in the Upper Rhineland."[68] The consequence of this for preaching was direct. Throughout Henry VIII's reign and even into Edward VI's, "we hear only occasionally of preachers who are able to do the kind of expository preaching that so many of the Continental Reformers did."[69] Instead they continued the medieval practice of dividing the text analytically, and applying it to various religious and moral questions.

This absence of a clean break from Scholastic preaching can be seen even among the Puritans. They tended not to follow the Continental Reformers in using the form of the patristic homily, that is, a running commentary on a passage of Scripture. "In England," Old explains, "the break between medieval homiletics and Reformation homiletics was not nearly as clear as it was on the Continent." "The Puritans," he says, "most frequently used the scholastic, analytical form."[70] "England," he continues, "never had anything like the patristic revival to which Rhenish Protestantism was heir."[71]

Old maintains that the Puritans attempted to establish the *lectio continua*. Their official orders of service (as noted above) show that. But the

68. Old, *Reading and Preaching*, 4:148.
69. Ibid., cf. *Reading and Preaching*, 5:29.
70. Ibid., 326.
71. Ibid.

Scholastic method made this difficult. "The scholastic sermon form slowed down the *lectio continua*. Rarely could one cover in one sermon more than a single verse of Scripture using this form."[72] The pace slowed to single verses, and even to multiple sermons on single verses. "What this ultimately meant was the finishing off of the *lectio continua* and the gradual development of thematic preaching."[73]

The Puritans, for the most part, maintained the "plain style" of the Continental Reformers. But they did so within a Scholastic analytical framework that made *lectio continua* preaching all but impossible to maintain.

As noted above, John Cotton described in the *New England Way* in 1642 the practice of reading a chapter from one testament in the morning and the other testament in the evening, each in addition to the reading of the text to be preached.[74] This had been significantly eclipsed by the next generation, as the expository reading was dropped in favor of the "sermon proper." Increase Mather was among those who influenced the New England churches away from *lectio continua*. He began to limit the Scripture reading to that which was to be preached, and urged others to do the same.[75] The Brattle Street Church was founded in 1699 with a number of liturgical reforms in mind, including the restoration of the Old Testament and New Testament readings, as recommended by the directory. However, few New England churches followed Brattle Street's example. The important point to be observed is that already by the 1690's what had been practiced in the 1630's had eroded and had to be revived by the Brattle Street Church.[76]

A generation later Cotton Mather, writing in his *Ratio Disciplinae*, provided a typical order of worship in his day (1726).

- announcements
- prayer
- Psalm sung
- reading of Scripture & sermon (*lectio selecta*)

72. Ibid., 327.
73. Ibid.
74. Old, *Reading & Preaching*, 5:172.
75. Ibid.
76. Ibid.

- short prayer
- Psalm sung
- benediction (typically the apostolic)[77]

Mather then discussed the matter of *lectio continua* Scripture reading, admitting a diversity of practice in New England. He acknowledged the position of John Cotton, who argued in 1645 (in his book *Singing of Psalms*) that the reading of Scripture was an "ordinance" of public worship distinct from preaching. Mather also notes that this is the position of the Westminster Directory. The New England churches, however, followed three different patterns:

1. Some read Scripture *lectio continua* without commentary.
2. Some read Scripture *lectio continua* with commentary.
3. Some only read the passage of Scripture to be preached.

Respecting the churches that only read the Scripture to be preached, he listed the following reasons:

1. They could see no precept or pattern in Scripture for reading without exposition.
2. Proper sermons typically include the reading of multiple passages of Scripture with the advantage that their use is in the context of their "place and use in divinity."[78]
3. While exposition by gifted men is to be preferred to bare reading, some ministers' gifts require a different manner of handling the word of God than sequential exposition.
4. Some chapters of the Bible are not appropriate for public reading.
5. Public reading of Scripture may lead to the neglect of Scripture reading in families.

Horton Davies maintains that Cotton Mather objects to "lections without commentary."[79] The present writer, however, can find no such objections.

77. Cotton Mather, *Ratio Disciplinae Frutrum Nov-Anglorum: A Faithful Account of the Discipline Professed & Practiced in the Churches of New England* (1726; repr. New York: Arno Press, 1972), 67.
78. Ibid., 64.
79. Davies, *American Puritans*, 298, n. 2.

Mather merely lists the various pros and cons, without committing himself to one side or the other. Indeed he claims that to refer to readings without commentary as "dumb readings" is "esteemed improper and indecent."[80] He concludes his review of the various approaches to Scripture reading saying,

> If there be not a perfect harmony in the churches about the manner of performing this duty, however there is perfect charity; It breeds no difference. Yea, that the Scriptures be publicly read, in some sense, it may be said, they are all agreed.[81]

Yet those wishing to limit the public reading to the preaching text ultimately carried the day, the arguments 1–5 above, apparently gaining universal approval. The preference for lengthy, highly analytical sermons among the Puritans and their descendents would seem to be the primary reason, the reason driving all other reasons, for the disappearance of *lectio continua* Scripture reading in English-speaking Reformed churches.

PUBLIC VERSUS PRIVATE

Old points to a second development in English Puritanism that tended to undermine *lectio continua*. This was the problem of the separation of the reading of the Word from the preaching of the Word. Often forced out of the regular parish services by political or ecclesiastical authorities, much Puritan *lectio continua* preaching was done at "lectures" held Sunday afternoon or midweek. Expository preaching became separated from worship, and the sermon from the lectionary. This was the case both among Anglicans as well as Puritans, whose preaching often was unrelated to the lectionary. Even among the emerging Congregationalist and Presbyterian churches the sermon was moved to the end of the service, separated from the Scripture lesson. The Scripture reading gradually came to lose its importance as a distinct element of public worship.[82]

Weekday Versus Sunday Lections

A third reason for the loss of the *lectio continua*, closely associated with the preceding, has to do with the distinction between weekday and

---

80. Mather, *Ratio*, 67.
81. Ibid., 67–68.
82. Old, *Reading & Preaching*, 4:328.

Sunday Scripture readings in both the Anglican and Puritan traditions. The Prayer Book lectionary, by Cranmer's design, took the congregation through the Old Testament once and the New Testament three times in a year (4 chapters a day in morning and evening prayer).[83] Cranmer was committed to the *lectio continua* in the weekday services. The dearth of qualified preachers or literate congregants (who could read the Bible for themselves) meant that the reading of Scripture was seen as a major means through which the Reformation would make progress in England. The designers of the 1549 and subsequent Prayer Books understood this. The English lectionary was "a serious attempt to guarantee the reading of the whole Bible through in the course of a year in such a way that the literary integrity of the different books (was) respected and the context of each passage is evident," writes Old.[84] But the Sunday lectionary followed a different course. The *lectio selecta* became the norm for the weekly Lord's Day communion services and holy days.

The Puritans, like the Continental Reformers, moved the daily service into the home. They came to make a distinction between the public reading of Scripture, for which the minister gave explanation and comment (the expository reading or sermon proper), and the private reading of Scripture, in which no comment was made.

A "simple reading, or 'dumb reading,' was deemed inadequate for a service of worship," for increasing numbers of New England's Puritans, notes Hambrick-Stowe in *The Practice of Piety*.[85] As we have seen, whenever Reformed Protestants in the English-speaking world had an opportunity to shape their own services, whether among the post-Restoration Presbyterians and Congregationalists in England, the Scots, or the Puritans in New England, "expository readings" of a chapter of the New Testament and the Old Testament became a feature of their worship. Supporting it were *lectio continua* readings in family worship for which reading without commentary was deemed acceptable. When the expository reading was dropped in later centuries in favor of the single long sermon upon a short text, it

---

83. Ibid., 151–55.

84. Ibid., 157.

85. Charles E. Hambrick-Stowe, *The Practice of Piety: Puritan Devotional Disciplines in Seventeenth-Century New England* (Chapel Hill, NC: University of North Carolina Press, 1982), 110; Old, *Reading & Preaching*, 4:328.

was done in the context of extensive *lectio continua* readings in homes, of which the M'Cheyne Lectionary is a surviving example. As noted, Cotton Mather refers to the sentiment in New England that *lectio continua* reading without commentary in public worship would undermine the same in family worship. It would "invite private Christians to neglect" their duty of reading Scripture "in private families."[86] Ironically, the prevalence of *lectio continua* in the daily services of the established church and in Puritan and dissenting homes tended to undermine the need for *lectio continua* reading in the Sunday services.

Time Constraints

The constraints of time under which public services were (and are) conducted must also be given significant consideration. As noted above, the Westminster Directory expressed concern that the expository reading be done with "regard . . . unto the time." The directory sought to prevent the sermon or some other ordinance from being "straitened" (i.e. reduced, restricted, shortened) or "rendered tedious" by lengthy comments on the Scripture reading. Horton Davies estimates that the Puritan worship service lasted three to three and a half hours. Even among the Puritans there were limits. As the second sermon grew to be one and a half to two hours in length, it eventually came to swallow up the expository reading.[87] The first "sermon" came to be seen as a redundancy, especially since Scripture reading could be done at home. Yet what was lost was the sequential, extended reading envisioned by the directory or as practiced the first generation in New England, among the Dissenters in England, and for several generations in Scotland.

Pietism

Fifth, the Pietistic movement of the seventeenth and eighteenth centuries brought a fresh concern for heart-felt religion and for conversions. Its concern for warm feelings, personal piety, devotional Bible study, and inspiration services was not well served by extended readings from obscure chapters of the Old Testament. Selected inspirational verses were better suited to these ends than were large chunks of Scripture

---

86. Mather, *Ratio*, 64.
87. Davies, *American Puritans*, 11.

313

read from, say, 1 Samuel. This preference for the inspirational is clear in more recent times in the pastoral manuals of Broadus and the *Leadership Handbook* cited above. Churches that would never have dreamed of adopting the Anglican lectionary nevertheless adopted a *lectio selecta* based upon evangelistic and inspirational criteria even as they abandoned the *lectio continua*.

As pietism developed into revivalism, and as churches increasingly adopted the revivalistic format, time-constraints further squeezed-out Scripture reading. Choirs, solos, duets, and other forms of "special music" had to be accommodated. Something had to give way to the needs of evangelism and inspiration. It was natural to reduce the Bible reading. The result of these trends, the long Puritan sermon, weekday *lectio continua* at home, the requirements of pietism, and the constraints of time, was that *lectio continua* public reading dropped out of the public worship of English-speaking Reformed Protestantism by the mid-nineteenth century. This was true of the descendants of New Light and Old Light churches of the eighteenth century, New School and Old School churches of the nineteenth century, and fundamentalist and modernist churches of the twentieth century. It is true of the whole English Dissenting, Puritan, and Scottish Presbyterian heritage. Across all these categories there was a curiously uniform neglect of extended *lectio continua* Scripture reading. The practice was not maintained nor revived in American, or English, or Scottish Protestantism, whether Presbyterian, Congregationalist, Baptist, or Methodist from the time of the beginning of its erosion in the early nineteenth century until the late twentieth century. *Lectio continua* preaching was maintained in some circles, *lectio continua* reading was not. Not until the liturgical reform movements of the mid to late twentieth century did *lectio continua* Scripture reading begin to get some attention again. The reintroduction of this plank from the Reformer's platform of church reform is one of the major needs of our day.

RECOVERY

How do we go about recovering the public reading of Scripture, specifically *lectio continua* Scripture reading in our churches? Consider the following.

1. *Read a chapter of each testament in each service,* as recommended by the Westminster Directory for the Public Worship of God (see above). By this we mean read not *slavishly* but *roughly* a chapter. Some chapters are long and need to be broken up into several pieces. Other sections of Scripture are not well-suited to the public reading, and so may need to be skipped over. In other words, the reading should be of *suitable* length. But the basic guideline should be a chapter per testament per service.

2. *Read the testament not being preached.* This guideline is proposed as a way of maintaining biblical balance. If the gospel of Matthew is being preached in the morning service, then read Old Testament books along with the text from Matthew being preached. If the books of Samuel and Kings are being preached in the evening, then read a gospel, Acts, or an epistle alongside of the Samuel/Kings text being preached.

3. *Read passages that are accessible to the congregation.* It would probably prove unwise to begin the implementation of a program of *lectio continua* readings in the book of Leviticus. It can be done, but it is not recommended. Start with the Gospels, Acts, Psalms, Epistles, Proverbs, or an Old Testament narrative.

4. *Consistent with this, skip over (with descriptive comments) exceptionally remote or difficult texts.* Passages such as Exodus 25–31 (describing the tabernacle and its furnishings, Joshua 15–21 (outlining the distribution of the Promised Land to the twelve tribes), 1 Chronicles 1–9 (genealogies), Nehemiah 3 (describing the placement of workers on the walls of Jerusalem) ordinarily are best handled with a summary comment while transitioning to the next text to be read.

5. *Vary scriptural types.* It would probably be unwise to plow through one Minor Prophet after another, or straight through Old Testament narrative from Genesis to Nehemiah. Instead, vary the diet. Move from gospel to Old Testament narrative to epistle to Old Testament poetry to Acts to Old Testament wisdom and so on.

6. *Provide brief introductions to books and chapters.* By "brief" we mean normally a few sentences lasting 15–45 seconds. A few comments

315

setting the stage of the text to be read or anticipating a difficulty in the text can do much to enhance the spiritual profitability of the reading.

7. *Read slowly, clearly, and with nuance.* J. C. Ryle credited the reading of Scripture in the context of worship as being instrumental in his own conversion. The text was Ephesians 2:8, described by J. I. Packer as skillfully read in church "with significant pauses, thus achieving great emphasis."[88] Scripture may be read with more or less skill. Our final concern is that care be taken to read the Scripture well. The reading should not be rushed. Neither should the reading drag. The text to be read should be studied carefully enough that it can be read with comprehension and nuance, enhancing the understanding of the congregation. There is a direct relationship between the skill with which Scripture is read and the value of that reading for the listeners. Edification, after all, is the goal at which we are aiming. Substantial portions of Scripture should be read in the assemblies of God's people because this is what God required of them in Bible times, what was practiced by the patristic church and Reformation-era Reformed churches, and above all, because the reading of Scripture edifies the people of God.

88. J. I. Packer, *Faithfulness and Holiness: The Witness of J. C. Ryle* (Wheaton, Illinois: Crossway Books, 2002), p. 27.

16

Global Kingdom Vision and the
Westminster Confession of Faith

S A M U E L   H .   L A R S E N [1]

IT IS OFTEN ALLEGED, even by friends of the Westminster tradition, that the Westminster Confession of Faith, along with the wider Protestant Reformation of which it was a part, lacked a global missions perspective and a vision for reaching all nations with the gospel.[2] Whether such

1. This lecture was given at the inauguration of Dr. Samuel H. Larsen into the Samuel Patterson Chair of Missions and Evangelism at Reformed Theological Seminary, Jackson, Mississippi. "Rev. Samuel B. Patterson, founding President of Reformed Theological Seminary, was a man of vision and warmhearted devotion to bringing the gospel of Jesus Christ to all. As I occupy the chair of missions and evangelism that has been named in his memory, my aspiration is to build upon Professor Patterson's legacy by engaging a biblical ontology, missiological perspective, and a discerning use of the social sciences in ways that will serve to advance the global Kingdom of the Lord Jesus Christ. The remarks that follow are offered in that spirit."

2. Gustav Warnack, *Outline of a History of Protestant Missions from the Reformation to the Present Time*, 3rd. English ed., ed. George Robson (New York: Fleming H. Revell, 1906) 19. Warnack states: "In Calvin, too, there is found no recognition of such a duty [on the part of the church to send out missionaries]. He does not, indeed, teach directly that already through the Apostles the Gospel has been preached in the whole world, but that Christ penetrates quickly, like the lightning from the east to the west, that he may call the nations everywhere into the church. Thus the extension of Christianity is still in progress, albeit the apostolate

impressions are valid is another matter, which leads us to the guiding question for the discussion that follows: Does the Westminster Confession of Faith overlook global missions?

In order to answer that question, it is important to understand the historical context of the Westminster Assembly (1645–46). The assembly was convened during the life-and-death struggle for the survival of the Protestant Reformation in England, Scotland, and Wales amid persecution by the Roman Catholic Church and the Stuart royal house. The counter-reformation would claim hundreds of thousands of Protestant lives across Europe. Just as Islam is today again recognized by many as the single greatest threat to Christianity since the fall of global Marxism, just so, in England and Scotland in the mid-seventeenth century, reactionary Roman Catholicism was viewed as the embodiment of the Antichrist and as the greatest threat to biblical Christianity.

At issue at that time were two fundamental matters, both absolutely foundational to global missions:

1. What is the gospel?
2. How is the gospel to be spread?

The Puritans, Congregationalists, and Presbyterians who participated in the Westminster Assembly's work addressed those core concerns under near-constant threat of royalist attack. Aware of their historical context, they worked with a sense of both gravity and urgency. Could they have said more about the global missionary task of the church? Most certainly, and we would do well in our own day to build upon their work toward that end. Nevertheless, the Westminster divines did not ignore global missions, as is sometimes assumed.

The original guiding question of the present discussion is, "Does the Westminster Confession of Faith overlook global missions?" In order to address that question, I propose to address three subsidiary questions:

---

was an extraordinary office, which as such has not been perpetuated in the Christian church." Although Warnack is aware of Calvin's involvement in sending Huguenot ministers to Brazil, he fails adequately to take into account that one of them, Jean de Lery, in a well-accredited historical account written in 1558 and first published shortly thereafter, records his being sent in 1556 (while studying theology under Calvin at the time) by the Church of Geneva as a missionary to Brazil specifically for the explicit purpose of bringing the gospel to aboriginal inhabitants as well as to European settlers.

1. What does the confession itself say concerning global missions?
2. How were the teachings of the confession actually given expression within the American colonies in the ministries of men who embraced it, such as John Eliott and David Brainerd, and, through them, pioneer missionaries such as Henry Martyn and William Carey?
3. How may the foundation laid by the confession be amplified and fleshed out in order to give more complete treatment of the biblical teaching regarding the global missionary task of the church?

In the following discussion, we will proceed to consider each of those three subsidiary questions in turn.

Confessional Statements Concerning Global Missions

We begin with our first subsidiary question: What does the confession itself say concerning global missions?

For the purposes of the present discussion, the form of the confession used will be the one adopted by the Presbyterian Church in America (PCA), which is substantially the same as the one adopted by the First General Assembly of the Presbyterian Church in the United States of America in 1789. Its primary difference from the original lies in its disallowing interference by the civil magistrate in ecclesiastical affairs and in its toning down of what some considered intemperately vitriolic anti-Roman Catholic language.

Eight chapters of the confession are of special interest with regard to global missions: 1, 7, 8, 10, 15, 21, 25, and 26.

WCF 1.8 affirms that "because these original tongues are not known to all the people of God, who have right unto, and interest in the Scriptures, and are commanded, in the fear of God, to read and search them, therefore they are to be translated into the vulgar language of every nation unto which they come. . . ." Implicit is the assumption that the Bible is capable of translation into the language of every people group (across cultural boundaries); explicit is the affirmation that the Scriptures "are to be" so translated, which presupposes carrying the Word of God to "every nation unto which they come" (i.e., global missions). Noteworthy is the phrase "all the people of God," which, in the context, embraces "every nation."

WCF 7.6 states, "Under the gospel, when Christ, the substance, was exhibited, the ordinances in which this covenant is dispensed are the preaching of the Word, and the administration of the sacraments of baptism and the Lord's Supper: which, though fewer in number, and administered with more simplicity, and less outward glory, yet, in them, it is held forth in more fullness, evidence, and spiritual efficacy, to all nations, both Jews and Gentiles; and is called the new testament." The sphere of the gospel ministry here clearly embraces "all nations."

WCF 8.5 states, "The Lord Jesus, by His perfect obedience, and sacrifice of himself, which he, through the eternal Spirit, once offered up unto God, hath fully satisfied the justice of his Father; and purchased, not only reconciliation, but an everlasting inheritance in the kingdom of heaven, for all those whom the Father hath given unto him." WCF 8.8 continues, "To all those for whom Christ hath purchased redemption, he doth certainly and effectually apply and communicate the same; making intercession for them, and revealing unto them, in and by the Word, the mysteries of salvation; effectively persuading them by his Spirit to believe and obey, and governing their hearts by his Word and Spirit; overcoming all their enemies by his almighty power and wisdom, in such manner, and ways, as are most consonant to his wonderful and unsearchable dispensation." The phrase "all those for whom Christ hath purchased redemption" must be understood in light of WCF 7.6 (see above).

WCF 10.4 reads, "... much less can men, not professing the Christian religion, be saved in any other way whatsoever, be they never so diligent to frame their lives according to the light of nature, and the laws of that religion they do profess. And, to assert and maintain that they may, is very pernicious, and to be detested." The authors were quite aware of the religion of Islam, of primal religion in the American colonies, and of medieval Roman Catholicism. The context (concerning effectual calling) makes clear that none anywhere are saved apart from the work of the Holy Spirit through the proclamation of the gospel. Implicit is the concern of Christ for the lost of all nations (again, cf. WCF 7.6), among whom are the elect, and the necessity of proclaiming the gospel to them.

WCF 15.1 reads, "Repentance unto life is an evangelical grace, the doctrine whereof is to be preached by every minister of the gospel, as well as that of faith in Christ." The acknowledged central duty of ministers of the gospel is to proclaim repentance and faith in Christ, which is the core of evangelism and is at the heart of missions.

WCF 21.6 states, "Neither prayer, nor any other part of religious worship, is now, under the gospel, either tied unto, or made more acceptable by any place in which it is performed, or towards which it is directed: but God is to be worshipped everywhere, in spirit and truth. . . ." In the context, the Confession refutes the notion that geographic location in any way either enhances or restricts the acceptability of worship, but the clear corollary is that all the earth is to be filled with the worship of God (cf. Ps. 67:7, Ps. 72:19).

The twenty-fifth chapter of the confession is especially rich. WCF 25.1 states that "The catholic or universal church, which is invisible, consists of the whole number of the elect, that have been, are, or shall be gathered into one, under Christ the Head thereof; and is the spouse, the body, the fullness of him that filleth all in all." WCF 25.2 goes on to state, "The visible church, which is also catholic or universal under the gospel (not confined to one nation, as before under the law), consists of all those throughout the world that profess the true religion; and of their children: and is the kingdom of the Lord Jesus Christ, the house and family of God, out of which there is no ordinary possibility of salvation." To this, WCF 25.3 adds, "Unto this catholic visible church Christ hath given the ministry, oracles, and ordinances of God, for the gathering and perfecting of the saints, in this life, to the end of the world: and doth, by His own presence and Spirit, according to his promise, make them effectual thereunto." WCF 25.5 further notes that "Nevertheless, there shall be always a church on earth, to worship God according to his will." Clearly, the confession envisions the boundaries of the kingdom of God, the church of Christ, to extend geographically worldwide, to the ends of the earth, and to the end of time.

In summary, the Westminster Confession of Faith painstakingly, accurately, and succinctly addressed the core issues foundational to global missions: What is the gospel? and How is the gospel to be spread? The syncretism that resulted in Spanish missions to the New World were in no small measure the result of Roman Catholicism's own answers to those questions. As we shall see, a very different approach would be taken by Protestant Reformed missionaries, especially those who were influenced by the Westminster Confession of Faith.

EARLY MISSIONARY PIONEERS

We therefore come to our second subsidiary question: How were the teachings of the confession actually given expression in the American colonies in the ministries of men who embraced it, such as John Eliot and David Brainerd, and, through them, pioneer missionaries such as Henry Martyn and William Carey?

In the seventeenth century, the principal colonies in the New World that belonged to England and Scotland were those in North America. There, Puritan settlers came into immediate contact with Indians of very different culture, worldview, and religion. Among the early intentional missionaries to the Indians of North America was John Eliot (1605–90), "the Apostle to the Indians."

The Long Parliament in 1649 chartered the first Protestant missionary society, which according to Latourette, "was, indeed, without exact counterpart in the earlier spread of Christianity or of any other religion."[3] It was the Society for the Propagation of the Gospel in New England, and a collection of nearly 12,000 pounds for the Society's purposes was received from counties, towns and parishes of England and Wales.[4] John Eliot, following the Mayhews, had begun to preach among the Indians in the vicinity of Boston in 1646, and his work was among the first supported by the new Society when it was founded in 1649. Eventually 30 villages of "praying Indians" were established, with a translation by Eliot of the New Testament in 1661 and of the Old Testament two years later. Although the villages were massacred during the upheaval of King Philip's War (1675–76), suffering from both marauding Indian bands and from blindly retaliating settlers, the pioneering work of John Eliot stands as a monument to the missionary vision of one who shared in the theology of the confession.

Following the Great Awakening of 1734–1735, David Brainerd (1718–1747) attended Yale for three years before serving among the Indians in North America until his early death, at age twenty-nine, from tuberculosis. Deeply influenced by the examples of John Eliot and John Sergeant, and by the ministry of Jonathan Edwards, he gave his life in a brief but intense itinerant preaching ministry among the Indians. His diary, edited and published

3. Kenneth Scott Latourette, *A History of the Expansion of Christianity* (New York: Harper, 1938), 44.
4. Ibid., 45.

posthumously by Jonathan Edwards, in turn profoundly influenced both Henry Martyn and William Carey.[5] Following ministry in India, Martyn completed the first translation of the Bible into Persian. Carey also served in India and has often been called the "Father of Modern Missions." The legacy of the confession has reverberated throughout the world through its direct and indirect influence upon leaders in world missions. It resulted in a very different legacy from that of Roman Catholic missions conducted in the wake of the Counter-Reformation. The resulting Protestant missions tended to reject syncretism and to emphasize personal repentance and faith in Christ, along with instruction in biblical knowledge and translation of the Scriptures into the local languages.

EARLY MISSIONARY PIONEERS—WHITHER NOW?

Our third subsidiary question remains to be addressed: How may the foundation laid by the Westminster Confession be amplified and fleshed out in order to give more complete treatment of the biblical teaching regarding the global missionary task of the church? The modern terminology of "global missions" has only become commonplace within about the last century. If the concepts are clearly present in the confession, it need not be faulted for using the vocabulary of its own time.

As the confession itself affirms, no single confession (or creed or pronouncement by a church council), being by its very nature only humanly crafted and not itself God-breathed Scripture, can claim to summarize fully and perfectly the whole counsel of God contained in the sixty-six canonical books of the Bible. What is amazing is, not that there are omissions in the Westminster Confession or topics which would benefit from greater explication and emphasis, but that the Westminster Assembly actually accomplished its work so very well. Arguably, no other document sets forth so clearly, cogently, and succinctly, the system of doctrine regarding salvation as does the Westminster Confession of Faith and its accompanying Larger and Shorter Catechisms.

Where, then, might we like to have the confession's testimony amplified or extended? Permit me to offer a few ideas that may serve to begin a

---

5. Stephen Neill, *A History of Christian Missions* (New York: Penguin, 1964), 226. Neill writes, "Brainerd died, but lived on in the lives of those, like William Carey and Henry Martyn, who found inspiration in his impassioned words."

continuing conversation on the matter. A formal amendment to the West-minster Confession, while not prohibited either by the document itself or by the Book of Church Order of the PCA, is perhaps not necessary. Never-theless, an accompanying statement may be helpful to make explicit what is implicit and to amplify what is sketchy in the confession. That statement might include the following kinds of things:

1. Explicit reference to the teleological and doxological culmination of the global task of bringing the gospel to the nations (cf. Mat-thew 24:14 and Revelation 7:9).
2. Acknowledgment that believers are God's "pilgrim people" in the world, with implications for stewardship of their time, efforts, and substance with respect to bringing God's salvation to the ends of the earth (Acts 13:47).
3. Recognition of the truth that reconciliation with God often brings about reconciliation with others, with resulting improvements in social justice (not in the reverse order).[6] Social concern is biblical; the social gospel is not.

Church courts have frequently adopted statements containing these or similar teachings. None, however, have been accorded constitutional status alongside the confession (which has rarely been amended) and the Book of Church Order (which, by contrast, has frequently been amended). Conferring upon a carefully worded statement such con-stitutional status is one way of bearing witness before the world, in a more enduring way, to the priority we understand Scripture gives to global missions. What our confession already points toward we would articulate more clearly. *Ecclesia reformata semper reformanda est* ("the Reformed church is always reforming").

6. Ibid., 297. Neill concludes, "The experiment has been tried in a great many countries; and the result has been to show that acceptance of the Gospel invariably comes before civiliza-tion, and not civilization before acceptance of the Gospel."

17

Martyn Lloyd-Jones on
Theology and Preaching

Robert L. Penny

A Theological Orientation: A Prerequisite to Preaching

Central to the method of examining the principles of expository preaching of Martyn Lloyd-Jones[1] is a consideration and understanding of his theological approach or orientation. His view of the relationship of theology and preaching would stand today, in most evangelical traditions, as atypical. Yet because of his view of the prominent role of theology in preaching, he would consider this orientation to be one of the ingredients of good expository preaching. He discussed this prerequisite in a general treatment of the content of the sermon and specifically under what *determines*

1. This essay is adapted from Robert Lee Penny, *An Examination of the Principles of Expository Preaching of David Martyn Lloyd-Jones* (D.Min. diss., Harding University, 1980). The editors of *20 Centuries of Great Preaching* include Lloyd-Jones as one of the leading preachers of the last century (one of eight so treated), apparently to be ranked among *all* who have gone before in the history of the church. Some of his lectures reveal that he was a careful student of the theology and practice of preaching in those preceding centuries. "David Martyn Lloyd-Jones," ed. Clyde E. Fant and William Pinson (Waco, TX: Word, 1971), 11:263–329.

content. His answer is that one's theology is very instrumental in governing content. One should give attention, therefore, to a consideration of his views on this principle.

Lloyd-Jones felt that the "evidence from the New Testament itself," which he took to be "supported and exemplified by the history of the Church," leads one to the belief that the "ultimate justification" for asserting "the primacy of preaching" is "theological."[2] He explained "the whole message" of the Bible "asserts this and drives us to this conclusion."[3] One can thus see how his theology has led him to a certain high view—"primacy"—of the role of preaching, but it also led him to a certain approach to the task and manner of the preparation and delivery of sermons. He gave his reasoning:

> The moment you consider man's real need, and also the nature of the salvation announced and proclaimed in the Scriptures, you are driven to the conclusion that the primary task of the Church is to preach and proclaim this, to show man's real need, and to show the only remedy, the only cure for it.[4]

In describing the connection between theology and preaching, Lloyd-Jones gave it as a "general proposition" that preaching "must always be theological, always based on a theological foundation."[5] In order to leave

2. David Martyn Lloyd-Jones, *Preaching and Preachers* (Grand Rapids: Zondervan, 1972), 64 (hereafter cited as *Preaching*). Lloyd-Jones said, "With the Puritans we stand for preaching. Their view of preaching . . . was governed by theology. One's view of preaching is ultimately not a matter of taste, but is an expression of one's theological standpoint, and ultimately one's view of the Gospel. This is something that I could demonstrate in history even before the Protestant Reformation." "Preaching," in *Anglican and Puritan Thinking* (Rushden, England: The Westminster Conference, 1977), 90. Hereafter cited as "Preaching." Lloyd-Jones's high regard for some elements of Puritan preaching, which may be seen throughout his lectures and writings, may find its ultimate rationale on these points: their *convictions* and *approach*.

3. Ibid. Lloyd-Jones said, "I am simply demonstrating the point that the basis of our view of preaching is always theological. All these men claimed, and the Puritans claimed, and all who believe the supremacy of preaching, have always claimed, is that this was our Lord's own method of teaching the Truth. Our Lord was a preacher, John the Baptist . . . was also a preacher primarily. In the book of Acts we find the same: Peter on the day of Pentecost got up and preached, and he continued to do so. The Apostle Paul was preeminently a great preacher. We see him preaching in Athens, as he declares the Truth to the Athenians." "Preaching," 91. This sounds much like a reference to or an exercise in the exegetical discipline known as biblical theology.

4. Ibid.

5. Ibid., 64.

no room for misunderstanding, Lloyd-Jones stated the proposition negatively: "There is no type of preaching that should be non-theological."[6]
Some might conceive that such a generalization could be made but that an
exception could also be made in connection with evangelistic preaching.
But Lloyd-Jones did not yield his thesis even on this point. Lloyd-Jones
believed evangelism also to be "highly theological."[7] If evangelistic preaching is not theological, Lloyd-Jones maintained, then it "is not evangelism
at all in any true sense."[8] He gave his rationale and application of his theory
when he said:

> I would be prepared to argue that in many ways evangelistic preaching
> should be more, rather than less theological than any other, and for good
> reason. Why is it that you call people to repent? Why do you call them
> to believe the gospel? You cannot deal properly with repentance without
> dealing with the doctrine of man, the doctrine of the Fall, the doctrine of
> sin and the wrath of God against sin. Then when you call men to come
> to Christ and to give themselves to Him, how can you do so without
> knowing who He is, and on what grounds you invite them to come to
> Him, and so on.[9]

Features

One should view the features of Lloyd-Jones's convictions on this
subject first from his negative statements and then from the positive. He
clarified his assertion by stating that preaching "is not lecturing on theology,
or on any aspect of theology."[10] Nor is anyone ever justified in imposing
"his system violently"[11] on any particular text. Some do violence with their
systematic theology. They wrongly derive a particular doctrine from a text.
The doctrine "may be true," but Lloyd-Jones objected that it "does not arise
from that particular text."[12]

Now we can follow Lloyd-Jones's positive statements on this matter.
He maintained that the preacher must have a "good grasp" of the whole

6. Ibid., 65.
7. Ibid.
8. Ibid.
9. Ibid.
10. Ibid.
11. Ibid., 66.
12. Ibid.

biblical message, a message that he understood formed a "unity."[13] He believed that the preacher ought to be well-versed in biblical theology which, to him, ultimately leads to systematic theology. Lloyd-Jones placed this priority on systematics when he said, "To me there is nothing more important in a preacher than that he should have a systematic theology, that he should know it and be well-grounded in it."[14] He believed that this should serve as a "background" and as a "controlling influence" in one's preaching.[15]

Lloyd-Jones believed in holding each message in its position of unity with the rest of Scripture and theology. Each message must reflect that it is "a part or an aspect of this total body of truth."[16] It is never something in "isolation."[17] To him this is the effect and meaning of the generally espoused interpretive principle "comparing Scripture with Scripture."

Lloyd-Jones believed that such a practice would preclude a certain danger to which many preachers are exposed when they deal with isolated texts or texts, for example, which are treated out of the sequence of the entire biblical book. He gave a warning:

> We should be particularly careful when we preach on isolated texts and deal with each one separately. The reason for that, of course, is that we may well find ourselves becoming guilty of contradictions. We deliver a message on the basis of one text, but because it is not related to others, and to the whole truth, when we come to deal with another text we may say something that contradicts what we have said in the first sermon.[18]

The "way to avoid that," Lloyd-Jones said, is "to be always theological."[19] Lloyd-Jones gave a summary of this method and approach:

13. Ibid. Admirers of Lloyd-Jones of the Reformed persuasion wonder if this could this be an allusion to "covenant theology."

14. Ibid.

15. Ibid.

16. Ibid.

17. Ibid. Some of these statements sound, to this writer, like those of the honoree of this volume during classroom lectures, doubtless because of identical convictions. That is what makes the subject of this essay so appropriate for this volume.

18. Ibid., 65.

19. Ibid.

The right use of systematic theology is, that when you discover a particular doctrine in your text you check it, and control it, by making sure that it fits into this whole body of biblical doctrine that is vital and essential.[20]

Lloyd-Jones understood this method as the fulfillment of the preacher's calling to deliver "all the counsel of God" (Acts 20:27). But he held, at the same time, that "we must always be textual."[21] Again, to clarify his position in regard to the relationship of theology and preaching, he stated at length:

> Perhaps I can clarify this by reminding you that it is obvious in New Testament times, and in the early days of the Christian Church, they did not preach in a manner that has become customary with us. They did not take a text out of the New Testament and analyze it and expound it and then apply it, because they did not have the New Testament. Well, what did they preach? They preached the great message that had been committed to them, this great body of truth, this whole doctrine of salvation. My argument is that this is what we should always be doing, though we do it through individual expositions of particular texts. That is, to me, in general the relationship between theology and preaching.[22]

Summary and Conclusion

One may now make some observations in the interests of clarity and in summary: (1) what has been discussed here is a matter which could be called a *principle* of expository preaching of Lloyd-Jones; (2) it is in the nature of an *orientation* to sermon preparation and content; (3) it is one that Lloyd-Jones apparently viewed as a *prerequisite* in order to achieve what he would call good expository preaching; (4) it is a principle he sees as *universally* important and believes that *all* preachers should be using this approach and that they should use it for *all* kinds of sermons; and (5) he viewed the use and practice of this approach as *apostolic*. He found great embodiments of this principle in two figures outstanding in the history of the church for their preaching. In a discussion of what he saw as the balance of Jonathan Edwards, he said:

20. Ibid., 66–67.
21. Ibid., 66.
22. Ibid., 67. For our Lord's practice refer to Richard Gaffin's essay in this volume.

In other words, what strikes one about Edwards as one looks at the man as a whole is the completeness, the balance. He was a mighty theologian and a great evangelist at the same time. How foolish we have become! The man was both as was the Apostle Paul. [Edwards] was a great pastor; he dealt with souls and their problems.

Lessons for Preachers

From this we may draw at least two apparent conclusions or lessons. *First*, whatever zeal or affection for the method and insights of biblical theology one might possess, a preacher must never allow a "theological amnesia" to come over him even momentarily. The doctrines of the biblical *didaka* must be his polar star. *Secondly*, preachers must always guard that "good deposit" that has been committed to them (2 Tim. 1:9, 14; Rom. 7:14).

THE PRIMACY OF PREACHING

A major approach of Lloyd-Jones that should be seen as cardinal to his principles of preaching is his idea of the *primacy* of preaching. By this suggestion, he means to call attention to the chief or central place that he advocated preaching holds or should hold in the calling and work of the minister. He made no reservations, conditions, or allowances when he stated, in no uncertain terms, that preaching is primary, "the chiefest thing of all," "the most important" aspect of the ministry.[23]

Lloyd-Jones held that the work of preaching is the "highest and greatest and most glorious calling to which anyone can ever be called." With this conviction of primacy, there was also the conviction of need, and as shall be seen shortly, of a dearth of true preaching our day. He would declare "without any hesitation" that the "most urgent need" in the Christian church today is "true preaching." Because it is the greatest

23. Lloyd-Jones, *Preaching*, 185–86. As long ago as 1964 Lloyd-Jones, in a lecture partly on George Whitefield, said, "Whitefield I believe is calling us back to preaching. I hope that I am not going to be misunderstood, but nothing can substitute for preaching. I am a great believer in reading; I get much of my greatest enjoyment in reading. But reading is no substitute for preaching; and to read a sermon and to listen to it being preached are not the same thing. . . .You need the 'lightning and the thunder and the rainbow.'" "John Calvin and George Whitefield," in *Able Ministers of the New Testament* (London: Puritan and Reformed Studies Conference, 1964), 96.

need for the church, he saw it also as "obviously the greatest need of the world also."[24]

With some idea of the general conviction and approach of Lloyd-Jones to the place of preaching, this essay shall proceed to survey his reasons for his near exclusive position or position on the primacy of preaching. First, he discussed two critical questions; second, he stated his thesis of the primacy of preaching and sought to demonstrate that it was established by three mandates: the biblical, the historical, and the theological. Third, he discussed what he perceived as current relevant issues and objections that could arise to challenge his thesis.

Two Critical Questions

First, there were two critical questions regarding preaching that Lloyd-Jones saw as current issues. The first is, "Is there any need of preaching?" On this question, Lloyd-Jones made the following three observations. He believed the very fact that one had to pose such a question stands as "the most illuminating commentary" on the "state of the Church at the present time." He felt that here is to be found the "chief explanation" of the "present more or less parlous condition" and "ineffectiveness of the Christian Church in the world today." He attributed this to a certain fogginess on the part of Christian people. He believed that "the main trouble" arose from the fact that "people are not clear in their minds as to what preaching really is."[25]

From this Lloyd-Jones went on to discuss the second critical question: "What is the cause of the present reaction against preaching?" He discussed general reasons, those affecting society as a whole, and then particular reasons relating to the church. A general reason had to do with what he called "Baldwinism." This is named for a late prime minister of England, Stanley Baldwin, who served during the 1920s and 1930s. Lloyd-Jones claimed that because Baldwin had no gift as a speaker or an orator, he discounted "the

---

24. Ibid., 9. In apparent agreement, Lloyd-Jones cited the conviction of the Puritan William Perkins: "William Perkins defines the business of preaching thus: 'It is to collect the Church and to accomplish the number of the elect.' That is the primary business of the Church. Its other function is 'to drive the wolves away from the folds of the Lord.'" "Preaching," 96.

25. Ibid., 9–10. Cf. Merrill Abbey's conviction that when words are put into a "message embodied in a convincing person, they become as powerful as any that the age of electronic media has produced." Merrill R. Abbey, *Communication in Pulpit and Parish* (Philadelphia: Westminster Press, 1973), 85. Abbey went on to say that among the "powerful media of our time, truth through personality is still a force of primary potency." Ibid.

value and importance of speech and oratory" and "conveyed the suggestion that if a man is a great speaker he is a man whom you cannot trust." The result was the promotion, and later prevalence, of a "new attitude towards oratory and eloquence and speaking worthy of the name," an attitude of "distrust of the orator." This is "Baldwinism."[26]

Lloyd-Jones also saw some reasons for the present reaction to preaching that related to the church itself. He did not hesitate to put in "the first position" the "loss of belief in the authority of the Scriptures" and a "diminution in the belief in the Truth." He saw this as the "main factor."[27]

The second reason Lloyd-Jones listed for the present reaction is the "reaction against what were called 'the great pulpiteers'" especially those of "the second half of the [nineteenth] century." Lloyd-Jones gave an example. He saw that the "man who was most typical in this respect in the U.S.A. was Henry Ward Beecher." Lloyd-Jones actually placed these preachers in a unique category. He said that they were "pulpiteers rather than preachers" and were "professionals" who possessed a good deal of the element of showmanship and who could occupy a pulpit and "dominate the people." To Lloyd-Jones they were an "abomination," men with whom "form became more important than substance" and the "oratory and the eloquence became things in and of themselves, and ultimately preaching became a form of entertainment."[28]

Lloyd-Jones listed the third reason relating to the church for the present reaction to preaching as a "wrong conception of what a sermon really is, and therefore of what preaching really is." He saw this as a result of several factors. First, there is the "printing and publication of sermons" which he held "has had a bad effect upon preaching." Second, there were the "essayists." He observed that the Scottish school of preachers began to give "great attention to literary and historical allusions and quotations." Actually, they were "essayists rather than preachers," but since they published those "essays as sermons, they were accepted as sermons." Third, there is a list of miscellaneous items that to him serve to encourage a wrong conception of what a sermon really is. He saw that ideas had crept in that what is needed is a "chat," an "address," or a "quiet talk," rather than a sermon.[29] The "service" came to be emphasized. He

26. Ibid., 11–13.
27. Ibid., 13.
28. Ibid., 13–15.
29. Some alert preachers, theologians, and observers recommend that we also cease today's common practice of referring to preaching as "sharing," perhaps as opposed to "declaring." Believing, perhaps, there is a danger of being guilty of the same fallacy.

observed "an increase in the element of entertainment in public worship." The "giving of testimonies" came in. Finally, Lloyd-Jones observed an "increasing emphasis upon 'personal work'. . . or 'counseling.' "[30]

Lloyd-Jones also saw some reasons for the present reaction to preaching that came from the non-church or para-church sector of Christianity. Those who believe one needs to "abandon the Church if we really are to propagate the Gospel" made up this group. Lloyd-Jones saw the influence of this group to be against preaching. They suggest, according to Lloyd-Jones, that one should "make a clean break with all this tradition which we have inherited," and in order to reach people, one should "mix with them," "live among them," "share our lives with them," and "show the love of God to them by just bearing one another's burdens and by being one of them." Further, this school would contend that missionaries, rather than preaching the truth as their primary aim, "should take ordinary jobs, mix among the people, and more especially, enter into their political and social affairs."[31] Lloyd-Jones observed that the above are factors that have led to the present reaction against true preaching.

A Thesis

Secondly, we are to observe Lloyd-Jones's thesis concerning preaching and its place in the ministry of the church and examine the three mandates which he saw as the basis of his thesis. He said that the "primary task of the Church and of the Christian minister is the preaching of the Word of God."[32] He saw the three-fold mandate for the validity of this thesis to lie in the *Bible, church history*, and *theology*.

Biblical Mandate

First, we will survey some of the summary statements that Lloyd-Jones perceived to be the biblical mandate for the primacy of preaching.

30. Ibid., 15–17.
31. Ibid., 18–19.
32. Ibid., 19. Cf. Baumann's similar conviction: "It is my conviction that preaching has the potential for significant influence in our electronic era if the preacher will be sensitive to the changes dictated by the sovereign movement of the Holy Spirit. God cannot be domesticated, limited by our programming, nor restricted to the method of preaching; yet there is insufficient evidence to indicate that imaginatively conceived, faithfully executed preaching, is not still the primary instrument chosen of God to proclaim the Good News of Christ." J. Daniel Baumann, *Introduction to Contemporary Preaching* (Grand Rapids: Baker, 1972), 12–13.

Although he claimed that he "could give evidence also from the Old Testament in the prophets," he confined himself only to the New Testament. Here he saw evidence in both the pre-resurrection and post-resurrection ministries of Christ. He understood the earthly ministry of the Lord to demonstrate a primary concern for preaching and teaching. For example, the miracles "were not His primary work, they were secondary." He discussed what he saw as the repeated emphasis of Jesus and implied that it was contrary to the present and popular concept of the place of social concerns in the total ministry of the church. After a summary examination of what one may call the "other worldly" aim of Jesus, Lloyd-Jones concluded:

> The teaching is the first thing, and [Jesus] reminded them that the Christian is the light of the world. . . . I suggest that in the Gospels, and in the life and ministry of our Lord Himself, you have this clear indication of the primacy of preaching and teaching.[33]

As for the post-resurrection ministry of Jesus, Lloyd-Jones saw the same emphasis in the apostles and the rest of the New Testament. Two examples he gave were the Great Commission and Pentecost. Of the former, he observed:

> [Christ] tells these chosen men that they are primarily to be "witnesses unto Me." That is to be their first great task. He is going to give them other powers, but their main business is to be witnesses unto Him.[34]

Apparently, Lloyd-Jones understood the concept of witness here as referring primarily to the verbal aspect of the function of a witness.

Of the many phenomena of Pentecost, Lloyd-Jones singled out one that he took to be very relevant to his thesis. He said that it is "interesting

---

33. Ibid., 20–21. Lloyd-Jones said, "Christianity is primarily a listening to God. God is speaking! Religion is man searching for God. Christianity is God seeking man, manifesting Himself to him, and drawing Himself unto him. This, I believe, is at the back of the Puritan idea of placing in the central position of the exposition of the Word of God in preaching." "Preaching," 95. Such statements seem to indicate a latent covenant theology, direct references to which in Lloyd-Jones, this writer has not discovered yet but adherence to which by most, if not all, of the contributors of this volume (as one may observe) is very pronounced.

34. Ibid., 22.

to observe" that "immediately after these men are filled with the Holy Spirit on the Day of Pentecost they begin to preach."[35]

Lloyd-Jones believed the most illuminating and "interesting statement of all" to be in Acts 6:2 which stands as a rationale for the institution of the diaconate. He applied that statement in such a way as to see in it a basis for the primacy of preaching today. He said, "I know of nothing that speaks more directly upon the present state and condition of the Church and what is her primary task." He gave his approach to the application of this passage:

> Surely the business of the Christian Church, and the leaders particularly, is to deal with this crying need [of the neglected] widows. Why go on preaching when people are starving and in need and are suffering? That was the great temptation that came to the Church immediately; but the Apostles under the leading and guidance of the Holy Spirit and the teaching they had already received, and the commission they had from their Master, saw the danger and they said, "It is not reason that we should leave the Word of God, and serve tables." This is wrong. We shall be failing in our commission if we do this. We are here to preach this Word, this is the first thing, "We will give ourselves continually to prayer and the ministry of the Word."[36]

Lloyd-Jones's application is that now these "priorities are laid down once and forever." He restated his thesis and some conclusions about preaching meant to apply to the contemporary scene:

> This is the primary task of the Church, the primary task of the leaders of the Church, the people who are set in this position of authority; and we must not allow anything to deflect us from this, however good the cause, however great the need.[37]

Another element that Lloyd-Jones saw in the biblical mandate for the primacy of preaching was the notion of the propagation of the truth. He saw this as *the* task of the church and the *specialty* of preaching. He pointed

35. Ibid.
36. Ibid., 23.
37. Ibid.

to Paul's statement in 1 Timothy 3:15 as supportive of this conviction and of his thesis:

> The Apostle Paul reminds Timothy that the Church is 'the pillar and the ground of the Truth.' She is not a social organization or institution, not a political society, not a cultural society, but 'the pillar and the ground of the Truth.'[38]

Historical Mandate

Secondly, we shall look at what Lloyd-Jones perceived as the historical mandate for the primacy of preaching. In this discussion, he shared his broad view of church history in relation to preaching and pointed to a particular period. Referring to his thesis and the biblical support that he gave for it, he said:

> All this is fully confirmed in Church history. Is it not clear, as you take a bird's eye view of Church history, that the decadent periods and eras in the history of the Church have always been those periods when preaching had declined? What is it that always heralds the dawn of a Reformation or a Revival? It is renewed preaching.[39]

Lloyd-Jones gave as examples the Reformation and periods of revival. He saw these as "notable periods of the greatest preaching that the Church has ever known." He believed that as that was true, "in the beginning as described in the book of Acts," so it was "also after the Protestant Reformation." He called Luther, Calvin, Knox, Latimer, and Ridley "great preachers."[40]

Theological Mandate

Thirdly, we shall observe the theological mandate that compelled Lloyd-Jones to the conviction of the central or primary place of preach-

---

38. Ibid., 24.

39. Ibid.

40. Ibid., 25. In another place Lloyd-Jones elaborated: "When you come to the Reformation itself this proposition needs no demonstration. Martin Luther was preeminently a great preacher. So was John Calvin. Let us not forget this. These men were first and foremost, regular preachers and great preachers. You cannot think of John Knox in Scotland for a moment without thinking of his great preaching and the way in which Mary, Queen of Scots, would tremble as she listened to him. She was more afraid of his preaching than the troops that the English sent to take her captive. The same was true of Zwingli in Switzerland." "Preaching," 90–91.

ing. He said that the "ultimate justification" for "asserting the primacy of preaching" is "theological." He felt that he could "argue" that the whole message of the Bible asserts this and drives toward this conclusion. He set about to present support from three areas of theology: (1) anthropology, (2) soteriology, and (3) ecclesiology.[41]

In his discussion of the doctrine of man, Lloyd-Jones took both a negative and positive turn. He showed a negative reaction to a prevailing approach in the ministry that he felt betrayed a wrong doctrine of man. He observed that many people try "to diagnose the human situation," and they come to the conclusion that man is merely "unhappy, man is the victim of circumstances." He saw that such people believe that man's primary need "is to have these things dealt with" and "to be delivered from them." But Lloyd-Jones felt that this was "too superficial a diagnosis of the condition of man." He felt that "man's real trouble" is that he is a "rebel against God and consequently under the wrath of God."[42]

The positive argument of Lloyd-Jones came in the form of an assertion of, and conclusion about, a New Testament statement regarding man:

> Now this is the biblical statement concerning him, this is the biblical view
> of man as he is by nature. He is "dead in trespasses and sins," that means
> spiritually dead. He is dead to the life of God, to the spiritual realm and
> to all the beneficent influences of that realm upon him.[43]

This seems to be the essence of this doctrine of man. The Reformed articles of faith known as the Westminster Confession of Faith and Catechisms and the Three Forms of Unity of the Dutch Reformed communions expound this doctrine more fully.

In soteriology, Lloyd-Jones emphasized the role which knowledge and truth play. He pointed to the Apostle Paul, who "describes salvation" in the words, "coming to a knowledge of the truth" (1 Tim. 2:4). He went on to

---

41. Ibid., 26.

42. Ibid., 27. Lloyd-Jones when interviewed in retirement pointed out: "The New Testament scholar, Professor R. V. G. Tasker, attended [Westminster Chapel] on Sunday nights; he forsook liberalism and told me that under my ministry he became convinced of original sin and the wrath of God, and that led to a complete change." Carl F. H. Henry, "Martyn Lloyd-Jones: From Buckingham to Westminster," *Christianity Today*, February 8, 1980: 157.

43. Ibid. Cf. W. H. Anderson's suggestion that the most fundamental problem for preaching today is the nature of man, rather than a materialistic culture or modern science. In "The Possibility of Biblical Preaching," *Christianity Today* 7 (June 1963): 868.

say, "Salvation is knowledge of the truth . . . ." Then he drew a conclusion that he applied directly to his thesis:

> If this is the greatest need of man, if his ultimate need is something that arises out of this ignorance of his which, in turn, is the result of rebellion against God, well then, what he needs first and foremost is to be told about this, to be told the truth about himself, and to be told of the only way in which this can be dealt with. So I assert that it is the peculiar task of the Church, and of the preacher to make all this known.[44]

To him, then, preaching as the propagation of truth is indispensable, and therefore, primary.

As a third and final locus of theology, Lloyd-Jones presented his findings in ecclesiology as support. He disagreed with what he called "the modern fallacy" which has "come into the Church" and "is influencing the thinking of many in the Church." He criticized this "notion" that "the business of the Church" is supposed to be "to make people happy, or to integrate their lives, or to relieve their circumstances and improve their conditions." In contrast, Lloyd-Jones's "case" is that "to do that is just to palliate the symptoms, to give temporary ease, and that it does not go beyond that."[45]

Lloyd-Jones believed that the primary purpose of the church was to seek to "put man into the right relationship with God, to reconcile man to God." He held that this is the *specialty* of the church and of preaching:

> The business of the Church, and the business of preaching—and she alone can do this—is to isolate the radical problems and to deal with them in a radical manner. This is specialist work; it is the peculiar task of the Church. . . . The Church is a special and specialist institution and this is a work that she alone can perform.[46]

CHALLENGES TO THE THESIS

Now we turn to consider Lloyd-Jones's discussion of the objections that he perceived to be challenges to his thesis. He gave evidence that he was not oblivious to contemporary positions, issues, and arguments in this

44. Ibid., 28–29.
45. Ibid., 30.
46. Ibid., 32.

area. He weighed them, and to his mind they lacked validity. In his treatise, he discussed the argument that the church and its ministry should seek to address and handle social problems, the argument that the ministry should focus on and handle personal problems, and a miscellaneous series of objections.

Handle Social Problems

Here we survey Lloyd-Jones's treatment of the argument that the church and its ministry should consider its main business to be the addressing and handling of social problems. He saw that behind this position was the notion that "the old evangelical preaching of the Gospel" was "too personal," and "too simple" and that this approach "did not deal" with "social problems and conditions." He saw this position as a "part" of the "liberal, modernist, higher critical view of the Scriptures and of our Lord." His observation was that while many today regard this as "so new" and as "the primary task of the Church," it is something that had been "tried with great thoroughness in the early part of [the twentieth] century." He believed that people from today's vantage are "entitled to ask," whether the efforts of this position "worked," "how effective they were," and "what they led to." He said that he had "no hesitation in asserting," that these efforts were "largely responsible for emptying the churches in Great Britain." He claimed, furthermore, that this approach actually has "the reverse effect from that which it sets out to achieve."[47]

Lloyd-Jones pointed to the Protestant Reformation as an example of a movement back to historic, biblical Christianity and to the primacy of preaching. His observation was that this movement gave "the greatest possible stimulus to science and scientific inquiry and study" and that it "did the same to literature and many other activities of man." He believed further that it encouraged the building of hospitals, education, and concern for the poor. "My argument is that when the Church performs her primary task these other things invariably result from it."[48]

Handle Personal Problems

Secondly, Lloyd-Jones had a controversy with those who believed that preachers "ought to preach less and spend more time in personal work and

47. Ibid., 33–35.
48. Ibid., 36.

339

counseling," in order to help more effectively those who are hurting with problems and sufferings. Regarding this, Lloyd-Jones held that "true preaching does deal with personal problems," so much so that "true preaching saves a great deal of time for the pastor." He wanted it to be noted that he was "speaking out of forty years of experience."[49]

Again, Lloyd-Jones gave an example that embodied his thesis of primacy and which apparently he believed answered the controversy:

> The Puritans are justly famous for their pastoral preaching. They would take up what they called "cases of conscience" and deal with them in their sermons; and as they dealt with these problems they were solving the personal individual problems of those who were listening to them.[50]

Lloyd-Jones's contention was that "personal counseling and all these other activities" are "meant to supplement the preaching, not to supplant it." These other things "must never be thought of as the primary work." Preaching should![51]

Miscellaneous Objectives

Thirdly, Lloyd-Jones discussed a series of four miscellaneous objections to his thesis. One objection he saw to his thesis of the primacy of preaching is, "Have not the times changed?" His answer was that "God has not changed," and "man has not changed." He explained:

> I know that there are superficial changes—we may dress differently, we may travel at four hundred miles an hour instead of four miles an hour—but man has not changed at all, and man's needs are exactly and precisely what they always have been.[52]

A second objection is, "Is not man too sophisticated and educated for preaching? Can it not be done better through reading and use of elec-

---

49. Ibid., 37. Cf. Lloyd-Jones's statement of experience in counseling in *The Christian Warfare* (Grand Rapids: Baker, 1976), 114. Cf. also Lloyd-Jones's statements in retirement concerning his own counseling, that he "spent well over an hour after service with individuals seeking conversion or counsel." Henry, "From Buckingham," 157.

50. Ibid.

51. Ibid., 40.

52. Ibid., 41.

tronic media?" To this, Lloyd-Jones had several reservations. He saw it as the "wrong approach" because it is "too individualistic." He believed it puts man "too much in control" because he can "switch it off." Then too, "that whole approach lacks the vital element of the Church." Of this last concept, he gave an explanation:

> We must recapture this notion that the whole Church is a part of this witness to the Gospel and its truth and its message. It is therefore most important that people should come together and listen in companies in the realm of the Church. . . . The very presence of a body of people in itself is a part of the preaching, and these influences begin to act immediately upon anyone who comes into a service.[53]

A third objection Lloyd-Jones treated is, "Cannot all this be done better by means of group discussions?" He gave his observation of the results of small group discussions and his four-fold rationale. He saw this method as one that "rarely succeeds" and one that has "very rarely been fruitful or effective as a means of winning people to the Christian faith."[54]

Lloyd-Jones then gave his four-fold rationale for his position. He said that the first and "all sufficient reason in itself" is that "God is not to be discussed or debated," as if he were "a philosophical proposition." His idea was that God "is Who He is and What He is," and that the attitude of a person "is more important than anything that [one does] in detail." A second reason was that in treating Christian topics such as God, the soul, eternity, etc., one is "dealing with the most serious and solemn matter in life." He, therefore, could not escape the conviction that the "very character and nature of the subject" demands that it "be placed" in the "most thoughtful and serious atmosphere that we know or can create."[55]

A third reason Lloyd-Jones gave as his rationale about small group discussions was that actually "debate or discussion or dialogue" is "impossible" because of the "spiritual ignorance of the natural man, the non-Christian." Having discussed 1 Corinthians 2:14, he went further to say that "the man who is not a Christian" is really "incapable of entering into a discussion about these matters." His fourth and final reason for his negative position on small groups

53. Ibid., 42–43.
54. Ibid., 46.
55. Ibid., 47–48.

as a substitute for preaching was based on Matthew 18:3. He observed that the "ultimate trouble" with the natural man "is his pride." He concluded, therefore, that "what the natural man" needs "above everything else" is "to be humbled." He believed that preaching was the tool to accomplish that end.[56]

The fourth and final objection against Lloyd-Jones's thesis of the primacy of preaching dealt with the results of his position. The objection is, "All this may be right in theory, but people will not come to listen, will they?" Lloyd-Jones contended the reverse; he saw that people "will come" and "they do come" when "it is true preaching." He acknowledged that it "may be slow work" and that it should be seen as a "long term policy." Yet his "whole contention" is "that it works, that it pays, and that it is honored" and "must be" because it is "God's own method."[57]

RECAPITULATION

A recapitulation seems to be in order. We have now surveyed another cardinal distinctive to the principles and practice of expository preaching according to Lloyd-Jones. He viewed the task of preaching as the *primary* task and function of the church and its ministry. Its *restoration* to that central and chief place he believed to be the *greatest* need of the hour. He wrestled with the reactions to preaching that persist today, he presented biblical, historical, and theological rationale for his thesis of primacy, and he debated miscellaneous objections to his thesis. In all of his discussion, he showed sympathy for the rationale behind an objection or argument. But then he revealed also a corresponding *impatience* with the failure of the methodology that had been used to bring about a solution. Preaching was thus set forth and seen to be the true and tried solution to the problems facing the church and the world. It seems, then, that he would advise pastors today to learn that *unless* they carry this conviction into their studies and into their pulpits, they will *never* achieve the desired biblical results.

CONCLUSION

Here we are given a major recommendation from Lloyd-Jones concerning a theological orientation and the prominent place of preaching.

56. Ibid., 49–50.
57. Ibid., 50–51.

It is clear that he viewed preaching as a *chief* task of the church. While he said that he was "not attempting to deal with all the aspects of a minister's work,"[58] such as pastoral visiting or pulpit prayers, etc., one may wonder how he viewed the presentation of the necessity of a variety of functions in the ministry of the church as suggested in Romans 12 and also in 1 Corinthians 12. He did, however, make the point that preaching is that which "controls everything and determines the character of everything else."[59] He seems to imply that preaching is the central function by which the others are to be determined.

58. Ibid., 185–86.
59. Ibid.

PART 5

History

To understand certain authors and certain philosophers, the intellectual life of the reader must be in harmony with theirs; so must there be an intimate affinity with the holy books to penetrate their mysteries. "The man that has not the Spirit of God," said Martin Luther, "does not understand one jot or tittle of the Scripture." Now that this condition was fulfilled [through Tyndale's English translation], the Spirit of God moved upon the face of the waters.[1]

—J. H. MERLE D'AUBIGNE

1. J. H. Merle d'Aubigne, *The Reformation in England* (Edinburgh: Banner of Truth, 1977), 1:247–48.

18

Confession out of Crisis: Historiography and Hope in the Westminster Assembly of Divines, 1643–52[1]

MICHAEL A. MILTON

OUR CRISIS

Several years ago, while working in church planting in the Midwestern United States, this writer realized that there was a crisis in the hearts of those who were confessionally Reformed, and in particular those Christians who hold that the confessional fruit of the Westminster Assembly of Divines of the seventeenth century is in fact as

1. The end date of the Westminster Assembly is frequently designated as 1649, which refers to the total of the 1163 sessions for its important business. The 1652 date refers to its final entry in its Minutes, March 25, 1652. According to Warfield, "In the ordinance convening the Assembly, it is commissioned to sit 'during this present Parliament, or until further order be taken by both the said houses.'" *The Westminster Assembly and Its Work*, in *The Works of Benjamin Breckenridge Warfield*, ed. Caspar Wistar Hodge, William Park Armstrong, and Ethelbert D. Warfield, (1932; repr., Grand Rapids: Baker, 2003), 6:3. See also William Barker's *Puritan Profiles* (Fearn, Ross-shire: Christian Focus, 1996), 6–8.

the crown of the greatest age of confessional exposition, the Protestant Reformation. No other similar documents have concentrated in them, and formulated with such precision, so much of the truth deposited in the Christian revelation.[2]

I had telephoned another Reformed pastor not too far from me to talk about some common projects that we could do together. The conversation began: "So are you encouraged in the work there?" My question was the lever that opened the valve to his heart and a flood of vile complaints began to surge forth:

"Are you kidding? This place is the den of Arminianism! The whole church is Arminian in this area and the people here, who called themselves Reformed, are up to their eyes in it—no, they are bathing in it! I try to preach Reformed doctrine but they will have none of it. The times that we are living in cannot bear strong teaching and cannot bear clear, biblical, Reformed doctrine!"

He was still breathing hard from letting out all of that. I was tempted to go to a Rogerian counseling follow up: "So, I am hearing you say that you are not encouraged," but I didn't.

But this poor fellow who cannot see how a clear Reformed confessional Christianity can make a go of it in today's world is surely not alone. Many today doubt whether the times we live in can indeed bear a theology that Robert L. Reymond calls a "systematic theology [of the Christian faith] that will pass biblical muster"[3] (and that is what we believe the confessional standards produced by the Westminster divines do in fact do). There can be no denying that the beginning of our twenty-first century is an age in crisis. This could be said of the world as a whole, but just confining our view to the West, and in particular to the English-speaking nations and Western Europe, no one can deny the erosion of vital common pillars. Our age is marked by an increasingly factious spirit in politics. While gridlock is to be expected in politics in any age, some are telling us that our age is particularly poisonous. Perhaps some would point to the so-called "Red State-Blue State" reality as a case in

2. John Murray, "The Westminster Standards," *The Calvin Forum*, 9 (1944), http://members.aol.com/RSICHURCH/standard.html (accessed Feb. 2, 2008).
3. Robert L. Reymond, *A New Systematic Theology of the Christian Faith* (Nashville: Thomas Nelson, 1998), xx.

point. In philosophy, our generation, coming out of the bloodiest century in world history, is no longer satisfied with the answer of modernism and has moved to a postmodern philosophical outlook that is confused about the issue of truth. Dr. Albert Mohler, in his 2004 plenary address at the Annual Meeting of the Evangelical Theological Society,[4] suggested that, in postmodernism, we have "now moved beyond a concern for truth . . . In a world of media invention and virtual reality, truth has become a distant category."[5] America is divided. And this division has had an enormous impact on popular culture. Thus, we have a "Fox News worldview" and a "CNN worldview" in the living rooms of our nation. In religion, this political, philosophical, and culture divide has produced or at least been partners to a new, widely accepted religious pluralism. "Plurality," David Tracy writes, "is a fact."[6] D. A. Carson has written about the realities and meanings of this new pluralism in the West in *The Gagging of God: Christianity Confronts Pluralism*. He writes of the relationship of immigration and the substantial rise in Hindus and Buddhists in Britain, Canada, and the United States. Carson paints a bleak picture of the situation in the West today:

> [The Eastern religions] are winning converts. The familiar cults are holding their own; some of them, like the Mormons, are growing fairly rapidly. Numerous studies document the rise of New Age religions and the revitalization of various forms of neo-paganism. Not long ago witches covens were virtually unknown; now they advertise in the newspapers. Current immigration patterns are bringing in more and more people with little heritage in the Judeo-Christian tradition, and this fact doubles the impact of the number of people within the country who for various reasons have lost or abandoned the tradition.[7]

The combination of secularization and new immigrant religion and revival of paganism, combined with a rising desire for mystical, experiential religion has produced a phenomenon, which Tom Beaudoin calls

---

4. R. Albert Mohler, "What Is Truth? Truth and Contemporary Culture," *The Journal of the Evangelical Theological Society* 48 (2005). See also Andreas J. Kèostenberger, *Whatever Happened to Truth?* (Wheaton, IL: Crossway Books, 2005).

5. Mohler, "What Is Truth," 63.

6. As cited in D.A. Carson, *The Gagging of God: Christianity Confronts Pluralism* (Grand Rapids: Zondervan, 1996), 13.

7. Ibid.

"virtual faith."[8] One gets all of the trappings of religion without any of the dogma. A recent sermon I heard captures this generation well: "Starbucks Spirituality."[9]

Added to all this cauldron of crisis in the West could be the deconstructionism in denominations. This phenomenon, which may be related to the others (indeed, it could be argued that all of our presenting trials are forever joined at the hips), is all about how traditional denominational structures continue to fragment. Members of the Presbyterian Church in America know all about this as our fellowship of congregations came about through the deconstruction, due to liberalism, of the old Presbyterian Church in the United States of America. It continues today in a renewed fashion with, say, the Episcopal Church USA from the fallout of the ordination of a practicing homosexual to the office of bishop. It seems that only a minority agree that this sort of deconstruction of liberalizing denominations is a "good thing." But there are other trends that suggest deconstruction is happening on another level altogether. Richard Lints, in his book, *The Fabric of Theology: A Prolegomenon to Evangelical Theology*,[10] believes that evangelicalism "has in recent decades squandered so much of its theological heritage that it is becoming harder and harder to define it primarily in theological terms."[11] Astute observers of the evangelical scene, such as George M. Marsden, David Wells, Iain Murray, and perhaps even Martin Marty,[12] agree that evangelicalism is in great flux as methodological interests, sociological interests, the rise of mega churches, as well as the older reasons for splitting—theological convictions—are driving churches into a "post denominational" future.[13]

8. Tom Beaudoin, *Virtual Faith: The Irreverent Spiritual Quest of Generation X* (San Francisco: Jossey-Bass Inc., Publishers, 1998).

9. Thomas Tewell, "Starbucks Spirituality!" (sermon, The Fifth Avenue Presbyterian Church, New York, NY, September 26, 1999).

10. Richard Lints, *The Fabric of Theology: A Prolegomenon to Evangelical Theology* (Grand Rapids: Eerdmans, 1993).

11. I quote from Don Carson's analysis of Lints' position as he offers it in *The Gagging of God*, 458.

12. I say, "even Martin Marty" because the noted ELCA Lutheran from the University of Chicago would not normally be quoted alongside Wells and Murray. In this case, as an observer of modern evangelicalism, he rates the listing! See his "Tensions Within Contemporary Evangelicalism: A Critical Appraisal" in *The Evangelicals: What They Believe, Who They Are, Where They Are Changing* (Nashville: Abington, 1975), 173, which is cited in Carson's *The Gagging of God*, 446.

13. See, for instance, Adair T. Lummis, "Brand Name Identity in a Post-Denominational Age: Regional Leaders' Perspectives on Its Importance for Churches" (paper, Annual Meetings of the

Some readers, too, may be tempted to say with my pessimistic Reformed friend, "The times that we are living in cannot bear strong teaching and cannot bear clear, biblical, Reformed doctrine!" This writer will concede that we are in a crisis of sorts. But he will not concede that clear, confessional Christianity as carefully, thoroughly, and most important of all, biblically systematized in our Westminster statements of faith, is done for. Indeed, what this writer hopes to show today is that when the 121 English Puritan ministers, six Scottish commissioners and thirty laymen—ten from the House of Lords and twenty from the House of Commons—met together from July 1, 1643 until February 22, 1649, they produced not only the greatest summary of the Christian faith the world has ever known before or since, but they did it under conditions not dissimilar to our own. Moreover, while I agree with J. I. Packer that the Puritans were "spiritual giants" and that we are, in contrast, spiritual dwarfs, it is the goal of this essay to show that we do not have to stay that way. Indeed, I want us to see that what may very well be the great era of preachers and preaching in the history of the church of Jesus Christ commenced under a crisis that was descriptive of Christopher Hill's book about that age: "The World Turned Upside Down."[14] I want us to see that the "Golden Era" of biblical faith was forged in a crisis. And I want us to see this because history has something to teach us. No. God has something to teach us. Let us consider their times.

PURITAN CRISIS

Political Factions

The Welsh preacher William Erbery said, "If madness be in the heart of every man (Eccles. 9.3), then this is the island of Great Bedlam. . . ."[15] He may have been speaking of the insane at Bedlam, England, but his whimsical statement also described the political situation in the realm.

Society for the Scientific Study of Religion, Columbus, OH, October, 2001), http://hirr.hartsem. edu/bookshelf/lummis_article1.html (accessed Feb. 2, 2008).

14. Christopher Hill, *The World Turned Upside Down; Radical Ideas during the English Revolution* (London: Temple Smith, 1972).

15. William Erbery, *The Mad Man's Plea* (1653), cited in Hill, *World Turned Upside Down*, 8.

People living in the early seventeenth century were simply not prepared for the wide spread political wars that consumed them. Despite the sixteenth-century Reformation, the institutions of king and church remained firm pillars in the architecture of English life. The unfolding events of the mid-seventeenth century caught them off guard. The squabbles between Parliament and king became a blood feud involving families in a way that we have known on our own soil during the American War Between the States. Historian Peter Lake's assessment seems right when he says,

> In the area of secular politics, seventeenth-century English people found the fact of political conflict very hard to accept and still harder to explain. In the face of it they resorted to the rhetoric of faction.[16]

Faction at the Top. First, the very throne of England was at stake. Charles I, with all due regard for the kinder portrait given by C. V. Wedgwood,[17] seemed bent by disposition, as well as by contemporary events that threatened him, toward the extremity of autocratic rule over an increasingly democratic minded people. Career-minded minions such as Archbishop William Laud—who has been judged "the greatest calamity ever visited upon the Church of England"[18]—served to cultivate the egomaniacal mind of the Stewart Royal. Civil War moved across the landscape of the Realm as a bloody testimony to the growing hatred in the land. "On the 6th February, 1649, the monarchy was abolished. And Parliament declared that the office of the king in this nation is unnecessary, burdensome and dangerous to the liberty, society and public interest of the people."[19] Nothing that we can imagine today in our partisan politics can compare to the act of regicide.

Political Faction in the Middle. If the political instability at the top had to do with the king, then we might say that political instabil-

16. Peter Lake, "Calvinism and the English Church 1570–1635," cited in Margo Todd, *Reformation to Revolution: Politics and Religion in Early Modern England, Rewriting Histories* (London: Routledge, 1995), 200.

17. See C. V. Wedgwood, *The Trial of Charles I* (London: Collins, 1964).

18. Patrick Collinson, *The Religion of Protestants: The Church in English Society, 1559–1625* (Oxford: Clarendon Press, 1984), 90.

19. This statement may be found at http://www.historylearningsite.co.uk/CharlesI_execution.htm (accessed Feb. 2, 2008).

ity existed in a great way in the "middle" as it had to do with authority and conflict within Puritanism itself. Indeed, the ascendancy of
Puritanism in England did not spell political calm, for the Puritans
were not all of one mind. Millenarian anarchist groups such as the
Fifth Monarchists, a broad "urban" group[20] gathered especially from
the Border countries, were as dissatisfied with Oliver Cromwell as
they were with Charles I. One frequently cited example of this unrest
within Puritanism involved both the pulpit and congregation of one
of the most beloved members of the Westminster Assembly, William
Gouge, and one of the most celebrated evangelists of the day (and we
might call him a church planter), Vavasor Powell. Powell, who had
been sent out by the Assembly to bring the Reformed faith (and the
ejection of Arminian Anglican clergy) to Wales, and Cromwell himself, was by now famous enough not only to preach to Parliament,
as he did, but to assume the pulpit of old Gouge. The story is this:
Cromwell became the Lord Protector of England on December 16,
1653. And on December 19, Vavasor Powell, who was being courted by
radical groups and moderate groups (and who was more mainstream
than some would like to admit) asked the congregation at Black Fri-
ars to go home and ask themselves if they would rather have Oliver
Cromwell to rule over them or Jesus Christ.[21] As indiscreet and pasto-
rally unproductive as this may have been (he was jailed by Cromwell
for the statement), Powell spoke for a growing constituency in Wales
and England. As Geoffrey Nuttal, Richard Greaves, and other Puritan
scholars such as R. Tudur Jones have shown, the "radical fringe" that
we may see in looking back, were not seen as such then.[22] While calmer

20. For more on the Fifth Monarchy Men see Louise Fargo Brown, *The Political Activities of the Baptists and Fifth Monarchy Men in England During the Interregnum* (Washington: American Historical Association, 1912) and B. S. Capp, *The Fifth Monarchy Men; a Study in Seventeenth-Century English Millenarianism* (London: Faber, 1972).

21. See Christopher Hill, *God's Englishman; Oliver Cromwell and the English Revolution* (New York: Harper & Row, 1970).

22. See especially Geoffrey Fillingham Nuttall and R. Buick Knox, *Reformation, Conformity and Dissent: Essays in Honour of Geoffrey Nuttall* (London: Epworth Press, 1977). Jones' contribution, "The Healing Herb and the Rose of Love: The Piety of Two Welsh Puritans" deserves careful reading by those who would too quickly dispense with Vavasor Powell and Morgan Llwyd as mere rebels. They were thorough going Puritans, with Vavasor Powell, in particular, rising as a great champion of covenant theology amidst the cacophony of heterodox voices in seventeenth-century Puritanism. Further study in the "Welsh Saints" would yield great rewards in understanding the glory of the Westminster

Scottish voices called for order, the situation down south grew worse and worse. It was in this political firestorm that the greatest Confession of Faith in the Christian church was born.

Political Faction at the Bottom. Using the language of historians who have made a case for understanding the times through "lower" historical studies—I am thinking of men like David Underdown and his *Revel, Riot, and Rebellion*—[23] the common people of the British Isles were less interested in the king's troubles than their own. "It's the economy stupid" would have been just as apropos then as it was when the irascible James Carville said it during Bill Clinton's presidency. And yet the people, likely more individualistic than we might first imagine, were troubled by kinsmen and their tales of a more free New England. They were troubled by allegiance to the older authority structures, which were at least comfortable and known. The Puritan movement was a movement of young intellectuals and the merchant class. While we might see them as dour, black-clad, spoilsports, the common folk would have seen them as upstarts and a sort of 1960s-like group, who were taking things a bit too far. And by the time the divines gathered in Westminster Abbey and retired to the Jerusalem Chamber to begin the work of bringing the church into conformity with the Reformed faith, more than 1,500 fathers, sons, and brothers had been lost at the Battle of Edgehill in the fall of 1642. By the following summer the Battle of

---

Assembly faith as it was produced in the crisis of political factionalism. See the following: David Davies, *Vavasor Powell: The Baptist Evangelist of Wales in the Seventeenth Century* (London: Alexander and Shepheard, 1896), R. Tudur Jones, *Vavasor Powell* (Abertawe: Gwasg John Penry, 1971), *The Life and Death of Mr. Vavasor Powell, That Faithful Minister and Confessor of Jesus Christ* (1671), Michael A. Milton, "The Application of the Theology of the Westminster Assembly in the Ministry of the Welsh Puritan, Vavasor Powell (1617–1670)" (PhD diss., The University of Wales, 1998), Geoffrey Fillingham Nuttall, *The Welsh Saints, 1640–1660: Water Cradock, Vavasor Powell, Morgan Llwyd* (University of Wales Press, 1957), Thomas Richards, *A History of the Puritan Movement in Wales: From the Institution of the Church at Llanfaches in 1639 to the Expiry of the Propagation Act in 1653* (London: National Eisteddfod Association, 1920), Glanmor Williams, *Welsh Reformation Essays* (Cardiff: University of Wales Press, 1967).

23. David Underdown, *Revel, Riot, and Rebellion: Popular Politics and Culture in England, 1603–1660* (Oxford: Clarendon Press, 1985). See also *Fire from Heaven: Life in an English Town in the Seventeenth Century* (New Haven, CT: Yale University Press, 1992); *A Freeborn People: Politics and the Nation in Seventeenth-Century England* (Oxford: Clarendon Press, 1996); and *Pride's Purge: Politics in the Puritan Revolution* (London: G. Allen & Unwin, 1985).

Marston Moor would consume more blood as the Royalist lost approximately 3,000 men, with 4,500 more taken prisoner. Cromwell's forces lost 500. As we have seen in our own day, even the strongest of political backbones gives way eventually to the cries of distraught mothers. The body bags change everything.

Culture Wars

When people talk about the so-called "Golden Era" of Puritanism, they do not often consider the cultural factions at work in the British society.[24] Most of us would freely admit that there have been tensions between Englishmen and Welshmen and Scotsmen and Irishmen since the coming of the Romans, but by the mid-seventeenth century the culture wars were way beyond that. Imagine a Larry King Live debate, not between Al Mohler and Rosie O'Donnell, but perhaps one of those free-for-alls, with multiple voices. There might be William Laud, advocating the use of statues of Jesus, gilded with gold, as being helpful for worship. On another side there would be the fathers of Ipswich who, according to historians like David Underdown, were renowned for hosting great carnivals.[25] Then, there would have been those who were dispensing with worship services in order to hold some bowling matches.[26] And they would all have been ganging up on a Puritan, say William Gurnall of Lavenham, near Ipswich. He would have drawn fire for his views on the use of statues in the sanctuary and his views of entertainment and sports replacing the priority of Sabbath worship. He would have appreciated art and fun as much as the next man, but in the poisonous cultural atmosphere of that day, he would have been branded an uncultured rogue trying to impose his cultural standards on everyone else. According to noted Puritan historian, Patrick Collinson, the Puritans had "hostility to mendacious art but not to art itself."[27] The Puritans were caricatured then, as now, however, as people who hated art, disliked literature, and avoided all sports.

24. See works such as Christopher Hill, *Society and Puritanism in Pre-Revolutionary England*, 2nd ed. (New York,: Schocken Books, 1967) and Derek Hirst, *Authority and Conflict: England, 1603–1658, The New History of England* (Cambridge, MA: Harvard University Press, 1986).

25. See Underdown, *Revel, Riot, and Rebellion*.

26. See, for example, the article, "Puritans at Play," http://www.sec.state.ma.us/mhc/mhcexh/musprv/nend/purplay/playidx.htm (accessed Feb. 2, 2008).

27. Patrick Collinson, "Protestant Culture and Cultural Revolution," in Todd, *Reformation to Revolution: Politics and Religion in Early Modern England*, 40.

The meeting of the Assembly of Divines at Westminster Abbey happened in the face of a nation teetering on the brink of implosion. The nation's institutions, which had held together the center of British life, were collapsing, and in their place one could see the emergence of libertines and anarchists, the resurgence of paganism (in some places like Wales and the border counties between England and Wales it never really went away), and the young Calvinists from Emmanuel College, Cambridge, a minor, albeit intellectually and financially stronger player, bringing their views to the table. Some have described the Puritan advances as having no culture of their own but "creating an iconoclastic holocaust of the culture which already existed."[28] What was happening in the midst of this? As Richard Cust has shown in his *News and Politics in Early Seventeenth-Century England*, "One of the more problematic issues currently being discussed by early seventeenth-century historians relates to the impact of news . . . ."[29]

The old media elites were giving way to a new, more democratic way of getting out the news. Dan Rather was out. Rush Limbaugh and Sean Hannity were in. Or, to be more accurate, "The old anchors were out and bloggers were in!" No one can conduct serious inquiry into seventeenth-century historiography without becoming aware of a seismic shift in culture due to the proliferation of pamphlets, tracts, sermons, and newsletters. Every group imaginable had them: Arminians, Calvinists, Levelers, Ranters, Diggers, Quakers. So pervasive were they that by the time of the restoration of the monarchy with Charles II, the Earl of Newcastle advised the new king that he should suppress newsletter-writers.[30] As the Internet has been credited with opening up the old Communistic countries to freedom of thought that eventually brought down the Soviet Empire, the seventeenth-century version of ground-swell, mass media fueled a cultural war within England and Wales that further divided the country.

As the divines gathered in 1643 for the first summer of their historic meetings, they sought to find biblical unity, form a radically Reformed view of Christ and culture, and propagate that view to a culturally splintered society.

---

28. Ibid., 34.
29. Richard Cust, "News and Politics in Early Seventeenth-Century England," in Todd, *Reformation to Revolution: Politics and Religion in Early Modern England*, 232.
30. Ibid., 233.

Religious Pluralism

One must also remember that the assembly came together in the midst of religious pluralism. " 'Pluralism' is a surprisingly tricky word in modern discussion,"[31] says D. A. Carson. But he provides a helpful, if not amazingly simple, definition of empirical pluralism by stating it is "the growing diversity in our culture."[32] No century could be more dramatically pluralistic than the seventeenth-century. By that I mean to say that when the older institutions gave way, it was like pulling away baseboard to reveal an army of termites eating away at the house. The deconstruction of the Church of England and the resulting competition between acceptable replacements—namely Presbyterians and Independents—revealed the underground world of mysticism, continuing revelation, and radical millenarianism within the broadest definitions of Christianity, as well as paganism, animism, superstition, and even a sort of emperor-worship in non-Christian religions. A number of historians have shown that these things never went away and that genuine conversion to Jesus Christ had not occurred in many places in British life. Indeed, a sort of cultural Christianity was pervasive whereby farmers, village artisans, and merchants could cloak themselves with respectable religious clothing in order to provide a livelihood, but kept their ancient religions alive in secret. When the lights went off these pagans played. And when the covering was removed they were discovered. Britain was not as Christian as once thought.

Denominational Deconstruction

Seventeenth-century England and Wales, like today, was undergoing denominational deconstruction. Indeed, the emergence of many of the groups that we know today started in those days. Quakers got their start then. Our Baptist friends owe their respectability to the gains made in the heady days of the English Civil War. This was, after all, the day of John Bunyan. And the Savoy Conference of 1658,[33] which built on the foundation of the Westminster Assembly from a Congregationalist

---

31. Carson, *The Gagging of God*, 13.

32. Ibid.

33. See Iain H. Murray, *The Reformation of the Church: A Collection of Reformed and Puritan Documents on Church Issues* (Edinburgh: Banner of Truth, 1965).

perspective,[34] drafted a *Declaration of Faith and Order* that has become an important document for independent-minded, Reformed Congregationalists to this day. This was the day of Independents such as Thomas Goodwin, Philip Nye, and Jeremiah Burroughs, who resisted both Anglicanism and Presbyterianism with equal vigor. Men like John Milton, who were at once Puritan and free-thinkers, who resisted the assembly and thought that the new presbyter was but the old priest writ large, remind us of the emergence of liberalism within evangelicalism. This was the day of the Fifth Monarchy Men, who were strong premillennialists, and worked actively to resist human governments so that Daniel's fifth, and final, monarchy could be realized in their day. The year 1666 loomed large in the minds of even respectable men in the assembly because of its "666" date, and the closer that day came the more pitched the eschatological fervor became. It is difficult to overestimate the crisis that this post-Church of England environment brought to the Christian people of that day. It is also difficult to imagine the uniformity of the Westminster Assembly's work without seeing answers to prayer in it all.

The Westminster Assembly produced its majestic Confession, Catechisms, and Directory for Public Worship in the most extreme and volatile political environment imaginable. It drew up the most concise and definitive documents describing the system of doctrine taught in the Holy Bible amidst political factionalism, cultural clashes, religious pluralism, and denominational deconstruction. It is vital for us today to remember how it happened.

OUR HOPE

And this is where the historiography of the Westminster Assembly becomes our hope. I would tell my Reformed friend back in the Midwest, as I would say to you, "Yes, we are in a crisis of faith in our day. Yes, Arminianism has become predominant in our day. Yes, postmodernism (as did modernism), secularism, pluralism, and factious forces within our fellowship threaten the historic faith once delivered to the saints. But if such a beautiful, biblical confession of faith that glorifies God, magnifies

---

34. See Peter Toon's "The Westminster and Savoy Confessions: A Brief Comparison" in *Journal of the Evangelical Theological Society* 15 (1972): 153–60.

the Lord Jesus Christ, and offers salvation through faith in him alone by the announcement of a grace unknown in this world, could be written in such a time as the convulsive seventeenth-century, then God can do it again. Congregations can grow that confess these truths. Ministers can enjoy the blessing of God in their preaching, evangelism, and counseling. The people of Christ who teach the catechism to their children may expect the truth to take root in the lives of a coming generation. We may also pray for and anticipate God's blessings upon us by sending out missionaries to re-sow the gospel in those areas of old Christendom now hit by the blight of postmodernity. Moreover, this faith we confess causes us to send young people who believe the faith of Westminster to the people groups of this world who have not heard of the wonder of God's grace and the beauty of our Savior Jesus Christ. We may pray for and wait for the divine watering of our generation to happen through God coming down and sending revival, for in the worst of times, when the Westminster Assembly met, God did these very things.

Yes, the seventeenth century was a "Golden Era" of preachers and of confessional faithfulness to the Word of God. But they were golden preachers and they had a golden confession because their faith was refined as gold in the consuming fires of controversy that not only rival the difficulties of our own day, but may in fact surpass it. Were not all the confessions crafted amid such circumstances? Have not all of our greatest statements of faith been hammered out on the anvil of trial and affliction?

J. I. Packer has written, "The Puritan point, which was first, of course, a New Testament point, was that Christians should know what their hope is and draw from it power to resist whatever discouragements and distractions present circumstances may produce."[35]

George Whitefield said it best, I think, in his preface to a reprint of John Bunyan's works in 1767: "Ministers never write or preach so well as when under the cross; the Spirit of Christ and of glory then rests upon them. It was this, no doubt, that made the Puritans . . . such burning and shining lights."[36]

Let us remember the Spirit-wrought words of Christ's own apostle, who suffered greatly and wrote to others who suffered: "In this you rejoice,

---

35. J. I. Packer, *A Quest for Godliness: The Puritan Vision of the Christian Life* (Wheaton, IL: Crossway, 1990), 334.

36. As cited in Ibid. , 23.

though now for a little while, as was necessary, you have been grieved by various trials, so that the tested genuineness of your faith—more precious than gold that perishes though it is tested by fire—may be found to result in praise and glory and honor at the revelation of Jesus Christ" (1 Peter 1:6–7).

This is, and shall be, the greatest fruit of the Westminster Assembly, and perhaps one of its greatest lessons for our time.

19

Preaching Christ in
Post-Reformation Britain

CHAD VAN DIXHOORN

THIS ESSAY TAKES for granted that ministers of the gospel are to preach Christ from both testaments, and well it might after O. Palmer Robertson has done so much to further this tradition in his own writings. In fact, in grateful acknowledgement of Professor Robertson's work, this festschrift in turn takes as its organizing point the hermeneutical, exegetical, and homiletical task of proclaiming Christ from the Old Testament. This essay seeks to celebrate a great man and advance a great topic by tracing briefly the history of Christ-centered biblical interpretation and the appropriation of this christological exegesis by Reformed exegetes and preachers. I will argue that by the post-Reformation period there were different types of Christ-centered preaching, one rooted more obviously in dogmatics, the other in typology.

BACKGROUND TO THE WESTMINSTER ASSEMBLY

The tradition in which O. Palmer Robertson has thrived as a Christian minister has long confessed the importance of preaching Christ.

361

When the Westminster Assembly was giving instructions to preachers, it stressed that although a preacher cannot "prosecute every doctrine which lies in his text" he is "wisely to make choice" of the "most needfull and seasonable" ones and, "amongst these, such as may most draw their souls to Christ, the fountain of light, holinesse and comfort." Furthermore "the servant of Christ, whatever his method" in preaching, is to always preach "plainly . . . lest the cross of Christ should be made of none effect." He is always to be "looking at the honour of Christ" and ensure "that all that he teacheth is the truth of Christ." When he is done preaching, he should "give thanks for the great love of God in sending his Son Jesus Christ unto us." These words are all found in the Assembly's Directory for Public Worship.[1] Similar sentiments were expressed later in the Westminster Larger Catechism. There we are reminded that "the Spirit of God maketh the reading, but especially the preaching of the word an effectual means of . . . drawing them unto Christ" and "of conforming them to his image, and subduing them to his will."[2] This is the task of the preacher because it is the center of Scripture, and so the Westminster Confession of Faith notes that the very words "old and new covenants" or "testaments" have primary reference to Jesus Christ and to his death.[3]

The Bible

Of course the Westminster divines were not the only or the first or the most important people to talk about preaching Christ. We see it first in the Bible itself, then in the church fathers and medieval doctors, and again at the time of the Reformation. The apostles preached Christ, and they say so repeatedly.[4] They learned this from the Lord Jesus Christ himself, and he made clear that he was not only to appear in the New Testament which was to be written, but also in the Old Testament that had been written. The apostles were to preach Christ. The prophets already had. The risen Lord addressed this very topic in Luke 24, where he rebukes two disciples for being foolish and slow to understand what the prophets spoke about himself (v. 25). Then, "beginning with Moses

---

1. *A Directory for the Publique Worship of God* (London: G. M. and I. F. for the Company of Stationers, 1645), 16–18.
2. Westminster Larger Catechism 155
3. Westminster Confession of Faith 7.4.
4. E.g., Acts 5:42; 17:3; 1 Cor. 1:23; 2 Cor. 4:5; Eph. 3:8; Phil. 1:15–18; Col. 1:27–28.

and all the Prophets he explained" what "all the Scriptures" said "concerning himself" (v. 27). And a third time, he taught them what "Moses, the Prophets and the Psalms" said about his death and resurrection, and about the graces which accompany this accomplished work: repentance and the forgiveness of sins (vv. 44–47). Christ's teaching clearly enunciates the importance of the Old Testament to the Christian church, and clearly teaches the church that Christ is preached by the apostles *and* by the prophets. As well, verses 44–47 in particular point the way forward to a fuller understanding of the way in which Christ was present in Moses, the Prophets, and the Psalms. These verses put forward the idea that the Old Testament bears witness to Christ not in some vague way, but as the Christ who died and rose again and the Christ through whom human repentance and divine forgiveness are possible. It suggests that the Old Testament, and not just the New, speaks about Christ as mediator and redeemer—it speaks of Christ and his benefits.

Christ-Centered Preaching: From the Church Fathers to the Post-Reformation Reformed Orthodox

For the first centuries of the church, preachers preached on any portion of Scripture, sometimes preaching on certain themes, sometimes marking special events or holy days, sometimes preaching expository sermons. The expository sermon came to flower in the fourth century with pulpit giants like Augustine of Hippo (354–430) and John Chrysostom of Antioch and Constantinople (c. 347–407) who preached through vast portions of the Bible, chapter after chapter. Augustine often provides profound reflections on a passage of Scripture. Chrysostom presents stunning insights, often giving something like soliloquies within his delightful monologues.

Even as expository preaching reached new heights during the lifetime of these great fourth- and fifth-century preachers, the church's festal calendars became increasingly elaborate, requiring specific readings from Scripture for seasons and Sundays of the year. Here I am indebted to Hughes Oliphant Old and his excellent study on *The Reading and Preaching of the Scriptures in the Worship of the Christian Church*. Old remarks that by "the beginning of the fifth century . . . the public reading of Scripture in the church of Jerusalem had become so complicated that a special manual was needed to explain which portions of Scripture were to be read at the elaborate festivities in the Holy City."[5] Here was the development of the lectionary. During this late patristic or early medieval period the Christian church, East and West, designed lectionaries to guide them in the reading of Holy Scripture.[6]

One feature of the lectionary was that it trimmed the public reading of the Scriptures to as little as two-fifths of the biblical canon.[7] Another feature was that it even more drastically cut the canon for preaching, stipulating that sermons were to come from the four Gospels only. As if that were not problematic enough, Old notes that the liturgy became so complicated that "the original purpose of preaching" began "to fall from sight. Instead of explaining the Scriptures the sermon explains the liturgy. We begin to get sermons on the meaning of Septuagesima Sunday or on the message of the third Sunday in Advent." And an increasing number of the church's sermons were "canned" sermons, repeated from year to year.[8] Obviously in such a situation preaching Christ from the Old Testament could not be a concern of the church for the simple reason that there was no preaching from the Old Testament at all.

Now there were exceptions to this general rule since some preachers delivered occasional sermons on biblical passages other than the four Gospels, usually for special events or in special situations. Thus leaders in some monastic traditions preached or lectured on a variety of biblical texts during the week. These medieval preachers, such as Bernard of Clairvaux (1090–1151) or Bonaventure (ca. 1217–1274), or Thomas Aquinas (ca. 1225–1274) even returned on occasion to the patristic tradition of expository preaching, expounding a book of the Bible passage by passage. But certainly most Christian preachers in the Middle Ages, East and West, would rarely venture out of the four Gospels.[9]

5. Hughes Oliphant Old, *The Reading and Preaching of the Scriptures in the Worship of the Christian Church*, vol. 2, *The Patristic Age* (Grand Rapids: Eerdmans, 1998), 135.

6. For the fourth and fifth century Jerusalem lectionary, see Old, *Reading and Preaching*, 2:135–66; for Byzantine, Gallican, Mozarabic, and variant Roman lectionaries, see Old, *The Reading and Preaching of the Scriptures in the Worship of the Christian Church*, vol. 3, *The Medieval Church* (Grand Rapids: Eerdmans, 1999), 67–72, 81–95, 99–109, 153–84, and 191–97.

7. Realizing that little Scripture was covered by the lectionary in one year, certain traditions adopted two or three year cycles of reading to increase exposure to the Bible among the laity.

8. Old, *Reading and Preaching*, 2:165–66. For criticism of medieval preaching, see A. Burgess, *An Expository Comment* (London: Printed by A. M. for Abel Roper, 1661), 559. Criticism of recycled sermons was standard among Puritans.

9. For most Orthodox churches and Roman Catholic congregations today a similar pattern would be found; wider variety exists among Lutherans and Anglicans, not all of whom continue to use a lectionary.

Christ-Centered Exegesis: From the Church Fathers to the Post-Reformation Reformed Orthodox

Preaching in the Middle Ages was thus largely restricted to the New Testament, and this preaching often had a Christ-centered focus only because the name of the Lord Jesus Christ is on almost every page in the Gospels. But where the lectionary virtually halted *preaching* from the Old Testament, it did not end reflection on Old Testament *exegesis* and the place of Christ in that Testament. This is where it is useful to move from Old's survey of preaching to Richard Muller's survey of holy Scripture. During the late medieval period there were different streams of exegetical thought or emphasis. For much of the medieval period all streams flowed from the *quadriga*, the four-fold exegesis of Scripture. The *quadriga* posited one literal or historical meaning and three spiritual meanings for every text of Scripture. Muller sees the history of medieval exegesis "amply" demonstrating that the *quadriga* "could result either in a movement away from or a gravitation toward the literal sense." Movement away from, or even disregard of, the literal and historical sense of a text concerned more literally minded exegetes like Hugh of St Victor (d. 1141), Albert the Great (c. 1206–80), or Thomas Aquinas (c. 1225–74). But for our purposes it is important to recognize that even when Aquinas lobbied for an increasingly literal exegesis of Scripture, he did see "various figures and symbols of Christ in the Old Testament as belonging to the spiritual sense." So too did major exegetes, like Nicholas of Lyra (d. 1349), who were cautious in their biblical interpretations but still "sought to retain the christological reading of the Old Testament."[10]

A focus on Christ in the Old Testament appears to have typified all schools of exegesis to the eve of the Reformation. This is more obviously the case where the fifteenth century experienced a decrease (although not the demise) of literal and historical exegesis. Muller, approving Jacques Verger's estimation of exegesis, sees a "collapse of exegetical labor in the universities" while, in Verger's own words, "the prestige of Lombard's Sentences as the basis of all theological instruction" kept rising.[11] Unsurprisingly, this led to increased New Testament readings of Old Testament texts, including Christ-centered readings. While we see Christ in these highly spiritualized

---

10. Richard A. Muller, *Post-Reformation Reformed Dogmatics: The Rise and Development of Reformed Orthodoxy, ca. 1520 to ca. 1725*, vol. 2, *Holy Scripture: The Cognitive Foundation of Theology*, 2nd ed. (Grand Rapids: Baker, 2003), 35–37, 57 (hereafter cited as *PRRD*).

11. Ibid., 58–59.

readings of the Old Testament, it is also the case that Muller can speak of humanists like Lefèvre d'Étaples (c. 1460–1536) holding to a "doctrine of *Christus solus*—Christ alone as the center and meaning of Scripture."[12] And Erasmus of Rotterdam "could declare that Christ was the *scopus*" of theology, and it has been argued, of Scripture.[13]

Christ-centered hermeneutics enjoyed a long history of dominance among exegetes and some noted advocates through the centuries, and the arrival of the Reformation apparently did little to change this. Luther, Calvin, and their contemporary Reformers join with their forebears in repeating the now established hermeneutical watchword—the "scope" or "center" of all of Scripture is Jesus Christ.[14] Little *appeared* to change, but it is significant that the Reformers seem to have been content to speak of the scope of Scripture either as Christ, or as "the gospel," using the two terms interchangeably.[15] Equally significant is the fact that the Reformers actually began to preach once again from both testaments. Even if, like Luther, some continued with the lectionary for weekly morning worship, they preached through other biblical books on Sunday evenings and during the week on a scale not seen since the days of the church fathers.[16] This practice continued during the era of the Early Reformed Orthodox (c. 1565–1640) and High orthodoxy, which begins at the time of the Westminster Assembly.[17]

THE WESTMINSTER DIVINES ON CHRIST-CENTERED EXEGESIS AND PREACHING

Preaching the Word of God

The authors of the Westminster Standards[18]—those confessional texts which summarize the doctrines which O. Palmer Robertson preaches, teaches and defends—were keen to communicate the importance of

---

12. Ibid., 61; see 59–61.

13. Ibid., 209.

14. Ibid., 206–13.

15. Ibid., 207.

16. Hughes Oliphant Old, *The Reading and Preaching of the Scriptures in the Worship of the Christian Church*, vol. 4, *The Age of the Reformation* (Grand Rapids: Eerdmans, 2002), 27–38, 148–57.

17. Muller, *PRRD*, 2:214–17, 218–23.

18. The Westminster Confession of Faith, the Westminster Larger Catechism and the Westminster Shorter Catechism.

preaching the whole counsel of God from the Scriptures only. Thus when he read about Ezekiel's practice of proclaiming all that the Lord had shown him, William Greenhill, an Independent, had little difficulty transferring the prophet's example into an imperative for ministers: they are to preach only and preach all that they learn at Christ's school (Ezek. 11:25).[19] Burgess puts forth the same standard when he says that preachers "must dresse every Sermon at the glasse [mirror] of the Word; they must preach as they read in Scripture."[20] He gives three reasons why the preacher is to preach only (and all of) what the Bible has to say, each building on Paul's exhortation in 1 Corinthians 3:10 that ministers take care how they lay their foundations.[21] The first reason to take care in preaching is God. It is his Word that ministers are purporting to preach; his honour is at stake, and he does not approve of man's thoughts being substituted for his. Faithful preaching calls for much humility, prayer and, of course, study on the part of the preacher who must be careful to speak biblical thoughts.[22] The second reason to take care in preaching is for man's sake. If God's words are not preached, the sermon loses all its use and effect. At best, it is hay and stubble—useless for spiritual nourishment, certainly not life-giving. At worst, parishioners come to drink at the fountain and are given poison. "Foolish and unwarrantable opinions and doctrines of men" are not "able to produce . . . gracious effects."[23] The third reason is closest to home: preach the whole Bible for the preacher's sake. Burgess points out that the preacher is given a ministry, not a "magistery." God, and not the preacher, can best determine what Christians need. The minister "may not be a Master to dictate and affirm what he pleaseth." Rather, he must imitate Paul and deliver to the people what he receives

---

19. William Greenhill, *An Exposition of the five first Chapters of the Prophet Ezekiel* (London; by Matthew Simmons for Benjamin Allen, 1645), vol. II. Cha11 Ver. 25. 473; (Edinburgh: Banner of Truth, 1994), 287; Stephen Marshall, according to his biographer, found "most content" or satisfaction in "preaching of Christ" but was sure that "bookes . . . never taught him to preach Christ." G. Firmin's preface in S. Marshall, *The power of the civil magistrate* (London: for Nathaniel Webb and William Grantham, 1657).

20. Anthony Burgess, *The Scripture Directory, for Church Officers and People* (London: Abraham Miller for T. U., 1659), 141.

21. The context of the Apostle's extended metaphor makes it clear that he has preaching ministries in view.

22. Burgess, *Scripture Directory*, 142. Burgess is equally careful in noting that the preacher is not to subtract from God's Word.

23. Ibid., 143, 142–43.

from the Lord (1 Cor. 11:23). If not, Burgess says, we "endanger our own selves" and others.[24] This, he says, would make the preacher "a snare to, or a murderer of other mens souls" and "the blood of the soul will cry more terribly, than the blood of the body."[25]

Preaching Christ

It seems to me that all of the Westminster Assembly's theologians or, in seventeenth-century parlance, "divines," were completely convinced of the truth of what Greenhill and Burgess were teaching: the minister must preach only and all of what God has said in his written Word. But they would never have considered such instruction sufficient for the preacher. Preachers must also heed the biblical counsel of William Perkins, uttered at the conclusion of his *Art of Prophesying*: "Preach one Christ, by Christ, to the praise of Christ."[26] The divines would not have driven a wedge between preaching what the Bible says and preaching Jesus Christ. Quite to the contrary, Christ cannot be preached from anything but the Bible. As Thomas Ford once commented, "I am not able to apprehend, how Gods works of creation, as sun, moon, and stars, etc. did preach Christ" to people.[27] That message was only found in Holy Scripture. And on the other hand, the whole Bible was about the Messiah, and therefore proper exegesis demanded Christ-centred preaching. Thus Burgess argues that "it's the main end and scope of the Scriptures only to exalt Christ, and the end of the Ministry should be the same with the end of the Scripture."[28] Burgess backs up his claim at length: "All the Prophets before Christ, they witnessed of the Messiah. . . . Abraham, though [he lived] so long before Christ's Incarnation, yet it's said, 'He saw Christ's day.'" The same was true in the Mosaic administration of the covenant: "All those Rammes, those Bullocks, those Goats, they all did typifie a Christ."[29]

---

24. Ibid., 143.
25. Ibid., 144.
26. William Perkins, *The Art of Prophesying* in *Works* (London: John Legatt, 1617), 2:673; (Edinburgh: Banner of Truth, 1996), 79.
27. Thomas Ford, *Autokatakritos or, the sinner condemned of himself* (London: for Edward Brewster, 1668), 41.
28. Burgess, *Scripture Directory*, 150.
29. Ibid. For the Old Testament ceremonial law preaching Christ, see also John Lightfoot, *Works* (London: W. R. for Robert Scot, Thomas Basset, Richard Chiswell and John Wright, 1684),

It is not surprising, then, following his exhortations to preach the whole Word of God that Burgess expounds the next verse in 1 Corinthians 3 in a christological fashion: "For other foundation can no man lay, than that is laid, which is Jesus Christ."[30] Burgess has much to say about preaching Christ, the church's one foundation. Christ is the "only foundation, in respect of knowledge and instruction."[31] Then moving from epistemology to ethics, he argues that "we must preach Christ the foundation of all strength and power, from whom we receive all ability to do any thing that is good."[32] The same applies for ecclesiology and kingdom theology, as Christ is "head of the Church," and "governeth all things."[33] Furthermore, "Christ is to be set up the only foundation, in respect of mediation and intercession with God."[34] Our "persons and duties" are accepted only through him. No inheritance or blessing comes without his "imputed righteousnesse."[35] Burgess is only beginning. "Christ is to be preached as the foundation of all fulnesse, for all our necessities and spiritual wants."[36] Christ is "the Fountain of all the happiness, joy and spiritual content the godly hearer can have. We are to preach Christ as the centre in whom all the lines of your hope, love, and desire are to meet. Thus Paul himself, 'I determined to know nothing but Christ crucified,' 1 Corinthians 2:2."[37] Christ is the one whom we are to expect to meet in the sacraments, prayer and the preaching of the Word.[38] And "lastly, We are to preach Christ, not only as the foundation of our approaches to God, but of all Gods gracious actions and visitations to us." By that Burgess means that "we are not only to come to God in Christs name, but to expect that God will come to us through Christ." For "God is in Christ, reconciling the world to himself" (2 Cor. 5:19).[39] Of course some might like to qualify just how Christ was reconciling the "world" when not everyone would be saved. The gospel offer needed to be offered with appropriate sensitivity

---

1:520; George Walker understood that Christ was to be preached in synagogues, *The doctrine of the Sabbath* (Amsterdam, By Richt Right press, 1638), 125–26.

30. Burgess, *Scripture Directory*, 145–56.

31. Ibid., 145.

32. Ibid., 146.

33. Ibid.

34. Ibid., 147.

35. Ibid.

36. Ibid., 148.

37. Ibid., 149.

38. Ibid., 149–50.

39. Ibid., 150. The text is erroneously cited as 2 Corinthians 1:19.

to biblical Reformed theology and scriptural teaching on the extent of the atonement, but preaching also needed to reflect the encouraging "tenour of the gospel."[40]

Echoing similar sentiments, Obadiah Sedgwick states that it is "but labour lost to set up anything but Christ." Ministers are "to bee much in preaching Christ." Again, "your labours in preaching, will come to little, perhaps to nothing, if it not be Christ, or some thing in reference to Christ, on which you so laboriously insist in preaching; 'My Kingdom,' said Christ, 'is not of this world,' John 18:36. So your business is not the business of the world; Go then and preach the Kingdom of God."[41] The preaching of Christ, he argues in outline, is the preacher's (1) proper work, (2) sufficient and full work, (3) honourable work, (4) excellent work, and (5) comfort. The preacher must be able to know on the judgment day that he has preached Christ.[42] So too does the missionary, Thomas Thorowgood would add. And the task of the hearers, in Thorowgood's case native North "Americans," was to enlarge their hearts to receive those who endeavour "to preach Christ."[43]

The explicitness of the stress to preach Jesus Christ varies, of course, among the divines. Philippé Delmé's (d. 1653) work on preaching mentions Christ only in passing,[44] Oliver Bowles gives the subject a chapter,[45] and Edward Reynolds a treatise.[46] Reynolds pursues the necessity of preaching Christ from every angle. The origin of the book is an extended sermon on Paul's comment to the Corinthians that he and his fellow preachers "preach not ourselves, but Christ Jesus the Lord, and ourselves your servants for Jesus' sake" (2 Cor. 4:5). Following his text, Reynolds explains in some detail that we are to preach and that we are not to preach ourselves, providing examples of how preachers often do make themselves the focus of their sermons.[47]

---

40. Ford, *The sinner condemned of himself*, 52–53.

41. Obadiah Sedgwick, *The Fountain Opened* (London: T.R. and E.M. for Adoniram Byfield, 1657), 371.

42. Ibid., 371–72.

43. Thomas Thorowgood, *Digitus Dei: New discoveryes; with sure arguments to prove that the Jews (a Nation) or People lost in the world for the space of near 200 years, inhabite now in America* (London: for Thomas Slater, 1652), preface to the reader.

44. Philippé Delmé, *The Method of Good preaching* (London: J. B., 1701), 19–20, 42–44, 49, 52.

45. Oliver Bowles, *De pastore evangelico tractatus* (London: Samuel Gellibrand, 1649), Lib. 2, Ca13; 79–85.

46. Edward Reynolds, *Preaching of Christ* (London: Tho. Ratcliffe for George Thomason, 1662).

47. Ibid., 1–24, esp. 19–24.

He then goes on to argue that Christ is "the author, the object, and the end of all" preaching. As the author, Christ is the one who sends a preacher on his mission, calling them internally and externally to the pulpit ministry. Christ separates preachers from other Christian persons, consecrating them for the work they are given. As King he gives his ambassadors instructions, chiefly the task to be agents of reconciliation in Christ's place. As the object, Christ is the matter and message of all our preaching. The law drives us to Christ. The gospel itself resides in Christ as can be seen in every article of the Apostle's Creed—we believe in the Father of Christ; we believe in the Holy Spirit of Christ; we believe in the holy catholic bride of Christ; we believe in communion with the subjects of the King, Christ Jesus; and of course we preach remission of sins through Christ alone, through his resurrection. Just as the law and gospel find their focus and substance in Christ, so too do all prayers and both sacraments. And as the end of all preaching, the preacher does all that he can to advance the interests and plans of Christ, the people of Christ, and ultimately the glory of Christ.[48]

The law and the gospel were important but delicate topics at and around the time of the assembly. Antinomians (none of whom would appreciate the label and not all of whom deserved it) were said to be announcing that Christians had no need of the Mosaic law; some held there was no place even for a moral law. In the midst of the debates over preaching, the entire assembly ground to a halt when it considered the Preaching committee's over-zealous suggestion that sermon applications challenge Antinomians without "the disheartening of weak Christians" by indiscrete ministers.[49] Comments by Burroughs indicate that, in his opinion at least, the worry about "indiscrete ministers" was well-founded. On more than one occasion he indicates that preaching was at times getting moralistic. A mere preaching "against the vanities and profits of this world" is really not "the main thing, nor the right method of preaching."[50] Elsewhere he complains that it is common now to "preach morallity." Of course, morality is in the sphere

---

48. Ibid., 24–39. For similar assertions that Christ is the "matter and the author of the gospel," the "sermon" and the "power," see Reynolds, *An explication of the hundreth and tenth Psalme* (London: Felix Kyngston for Robert Bostocke, 1632), 249–50.

49. John Lightfoot, *Journal*, in *Works*, ed. J. R. Pitman (London: J. F. Dove, 1825), 13:280. The motion was sent back to the committee for further work.

50. Jeremiah Burroughs, *Gospel-Remission: or; A Treatise shewing, that True Blessedness consists in Pardon of Sin* (London: for Dorr. Newman, 1668), 77; (Morgan, PA: Soli Deo Gloria, 1995), 112–13.

of preaching, but is not a replacement for the gospel. "The great point that al ministers ought to aim at is the great point of reconciliation, and that is to be preacht."[51]

From a different generation, and preaching from a different text, Gouge preached the same message: Ephesians 6:19 records the Apostle Paul asking the saints to pray "that utterance may be given unto me, that I may open my mouth boldly, to make known the mystery of the gospel." Gouge deduced from the apostle's example that "the Gospell is the proper object of preaching." He tells his hearers that the Great Commission was a commission to preach the gospel. And he appeals to the letter to the Romans and notes that those who are called beautiful are the ones who preach the gospel (Rom. 10:15), and he quotes Romans 1:16, which states that "the Gospell is the power of God unto Salvation."[52] Goodwin concurs. Alluding to Romans 10:15, he submits that preachers would "add more beauty to their own feet" if they would preach more of the gospel and less of "truths of less moment."[53] And Cornelius Burges would note, just before the restoration of Charles II, that Bishops might add some credibility to their "Pomp" and "perpetual state of honour and dignity above their brethren" if they would occasionally "preach Christ to his flock."[54] "Quenching all zeale in preaching Christ," Thomas Wilson told a gathering of the House of Commons, is as great a sin in England as it was in the days of "the High-priest and his complices" who opposed Jesus and his disciples.[55] Nothing is more important than preaching Christ and, for Stephen Marshall, all "divisions and subdivisions in other matters of religion" are secondary in comparison. For "as long as each form [of government] carries people to the Word, houlds out Christ in his Word, Christ in preaching, Christ in the sacraments, there is food for souls."[56] Really, only the devils should be excluded from preaching Christ, as we learn from the example of the Savior in Mark 1:34.[57]

---

51. Jeremiah Burroughs, *Gospel-Reconciliation: or, Christ's Trumpet of Peace to the World* (London: Peter Cole, 1657), 270–71; (Morgan, PA: Soli Deo Gloria, 1997), 246.

52. William Gouge, *Whole Armour*, in *Works*, (London: J. Beale for J. Grismond, 1626–27), 255.

53. Thomas Goodwin, *Works* (Eureka, CA: Tanski Publications, 1996), 11:228.

54. Charles Burges, *No sacrilege nor sin to alienate or purchase Cathedral lands* (London: James Cottrel, 1660), 11.

55. Thomas Wilson, *Davids zeale for zion* (London: for John Bartlet, 1641), 19.

56. Stephen Marshall, *The Life of Christ* in *Works* (London: Peter Cole and Edward Cole, 1661), 57.

57. Lightfoot, citing the opinion of unnamed divines in *Works*, 1:642.

In the end, the reason for all the emphasis on Jesus Christ rested on the fact that they were his ambassadors and not another's. Christ came into the world saying "I am the way, the truth and the life." He said he was the "bread of life" that "came down from heaven." He preached himself as good news to the world. His ambassadors were given the same commission. These were the key notes that Anthony Burgess struck in his discussion of the subject. And this was no new thing. "All the Prophets were Prophets of Christ," Burgess writes, and "all the Officers in the New Testament, are the Officers of Christ."[58] Burroughs also highlights the fact that it is not only the main task of preachers to preach "gospel reconciliation," but that "it is their commission to preach that especially."[59] It is little wonder, then, that after studying John 1:6–9, John Arrowsmith found his ideal model in John the Baptist, the last prophet of the old era, whom the Apostle John commends as one who bore witness to the Light, always emphasizing that Christ must increase while he must decrease.[60] True ministers, Arrowsmith writes, "set up Christ in their ministry; they are content themselves to stand in the crowd, and to lift up Christ upon their shoulders; content, not to be seen themselves, so Christ be exalted."[61]

Ways of Preaching Jesus Christ and the Gospel

1. Dogmatic or Theological Ways to Christ. For most divines, the concept of preaching "Christ" appears to be interchangeable with the idea of preaching the "gospel," the good news about Christ. This meant, on the one hand, that if a Westminster divine was preaching Christ, he would usually preach Christ as Savior and mediator. And it meant, on the other hand, that if he was preaching the gospel, he would preach a gospel with Christ and his benefits—all the treasures and blessings and privileges that accompany a saving union or relationship with Jesus Christ.

But just how did the divines think that Christ or the gospel was to be preached? After all, there are vast parts of the Bible which do not mention

---

58. Burgess, *Scripture Directory*, 145.

59. Burroughs, *Gospel Reconciliation*, 246.

60. John Arrowsmith, *Theanthropos or God-Man: being an exposition upon the first eighteen verses of the first chapter of the gospel according to John* (London: for Humphrey Moseley & William Wilson, 1660), 103.

61. Arrowsmith, *God-Man*, 104; see also 112–13. See also E. Reynolds, *A sermon preached before the king* (London: Jo. Cotterel for Philemon Stephens, 1669), 35–36; and Reynolds, *Preaching of Christ*, 24–33.

Christ by name or the gospel by subject. It seems to me that the actual way in which the divines preached Christ was often theologically or dogmatically driven. Of course this should not be surprising as the dominant method of preaching, laid out by William Perkins, was of the exegesis of a biblical text, followed by the identification of the text's major doctrine (often more than one), the uses of the doctrine, and then a further application of those doctrines.[62] It is important to recognize that there is considerable variety in the execution of this format, as Philippé Delmé argues in his work on the subject.[63]

The simplest form that this doctrinal preaching took was Luther's, where timeless principles of "law" and "gospel" were pitted against each other. With this approach, the preacher would first identify one or more laws (or precepts or godly character traits) in a biblical text, then carefully convince the congregation that they fall short of that perfect standard, and finally show how Christ is the solution to the problem as the gracious Savior of sinners. This type of hermeneutic was understood as only an application of a basic reformational principle. Certainly the principle and hermeneutic should be distinguished: a large number of divines accepted the hermeneutic and applied it in their preaching; virtually all divines accepted the principle and would commonly speak of the law "as a preparative unto the Gospell"; where the law is a "schoole-master to bring us unto Christ" (Gal. 3:24).[64]

62. William Perkins, *The Art of Prophesying*, in *Works*, 2:645–73, esp. 673; (Edinburgh: Banner of Truth, 1996), 1–79, esp. 79. Drawing a direct line between William Perkins and the Westminster Assembly, J. I. Packer writes that the Puritan "principles in preaching, first formulated by Perkins in his *Arte of Prophecying*, found their best balanced expression in the Westminster Assembly's Directory for the Public Worship of God." See J. I. Packer, *Quest for Godliness* (Wheaton, IL: Crossway Books, 1990), 280. John F. Wilson argues that during the civil war the "plain style" of the preachers appointed by Parliament "may be traced back to their patriarch, William Perkins." John Wilson makes an explicit connection between Perkins' preaching instructions and those found in the Assembly's Directory. See J. F. Wilson, *Pulpit in Parliament* (Princeton: Princeton University Press, 1969), 139, 141–42; c.f. R. M. Norris, "The Preaching of the Assembly," in *To Glorify and Enjoy God: A Commemoration of the Westminster Assembly*, ed. J. L. Carson and D. W. Hall (Edinburgh: Banner of Truth, 1994), 67–68; Horton Davies, *Worship and Theology in England: From Andrewes to Baxter and Fox, 1603–1690* (Princeton: Princeton University Press, 1975), 163–64.

63. Delmé, *The Method of Good Preaching*, 1–7.

64. Gouge, *Whole Armour*, 254. Perhaps Richard Vines was trying to communicate the same idea when he reflected on the time "when Paul was required by Felix to preach to him the faith of Christ." Vines finds it interesting that the Scriptures record the Apostle preaching of "righteousness, temperance, and judgement to come, whereat Felix trembled."(Acts 24:25). See Richard Vines, *Gods drawing and mans coming to Christ* (London: for Abel Roper, 1662), 181. But it is

For the Reformed ministers at Westminster, this preparatory use of the law by no means excluded other uses of the law. That is to say, when applied by the Reformed orthodox, this law-gospel principle did not usually result in the denigration of the law. It was still needed in the Christian life. In fact, there is "scarce any Heretique ever so besotted as to preach Christ" for all persons irrespective of repentance and obedience. Indeed, Anthony Burgess, continued, "if I be Calvinist, Arminian, or any other way, I cannot have any quietnesse, or look for any comfort till I and my sins are divided."[65] In his estimation, "to preach Christ, or faith, or grace, or the benefit of the Sacraments so, as that a godly, exact and diligent walking and workiug [sic] is excluded, is to preach another Christ, another gospel then we have received."[66]

Burgess willingly employed a law-gospel hermeneutic at times and would preach law-gospel sermons, but he consciously attempted to develop a more rounded form of preaching which, in spite of his protests to the contrary, can probably be best called "doctrinal preaching." Particularly relevant is his sermon on 2 Corinthians 1:19 entitled, "Christ the Alpha and Omega of all preaching." There Burgess explained to his hearers that there were different understandings of "preaching Christ." By the phrase some "understand the doctrine [or teaching] of Christ," some "Christ and the doctrine of Christ" and some, including Burgess, believe that "Christ onely is to be the subject of all our preaching."[67]

As Burgess saw it, "the subject of the whole Scripture is Christ: The whole Word of God tends to the exalting of Christ." And "when we preach of faith, of repentance, of a godly life, these are but the ladders (as it were) to tread upon, that you may lay hold on Christ."[68] In asserting this, Burgess is probably trying to distance himself from those who preach on doctrines like faith and repentance, or perhaps on the Sermon on the Mount or the Lord's prayer, and manage not to present Jesus Christ and the way of salvation in

---

also possible that Vines so wanted to elevate the law that he was contesting the maxim that only the gospel converts sinners.

65. Anthony Burgess, *CXLV expository sermons upon the whole 17th chapter of the Gospel according to John* (London: Abraham Miller for Thomas Underhill, 1656), 243.

66. Ibid., 127.

67. Anthony Burgess, *An expository comment, doctrinal controversal [sic] and practical upon the whole first chapter of the second epistle of St Paul to the Corinthians* (London: A. M. for Abel Roper, 1661), 556–57.

68. Ibid., 557.

their sermons. Yet even as he measures out the distance between preaching Christ and preaching about faith or repentance, Burgess effectively argues the case for preaching Christ in Scripture *by means of doctrines* associated with Christ. Stated differently, if one listens to Burgess's discussion, or to his actual sermons, the accent of his preaching falls on biblical doctrine and not on biblical typology.

This is usefully illustrated by Burgess in his enumeration of four ways of preaching Christ.[69] In each case, the link that Burgess finds between the text of Scripture to the Christ he preaches is, in fact, a doctrinal one. In the first and easiest way, one preaches Christ when the historical "Jesus of Nazareth," the one "who was crucified at Jerusalem," and the fulfillment of prophecy, is preached. Here preaching Christ is at its simplest. A direct prophecy in the Old Testament or a reference to Jesus in the New Testament speaks of Christ, and so he is preached. The second way of preaching of Christ is to preach Christology, "God and man," "both his natures." Here, and only here, does Burgess appear to open the door to the possibility of preaching an ontological Christ without a discussion of the economic Christ. But in the particular example that he supplies, Burgess explains Christology much as Anselm does, even asking "*Cur Deus sit homo*," and then linking his discussion of the doctrine of the incarnation with the doctrine of the atonement. In his third way of preaching Christ, Burgess recommends focusing on Christ in his person and offices, explaining his two natures and his work as prophet, priest, and king. Here there is an inevitable blending of doctrinal preaching and what I will call typological preaching. After all, "the man" Jesus, and priests and prophets and kings are not merely doctrinal terms; they are also types and figures. Thus doctrinal connections to Christ of this third type often mingle with the type of Christ-centered preaching that I will discuss below. The fourth way to preach Christ is to set him up "as the King and Lord of his Church, to whose lawes and commands we are wholly to submit" lest we meet him one day as an angry judge. Burgess justifies this method as necessary in the face of Antinomian errors about the law, and misinterpretations of Scripture. And so "the law is preached, hell and damnation are preached, that so Christ may be the more welcome, that so the grace of the gospel may be the more conspicuous." Of course this final way of preaching Christ is identical to the law-gospel method discussed

---

69. The text misnumbers these four ways as five.

above.[70] With these four ways of preaching Christ, Anthony Burgess presents a nuanced form of theological connectivity to Christ which can be effected from any passage of Scripture. And it seems similar to that advocated by Obadiah Sedgwick, who was content to remind his readers that "labours in preaching, will come to little, perhaps to nothing, if it not be Christ, or *some thing in reference to Christ*" that is preached.[71]

2. *Typological Preaching.* Burgess's method was probably dominant among the divines (although the sermon structures of the divines awaits careful bibliographical research and nuanced description). But not everyone at the assembly liked doctrinal preaching. This can be seen in the assembly's debates, for some opposed the idea that the Perkinsian form of preaching should be recommended in the assembly's own directory for worship, some divines even opposing it strongly enough to record their negative votes.[72] But opposition, or at least a distance, from doctrinal preaching can also be seen in the exegesis of the divines. Certainly there was more than one understanding of how one moves from the text of

70. Burgess, *An expository comment*, 557–60, 690–91.

71. Sedgwick, *The Fountain Opened*, 371. Emphasis added.

72. Some assembly-men, such as Anthony Tuckney, were opposed to one style of sermon and particularly the traditional "Plain style" of preaching. Tuckney objected to those who were "considering the tying of a preacher to the forme of doctrine, reason & use." See the Minutes of the Westminster Assembly (Dr Williams's Library, London, MS 38.2, fo. 90r), as transcribed in C. B. Van Dixhoorn, "Reforming the Reformation: theological debate at the Westminster Assembly, 1643–1652" (PhD diss., University of Cambridge, 2004), vols. 3–7. Lightfoot records that both Thomas Gataker and William Gouge joined in Tuckney's protest "concerning the prescription of preaching by doctrine, reason, and use, as to strait for the variety of gifts, and occasion doth claim liberty." Their arguments had some effect as the assembly decided on "an addition in the close or preface, that this method is not to be prescribed to every man, nor upon every occasion, but is recommended upon the experience of the benefit that hath accrued by it." Lightfoot adds that "it cost a good deal of time before we could find terms for it." See J. Lightfoot, *Works*, 13:278. The three-volume folio of the minutes of the Westminster Assembly cited here contains approximately 530,000 words and survives in Dr. Williams's Library, London, the pre-eminent library for the study of Puritanism and nonconformity. It spans the years 1643 to 1652, covering the Westminster Assembly's formal debates (1643–49) and the proceedings of the "rump" committee which continued to ordain ministers after the assembly had completed its major tasks (1649–52). Approximately one third of the assembly's minutes were printed in the nineteenth century. The author is currently preparing an 880,000 word critical text of *The Minutes and Papers of the Westminster Assembly, 1643–1652* to be published by Oxford University Press. The late Emeritus Professor David F. Wright of New College, Edinburgh, was the project's founder, consulting editor, and chair of the advisory board. The current chair of the advisory board is Professor John Morrill of the University of Cambridge.

Scripture to the person and work of Christ. All of this is to say that there is another stream of interpretation that feeds into the pool the divines used as a sample for this study—the "typological" stream. This method of preaching Christ focuses, by way of emphasis, on pictures and types. To use Burgess's taxonomy of Christ-centered preaching as a reference point, typological preaching expands on Burgess's first way of preaching Christ, while not ignoring the minor note struck in Burgess's second way of preaching Christ.

Perhaps the best way of explaining this kind of preaching is to provide an example. Although it is a meditation and not a sermon *per se*, Charles Herle, prolocutor of the Westminster Assembly after William Twisse, provides a vivid example of the textual approach to seeing Christ in the Scripture. In his study, Herle reflects on Christ's "bloody sweat" in the Garden of Gethsemane, mentioned in Luke 22:44. This bloody sweat probably meant that sweat was pouring off Christ's body as blood would pour off a wounded man. Two hundred years later Dionysius of Alexandria said that "sweating blood" was still a current expression in his day and referred to "intense pain and distress." He said that people also referred to weeping "tears of blood," and that it meant the same thing.[73] Whatever the precise meaning of the term, this was extraordinary suffering. Who would have expected that the Son of God would need angelic help, and yet still suffer so? Some early Christians may well have found this embarrassing—they wanted a more courageous Savior. Some ancient manuscripts even leave this passage out, but Herle had no problems with the text's authenticity. On the contrary, he finds it rich in meaning for Christians.

In "sweat and blood" Herle finds "the two best emblemes of labour and passion, of doing and suffering, and so, the best epitomes, or (if you will) journals of our Saviour's life and death." This is the case because "both made up the travailes of his soule; the first he wrote in sweat, the other in blood." After all, what was his life other than "a continued sweat of passive action, *Hee went about always doing good.*" And "his death, what, but as incessant a bloodshed of active passion? *hee powred out his soule to death.*" Herle not only can find hints of the doctrines of the active and passive obedience of Christ in this passage, but he also cannot "find any two things in nature that may better serve for the indexes, or rather seales, of those his two Testaments"

---

73. Dionysius the Great, *The Works of Dionysius. Exegetical Fragments*, in *Ante-Nicene Fathers* (Peabody, MA: Hendrickson, 1994), 6:115.

than these two, "sweat and blood." Just think "of the Law, *working out in sweat salvation with feare and trembling.*" Just think "of the Gospell, buying it out with blood in price and value." It was "in these two therefore" that Christ did "beginne his passion, it being to bee the execution of both those Testaments; the complement of the one, and supplement of the other."

But in the wording of the passage we find indications of a "further mysterie." If Herle's language and the printer's italicization and punctuation can be overcome, then follow him as he considers that "in these two (Sweat and Blood) begins this our second *Adams* execution, because in these two (upon the matter) begins the first *Adams* sentence; the *Sweat of his browes*, whereby hee must *live the life*; the blood of mortality, whereby hee must *dye the death.*" Further significance is found in the two gardens: "that mans ransome and ruine might hold yet a more thorough proportion, both are in a Garden, that as in a Garden man had played the wanton with Gods bounty, so in a Garden too, this more then man might play the Champion with Gods fury; it was in a Garden, that God sought man sold to the devill for an apple, *Adam where art thou?* and 'tis here in the Garden too, that men seeke God sold by a devill, for as very a trifle: *whom seeke ye? Jesus of Nazareth.*" The parallels, and thus the potential types, are not insignificant. "In each Garden wee read of a drawne sword; in that by the Cherubim, in this, by Peter; that flames, but this wounds; that but menaces, but this maimes." In the end, "what was in that Garden but threatend to the first Adam, that was in this Garden suffered by the second; the difference is this, in that first Garden, the sword is still hostily brandished, a flaming sword that turned every way, in this second 'tis peaceably put up, Peter put up thy sword." But "nor shall the difference of these two Gardens bee of lesse comfort then is their concord," for "though in that first Garden of Paradise, the sword still keepes the dispossessed posterity of Adam from ever (here) returning thither"—for we "must first passe under the Angels sword, the stroke of death"—"yet to this latter Garden of redemption on a better Paradise to us, wee have free and safe accesse." There "no sword heere threatens, no Angell keepes the doore." Quite the opposite, for he "who is the Angell of the Covenant, both doore of the Fold, and Keeper of the doore, and that with that irresistible key of David, cryes here, *come unto mee all,* in a word, as at first in a Garden man was doom'd by God, *to earne his bread for life by his sweat,* so in a Garden here God earnes for man the *bread of life* by his Sweat too; nor is it of the browes only as that, but of the whole body, yea and soule too." And this is a redemption for all types of sinners, "that herein bloody murederous Caine might have bathed his purple soule as well as idle luxurious *Adam* his." Yes, "here's for both, both, *blood and sweat*: and that in the strange abundance of a shoure [i.e., a shower]; nor is it a dewie misty one, but of great drops running downe through his clothes to the ground."

Herle then turns to a common theme in Christology, asserting that "the least drop of this blood thus dignified by that enriching interest of union: it hath with the God-head, were of price enough, had he so pleased, to have ransomed as many worlds of men, as there bee men in this." He is left wondering why Jesus Christ is so "prodigall of his blood thus precious?" Why does he invert "that prophesie of *all nations flowing unto him*, by thus profusely flowing at once to all nations." The answer is that we have "all of us sinned, and all of us against all the whole Law, in all the whole man: and therefore so full, so proportionate shall bee the satisfaction, that hee *who is all in all and for all*, will answereably bleed throughout all the whole body." And "nor will this our Eliah thinke, this his selfe-sacrifice *once offered for all*, complete enough, unlesse he first drench it in a floud [i.e., flood] of his owne sweat and blood. But, nor is the cure lesse strange then the Physicke: the Method then the Medicine." Who can understand it? "Ours was the fever, and doth hee bleed? oft times a bleeding in the head (Physitians say) is best stopt by striking a veine in the foot, but here the malady is in the foot, the remedy in the head." We can only conclude that "the spirituall blood of Sin, holds a contrary course to that of the body, it flowes upward against Heaven." Perhaps this adds new significance to God's charge against Cain, that "*the voice of thy brothers blood cries up to Heaven*." And so "to cure that spiritual bloody Issue of the foot, sinne, must the head thus bleed for it." This deserves qualification of course: "must (I say) not out of any necessity on his side, more then that of his owne decree and promise, all the necessity, at least the need, was ours."[74]

Herle demonstrates that exegesis of a passage can be much enriched by dwelling on the inspired text and its language. From this passage and its context he vividly expounds the gospel and creatively touches on justification, the unity of the two testaments, the nature of the atonement, Christology, and the extent of the atonement. He illustrates his exposition with

---

74. Charles Herle, *Contemplations and devotions on the severall passages of our blessed Saviour's death* (London: Aug. Mat. for Humphrey Robinson, 1631), 1–9.

reference to medicine, implying that Christ as our Savior is our Physician. Herle's exegesis will probably evoke a wide range of responses from modern preachers, but the point here is that here he attempts to communicate the sense of the passage not by extracting a doctrine and then enumerating its uses, but by meditating on the wording of the text and its use throughout Scripture. Herle's method of communicating these doctrines is not driven so much by the doctrines themselves as by the text of Scripture. And yet, notably, Herle shows that typological sensitivity need not lead to an impoverishment of theology. It can actually lead to its enrichment.

REFLECTIONS ON PREACHING

Anthony Burgess on Preaching Christ

Arguably a stress on Christ-centered preaching is a Reformed hallmark, and the additional stress on preaching Christ from the Old Testament almost a Reformed distinctive. Yet in spite of appearances, this brief essay did not attempt to set Christ-centered preaching in its historical context in order to permit a few pages of back-slapping for Reformed preachers. On the contrary, it seems that many Reformed preachers, both past and present (including the author of this essay), could benefit from more careful reflection on the meaning of the Lord Jesus Christ's words in Luke 24. How is Christ present in the Scriptures? And how are we to preach Christ?

It is undeniable that Anthony Burgess's comment about his own day is true in ours: some preach doctrines—even doctrines relating to Christ such as his preincarnate existence, christophanies, or the relationship between his two natures and one person—but do not preach Christ in the sense that our Savior intended. It is worth asking, are preachers preaching Christ when they discuss his person only, apart from his benefits? When Jesus pointed to what the Old Testament said about himself, was he only asserting that we could go to Moses or the Psalms or the Prophets to learn Christology? Jesus specifically told his disciples that they should search "Moses, the Prophets and the Psalms" not only to find out about the great accomplishment of redemption in his suffering and resurrection, but also the application of that redemption in repentance and forgiveness. Jesus himself indicates that the Old Testament points to him as a "Christ" (vv. 26, 46). The same surely applies to the Scriptures written by Christ's apostles after his ascension.

381

Again, the point here is not that we should not see and preach classic Christology in the Old Testament, but that in Luke 24 Jesus was most likely telling his disciples that they could (and should have!) seen a saving, mediating Christ in the Old Testament. And so if we are to preach Christ from the Old Testament, we should preach more than classical Christology.

But perhaps we should even be more radical and question whether in Luke 24 Christ was telling his people to connect the dots between Christian doctrine and Christ himself. I for one believe that we can and must connect all "doctrinal dots" to Jesus Christ, but I doubt that Luke 24 has this sort of exercise in mind. That is to say, I think we can question whether Luke 24 supports the Perkinsian method of doctrine, use and application. Of course it is possible to find doctrines in the text of Scripture. This is easily illustrated in the simple law-gospel approach to preaching which quickly fits any text into an edifying grid and drastically reduces sermon preparation time. This is also illustrated by those gifted preachers, past and present, who either profoundly edify their people (and later readers) with more sophisticated (but often very accessible) doctrinal connections between the text and Christ.[75] And it is sadly illustrated by those who, wearyingly, somehow leave their congregations each week with messages on the sovereignty of God or the evils of popery. But although many, perhaps most, have utilized primarily doctrinal approaches to preaching Christ, this author recommends that we spend more time on the text of Scripture and attempt to pay more attention to the vivid types and pictures presented to us in God's Word.

The point here is not that Anthony Burgess is unedifying to read or unbiblical in his doctrine. In this writer's estimation he is profoundly edifying and robustly biblical in his theology. The point is simply to ask if Jesus Christ was actually saying that the *Scriptures speak* of him, or if all *theology connects* to him, or if we should draw a distinction between the two.

It seems to me that, at the very least, if it is the task of the ambassador to proclaim and explain and apply the word of Christ to his subjects, then that explanation before the people should usually seek to linger over the text of the proclamation as it is given in the Bible, and not to rush through Scripture or launch from it to get to greater things. In other words, God's people should leave a sermon on the first chapter of Matthew not only with a fuller understanding of the incarnation, but with a fuller understanding of

75. A blend of these views is popularized in Bryan Chapell, *Christ-centered Preaching*, 2nd ed. (Grand Rapids: Baker, 2005).

the first chapter of Matthew—perhaps a method of typological preaching closer to what Charles Herle exemplified, than to what Burgess explained.

Doctrinal Preaching Yesterday and Today

1. Concerns with Typological Preaching. Typological preaching raises a host of questions. If one is to try and seek out the significance of words and pictures used or cited or developed in the biblical text, how do we know when to stop? Did Herle know when to stop? What are the controls on the typological method as described? Parsons in the doctrinal preaching school who do pay attention to types and symbols tend to be very cautious. They are usually comfortable with using more obvious types and symbols, especially those actually identified in the New Testament as such. But like John Calvin, Henry Ainsworth, or Matthew Poole, they often "de-emphasize Christological readings of the Old Testament," or perhaps both testaments. [76]

Of course there is a reason why some who preach doctrinally are concerned about the potential pitfalls of some who preach typologically. First, a subset of those who attempt typological preaching give boring Bible tours that make their hearers conscious of every tick of the clock. Second, some who preach typological sermons not only denigrate doctrinal sermons, but doctrine itself. Third, some who champion typology appear to lack any form of restraint—the newer and wilder the better. They ultimately make the Bible look inaccessible and mysterious, requiring a new caste of literary priests to open the way of salvation for us. After all, isn't the Bible supposed to be simple? How right the Westminster divines were to say that "those things which are necessary to be known, believed, and observed for salvation" are not beyond our grasp. Every aspect of the gospel is "clearly propounded, and opened in some place of Scripture or other." Truly, "not only the learned, but the unlearned" can understand these things and, we might add, explain them to others. We only need to use the Word of God properly—reading it carefully and listening to it prayerfully.[77] This is not always exemplified in the preaching of those who are preoccupied with the types and pictures of the Bible.

76. For the Old Testament exegesis of these theologians (and others), see Muller, *PRRD*, 2:449.
77. Westminster Confession of Faith 1.7

2. Response to Concerns. And yet, taking the last objection first, we must remember that Bible reading is not always easy. On the one hand, certain parts of Scripture are harder to read than others. The apostle Peter himself said "some things" written by the apostle Paul are "hard to be understood." Any reader of the Bible, even a reader who has read the Bible for many years, knows that "all things in Scripture are not alike plain in themselves," as the Westminster Confession states. On the other hand, it is just as true that we all read the Bible at different levels and so, as the confession puts it, the Scripture is not "alike clear unto all." Some Christians understand the Bible better than other Christians. Some have just entered the Bible for the first time. There are things they have seen but do not yet understand. There are many doors which they have not yet opened and many corners which they have yet to explore. We are not all seasoned saints. We are not all teachers. Few, like Palmer Robertson, are both.

Given that certain portions of the Bible are difficult, especially for some people (including preachers), it is important to be humble in approaching the Bible and admit that what may seem obscure and difficult to us may still be correct. We must not reject an interpretation of the Bible simply because it is difficult to understand, either for us, or even for everyone. On the contrary, we should remember that this is God's revelation of himself, and we should not expect that everything revealed about God, nor the way in which God has revealed everything, will be easy for us to grasp. This applies, of course, to the typology of the Bible. Knowing how to apply biblical typology requires biblical wisdom. Ultimately we must remember to distinguish between the abuse of the thing and the thing itself. Bad as the bathwater may sometimes be, we need to keep the proverbial baby safe.

Second, although some modern defenders of typological preaching are attackers of theology, this has not always been the case and never needs to be the case. Herle was very able and willing to teach theology as he preached, albeit not by topical discussions of theology inserted in his sermons. But such discussions do not need to appear in every sermon. They can appear in some sermons (and certainly in all sermons on those texts which actually discuss doctrinal loci). And such discussions can appear in the church's catechesis and training of its members outside its worship services.

Third, typological preaching can be abused and become wearying but, all things considered, there is such variety in biblical phrasing and expression that it need not be the case. And it should be mentioned that many doctrinal sermons can also be wearying, especially when a preacher somehow manages to find and then ride his favorite doctrinal hobbyhorse from almost every biblical text.

Typological Preaching Yesterday and Today

Practical issues aside, one of the real differences between doctrinal and textual preaching is that those in the textual tradition are willing to see our Lord's and the apostles' exegesis as a pattern that can actually be imitated by preachers today. Rather than seeing the New Testament as merely the God-given depository of all legitimate (or safe) types for the preacher to use, typological preachers find in the New Testament a blueprint for do-it-yourself typological sermons. They are willing (in fact obliged) to try themselves to identify types and symbols imbedded by God in his Word. Like Peter Martyr Vermigli, Cocceius, Charles Herle, or Matthew Henry they use the Bible's pictures and metaphors to link Moses and the Psalms and the Prophets to one another, and ultimately to tether the whole of the Bible to Jesus Christ.[78]

Mining these treasures of the Bible is difficult work. Taking the diamonds that we find and presenting them to God's people in a way that magnifies God rather than merely dazzling his people, is also difficult work. Leading people to the Savior from any passage in the Bible is difficult work, but it is not impossible. And here I turn once more to the object of this festschrift, for O. Palmer Robertson has shown us time and again how very edifying and instructive it is to search out fully the depths of God's Word. There is no theological topic in most confessions or systematic theologies for "Israel" or "Land." And yet how much we learn about God, his Word, his ways, and the Savior for sinners, through Palmer Robertson's *The Israel of God.*

Among those who preach or who would like to preach typologically, there are some personal differences. Some may be concerned about restraint. For them, biblical pictures, types, and words throw up innumerable connections and they need to select carefully from among them the ones that are most central to the passage that is to be preached. But others are not looking for more restraint, but freedom and sanctified imagination. They read the

---

78. For the Old Testament exegesis of these theologians (and others), see Muller, *PRRD*, 2:449.

Charles Herles or Palmer Robertsons of this world and see the importance of a greater sensitivity to biblical types and images, but it does not seem to click for them. Perhaps they have even read the right books and heard the right lectures, but struggle to put it into practice. They only wish when they were coming to the text of Scripture that there was a concise commentary series that focused on preaching Christ from both testaments—after all, there are commentary series for exegesis and for application and for pretty much everything else. For those preachers who need help to employ biblical types and pictures, there are at least three lessons to learn from the Westminster divines, two positive, and one negative.

In the first place, we need to consider the size of the text that we have chosen to preach. Unfortunately this is where some Westminster divines serve as a negative example. Although it is pious to say that every letter, syllable, or word of Scripture speaks of Christ, it is functionally useless for the purpose of exegesis and preaching. The almost embarrassingly simple reason we are not finding Christ in some texts is that the text selected for preaching is simply too brief. The extreme form of this problem in preaching can be seen today when some preachers try to preach, or pretend to preach, sermons from the word "and" or "but." Of course, if they were really doing so, they could as easily preach from a dictionary.[79] But today's practice was probably learned from the past where preachers chose mere fragments of sentences and expounded them word by word. Such was the case with Jeremiah Burroughs, who would preach whole sermon series on a brief phrase, such as Isaiah 66:2, "and that trembleth at my Word."[80] In truth, Christ is in the Scriptures in coherent thoughts expressed in sentences, and more probably in paragraphs, whole narratives, or whole psalms. Paying attention to *genre* and legitimate literary units in the Bible increases the chance that one is going to find Christ in a legitimate, preachable pericope of Scripture. Doubtless this rule requires expansion and qualification around its edges, but this writer is sure that its center will hold.

And yet it is the case that some preachers know the Scripture and have a legitimate section of Scripture in front of them and they will still struggle

79. Thankfully, whether they see it or not, these preachers are usually connecting two or more biblical themes and those themes or ideas, not a single conjoining word in the passage, provides the text of their sermon.

80. Jeremiah Burroughs, *Gospel-fear, or, The heart trembling at the word of God evidenceth a blessed frame of spirit delivered in several sermons from Isa. 66, 2 and 2 Kings 22, 14* (London: J. D. for B. Aylmer, 1674); (Morgan, PA: Soli Deo Gloria, 1991).

to see those types and figures which point to Christ. So in the second place, we should read good examples of typologically sensitive exegesis. Here the church fathers, some Reformers, some Puritans, and Palmer Robertson are very helpful. For example those church fathers who wrote before the rise of the lectionary provide examples of preaching from both testaments that evidence a robust awareness of biblical typology; those who wrote after the lectionary often do the same, albeit usually from the Gospels only. Of course, not all types in the Fathers point to Christ. And often the typology suggested by the creative genius of the fathers needs some restraint. But for preachers for whom restraint comes with ease and creativity comes with difficulty, the creativity of the Fathers, used with restraint, can prove to be a real God-send—a type of training ground for preachers whose imagination is tired, or simply underdeveloped. Later examples are also helpful, not least those found in some of the writings of some of the Westminster divines or Matthew Henry, Geerhardus Vos, or O. Palmer Robertson.

Finally, every preacher needs to be saturated in the Scriptures. This is true because the Scriptures are God's gift to his people. In his goodness and wisdom God used his great power to commit his revelation about salvation into a written form. He gave us the Bible. There are many reasons why God might have done this, but among them are certainly the reasons mentioned in the Westminster Confession. God wanted to "better preserve" and propagate his truth. And he wished to firmly establish the church against its untiring opponents: the corruption of our own flesh, the malice of Satan, and the malice of the world. And so this revelation is "most necessary." What else could it be? After all, it reveals a "knowledge of God" and a knowledge of what is "necessary for salvation," and it is useful for building up the church and defending us from our enemies. The Scriptures are necessary for the spiritual health of Christian people, and necessary for the very existence of the church and its doctrine. And that means a great deal to God's people. How much we owe to God that he gave his church his Word. He did not need to reveal himself, but he did it for us. The Bible is a great gift to all Christians, but it is especially a great gift to preachers. It is not only the source of life for us and the matter for all our sermons, it should also be the greatest help in writing sermons. Charles Herle could draw on a wide variety of texts to illustrate and explain his passage and to preach Christ because he had a preacher's knowledge of Scripture. This kind of knowledge cannot be gained by paper or electronic concordances. Indeed, the concordances at the time of the Westminster divines were incomplete and expensive to own. A proper understanding of biblical typology requires prayerful travel through the pages of Scripture for the whole of our Christian pilgrimage. Only then can we begin to know the mind of the author, and compare and connect texts of Scripture as we ought.

CONCLUSIONS

The impetus to find Christ in the Scriptures is primarily a biblical one, and so it has also become the confessional air that Reformed people breathe. But it appears from this study that there are different paths to Christ, some primarily doctrinal, others primarily typological. This essay has suggested that the latter appears more biblical, and has sought to add a few more voices to the current conversation about preaching. But this suggestion is made with a catholic and not a partisan intent. The way in which we preach Christ is not unimportant, but the main matter is that we preach Christ. Some preach Christ one way, some another. But, to paraphrase the apostle Paul, "the important thing is that in every way"—whether doctrinally or typologically or in some other way—"Christ is preached." It is the preaching of Christ and all his benefits that will bring honour to the Son by the Holy Spirit, which will in turn bring all glory to the Father.

Here the concluding comments of Edward Reynolds are useful. It was Reynolds's insistent note that every minister ought to "preach Christ Jesus" as Lord and Savior: "determine to know nothing among your people but Christ crucified, let his name and grace, his spirit and love triumph in the midst of all your Sermons." Surely Reynolds was wise to counsel young preachers to make Christ their "great end . . . to glorifie him in the hearts, to render him amiable and precious in the eyes of his people; to lead them to him as a Sanctuary to protect them, a propitiation to reconcile them, a treasure to enrich them, a Physician to heal them, an Advocate to present them and their services unto God." Christ is all things for his people. Christ offers himself to us "as wisdom to counsel, as righteousnesse to justifie, as sanctification to renue, as redemption to save, as an inexhausted fountain of pardon, grace, comfort, victory, glory. Let Christ be the Diamond to shine in the bosom of all your Sermons." Preaching Christ should be done for the sake of those who hear, but it should primarily be done "for Jesus sake, if you love Jesus." This is an argument which Jesus himself uses with Peter.

"If you would have Jesus love you, if you tender his sheep, if you regard his command, if you fear his wrath, if you value his salvation, study the price of souls, snatch souls out of the fire, forewarn souls of the wrath to come, be humble, be faithful, be painful, be pitiful towards the souls of men." In short, "set forth Christ's excellency unto the souls of your hearers, that you may be able to say to him at his coming, as he to his Father, Behold me and the children whom thou hast given me. Thus doing, you shall both save your selves and them that hear you."[81]

81. Reynolds, *Preaching of Christ*, 46, 48.

20

The History of the American Presbyterian Church and the Struggle for Religious Freedom

Morton H. Smith

THE YEAR 2006 marked the three hundredth anniversary of the founding of the first Presbytery on the American shores. It is fitting for us to look back to that history in order to understand something of the roots of present-day Presbyterianism in the United States. In this essay I will make a brief survey of the early settlements of Presbyterians, and the establishment of Presbyterianism in America. I will devote particular attention to the relation of Virginia, the first English colony in America, to Presbyterianism. The reason for this focus is the significant steps that were taken in the struggle for the recognition of the right of all citizens to be allowed to worship according to their individual consciences. Of particular interest is the part played by Presbyterians in the development of the concept of the separation of church and state by the state in Virginia as she moved to statehood, which became the basis for the First Amendment to the Constitution of the United States of America.

THE PLANTING OF PRESBYTERIANISM IN AMERICA

The Chesapeake Colonies

Virginia. The first permanent English settlement on the American shores was at Jamestown, Virginia, in 1706. It was the beginning of the Chesapeake settlements, or the Chesapeake society. The Jamestown settlement was essentially a Puritan colony, and thus the first preachers in the colony were of the Puritan viewpoint. The Puritan movement in England was a movement to purify the Anglican Church's worship and doctrines. Henry VIII had seen the rise of Protestantism on the continent as a means of breaking with the power of Rome. His break was not primarily religious. His son, Edward VI aligned himself with the religious reformation. Mary had sought to return England to Roman Catholicism, whereas Elizabeth adopted only a moderate reforming attitude.

When James VI of Scotland assumed the English throne as James I, the Puritans had hoped he would favor their full reformation of the Church. He continued the more moderate reform. The Puritans remained as a strong party in England during his reign. The Virginia company was made up of Puritans. According to George M. Brydon, all of the ministers brought to the colony before 1624 under the Virginia Company were Puritan in their sympathies.[1] There was a minister with the first settlement, the Rev. Robert Hunt.[2]

The Rev. Alexander Whitaker, son of William Whitaker, Regius Professor of Divinity at Cambridge, who was a Presbyterian in his convictions, came in 1611, and served the Parishes of Bermuda Hundred on the south side of the James, and Henrico north of the James. "Like his father, Whitaker had strong puritan leanings."[3] He was succeeded by the Rev. George Keith, a Scotsman, who was a Presbyterian in practice. A number of Puritan dissenters came to Virginia, settling on the south side of the James. There were groups with ministers in the area of modern day Norfolk. In 1641 three New England ministers came to Virginia, and ministered to the Puritans of the colony.

1. George MacLaren Brydon, *Virginia's Mother Church and the Political Conditions under Which It Grew* (Richmond: Virginia Historical Society, 1947), 1:18, as cited by Ernest Trice Thompson, *Presbyterians in the South* (Richmond: John Knox Press, 1963), 1:12.

2. Richard L. Morton, *Colonial Virginia* (Chapel Hill, NC: University of North Carolina Press, 1960), 1:9.

3. Matthew Page Andrews, *Virginia, The Old Dominion* (New York: Doubleday, Doran and Company, Inc., 1937), 63.

The Virginia Company's charter prescribed that "the word and services of God be preached, planted and used according to the rites and doctrines of the Church of England." There was no bishop to enforce this in the colony, and thus there was more freedom than later existed. The control of the Company was in the hands of the Puritans until the revocation of the charter in 1624. The Company had on occasion assisted Puritan ministers, who were unwilling to conform to rules laid down by the Church, to find refuge in the new colony of Virginia. This angered King James, who thus revoked the charter. There were Puritans settled around the Norfolk area, though no particular congregation can claim a direct lineage from these early non-conformist groups. We may assume they were essentially Presbyterian. A number of Scottish settlers came during the seventeenth century, who settled along the Elizabeth River, near the present Norfolk. Others settled along the Rappahannock, James, and Potomac Rivers.

With the assumption of royal control of the colony in 1624, an act of conformity was passed. As the Puritan cause prospered in England, Governor Sir William Berkeley became more and more repressive in Virginia. When on January 29, 1649, Charles I, was executed, Gov. Berkeley and the General Assembly of the Colony became more rigid against all non-conformists, some 300 to 600 Virginia Puritans accepted the special invitation of Maryland Governor William Stone, formerly a Puritan leader in Northampton County, VA, to move to Maryland. Many moved to Anne Arundel County, Maryland, near Annapolis. Richard Warfield, B. B. Warfield's immigrant ancestor, came to Anne Arundel County directly from England in 1659. He was of Puritan conviction.

Scotch-Irish began to settle around the Chesapeake Bay as early as 1665. A definite Scotch-Irish settlement was found in Maryland by 1680. Not welcome in Virginia, they settled in Maryland, where they were welcomed. A number of them settled on the Eastern Shore, where Francis Makemie was later to labor. One of them, by the name of Robert Harper, moved further inland, up the Potomac, to the junction of the Shenandoah River with the Potomac. He established a ferry there, which gave its name to the settlement.

Maryland. Maryland was established as a Roman Catholic colony in 1632 under a grant from Charles I. With the coming of the Civil War in England (1642–1649), and the dominance of the Protestants under

Oliver Cromwell (1649–1658), Maryland received a large number of Puritan immigrants. Due to the restrictive policies of Virginia requiring the support of the Church of England, many dissenters, who had first settled there, also moved to Maryland.

In order to protect the Roman Catholics in the colony, The Maryland Toleration Act, also known as "The Act Concerning Religion," was passed in 1649 by the colonial assembly of the Province of Maryland mandating religious toleration for all who professed Christianity. As the first such law, in the colonies, it is often seen as a precursor to the First Amendment.[4] The result was that Maryland became the most religiously diverse of the English colonies. This law protected Christians; it made denying the divinity of Jesus a capital crime. After the restoration of the kings in England, Maryland sought to establish the Anglican Church for the colony. This was accomplished in 1692.

The Mid-Atlantic Colonies

New York. Though the Puritans of New England were generally Congregationalists, a number of them, particularly in Connecticut, favored Presbyterian polity. New York was first settled by the Dutch, who were generally Reformed in doctrine and Presbyterian in polity. Generally the Presbyterians of New England were absorbed into the established Congregational churches of both Massachusetts and Connecticut. Some migrated to New York. The Rev. John Young moved from New England to Long Island and established a church at Southold in 1640. Abraham Pierson, a graduate of Cambridge, labored first at Lynn, Massachusetts. From there he moved to South Hampton, Long Island, and eventually to Newark, New Jersey, where he established the first Puritan Church in that State. Early New Jersey settlements also included some Puritans from Connecticut. Newark included such an element as well as some Scottish settlers, who established the Presbyterian Church there in 1667–68. Francis Doughty led a group from Long Island to Manhattan and established the first Presbyterian congregation in New Amsterdam in 1643. After five years of ministry there, he went to Virginia and Maryland about 1650. By the time that New Amsterdam was taken by the English in 1664, there were six Puritan or Presbyterian congregations.

4. For the text of The Maryland Toleration Act see "The Maryland Toleration Act (1649)," http://odur.let.rug.nl/~usa/D/1601-1650/maryland/mta.htm (accessed March 31, 2008).

New Jersey. Further south along the Delaware River the settlement of Fairfield, New Jersey, was established by people from Fairfield, Connecticut, around 1680 under their pastor, Thomas Bridge. The Fairfield Church of Fairton, New Jersey, now in the PCA, traces its origins to this settlement. This congregation is found on the rolls of the first Presbytery of Philadelphia in 1707. A number of Puritans and Presbyterians moved from New England and New York, where there were various strictures against them, to New Jersey. Elizabethtown and Woodbridge were thus settled about 1680. In 1685 a group of Scots immigrated to Woodbridge under the Rev. George Scott, who had been imprisoned for his fidelity to Presbyterian principles.

Pennsylvania and Delaware. The earliest record of Presbyterians in Delaware is a congregation at Lewes under the Rev. Samuel Davis. There was correspondence with the ministers of Boston, and two men were sent. The Rev. John Wilson went to New Castle, Delaware, while the Rev. Benjamin Woodbridge went to Philadelphia. The latter was succeeded by the Rev. Jedediah Andrews in 1698. He served as the only Presbyterian pastor in Philadelphia for a number of years. He was to become a member of the first presbytery. Pennsylvania was, of course, established as a Quaker colony, but they allowed others to settle in the colony. Since the Quakers were pacifists, they welcomed settlers of other persuasions, to settle as a buffer between them and those who might attack them. Large numbers of Germans settled in what is now central Pennsylvania as a buffer between the Indians and the Quaker settlements.

In the eighteenth century large numbers of Scotch-Irish entered America through New Castle and Philadelphia. A string of Presbyterian communities and churches developed along the Mason and Dixon line from the Delaware River to the Susquehanna as a buffer between Roman Catholic Maryland and the Quakers. Large numbers of the Scotch-Irish stopped in these settlements for a period and then moved on to more promising areas. Many moved westward to western Pennsylvania, where there is still a strong element of Presbyterianism. Others turned southward, following the "Philadelphia Wagon Road" through the Valley of Virginia into the Carolinas south to Georgia, and southwest to East Tennessee and Kentucky. This was the main source of the settlers of the backcountry of these regions. With the opening of the Northwest Territory after the

American War for Independence, many Presbyterians moved westward into this territory from New York and Pennsylvania.

The Southern Colonies

The Carolina Lowlands—South Carolina and Georgia. The second southern society was an entirely different settlement that took place in what is called he Carolina lowlands, with Charleston, founded in 1670, as the central city. The earliest records of Reformed worship in that area are of the French Huguenots, who arrived in 1680. The last will and testament of a certain Caesar Mozé reveals that there must have been a French church in the Charleston area as early as 1687. Three shiploads of French Huguenot colonists had landed on the Carolina coast in 1669, thus beginning the permanent French colonization of South Carolina. The first large company arrived in 1680, and five years later, with the revocation of the Edict of Nantes, a larger migration of French Huguenots took place until the end of the century. Thompson said that though their numbers were only about a tenth of the white population of the colony, they prospered and were of great influence in the colony. "Their influence in the colony, far out of proportion to their numbers, was due to their high moral and intellectual fiber, emerging from the fires of persecution, and to the disciplines of their misfortunes."[5] In the course of time large numbers of the Huguenots were assimilated into the Church of England. This took place for several reasons. First, there was pressure upon them to assimilate into the English-speaking world. Second, their liturgy was closer to the Anglican liturgy than to the simple Puritan form of worship of the Presbyterians. Third, there is evidence that social and economic pressures were brought upon the Huguenots to conform to the Anglican Church.

A whole colony of New Englanders from Dorchester, Massachusetts, moved to South Carolina to found a Congregational Church at Dorchester in 1696. Between 1752 and 1771 much of this group transplanted itself to Liberty County, Georgia, and established Midway Church. From this Congregational church a large number of young men were fed into the ministry of various denominations. The Presbyterians received some thirty, including Thomas Goulding, first professor at Columbia Seminary, and Daniel Baker, the great Presbyterian evangelist to the old Southwest. Four

5. Thompson, *Presbyterians in the South*, 1:30.

Presbyterian Churches grew out of this church, which died after the War between the States: Walthourville, Flemington, Dorchester, and Midway (a Negro Church).

A church made up of Puritans from both England and New England, Scottish Presbyterians, Scotch-Irish Presbyterians, and French Huguenots was established in Charleston about 1690. It went under various names such as the Presbyterian Church, the White Meeting, the Independent Church, the New England Meeting, and the Circular Church. The first pastor was Benjamin Pierpont from New England. He was succeeded by John Cotton, also of New England. After his death Archibald Stobo, a Scot, became the pastor. The congregation became divided over the issue of Presbyterian government, which Stobo advocated. He resigned in 1704 and helped to organize several Presbyterian churches, including the churches at Wilton, Pon-Pon, James Island, and Cainhoy. A 1710 pamphlet gives the percentages of different church groups in South Carolina as follows: Presbyterian, including Congregationalists and Huguenots 45 percent, Anglicans 42.5 percent, with the Baptists at 10 percent and Quakers at 2.5 percent. Though the Presbyterian or Reformed group outnumbered the others at this time, the Anglicans had the advantage of tax support to build their buildings. The English Society for the Propagation of the Gospel sent twelve Episcopal missionaries to the colony. Stobo kept the Presbyterian cause alive by obtaining a few ministers from Scotland. The migration from Scotland and Northern Ireland continued to add to their cause as well.

Under Stobo's leadership, together with two Scottish ministers, Hugh Fisher and John Witherspoon, an independent presbytery developed in the Charleston area around 1722. (This presbytery passed out of existence at the time of the Revolution, and its records were lost.) This presbytery required subscription to the Westminster Confession of Faith, as indicated in correspondence regarding the Rev. Josiah Smith of Cainhoy, who was excluded in 1730, because of his refusal to subscribe. The pastor of the Independent Church of Charleston was opposed to subscription. The result was that in 1731 twelve families of that congregation withdrew to form the Scotch or First Presbyterian Church of Charleston. Churches like the First Presbyterian Church continued as independent Presbyterian churches until they eventually united with the mainline Presbyterian denomination. Dr. Thompson has a note to the effect that a new Charleston Presbytery was established in 1790, following the War for Independence. It sought union with the Presbyterian General Assembly in 1800, 1804, and 1811, but refused to be incorporated into the Synod of the Carolinas, and thus were refused reception by the assembly. This presbytery appears to have ceased to exist sometime after 1811.

The independency of spirit reflected in the Charleston-Savannah area has been characteristic of much Southern thought. No doubt it was forced on the early Presbyterians of this southern region simply by their distance from the rest of the American Presbyterians, but it was to leave a mark on the South Carolina Presbyterian mind. The people of this same area were to disagree with their brethren in 1837–38 and thus form the Independent Presbyterian denomination, which went its own way until the War between the States overshadowed their differences and brought about a union with other Southern Presbyterians.

Before leaving the Carolina lowlands, we should take note of the first colony of Scotch-Irish to settle in the region. They settled in the Williamsburg Township, near the Santee River, at what is now known as Kingstree. Thompson cites Professor R. L. Merriwether's description of these settlers: "The Williamsburgers . . . constituted a social unit of unusual strength and vigor. . . . Their chief bond was their church. . . . They were a Scotch Puritan community set down in a more easy going English plantation province. Their high standards of conduct and education, their social compactness and their remarkable vigor were valuable aids to South Carolina progress."[6]

Presbyterians also settled in the coastal areas of Georgia. As early as 1735 the Rev. John McLeod and a number of Scottish Highlanders settled in Darien, Georgia. This was a community somewhat inland from Savannah and served as a defense against the Spanish and the Indians. A Presbyterian church was established there. At Savannah a number of Scots, Scotch-Irish, French, and Swiss Calvinists joined together in 1755 to form the Independent Meeting in Savannah, which continues to this day as the Independent Presbyterian Church of Savannah. This church was established in association with the Church of Scotland. Its grant of land from George II states that it is to be used for such, "as are or shall be professors of the Doctrines of the Church of Scotland, agreeable to the Confession of Faith . . . ."[7] Its

---

6. Ibid., 36.

7. Anonymous: *History of the Independent Church and Sunday School, Savannah, Ga.* (Savannah: N. Nichols, 1882). Its present pastor, the Rev. Terry Johnson, is a minister of the PCA and a contributor to this volume.

first pastor was John Joachin Zubly, a very able man. Though this congregation remains independent, it has drawn its pastors from the Southern Presbyterian Church.

It is worth taking note of the fact that George Whitefield, who had established an orphanage at Savannah, and who traveled the American colonies for support for this orphanage, was not warmly received by the Presbyterians of the Charleston Presbytery. His impact, which was so great in the Presbyterian churches of the middle colonies, was thus not felt as strongly among the Presbyterians of the Carolina low country. This may account, in part, for the failure of Presbyterianism to grow and prosper in this region. The impact of the New Side Presbyterianism was to be felt far more intensely in the backcountry.

Eastern North Carolina—The Cape Fear River Area. A number of highland Scots settled the Cape Fear River area of North Carolina in 1732. Scottish Presbyterianism was thus established in this region. By the American War for Independence, twelve thousand Highlanders were in this area. It was largest Highlander settlement in the Colonies. They were induced to migrate due to the changes in Scotland following the battle of Culloden 1746. The first minister was James Campbell who came to Cross Creek from Pennsylvania in 1757. He first identified with the Presbytery of Charleston, but due to his inability to attend their meetings, transferred to Orange Presbytery in North Carolina.

The fact that most of the Highlanders spoke only Gaelic (which continued to be used in some of the church till after the War Between the States) protected them from the near-by Baptist missionaries at Sandy Creek and kept them faithful to Presbyterian Calvinism during the many years when they were without the ministrations of a regular pastor. Their custom of family worship also kept their faith alive. Children learned the catechism from their elders and the church officers examined them frequently on it. Before each hearth where there was reverence for the forms of the Scotch church, the whole family read the Bible aloud every day and repeated the Shorter Catechism.[8]

Charles Hodge concludes his survey of these early settlements of America with the following:

8. G. G. Johnson, as cited by Thompson, *Presbyterians in the South*, 1:37.

From this slight and imperfect view of the several classes of people by whom our country was settled, it is evident that a broad foundation for the Presbyterian Church was laid from the beginning. The English Puritans were all Calvinists, and many of them Presbyterians. The Dutch were Calvinists and Presbyterians; a moiety, at least of the Germans were of the same class. All the French Protestants were Calvinists and Presbyterians, and so, of course, were the Scotch and Irish.[9]

PLANTING OF PRESBYTERIANISM IN THE BACK COUNTRY

A third and somewhat later development was what is known as the back country of the South, which stretched from the Potomac south to Georgia along the Appalachian chain of mountains, including the piedmont to the east of the Blue Ridge, and the Valley of Virginia, which lies between the Blue Ridge and the Allegheny mountains, and East Tennessee, which lies west of the first range of the Appalachians.

The Back Parts consisted of an irregularly shaped area running southwest from Mason and Dixon's line for more than 600 miles to just beyond the southern banks of the Savannah River and varying from 20 to 160 miles in width. Beginning west of the Monocacy River with Frederick County, Maryland, it included the Great Valley and that portion of the Virginia Piedmont west of a line from Charlottesville due south to the North Carolina boundary, as well as the North and South Carolina Piedmont between the fall line and the Great Smokies. In extent this was the largest territory from the Chesapeake and Carolina countries combined.[10]

Prior to 1730 the backcountry was virtually unoccupied. By the beginning of the War for Independence, it was occupied by more than a million inhabitants. It was settled largely by Scotch-Irish and Germans. In the Valley of Virginia, the Scotch-Irish settled from Augusta County south to Big Lick (Roanoke). From there the stream of settlers divided, with many going southward into the piedmont area of North Carolina, and then westward along the foot of the mountains into South Carolina and Georgia. The other

---

9. Charles Hodge, *Constitutional History of the Presbyterian Church in the United States of America* (Philadelphia: William S. Martien, 1839), 59.

10. Carl Bridenbaugh, *Myths and Realities: Societies of the Colonial South* (Baton Rouge: Louisiana State University Press, 1952), 120.

stream proceeded southwesterly through what is now southwest Virginia into East Tennessee. With them came the Presbyterian Church into both of these regions. Included in these Scotch-Irish streams were the ancestors of Andrew Jackson, John C. Calhoun, Abraham Lincoln, and Jefferson Davis.

Thompson describes the Scotch-Irish thus:

> But the Scotch-Irish were more venturesome than the Germans, more venturesome indeed than any other people who had come hitherto to America. Their earliest groups settled near Martinsburg and Shepherd-stown in present-day West Virginia; others along the Opequon and Ca-capon creeks in the vicinity of Winchester. The great majority, however, moved farther up the Valley. While the Germans congregated near the lower end of the Valley, the Scotch-Irish pushed on in larger numbers to its farther extremities and on through the water gaps of the Blue Ridge into the Piedmont. Within a dozen years there were "congregations" of Presbyterians at points in Berkeley, Jefferson, Hardy, Rockingham, Augusta, Rockbridge, Botetourt, Charlotte, Prince Edward, and Campbell counties. By 1775 the had settled on the barks of the Holston and the Clinch and stood at the threshold of the Cumberland Gap.[11]

Between 1725 and 1776 a major migration of Scotch-Irish came to America. Some entered by way of New York and New England. Others came through Charleston and settled Williamsburg, South Carolina, but by far the largest stream came via the Delaware River through New Castle or Philadelphia. Some 30,000 came between 1771 and 1773. By the beginning of the War for Independence, there were some 500,000 Scotch-Irish in America, about one-sixth of the entire population. Most of these immigrants were Presbyterians, and this period saw the rapid development of the Presbyterian Church on these shores.

From 1750 on a steady stream flowed into the colony, drawn by the favorable reports of the pioneers and encouraged by the colonial authorities, who hoped that they would protect the older communities from the Indians. They came driving their cattle, hogs, and horses before them, until the whole country from what is now Raleigh to Morganton was filled with them. Meanwhile other Scotch-Irish pioneers turned westward from the fertile plains of North Carolina into the wilderness beyond the mountains,

---

11. Thompson, *Presbyterians in the South*, 1:46.

where later, along the banks of the Watauga, French Broad, and Clinch, would be laid the foundations of the present state of Tennessee.

By 1750 the stream had begun to flow into the South Carolina Piedmont and into upland Georgia. In 1768 a missionary from the Synod of New York and Philadelphia discovered thirty-eight Presbyterian settlements in South Carolina and five Presbyterian settlements in Georgia, possessing from twenty to five hundred families each.[12]

With the coming of the large migration of the Scotch-Irish, pressure was brought on Virginia to allow these new settlers to have freedom of conscience to worship God according their own understanding. Many of the Scots and of the Scotch-Irish had migrated to America to be able to worship freely, without governmental interference.

Of particular interest was the migration of John Caldwell, an immigrant from Northern Ireland, who was a ruling elder in one of the Pennsylvania Churches, to what is now Charlotte County, Virginia, east of the Blue Ridge. It was Caldwell who initiated the action in the Synod of the Presbyterian Church that resulted in correspondence with the governor of Virginia.[13] Upon a motion made by ruling elder John Caldwell, the Synod of the Presbyterian Church recognized the need for an open policy by Virginia adopted a resolution, which was addressed to the governor of Virginia. The letter was carefully framed.

To the honourable William Gooch, Esquire, Lieutenant Governor of the Province of Virginia, the humble address of the Presbyterian ministers convened in Synod, May 28th, 1738 &c.

May it please your honour, we take leave to address you in behalf of a considerable number of our brethren who are meditating a settlement in the remote parts of your government, and are of the same persuasion with The Church of Scotland. We thought it our duty to acquaint your honour with their design, and to ask your favor in allowing them the liberty of their consciences, and of worshipping God in a way agreeable to the principles of their education. Your honour is sensible that those of our profession in Europe have been remarkable for their inviolable attachment to the Protestant succession, in the illustrious house of Hanover, and have upon all occasions manifested an unspotted fidelity to our gracious

12. Ibid., 1:47.
13. John Caldwell was the ancestor of John Caldwell Calhoun.

sovereign King George, and we doubt but these our brethren will carry the same loyal principles to the most distant settlements where their lot may be cast, which will ever be influence them to the most dutiful submission to our government which is placed over them. This we trust will recommend them to your honour's countenance and protection and merit the free enjoyment of their civil and religious liberties. We pray for the Divine blessing upon your person and government, and beg leave to subscribe ourselves your honour's most humble and obedient servants.[14]

This synod sent the letter by the hand of the Rev. James Anderson, who had served pastorates in New York and Pennsylvania. Major William Gooch (1681–1751) came to Virginia as Lieutenant Governor in 1727. According to William Henry Foote, his roots were in Scotland, and he had been educated there.[15] He had a twenty-two year regime as governor, which was generally peaceful. During his governorship, the western parts of Virginia were opened. "Although his predecessor, Alexander Spotswood, led the Knights of the Golden Horseshoe into the Shenandoah Valley, it was William Gooch's policy as governor which really opened the way for westward development of the colony."[16] A recent Virginia historian observes, "It was official policy at Williamsburg to invite members of dissenting faiths into the trans mountain region. The colonial government realized, among other things, that the fighting Scotch-Irish, in particular, would be extremely useful on the frontier as bulwarks against the Indians and the French."[17]

Upon receipt of the letter from the Presbyterian Synod, Governor Gooch sent Mr. Anderson back with a letter addressed to the Synod of Philadelphia, dated November 4, 1738.

... And as I have always inclined to favor the people who have lately removed from other provinces, to settle on the western side of our great

---

14. "Minutes of the Synod of Philadelphia, 1719–1724." *Minutes of the Presbyterian Church in America 1706–1788*, edited Guy S. Klett (Philadelphia: Presbyterian Historical Society, 1976), 158 (language modernized).

15. Richard L. Morton, recognized as a good historian, in his *Colonial Virginia* quotes Foote to this effect, and makes no comment on the accuracy of the statement. The present author has not been able to verify this statement. Morton does seem to have been familiar with the Westminster Confession as the doctrinal standard of the Presbyterians.

16. Katharine L. Brown, *New Providence Church, 1746–1996, A History* (Raphine, VA: New Providence Presbyterian Church, 1996), 23.

17. *Virginia, The New Dominion* (New York, Doubleday & Company, Inc., 1971), 99.

mountains; so you may be assured, that no interruption shall be given to any minister of your profession who shall come among them, so as they conform themselves to the rules prescribed by the act of toleration in England by taking the oaths enjoined thereby, and registering the places of their meeting, and behave themselves peaceably towards the government.[18]

The three requirements of the governor reflect the Act of Toleration in England adopted in 1689.

This correspondence between the Presbyterian Church and the governor of Virginia took place prior to the division of the church between the Old Side and New Side, which took place in 1741. This division was the result of different views toward the Great Awakening and the Log College. The undivided Presbyterian Church had planted churches in Virginia. The earliest church in the Valley of Virginia was Opeckon, near present-day Winchester, Joist Hite moved there from Pennsylvania with a number of Presbyterian families. In 1735, William Hoge moved from Pennsylvania to Opeckon. The first meetinghouse was built on property he gave for the purpose. On the east side of the Blue Ridge, there was a settlement in Albermarle County, and also the Buffalo and Cub Creek Churches in Prince Edward, and Charlotte Counties.

The Old Stone Augusta Church, near Staunton, was settled by the Rev. John Craig in 1740. He also pastored the Tinkling Springs Church near present-day Fishersville. Alexander Miller came to assist the work in Augusta County. These were from Donegal Presbytery, which remained in the Old Side Church. John Thompson served in the Valley for a while, and then at Buffalo Church, near Farmville. He was also Old Side. Wesley Gewehr said of these congregations:

> The four settled ministers in the western counties belonged to the Old Side Presbytery of Donegal in Pennsylvania, and they were not apostles of the Great Awakening which was extending over the colonies in the decade of the 'forties. As we have seen, their group represented the strict wing of the Church and was opposed to many features of the great religious revival. It remained, therefore, for others to carry into the Old Dominion those ideas which were to make Presbyterianism an evangelical force. These were

18. "Minutes of the Synod," 168.

the New Light missionaries of the school of the Tennents and Whitefield. Their chief successes were in eastern Virginia, which they made the real center of the Great Awakening in the South.[19]

A number of the New Side ministers visited the Scotch-Irish settlements on both sides of the Blue Ridge in Virginia. They included Samuel and John Blair, John Roan, Samuel Finley, and Gilbert and William Tennent. In 1746 John Bair organized churches at North Mountain, Timber Ridge and the Forks of the James, all in Augusta County (now Rockbridge County). In 1741, William Robinson, who had been ordained by New Brunswick Presbytery (the mother Presbytery of the New Side Church), was sent to visit western Virginia and North Carolina. He came in 1743 to Hanover County, where there were a number of individuals who had been affected by the preaching of Whitefield, and were holding meetings to read sermons of Whitefield and Luther's commentary on Galatians. Robinson's visit was "momentous." "Hitherto missionary activities of the Presbyterian Church had been confined to Presbyterian communities. But in Hanover, Presbyterianism entered into a larger work; it was the first church to bring the revival and so to break the hold of the Establishment in eastern Virginia."[20] The result was the call of Samuel Davies, who was educated by Samuel Blair at Faggs Manor, to become pastor of these dissenters. His labors extended from the Pole Green Church in Hanover to Cub Creek in Charlotte County. On December 3, 1755, Hanover Presbytery was formed at the Pole Green Church in Hanover County. "The new presbytery included the greater part of Virginia (the churches in the lower Valley belonged to Donegal Presbytery) and extended indefinitely to the south and west. Except for the independent and languishing presbytery in the Carolina lowlands, it was the first presbytery to be organized in any of the Southern colonies. From it the Southern Presbyterian Church was in large part to take its rise."[21] With the healing of the division between the Old and New Side Churches in 1758, the earlier Old Side Churches in Virginia of Donegal Presbytery were incorporated into Hanover Presbytery.

---

19. Wesley M. Gewehr, *The Great Awakening in Virginia, 1740–1790* (Durham, NC: Duke University Press, 1930), 45.

20. Thompson, *Presbyterians in the South*, 1:53.

21. Ibid., 1:59.

Under the leadership of John Caldwell, a number of Scotch-Irish established the Buffalo congregation in Prince Edward County, and Cub Creek Church in Charlotte County. These congregations were to become a part of the first presbytery in the South. When Samuel Davies came to Hanover under the direction of Newcastle Presbytery of the New Side Presbyterian Church, being aware of the charges leveled against John Roan for preaching without a license, he went first to Williamsburg to petition the General Court for a license to minister in Hanover at four meeting houses. The license was granted on April 14, 1747:

> On petition of Samuel Davies a Dissenting Minister, who, this day in Court took the usual oaths to his Majesty's person and government, and subscribed the Test, and likewise publicly declared his assent thereunto, he is allowed to assembly and meet any congregation of Dissenters, at the several meeting-houses, on the lands of Samuel Morris, David Rice, and Stephen Leacy, in Hanover county, and on the lands of Thomas Watkins in Henrico county, without molestation, they behaving in a peaceable manner, and conforming themselves according to the directions of the acts of parliament in that behalf made.[22]

Thus we see the recognition by the government of the colony of Virginia of the Presbyterians as falling under the protection of the Act of Toleration. Samuel Davies established the first presbytery in Virginia in December, 1755. This was the mother presbytery of all of the Southern Presbyterian presbyteries. It included the whole of the Virginia colony.

Francis Makemie stands as the father of the Presbyterian Church in America, Davies as the apostle of Virginia.

> To no one man in a religious point of view, does the State owe as much; no one can claim a more affectionate remembrance by Christian people. His residence in the State is an era in its history.... The sole supremacy of Christ in the Church—the authority of the Word of God—the equality of the ministers of religion,—and individual rights of conscience—principles for which he pled before the General Court ... are now a part and parcel of the religious and political creed of an overwhelming majority of the citizens of the "Ancient Dominion."[23]

22. Foote, cited in Ibid., 160.
23. William Henry Foote, *Sketches of Virginia, Historical and Biographical* (1850; repr., Richmond: John Knox Press, 1966), 1:304.

The Presbyterian Church Organized

The First Presbytery

The first organization of Presbyterianism in America took place, a century after the first settlement at Jamestown, under the leadership of the Rev. Francis Makemie, who came to America in 1683. He was of Scottish ancestry and a graduate of the University of Edinburgh during the "killing time" in Scotland. He was received by the Presbytery of Laggan in Northern Ireland in 1680 and ordained as a missionary to America in 1681, after professing "his adherence to the truth professed in the Reformed Churches against 'Popery, Arminianism, prelacy, Erastianism, Independency and whatever else is contrary to sound doctrine and the power of godliness.' "[24]

His first ministry on American shores was in the present Norfolk, Virginia, area. The first organized Presbyterian congregation there was registered with Makemie, called a dissenter minister, August 15, 1692. This congregation did not continue. He later settled in Accomac County, Virginia, on the Eastern Shore. He received a license to preach from the County of Accomac, on the basis of a similar license he had received in Barbados. His home in Pocomoke and another house he owned in Onancock were designated as preaching points. During this period, he published a Catechism expounding the faith of the Westminster Confession. He founded the Rehoboth and Snow Hill Churches in Maryland, which still exist. He also established four other churches, namely, Manokin, Wicomico, Pitts Creek, and Buckingham.

Makemie returned to England to gain support and to recruit two other ministers to come to America with him. They were John Hampton of Northern Ireland and George McNish of Scotland. They were eventually licensed in Maryland and took charge of four of the six churches Makemie had founded. In 1706 Makemie, Hampton, and McNish, together with a Mr. Taylor of Maryland, and three other ministers, Jeddidiah Andrews of Philadelphia, John Wilson, and Samuel Davis of Delaware formed a presbytery, called by Makemie "A Meeting of Ministers."

Charles Augustus Briggs describes the nature of American Presbyterianism thus:

24. As cited by Thompson, *Presbyterians in the South*, 1:21.

The American Presbyterian Church began historically at the bottom, and only by degrees did it rise into the magnificent system which we now behold. It was not a reconstruction of an old Papal system into a new Presbyterian system, as in Scotland. It was a free and natural growth in accordance with the preferences of the congregations themselves. American Presbyterianism was born and nurtured and reached its maturity in freedom. It developed naturally in accordance with the circumstances of the country. It was not imposed upon the people by civil or ecclesiastical tribunals.[25]

Briggs speaks later of the fact that the interest of Presbyterians in religious liberty grew out of struggle against injustice and tyranny, "It was the external struggle against civil injustice and tyranny, and the internal struggle with narrowness, intolerance, and bigotry that made Presbyterianism in America the champion of civil and religious."[26]

The first page of the record of "A Meeting of Ministers" is missing, and thus the basis of their union is not known, though it is clear that all were committed Presbyterians, and no doubt intended to include only such as agreed with them. The first of the remaining pages of minutes record the trials and ordination of Mr. John Boyd, which took place in December, 1706. He was a native of Scotland and labored at Freehold and Middletown, New Jersey, where he died, in 1708. It appears from the record that there were some fifteen congregations associated with this first presbytery; two were in Virginia, six in Maryland, five in Pennsylvania and Delaware, and two in New Jersey.

The basis of the union of the presbytery is unknown, due to the loss of the first page of the minutes. It has been suggested that it was based on the personal knowledge that the men had of each other. They would have known each other as all being Presbyterians in accord with the Westminster Confession from their earlier meeting for the ordination of Jedidiah Andrews. They were now meeting more formally, and determined to have annual meetings. Knowing each other to be in accord with the Westminster Standards, it may be assumed that some commitment to these standards would have been the basis of their union. It has been suggested that since

---

25. Charles Augustus Briggs, *American Presbyterianism, Its Origin and Early History Together with an Appendix of Letters and Documents, Many of Which Have Recently Been Discovered*, (New York: Charles Scribner's Sons, 1885), 131.

26. Ibid., 289

they regarded themselves as a branch of the Church of Scotland, there was no need for a formal adoption of a constitution.[27]

Makemie speaks of his own ordination,

> I am constrained to justify my office from these uncharitable calumnies, and, that grace might be magnified, by giving this relation, in the sight of an all-seeing and all-present God; that, ere I received the imposition of hands, in that scriptural and orderly way of separation unto my holy and ministerial calling, I gave requiring satisfaction, to godly, learned and judicious discerning men, of a work of grace and conversion wrought in my heart, by the Holy Spirit, in my fourteenth year, by and from the pains of a godly schoolmaster, who used no small diligence in gaining tender souls to God's service and fear; since which time, to the glory of God's free grace be it spoke, I have had the sure experiences of God's dealings with me, according to his infinite and unerring wisdom, for my unspeakable comfort.[28]

If it is accurate to affirm that they considered themselves as a branch of the Church of Scotland, then the matter of subscription to the Westminster Standards was assumed. They make no mention of this understanding in letters addressed to the Church or Scotland or of Ireland. John Thompson, when he argued for the adoption of the standards (see below) says that he did not know of any binding doctrinal standards to be in existence in the American Church.

Though the records are silent on the question of subscription, it is quite clear that the distinct design of the fathers of our church, in organizing themselves into a presbytery, was the erection of an evangelical society to serve as organ for the propagation of the gospel in America. In a letter, addressed to Sir Edmund Harrison of London, in May, 1709, they set forth the deplorable spiritual condition of the colonies and urged the Christian people of London to come to their help:

> The negotiation begun and encouraged by a fund, in the time when our worthy friend, Mr. Makemie, now deceased, was with you, for evangeliz-

---

27. Unknown author from Web page entitled "History of American Presbyterianism, Lesson 1: The Adopting Act," http://www.americanpresbyterianchurch.org/the_adopting_act.htm (accessed March 31, 2008).

28. Francis Makemie, *An Answer to George Keith's Libel agaist a Catechism Published by Francis Makemie*, (Boston: Benjamin Harris, 1694) found in Boyd S. Schlenther, *The Life and Writings of Francis Makemie*, (Philadelphia: The Presbyterian Historical Society, 1971), 52.

ing these colonies, was a business exceeding acceptable to a multitude of people, and was likely to have been of great service, if continued; which makes us much grieved that so valuable a design was so soon after its beginning, laid aside. The necessity of carrying on the same affair being as great, if not greater, now, than it was then, we hope that our patrons in London will revive good and important a work, and not let it lie buried under the ashes.... That our evangelical affairs may be the better managed, we have formed ourselves into a Presbytery, annually to be convened at this city; at which times, it is a sore distress and trouble unto us, that we are not able to comply with the desires of sundry places, crying unto us for ministers, to deal forth the word of life unto them. Therefore, we must earnestly beseech you, in the bowels of our Lord, to intercede with the ministers of London, and other well-affected gentlemen, to extend their charity and pity to us, and to carry on so necessary and glorious a work.[29]

The presbytery considered itself an evangelical society, designed to spread the gospel throughout America. By forming into a presbytery, it was their intent to conduct their affairs under their own supervision, without having to depend upon the churches in Great Britain. Their appeals to the Presbytery of Dublin, to the London ministers, and to the Synod of Glasgow was not that of subjection to them, but an appeal for more ministers, and for financial support to carry out their mission.

Following the formation of the presbytery, Makemie visited New York, where he preached a sermon at the invitation of some of the residents of the city. He was arrested and charged with breaking the laws of New York. His case was carried over a year. He wrote a letter defending the right to preach.

William Henry Foote gives an assessment of Francis Makemie:

Looking at him as he appears in Virginia, aside from his education, he appears to be the most singular man of his day; his course cannot be well understood. That he had principles of religion and morality of great energy and unchangeable power is evident. And it is equally evident that they were not, what was malignancy, or in more modern times, radicalism, or personal ambition, or enthusiasm, or bigotry, or Jesuitical adherence to party. The current of his life flowed like a pure stream from an abiding equable fountain.[30]

29. *Minutes of the Presbyterian Church*, 73.
30. Foote, *Sketches of Virginia*, 1:85.

Elsewhere Foote says, "The facts and principles that sustained Makemie in Somerset and Accomack have been felt through all the South and West. He stands first in the list of names that shine as a galaxy in the Ecclesiastical horizon; and as a defender of civil liberty and equal rights in America he had no superior."[31] This is high praise indeed regarding one who is only remembered for having started the first American presbytery.

Boyd S. Schlenther gives the following assessment of Makemie as the "father of American Presbyterianism: "In his twenty-five years in the New World Francis Makemie had become colonial Presbyterianism's chief exponent, its leading literary apologist, main defender of its liberties, foremost overseer of its congregations, and the moving force in the formation of its first presbytery."[32]

Charles Hodge argued for the orthodoxy of the first presbytery:

> As it regards doctrines, the point to be ascertained is whether the Presbyterian church was a Calvinistic body, and required adherence to that system of doctrines as a condition of ministerial communion, or whether it demanded nothing more than assent to the essential doctrines of the gospel. . . . That our church has from the beginning required adherence to Calvinism as a condition of ministerial communion, can be made very clearly to appear. It is admitted that the Presbytery required of its members what it considered soundness in the faith, or orthodoxy. The only question then is, what was orthodoxy in the estimation of the founders of the church? Was it faith in the essential doctrines of the gospel? or was it faith in that system of doctrines, which, for convenience' sake, has obtained the name of Calvinism? . . . It seems a matter of supererogation to prove that men educated towards the close of the seventeenth, or the beginning of the eighteenth century, in Scotland, Ireland, or New England, regarded Calvinism as the true doctrine of the Scriptures, and considered any essential deviation for it as a disqualification for the work of the ministry. . . . It is to be remembered that the great majority of the early ministers of our church were either ordained or licensed before they became connected with it. The very testimonials, which they brought with them, if they came from Scotland or Ireland, stated explicitly that they had adopted

31. Ibid., p. 63, Foote gives a full account of Makemie's trial in New York to demonstrate his stand for freedom.

32. Boyd S. Schlenther, ed., *The Life and Writings of Francis Makemie* (Philadelphia: The Presbyterian Historical Society, 1971), 28.

the Westminster Confession of Faith; if they came from New England, they brought evidence of their Calvinism just as unequivocal. . . .

The single consideration then, that all the early ministers of our church came from places where Calvinism not only prevailed, but where it was strenuously insisted upon, is, in the absence of any evidence to the contrary, sufficient to prove that they were not so singular, or so much in advance of the spirit of their age, as to bring down their demands to the low standard of absolutely essential doctrines. . . . There can be no stronger evidence of the Calvinistic character of the church, than that the new test of orthodoxy was universally admitted, and that there was not a single member of the Synod who objected to any article in the [Westminster] Confession of Faith except that which related to the power of the civil magistrate in matters of religion. That article was by common consent discarded; all the others were cordially adopted.[33]

This first presbytery was divided into four in 1716 to form the first Presbyterian Synod in America. This was necessary due to the increased number of congregations and the geographical spread of the Church. In 1717 the first meeting of the synod took place. The synod was composed of the Presbyteries of Long Island, Philadelphia, New Castle (Maryland and Delaware), and Snow Hill (Eastern Shore of Maryland). This last presbytery appears never to have been formally organized. Presbyterianism had not prospered in Maryland after 1690, when the Church of England became the established Church of the Colony. Many of the Puritans and Presbyterians of Maryland conformed to the Church of England. There were no churches south of Maryland now a part of this Synod. The Makemie churches of Accomac County, Virginia, had not survived after his death. The church on the Elizabeth River was without pastor and had never associated itself with the presbytery or synod.

The Expanding Church

As we have seen above, the first presbytery was formed in 1706 at Philadelphia. Other than the isolated groups in eastern North Carolina, the lowlands of South Carolina, and a few isolated congregations in Maryland and Virginia, the Presbyterian church was not well established in the South

33. Hodge, *Constitutional History*, 84–88.

411

at the time of the founding of the first presbytery. This was largely due to the fact that the southern colonies established the Church of England. In this section I shall consider something of the expansion of the Presbyterian church, particularly as it affected the South.

To begin with William Tennent's Log College at Neshaminy in Pennsylvania may seem a strange starting place to consider the growth of the church, particularly in the South. As one recognizes the impact of the Log College, and the various academies that sprang up, which fed a good number of men into the ranks of the ministry of the Presbyterian Church, the relevance of these schools becomes apparent. This, coupled with the Great Awakening and the subsequent revivals, which spread through the South, became a major factor in the growth of Presbyterianism in these regions.

The Log College

In 1726 William Tennent was settled at the Neshaminy Presbyterian Church in Bucks County, Pennsylvania, about twenty-eight miles north of Philadelphia, on the road between Philadelphia and New York. He had four sons whom had been educating for the ministry. With his move to Neshaminy, he built a log building approximately twenty feet square in which to conduct classes, not only for his sons, but also for other young men interested in entering the ministry. Archibald Alexander speaks of this building thus: "Though humble and even despicable in its external appearance, [it] was an institution of unspeakable importance to the Presbyterian church, in this country."[34] This was the first school designed for the education of Presbyterian ministers on the American shores. Prior to this all the ministers of the American Presbyterian Church had been educated either in Scotland, Ireland, or New England. Tennent himself had been educated in Ireland. Among those who attended the Log College were Tennent's four sons: Gilbert, William Jr., John, and Charles. Others who attended were Samuel Blair, John Blair, Samuel Finley, William Robinson, John Rowland, Charles Beatty, Samuel Davis, John Rodgers, Alexander McWhorter, Alexander Cumming, and James Waddell.[35]

---

34. Archibald Alexander, *Biographical Sketches of the Founder, and Principal Alumni of the Log College* (Princeton: J. T. Robinson, 1845), 22.

35. Thomas Murphy, *Presbytery of the Log College* (Philadelphia: Presbyterian Board of Publication and Sabbath-School Work, 1889), 78.

Alexander describes the spiritual condition of the American Presbyterian churches at that time:

It may be proper to remark, in this place, that from all the accounts which we have, it appears, that at this time, the state of vital piety was very low in the Presbyterian church in America. And the same was true of the churches in New England. And this was remarkably the fact in regard to Great Britain. The ministers composing the Presbyterian church, in this country, were sound in the faith, and strongly attached to the Westminster Confession of Faith and Catechisms, as were also their people; and there were no diversities or contentions among them respecting the doctrines of the gospel; but as to the vital power of godliness, there is reason to believe, that it was little known or spoken of. Revivals of religion were nowhere heard of, and an orthodox creed, and a decent external conduct were the only points on which inquiry was made, when persons were admitted to the communion of the church. Indeed, it was very much a matter of course for all who had been baptized in infancy, to be received into full communion at the proper age, without exhibiting or possessing any satisfactory evidence of a change of heart, by the supernatural operations of the Holy Spirit. And the habit of the preachers was, to address their people as though they were all pious, and only needing instruction and confirmation. It was not a common thing to denounce the terrors of a violated law, and to insist on the absolute necessity of regeneration. Under such a state of things, it is easy to conceive, that in a short time vital piety may have almost deserted the church, and that formality and "dead orthodoxy" be all that was left of religion. And nothing is more certain, than that when people have sunk into this deplorable state, they will be disposed to manifest strong opposition to faithful, pointed preaching; and will be apt to view every appearance of revival with an unfavorable eye. Accordingly, when God raised up preachers, animated with a burning zeal, who laboured faithfully to convince their hearers of their ruined condition, and of the necessity of a thorough conversion from sin, the opposition to them, both in Great Britain and this country, was violent. The gospel, among people in such a condition, is sure to produce strife and division, between those who fall under its influence, and those whose carnal minds urge them to oppose it. It was in such a state of the church that Mr. Tennent came to this country. What his own course of religious experience had been, we have no information; but he seems to have imbibed a warm, evangelical spirit, and to have been, in this country, distinguished for his zeal and efforts in promoting vital piety. [36]

We are indebted to the journals of George Whitefield, who visited with William Tennent on his trips to Philadelphia, for a first hand description of the Log College and its activities. Alexander gives the following account of the contact between Tennent and Whitefield:

> When Mr. Whitefield first visited Philadelphia, Mr. Tennent lost no time in calling upon him. Though he lived nearly thirty miles from Philadelphia, yet no sooner did he hear of the arrival of this evangelical and successful preacher, than taking with him some of his pious friends, he repaired to the city, and from Mr. Whitefield's Journal, we learn, that the visit was very acceptable to him; for he says, "At my return home, [from visiting a family] was much comforted by the coming of one Mr. Tennent, an old gray-headed disciple and soldier of Jesus Christ. He keeps an academy about twenty miles from Philadelphia, and has been blessed with four gracious sons, three of which have been, and still continue to be, eminently useful in the church of Christ. He brought three pious souls along with him, and rejoiced me by letting me know how they had been spoken evil of for their Master's sake. He is a great friend of Mr. Erskine, of Scotland; and as far as I can learn, both he and his sons, are secretly despised by the generality of the synod, as Mr. Erskine and his friends are hated by the judicatories of Edinburgh, and as the Methodist preachers (as they are called) are, by their brethren in England." This testimony of Mr. Whitefield goes to show, that the course pursued by old Mr. Tennent and his sons, was different from that of the other ministers of the synod, to whom he stood in the same relation, as Whitefield, Wesley, and their coadjutors, to the great body of the clergy in England. Mr. Whitefield, on his return from New York, went to Neshaminy, and spent some days with Mr. Tennent.[37]

Here again we are glad to have the opportunity of using the very words of Whitefield.

> Nov. 22. [1739.] Set out for Neshaminy, (twenty miles distant from Trent Town,) where old Mr. Tennent lives, and keeps an academy, and where I

36. Ibid., 22–24.
37. Alexander, *Log College*, 18.

414

was to preach, today, according to appointment. About 12 [o'clock] we came thither, and found about three thousand people gathered together, in the meeting-house yard. Mr. William Tennent, [jr.] an eminent servant of JESUS CHRIST, because we staid beyond the time appointed, was preaching to them. When I came up, he soon stops; sung a psalm, and then I began to speak, as the Lord gave me utterance. At first, the people seemed unaffected, but in the midst of my discourse, the power of the LORD JESUS came upon me, and I felt such a struggling within myself for the people, as I scarce ever felt before. The hearers began to be melted down immediately, and to cry much; and we had good reason to hope the LORD intended good for many. After I had finished, Mr. Gilbert Tennent gave a word of exhortation, to confirm what had been delivered. At the end of his discourse, we sung a psalm, and dismissed the people with a blessing, O that the people may say amen to it! After our exercises were over we went to old Mr. Tennent's, who entertained us like one of the ancient patriarchs. His wife, to me seemed like Elizabeth, and he like Zachary; both, as far as I can learn, well, in all the commandments and ordinances of the LORD—blameless. Though God was pleased to humble my soul, so that I was obliged to retire for a while; yet we had sweet communion with each other, and spent the evening in concerting what measures had best be taken, for promoting our dear LORD'S kingdom. It happened very providentially, that Mr. Tennent and his brethren are appointed to be a presbytery, by the synod, so that they intend bringing up gracious youths, and sending them out from time to time, into the LORD'S vineyard. The place, wherein the young men study now is, in contempt, called, THE COLLEGE, &c. Friday, Nov. 23, parted with dear Mr. Tennent, and his other worthy fellow-labourers; but promised to remember each other publicly in our prayers.[38]

From the preceding extract we see that William Tennent was highly regarded by George Whitefield. It is evident that they held similar views regarding the gospel. Tennent was openly in favor of the Great Awakening. He was a classical scholar, which was recognized by his contemporaries. The Hon. Elias Boudinot, LL.D., who knew him well, says, "that he was well skilled in the Latin language, that he could speak and converse in it with as much facility, as in his vernacular tongue, and also, that he was a proficient in the other ancient languages."[39]

38. Ibid., 19.
39. Ibid., 27.

Alexander assesses William Tennent's work in the following words:

Mr. Tennent, as far as we know, never published any thing. We have, therefore, no means of ascertaining his abilities as a writer; but the benefit he conferred on the church by his school can never be forgotten. The Presbyterian church is probably not more indebted for her prosperity, and for the evangelical spirit that has generally pervaded her body, to any individual, than to the elder Tennent. Some men accomplish much more by those whom they educate, than by their own personal labours. This should be an encouragement to such ministers as are obliged to resort to teaching for their own support. If they are so favored as to be the means of bringing forward a few pious youth, and preparing them for the ministry, they may do more good than if their whole lives had been spent in doing nothing else but preaching the Gospel. And it is good policy for Presbyterian ministers to establish schools, in their charges, wherever they are needed. And this they may do, without subjecting themselves to the drudgery of teaching, all the time. Pious young men might be found, to whom such a situation would be a favor. And such institutions are often necessary to enable a minister to educate his own sons. When the means of acquiring a liberal education are brought to the doors of the people, many will avail themselves of the privilege, who would never have thought of going abroad for the same purpose. The truth of this remark has been verified in almost every place where a good school has been established.[40]

Other Academies and Their Graduates

The academy idea spread through the graduates of the Log College. Many of them established their own academies at the churches they served. One such academy that was to affect the South was the one established by Samuel Blair at Faggs Manor Church between West Chester and Oxford, Pennsylvania. Faggs Manor Academy was a classical college and theological seminary similar to the Log College. It grew rapidly, and became a source of great blessings at that time. Its influence was extended very widely. Among its graduates were Samuel Davies, Alexander Cumming, John Rodgers, James Finley, and Hugh Henry.

Robert Smith, a graduate of Faggs Manor who married the sister of Samuel Blair, founded Pequa Academy. Among the graduates of Pequa were

40. Alexander, *Log College*, 22–23.

John Caldwell, who settled in Charlotte County, Virginia, Samuel Stanhope Smith, and John Blair Smith, sons of Robert Smith. The Smiths became the first and second presidents of Hampden-Sydney College in Virginia.

William Robinson was trained at the Log College. He became an itinerant preacher who made extended tours to the South:

> Like a bright meteor he swept over the land, blazing in the light of God wherever he went. Through the sparsely settle regions of Pennsylvania, away to its western forests, through the whole of New Jersey, Delaware, and Maryland, and down the Great Valley of Virginia, and over the Blue Ridge region, through Albermarle and Augusta and other counties of the same state, through many of the larger towns of North Carolina, he hastened. To the Indians wherever he could find them, to terrified settlers flying from the butchery of the savages, to noisy gatherings of the Negroes, he pressed with the tidings of salvation."[41]

In 1743 he was invited to Hanover, Virginia, where he began preaching on four successive days. An eyewitness account says, "There is reason to believe there was as much good done by those four sermons as by all the sermons preached in these parts before or since."[42]

John Blair, the brother of Samuel Blair, served at Faggs Manor for nine years. He then went to Princeton to serve as acting president until John Witherspoon came from Scotland. Samuel Finley was born Northern Ireland in 1715 of Scottish descent. He came to America at the age of nineteen. He attended the Log College. He was licensed in 1740 and served as an evangelist in New Jersey. In 1744, at the age of twenty-nine, he accepted the call of the church at Nottingham, Maryland, a church later served by A. A. Hodge. In 1761 Finley was elected to the presidency of Princeton College. Archibald Alexander describes the academy at Nottingham:

> In this place he instituted an academy, with the view, chiefly, of preparing young men for the gospel ministry. This school was conducted with admirable wisdom and success, and acquired a higher reputation than any other in the Middle States, so that students from a distance were attracted to it.

41. Ibid.

42. William B. Sprague, *Annals of the American Pulpit or Commemorative Notices of Distinguished American Clergymen of Various Denominations* (New York: Robert Carter and Brothers, 1858), 3:93.

Some of the most distinguished men in our country laid the foundation of their eminence and usefulness in this academy. At one time there was a cluster of such young men who all were afterward distinguished, and some of them among the very first men in the country, as the following names will show: Governor Martin of North Carolina; Dr. Benjamin Rush of Philadelphia; the Rev. James Waddel, D.D., of Virginia; Governor Henry of Maryland; and the Rev. William M. Tennent of Abington, Pennsylvania. It would not be easy in any country to find such a constellation in one school at the same time.[43]

Samuel Davies was educated by Samuel Blair at Faggs Manor Academy. Davies may properly be called the "Father of Southern Presbyterianism," since his labors brought about the establishment of the mother presbytery of the South, namely, Hanover Presbytery. He labored in Virginia from 1747 to 1759, and convened the first meeting of the Presbytery of Hanover on December 3, 1755, at the direction of the Synod of New York. The effect of his ministry was diffused over all of Virginia and North Carolina. He held the Westminster Confession and Catechisms in the highest esteem. It was his regular practice to teach the Shorter Catechism to all of his members and to have it recited at the worship service on Sunday.

William Henry Foote, writing a century later, in 1850, speaks of William Robinson and Samuel Davies and of their teachers, the Tennents and the Blairs, as laying a foundation that "had a controlling influence over Virginia Presbyterians in creed and practice" to his day. He says:

> From the time of these men, the Virginia ministers and people have believed in awakenings,—in spiritual exercises in religion,—in the power of godliness in men's hearts and lives. From deep conviction they have been believers in the depravity of human nature,—the sovereignty of God,— original sin,—and the absolute necessity of the new birth. Hoping for justification by the righteousness of Christ made theirs by faith, believing it would be safe to appear in it, in the judgment to come, ministers and people rejoiced in the unseachable riches of Christ, through trials and difficulties that would make ordinary spirits tremble and quit the field. By the help of God they have left us a good report.[44]

43. Alexander, *Log College*, 206.
44. Foote, *Sketches of Virginia*, 1:146.

In 1746 John Blair organized churches at North Mountain, New Providence, Timber Ridge, and the Fork of the James, which became the nucleus of Lexington Presbytery. It was out of the New Providence and Timber Ridge Churches that Liberty Hall Academy, the predecessor of Washington College (now Washington and Lee University), was to come. William Graham was the first presbytery-appointed teacher at the academy. He taught Archibald Alexander, the founding professor of Princeton Seminary. Others who came from this school were Moses Hoge, John Holt Rice, and George Addison Baxter. Hoge was the first professor of theology at Hampden-Sydney, appointed by the Synod of Virginia. Rice succeeded him, and founded Union Seminary. Baxter was professor of theology there at the time of the Old School-New School division of 1837.

The Old Side–New Side Division (1741–58)

A controversy arose that was to divide the church in 1741 between the Old Side Synod of Philadelphia and what later became the New Side Synod of New York. This division occurred, in part, as a result of the great revivals of George Whitefield and his followers and the development of the "log colleges" and academies for the training of ministers. Some historians have suggested that the New Side was looser in its theology, in the same way that the New School of the next century was, but this interpretation is highly suspect.[45]

Thomas Murphy, pastor of the Frankford Presbyterian Church of Philadelphia, in his *The Presbytery of the Log College: or, The Cradle of the Presbyterian Church in America* says this of the Old Side–New Side controversy:

> In the beginning it should be distinctly stated and understood that there were no doctrinal differences. This should be made the more emphatic from the disposition sometimes found to connect this first great division

45. See Leonard Trinterud, *The Forming of an American Tradition: A Re-examination of Colonial Presbyterianism* (Philadelphia: Westminster Press, 1949), who has been somewhat uncritically followed by historians like George M. Marsden, *The Evangelical Mind and the New School Presbyterian Experience* (New Haven, CT: Yale University Press, 1970), and D. G. Hart in *Colonial Presbyterianism: Old Faith in a New Land: Commemorating the 300th Anniversary of the First Presbytery in America*, ed. S. Donald Fortson, Princeton Theological Monograph Series 71 (Eugene, OR: Pickwick Publications, 2007).

of the Church with the subsequent one of the Old and New Schools. There was, in fact, no relation or connection whatever between the two, as many of those who sympathized with the New Light side in the first controversy were just as strong in their sympathy with the Old School side of the latter controversy, and the contrary. We repeat that there were no contentions about doctrines connected with this schism. We read of no such debates.[46]

One of the reasons for the division in 1741 was the non-Presbyterian conduct of some of the New Side men, who were promoting the revivals that has started under George Whitefield's visit to the area. Doctrinally the New Side group held to the full subscription to the Westminster Standards as reflected in the action of the first meeting of the separated presbyteries:

> A more important evidence is to be found in the 'Declaration of the conjunct Presbyteries of New Brunswick and New Castle,' issued immediately after the schism. Those Presbyteries say: 'We think it proper, for the satisfaction of all concerning us, and as a due testimony to the truth of God, to declare and testify to the world our principles and sentiments in religion, according to which we design, through divine grace, ever to conduct ourselves, both as Christians, and as ministers, and as ruling elders.
>
> And, first, as to the doctrines of religion, we believe with our heart, and profess and maintain with our lips, the doctrines summed up and contained in the Confession of Faith, and Larger and Shorter Catechisms, composed by the reverend assembly of divines at Westminster, as the truths of God revealed and contained in the holy Scriptures of the Old and New Testaments; and do receive, acknowledge, and declare the said Confession of Faith and Catechisms to be the confession of our faith; yet so as that no part of the twenty third chapter of said Confession shall be so construed as to allow civil magistrates, as such, to have any ecclesiastical authority in Synods, or church judicatories, much less the power of a negative voice over them in their ecclesiastical transactions; nor is any part of it to be understood as opposite to the memorable revolution and the settlement of the crown and of the three kingdoms in the illustrious house of Hanover.[47]

Hodge commented:

46. Murphy, *Presbytey of the Log College*, 158–59.
47. Hodge, *Constitutional History*, 2:189.

The exception here made to certain parts of the twenty-third chapter, proves the adoption of all the rest. This is as strict an adoption of the Confession of Faith as was ever made by any Synod in our church. Besides this decisive declaration, reference might be made to the fact, that during all the protracted negotiations for a union, there was not a word said about doctrinal differences. Each Synod spoke of the other as holding the same system of doctrines.[48]

It appears from this history that the great schism was not the result of conflicting views as to doctrine. It was the result of alienation of feeling produced by the controversies relating to the revival.[49]

When the Synod of New York was formed in 1745, the members agreed, *inter alia*, on the following plan and foundation of their synodical union:

They agree that the Westminster Confession of Faith, with the Larger and Shorter Catechisms, be the public confession of their faith in such manner as agreed unto by the Synod of Philadelphia, in the year 1729; and to be inserted in the latter end of this book. And they declare their approbation of the Directory of the Assembly of Divines at Westminster, as the general plan of worship and discipline.[50]

In 1751 the Synod of New York declared as follows:

The Synod being informed of certain misrepresentations concerning the constitution, order and discipline of our churches, industriously spread by some of the members of the Dutch congregations, interspersed among or bordering upon us, with design to prevent occasional or constant communion of their members with our churches; to obviate all such misrepresentations, and to cultivate a good understanding between us and our brethren of the Dutch churches, we do hereby declare and testify our constitution, order, and discipline, to be in harmony with the established church of Scotland. The Westminster Confession, Catechisms, and Directory for public worship and church government adopted by them, are in like manner received and adopted by us. We declare ourselves united with that church in the same faith, order and discipline.[51]

48. Ibid.
49. Ibid., 207.
50. Ibid., 233.
51. *Minutes of the Presbyterian Church*, 245.

421

The Old Side adopted the standards also:

> That every member of this Synod, whether, minister or elder, does sincerely and heartily receive, own, acknowledge, or subscribe the Westminster Confession of Faith, the Larger and Shorter Catechisms, as the confession of his faith, and the Directory, as far as circumstances allow and admit in this infant church, for the rule of church order. Ordered, that every session do oblige their elders to do the same at their admission. This was readily approved, nemine contradicente.[52]

Hodge commented:

> Hitherto the adoption of the Confession of Faith had been required only of ministers. It was now required of elders, and that with evident propriety. They are entitled, as members of Presbytery, to sit in judgment on the doctrinal knowledge of candidates for ordination, and on the orthodoxy of ministers. This regulation, therefore, still continues a part of the constitution of the church.[53]

According to Murphy, the following matters were agitating the church at the time of the schism of 1741. First, the seasons of the quickening of the Holy Spirit in the churches under Whitefield two years earlier, and under the continued ministry of the Log College men, was the occasion that Satan used to sow discord in the church, with his strange possessions and afflictions. Second, was the existence of the Log College, which admittedly did not teach a full academic course of studies in preparing men for the ministry. The Log College was openly admitted to be an emergency measure, and not designed to give the full classical education. Third, the different mind-sets of the Scotch-Irish, with their thorough training and their love for order over against the New England element with its ardent life and intense energy. Fourth, the lack of clarity that existed in the young church as to the rights and duties of the various branches of the ecclesiastical system was cause for tension in the church. What was the duty of presbytery to presbytery, and to the synod, and to the local congregations. Murphy points out that none of these causes

---

52. Ibid., 223.
53. Hodge, *Constitutional History*, 2:224.

was the subject of formal controversy, but they all existed and became the grounds of fermentation and increasing irritation.[54]

There were several specific causes for the disruption. First, there was the difference in practice of the Old Side and the New Side regarding the admission to the Lord's Table. The Old Side practice was to admit nearly all who had been baptized to the Table without pressing the matter of an evidence of the new birth. The New Side tended to the opposite extreme, insisting that the instant of conversion must be known, tangible and very apparent and accompanied by various manifestations. Certain means to produce the impressive manifestations of the change were used, which gave rise to controversy.[55]

The second cause of the disruption was the intrusion of the New Side people into other congregations and even into other presbyteries than their own, preaching with utmost zeal. They felt impelled to go anywhere, regardless of ecclesiastical boundaries, to awaken the backsliding and the careless. The Old Siders deemed this an affront and a reflection of their fidelity as ministers. "The ardent revivalist would not be restrained, and the others became more and more exasperated."[56]

Archibald Alexander describes the situation thus:

> Gilbert Tennent and Samuel Blair were men of invincible firmness. They were the leaders in this warfare. They saw a great harvest before them, and the Lord seemed to attend their labors everywhere with a blessing; and they were led to think that mere forms of order and regulations of ecclesiastical bodies were of trivial importance compared with the advancement of the Redeemer's kingdom and the salvation of souls. They felt, as did the apostles and the first Reformers, that they were called to go everywhere preaching the gospel, without regard to prescribed limits of Presbyteries or congregations, especially as they observed that many pastors neglected to inculcate on their hearers the necessity of a change of heart, and that the people were as really perishing for lack of knowledge as they were under Jewish or Popish instructors. They felt themselves bound, therefore, to preach far and wide wherever the people would hear them.[57]

54. Murphy, *Presbytery of the Log College*, 160–63.
55. Ibid., 163.
56. Ibid., 164.
57. Alexander, *Biographical Sketches*, 70.

The third cause for the division was the issue of theological education. The Old Side men objected to the Log College men, who did not
have the requisite college degree in addition to their theological training.
The Log College men, on the other hand, stressed the godliness and true
piety of the candidate was of the highest importance for a minister to have.
The synod passed a rule that all candidates would have to be examined
by the synod, or one of its committees, to determine if they had proper
educational background, either the bachelor's degree, or its equivalent
from a private education, before they could be licensed or ordained by a
presbytery. The Presbytery of New Brunswick in 1739 deemed the action
of the synod to be a usurpation of Presbytery powers and proceeded to
license a student from the Log College. Their reasoning was "that it is a
false hypothesis that the majority of any church judicatory has a power
committed to them by Christ to make new rules about religious matters,
which shall be binding on those who conscientiously dissent from them;
even though the majority judges the rules to be not against but agreeable
to the word and serviceable to religion."[58] They held that "since Christ has
given to presbyteries the power of ordination, the rule was unwarrantable
interference with their privileges."[59] Hodge indicates that the presbytery
at this juncture failed to recognize that as a constituent part of a larger
body. "The question was not, what a presbytery considered in itself might
do, but what a presbytery making a constituent part of a whole church
might properly do.... If to secure this object [soundness of character and
orthodoxy of members], the synod agreed that all who are admitted to
this sacred truth should have certain qualifications; all the members are
bound to submit or to leave the body."[60] The synod debated the matter for
a day, and then reaffirmed its action. The synod refused to recognize this
action of the presbytery. The result was the withdrawal of the Presbytery
of New Brunswick in 1741. Eventually, in 1745 the Synod of New York
was formed made up of the Presbyteries of New York, New Castle, and
New Brunswick as the New Side Synod.

Hodge comments on the schism thus:

58. Webster, Charles, *A History of the Presbyterian Church in America, from its Origin until
the Year 1760, with Biographical Sketches of Its early Minister* (Philadelphia: Joseph M. Wilson,
1857), 139.

59. Hodge, *Constitutional History,* 2:109.

60. Ibid., 110.

It must be borne in mind that, at this period, the synod was not only the highest judicatory of the church, but it included all the presbyteries. Its determinations or acts, therefore, were of the same nature with our constitutional rules when adopted by a majority of the presbyteries. They were the expression of the will of the whole church. In the particular case under consideration, all the presbyteries, without an exception, sanctioned the rule in question because it was adopted before the organization of the Presbytery of New Brunswick. And when that presbytery objected, there were four presbyteries for the rule and one against it. The conduct of the New Brunswick Presbytery . . . [was]an obvious breach of faith; it [was] a violation of the compact which the presbyteries have bound themselves to observe. And when any presbytery ordains any man who has not the constitutional qualifications as to learning, orthodoxy, or experimental religion, a positive and grievous wrong is inflicted on all the other presbyteries.[61]

Happily this schism was healed in 1758. The Rev. Gilbert Tennent had preached a sermon warning of the danger of an unconverted ministry in 1741. He came forward and apologized to the Old Side men, indicating that he had not intended to say any of them were unconverted. Here we see the "greatness" of a man who was willing to admit his error, and to apologize for it. It helped to heal the breach between the two sides. The Synods of Philadelphia and New York came back together on May 29, 1758, on the basis of a plan of union having been considered and approved by both Synods. It was declared in this joint meeting that "both Synods continue to profess the same principles of faith, and adhere to the same form of worship, government, and discipline,"[62] and the plan on the basis of which they united in one body under the name of the Synod of New York and Philadelphia provided, *inter alia*, as follows:

> I. Both Synods having always approved and received the Westminster Confession of Faith, and Larger and Shorter Catechisms, as an orthodox and excellent system of Christian doctrine, founded on the Word of God, we do still receive the same as the confession of our faith, and also adhere to the plan of worship, government, and discipline, contained in the Westminster Directory, strictly enjoining it on all our members and

61. Ibid., 112.
62. Ibid., 286.

probationers for the ministry, that the preach and teach according to the form of sound words in said Confession and Catechisms, and avoid and oppose all errors contrary thereto. . . .

VI. That no Presbytery shall license or ordain to the work of the ministry, any candidate until he . . . declare his acceptance of the Westminster Confession and Catechisms as the confession of his faith, and promise subjection to the Presbyterian plan of government in the Westminster Directory.[63]

THE FIRST GENERAL ASSEMBLY IN 1789

The First General Assembly in 1789 rewrote the parts of the confession that had given difficulty in the act of 1729. They also rewrote chapter 31 and deleted a phrase from the Larger Catechism question 109. From that time, full subscription was expected of all of the confession and catechisms of the church.

THE STRUGGLE FOR RELIGIOUS FREEDOM

Dr. Ernest Trice Thompson opens his chapter on "The Struggle for Religious Freedom" with the following observation:

At the beginning of the American Revolution separation of church and state was not to be found in any sovereign nation . . . . It was the struggle for complete religious liberty in Virginia which clarified the meaning of the principle and brought it to the attention of the nation, so that it was finally adopted as Article I of the Bill or Rights.[64]

Generally the credit for the separation of church and state is given to James Madison and Thomas Jefferson. Jefferson was a Deist, whose ideas of freedom and democracy came from the Age of Reason. James Madison, on the other hand, was reared in the Episcopal Church and educated at the College of New Jersey under John Witherspoon. John M. Mecklin in his *The Story of American Dissent* says, "It is at least possible that Madison was

63. Ibid., 286–87.
64. Thompson, *Presbyterians of the South*, 1:97.

imbued with the idea of separation of church and state by Witherspoon, who brought to Princeton a strong antipathy to a state-controlled church as a result of his fight with the Moderates in Scotland."[65] Since the colony of Virginia had had for over a century an established church, namely the Church of England, or the Episcopal Church, it was natural that the issue was raised as to whether this would continue, now that Virginia had become an independent state. The debate began in 1776 and continued until 1785. Thomas Jefferson, who was a member of the Virginia Assembly, sided with the dissenting churches in advocating the non-establishment of any church. Anson Phelps Stokes in his work *Church and State in the United States* suggests that the ministers of the dissenting churches, namely, the Baptists and Presbyterians, cleared the ground for Jefferson's act to pass. Patrick Henry, then a member of the assembly, advocated the continued establishment, or at least the public support of the Episcopal Church. Due to his great popularity and ability to sway his listeners by oratory, the outcome was far from easily settled. The Presbytery of Hanover, representing all Virginia Presbyterians, addressed the assembly with resolutions in 1776, 1777, twice in 1784, and once in 1785. Dr. Thompson gives an account of the various acts of the assembly and of the presbytery from 1772 to 1787.

In the first memorial of 1776, signed by John Todd, pastor in Louisa County and moderator of the presbytery started its running argument with the legislators. The presbytery stated the biblical ground for the independence of the church from the state thus:

> Neither can it be made to appear that the gospel needs any such civil aid. We rather conceive that when our blessed Savior declares his kingdom is not of this world, he renounces all dependence upon State power, and as his weapons are spiritual, and were only designed to have influence on the judgment and heart of man, we are persuaded that if mankind were left in the quiet possession of their unalienable rights and privileges, Christianity, as in the days of the Apostles, would continue to prevail and flourish in the greatest purity by its own native excellence and under the all disposing providence of God.
>
> We would humbly represent that the only proper objects of civil government are the happiness and protection of men in the present state of existence, the security of the life, liberty, and property of the citizens, and

65. As cited in Ibid.

to restrain the vicious and encourage the virtuous by the wholesome laws, equally extending to every individual. But that the duty which we owe to our Creator and the manner of discharging it, can only be directed by reason and conviction, and as nowhere recognizable but at the tribunal of the universal judge.

Therefore, we ask no ecclesiastical establishments for ourselves; neither can we approve of them when granted to others.[66]

Having experienced in Scotland the inequities and inconveniences of being dissenters, Presbyterians joined others, notably the Baptists, to dis-establish the Anglican Church in Virginia. The passage of separation of church and state was not a foregone conclusion, since it broke with over a millennium of western Christian tradition. The Anglicans were still strong in the legislature.[67]

The Presbytery of Hanover met at Timber Ridge, October 27, 1784. The Rev. John Blair Smith, President of Hampden-Sydney College, in accord with an action of last meeting of presbytery, produced a copy of the memorial presented to the last sessions of the State General Assembly, complaining of certain infringements on our religious liberty. The presbytery approved the memorial and ordered it to be recorded in the presbytery book, and ordered that it to be sent to the current session of the assembly.

The presbytery refers to the proposed assessment in such a way as to suggest they agreed with it. This was probably due to the general feeling that was abroad in the state, that in order to preserve religion, the state needed to assess its citizens for its support. It appears that most Virginia Presbyterians opposed such an assessment. It has been suggested that John Blair Smith was the primary author of this resolution. He was a close neighbor of Patrick Henry, who defended the idea of the assessment. Mr. Smith may have thus been influenced to accept the idea of assessment by Mr. Henry. The assembly did not pass the assessment, but delayed action for the response of the people.

When the Presbytery of Hanover met at Bethel in Augusta County, May 19, 1785, the question was raised with the presbytery as to whether

66. Foote, *Sketches of Virginia*, 1:324.

67. James H. Smylie, "From Revolution to Civil War (1776–1861)," *Virginia Presbyterians in American Life: Hanover Presbytery (1755–1980)* (Richmond, VA: Hanover Presbytery, 1982), 50–51.

it approved the kind of assessment that the assembly had proposed. The presbytery voted unanimously against such a measure and sent a resoultion to this effect to the assembly. The presbytery then did *quite* an *unusual thing*. It called a general convention of all the Presbyterians of Virginia to meet at Bethel on August 10, 1785, so that the concensus of all the Presbyterians could be expressed to the Virginia Assembly. This convention adopted a lengthy communication indicating their desire for the state to adopt a position of full freedom of religion.

The Rev. John B. Smith received permission to be heard before the Committee of the Whole House of the Virginia Assembly. He spoke on three successive days against the general assessment bill. In him were combined the powers of logic and declamation. Self-possessed, he was fervid in debate. Governor Patrick Henry's argument in favor of a general assessment, joined to his personal character, had, for a time, drawn Mr. Smith and William Graham to favor the bill. But further reflection on the ultimate bearing of the bill led them to take the opposition to the governor. With the strong actions of both the Presbytery and the general Convention of the Presbyterians of Virginia, John Blair Smith knew, when he appeared before the Committee of the Whole, that he represented the whole Presbyterian population in the state, and that he also represented the opinions and decisions of the numerous Baptists. He pled the principles of natural law, and the purity of morals and religion involving the welfare of the state. James Madison knew that he spoke the opinions of all the dissenters, and of many that were not dissenters from the religion of the state, and he pled the principles of natural law and of political rights, that men's thoughts were free in religion as in politics.

As a result of such strong arguments, representing such a large number of the citizens of the state, the assembly adopted the following bill proposed by Thomas Jefferson, who was a Deist, and not a Christian:

"An Act for Establishing Religious Freedom"

Whereas, Almighty God hath created the mind free;—that all attempts to influence it by temporal punishments or burthens, or by civil incorporations, tend only to beget habits of hypocrisy and meanness, and are a departure from the plan of the holy Author of our religion, who, being Lord both of body and mind, yet chose not to propagate it by coercions on either, as was in his almighty power to do;-that the impious presumptions of legislators and rulers, civil and ecclesiastical, who being themselves but fallible and uninspired men, have assumed dominion over the faith of others, setting up their own opinions and modes of thinking as the only true and infallible, and as such endeavouring to impose them on others, hath established and maintained false religions over the greater part of the world, and through all time ;-that to compel a man to furnish contributions of money for the propagation of opinions which he disbelieves, is sinful and tyrannical; that even the forcing him to support this or that teacher of his own religious persuasion, is depriving him of the comfortable liberty of giving his contributions to the particular pastor whose morals he would make his pattern, and whose powers he feels most persuasive to righteousness, and is withdrawing, from the ministry, those temporary rewards, which, proceeding from an approbation of their personal conduct, are an additional incitement to earnest and unremitting labours for the instruction of mankind;-that our civil rights have no dependence on our religious opinions, any more than our opinions in physics and geometry;-that therefore the proscribing any citizen as unworthy the public confidence, by laying upon him an incapacity of being called to offices of trust or emolument, unless lie profess or renounce this or that religious opinion, is depriving him injuriously of those privileges and advantages to which, in common with his fellowcitizens, he has a natural right;-that it tends only to corrupt the principles of that religion it is meant to encourage, by bribing with a monopoly of worldly honours and emoluments those who will externally profess and conform to it;-that though indeed those are criminal who do not withstand such temptations, yet neither are those innocent who lay the bait in their way;-that to suffer the civil magistrate to intrude his powers into the field of opinion, and to restrain the profession or propagation of principles, on supposition of their ill tendency, is a dangerous fallacy, which at once destroys all religious liberty, because he being, of course, judge of that tendency, will make his opinions the rule of judgment, and approve or condemn the sentiments of others only as they shall square with or differ from his own;-that it is time enough for the rightful purposes of civil government, for its officers to interfere when principles break out into overt acts against peace and good order;-and finally, that truth is great, and will prevail, if left to herself; that she is the proper and sufficient antagonist to error, and has nothing to fear from the conflict, unless by human interposition disarmed of her natural weapons, free argument and debate, error ceasing to be dangerous when it is permitted freely to contradict them.

2d. Be it enacted by the General Assembly, That no man shall be compelled to frequent or support any religious worship, place, or ministry whatsoever, nor shall be enforced, restrained, molested, or burthened in his body or goods, nor shall otherwise suffer on account of his religious opinions or belief; but that all men shall be free to profess, and by argument to maintain, their opinion in matters of religion, and that the same shall in no wise diminish, enlarge, or affect their civil capacities.

3d. And though we well know that this Assembly, elected by the people for the ordinary purposes of legislation only, have no power to restrain the acts of succeeding Assemblies, Constituted with powers equal to our own; and that, therefore, to declare this act to be irrevocable, would be of no effect in law; yet we are free to declare, and do declare, that the rights hereby asserted are of the natural rights of mankind, and that if any act shall be hereafter passed to repeal the present, or to narrow its operation, such act will be an infringement of natural right.[68]

We may not be able to know for certain just how much influence the resolutions from the Presbyterians may have had on the assembly, but it is clear that the Presbyterians were in favor of religions freedom. They had come to this country for the express purpose of enjoying religious freedom, and from their beginnings in America they maintained this position, as seen in the position taken by Francis Makemie. Much of what is taken for granted today as normal was brought to this country and planted here by Scottish and Scotch-Irish Presbyterians. The action of the Virginia Assembly gave impetus to the First Amendment of the Bill of Rights to the Constitution of the United States, under which all Americans live today. It was certainly not an act to remove all religion from the life of the nation, but was intended to preserve the freedom of every individual in the practice of his religion.

---

68. *The Virginia Statute for Religious Freedom: Its Evolution and Consequences in American Public Life*, ed. Merrill D. Peterson and Robert C. Vaughan (Cambridge: Cambridge University Press, 1988), xvii–xviii.

21

Mercy Ministries in the Post-Bellum South: Care for the Poor and Palmer Orphanage, 1894–1920

R O B E R T   L .   P E N N Y

AFTER THE WAR Between the States, the South was very poor. Yale University Sterling Professor of History, C. Vann Woodward, in his seminal study *Origins of the New South, 1877–1913*, specifically anticipated the problem towards which this study is directed when he quoted historian Arnold Toynbee as part of the front matter of the book.

> I remember watching the Diamond Jubilee procession [in Britain] myself as a small boy. I remember the atmosphere. It was: Well, here we are on top of the world, and we have arrived at this peak to stay there—forever! This is, of course, a thing called history, but history is something unpleasant that happens to other people. We are comfortable outside all that. I am sure if I had been a small boy in New York in 1897 I should have felt the same. Of course, if I had been a small boy in 1897 in the Southern part of the United States, I should not have felt the same; I should then

432

have known from my parents that history had happened to my part of the world.[1] [emphasis added]

This statement provides both an excellent introduction to and a precise context for this study of a challenge that did not go unmet by a Presbyterian church in the South. First Presbyterian Church (PCUS) of Columbus, Mississippi,[2] saw the challenge of poverty and set about to meet the need. Through the assistance of pastoral leadership and a true ecumenical spirit in the community, it sought to meet the need of the hour.

Professor James H. Smylie, a Southern Presbyterian church historian, attempts to help history students to assess the dimensions of this challenge in his appropriately titled article, "The Burden of Southern Church Historians: World Mission, Regional Captivity, and Reconciliation." One perspective that he shared with Woodward was that Southerners have had to live with "several problems not generally shared by the nation—for example, poverty amid prosperity, failure in a success oriented culture." He believed that church historians must be active in investigating "these burdens" and pointing to reconciling perspectives. For example, regarding ethics they must "agonize over the regional, national, and international dimensions of poverty, racism, and war." They must be careful not to "become entrapped" in a history that "may seem meaningless." Smylie's predecessors, Robert L. Dabney, Thomas Peck, and Thomas Cary Johnson, set an example because they too saw that history, and the Providence that moves it, could be "something unpleasant" and a challenge. Smylie set forth the precept that assessment of the church's history in the modern world will be adequate only "if we can relate past and present in a continuum, and in such a way as to

---

1. C. Vann Woodward, *Origins of the New South, 1877–1913*, A History of the South, ed. Wendell Holmes Stephenson and F. Merton Caulter (Baton Rouge: Louisiana State University Press and the Littlefield Fund for Southern History, University of Texas, 1971), 9:xiii.

2. In the early 1970s, approximately two-thirds of this congregation at a regularly called and legal congregational meeting voted to change its affiliation to the new Presbyterian Church in America (PCA). A settlement was reached with the dissenting one-third, allowing the larger group to retain the church facilities on Main Street and the interest in Palmer Home for Children and the smaller group to receive a five-acre site in another part of town and some financial assets. Since the issues that brought about this division occurred eighty years later, all references in the text will be to the original First Presbyterian Church. The PCA majority group eventually took the name Main Street Presbyterian Church. The smaller group took the name First Presbyterian Church and remained affiliated with the Presbyterian Church in the United States of America (PCUSA), a successor of the original Presbyterian Church in the United States (PCUS). The latter was the updated name of the Presbyterian Church in the Confederate States.

open new possibilities for the future." That will be a goal of this study. One must bear in mind Smylie's additional warning regarding that which will one day assess these efforts:

> Our children and our children's children will rise up someday and assess the way we have carried our burdens, just the way we have judged our predecessors. . . . We may set their teeth on edge.[3]

The story of how First Presbyterian Church of Columbus was inspired to launch, and did successfully launch, a ministry to destitute children is an encouraging one about meeting this kind of need. Historian Pete Daniel also pointed out the specific economic context:

> As the South entered the twentieth century, it carried the burdens of its history – defeat in war, a race and class system, poverty, and the recent failure of the Populist movement.[4]

This ministry involved carrying the burden of Southern history because it had to do with altering the harsh effects of that history in the lives of some of its youngest and most helpless victims, boys and girls without parents. This story may serve as a case study on how to go about bringing a redemptive dimension to the problems of contemporary society, especially in the South. Thus, the purpose of this study is to tell the story of the beginning and development of the ministry of First Presbyterian Church of Columbus, Mississippi, to poor, destitute children, which came to be known as Palmer Orphanage. What were the motivation, purpose, and result of this ministry? The present writer is aware, having served as senior pastor of this church for over eight years (1979–88), that Paul's admonition in Galatians 6:2 became their mandate: "Bear one another's burdens, and so fulfill the law of Christ."

The honoree of this volume, O. Palmer Robertson, has spent a large portion of his career in Africa with similar motives in the training of native

---

3. James H. Smylie, "The Burden of Southern Church Historians: World Mission, Regional Captivity, and Reconciliation," *Journal of Presbyterian History* 46 (December 1968): 276, 305–7. Smylie, at the time of the publication of this article, was a professor of church history at Union Theological Seminary, Richmond, Virginia.

4. Pete Daniel, *Standing at the Crossroads: Southern Life Since 1990* (New York: Hill and Wang, 1969), 3.

pastors who will be equipped with the redemptive and reconciling word of the gospel to do the same in their countries of Liberia, Malawi, and now Uganda.[5] Those of us who know him are confident that the same Reformed faith and love that burned in the hearts of Drs. Dabney, Palmer, Thornwell, Johnson, and their successors also beats in the heart of Palmer Robertson. Therefore, the recounting of this story has a second purpose as well.

PHASE ONE: ORGANIZATION AND LEGAL CONSOLIDATION

Dr. Horace Villee, pastor of First Presbyterian Church from 1949–1971, was on the mark when he said that in the session meeting on Tuesday, September 11, 1884, a "momentous decision" was made. It was the decision to name their new organization for the care of poor, homeless orphans, "The Palmer Orphanage," and to go public by seeking the advice and counsel of the presbytery and the synod regarding their new venture.[6]

The Rev. William States Jacobs had only just arrived as pastor. This young pastor, only two years out of seminary, had "inspired" the ruling elders, deacons, and church trustees with a "vision of an institution that would stamp its Christian influence upon the lives of countless children who might find there a home that would be denied them otherwise." Jacobs was the son of Rev. William Plummer Jacobs who was the founder (in 1883) of Thornwell Orphanage, Clinton, South Carolina. Villee made an appropriate, and probably accurate, observation when he reported that William's youth spent at Thornwell was "largely responsible for his desire to see a similar institution established when he became a minister of the Gospel himself."[7]

5. In January 2006, while lecturing at African Bible College, Uganda, this writer made a weekend expedition to northern Uganda with Palmer Robertson, the Rev. Paul Chinchen, Chancellor of ABC, Malawi, and other U.S. pastors to observe the needs of orphaned children in refugee camps in Lira, Gulu, etc. These orphans, called "Night Children" because at dark they flee their homes to sleep in Christian centers of refuge in and near Gulu, are left in the wake of murdered, raped, and pillaged parents, at the hands of the rogue terrorist Joseph Kony and his guerilla army, ironically called the Lord's Resistance Army (LRA) of the Ten Commandments. Cf. J. Carter Johnson, "Deliver Us from Kony," *Christianity Today* (January 1, 2006).

6. Horace L. Villee, "Brief History of Palmer Orphanage, December 10, 1950. First Presbyterian Church, Columbus, Mississippi," Library of the Main Street Presbyterian Church, 1. No doubt, much of this story is oral tradition, but there existed contemporarily first-hand links with parties involved in the organization of the home.

7. Ibid.

A detailed account of what long-time Palmer trustee and board secretary-treasurer William J. Love called the "Period of Beginning and Development, 1894–1920" is now in order.[8] For convenience, these years may be divided into two sub-periods: 1894–1901, Organization and Legal Consolidation; and 1902–1920, Cooperation: Larger Ministry and Development.

The first sub-period, "Organization and Legal Consolidation," began with the first meeting in which the subject of a ministry to orphan children was brought up, on July 17, 1894. The minutes of both the church session and the orphanage board carry the critical resolution, which was adopted:

> WHEREAS, it is believed that the time is auspicious for the effort to establish within the bounds of this synod an orphanage and the necessary educational facilities to be attached thereto and looking to the many advantages within the bounds of this church for the establishment of such in institution; therefore, be it
>
> RESOLVED, that the suggestion made by our Pastor Rev. W. S. Jacobs to that effect meets with our cordial approbation and we will aid earnestly in promoting the enterprises.[9]

The local church session concluded by requesting ruling elder J. A. Orr to draw up a charter "under which we may most effectively carry out the objects of the organization as provided for by the laws of [the state of] Mississippi."[10]

The approval of the local board of deacons would be sought. The church session met jointly with them on the next day, July 18. After the subject of establishing the orphanage was "fully discussed" and "on motion of Deacon John P. Mayo," it "was resolved that the Board of Deacons cooperate with the session in carrying out the objects named," by a unanimous vote among the deacons only. Then a joint resolution was proposed and adopted.[11]

Apparently, there was in existence at this point a Ladies' Orphanage Association of Columbus because there is a reference to it in the session

8. William J. Love, "Palmer Orphanage: Its Origin, History, and Financial Structure, December 20, 1953," Library of Main Street Presbyterian Church, Columbus, Mississippi, 23.

9. "Minutes of the Session of First Presbyterian Church, Columbus, Mississippi, 1894–1920, Library of Main Street Presbyterian Church, Columbus, Mississippi; 110; "Minutes of the Board of Trustees, Palmer Orphanage, Columbus, Mississippi, 1894–1920," Photocopy in the Library of Main Street Presbyterian Church, Columbus, Mississippi, 1–2.

10. "Session Minutes," 110–11.

11. Ibid., 111; "Board Minutes," 2.

minutes of August 14, 1894. There was a motion proposed by ruling elder J. A. Neilson and adopted that the session "say to the Ladies of the Orphanage Association of Columbus, Mississippi, that the session are heartily in accord with them and ready to cooperate with them in the movement now inaugurated to found an Orphan Asylum in the city."[12]

Another significant meeting was held on the night of August 31, 1894, which only the board minutes record. It was held "in the Pastor's study of First Presbyterian Church" and to this meeting "all the officials [elders and deacons] of that church were invited." The pastor-moderator, Rev. Jacobs, seven ruling elders, two deacons, and the Sunday school superintendent were present. The following resolution was adopted:

> RESOLVED: That we the Elders, Deacons, and Trustees of the Columbus [First] Presbyterian Church whose names are hereunto signed organize ourselves into a Board of Trustees to found an orphanage in the city of Columbus, Mississippi.[13]

At the next meeting on September 11, 1884, the board decided on a name and its first slate of officers. The official name was to be "The Palmer Orphanage." This was done in honor of Dr. Benjamin Morgan Palmer, the pastor of First Presbyterian Church of New Orleans (1856–1902), who was then a member of the Synod of Mississippi.[14] Villee explained further that Dr. Palmer was the first moderator of the newly organized General Assembly of the Confederate States of America in 1861. He was, like Dr. James Henley Thornwell, a prominent theologian (and secessionist) after whom the Thornwell Orphanage was named, and a leader of Presbyterians in the South. Dr. C. W. Grafton, prominent pastor and historian of Presbyterianism in Mississippi, remarked that the naming of the home for Palmer was a "happy thought" because the two men were friends and

---

12. "Session Minutes," 113.

13. "Board Minutes," 2–3. A marginal note, in longhand, attests: "Elders, Deacons, and Trustees form the Board of Trustees." It is significant that there are no corresponding session minutes of this meeting.

14. Synods were larger judicatories comprised of all the presbyteries of one or more states, one purpose for which was joint ministries. At that time the southern part of Louisiana, encompassing New Orleans, was a part of the Synod of Mississippi. This was not unusual. Georgia and South Carolina comprised the synod that sent some of the original missionary personnel to south Mississippi. That synod also founded the [James Henley] Thornwell Orphanage in South Carolina.

closely associated in ecclesiastical life; and this completed "the binding together [of] two great names in caring for poor and needy orphans."[15]

A nominating committee presented a slate and the following officers were elected: Rev. W. S. Jacobs, president; Mr. S. H. Ayres, treasurer; and Mr. W. A. Campbell, secretary. Other business at this meeting pertained to fund-raising and public relations. The Presbytery of Tombeckbee (Tombigbee) and the Synod of Mississippi were to be notified of the organization and requested "to authorize at least one collection annually for this Institution." One trustee was assigned to write to *The Southwestern Presbyterian*, a church periodical whose headquarters were in New Orleans, in order "to bring the matter fully before the churches of the Synod of Mississippi." Another action was the appointment of a committee of three persons "to formulate plans to make a systematic canvass of Columbus and surrounding country in the interest of this Orphanage."[16]

The next board meeting took place three months later on Wednesday, December 12, 1894, "after the [church's] regular prayer meeting," and "all who felt interested" were asked to remain for the meeting "as there would be no secrets." The matter of soliciting "subscriptions to the orphanage," by "ladies and gentlemen," from "the several churches of the city" was discussed. It was decided to appoint a committee of three which would, "in consultation with members of the other churches," appoint committees from each of these churches "to solicit subscriptions and contributions in the several wards of the city and that these committees shall be composed of ladies and gentlemen."[17]

The next recorded meeting on March 13, 1897, had been called in order "to go forward in the work of building up this orphanage" because "the time had come to act." The board president, Rev. Jacobs, read a list of committees and names of people from local churches, which were to solicit

15. Love, "History," 11; Horace L. Villee, "Remarks Concerning Palmer Orphanage, Columbus, Mississippi; April 3. 1952," Columbus Kiwanis Club; Library of Main Street Presbyterian Church, Columbus, Mississippi, 3; Villee, "Brief History," 2; and Cornelius Washington Grafton, "History of the Mississippi Synod of the Presbyterian Church," (State Archives, Jackson, Mississippi, 1927), 649.

16. "Session Minutes," 115–16; "Board Minutes," 4–6. It is interesting to note that W. A. Campbell was concurrently the clerk (secretary) of the session and secretary of the board. Since the handwritten board minutes appear to have a neater, more deliberate appearance, rather than the hurried hand of those of the session, Campbell probably later transcribed the board minutes from those of the session. But strangely, on this meeting, the session minutes are fuller.

17. "Board Minutes," 7–8.

in each church: the Presbyterian Church, the Methodist Church, the Baptist Church, the Cumberland Presbyterian Church, the Christian Church, the Episcopal Church, the Jewish Synagogue, the Catholic Church, and the "outsiders." A motion carried providing that "all the ministers of the various churches of this city be made *ex officio* members of the Palmer Orphanage Association." An invitation to the public meeting in the following week was to be sent and read in all the local churches. At the other three meetings of 1885, the board discussed and adopted the charter written by trustee J. A. Orr and adopted the constitution and by-laws written by a committee. It is worth noting that a certain "Rabbi Hertz" was in attendance at one of those meetings.[18]

During the next three years the board was absorbed in the routine matters of constructing facilities. This involved them in the purchase of land, securing the services of an architect, engaging building contractors, and so forth. They continued to expand their efforts at solicitation and launched a periodical for this purpose.[19]

Over the next two years there were further actions toward organization and consolidation. By the meeting of January 4, 1899, the first superintendent was on hand, the Rev. Benjamin Franklin Bedinger. The founding board president, W. S. Jacobs, had resigned in order to accept a call to another church. "Matrons" were hired to serve as house-parents. The first children were taken into the home, and some joined First Presbyterian Church. The church authorized Sunday school and Thanksgiving Day offerings for the Orphanage. One of the new buildings was to be named for the Mississippi Christian youth society known as "The Christian Endeavor," if that society would "donate as much as five hundred dollars toward its erection." C. H. Ayres resigned as treasurer and A. E. Love was elected to take his place. Mr. Bedinger resigned at the June 4 meeting but no reason is given. At the next meeting the Rev. Dunbar H. Ogden, the new pastor of First Presbyterian Church, was in attendance. A treasurer's report appeared:

Receipts: $4003.51
Expenditures: $3783.42
Balance in Bank: $329.04[20]

18. Ibid., 14–18.
19. Ibid., 19–38.
20. Ibid., 39–55; "Session Minutes," 194–244

The issue of parental visitation arose and was handled by the adoption of a rule providing that "no parent be allowed to remain for more than one day and night." Mr. W. T. Caldwell was elected as the second superintendent. Students from the Industrial Institute and College (forerunner of Mississippi University for Women) gave contributions of seventy-seven dollars. Authorization was given for the construction of sheds for the protection of stock. Miss Clara Swoope of Allendale, Mississippi, was hired as a matron. Mr. Caldwell's resignation was tendered and later accepted. A new school building was erected. A committee was appointed to prepare a report for the Synod of Mississippi. Rev. H. E. McClure of Lafayette, Georgia, was elected as the third superintendent. With these events Palmer Orphanage began and found legal establishment.[21]

PHASE TWO: COOPERATION: LARGER MINISTRY AND DEVELOPMENT

A new era began for the orphanage in 1902, the sub-period of cooperation: large ministry and development, 1902–20. A committee had already been appointed to make contact with the Synod of Mississippi. The minutes of the board of May 2, 1902, reveal that the current board president, the Rev. D. H. Ogden, "was instrumental to write [to a] committee appointed by the synod to meet with the trustees of the Orphanage" in early June 1902. The same authorizing motion went on to state that "all trustees be requested to be present at a called meeting on May 19, 1902."[22]

This was not to be the orphanage's first contact with or recognition by the Synod of Mississippi. In 1894, the Rev. W. S. Jacobs had addressed the synod concerning the local efforts to launch an orphanage. The synod responded with the following resolution:

> Synod has heard with much pleasure from Rev. W. S. Jacobs, of the attempt to establish and Orphanage in the city of Columbus, Mississippi. We regard it is a cause of rejoicing that, in the midst of these stringent times, God has caused the riches of his grace to abound in liberality towards the originating of this enterprise. . . . This cause of the orphan is especially dear to the God of the widow and orphan.[23]

21. "Board Minutes," 56–95.
22. Ibid., 98.
23. Quoted in Villee, "Remarks," 1.

The synod resolution went on to give "its hearty approval to the scheme of the Columbus brethren" and to express eloquently their pleasure that:

> The institution is to bear the name of a brother who has long been among us, wise in counsel and valiant for truth, and we trust the at the Palmer Orphanage is entering upon a career of great usefulness, and will prove a worthy co-laborer with its kindred institute in South Carolina. May the mantles of Thornwell and Palmer, who were one in the faith of our fathers, one in hope and love, rest upon those who are moving in this good work, and inspire them with untiring zeal in their self-sacrificing labors.[24]

Finally, at the same meeting, the synod invoked "God's blessing upon the orphanage" and "reverently commend[ed] it to the prayers and benefi-ciations of all those who loved the Master's name."[25]

At the 1895 meeting of the synod, other actions were taken to assist the efforts of the orphanage:

1. That Synod allow a representative of the institution to visit churches within the bounds of Synod at the pleasure of session and pastor.

2. That Synod allow circulars to be issued to churches with the approval of Synod, urging them to take a collection on Thanksgiv-ing for Palmer Orphanage unless pledged to some other cause.[26]

Thus, the stage was set for the board meeting on May 19, 1902. A resolution was moved, seconded, and carried that "the trustees of the Palmer Orphanage tender it to the Synod of Mississippi with certain conditions." One condition adopted for the transfer "shall be that as long as it is an orphanage, it shall be in Columbus, Mississippi." The committee appointed to work out the legal matters was "to secure [a] joint contract with the Synod of Mississippi in the management." At the meeting of November 5, 1902, a committee was appointed to compile a statement of the condition of the home. It reported on November 12, 1902, at which time its report

24. Ibid.
25. Ibid.
26. Ibid.

was accepted and completed in order to present it to the synod. A copy was to be sent to the Synod of Louisiana.[27]

At the November 24 meeting, the committee appointed to work on legal arrangements reported to the board:

> The amended charter was read and on motion was adopted by a vote, and on motion the following three (3) trustees were elected: John A. Snell for the term of one (1) year and A. E. Love for a term of two (2) years and for the term of three (3) Rev. D. H. Ogden.[28]

A further provision regarding election of trustees adopted at the same meeting is important and deserves to be given in full:

> Moved, seconded, and carried that the annual elections hereafter be the first Monday of November and that elections of trustees each year be by the officers of the First Presbyterian Church of Columbus, Mississippi.[29]

In 1902, the Synod of Mississippi heard and adopted the report of its committee appointed "to confer with the trustees of Palmer Orphanage as to what was necessary to establish a closer relationship between this body and that institution." It adopted what was basically the original charter, except for the inclusion of the name of the Synod of Mississippi and the incorporators and trustees it named at this meeting. Two-thirds interest in the orphanage was transferred to the synod, while the church retained one-third interest.[30]

What is noteworthy here is the report to the synod as to the current condition of the orphanage. The real property consisted of eighteen acres of land and two brick buildings. It also had outbuildings "together with the usual equipment of a small farm" all at an "estimated value of $12,000.00." Residing at the home at this time were thirty-nine children, twenty boys and nineteen girls, who experienced during the year no "serious sickness." It was reported that the children are "happy" and "for the most part well-behaved," and do "their work well and cheer-

---

27. "Board Minutes," 105–6.

28. Ibid., 207.

29. Ibid.

30. "Minutes of the Synod of Mississippi of the Presbyterian Church in the United States, 1902," Photocopy in the Library of Main Street Presbyterian Church, 94–98.

fully." The staff were: the Rev. H. W. McClure, superintendent; Mrs. H. E. McClure, matron; Miss Clara Swoope, assistant matron; and Miss M. E. Baird, teacher. A nine-month school was maintained with thirty-five children enrolled. The oldest girl was taking a course at I.I.C., and three of the children were reported as being too young for school. The school was "graded" and "under the supervision of the superintendent of city schools." Religious instruction consisted of "daily training in the Scriptures and Catechisms."[31]

The Christian Endeavor Building was reported to have been completed at a cost of thirty-three hundred dollars; it was a combined chapel and boy's dormitory. Concerning the current financial condition, it was reported that "all obligations are met monthly" and the orphanage was "free of all debt save the amount due on the new building." The reason given for this was "the liberality of churches, Sabbath schools, and individuals interested in the work." The report concluded with a recommendation and acknowledgment:

> We believe that the work is in better condition now than ever before in its history and we ask the Synod continue its support, recommending to the churches and Sabbath schools that offerings be made for this cause as frequently as possible, but especially at Thanksgiving season.
>
> We would acknowledge the blessing of God as he has enabled us to carry forward this work, and has given us so many evidences of his presence and tokens of his love.[32]

The first meeting of the board, after merger and reorganization, was held on January 26, 1903. The following officers were elected: the Rev. J. E. Jones, president; the Rev. D. H. Ogden, vice-president; and Mr. A. E. Love, secretary-treasurer. The first issue of importance was to determine "whether the property was in the name of the individual corporators or of the corporation." It was reported at the next meeting on May 4 that "the committee had examined the records and found that the property of the Palmer Orphanage was in the name of the corporation." At these two meetings an executive committee was appointed, a

31. Ibid.
32. Ibid.

constitution and by-laws were adopted, and routine matters of business were handled.[33]

The first year of cooperation seemed to be a success. The superintendent reported to the synod meeting of 1903 in glowing terms:

> In this, my first annual report as Superintendent of Palmer Orphanage . . . I desire to thank God for his goodness and blessings upon the orphanage. This has been a year of progress along many lines for the orphanage. We were in debt at the beginning of the year, but by the generosity of the people the debt has been paid and some improvement made.[34]

The food provision for the orphanage seemed abundant as "garden and field crops have been all we could ask," 150 bushels of sweet potatoes were "put up," and five hogs made "about 1,000 pounds of meat." Wood and coal were supplied at "exceedingly low" prices. The children numbered fifty-three, and only one case of serious sickness was reported. The school was "successfully taught by our assistants in that department." The superintendent expressed both thanks to friends and the hope that "they will remember us in the future in this work of caring for the fatherless and destitute." The financial report (for 1902) showed receipts of $4,512.72, disbursements of $3,675.00, and a building fund of $1,060.00. [35]

The synod's response was equally positive:

> We have examined the report of the Board of Trustees. We note with pleasure and gratitude to God the continued success and prosperity of our orphanage.
>
> Many manifestations of God's blessings rest upon the institution. . . . We regard this work as a sacred trust committed to us by the great Head of the Church and as such is worthy of our sympathy and support. Surely there is no grander work closer to the heart of our Master than caring for the orphans of our church.[36]

33. "Board Minutes," 113–16.

34. Ibid., 123–25.

35. Ibid.

36. "Minutes of the Synod of Mississippi of the Presbyterian Church in the United States, 1903," Photocopy in the Library of Main Street Presbyterian Church, Columbus, Mississippi, 153.

Another major influence in the development of Palmer Orphanage in this sub-period was the inclusion of the Synod of Louisiana in the ministry and management. It received a one-third interest from the Synod of Mississippi. The board, at its meeting on November 2, 1903, resolved that:

> Synod be requested by the Board to adopt such measures as Synod deem best to continue and enlarge the interest of the Synod of Louisiana in the work of Palmer Orphanage.[37]

The Synod of 1903 complied and adopted a recommendation:

> That the Louisiana Synod be conferred with and in the event representation on our Board is desired, that our charter be so amended as to provide for ten trustees and that the tenth be elected from that Synod.[38]

This merger took place and the board, on May 8, 1906, heard and adopted a report from J. A. Orr stating that "the charter had been changed and that the Synod of Louisiana had elected Rev. J. H. Dale of New Orleans as a trustee."[39]

Meanwhile, the life of First Presbyterian Church was being affected by the presence and growth of the orphanage's ministry. The church session minutes reflect it in several entries. New members were received from Palmer and the children sat as a body in the church gallery. The pastor provided monthly preaching and weekly prayer meeting at Palmer, until a chaplain was jointly retained for Palmer and a local city mission. The chaplain started a mission Sunday school at Palmer. The church pledged fifty dollars toward a new kitchen at Palmer. The church agreed to pay six dollars for additional benches for the new mission Sunday school at Palmer. The Rev. J. V. Hill, the new pastor, was elected a trustee.[40]

During the remaining years of this period the board took two significant actions, which would prove to enhance for many years the ministry of the home. On November 7, 1905, it elected the Rev. William F. Frierson as superintendent. Mr. Frank P. Phillips was elected in 1917 as a trustee, a representative from the church, according to a report to the board received

37. "Board Minutes," 122.
38. "Synod Minutes, 1903," 153.
39. "Board Minutes," 143–44.
40. "Session Minutes," 63–123.

from the church's clerk of session. Frierson would serve as superintendent for nearly fifteen years. His son would succeed him and serve for over thirty years. Phillips would be a generous benefactor during the second period of Palmer's history 1921–1939, called by Love, "The Period of Hardship and Retrenchment." Robin Weaver, Sr., a late elder emeritus in the church and a trustee for over thirty years (who as an attorney did *gratis* legal work for the orphanage), reported on Phillips' benevolence following the stock market crash of 1929. Phillips once told Superintendent John Frierson, "John, you go ahead and write the checks as usual for Palmer Orphanage for whatever is needed and, at the end of the month, if there's any deficit, I'll make it up."[41]

LIFE AT THE ORPHANAGE

What was life at the orphanage actually like, and how well was the challenge of poverty and redemption met? Racial integration and dealing forthrightly with the problems of illegitimacy were avoided and obviously not contemplated at the time. The original charter of 1894 and the amended charter of 1902, as adopted by the Synod of Mississippi, gave the following purposes for the Palmer Orphanage Corporation:

> The purposes for which it is created are to support, rear, train, discipline, maintain, and educate white orphans, or children of reputable parents, one of whom is dead.[42]

During the period from its founding in 1895 to 1920, the orphanage had retained five superintendents. Four were ministers and the fifth was a minister's son and lawyer; this would obviously indicate that religious instruction and influence was to be a primary emphasis:[43]

- Rev. Benjamin Franklin Bedinger, D.D., 1897–1900
- Rev. W. T. Caldwell, 1900–1901

41. "Board Minutes," 138–39, 188; and Robin Weaver, Sr., "Sesquicentennial History of The Presbyterian Church of Columbus, Mississippi, and Several Episodes of Interest Concerning the Same, May 3, 1979," Library of Main Street Presbyterian Church, Columbus, Mississippi, 9.
42. "Synod Minutes, 1902," 97–98.
43. John F. Frierson, "Palmer Orphanage," In *The Presbyterian Work in Mississippi*, ed. Fred R. Graves (Sumner, MS: The Sentinel Press, 1927), 88; Villee, "Remarks," 2.

- Rev. H. E. McClure, 1901–1905
- Rev. W. V. Frierson, 1905–1919
- Mr. John F. Frierson, 1919–1950

By the end of 1926, the closest date for which information is available, the property of the orphanage consisted of one hundred ten acres of land, "all in one block except for ten acres across the road." There were four principal "brick veneered buildings": a girls' dormitory (Lindamood Building), which included a dining room and kitchen; a boys' dormitory (Christian Endeavor Building), a school building, and a superintendent's home. The entire properties were estimated in 1926 to be worth eighty-five thousand dollars.[44]

In 1926, Superintendent John Frierson reported that there were over seventy-five children in the orphanage, "ten more girls than boys" and that "this is the capacity of the institution." The staff consisted of one superintendent, four matrons, and two teachers. The children did "the principal part of the work in the institution." The girls did "the domestic work in the home" and the boys did "work in the gardens and the farm and in the dairy."[45]

The orphanage maintained at this time a school with two teachers, which went through the sixth grade. Above this, the children attended the Columbus public schools. Many girls went on to attend Mississippi State College for Women (now University). Many boys went on to attend Mississippi State College (now University), University of Mississippi, Southwestern at Memphis (now Rhodes College), and Davidson College.[46]

Was the financial support during this period adequate? William J. Love, long-time trustee, secretary-treasurer of the board, and son of an early trustee, did an exhaustive, year-by-year study of the financial condition and structure of the orphanage. He reported to the board and the Synod of Mississippi on his findings in a well done, but unpublished report dated December 20, 1953. Here is a reproduction of his table of findings:

1902—All obligations met

1903—No outstanding bills

44. Frierson, "Palmer," 88; Love, "History," 5.
45. Frierson, "Palmer," 88.
46. John F. Frierson, "Valedictory of John F. Frierson to the Synod of Mississippi; September 27, 1950," Library of Main Street Presbyterian Church, Columbus, Mississippi.

1904—Balance on hand—$197.62
1905—New building begun
1906—Laundry built; endowment of $1,200.00
1908—Debt of $270.00
1909—$1,200.00 worth of improvements
1910—Small debt
1911—Receipts $7,637.01; Debt of $1,217.42
1914—Receipts $10,143.83; Debt of $1,740.17
1917—Receipts $13,035.67; Cash on hand $758.82
1918—Receipts $10,754.27; Cash on hand $394.27
1919—Receipts $17,914.40; Cash on hand $2,060.56
1920—Debt of $1,237.54
1921—Receipts of $21,359.02; Cash on hand $576.92
1922—Receipts of $15,529.43; Debt of $1,574.62.[47]

The orphanage to this point "never had a personal solicitor in the field." Superintendent Frierson indicated in 1926 the sources of their financial support:

The institution belongs to the Presbyterians of Mississippi and Louisiana, and those who are in charge of the work appreciate very much the splendid cooperation and support that they have received through all these years and only bespeak a little more liberal support for their current expenses.[48]

Later, in 1950, Superintendent Frierson would acknowledge, "The churches, Sabbath schools, auxiliaries, and individuals have, by friendship, moral support and contributions, made this work possible."[49]

Results

What were the results of these early efforts and their developments? Love reported in 1953 that "during the period of its existence (Palmer) has served some six hundred to eight hundred children." About "sixty young men and women served in the military forces of the country in World War

47. Love, "History," 23.
48. Frierson, "Palmer," 87, 89.
49. Frierson, "Valedictory," 3.

II." Many "occupy humble places in the world of business" and some occupy "honorable positions in all walks of life." Some attained distinction:

> One boy is now a doctor in Siam [Thailand]; one girl is connected with the State Department in Paris; and another girl, a graduate of M.S.C.W. with highest honors, studied abroad on a Rotary Fellowship and is now an officer in the Waves.[50]

In 1950, Superintendent Frierson gave a summary about the alumni:

> The alumni of Palmer Orphanage are throughout the length and breadth of the land, and in foreign countries—Japan, France, New York, Washington, D.C., New Jersey, Seattle, Chicago, Detroit, Minneapolis, Des Moines, Pueblo, Florida, Tennessee, Alabama and a half a dozen cities in California. They are throughout Mississippi, Jackson, Gulfport, Meridian, Clarksdale, Greenville, and elsewhere. More than 450 have passed through the institution since I have been associated with it.[51]

Love, who was associated with the home for its first half century and who had an intimate knowledge of its affairs, first, through his father's association as a trustee and then through his own and aforementioned exhaustive study could state:

> The children have never wanted for the necessities of life, for good schooling as long as they were able and willing to take it, and for proper religious instruction.[52]

CONCLUSION

Were the efforts of First Presbyterian Church of Columbus, Mississippi, effective or successful to alleviate the poverty and suffering typical of Southern society following the War Between the States? It appears that their efforts to launch a ministry to destitute children without parents were notably effective, at least through the period which passed under observation,

50. Love, "History," 23.
51. Frierson, "Valedictory," 2. Frierson's years as superintendent were 1919–50.
52. Love, "History," 29.

1895–1920. Not only was the effort successful, but it stands as an inspiring example of how today's church, standing at the "crossroads" as every generation in the American South does, may go about facing the challenges to human life and the "burdens" confronting Southern culture today and doing it with redemptive and reconciling dimension.[53]

Thus, we are again reminded of the truth of the words of the popular Christian hymn "Lead On, O King Eternal," that echo the teachings of Christ the Redeemer:

> Lead on, O King eternal, till sin's fierce war shall cease,
> and holiness shall whisper the sweet amen of peace;
> for not with swords loud clashing, nor roll of stirring drums,
> but deeds of love and mercy, the heavenly kingdom comes.

---

53. The honoree of this volume added his efforts in a teaching ministry to one new ministry in the American South, Reformed Theological Seminary; one in Florida, Knox Theological Seminary; and three in Africa, African Bible Colleges in Liberia, Malawi, and Uganda, thus serving destitute areas. Though not always in the South, Robertson's labors reflect a desire to help establish institutions that will be characterized by a redemptive and reconciling mission and dimension. However, Robertson was a bold preacher for reconciliation with African-Americans and an opponent of all forms of racial discrimination. His ministry has always been a voice for inclusion and his labors in Africa bespeak a dedication to that emphasis.

PART 6

Tributes

22

Reformed Theological Seminary

ROBERT C. CANNADA JR.

PALMER ROBERTSON only taught at Reformed Theological Seminary for one year while I was a student, but I remember him as perhaps the best classroom professor I had. Both his style of teaching and his content were outstanding.

All of his students through the years certainly appreciate his explanation of the covenants throughout the Bible and his illustration of the lazy V to explain the progressive (expanding, complimentary, non-contradicting) unfolding of God's revelation through the biblical covenants over time. I remember this concept particularly from Palmer's course on the book of Hebrews. I will always remember that course and the profound impact it had on my understanding and appreciation for the relationship between the Old Testament and the New Testament, especially the fulfillment of all things in Jesus Christ, our "better" prophet, priest, and king.

I also remember in particular Palmer's prayers in class. He used a great deal of Scripture and specific biblical terminology in his prayers and this encouraged me immensely in my own approach to the throne of grace.

Palmer has been a blessing to several Reformed seminaries and to the church at large. Palmer and I were nurtured in the same home church, First Presbyterian in Jackson, Mississippi; and I am pleased that we share the same heritage and commitment to Reformed theology and ministry. May our Lord continue to bless him and use him as a blessing.

23

Covenant Theological Seminary

WILLIAM S. BARKER II

PALMER ROBERTSON served on the faculty of Covenant Theological Seminary from 1980 to 1985, during most of which time I was president of the seminary (1977–84). At that time Covenant represented a strong historic (non-dispensational) premillennial tradition. Although some amillennialists had previously served on the faculty, Palmer, as a professor of Old Testament teaching the prophetical books, would be the first "amil" to teach in the area of eschatology. So his interview with the faculty was bound to be interesting. His presentation of himself and his views was so positive that, as he left the faculty lounge for our discussion and vote, I overheard one of our staunchest veteran "premils" whisper to another one: "Pure gold!"

Palmer was the second member of the Presbyterian Church in America (PCA) to join the faculty of Covenant, which was the denominational seminary of the Reformed Presbyterian Church, Evangelical Synod, which would join, and be received by, the PCA in 1982 (the first was David Calhoun in 1979). His *Christ of the Covenants* had just been published in 1980. That book's ready acceptance, along with his messages in chapel, won the favor of both students and colleagues and contributed to the happy joining and receiving of the two denominations.

When Palmer came to Covenant Seminary, he had been one of the outspoken leaders in opposition to a colleague's views on justification at Westminster Theological Seminary. In my presidential interview with Palmer, I indicated that I did not want this controversy imported into Covenant Seminary, where there was no disagreement with the Westminster Confession and Catechisms on the doctrine of justification. During my tenure as president, I believe that Palmer honored this commitment. Always one who combined his academic pursuits with churchmanship, Palmer's church concerns eventually became part of some tension within the faculty and administration and led, after several fruitful years at Covenant, to his joining the faculty of Knox Seminary.

Our personal friendship has continued over the years, and I rejoice in this volume's tribute to Palmer Robertson's service for our Lord.

24

Knox Theological Seminary

MICHAEL A. MILTON

IT IS MY HONOR to submit my paper for inclusion in this book for my friend, Dr. O. Palmer Robertson. Dr. Robertson is truly a theologian for all seasons. Having served on the faculties of the most notable Reformed schools of theology in America, as well as having been a missionary and pastor, he has become the living archetype of the pastor-scholar that best serves the training of pastors, teachers, and missionaries for the church of our Lord Jesus Christ.

As the administrator of Knox Theological Seminary during part of the time Dr. Robertson taught there, I observed, firsthand, his several unique gifts woven together under the singular headship of his Savior Jesus Christ to produce students whose hearts and heads were filled with the wonder of justification by faith alone through Christ alone by God's grace alone. The doctrine of God's covenants has never been so ably taught as the very plan of salvation than when this man has taught it. But even more—Dr. Robertson taught it as *the* plan of salvation, not as a theorist holding forth an idea *about* God, but as an evangelist personally convinced of this truth, having been sent *from God*, and holding forth the Word of life to those who would receive Jesus Christ as Lord.

Thus, our students left Knox with hearts on fire for Christ and his covenant. They were trained to hold forth these doctrines as that Word from another *world* which would draw sinners forth from "this present evil age" like brands plucked from the burning and make them to be adopted sons and daughters of our covenant God. This Palmer Robertson did in the classroom, in the counseling room (often his home), and in the pulpit of Coral Ridge Presbyterian Church as, arguably, the church's most popular guest preacher.

Scholar. Teacher. Evangelist. Pastor. Counselor. Preacher. Friend. Husband. Father. Grandfather. Thank God for such a witness in our day! How I praise the Lord for giving us such an example! I now join with many others in giving thanks to God for this choice servant of Christ who takes his place alongside Hodge and Palmer, Breckenridge and Thornwell—men who were, like our man, theologians for all seasons.

25

New Geneva Theological Seminary

DOMINIC A. AQUILA

IN GOD'S PROVIDENCE, I had the privilege of meeting Palmer Robertson over forty years ago. Since that time our lives and ministries intersected in special ways. We first met when Palmer was pastor of Picayune Presbyterian Church in Picayune, Mississippi, and I was a student at Belhaven College. We served on a committee of the Synod of Mississippi that oversaw campus ministries.

Shortly afterwards, Palmer was called to Reformed Theological Seminary (RTS) in Jackson to teach Old Testament, and I was privileged to study under him. One of the more popular courses at RTS was Palmer's "Old Testament Biblical Theology," which was a third-year class. When my class heard that Palmer had accepted a call from Westminster Seminary in Philadelphia, we petitioned the faculty to allow us to take OTBT in our second year since he would be gone by our last year. In order to accommodate this schedule change the class had to meet at 7:00 a.m. four days a week for the entire year.

When I was called to a church in Richmond, Virginia, Palmer preached the sermon at my ordination service. While we had less frequent opportunities to meet after my ordination, years later we connected again when Palmer was invited to teach Old Testament at Knox Seminary in Ft. Lauderdale, Florida, where I was on the board and taught some classes.

However, what stands out more to me than a good friendship is Palmer's commitment to Scripture and to the centrality of Christ in the flow of God's redemptive history. Learning the wonders of redemptive history from Palmer was, I suspect, like the experience of the two men on the road to Emmaus on the first Easter. Christ came alongside of them and heard their lament that someone had taken the body of Jesus from the tomb; they could not understand it. Jesus chastened them and then we read, " 'How foolish you are, and how slow of heart to believe all that the prophets have spoken! Did not the Christ have to suffer these things and then enter his glory?' And beginning with Moses and all the Prophets, he explained to them what was said in all the Scriptures concerning himself" (Luke 24:25–27). Later on they remarked, "Were not our hearts burning within us while he talked with us on the road and opened the Scriptures to us?"

Palmer Robertson loves the Bible of Jesus and the Jesus of the Bible. By preaching this central truth, sinners will be confronted with God's gracious gift of his Son, the only Savior of God's people.

26

African Bible Colleges

W. WILSON BENTON

DR. O. PALMER ROBERTSON has been extremely supportive of and intimately involved with African Bible Colleges (ABC) since this organization's conception and birth. As brother-in-law and brother to the ABC founders, Jack and Nell Chinchen, respectively, Dr. Robertson gave vital encouragement to the vision in its embryonic stage, and has continued to lend his expertise and experience as the dream has become a reality, first in Liberia, then in Malawi, and now in Uganda. Quickly, however, his contribution increased from welcomed advice to crucial participation; first as an occasional semester lecturer in Liberia to a full-time professor of Old Testament, biblical theology, systematic theology, and homiletics in Malawi to the president of the Uganda campus, which is thriving under his leadership. It is well within the mark to say that Robertson has been an indispensable expression of God's grace in the planting, growth, development, and ever-increasing ministry of African Bible Colleges.

My fellow members of the Board of Trustees join me in extending to Palmer Robertson our sincere gratitude for his service, our heartfelt congratulations on the celebration of his seventieth birthday, and our earnest prayers for his continued health, labors of love, and faithful proclamation of God's truth.

461

Appendix: Select Bibliography of O. Palmer Robertson

PAUL AUSTIN

BOOKS AND COMMENTARIES

"A People of the Wilderness: The Concept of the Church in the Epistle to the Hebrews." ThD diss., Union Theological Seminary, 1966.

The Christ of the Covenants. Phillipsburg, NJ: Presbyterian and Reformed, 1980.

Covenants: God's Way with His People. Philadelphia: Great Commission, 1987.

Covenants Leader's Guide: A Teaching Manual for Use in Adult Study Groups. Philadelphia: Great Commission, 1987.

The Books of Nahum, Habakkuk, and Zephaniah. NICOT. Grand Rapids: Eerdmans, 1990.

Jonah: A Study in Compassion. Edinburgh: Banner of Truth, 1990.

The Final Word: A Biblical Response to the Case for Tongues and Prophecy Today. Edinburgh: Banner of Truth, 1993.

Psalms in Congregational Celebration. Darlington: Evangelical Press, 1995.

Prophet of the Coming Day of the Lord: The Message of Joel. Darlington: Evangelical Press, 1995.

Understanding the Land of the Bible: A Biblical-Theological Guide. Phillipsburg, NJ: P&R, 1996.

The Israel of God: Yesterday, Today, and Tomorrow. Phillipsburg, NJ: P&R, 2000.

The Genesis of Sex: Sexual Relationships in the First Book of the Bible. Phillipsburg, NJ: P&R, 2002.

Coming Home to God. Darlington: Evangelical Press, 2003.

The Current Justification Controversy. Unicoi, TN: Trinity Foundation, 2003.

The Christ of the Prophets. Phillipsburg, NJ: P&R, 2004.

ARTICLES IN WORKS OF COMPOSITE AUTHORSHIP

"The Outlook for Biblical Theology." In *Toward a Theology for the Future*, ed. David F. Wells and Clark H. Pinnock, 65–76. Carol Stream, IL: Creation, 1971.

"Is There a Distinctive Future for Ethnic Israel in Romans 11?" In *Perspectives on Evangelical Theology*, ed. Kenneth S. Kantzer and Stanley N. Gundry, 209–27. Grand Rapids: Baker, 1979.

"Hermeneutics of Continuity." In *Continuity and Discontinuity: Perspectives on the Relationship between the Old and New Testaments: Essays in Honor of S. Lewis Johnson Jr.*, ed. John S. Feinberg, 89–108. Westchester, IL: Crossway, 1988.

"A New Covenant Perspective on the Land." In *The Land of Promise: Biblical, Theological and Contemporary Perspectives*, ed. Philip Johnston and Peter Walker, 121–41. Downers Grove, IL: InterVarsity, 2000.

"Leaving the Shadows: The Land from a Reformed Covenantal Perspective." In *The Bible and the Land*, ed. Lisa Loden, Peter Walker and Michael Wood, 65–82. Jerusalem: Musalaha, 2000.

"Definite Atonement." In *After Darkness, Light: Distinctives of Reformed Theology*, ed. R.C. Sproul Jr., 95–110. Phillipsburg, N.J.: P&R, 2003.

"The Holy Spirit in the Westminster Confession of Faith." In *The Westminster Confession into the 21st Century: Essays in Remembrance of the 350th Anniversary of the Westminster Assembly*, ed. J. Ligon Duncan III., 57–99. Fearn, Ross-shire: Christian Focus, 2003.

Journal and Magazine Articles

"Which is Right?" *The Presbyterian Journal* 29, no. 4 (May 27, 1970): 10–11.

"Words and The Word." *The Presbyterian Journal* 31, no. 14 (August 2, 1972): 11.

"Straw Men vs. Scripture." *The Presbyterian Journal* 31, no. 29 (November 15, 1972): 9–11.

"If Ever—Now!" *The Presbyterian Journal* 32, no. 11 (July 11, 1973): 7–8.

"Shipwreck and the Great Commission." *The Presbyterian Journal* 32, no. 21 (September 19, 1973): 11.

"Tongues Today?" *The Presbyterian Journal* 32, no. 46 (March 13, 1974): 7–8.

"Unquestionably a Revelation Phenomenon," *The Presbyterian Journal*, 33, no. 31 (November 22, 1974): 8–9.

"Who Should Send Them?" *The Presbyterian Journal* 33, no. 53 (April 30, 1975): 11, 18.

"Presbyteries: Send Missionaries." *The Presbyterian Journal* 34, no. 12 (July 23, 1975): 10.

"Tongues: Sign of Covenantal Curse and Blessing." *Westminster Theological Journal* 38, no. 1 (Fall 1975): 43–53.

"Current Reformed Thinking on the Nature of the Divine Covenants." *Westminster Theological Journal* 40, no. 1 (Fall 1977): 63–76.

"God Justifies the Ungodly." *The Presbyterian Journal* 38, no. 26 (October 24, 1979): 10–11.

"One with Christ." *The Presbyterian Journal* 38, no. 37 (January 9, 1980): 10–12, 18.

"Genesis 15:6: New Covenant Expositions of an Old Covenant Text." *Westminster Theological Journal* 42, no. 2 (Spring 1980): 259–89.

"Justified by Works?" *The Presbyterian Journal* 38, no. 52 (April 23, 1980): 12–13, 22.

"The PCA—Past, Present and Future." *The Presbyterian Journal* 39, no. 16 (August 20, 1980): S6–S8.

"The Old Testament's John 3:16." *The Presbyterian Journal* 39, no. 47 (March 25, 1981): 7.

"Daniel P. Fuller's Gospel and Law, Contrast or Continuum? (A Review Article)." *Presbyterion* 8, no. 2 (Fall 1982): 84–91.

"The Justified (By Faith) Shall Live By His Steadfast Trust – Habakkuk 2:4." *Presbyterion* 9, nos. 1–2 (Spring–Fall 1983): 52–71.

"Biblical Presbyterianism and The Faith Once Delivered." *Session to Session* 1, no. 1 (April/May 1987): 1–2.

"Cornelius Van Til Sleeps: A Tribute to His Living." *Session to Session* 1, no. 1 (April–May 1987): 3.

"Abortion, Civil Disobedience, and the Christian." *Session to Session,* 1, no. 2 (June–July 1987): 1–2.

"Hold to the Heritage." *Session to Session* 1, no. 3 (August–September 1987): 2–3.

"Bill Moyers and the Reconstructionists." *Session to Session* 1, no. 5 (December–January 1988): 1, 3.

"A Handbook for Ruling Elder Involvement in the General Assembly of the Presbyterian Church in America." *Session to Session* 2, no. 1 (February–March 1988): 1–2.

"Morton Howison Smith: A Word of Appreciation," *Session to Session* 2, no. 2 (April–May 1988): 1, 4.

"A Protest in Response to the 'Summary Positions' Paper on Church/State Relations Adopted by the 16th General Assembly of the Presbyterian Church in America." In *Minutes of the Sixteenth General Assembly of the Presbyterian Church in America, June 6–10, 1988,* by the Committee for Christian Education and Publications, 206–7. Atlanta: The Committee for Christian Education and Publications, 1988.

"Bill Rose and Our Reaffirmations." *Session to Session* 2, no. 4 (August–September 1988): 1–2.

"Perceiving the Passion in Central Europe." *Session to Session* 3, no. 2 (April–May 1989): 1–2.

"The Assembly that Dared Say No." *Session to Session* 3, no. 3 (June–July 1989): 1–2.

"A Vision for the Decade." *Session to Session* 3, no. 6 (December–January 1990): 1–2.

"Leave Well Enough Alone." *Session to Session* 4, no. 4 (August–September 1990): 1–2.

"Prophecy Today?" *The Banner of Truth* 323/4 (August–September 1990):12–26.

"Reflections on the New Testament Testimony Concerning Civil Disobedience." *Journal of the Evangelical Theological Society* 33, no. 3 (September 1990): 331–51.

"The Day the Sun Stood Still" *Session to Session* 4, no. 6 (December–January 1991): 1–4.

"The Covenant and History." *Tabletalk* 15, no. 3 (March 1991): 30.

"The Divine Court's Decision about Abortion." *Session to Session* 5, no. 3 (June–July 1991): 1, 3–5.

"Tongues Today?" *The Banner of Truth* 337 (October 1991): 9–28.

"A Christian Perspective on AIDS, Part I." *Session to Session* 5/6, no. 6/1 (December 1991–March 1992): 6–8.

"A Christian Perspective on AIDS, Part II." *Session to Session* 6, no. 2 (April–June 1992) 3–4.

"Denigration of Prophecy." *The Banner of Truth* 346 (July 1992): 10–11, 27.

"Christ's Work in Song." *Tabletalk* 18, no. 1 (January 1994): 25–26.

"The Messiah Foretold." *Tabletalk* 18, no. 2 (February 1994): 29–30.

"The Lord's Name Is to Be Praised." *Tabletalk* 18, no. 3 (March 1994): 28–29.

"Who Is This 'Son of Man'?" *Tabletalk* 18, no. 4 (April 1994): 26–27.

"Satisfaction in Him Alone." *Tabletalk* 18, no. 5 (May 1994): 30–31.

"Put Your Trust in the Son." *Tabletalk* 18, no. 6 (June 1994): 28–29.

"Judgments Divine and Human." *Tabletalk* 18, no. 7 (July 1994): 26–27.

"Brothers in the Family of God." *Tabletalk* 18, no. 8 (August 1994): 29–30.

"Atheism: A Fool's Pursuit." *Tabletalk* 18, no. 9 (September 1994): 27–28.

"A Journey to God's House." *Tabletalk* 18, no. 10 (October 1994): 25–26.

"Giving Thanks to the Lord." *Tabletalk* 18, no. 11 (November 1994): 44–45.

"Holding All Authority." *Tabletalk* 18, no. 12 (December 1994): 42–43.

"The Promise of the Gospel." *Tabletalk* 19, no. 5 (May 1995): 15, 53.

"Giving Thanks to the Lord." *Evangelical Times* 29, no. 5 (May 1995): 7.

"Christ the Prophet in Deuteronomy 18." *Evangelical Times* 29, no. 7 (July 1995): 15.

"Thoughts on Theological Education: An Interview with Dr. O. Palmer Robertson." Interview by Byron Snapp and Pete Hurst. *The Presbyterian Witness* 9, no. 3 (Summer 1995): 12–18.

"The Lord Will Provide." *Tabletalk* 20, no. 12 (December 1996): 12–13, 52.

"Coronation Day." *Tabletalk* 22, no. 6 (June 1998): 8–10, 52.

"Why on Sunday?" *Evangelical Times* 33, no. 4 (April 1999): 19.

"Eschatology 1. The End of the World." *Evangelical Times* 33, no. 5 (May 1999): 17.

"Eschatology 2. The Rapture." *Evangelical Times* 33, no. 6 (June 1999): 12.

"Eschatology 3. The Millennium." *Evangelical Times* 33, no. 7 (July 1999): 21.

"Eschatology 4. The Future of the Jews." *Evangelical Times* 33, no. 8 (August 1999): 23.

"Have You Been Baptised in the Spirit? Part 1." *Evangelical Times* 33, no. 10 (October 1999): 19.

"Have You Been Baptised in the Spirit? Part 2." *Evangelical Times* 33, no. 11 (November 1999): 34.

"Jesus Will Come Again." *Evangelical Times* 33, no. 12 (December 1999): 17.

"The Sign of the Covenant." *Tabletalk* 25, no. 1 (January 2001): 38–39.

"The Renewal of the Covenant." *Tabletalk* 25, no. 2 (February 2001): 26–37.

"The Day the Sun Stood Still." *Tabletalk* 25, no. 3 (March 2001): 41–42.

"A Theologian of the Heart." *Tabletalk* 25, no. 4 (April 2001): 39–40.

"The Lot and the Land." *Tabletalk* 25, no. 5 (May 2001): 37–38.

"The Loss of the Land." *Tabletalk* 25, no. 6 (June 2001): 41–42.

"The Sadness of Syncretism." *Tabletalk* 25, no. 7 (July 2001): 39–40.

"Women of Prayer." *Tabletalk* 25, no. 8 (August 2001): 36–37.

"The Foolishness of Favoritism." *Tabletalk* 25, no. 9 (September 2001): 40–41.

"Preserve Your Consecration." *Tabletalk* 25, no. 10 (October 2001): 38–39.

"Chaos without a King." *Tabletalk* 25, no. 11 (November 2001): 36–37.

"Days of Chaos." *Tabletalk* 25, no. 12 (December 2001): 40–41.

"The Wind Blows Where It Wills." *Tabletalk* 28, no. 7 (July 2004): 12–15.

TRANSLATED WORKS

Las Lenguas: Señal de Maldición y Bendición del Pacto [*Tongues: Sign of Covenantal Curse and Blessing* in Spanish]. Translated by Jorge Zamora. Grand Rapids: Subcomisión Literatura Cristiana de la Iglesia Cristiana Reformada, 1977.

"Espantajos vs. las Escrituras." [*Straw Men vs. Scripture* in Spanish]. Translated by Carmen Alejandro de Giráu. *Heraldo de Gracia* 2 (April–June 1986): 3–9.

Ingyo Ingel [*Prophet of the Coming Day of the Lord: The Message of Joel* in Korean]. Seoul: Pastoral Resource Press, 1996.

Terra de Deus: O Significado das Terras Bíblicas Para os Planos e Propósitos de Deus [*Understanding the Land of the Bible: A Biblical-Theological Guide* in Portugese]. Translated by Hope Gordon Silva. São Paulo: Editora Cultura Cristã, 1998.

Khristos Bozhix Zavetov [*The Christ of the Covenants* in Russian]. Odessa: Godeistvize, 2002.

A Palavra Final: Reposta Bíblica à Questão das Línguas e Profecias Hoje [*The Final Word: A Biblical Response to the Case for Tongues and Prophecy Today* in Portugese]. Translated by Valter Graciano Martins. São Paulo: Editora Os Puritanos, 1999.

Geneza relatiei intime dintre barbat si femeie: Relatiei sexuale mentionate in prima carte a Bibliei [*The Genesis of Sex: Sexual Relationships in the First Book of the Bible* in Romanian]. Translated by Dorin Pantea. Oradea: Faclia, 2002.

O Cristo dos Pactos [*The Christ of the Covenants* in Portugese]. Translated by Américo Justiniano Ribeiro. São Paulo: Editora Cultura Cristã, 2002.

Bozhiat Izrail: Minalo, Nactoishte, Budeshte. [*The Israel of God: Yesterday, Today, and Tomorrow* in Bulgarian]. Translated by Miraslava Zareva. Sofia: Dynamic Consulting, 2002.

Khristos v Zavetite [*The Christ of the Covenants* in Bulgarian]. Translated by Snezhana Slavkova. Sofia: Dynamic Consulting, 2002.

Kyeyak sinhak kwa Kurisudo [*The Christ of the Covenants* in Korean]. Translated by Kim Ui-won. Seoul: Kidokkyo Munso Songyohoe, 2002.

Cesta K Bohu [*Coming Home to God* in Slovak]. Translated by Peter Juro. Pezinok: Ordo Salutis, 2004.

O Israel de Deus: Passado, Presente e Futuro [*The Israel of God: Yesterday, Today, and Tomorrow* in Portugese]. Translated by Denise Avalone. São Paulo: Editora Vida, 2005.

Dominic A. Aquila is president of New Geneva Theological Seminary in Colorado Springs, Colorado, and served as moderator of the 34th General Assembly of the Presbyterian Church in America.

Paul Austin is librarian and professor of Bible at African Bible College, Kampala, Uganda.

William S. Barker II is professor emeritus of church history at Westminster Theological Seminary in Philadelphia and past president of Covenant Theological Seminary in St. Louis, where he also serves as an adjunct professor.

W. Wilson Benton is interim senior minister at Christ Presbyterian Church in Nashville, Tennessee; former senior minister at Kirk of the Hills Presbyterian Church in St. Louis; and member of the board of trustees of the African Bible Colleges.

Robert C. Cannada Jr. is chancellor of Reformed Theological Seminary.

J. Knox Chamblin is professor emeritus of New Testament at Reformed Theological Seminary in Jackson, Mississippi.

Chad Van Dixhoorn is the executive director and general editor of the Westminster Assembly Project, Cambridge, England, and is a member of the faculty of history at the University of Cambridge.

Jane Kincannon Robertson Dodds is a freelance artist and the oldest of the three daughters of Palmer Robertson.

Richard B. Gaffin Jr. is Charles Krahe Professor of Biblical and Systematic Theology at Westminster Theological Seminary in Philadelphia.

Terry L. Johnson is senior minister of Independent Presbyterian Church in Savannah, Georgia.

Douglas F. Kelly is Richard Jordan Professor of Systematic Theology at Reformed Theological Seminary in Charlotte, North Carolina, and former professor of systematic theology at Reformed Theological Seminary in Jackson, Mississippi.

Simon J. Kistemaker is professor emeritus of New Testament at Reformed Theological Seminary in Orlando, Florida, and former professor of New Testament at Reformed Theological Seminary in Jackson, Mississippi.

George W. Knight III is chairman of the board of trustees of Greenville Presbyterian Theological Seminary in Greenville, South Carolina, and former professor of New Testament at Covenant Theological Seminary in St. Louis.

Samuel H. Larsen is Samuel Patterson Professor of Missions and Evangelism and vice president for international doctoral programs at Reformed Theological Seminary in Jackson, Mississippi.

Michael A. Milton is president of Reformed Theological Seminary in Charlotte, North Carolina; former senior minister at First Presbyterian Church in Chattanooga, Tennessee; and former administrator at Knox Theological Seminary in Fort Lauderdale, Florida.

Robert L. Penny is vice president for development at Reformed Theological Seminary in Jackson, Mississippi, and former minister of evangelism and discipleship at First Presbyterian Church in Hattiesburg, Mississippi.

Richard D. Phillips is senior minister of Second Presbyterian Church in Greenville, South Carolina; member of the board of directors of the Alliance of Confessing Evangelicals; chairman of the Philadelphia Conference on Reformed Theology; and co-editor of the Reformed Expository Commentary series.

Joseph A. Pipa Jr. is president and professor of historical and systematic theology at Greenville Presbyterian Theological Seminary in Greenville, South Carolina.

W. Duncan Rankin is senior minister of Covenant Presbyterian Church in Oak Ridge, Tennessee; adjunct professor of systematic theology at Reformed Theological Seminary in Jackson, Mississippi; and member of the board of directors of GRACE.

Robert L. Reymond is professor of systematic theology at Knox Theological Seminary in Fort Lauderdale, Florida.

Benjamin Shaw is professor of Old Testament at Greenville Presbyterian Theological Seminary in Greenville, South Carolina.

Morton H. Smith is professor of systematic theology at Greenville Presbyterian Theological Seminary in Greenville, South Carolina; former professor of systematic theology at Reformed Theological Seminary in Jackson, Mississippi; and former professor of Bible at Belhaven College in Jackson, Mississippi.

Bruce K. Waltke is professor of Old Testament at Reformed Theological Seminary in Orlando, Florida, and professor emeritus of biblical studies at Regent College in Vancouver, British Columbia.

Guy Prentiss Waters is associate professor of New Testament at Reformed Theological Seminary in Jackson, Mississippi.

C. N. Willborn is professor of historical and biblical theology at Greenville Presbyterian Theological Seminary in Greenville, South Carolina.